CompTIA A+ Core 2 Exam Guide to Operating Systems and Security, Tenth Edition, Jean Andrews, Joy Dark, Jill West

SVP, Skills Product Management: Jonathan Lau

Product Director: Lauren Murphy

Product Team Manager: Kristin McNary

Product Manager: Amy Savino

Product Assistant: Thomas Benedetto

Executive Director, Content Design: Marah Bellegarde

Director, Learning Design: Leigh Hefferon

Learning Designer: Natalie Onderdonk

Senior Marketing Director: Michele McTighe

Associate Marketing Manager: Cassie Cloutier

Product Specialist: Mackenzie Paine

Director, Content Delivery: Patty Stephan

Senior Content Manager: Brooke Greenhouse

Digital Delivery Lead: Jim Vaughey

Designer: Erin Griffin

Cover Designer: Joseph Villanova

Cover image: iStockPhoto.com/photoart23D

Production Service/Compositor: SPi-Global

For product information and technology assistance, contact us at
**Cengage Customer & Sales Support, 1-800-354-9706
or support.cengage.com.**

For permission to use material from this text or product, submit all requests online at **www.cengage.com/permissions.**

Library of Congress Control Number: 2018953405

ISBN: 978-0-357-10850-5

Cengage
20 Channel Center Street
Boston, MA 02210
USA

Cengage is a leading provider of customized learning solutions with employees residing in nearly 40 different countries and sales in more than 125 countries around the world. Find your local representative at: **www.cengage.com.**

Cengage products are represented in Canada by Nelson Education, Ltd.

To learn more about Cengage platforms and services, register or access your online learning solution, or purchase materials for your course, visit **www.cengage.com.**

Notice to the Reader
Publisher does not warrant or guarantee any of the products described herein or perform any independent analysis in connection with any of the product information contained herein. Publisher does not assume, and expressly disclaims, any obligation to obtain and include information other than that provided to it by the manufacturer. The reader is expressly warned to consider and adopt all safety precautions that might be indicated by the activities described herein and to avoid all potential hazards. By following the instructions contained herein, the reader willingly assumes all risks in connection with such instructions. The publisher makes no representations or warranties of any kind, including but not limited to, the warranties of fitness for particular purpose or merchantability, nor are any such representations implied with respect to the material set forth herein, and the publisher takes no responsibility with respect to such material. The publisher shall not be liable for any special, consequential, or exemplary damages resulting, in whole or part, from the readers' use of, or reliance upon, this material.

Printed in the United States of America
Print Number: 01   Print Year: 2019

CompTIA A+ Core 2 Exam Guide to Operating Systems and Security

TENTH EDITION

Jean Andrews, Joy Dark, Jill West

CENGAGE
Learning®

Australia • Canada • Mexico • Singapore • Spain • United Kingdom • United States

Table of Contents

CHAPTER 4

Maintaining Windows. **183**

CHAPTER 5

Troubleshooting Windows After Startup. **249**

CHAPTER 6

Troubleshooting Windows Startup. . . . **317**

CHAPTER 7

Securing and Sharing Windows Resources 371

CHAPTER 8

Security Strategies and Documentation 437

CHAPTER 9

Supporting Mobile Devices 479

CHAPTER 10

macOS, Linux, and Scripting 545

APPENDIX A

Safety Procedures and Environmental Concerns 607

APPENDIX B

Entry Points for Startup Processes. . . . 625

APPENDIX C

CompTIA Acronyms. 629

Glossary. 639

Index. 693

COMPTIA A+ CORE 2 (220-1002) EXAM OBJECTIVES MAPPED TO CHAPTERS

CompTIA A+ Core 2 Exam Guide to Operating Systems and Security, Tenth Edition fully meets all of the CompTIA's A+ Core 2 (220-1002) Exam Objectives.

COMPTIA A+ CORE 2 (220-1002)

1.0 OPERATING SYSTEMS

1.1 Compare and contrast common operating system types and their purposes.

Objectives	Chapter	Primary Section
• 32-bit vs. 64-bit	2	How to Plan a Windows Installation
- RAM limitations	2	How to Plan a Windows Installation
- Software compatibility	2	How to Plan a Windows Installation
• Workstation operating systems	10	Linux Operating System
- Microsoft Windows	10	Linux Operating System
- Apple Macintosh OS	10	Linux Operating System
- Linux	10	Linux Operating System
• Cell phone/tablet operating systems	9	Mobile Device Operating Systems
- Microsoft Windows	9	Mobile Device Operating Systems
- Android	9	Mobile Device Operating Systems
- iOS	9	Mobile Device Operating Systems
- Chrome OS	9	Mobile Device Operating Systems
• Vendor-specific limitations	10	Linux Operating System
- End-of-life	10	Linux Operating System
- Update limitations	10	Linux Operating System
• Compatibility concerns between operating systems	10	Linux Operating System

1.2 Compare and contrast features of Microsoft Windows versions.

Objectives	Chapter	Primary Section
• Windows 7	1	Windows Interfaces
• Windows 8	1	Windows Interfaces
• Windows 8.1	1	Windows Interfaces
• Windows 10	1	Windows Interfaces
• Corporate vs. personal needs	1	Windows Interfaces
- Domain access	1	Windows Interfaces
- BitLocker	1	Windows Interfaces
- Media center	1	Windows Interfaces
- Branchcache	1	Windows Interfaces
- EFS	1	Windows Interfaces
• Desktop styles/user interface	1	Windows Interfaces

1.3 Summarize general OS installation considerations and upgrade methods.

Objectives	Chapter	Primary Section
• Boot methods	2	How to Plan a Windows Installation
- USB	2	Installing Windows 10, Windows 8.1, and Windows 7
- CD-ROM	2	Installing Windows 10, Windows 8.1, and Windows 7
- DVD	2	Installing Windows 10, Windows 8.1, and Windows 7
- PXE	2	How to Plan a Windows Installation

Objectives	Chapter	Primary Section
- Solid state/flash drives	2	Installing Windows 10, Windows 8.1, and Windows 7
- Netboot	10	macOS for Macintosh Computers
- External/hot-swappable drive	2	How to Plan a Windows Installation
- Internal hard drive (partition)	6	Options to Reinstall Windows
• Type of installations	2	How to Plan a Windows Installation
- Unattended installation	2	Special Concerns When Working in a Large Enterprise
- In-place upgrade	2	How to Plan a Windows Installation
- Clean install	2	How to Plan a Windows Installation
- Repair installation	6	Options to Reinstall Windows
- Multiboot	2	Installing Windows 10, Windows 8.1, and Windows 7
- Remote network installation	2	Special Concerns When Working in a Large Enterprise
- Image deployment	2	Special Concerns When Working in a Large Enterprise
- Recovery partition	6	Options to Reinstall Windows
- Refresh/restore	6	Options to Reinstall Windows
• Partitioning	4	Managing Files, Folders, and Storage Devices
- Dynamic	4	Managing Files, Folders, and Storage Devices
- Basic	4	Managing Files, Folders, and Storage Devices
- Primary	4	Managing Files, Folders, and Storage Devices
- Extended	4	Managing Files, Folders, and Storage Devices
- Logical	4	Managing Files, Folders, and Storage Devices
- GPT	4	Managing Files, Folders, and Storage Devices
• File system types/formatting	4	Managing Files, Folders, and Storage Devices
- ExFAT	4	Managing Files, Folders, and Storage Devices
- FAT32	4	Managing Files, Folders, and Storage Devices
- NTFS	4	Managing Files, Folders, and Storage Devices
- CDFS	4	Managing Files, Folders, and Storage Devices
- NFS	4	Managing Files, Folders, and Storage Devices
- ext3, ext4	10	Linux Operating System
- HFS	10	macOS for Macintosh Computers
- Swap partition	10	Linux Operating System
- Quick format vs. full format	2	Installing Windows 10, Windows 8.1, and Windows 7
• Load alternate third-party drivers when necessary	2	How to Plan a Windows Installation
• Workgroup vs. Domain setup	1	How Windows Controls Access to Network Resources
• Time/date/region/language settings	2	Installing Windows 10, Windows 8.1, and Windows 7
• Driver installation, software, and Windows updates	2	What to Do After a Windows Installation
• Factory recovery partition	6	Options to Reinstall Windows
• Properly formatted boot drive with the correct partitions/format	6	Tools for Least Invasive Solutions
• Prerequisites/hardware compatibility	2	How to Plan a Windows Installation
• Application compatibility	2	How to Plan a Windows Installation
• OS compatibility/upgrade path	2	How to Plan a Windows Installation

1.4   Given a scenario, use appropriate Microsoft command-line tools.

Objectives	Chapter	Primary Section
• Navigation	4	Using a Command-Line Interface (CLI)
- dir	4	Using a Command-Line Interface (CLI)
- cd	4	Using a Command-Line Interface (CLI)
- ..	4	Using a Command-Line Interface (CLI)
• ipconfig	3	Troubleshooting Network Connections
• ping	3	Troubleshooting Network Connections

Objectives	Chapter	Primary Section
• tracert	3	Troubleshooting Network Connections
• netstat	3	Troubleshooting Network Connections
• nslookup	3	Troubleshooting Network Connections
• shutdown	4	Using a Command-Line Interface (CLI)
• dism	5	Best Practices to Troubleshoot Windows-Related Problems
• sfc	5	Best Practices to Troubleshoot Windows-Related Problems
• chkdsk	5	Best Practices to Troubleshoot Windows-Related Problems
• diskpart	6	Tools for Least Invasive Solutions
• taskkill	5	Application Errors and Crashes
• gpupdate	7	Using Active Directory Domain Services
• gpresult	7	Using Active Directory Domain Services
• format	4	Using a Command-Line Interface (CLI)
• copy	4	Using a Command-Line Interface (CLI)
• xcopy	4	Using a Command-Line Interface (CLI)
• robocopy	4	Using a Command-Line Interface (CLI)
• net use	3	Troubleshooting Network Connections
• net user	3	Troubleshooting Network Connections
• [command name] /?	4	Using a Command-Line Interface (CLI)
• Commands available with standard privileges vs. administrative privileges	4	Using a Command-Line Interface (CLI)

1.5 Given a scenario, use Microsoft operating system features and tools.

Objectives	Chapter	Primary Section
• Administrative	5	
- Computer Management	5	Concepts and Windows Tools for Solving Problems with Windows, Applications, and Hardware
- Device Manager	2	What to Do After a Windows Installation
- Local Users and Groups	7	Controlling Access to Folders and Files
- Local Security Policy	7	Securing a Windows Personal Computer
- Performance Monitor	5	Best Practices to Troubleshoot Windows-Related Problems
- Services	5	Slow Startup and Slow Performance
- System Configuration	5	Best Practices to Troubleshoot Windows-Related Problems
- Task Scheduler	5	Slow Startup and Slow Performance
- Component Services	5	Application Errors and Crashes
- Data Sources	5	Application Errors and Crashes
- Print Management	5	Troubleshooting Hardware Problems in Windows
- Windows Memory Diagnostics	5	Best Practices to Troubleshoot Windows-Related Problems
- Windows Firewall	7	Securing a Windows Personal Computer
- Advanced Security	7	Securing a Windows Personal Computer
- Event Viewer	5	Best Practices to Troubleshoot Windows-Related Problems
- User Account Management	7	Controlling Access to Folders and Files
• MSConfig	5	Best Practices to Troubleshoot Windows-Related Problems
- General	5	Best Practices to Troubleshoot Windows-Related Problems
- Boot	5	Best Practices to Troubleshoot Windows-Related Problems
- Services	5	Best Practices to Troubleshoot Windows-Related Problems
- Startup	5	Best Practices to Troubleshoot Windows-Related Problems
- Tools	5	Best Practices to Troubleshoot Windows-Related Problems
• Task Manager	5	Best Practices to Troubleshoot Windows-Related Problems
- Applications	5	Best Practices to Troubleshoot Windows-Related Problems
- Processes	5	Best Practices to Troubleshoot Windows-Related Problems
- Performance	5	Best Practices to Troubleshoot Windows-Related Problems
- Networking	5	Best Practices to Troubleshoot Windows-Related Problems
- Users	5	Best Practices to Troubleshoot Windows-Related Problems

Objectives	Chapter	Primary Section
• Disk Management	4	Managing Files, Folders, and Storage Devices
- Drive status	4	Managing Files, Folders, and Storage Devices
- Mounting	4	Managing Files, Folders, and Storage Devices
- Initializing	4	Managing Files, Folders, and Storage Devices
- Extending partitions	4	Managing Files, Folders, and Storage Devices
- Splitting partitions	4	Managing Files, Folders, and Storage Devices
- Shrink partitions	4	Managing Files, Folders, and Storage Devices
- Assigning/changing drive letters	4	Managing Files, Folders, and Storage Devices
- Adding drives	4	Managing Files, Folders, and Storage Devices
- Adding arrays	4	Managing Files, Folders, and Storage Devices
- Storage spaces	4	Managing Files, Folders, and Storage Devices
• System utilities	5	Slow Startup and Slow Performance
- Regedit	5	Using a Command-Line Interface (CLI)
- Command	4	Application Errors and Crashes
- Services.msc	5	Concepts and Windows Tools for Solving Problems with
- MMC	5	Windows, Applications, and Hardware
		Remote Connections
- MSTSC	4	Windows Tools for Users and Technicians
- Notepad	1	Windows Tools for Users and Technicians
- Explorer	1	Windows Tools for Users and Technicians
- Msinfo32	1	Troubleshooting Hardware Problems in Windows
- DxDiag	5	Managing Files, Folders, and Storage Devices
- Disk Defragmenter	4	Best Practices to Troubleshoot Windows-Related Problems
- System Restore	5	What to Do After a Windows Installation
- Windows Update	2	

1.6   Given a scenario, use Microsoft Windows Control Panel utilities.

Objectives	Chapter	Primary Section
• Internet Options	7	Securing a Windows Personal Computer
- Connections	7	Securing a Windows Personal Computer
- Security	7	Securing a Windows Personal Computer
- General	7	Securing a Windows Personal Computer
- Privacy	7	Securing a Windows Personal Computer
- Programs	7	Securing a Windows Personal Computer
- Advanced	7	Securing a Windows Personal Computer
• Display/Display Settings	5	Troubleshooting Hardware Problems in Windows
- Resolution	5	Troubleshooting Hardware Problems in Windows
- Color depth	5	Troubleshooting Hardware Problems in Windows
- Refresh rate	5	Troubleshooting Hardware Problems in Windows
• User Accounts	7	Controlling Access to Folders and Files
• Folder Options	1	Windows Tools for Users and Technicians
- View hidden files	1	Windows Tools for Users and Technicians
- Hide extensions	1	Windows Tools for Users and Technicians
- General options	1	Windows Tools for Users and Technicians
- View options	1	Windows Tools for Users and Technicians
• System		
- Performance (virtual memory)	5	Slow Startup and Slow Performance
- Remote settings	4	Remote Connections
- System protection	4	Backup Procedures
• Windows Firewall	7	Securing a Windows Personal Computer
• Power Options	1	Windows Tools for Users and Technicians
- Hibernate	1	Windows Tools for Users and Technicians

Objectives	Chapter	Primary Section
- Power plans	1	Windows Tools for Users and Technicians
- Sleep/suspend	1	Windows Tools for Users and Technicians
- Standby	1	Windows Tools for Users and Technicians
• Credential Manager	7	Securing a Windows Personal Computer
• Programs and features	2	What to Do After a Windows Installation
• HomeGroup	1	How Windows Controls Access to Network Resources
• Devices and Printers	2	What to Do After a Windows Installation
• Sound	1	Windows Tools for Users and Technicians
• Troubleshooting	5	Concepts and Windows Tools for Solving Problems with Windows, Applications, and Hardware
• Network and Sharing Center	1	How Windows Controls Access to Network Resources
• Device Manager	2	What to Do After a Windows Installation
• BitLocker	7	Securing a Windows Personal Computer
• Sync Center	7	Controlling Access to Folders and Files

1.7 Summarize application installation and configuration concepts

Objectives	Chapter	Primary Section
• System requirements	2	What to Do After a Windows Installation
- Drive space	2	What to Do After a Windows Installation
- RAM	2	What to Do After a Windows Installation
• OS requirements	2	What to Do After a Windows Installation
- Compatibility	2	What to Do After a Windows Installation
• Methods of installation and deployment	2	What to Do After a Windows Installation
- Local (CD/USB)	2	What to Do After a Windows Installation
- Network-based	2	What to Do After a Windows Installation
• Local user permissions	2	What to Do After a Windows Installation
- Folder/file access for installation	2	What to Do After a Windows Installation
• Security considerations	2	What to Do After a Windows Installation
- Impact to device	2	What to Do After a Windows Installation
- Impact to network	2	What to Do After a Windows Installation

1.8 Given a scenario, configure Microsoft Windows networking on a client/desktop.

Objectives	Chapter	Primary Section
• HomeGroup vs. Workgroup	1	How Windows Controls Access to Network Resources
• Domain setup	1	How Windows Controls Access to Network Resources
• Network shares/administrative shares/mapping drives	7	Controlling Access to Folders and Files
• Printer sharing vs. network printer mapping	7	Securing a Windows Personal Computer
• Establish networking connections	3	Connecting a Computer to a Local Network
- VPN	3	Connecting a Computer to a Local Network
- Dial-ups	3	Connecting a Computer to a Local Network
- Wireless	3	Connecting a Computer to a Local Network
- Wired	3	Connecting a Computer to a Local Network
- WWAN (Cellular)	3	Connecting a Computer to a Local Network
• Proxy settings	7	Securing a Windows Personal Computer
• Remote Desktop Connection	4	Remote Connections
• Remote Assistance	4	Remote Connections
• Home vs. Work vs. Public network settings	1	How Windows Controls Access to Network Resources
• Firewall settings	7	Securing a Windows Personal Computer
- Exceptions	7	Securing a Windows Personal Computer
- Configuration	7	Securing a Windows Personal Computer
- Enabling/disabling Windows Firewall	7	Securing a Windows Personal Computer

Objectives	Chapter	Primary Section
• Configuring an alternative IP address in Windows	3	Connecting a Computer to a Local Network
- IP addressing	3	Connecting a Computer to a Local Network
- Subnet mask	3	Connecting a Computer to a Local Network
- DNS	3	Connecting a Computer to a Local Network
- Gateway	3	Connecting a Computer to a Local Network
• Network card properties	3	Connecting a Computer to a Local Network
- Half duplex/full duplex/auto	3	Connecting a Computer to a Local Network
- Speed	3	Connecting a Computer to a Local Network
- Wake-on-LAN	3	Connecting a Computer to a Local Network
- QoS	3	Connecting a Computer to a Local Network
- BIOS (on-board NIC)	3	Connecting a Computer to a Local Network

1.9 Given a scenario, use features and tools of the Mac OS and Linux client/desktop operating systems.

Objectives	Chapter	Primary Section
• Best practices		
- Scheduled backups	10	macOS for Macintosh Computers
- Scheduled disk maintenance	10	macOS for Macintosh Computers
- System updates/App Store	10	macOS for Macintosh Computers
- Patch management	10	macOS for Macintosh Computers
- Driver/firmware updates	10	macOS for Macintosh Computers
- Antivirus/Anti-malware updates	10	macOS for Macintosh Computers
• Tools		
- Backup/Time Machine	10	macOS for Macintosh Computers
- Restore/Snapshot	10	macOS for Macintosh Computers
- Image recovery	10	macOS for Macintosh Computers
- Disk maintenance utilities	10	macOS for Macintosh Computers
- Shell/Terminal	10	macOS for Macintosh Computers
- Screen sharing	10	macOS for Macintosh Computers
- Force Quit	10	macOS for Macintosh Computers
• Features		
- Multiple desktops/Mission Control	10	macOS for Macintosh Computers
- Key Chain	10	macOS for Macintosh Computers
- Spot Light	10	macOS for Macintosh Computers
- iCloud	10	macOS for Macintosh Computers
- Gestures	10	macOS for Macintosh Computers
- Finder	10	macOS for Macintosh Computers
- Remote Disc	10	macOS for Macintosh Computers
- Dock	10	macOS for Macintosh Computers
- Boot Camp	10	macOS for Macintosh Computers
• Basic Linux commands		
- ls	10	Linux Operating System
- grep	10	Linux Operating System
- cd	10	Linux Operating System
- shutdown	10	Linux Operating System
- pwd vs. passwd	10	Linux Operating System
- mv	10	Linux Operating System
- cp	10	Linux Operating System
- rm	10	Linux Operating System
- chmod	10	Linux Operating System
- chown	10	Linux Operating System
- iwconfig/ifconfig	10	Linux Operating System
- ps	10	Linux Operating System
- su/sudo	10	Linux Operating System

2.0 SECURITY

2.1 Summarize the importance of physical security measures.

2.2 Explain logical security concepts.

2.3   Compare and contrast wireless security protocols and authentication methods.

Objectives	Chapter	Primary Section
• Protocols and encryption	3	Setting Up a Multifunction Router for a SOHO Network
- WEP	3	Setting Up a Multifunction Router for a SOHO Network
- WPA	3	Setting Up a Multifunction Router for a SOHO Network
- WPA2	3	Setting Up a Multifunction Router for a SOHO Network
- TKIP	3	Setting Up a Multifunction Router for a SOHO Network
- AES	3	Setting Up a Multifunction Router for a SOHO Network
• Authentication	8	Protecting Network Resources
- Single-factor	8	Protecting Network Resources
- Multifactor	8	Protecting Network Resources
- RADIUS	8	Protecting Network Resources
- TACACS	8	Protecting Network Resources

2.4   Given a scenario, detect, remove, and prevent malware using appropriate tools and methods.

Objectives	Chapter	Primary Section
• Malware	8	Dealing with Malicious Software on Personal Computers
- Ransomware	8	Dealing with Malicious Software on Personal Computers
- Trojan	8	Dealing with Malicious Software on Personal Computers
- Keylogger	8	Dealing with Malicious Software on Personal Computers
- Rootkit	8	Dealing with Malicious Software on Personal Computers
- Virus	8	Dealing with Malicious Software on Personal Computers
- Botnet	8	Dealing with Malicious Software on Personal Computers
- Worm	8	Dealing with Malicious Software on Personal Computers
- Spyware	8	Dealing with Malicious Software on Personal Computers
• Tools and methods	8	Dealing with Malicious Software on Personal Computers
- Antivirus	8	Dealing with Malicious Software on Personal Computers
- Anti-malware	8	Dealing with Malicious Software on Personal Computers
- Recovery console	8	Dealing with Malicious Software on Personal Computers
- Backup/restore	8	Dealing with Malicious Software on Personal Computers
- End user education	8	Dealing with Malicious Software on Personal Computers
- Software firewalls	8	Dealing with Malicious Software on Personal Computers
- SecureDNS	8	Protecting Network Resources

2.5   Compare and contrast social engineering, threats, and vulnerabilities.

Objectives	Chapter	Primary Section
• Social engineering		
- Phishing	8	Protecting Network Resources
- Spear phishing	8	Protecting Network Resources
- Impersonation	8	Protecting Network Resources
- Shoulder surfing	8	Protecting Network Resources
- Tailgating	8	Protecting Network Resources
- Dumpster diving	8	Protecting Network Resources
• DDoS	8	Dealing with Malicious Software on Personal Computers
• DoS	8	Dealing with Malicious Software on Personal Computers
• Zero-day	8	Dealing with Malicious Software on Personal Computers
• Man-in-the-middle	8	Dealing with Malicious Software on Personal Computers
• Brute force	7	Securing a Windows Personal Computer
• Dictionary	8	Dealing with Malicious Software on Personal Computers
• Rainbow table	8	Dealing with Malicious Software on Personal Computers
• Spoofing	8	Dealing with Malicious Software on Personal Computers
• Non-compliant systems	8	Dealing with Malicious Software on Personal Computers
• Zombie	8	Dealing with Malicious Software on Personal Computers

2.6 Compare and contrast the differences of basic Microsoft Windows OS security settings.

Objectives	Chapter	Primary Section
• User and groups	7	Controlling Access to Folders and Files
- Administrator	7	Controlling Access to Folders and Files
- Power user	7	Controlling Access to Folders and Files
- Guest	7	Controlling Access to Folders and Files
- Standard user	7	Controlling Access to Folders and Files
• NTFS vs. share permissions	7	Controlling Access to Folders and Files
- Allow vs. deny	7	Controlling Access to Folders and Files
- Moving vs. copying folders and files	7	Controlling Access to Folders and Files
- File attributes	7	Controlling Access to Folders and Files
• Shared files and folders	7	Controlling Access to Folders and Files
- Administrative shares vs. local shares	7	Controlling Access to Folders and Files
- Permission propagation	7	Controlling Access to Folders and Files
- Inheritance	7	Controlling Access to Folders and Files
• System files and folders	7	Controlling Access to Folders and Files
• User authentication	7	Securing a Windows Personal Computer
- Single sign-on	7	Securing a Windows Personal Computer
• Run as administrator vs. standard user	5	Concepts and Windows Tools for Solving Problems with Windows, Applications, and Hardware
• BitLocker	7	Securing a Windows Personal Computer
• BitLocker To Go	7	Securing a Windows Personal Computer
• EFS	7	Securing a Windows Personal Computer

2.7 Given a scenario, implement security best practices to secure a workstation.

Objectives	Chapter	Primary Section
• Password best practices	7	Securing a Windows Personal Computer
- Setting strong passwords	7	Securing a Windows Personal Computer
- Password expiration	7	Securing a Windows Personal Computer
- Screensaver required password	7	Securing a Windows Personal Computer
- BIOS/UEFI passwords	7	Securing a Windows Personal Computer
- Requiring passwords	7	Securing a Windows Personal Computer
• Account management	7	Controlling Access to Folders and Files
- Restricting user permissions	7	Controlling Access to Folders and Files
- Logon time restrictions	7	Using Active Directory Domain Services
- Disabling guest account	7	Using Active Directory Domain Services
- Failed attempts lockout	7	Using Active Directory Domain Services
- Timeout/screen lock	7	Using Active Directory Domain Services
- Change default admin user account/password	7	Using Active Directory Domain Services
- Basic Active Directory functions	7	Using Active Directory Domain Services
○ Account creation	7	Using Active Directory Domain Services
○ Account deletion	7	Using Active Directory Domain Services
○ Password reset/unlock account	7	Using Active Directory Domain Services
○ Disable account	7	Using Active Directory Domain Services
• Disable autorun	7	Securing a Windows Personal Computer
• Data encryption	7	Securing a Windows Personal Computer
• Patch/update management	4	Scheduling Preventive Maintenance

2.8 Given a scenario, implement methods for securing mobile devices.

Objectives	Chapter	Primary Section
• Screen locks	9	Securing a Mobile Device
- Fingerprint lock	9	Securing a Mobile Device
- Face lock	9	Securing a Mobile Device
- Swipe lock	9	Securing a Mobile Device
- Passcode lock	9	Securing a Mobile Device
• Remote wipes	9	Securing a Mobile Device
• Locator applications	9	Securing a Mobile Device
• Remote backup applications	9	Securing a Mobile Device
• Failed login attempts restrictions	9	Securing a Mobile Device
• Antivirus/Anti-malware	9	Securing a Mobile Device
• Patching/OS updates	9	Securing a Mobile Device
• Biometric authentication	9	Securing a Mobile Device
• Full device encryption	9	Securing a Mobile Device
• Multifactor authentication	9	Securing a Mobile Device
• Authenticator applications	9	Securing a Mobile Device
• Trusted sources vs. untrusted sources	9	Securing a Mobile Device
• Firewalls	9	Securing a Mobile Device
• Policies and procedures	9	Securing a Mobile Device
- BYOD vs. corporate-owned	9	Securing a Mobile Device
- Profile security requirements	9	Securing a Mobile Device

2.9 Given a scenario, implement appropriate data destruction and disposal methods.

Objectives	Chapter	Primary Section
• Physical destruction	8	Protecting Network Resources
- Shredder	8	Protecting Network Resources
- Drill/hammer	8	Protecting Network Resources
- Electromagnetic (Degaussing)	8	Protecting Network Resources
- Incineration	8	Protecting Network Resources
- Certificate of destruction	8	Protecting Network Resources
• Recycling or repurposing best practices	8	Protecting Network Resources
- Low-level format vs. standard format	8	Protecting Network Resources
- Overwrite	8	Protecting Network Resources
- Drive wipe	8	Protecting Network Resources

2.10 Given a scenario, configure security on SOHO wireless and wired networks.

Objectives	Chapter	Primary Section
• Wireless-specific	3	Setting Up a Multifunction Router for a SOHO Network
- Changing default SSID	3	Setting Up a Multifunction Router for a SOHO Network
- Setting encryption	3	Setting Up a Multifunction Router for a SOHO Network
- Disabling SSID broadcast	3	Setting Up a Multifunction Router for a SOHO Network
- Antenna and access point placement	3	Setting Up a Multifunction Router for a SOHO Network
- Radio power levels	3	Setting Up a Multifunction Router for a SOHO Network
- WPS	3	Setting Up a Multifunction Router for a SOHO Network
• Change default usernames and passwords	3	Setting Up a Multifunction Router for a SOHO Network
• Enable MAC filtering	3	Setting Up a Multifunction Router for a SOHO Network
• Assign static IP addresses	3	Setting Up a Multifunction Router for a SOHO Network
• Firewall settings	3	Setting Up a Multifunction Router for a SOHO Network
• Port forwarding/mapping	3	Setting Up a Multifunction Router for a SOHO Network

Objectives	Chapter	Primary Section
• Disabling ports	3	Setting Up a Multifunction Router for a SOHO Network
• Content filtering/parental controls	3	Setting Up a Multifunction Router for a SOHO Network
• Update firmware	3	Setting Up a Multifunction Router for a SOHO Network
• Physical security	3	Setting Up a Multifunction Router for a SOHO Network

3.0 SOFTWARE TROUBLESHOOTING

3.1   Given a scenario, troubleshoot Microsoft Windows OS problems.

Objectives	Chapter	Primary Section
• Common symptoms		
- Slow performance	5	Slow Startup and Slow Performance
- Limited connectivity	5	Troubleshooting Hardware Problems in Windows
- Failure to boot	6	Troubleshooting Specific Windows Startup Problems
- No OS found	6	Troubleshooting Specific Windows Startup Problems
- Application crashes	5	Application Errors and Crashes
- Blue screens	6	Troubleshooting Specific Windows Startup Problems
- Black screens	6	Troubleshooting Specific Windows Startup Problems
- Printing issues	5	Troubleshooting Hardware Problems in Windows
- Services fail to start	5	Application Errors and Crashes
- Slow bootup	5	Slow Startup and Slow Performance
- Slow profile load	6	Troubleshooting Specific Windows Startup Problems
• Common solutions		
- Defragment the hard drive	4	Managing Files, Folders, and Storage Devices
- Reboot	6	Troubleshooting Specific Windows Startup Problems
- Kill tasks	5	Application Errors and Crashes
- Restart services	5	Application Errors and Crashes
- Update network settings	5	Troubleshooting Hardware Problems in Windows
- Reimage/reload OS	6	Troubleshooting Specific Windows Startup Problems
- Roll back updates	6	Troubleshooting Specific Windows Startup Problems
- Roll back device drivers	6	Troubleshooting Specific Windows Startup Problems
- Apply updates	6	Troubleshooting Specific Windows Startup Problems
- Repair application	5	Application Errors and Crashes
- Update boot order	6	Troubleshooting Specific Windows Startup Problems
- Disable Windows services/applications	5	Application Errors and Crashes
- Disable application startup	5	Application Errors and Crashes
- Safe boot	5	Best Practices to Troubleshoot Windows-Related Problems
- Rebuild Windows profiles	6	Troubleshooting Specific Windows Startup Problems

3.2   Given a scenario, troubleshoot and resolve PC security issues.

Objectives	Chapter	Primary Section
• Common symptoms		
- Pop-ups	8	Dealing with Malicious Software on Personal Computers
- Browser redirection	8	Dealing with Malicious Software on Personal Computers
- Security alerts	8	Dealing with Malicious Software on Personal Computers
- Slow performance	8	Dealing with Malicious Software on Personal Computers
- Internet connectivity issues	8	Dealing with Malicious Software on Personal Computers
- PC/OS lockup	8	Dealing with Malicious Software on Personal Computers
- Application crash	8	Dealing with Malicious Software on Personal Computers
- OS updates failures	8	Dealing with Malicious Software on Personal Computers

Objectives	Chapter	Primary Section
- Rogue antivirus	8	Dealing with Malicious Software on Personal Computers
- Spam	8	Dealing with Malicious Software on Personal Computers
- Renamed system files	8	Dealing with Malicious Software on Personal Computers
- Disappearing files	8	Dealing with Malicious Software on Personal Computers
- File permission changes	8	Dealing with Malicious Software on Personal Computers
- Hijacked email	8	Dealing with Malicious Software on Personal Computers
○ Responses from users regarding email	8	Dealing with Malicious Software on Personal Computers
○ Automated replies from unknown sent email	8	Dealing with Malicious Software on Personal Computers
- Access denied	8	Dealing with Malicious Software on Personal Computers
- Invalid certificate (trusted root CA)	8	Dealing with Malicious Software on Personal Computers
- System/application log errors	8	Dealing with Malicious Software on Personal Computers

3.3 Given a scenario, use best practice procedures for malware removal.

Objectives	Chapter	Primary Section
1. Identify and research malware symptoms.	8	Dealing with Malicious Software on Personal Computers
2. Quarantine the infected systems.	8	Dealing with Malicious Software on Personal Computers
3. Disable System Restore (in Windows).	8	Dealing with Malicious Software on Personal Computers
4. Remediate the infected systems.	8	Dealing with Malicious Software on Personal Computers
a. Update the anti-malware software.	8	Dealing with Malicious Software on Personal Computers
b. Scan and use removal techniques (safe mode, pre-installation environment).	8	Dealing with Malicious Software on Personal Computers
5. Schedule scans and run updates.	8	Dealing with Malicious Software on Personal Computers
6. Enable System Restore and create a restore point (in Windows).	8	Dealing with Malicious Software on Personal Computers
7. Educate the end user.	8	Dealing with Malicious Software on Personal Computers

3.4 Given a scenario, troubleshoot mobile OS and application issues.

Objectives	Chapter	Primary Section
• Common symptoms	9	Troubleshooting Mobile Devices
- Dim display	9	Troubleshooting Mobile Devices
- Intermittent wireless	9	Troubleshooting Mobile Devices
- No wireless connectivity	9	Troubleshooting Mobile Devices
- No Bluetooth connectivity	9	Troubleshooting Mobile Devices
- Cannot broadcast to external monitor	9	Troubleshooting Mobile Devices
- Touch screen non-responsive	9	Troubleshooting Mobile Devices
- Apps not loading	9	Troubleshooting Mobile Devices
- Slow performance	9	Troubleshooting Mobile Devices
- Unable to decrypt email	9	Troubleshooting Mobile Devices
- Extremely short battery life	9	Troubleshooting Mobile Devices
- Overheating	9	Troubleshooting Mobile Devices
- Frozen system	9	Troubleshooting Mobile Devices
- No sound from speakers	9	Troubleshooting Mobile Devices
- Inaccurate touch screen response	9	Troubleshooting Mobile Devices
- System lockout	9	Troubleshooting Mobile Devices
- App log errors	9	Troubleshooting Mobile Devices

3.5 Given a scenario, troubleshoot mobile OS and application security issues.

Objectives	Chapter	Primary Section
• Common symptoms	9	Troubleshooting Mobile Devices
- Signal drop/weak signal	9	Troubleshooting Mobile Devices
- Power drain	9	Troubleshooting Mobile Devices
- Slow data speeds	9	Troubleshooting Mobile Devices
- Unintended Wi-Fi connection	9	Troubleshooting Mobile Devices
- Unintended Bluetooth pairing	9	Troubleshooting Mobile Devices
- Leaked personal files/data	9	Troubleshooting Mobile Devices
- Data transmission over limit	9	Troubleshooting Mobile Devices
- Unauthorized account access	9	Troubleshooting Mobile Devices
- Unauthorized location tracking	9	Troubleshooting Mobile Devices
- Unauthorized camera/microphone activation	9	Troubleshooting Mobile Devices
- High resource utilization	9	Troubleshooting Mobile Devices

4.0 OPERATIONAL PROCEDURES

4.1 Compare and contrast best practices associated with types of documentation.

Objectives	Chapter	Primary Section
• Network topology diagrams	8	Best Practices for Documentation and Security Policies
• Knowledge base/articles	8	Best Practices for Documentation and Security Policies
• Incident documentation	8	Best Practices for Documentation and Security Policies
• Regulatory and compliance policy	8	Best Practices for Documentation and Security Policies
• Acceptable use policy	8	Best Practices for Documentation and Security Policies
• Password policy	8	Best Practices for Documentation and Security Policies
• Inventory management	8	Best Practices for Documentation and Security Policies
- Asset tags	8	Best Practices for Documentation and Security Policies
- Barcodes	8	Best Practices for Documentation and Security Policies

4.2 Given a scenario, implement basic change management best practices.

Objectives	Chapter	Primary Section
• Documented business processes	8	Best Practices for Documentation and Security Policies
• Purpose of the change	8	Best Practices for Documentation and Security Policies
• Scope the change	8	Best Practices for Documentation and Security Policies
• Risk analysis	8	Best Practices for Documentation and Security Policies
• Plan for change	8	Best Practices for Documentation and Security Policies
• End-user acceptance	8	Best Practices for Documentation and Security Policies
• Change board	8	Best Practices for Documentation and Security Policies
- Approvals	8	Best Practices for Documentation and Security Policies
• Backout plan	8	Best Practices for Documentation and Security Policies
• Document changes	8	Best Practices for Documentation and Security Policies

4.3 Given a scenario, implement basic disaster prevention and recovery methods.

Objectives	Chapter	Primary Section
• Backup and recovery	4	Backup Procedures
- Image level	4	Backup Procedures
- File level	4	Backup Procedures
- Critical applications	4	Backup Procedures
• Backup testing	4	Backup Procedures
• UPS	4	Backup Procedures
• Surge protector	4	Backup Procedures
• Cloud storage vs. local storage backups	4	Backup Procedures
• Account recovery options	6	Troubleshooting Specific Windows Startup Problems

4.4 Explain common safety procedures.

Objectives	Chapter	Primary Section
• Equipment grounding	Apx A	Protecting the Equipment
• Proper component handling and storage	Apx A	Protecting the Equipment
- Antistatic bags	Apx A	Protecting the Equipment
- ESD straps	Apx A	Protecting the Equipment
- ESD mats	Apx A	Protecting the Equipment
- Self-grounding	Apx A	Protecting the Equipment
• Toxic waste handling	Apx A	Protecting the Environment
- Batteries	Apx A	Protecting the Environment
- Toner	Apx A	Protecting the Environment
- CRT	Apx A	Protecting the Environment
- Cell phones	Apx A	Protecting the Environment
- Tablets	Apx A	Protecting the Environment
• Personal safety	Apx A	Protecting Yourself
- Disconnect power before repairing PC	Apx A	Protecting Yourself
- Remove jewelry	Apx A	Protecting Yourself
- Lifting techniques	Apx A	Protecting Yourself
- Weight limitations	Apx A	Protecting Yourself
- Electrical fire safety	Apx A	Protecting Yourself
- Cable management	Apx A	Protecting Yourself
- Safety goggles	Apx A	Protecting Yourself
- Air filter mask	Apx A	Protecting Yourself
• Compliance with government regulations	Apx A	Protecting the Environment

4.5 Explain environmental impacts and appropriate controls.

Objectives	Chapter	Primary Section
• MSDS documentation for handling and disposal	Apx A	Protecting the Environment
• Temperature, humidity level awareness, and proper ventilation	Apx A	Protecting the Equipment
• Power surges, brownouts, and blackouts	Apx A	Protecting the Equipment
- Battery backup	Apx A	Protecting the Equipment
- Surge suppressor	Apx A	Protecting the Equipment
• Protection from airborne particles	Apx A	Protecting the Equipment
- Enclosures	Apx A	Protecting the Equipment
- Air filters/mask	Apx A	Protecting Yourself
• Dust and debris	Apx A	Protecting the Equipment
- Compressed air	Apx A	Protecting the Equipment
- Vacuums	Apx A	Protecting the Equipment
• Compliance to government regulations	Apx A	Protecting the Environment

4.6 Explain the processes for addressing prohibited content/activity, and privacy, licensing, and policy concepts.

Objectives	Chapter	Primary Section
• Incident response	8	Best Practices for Documentation and Security Policies
- First response	8	Best Practices for Documentation and Security Policies
○ Identify	8	Best Practices for Documentation and Security Policies
○ Report through proper channels	8	Best Practices for Documentation and Security Policies
○ Data/device preservation	8	Best Practices for Documentation and Security Policies

Objectives	Chapter	Primary Section
- Use of documentation/documentation changes	8	Best Practices for Documentation and Security Policies
- Chain of custody	8	Best Practices for Documentation and Security Policies
○ Tracking of evidence/documenting process	8	Best Practices for Documentation and Security Policies
• Licensing/DRM/EULA	8	Best Practices for Documentation and Security Policies
- Open-source vs. commercial license	8	Best Practices for Documentation and Security Policies
- Personal license vs. enterprise licenses	8	Best Practices for Documentation and Security Policies
• Regulated data	8	Best Practices for Documentation and Security Policies
- PII	8	Best Practices for Documentation and Security Policies
- PCI	8	Best Practices for Documentation and Security Policies
- GDPR	8	Best Practices for Documentation and Security Policies
- PHI	8	Best Practices for Documentation and Security Policies
• Follow all policies and security best practices	8	Best Practices for Documentation and Security Policies

4.7 Given a scenario, use proper communication techniques and professionalism.

Objectives	Chapter	Primary Section
• Use proper language and avoid jargon, acronyms, and slang, when applicable	1	What Customers Want: Beyond Technical Know-How
• Maintain a positive attitude/project confidence	1	What Customers Want: Beyond Technical Know-How
• Actively listen (taking notes) and avoid interrupting the customer	1	What Customers Want: Beyond Technical Know-How
• Be culturally sensitive	1	What Customers Want: Beyond Technical Know-How
- Use appropriate professional titles, when applicable	1	What Customers Want: Beyond Technical Know-How
• Be on time (if late, contact the customer)	1	What Customers Want: Beyond Technical Know-How
• Avoid distractions	1	What Customers Want: Beyond Technical Know-How
- Personal calls	1	What Customers Want: Beyond Technical Know-How
- Texting/social media sites	1	What Customers Want: Beyond Technical Know-How
- Talking to coworkers while interacting with customers	1	What Customers Want: Beyond Technical Know-How
- Personal interruptions	1	What Customers Want: Beyond Technical Know-How
• Dealing with difficult customers or situations	1	What Customers Want: Beyond Technical Know-How
- Do not argue with customers and/or be defensive	1	What Customers Want: Beyond Technical Know-How
- Avoid dismissing customer problems	1	What Customers Want: Beyond Technical Know-How
- Avoid being judgmental		
- Clarify customer statements (ask open-ended questions to narrow the scope of the problem, restate the issue, or question to verify understanding)	1	What Customers Want: Beyond Technical Know-How
- Do not disclose experiences via social media outlets	1	What Customers Want: Beyond Technical Know-How
• Set and meet expectations/timeline and communicate status with the customer	1	What Customers Want: Beyond Technical Know-How
- Offer different repair/replacement options, if applicable	1	What Customers Want: Beyond Technical Know-How
- Provide proper documentation on the services provided	1	What Customers Want: Beyond Technical Know-How
- Follow up with customer/user at a later date to verify satisfaction	1	What Customers Want: Beyond Technical Know-How
• Deal appropriately with customers' confidential and private materials	1	What Customers Want: Beyond Technical Know-How
- Located on a computer, desktop, printer, etc.	1	What Customers Want: Beyond Technical Know-How

4.8 Identify the basics of scripting.

Objectives	Chapter	Primary Section
• Script file types	10	Scripting Software and Techniques
- .bat	10	Scripting Software and Techniques
- .ps1	10	Scripting Software and Techniques
- .vbs	10	Scripting Software and Techniques
- .sh	10	Scripting Software and Techniques
- .py	10	Scripting Software and Techniques
- .js	10	Scripting Software and Techniques
• Environment variables	10	Scripting Software and Techniques
• Comment syntax	10	Scripting Software and Techniques
• Basic script constructs	10	Scripting Software and Techniques
- Basic loops	10	Scripting Software and Techniques
- Variables	10	Scripting Software and Techniques
• Basic data types	10	Scripting Software and Techniques
- Integers	10	Scripting Software and Techniques
- Strings	10	Scripting Software and Techniques

4.9 Given a scenario, use remote access technologies.

Objectives	Chapter	Primary Section
• RDP	14	Remote Connections
• Telnet	10	Linux Operating System
• SSH	10	Linux Operating System
• Third-party tools	10	Linux Operating System
- Screen share feature	10	Linux Operating System
- File share	10	Linux Operating System
• Security considerations of each access method	10	Linux Operating System

Introduction: CompTIA A+ Core 2 Exam Guide to Operating Systems and Security

CompTIA A+ Core 2 Exam Guide to Operating Systems and Security, Tenth Edition was written to be the very best tool on the market today to prepare you to support users and their resources on networks, desktops, laptops, mobile devices, virtual machines, and in the cloud. The text has been updated to include the most current hardware and software technologies; this book takes you from the just-a-user level to the I-can-fix-this level for software, networks, and virtual computing infrastructures. It achieves its goals with an unusually effective combination of tools that powerfully reinforce both concepts and hands-on, real-world experiences. It also provides thorough preparation for the content on the new CompTIA A+ Core 2 Certification exam. Competency in using a computer is a prerequisite to using this book. No background knowledge of electronics or networking is assumed. An appropriate prerequisite course for this book would be a general course in computer applications.

This book includes:

- *Several in-depth, hands-on projects* at the end of each chapter that invite you to immediately apply and reinforce critical thinking and troubleshooting skills and are designed to make certain that you not only understand the material, but also execute procedures and make decisions on your own.
- *Comprehensive review and practice end-of-chapter material*, including a chapter summary, key terms list, critical thinking questions that focus on the type of scenarios you might expect on A+ exam questions, and real-world problems to solve.
- *Step-by-step instructions* on installation, maintenance, optimization of system performance, and troubleshooting.
- A *wide array of photos, drawings, and screenshots* support the text, displaying in detail the exact software and hardware features you will need to understand to set up, maintain, and troubleshoot physical and virtual computers and small networks.

In addition, the carefully structured, clearly written text is accompanied by graphics that provide the visual input essential to learning and to help students master difficult subject matter. For instructors using the book in a classroom, instructor resources are available online.

Coverage is balanced—while focusing on new technologies and software, including virtualization, cloud computing, the Internet of Things, and Windows 10, the text also covers the real world of an IT support technician, where some older technologies remain in widespread use and still need support. For example, the text focuses on Windows 10, the most popular OS for desktops and laptops, but also covers Windows 8/7, macOS, and Linux for desktops, and Android, iOS, Windows Mobile, and Chrome OS for mobile devices. Other covered content that is new with the A+ Core 2 exam includes change management best practices, scripting, SSH, and Windows Server Active Directory.

This book provides thorough preparation for CompTIA's A+ Core 2 Certification examination. This certification credential's popularity among employers is growing exponentially, and obtaining certification increases your ability to gain employment and improve your salary. To get more information on CompTIA's A+ certification and its sponsoring organization, the Computing Technology Industry Association, see their website at *www.comptia.org*.

FEATURES

To ensure a successful learning experience, this book includes the following pedagogical features:

- ▲ *Learning Objectives.* Every chapter opens with a list of learning objectives that sets the stage for you to absorb the lessons of the text.
- ▲ *Comprehensive Step-by-Step Troubleshooting Guidance.* Troubleshooting guidelines are included in almost every chapter. In addition, Chapter 5 focuses on troubleshooting Windows after startup; Chapter 6 covers troubleshooting Windows problems that occur during startup, and Chapter 9 covers troubleshooting mobile devices.
- ▲ *Step-by-Step Procedures.* The book is chock-full of step-by-step procedures covering subjects from operating system installations and maintenance to troubleshooting the boot process or a failed network connection and optimizing system performance.
- ▲ *Visual Learning.* Numerous visually detailed photographs, three-dimensional art, and screenshots support the text, displaying hardware and software features exactly as you will see them in your work.
- ▲ *CompTIA A+ Table of Contents.* This table of contents gives the chapter and section that provides the primary content for each certification objective on the A+ Core 2 exam. This is a valuable tool for quick reference.
- ▲ *Applying Concepts.* These sections offer real-life, practical applications for the material being discussed. Whether outlining a task, developing a scenario, or providing pointers, the Applying Concepts sections give you a chance to apply what you've learned to a typical computer or network problem, so you can understand how you will use the material in your professional life.

A+ Icons. All of the content that relates to CompTIA's A+ Core 2 Certification exam is highlighted with a blue A+ icon. The icon notes the exam name and the objective number. This unique feature highlights the relevant content at a glance, so that you can pay extra attention to the material. Content that also applies to the A+ Core 1 (220-1001) exam is highlighted with a green A+ icon.

Notes. Note icons highlight additional helpful information related to the subject being discussed.

A+ Exam Tip Boxes. These boxes highlight additional insights and tips to remember if you are planning to take the CompTIA A+ exams.

Caution Icons. These icons highlight critical safety information. Follow these instructions carefully to protect the computer and its data and to ensure your own safety.

OS Differences. These boxes point you to the differences among Windows 10, Windows 8, and Windows 7.

- ▲ *End-of-Chapter Material.* Each chapter closes with the following features, which reinforce the material covered in the chapter and provide real-world, hands-on testing:
  - ▲ *Chapter Summary:* This bulleted list of concise statements summarizes all major points of the chapter.

▲ *Key Terms:* The content of each chapter is further reinforced by an end-of-chapter key term list. The definitions of all terms are included with this text in a full-length glossary.

▲ *Thinking Critically Questions:* You can test your understanding of each chapter with a comprehensive set of "Thinking Critically" questions to help you synthesize and apply what you've learned in scenarios that test your skills at the same depth as the A+ exam.

▲ *Hands-On Projects:* These sections give you practice using the skills you have just studied so that you can learn by doing and know you have mastered a skill.

▲ *Real Problems, Real Solutions:* Each comprehensive problem allows you to find out if you can apply what you've learned in the chapter to a real-life situation.

▲ *Student Companion Site.* Additional content included on the companion website includes Electricity and Multimeters, and FAT Details. Other helpful online references include Frequently Asked Questions, and a Computer Inventory and Maintenance form.

WHAT'S NEW IN THE TENTH EDITION

Here's a summary of what's new in the *Tenth Edition*:

▲ Content maps to all of CompTIA's A+ Core 2 exam.

▲ There is now more focus on A+, with non-A+ content moved online to the companion website or eliminated.

▲ The chapters focus on Windows 10 with some content about Windows 8/7.

▲ New content is added (all new content was also new to the A+ Core 2 exam).

   ▲ Windows 10 is added. Operating systems covered now include Windows 10, Windows 8, and Windows 7. New content on Linux, macOS, and mobile operating systems (Android, iOS, Windows Phone, and Chrome OS) is added.

   ▲ New content on Active Directory Domain Services is covered in Chapter 7.

   ▲ New content on understanding and writing scripts is covered in Chapter 10.

   ▲ Enhanced content on supporting mobile devices (including the Android OS, iOS, Windows Phone, and Chrome OS) is covered in Chapter 9.

   ▲ Hands-On Projects in several chapters use virtual machines so that you get plenty of practice using this essential cloud technology.

   ▲ New content on change management, network topology diagrams, regulatory and compliance policies, acceptable use policies, inventory management, and regulated data is covered in Chapter 8.

   ▲ The Internet of Things (IoT) and how to set up a smart home are covered in Chapter 9.

   ▲ Content on supporting and troubleshooting laptops is integrated throughout the text.

FEATURES OF THE NEW EDITION

Chapter **objectives** appear at the beginning of each chapter, so you know exactly what topics and skills are covered.

A+ Exam Tips include key points pertinent to the A+ exams. The icons identify the sections that cover information you will need to know for the A+ certification exams.

CHAPTER 7

Setting Up a Local Network

After completing this chapter, you will be able to:

- Describe network types and the Internet connections they use
- Connect a computer to a wired or wireless network
- Configure and secure a multifunction router on a local network
- Troubleshoot network

In this chapter, you learn about the types of networks and the technologies used to build networks. You also learn to connect a computer to a network and how to set up and secure a small wired or wireless network.

This chapter prepares you to assume total responsibility for supporting both wired and wireless networks in a small office/home office (SOHO) environment. Later, you'll learn more about the hardware used in networking, including network devices, connectors, cabling, networking tools, and the types of networks used for Internet connections. Let's get started by looking at the types of networks you might encounter as an IT support technician and the types of connections they might use to connect to the Internet.

★ **A+ Exam Tip** Much of the content in this chapter applies to both the A+ Core 1 220-1001 exam and the A+ Core 2 220-1002 exam.

⚡ **Caution** If sensitive data is on the hard drive, know that a quick or full format will not actually erase this data from the drive; hackers have been known to be able to read such data even after the volume is formatted. To actually erase the data, you can use a zero-fill utility available from hard drive manufacturers. This software overwrites everything on the drive with zeroes. You learn more about zero-fill utilities in Chapter 8.

>> HANDS-ON PROJECTS

Hands-On | Project 1-1 Practicing Using the Quick Launch Menu

Do the following to practice using the Quick Launch menu:

1. Click the **Power** icon on the Start menu. What are the options on the Power icon menu?
2. Open the **Quick Launch** menu, and practice using several options on the menu. What are the submenu items that appear when you point to *Shut down or sign out*?
3. Click **Power Options** on the Quick Launch menu. The Settings app opens to the Power & sleep page. Sometimes you need to use links in the Settings app to navigate to the control panel applets and find more options. Find the settings in the Power Options window that allow you to change the options available in the *Shut down or sign out* menu.
4. Go to the **Start** menu. Click your account icon on the left side of the Start menu. What options appear in the drop-down menu? Try the Lock and Sign out options, and describe what each option does.

Hands-On | Project 1-2 Creating Shortcuts

Do the following to practice creating shortcuts on the Windows desktop:

1. Open Windows 10/8 File Explorer or Windows 7 Windows Explorer and create a folder called **Temp** under the root directory of the hard drive. List the steps you took.
2. Add a subfolder to Temp called **MyFiles**. List the steps you took.
3. Create a text file named **Text1.txt** in the MyFiles folder. List the steps you took.

Cautions identify critical safety information.

Hands-On Projects provide practical exercises at the end of each chapter so that you can practice the skills as they are learned.

Notes indicate additional content that might be of student interest or information about how best to study.

APPLYING | CONCEPTS   SELF-CONTROL

Jack had a bad day on the phones at the networking help desk in Atlanta. An electrical outage coupled with a generator failure had caused servers in San Francisco to be down most of the day. The entire help-desk team had been fielding calls all day explaining to customers why they did not have service and giving expected recovery times. The servers were finally online, but it was taking hours to get everything reset and functioning. No one had taken a break all afternoon, but the call queue was still running about 20 minutes behind. Todd, the boss, had asked the team to work late until the queue was empty. It was Jack's son's birthday and his family was expecting Jack home on time. Jack moaned as he realized he might be late for Tyler's party. Everyone pushed hard to empty the queue. As Jack watched the last call leave the queue, he logged off, stood up, and reached for his coat.

> 📝 **Notes** These instructions assume you are using a mouse and keyboard. If you're using a touch screen, simply tap instead of clicking, press and hold instead of right-clicking, double-tap instead of double-clicking, and swipe to scroll the screen to the right, left, up, or down.

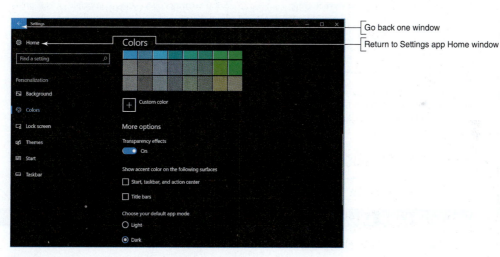

Figure 1-39   Dark app mode is ideal for low-light conditions

Applying Concepts sections provide practical advice or pointers by illustrating basic principles, identifying common problems, providing steps to practice skills, and encouraging solutions.

Visual full-color graphics, photos, and screenshots accurately depict computer hardware and software components.

Chapter Summary bulleted lists of concise statements summarize all major points of the chapter, organized by primary headings.

>> CHAPTER SUMMARY

Securing a Windows Personal Computer

▲ A long password is a strong password.

▲ Use Local Group Policies (gpedit.msc) and Local Security Policies (secpol.msc) to secure a Windows computer.

▲ The Internet Options dialog box is used to manage many Internet Explorer settings. Proxy settings are managed using the Connections tab, and add-ons are managed using the Programs tab.

▲ Encrypting File System (EFS) encrypts files and folders on an NTFS file system. BitLocker Drive Encryption encrypts an entire volume on a hard drive. Both are available on business and professional editions of Windows.

>> KEY TERMS

For explanations of key terms, see the Glossary for this text.

Active Directory (AD)	Everyone group	Local Security Policy	principle of least privilege
Active Directory Domain Services (AD DS)	folder redirection	local shares	privileges
ActiveX control	forest	Local Users and Groups	Remote Admin share
administrative shares	gpresult	mapping	Resultant Set of Policy (RSoP)
Administrators group	gpupdate	multifactor authentication (MFA)	Server Manager
Anonymous users	Group Policy	Network File System (NFS)	share permissions
Authenticated Users group	Group Policy Object (GPO)	Network Places Wizard	strong password
BitLocker Drive Encryption	Guests group	network share	Sync Center
BitLocker To Go	hidden share	NTFS permissions	TPM (Trusted Platform Module)
brute force attack	Home folder	organizational unit (OU)	Users group
defense in depth	inherited permissions	permission propagation	Windows Firewall
Encrypting File System (EFS)	Internet Options	permissions	
	Local Group Policy	Power Users group	

>> THINKING CRITICALLY

These questions are designed to prepare you for the critical thinking required for the A+ exams and may use content from other chapters and the web.

1. Your organization has set up three levels of classification for data accessed by users on a small network:
   ▲ Low security: Data in the C:\Public folder
   ▲ Medium security: Data in a shared folder that some, but not all, user groups can access
   ▲ High security: Data in a shared and encrypted folder that requires a password to access. The folder is shared only to one user group.

Key Terms are defined as they are introduced and listed at the end of each chapter. Definitions can be found in the Glossary.

Thinking Critically sections require you to analyze and apply what you've learned.

>> REAL PROBLEMS, REAL SOLUTIONS

REAL PROBLEM 1-1 Using Windows Help and Support

The best IT support technicians are the ones who continually teach themselves new skills. You can teach yourself to use and support Windows by using the web, a couple of apps in Windows 10 called Get Help and Tips, or the Windows Help and Support utility in Windows 8/7. To start the apps in Windows 10, type **get help** in the search box or type **tips** in the search box. In Windows 8, type **Help and Support** on the Start screen. In Windows 7, click **Start** and then click **Help and Support**. If you are connected to the Internet, clicking links can take you to the Microsoft website, where you can find information and watch videos about Windows.

Do the following to research a topic so you can become an independent learner about Windows:

1. The Windows 10/8/7 Snipping Tool can help you take screenshots of the Windows desktop. These screenshots are useful when documenting computer problems and solutions. Use Get Help or Windows Help and Support to find out how to use the Snipping Tool. Use it to take a screenshot of your Windows desktop. Save the screenshot into a file on a USB flash drive or on the hard drive. Print the file contents.

2. Access the *support.microsoft.com* website for Windows support. Save or print one article from the Knowledge Base that addresses a problem when installing Windows 10/8/7.

3. Search the web to learn the purpose of the pagefile.sys file. What website did you use to find your answer? Why is the Microsoft website considered the best source for information about the pagefile.sys file?

REAL PROBLEM 1-2 Documenting How to Use Windows

This problem requires a microphone, and a webcam would also be useful. Make a screen recording with a voiceover to teach end users how to use Windows. Do the following:

1. Screencast-O-Matic offers free software to make a screen recording with voice and video. Go to *screencast-o-matic.com* and launch the online video recording software. You might be required to download and install the software.

2. Select a Windows feature to explain. For example, you can explain how to open and close an app, install or uninstall an app, create a shortcut, empty the Recycle Bin, or use the Start menu. You or your instructor might have other ideas.

3. Use the Screencast-O-Matic software to make a screen recording that explains how to use the Windows feature you selected. The recording should be no longer than three minutes. Explain the steps as you go. The software records your screen movements, your voice if a microphone is detected, and video if a webcam is detected.

4. View the video. If you see a problem, record it again. When you're satisfied with your video, save it as an MP4 file.

Real Problems, Real Solutions allow you to apply what you've learned in the chapter to a real-life situation.

WHAT'S NEW WITH COMPTIA® A+ CERTIFICATION

The CompTIA A+ certification includes two exams, and you must pass both to become CompTIA A+ certified. The two exams are Core 1 (220-1001) and Core 2 (220-1002).

Here is a breakdown of the domain content covered on the two A+ exams.

This text covers content on the Core 2 (220-1002) exam. Content on the Core 1 (220-1001) exam is covered in the companion text, *CompTIA A+ Exam Guide to Computing Infrastructure*.

CompTIA A+ 220-1001 Exam	
Domain	**Percentage of Examination**
1.0 Mobile Devices	14%
2.0 Networking	20%
3.0 Hardware	27%
4.0 Virtualization and Cloud Computing	12%
5.0 Hardware and Network Troubleshooting	27%
Total	100%

CompTIA A+ 220-1002 Exam	
Domain	**Percentage of Examination**
1.0 Operating Systems	27%
2.0 Security	24%
3.0 Software Troubleshooting	26%
4.0 Operational Procedures	23%
Total	100%

INSTRUCTOR'S MATERIALS

Please visit *cengage.com* and log in to access instructor-specific resources on the Instructor Companion Site, which includes the Instructor's Manual, Solutions Manual, Test creation tools, PowerPoint Presentation, Syllabus, and figure files.

Instructor's Manual: The Instructor's Manual that accompanies this textbook includes additional instructional material to assist in class preparation, including suggestions for classroom activities, discussion topics, and additional projects.

Solutions: Answers to the end-of-chapter material are provided. These include the answers to the Thinking Critically questions and to the Hands-On Projects (when applicable), as well as Lab Manual Solutions.

Cengage Learning Testing Powered by Cognero: This flexible, online system allows you to do the following:
- Author, edit, and manage test bank content from multiple Cengage Learning solutions.
- Create multiple test versions in an instant.
- Deliver tests from your LMS, your classroom, or wherever you want.

PowerPoint Presentations: This book comes with Microsoft PowerPoint slides for each chapter. These are included as a teaching aid for classroom presentation, to make available to students on the network for chapter review, or to be printed for classroom distribution. Instructors, please feel at liberty to add your own slides for additional topics you introduce to the class.

Figure Files: All of the figures in the book are reproduced on the Instructor Companion Site. Similar to the PowerPoint presentations, these are included as a teaching aid for classroom presentation, to make available to students for review, or to be printed for classroom distribution.

TOTAL SOLUTIONS FOR COMPTIA A+

MINDTAP FOR A+ CORE 2 EXAM GUIDE TO OPERATING SYSTEMS AND SECURITY, TENTH EDITION

MindTap is an online learning solution designed to help students master the skills they need in today's workforce. Research shows employers need critical thinkers, troubleshooters, and creative problem-solvers to stay relevant in our fast-paced, technology-driven world. MindTap helps you achieve this with assignments and activities that provide hands-on practice, real-life relevance, and certification test prep. Students are guided through assignments that help them master basic knowledge and understanding before moving on to more challenging problems.

MindTap activities and assignments are tied to CompTIA A+ certification exam objectives. Live, virtual machine labs allow learners to practice, explore, and try different solutions in a safe, sandbox environment using real Cisco hardware and virtualized Windows, Linux, and UNIX operating systems. The Adaptive Test Prep (ATP) app is designed to help learners quickly review and assess their understanding of key IT concepts. Learners have the ability to test themselves multiple times to track their progress and improvement. The app allows them to filter results by correct answers, by all questions answered, or only by incorrect answers to show where additional study help is needed.

You can test students' knowledge and understanding with graded pre- and post-assessments that emulate the A+ certification exams. Module tests and review quizzes also help you gauge students' mastery of the course topics.

Readings and videos support the lecture, while "In The News" assignments encourage students to stay current with what's happening in the IT field. Reflection activities require students to problem-solve for a real-life issue they would encounter on the job and participate in a class discussion to learn how their peers dealt with the same challenge.

MindTap is designed around learning objectives and provides the analytics and reporting so you can easily see where the class stands in terms of progress, engagement, and completion rates. Use the content and learning path as is or pick and choose how our materials will wrap around yours. You control what the students see and when they see it. Learn more at *http://www.cengage.com/mindtap/*.

- ◢ Instant Access Code: (ISBN: 9780357108314)
- ◢ Printed Access Code: (ISBN: 9780357108321)

LAB MANUAL FOR A+ CORE 2 EXAM GUIDE TO OPERATING SYSTEMS AND SECURITY, TENTH EDITION

The Lab Manual, now part of your MindTap course, contains over 120 labs to provide students with additional hands-on experience and to help prepare for the A+ exam. The Lab Manual includes lab activities, objectives, materials lists, step-by-step procedures, illustrations, and review questions.

ACKNOWLEDGMENTS

Thank you to the wonderful people at Cengage who continue to give their best and go the extra mile to make the books what they are: Kristin McNary, Amy Savino, and Brooke Greenhouse. We're grateful for all you've done. Thank you, Dan Seiter, our Developmental Editor extraordinaire, for upholding us with your unwavering, calm demeanor in the face of impossible schedules and inboxes, and to Karen Annett, our excellent copyeditor/proofreader. Thank you, Danielle Shaw, for your careful attention to the technical accuracy of the book.

Thank you to all the people who took the time to voluntarily send encouragement and suggestions for improvements to the previous editions. Your input and help is very much appreciated. The reviewers of this edition provided invaluable insights and showed a genuine interest in the book's success. Thank you to:

Craig Brigman – Liberty University

Kimberly Perez – Tidewater Community College

To the instructors and learners who use this book, we invite and encourage you to send suggestions or corrections for future editions. Please write to the author team at *jean.andrews@cengage.com*. We never ignore a good idea! And to instructors, if you have ideas for how to make a class in A+ Preparation a success, please share your ideas with other instructors! You can find us on Facebook at *http://www.facebook.com/JeanKnows*, where you can interact with the authors and other instructors.

This book is dedicated to the covenant of God with man on earth.

Jean Andrews, Ph.D.

Joy Dark

Jill West

ABOUT THE AUTHORS

Jean Andrews has more than 30 years of experience in the computer industry, including more than 13 years in the college classroom. She has worked in a variety of businesses and corporations designing, writing, and supporting application software; managing a help desk for computer support technicians; and troubleshooting wide area networks. She has written numerous books on software, hardware, and the Internet, including the best-selling *CompTIA A+ Core 1 Exam Guide to Computing Infrastructure, Tenth Edition,* and *CompTIA A+ Core 2 Exam Guide to Operating Systems and Security, Tenth Edition.* She lives in northern Georgia.

Joy Dark has worked in the IT field as a help-desk technician providing first-level support for a company with presence in 29 states, a second-tier technician in healthcare IT, and an operations specialist designing support protocols and structures. As a teacher, Joy has taught online courses in IT and has taught English as a Second Language in the United States and South America. She has helped write several technical textbooks with Jean Andrews. She also creates many photographs used in educational content. Joy lives in northwest Georgia with her two daughters and Doberman dog.

Jill West has taught K thru college using a flipped classroom approach, distance learning, hybrid teaching, and educational counseling. She currently teaches computer technology courses at Georgia Northwestern Technical College, both online and in the classroom. She regularly presents on CompTIA certification courses at state and national conferences and international webinars. Jill and her husband Mike live in northwest Georgia, where they homeschool their four children.

READ THIS BEFORE YOU BEGIN

The following hardware, software, and other equipment are needed to do the Hands-On Projects in each chapter:

- ▲ You need a working computer on which you can install an operating system.
- ▲ Troubleshooting skills can better be practiced with an assortment of nonworking expansion cards that can be used to simulate problems.
- ▲ Windows 10 Pro is needed for most chapters. In addition, macOS is used in Chapter 10.
- ▲ Internet access is needed for most chapters.
- ▲ An iOS or Android smartphone or tablet is needed for Chapter 9.
- ▲ A SOHO router that includes a wireless access point is needed for Chapter 3.

> ⚡ **Caution** Before undertaking any of the lab exercises, starting with Chapter 1, please review the safety guidelines in Appendix A.

Windows Versions and Customer Service

After completing this chapter, you will be able to:

- Use Windows to interface with users, files and folders, applications, and hardware
- Use Windows tools to explore, examine, and support the system
- Explain the various ways Windows secures resources on the network and secures a network connection
- Support customers with professionalism and respect, in addition to your technical skills

Like many other computer users, you have probably used your personal computer to play games, update your Facebook profile, write papers, or build Excel worksheets. This text takes you from being an end user of your computer to becoming an information technology (IT) support technician able to support all types of personal computers. The only assumption made here is that you are a computer user—that is, you can turn on your machine, load a software package, and use that software to accomplish a task. No experience in electronics is assumed.

As an IT support technician, you'll want to become A+ certified, which is the industry standard certification for IT support technicians. This text prepares you to pass the A+ 220-1002 Core 2 exam by CompTIA (*comptia.org*). Its accompanying text, "CompTIA A+ Core 1 Exam Guide to Computing Infrastructure," prepares you to pass the A+ 220-1001 Core 1 exam. Both exams are required by CompTIA for A+ certification.

In this chapter, you learn about the versions of Microsoft Windows and how this operating system provides an interface between users and applications and between applications and hardware devices. You learn to use several Windows tools and utilities that are useful to view and manage storage devices, examine a system, and troubleshoot simple problems with hardware and applications. Finally, you learn about interpersonal skills (people skills, sometimes called soft skills) needed by an IT support technician.

★ **A+ Exam Tip** In this text, you learn about Windows 10, Windows 8.1, Windows 8.0, and Windows 7. All these operating systems are covered on the A+ Core 2 exam. In the text, we use Windows 8 to refer to Windows 8.0 and Windows 8.1.

WINDOWS INTERFACES

**A+
CORE 2
1.2**

An operating system (OS) is software that controls a computer. In general, you can think of an operating system as the middleman between applications and hardware, between the user and hardware, and between the user and applications (see Figure 1-1).

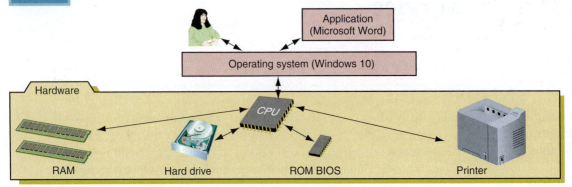

Figure 1-1   Users and applications depend on the OS to relate to all applications and hardware components

Several applications might be installed on a computer to meet various user needs, but a computer really needs only one operating system. Although there are important differences among them, all operating systems share the following four main functions:

▲ *Function 1:* Provide a user interface

    ▲ Performing storage and housekeeping procedures requested by the user, such as reorganizing a hard drive, deleting files, copying files, and changing the system date

    ▲ Providing a way for the user to manage the desktop, hardware, applications, and data

▲ *Function 2:* Manage files

    ▲ Managing files on hard drives, DVD drives, CD drives, USB flash drives, and other drives

    ▲ Creating, storing, retrieving, deleting, and moving files

▲ *Function 3:* Manage hardware

    ▲ Managing the BIOS/UEFI (programs permanently stored on hardware devices)

    ▲ Managing memory, which is a temporary place to store data and instructions as they are being processed

    ▲ Diagnosing problems with software and hardware

    ▲ Interfacing between hardware and software (that is, interpreting application software needs to the hardware and vice versa)

▲ *Function 4:* Manage applications

    ▲ Installing and uninstalling applications

    ▲ Running applications and managing the interface to the hardware on behalf of an application

Windows 10 is the latest Microsoft operating system and is an upgrade to Windows 8, which was preceded by Windows 7. Windows 8.1 is a free update or release of the original Windows 8. Every IT support technician needs to be a power user of Windows 10 and familiar with Windows 8/7.

> ✎ **Notes** This chapter assumes Windows 10 is already installed on your computer, and it would be helpful if you have access to the Windows 8 and Windows 7 operating systems as you work your way through this chapter. If Windows is not yet installed, read Chapter 2 and install Windows 10, 8, or 7. Then you can return to this chapter to learn how to use the OS.

Every Windows OS offers a **graphical user interface (GUI**; pronounced "GOO-ee") that uses graphics instead of a command-driven interface. Windows 10 offers two graphical user interfaces—the desktop and Tablet mode via a feature called Continuum. Windows 8 has two graphical user interfaces—the modern interface and the desktop. Windows 7 offers one graphical user interface, the desktop. We next examine these interfaces.

> ✎ **Notes** The figures and steps in this text use Windows 10 Professional, Windows 8.1 Professional, and Windows 7 Professional. If you are using a different edition of Windows 10, 8, or 7, your screens and steps may differ slightly from those presented here.

WINDOWS 10 INTERFACE

A+
CORE 2
1.2

Let's take a quick look at the Windows 10 desktop and Start menu, as well as other features you'll find useful when supporting Windows 10.

WINDOWS 10 DESKTOP

The application and utility hub in Windows 10 is the Start menu on the desktop (see Figure 1-2). Tools used by technicians to support, secure, and troubleshoot Windows, as well as productivity software such as Microsoft Office, QuickBooks, and Dreamweaver, can be accessed from the Start menu, desktop, and taskbar. The **taskbar** is normally located at the bottom of the Windows desktop, displaying information about open programs and providing quick access to others. By default, Windows 10 pins the Task View, Microsoft Edge, File Explorer, and Store icons in the Quick Launch toolbar on the left side of the taskbar. Click an icon to open the program. An open application displays a program icon in the taskbar to the right of the toolbar; if a pinned application is open, it is underlined.

Figure 1-2 Windows 10 uses a Start menu with live tiles

The Windows 10 Start menu has **live tiles** on the right side of the menu that offer continuous real-time updates. Click a tile or program name to open its app. The left side of the Start menu includes lists of: (1) recently added apps, if there are any, (2) apps used most often, (3) suggested apps for downloading from the Windows Store, and (4) an alphabetical list of all apps available on the computer. To expand the view of the links on the left side of the Start menu, click the three horizontal bars (sometimes called a hamburger button) at the top-left corner of the menu, as shown in Figure 1-2.

The bottom-left corner of the Start menu has a few icons that you can use to access important functions. Click the **Account** icon to change account settings, lock Windows, or sign out of Windows. Other icons allow you to access File Explorer, the Settings app, and the Power menu. Click the **Power** icon to put the computer in sleep mode, shut it down, or restart.

> ✎ **Notes** To customize the Start menu, open the Start menu and click the **Settings app** icon. In the Settings app, open the **Personalization** group and select **Start**. If you prefer to use the Windows 8 Start screen in Windows 10, apply the full-screen Start menu option in the Personalization group of the Settings app.

The notification area, also called the system tray or systray, is located on the right side of the taskbar by default and displays open services. A service is a program that runs in the background to support or serve Windows or an application. The services in the notification area include the volume or sound control and network connectivity.

To launch a program from the desktop, use one of these methods:

▲ *Start menu.* Click the **Start** button and find the program in the list of all programs on the left, or find the pinned app or a live tile on the right. To pin an app to the Start menu, find the app in the alphabetical apps list, right-click the app tile, and click **Pin to Start**. To unpin an app from the Start menu, right-click the pinned app tile and click **Unpin from Start**.

▲ *Windows 10 search box with Cortana.* Cortana is the new voice-enabled search feature of Windows 10 and is accessed using the search box on the taskbar (shown earlier in Figure 1-2). If you know the name of the program file, you can type that name in the search box and press **Enter**, or click the microphone button to the right of the search box and then say the command to Cortana. For example, the program name of the Notepad text editor is notepad.exe. When you type **notepad** in the search box and press **Enter**, the Notepad window opens. (Windows assumes the file extension for a program is .exe, so it's not necessary to type the extension.) Alternatively, you can click the microphone button and then say, "**Open Notepad**." The Notepad window opens.

▲ *Quick Launch menu.* To launch most Windows support tools, right-click the **Start** button to display the Quick Launch menu (see Figure 1-3) and then click an item to open it. You can also press **Win+X** to launch the menu from anywhere in Windows 10.

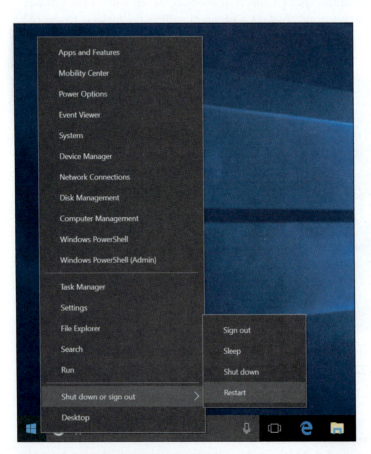

Figure 1-3 Use the Quick Launch menu from anywhere in Windows to access useful Windows utilities and screens

Here are some important items on the Quick Launch menu. You'll learn to use these and other items on the menu in this chapter and later chapters:

▲ Use the Settings app to change Windows settings. To change more advanced settings, you'll need to use the Control Panel. You'll have a chance to explore the Settings app and Control Panel later in this chapter.

▲ To repair, update, and uninstall installed apps, use the Apps & Features window, which can also be found in the Settings app. The window also has a link to the Programs and Features window, which you can use to turn Windows features on or off.

▲ The System link opens the About page in the Settings app to display information about the system and gives links to many more tools to manage settings (see Figure 1-4). The About page replaces the System window of earlier versions of Windows, although you can still find the System window in Control Panel.

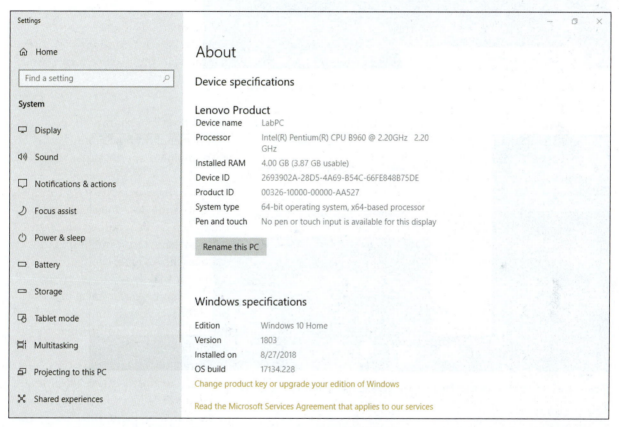

Figure 1-4 The About page in the Settings app displays the same information found in the System window

▲ Windows PowerShell and Windows PowerShell (Admin) provide a command-line interface where you can process small PowerShell programs called cmdlets. Earlier versions of Windows provided Command Prompt and Command Prompt (Admin) options on the Start menu, which open a command-line interface to enter Windows commands. You learn to use PowerShell and Command Prompt windows in Chapter 4.

▲ Notice the *Shut down or sign out* item near the bottom of the Quick Launch menu in Figure 1-3. When you point to it, you see submenu items that always include Shut down, Sign out, and Restart. Depending on your system configuration, you might also see Sleep or Hibernate.

▲ *Pin to taskbar.* For a program you use often, you can add its icon to the taskbar on the desktop, which is called **pinning** to the taskbar. Right-click an app on the Start menu to see the app's shortcut menu (see Figure 1-5). If necessary, click **More**, then click **Pin to taskbar**. You can also open a program, right-click the program's icon in the taskbar, and then click **Pin to taskbar** (see Figure 1-6).

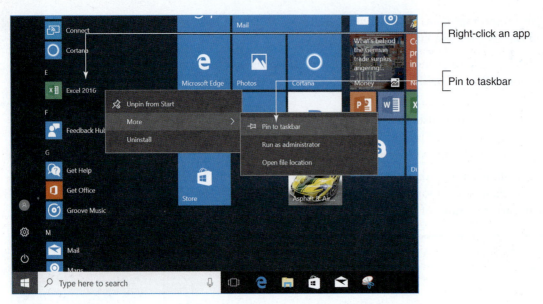

Figure 1-5   Right-click an app to pin it to the taskbar from the Start menu

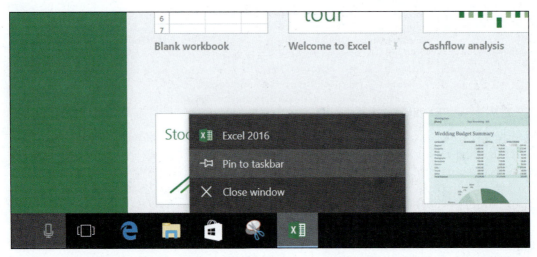

Figure 1-6   Right-click an icon for an open app and then pin it to the taskbar

▲ *Double-click the program file name in File Explorer.* File Explorer allows you to view and manage files and folders on your computer or the network. To open File Explorer, click the **File Explorer** icon in the taskbar or the Quick Launch menu. You can launch a program by double-clicking the program file name in File Explorer.

▲ *Shortcut on the desktop.* You can place a shortcut to a program on the desktop and then double-click the shortcut to launch the program. You learn to create shortcuts later in this chapter.

▲ *Run box or search box.* If you know the name of the program file, you can open the Quick Launch menu and click **Run**. The Run box appears, as shown in Figure 1-7. Type the name of the program file and press **Enter**. For example, the program file name of the Notepad text editor is notepad.exe. When you type **notepad** in the Run box and press **Enter,** the Notepad window appears. (Windows assumes the file extension for a program is .exe, so it's not necessary to type the extension.) You can also enter **notepad** in the Windows 10 search box to launch the program.

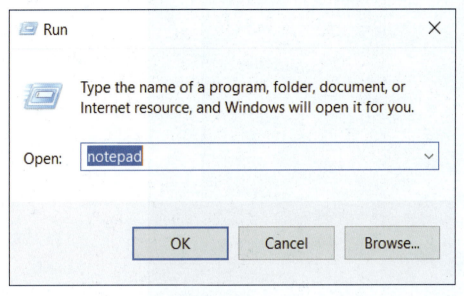

Figure 1-7 Use the Run box to launch a program

Here are a few tips about managing windows on the desktop:

◢ Drag the title bar of a window to move the window. Use the buttons in the upper-right corner to resize, maximize, minimize, and close a window.
◢ Drag a window to the top of the screen to maximize it. Drag the window downward on the screen to return it to its original size. Drag a window to the right or left of the screen so that it snaps to the side of the screen and fills that half of it. Drag a window to a corner of the screen so that it snaps to a quarter-size of the screen in that corner.
◢ Press and shake (drag back and forth quickly) the title bar of a window to minimize all other windows except the one you shake. Shake again to restore the size of the other windows.

WINDOWS 10 FEATURES

Here's a brief list of Windows 10 features that apply mainly to the end user:

◢ *Action Center.* The new Action Center in Windows 10 is used to toggle several Windows features on and off, access the Settings app, and view notifications. In Windows 10, you open the Action Center by clicking the Action Center icon next to the date and time in the taskbar (see Figure 1-8). Windows 8 has an Action Center that is much more powerful than the Windows 10 Action Center. The Windows 10 version of the Windows 8 Action Center is called Security and Maintenance and can be found in the Windows 10 Control Panel.

Figure 1-8   The Action Center is used for accessing Security and Maintenance and other
Windows features

▲ *Cortana.* Windows 10's digital assistant, Cortana, can learn your speech, handwriting patterns, and
typing history to assist with user input. Access Cortana using the search box on the taskbar (see
Figure 1-9). Cortana speaks using a woman's voice, so she is often referred to using a female pronoun.
Cortana can, for example, help you search your computer for a file, compose an email, search the
Internet, or even check the weather.

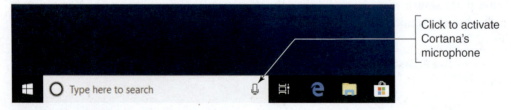

Click to activate
Cortana's
microphone

Figure 1-9   Access Cortana by typing or speaking to her

▲ *Snap Assist.* Windows 8 introduced Snap Assist, which makes it easy to snap windows to the left or right side of the screen, but this was a problem for Windows 8 modern apps that needed the entire screen. To allow for more flexibility, Snap Assist in Windows 10 allows for half and quadrant snapping, so a window can take up all of the screen, half of it, or only a quarter. Windows 10 apps are now contained in windows that float on the desktop and can be snapped to an edge or corner.

▲ *Task View.* To help organize applications opened on the desktop, Windows 10 uses Task View to create multiple virtual desktops so you can flip through to the desired desktop as needed (see Figure 1-10). For example, if you are paying bills, writing a paper, and surfing the Internet, you can put those three tasks on separate desktops. On desktop 1, you can open relevant web browsers and budgeting software. On desktop 2, open Microsoft Word, OneNote, and web browsers for research. On desktop 3, open web browsers to keep up with social media and news. To open a new desktop, click the **Task View** icon on the taskbar (refer back to Figure 1-2), and then click **New desktop**. The keyboard shortcut to toggle your open desktops is **Ctrl+Win+arrow left** or **arrow right**. To close a desktop, click the Task View icon and close its Desktop thumbnail in the pane just above the taskbar.

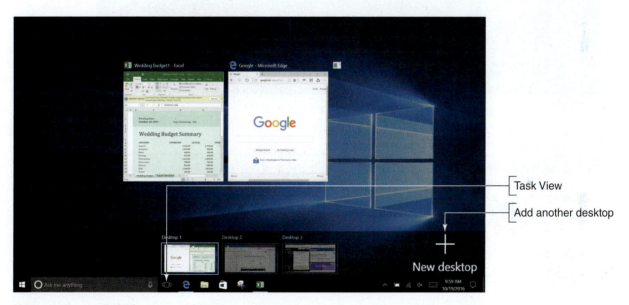

Figure 1-10   Use Task View to organize your open apps

APPLYING | CONCEPTS   SIGNING IN TO WINDOWS 10 AND USING THE WINDOWS 10 INTERFACE

Windows 10 is designed to flow between touch screen and desktop interfaces. Follow these steps to learn how to sign in to Windows 10 and manage apps:

1. When you start up a Windows 10 computer, you see the lock screen. Click anywhere on the screen and the sign-in screen appears (see Figure 1-11). To sign in, select a user account and enter the account password. The desktop appears.

(continues)

Figure 1-11   The Windows sign-in screen

> **✎ Notes** These instructions assume you are using a mouse and keyboard. If you're using a touch screen, simply tap instead of clicking, press and hold instead of right-clicking, double-tap instead of double-clicking, and swipe to scroll the screen to the right, left, up, or down.

2. To open an app, click the **Start** icon, and then click the app tile on the Start menu.

3. Using the Start menu, open a second app.

> **✎ Notes** In Windows, there are multiple ways to do the same thing. For example, to open the Start menu, (1) click the **Start** button or (2) press the Windows key on the keyboard.

4. Use Snap Assist to snap a window to the left or right side or a corner of the screen so a second window can share it. To snap a window, press and drag the title bar of the window to the left or right side of the screen. When you release the window, it snaps to the side, and then you can snap a second app to the other side of the screen. You can press and drag the vertical bar between the two windows to adjust the window sizes (see Figure 1-12).

> **✎ Notes** To snap windows, your screen resolution must be at least 1024 × 768.

(continues)

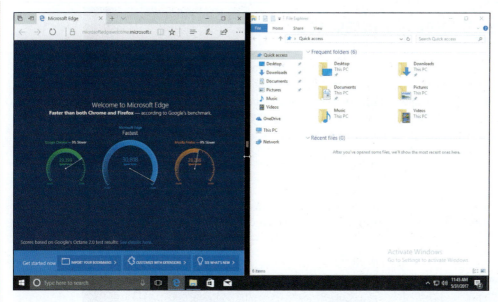

Figure 1-12 Two app pages on the screen

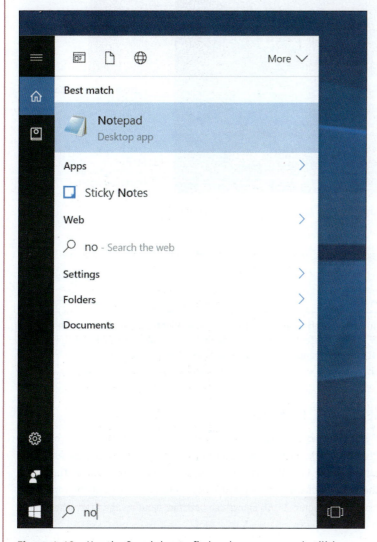

Figure 1-13 Use the Search bar to find and open apps and utilities

5. Open and close three other apps using these two methods:

   ◢ Open the Start menu and click a tile in the alphabetical list of programs on the left.

   ◢ In the Search bar, type the name of the app you want to open. As you type, search results appear above the Search bar. For example, when **no** is typed in the Search bar in Figure 1-13, Notepad appears as the best match. Other possible search results are also listed. You can click any app in the search results to open it. By default, the Search feature searches for apps, Windows settings, files, web images, and web videos. If you click an item under the *Web* heading, Edge opens to search online.

6. To see thumbnails of open apps that are not visible on the screen, click **Task View** in the taskbar (refer to Figure 1-10).

7. To close a selected app, move your pointer to the top of the screen. A menu bar appears if it was hidden. Click the red **X** on the far right of the menu bar.

8. Close all open apps.

WINDOWS | 8 MODERN INTERFACE

**A+
CORE 2
1.2**

The Windows 8 **modern interface**, also called the Windows 8 interface and formerly called the **Metro User Interface** or **Metro UI**, presents the Start screen to the user. The **Start screen** contains tiles that represent lean apps, which use few system resources and are designed for social media, social networking, and the novice end user (see Figure 1-14). Click a tile to open its app. Some apps use live tiles. For example, the People app has a live tile to make it easy to keep up with updates on Facebook, LinkedIn, and Twitter.

> ✎ **Notes** Remember that in this text, we use Windows 8 as an umbrella term to cover Windows 8.0 (the first release of Windows 8) and Windows 8.1 (the free update to Windows 8.0).

Figure 1-14 The Windows 8 Start screen is used to view app tiles and to open apps

The modern interface uses pages in comparison to the windows used on the desktop. The interface is specifically designed for touch screens.

> ✎ **Notes** To conserve system resources, you can turn off a Windows 10/8 live tile. Right-click the tile on the Start screen and then click **Turn live tile off** in the shortcut menu that appears. You can also use Task Manager to find out how the app is affecting overall system performance. You learn to use Task Manager in Chapter 5.

THE CHARMS BAR AND THE SETTINGS CHARM

The **charms bar** appears on the right side of any Windows 8 screen when you move your pointer to a right corner (see Figure 1-15A). It gives handy access to common tasks such as returning to the Start screen, searching for content, connecting to a wireless network, personalizing the Start screen, and changing other Windows settings. In the charms bar, click a **charm** to select it. The Settings charm can be particularly useful, and items at the top of the Settings pane can change depending on the situation. Figure 1-15B shows the Settings pane on the Start screen, and Figure 1-15C shows the Settings pane on the desktop.

(continues)

Figure 1-15   (A) The charms bar, (B) the Settings pane on the Start screen, and (C) the Settings pane
on the desktop

> ✎ **Notes**   With the first release of Windows 8, many users complained that important items like the charms bar
> were difficult to find and not intuitive to use. As a result, beginning with Windows 8.1, Microsoft added tips that
> randomly appear on screen to help users learn how to use the new interface.

THE POWER ICON

Use the Power icon in the upper-right corner of the Start screen to shut down or restart the computer. Click the
Power icon, and then click an item in the menu that appears (see Figure 1-16). The items on this menu always
include Shut down and Restart, and, depending on the configuration, might also include Sleep and Hibernate.

Figure 1-16   Use the Power icon at the top of the Start screen to shut down
or restart the system

(continues)

WINDOWS 8 DESKTOP

To access the Windows 8 desktop, click the Desktop tile on the Start screen. When you move your pointer to a right corner of the desktop screen, the charms bar appears, as shown in Figure 1-17. Click the **Start** charm in the charms bar to return to the Start screen. Alternately, you can click the Start button in the taskbar to return to the Start screen.

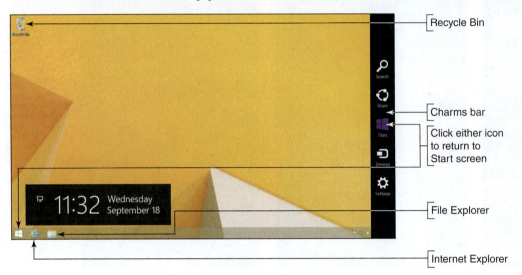

Recycle Bin

Charms bar

Click either icon to return to Start screen

File Explorer

Internet Explorer

Figure 1-17 The Windows 8 desktop with the charms bar in view

> ✎ **Notes** According to Microsoft terminology, you *sign in* to Windows 10/8 and *log on* to Windows 7.

> ↻ **OS Differences** The Windows 7 desktop provides a 3D user interface called the **Aero user interface** that gives a glassy appearance (see Figure 1-18). The Windows 7 desktop can have **gadgets**, which are mini-apps that provide information such as the time, date, news headlines, or weather. You can open programs by using the Start menu, shortcuts on the desktop, or icons in the taskbar. For example, to open Windows 7 Windows Explorer, click its icon in the taskbar. File Explorer in Windows 10/8 is called **Windows Explorer** in Windows 7.

Figure 1-18 The Windows 7 desktop using the Aero interface has a glassy, transparent look

CHOOSING A WINDOWS EDITION

A+ CORE 2 1.2 Microsoft offers several editions of each version of Windows. Here are the most important ones:

◢ Important Windows 10 editions for personal computers include Windows 10 Home, Windows 10 Pro, Windows 10 Enterprise, and Windows 10 Education. Home editions for Windows are intended for laptops and desktop computers in a home or small office. Pro, Enterprise, and Education editions are designed to work in large organizations and enterprises. Enterprise editions allow for volume licensing. Education editions are less expensive editions for those who can prove they qualify for the educational discounts.

◢ Windows 8 options are Windows 8.1 Core (the Home version), Windows 8.1 Pro, and Windows 8.1 Enterprise.

◢ Windows 7 options are Windows 7 Home Basic and Premium, Windows 7 Professional, and Windows 7 Enterprise.

> ★ **A+ Exam Tip** The A+ Core 2 exam expects you to be able to compare and contrast which version and edition of Windows is best in a given scenario, including Windows 10, Windows 8.1, Windows 8.0, and Windows 7 personal and corporate editions.

When deciding among Windows 10, Windows 8, or Windows 7 for a new installation, select Windows 10 if possible because Microsoft support for its latest OS will last longer, and Windows 10 improves in many ways on Windows 8 and Windows 7.

When faced with choosing an edition of Windows 10/8/7, consider the purposes for using Windows. Is the computer intended for corporate or personal use? Different editions offer different features. The professional editions have more features that are more useful in a corporate setting, which is why these editions are more expensive. Consider the following features that the user or organization might require; they are all available on the Windows 10/8/7 Pro, Education, Business, and Ultimate editions, but are not available in the Home editions:

◢ *Domain access.* If the computer connects to a corporate or educational network to access network resources, it requires access to a Windows domain, which manages resources on the network. How to join a domain is covered later in this chapter.

◢ *BitLocker.* BitLocker encrypts an entire volume on a drive to protect the data and can provide full hard drive encryption. This level of security is often required by corporations to secure a computer and its data and settings before the computer is allowed to connect to and access resources on a corporate network.

◢ *Encryption File System (EFS).* EFS encrypts files and folders to protect the data. Although not as secure as full drive encryption, EFS is sometimes required by individuals and corporations to protect the data on a computer's hard drive.

◢ *Branchcache.* Branchcache optimizes content access over a wide area network (WAN) by retrieving content from remote servers and caching it on local servers for better access. The feature is sometimes required to optimize accessing resources on remote corporate networks.

◢ *Media Center.* Media Center is a digital video recorder and media player originally offered as part of earlier editions of Windows, including Windows 7 Professional. It was also available as a paid add-on in Windows 8 Pro. However, it is deprecated (no longer available) starting with Windows 10.

Now that you're familiar with the Windows interfaces and editions, let's learn to use several tools that are helpful to both users and technicians.

WINDOWS TOOLS FOR USERS AND TECHNICIANS

A+
CORE 2
1.2, 1.3,
1.5, 1.6,
1.8

All users need to know how to use File Explorer or Windows Explorer. In addition, a technician needs to know how to use the Control Panel, Power Options, System window, System Information window, and for Windows 8/7, the Action Center. All these tools are covered in this part of the chapter.

WINDOWS 10/8 FILE EXPLORER AND WINDOWS 7 WINDOWS EXPLORER

A+
CORE 2
1.6

You open Windows 10/8 File Explorer or Windows 7 Windows Explorer in these ways:

▲ Click the yellow File Explorer or Windows Explorer icon in the taskbar. If an Explorer window is already open, it becomes the active window. To open an additional instance of Explorer, right-click the File Explorer icon and click **File Explorer**. Having two instances of Explorer open makes it easy to drag and drop files and folders from one location to another.

▲ For Windows 10, press **Win+X** or right-click the Start button to open the Quick Launch menu, and then click **File Explorer**. From the Windows 8 desktop, open the Quick Launch menu (press **Win+X**) and click **File Explorer** in the menu. For Windows 7, right-click **Start** and select **Open Windows Explorer** from the menu that appears. If an Explorer instance is already open, a new instance of Explorer is created.

▲ For Windows 10, enter **explorer** in the search box. For Windows 8, open the Quick Launch menu, click **Run**, and enter **explorer** in the Run box. For Windows 7, click **Start** and enter **explorer** in the search box. You can use this method to open multiple instances of Explorer.

▲ In Windows 10, click the **microphone** button in the search box on the taskbar. Tell Cortana to "**Open File Explorer.**" If an Explorer window is already open, it becomes the active window.

The Windows 10/8 File Explorer window has tabs near the top that open ribbons (see Figure 1-19). These tabs can change depending on the situation. You click a tab to see its ribbon or a drop-down menu that appears with more tools. The Home ribbon is shown in the figure. The left pane in Windows 10 is called the Quick access area; pin often-used folders in this area to quickly access them. In Windows 8/7, this area is called Favorites. The Windows 7 Windows Explorer window doesn't use ribbons (see Figure 1-20).

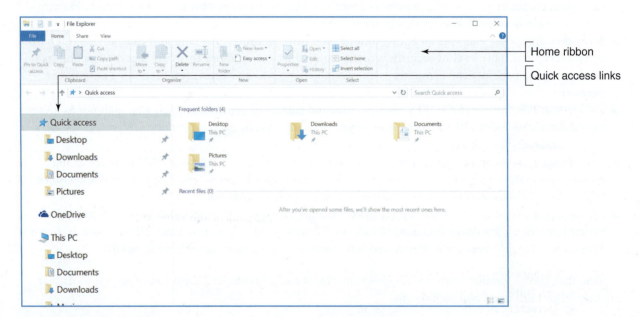

Figure 1-19 The Windows 10 File Explorer window with the Home ribbon shown

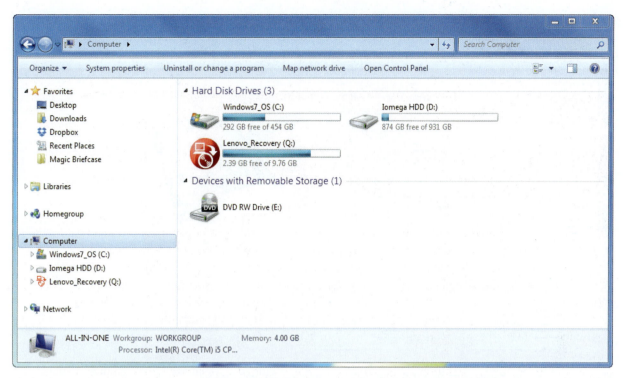

Figure 1-20 The Windows 7 Windows Explorer window with the Computer item selected in the left pane

---

APPLYING | CONCEPTS   **USING QUICK ACCESS IN FILE EXPLORER**

In Windows 10 File Explorer, shortcuts to Desktop, Downloads, Documents, and Pictures are pinned to the Quick access list by default. Pinned shortcuts remain in the list until you remove them. Shortcuts to recently used items appear in the list, and then disappear in time if they are no longer being used. If you want an item to remain in the Quick access list, you can pin it.

Follow these steps to pin a folder to the Quick access list:

1. Create a new folder on the desktop, and change the folder name to **Projects**. To create the folder, right-click the desktop, select **New** in the shortcut menu, and click **Folder**. You can then rename the folder.

2. Open **File Explorer**. Click **Quick access** in the left pane to view Quick access items in the main folder window. The top section lists frequently used folders (Frequent folders) and the bottom section lists recently used files (Recent files). Notice Frequent folders are also listed in the left pane of the File Explorer window.

3. Drag and drop the Projects folder into the Quick access Frequent folders section. Notice that a shortcut to the Projects folder now appears under *Quick access* in the left pane, with a pin icon next to its name.

4. Right-click the **Projects** folder under Quick access in the left pane or in the Quick access view and select **Unpin from Quick access**.

Let's see how to use the Explorer windows to manage files and folders and other system resources.

FILES AND DIRECTORIES

Every OS manages a hard drive, optical drive, USB drive, or other type of drive by using directories (also called folders), subdirectories, and files. The drive is organized with a single root directory at the top of the hierarchical structure of subdirectories, as shown in Figure 1-21. The exception to this rule is a hard drive because it can be divided into partitions that can have more than one volume, such as drive C: and drive D:, on the same physical hard drive (see Figure 1-22). For a volume, such as drive C:, the root directory is written as C:. Each volume has its own root directory and hierarchical structure of subdirectories. You can think of volumes as logical drives within the one physical drive.

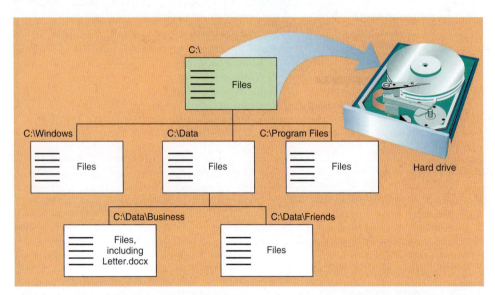

Figure 1-21   Storage devices such as a USB drive, DVD, or hard drive are organized into directories and subdirectories that contain files

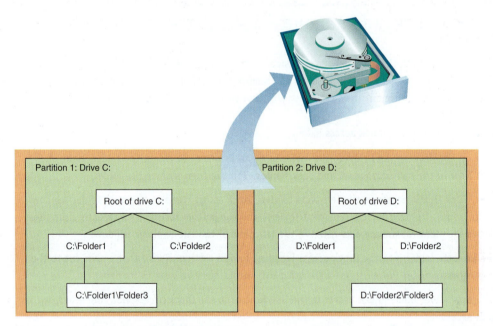

Figure 1-22   A hard drive can be divided into one or more partitions that can each contain a volume such as drive C: or drive D:

As shown in Figure 1-21, the root directory can hold files or other directories, which can have names such as C:\Data. These directories, called subdirectories, child directories, folders, or subfolders can have other directories listed in them in turn. Any directory can have files and other subdirectories listed in it; for example, Figure 1-21 shows that one file on drive C: is C:\Data\Business\Letter.docx. In this path to the file, the C: identifies the volume and is called the drive letter. Drive letters used for a hard drive, CD, USB drive, or DVD are C:, D:, E:, and so forth.

When you refer to a drive and directories that are pointing to the location of a file, as in C:\Data\Business\Letter.docx, the drive and directories are called the **path** to the file (see Figure 1-23). The first part of the name before the period is called the **file name** (Letter), and the part after the period is called the file extension (.docx). A **file extension** indicates how the file is organized or formatted, the type of content in the file, and what program uses the file. For example, the .docx file extension identifies the file type as a Microsoft Word document file. By default, Windows does not display file extensions in Explorer. How to display these extensions is coming up.

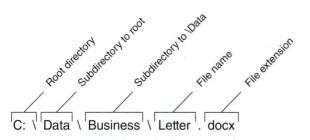

Figure 1-23 The complete path to a file includes the volume letter, directories, file name, and file extension; the colon, backslashes, and period are required to separate items in the path

NAVIGATE THE FOLDER STRUCTURE

When working with the File Explorer or Windows Explorer window, these tips can make your work easier:

◢ Click or double-click items in the left pane, called the **navigation pane**, to drill down into these items. The folders or subfolders appear in the right pane. You can also double-click folders in the right pane to drill down. When you click the arrow on the left side of a folder in the navigation pane, its subfolders are listed underneath it in the pane.

◢ To control how files and subfolders appear in the right pane of Windows 10/8, click one of the icons in the lower-right corner to select Thumbnail view or Details view (see Figure 1-24A). For Windows 7, click the View icon in the menu bar and select your view (see Figure 1-24B).

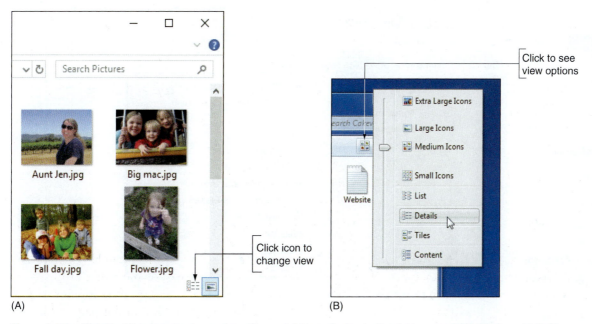

(A)   (B)

Figure 1-24 Click the View icon to change how files and folders display in the right pane of (A) Windows 10/8 File Explorer or (B) Windows 7 Windows Explorer

◢ To control the column headings that appear in Details view, right-click a column heading and select the headings that you want to appear (see Figure 1-25). To control which column is used to sort items in Details view, click a column heading.

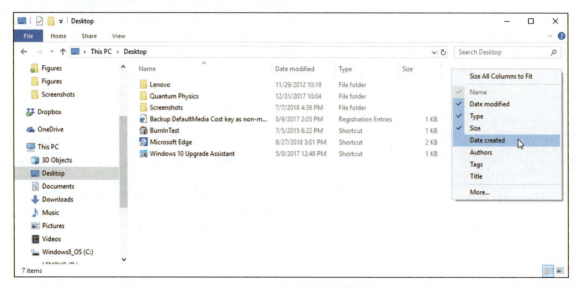

Figure 1-25   Right-click a column heading to select columns to display in Details view

◢ To search for a folder or file, use the search box in the upper-right corner of the window.
◢ Use the forward and back arrows in the upper-left corner to move forward and backward to previous views.
◢ Click a right arrow in the path displayed in the address bar at the top of the Explorer window to see a drop-down list of subfolders (see Figure 1-26). Click one to move to the subfolder.

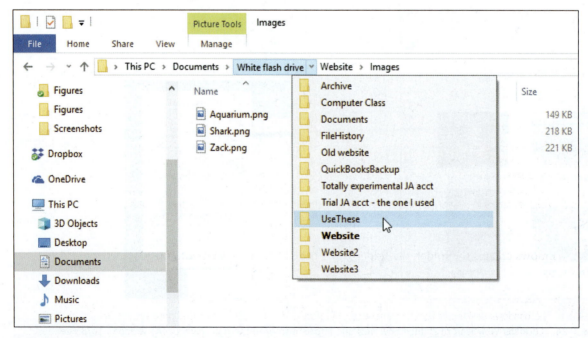

Figure 1-26   Click a right arrow in the address bar to move up the folder tree and down to a new folder

CREATE A FOLDER

To create a folder, first select the folder you want to use as the parent folder. (Remember that a parent folder contains the child folder.) Next, use one of these methods to create the new folder:

▲ In Windows 10/8, select the **Home** ribbon and click **New folder**. In Windows 7, click **New folder** on the menu bar.

▲ Right-click in the white area of the right pane and point to **New** in the shortcut menu. The menu in Figure 1-27 appears. Click **Folder** to create a regular folder or click **Compressed (zipped) Folder** to create a compressed folder.

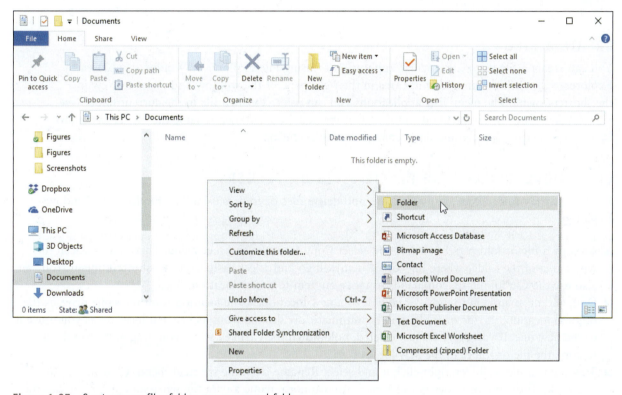

Figure 1-27 Create a new file, folder, or compressed folder

> ✎ **Notes** A **compressed (zipped) folder** has a .zip extension. Any file or folder that you put in this folder will be compressed to a smaller size than normal. A compressed folder is often used to make files smaller so they can more easily be sent by email. When you remove a file or folder from a compressed folder, the file or folder is uncompressed back to its original size. In general, Windows treats a compressed folder more like a file than a folder.

After Windows creates the folder, the folder name is highlighted so that you can rename it (see Figure 1-28).

> ✎ **Notes** The Windows desktop is itself a folder and is located at C:\Users*username*\Desktop. For example, if the user, Anne, creates a folder named Downloads on her desktop, the folder is located at C:\Users\Anne\Desktop\Downloads.

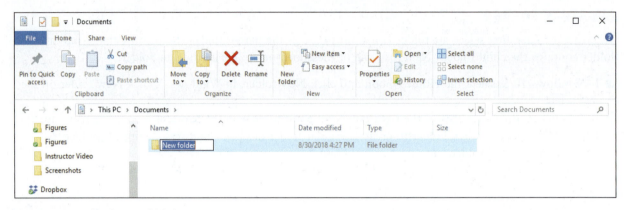

Figure 1-28 Edit the new folder's name

CREATE A FILE

You can create a file using a particular application or using File Explorer or Windows Explorer. In Explorer, right-click the unused white area in the right pane of the window and point to **New** in the shortcut menu. The menu lists applications you can use to create a file in the current folder (see Figure 1-27). Click the application and the file is created. You can then rename the file. However, to keep the proper file association, don't change the file extension.

COPY, MOVE, RENAME, OR DELETE FILES OR FOLDERS

Use these handy tips to copy, move, rename, and delete files or folders using File Explorer or Windows Explorer:

▲ To copy a file or folder, right-click it and select **Copy** from the shortcut menu. Then right-click in the white area of the folder where the copied item will go and select **Paste** from the shortcut menu. You can also use the Cut and Paste commands to move an item to a new location.

▲ Drag and drop an item to move or copy it to a new location. If the location is on the same drive as the original location, the file or folder will be automatically deleted from its original location as you move it to the new one. If you don't want it deleted, hold down the **Ctrl** key while you drag and drop the item to copy the file or folder to the new location.

▲ To rename a file or folder, right-click it and select **Rename** from the shortcut menu. Change the name and click off the file or folder to deselect it. You cannot rename a data file when an application has the file open, and you can't rename a program file when the program is running; first close the data file or program and then rename it.

▲ To delete a file or folder, select the item and press the **Delete** key, or right-click the item and select **Delete** from the shortcut menu. The deleted file or folder and all its contents, including subfolders, is sent to the Recycle Bin.

▲ To select multiple items to delete, copy, or move at the same time, hold down the **Shift** or **Ctrl** key as you click. To select several adjacent items in a list, click the first item and **Shift-click** the last item. To select nonadjacent items in a list, hold down the **Ctrl** key as you click each item.

Files deleted from the hard drive are stored in the Recycle Bin on the desktop. Emptying the Recycle Bin will free up your disk space by permanently deleting the files. To empty the Recycle Bin, right-click the bin and select **Empty Recycle Bin** from the shortcut menu.

> ✏ **Notes** In this chapter, you use File Explorer or Windows Explorer to create, copy, move, delete, and rename files and folders. In Chapter 4, you will learn that you can do the same tasks using commands from a command prompt.

CREATE A SHORTCUT

To create a shortcut on the Windows desktop to a data file or program, use File Explorer or Windows Explorer to locate the data file or program file, right-click it, and click **Create shortcut** in the menu that appears. For example, in Figure 1-29, you can see that a shortcut to the C:\Windows\System32\notepad.exe program is about to be placed on the Windows desktop.

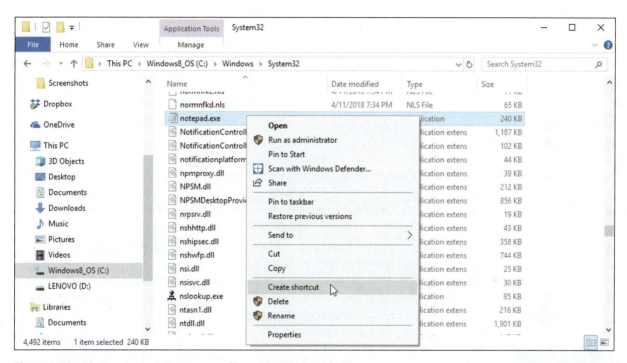

Figure 1-29 Place a shortcut to a program file on the Windows desktop

CONTROL PANEL

A+
CORE 2
1.2, 1.6

Control Panel is a window containing several small utility programs called applets that are used to manage hardware, software, users, and the system. (In general, a utility program is used to maintain a system or fix a computer problem.) To access Control Panel in Windows 10, type **Control Panel** in the search box on the taskbar. In Windows 8, right-click **Start** and click **Control Panel**. In Windows 7, click **Start** and click **Control Panel**.

By default, Control Panel appears in **Category view** where utilities are grouped by category. To switch to **Classic view**, click **Category** and select either Large icons or Small icons. Figure 1-30 shows the Windows 10 Control Panel in Small icons view. Use the search box in the title bar to help find information and utilities in Control Panel.

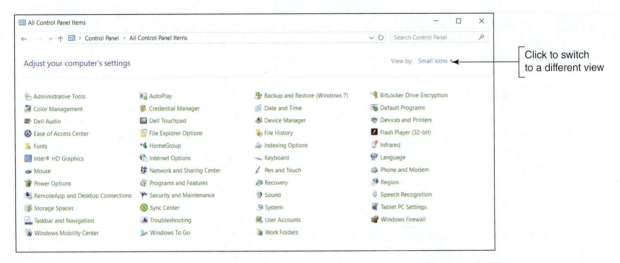

Figure 1-30   Many technicians prefer to use Control Panel in Classic view to more easily access utilities

Here is a short list of some of the applets in Control Panel. Later in the text, you learn about other Control Panel applets:

▲ The Sound applet is used to select a default speaker and microphone and adjust how Windows handles sounds. To control volume, use the volume icon in the taskbar.

▲ The Network and Sharing Center is a tool for viewing basic network information and setting up connections.

▲ HomeGroup is in the Windows 8/7 Control Panel but is not supported by Windows 10. A homegroup allows Windows 8/7 computers on a small network to share resources.

▲ The Power Options applet is used to select or customize a power plan for your computer.

▲ The Windows 10 File Explorer Options applet or Windows 8/7 Folder Options applet lets you change how files and folders are displayed in File Explorer or Windows Explorer.

> ★ **A+ Exam Tip**   The A+ Core 2 exam expects you to be able to use Control Panel utilities such as Folder Options, System, Power Options, HomeGroup, and the Network and Sharing Center when given a scenario.

WINDOWS 10 FILE EXPLORER OPTIONS OR WINDOWS 8/7 FOLDER OPTIONS

**A+
CORE 2
1.6**

The Windows 10 File Explorer Options applet or the Windows 8/7 Folder Options applet in Control Panel can be used to view and change options assigned to folders. These options control how users view the files in the folder and what they can do with these files. In File Explorer or Windows Explorer, Windows has an annoying habit of hiding file extensions if it knows which application is associated with a file extension. For example, just after installation, it hides .exe, .com, .sys, and .txt file extensions, but does not hide .docx, .pptx, or .xlsx file extensions until the software to open these files has been installed. Also, Windows really doesn't want you to see its own system files, and it hides these files from view until you force it to show them.

APPLYING | CONCEPTS   CHANGING FILE EXPLORER OPTIONS

A technician is responsible for solving problems with system files (files that belong to the Windows operating system) and file extensions. To fix problems with these files and extensions, you need to see them first. To change File Explorer options so you can view system files and file extensions in Windows 10/8/7, do the following:

1. Open **Control Panel** and, if necessary, change the view to **Small icons** view. For Windows 10, click **File Explorer Options**. For Windows 8/7, click **Folder Options**. The File Explorer Options or Folder Options dialog box appears. Even though the name is different, the dialog box works the same in Windows 10 and Windows 8/7. Figure 1-31A shows the box for Windows 10 with the General tab selected. On the General tab, you can change settings for how Explorer navigates folders and handles the navigation pane.

> ✎ **Notes** In Windows, the difference between a window and a dialog box is that a window can be resized, but a dialog box cannot.

2. Click the **View** tab. Scroll down in the Advanced settings group and make these selections to show hidden information about files, folders, and drives, as shown in Figure 1-31B:

   ◢ Select **Show hidden files, folders, and drives**.
   ◢ Uncheck **Hide extensions for known file types**.
   ◢ Uncheck **Hide protected operating system files (Recommended)** and respond to the Warning box.

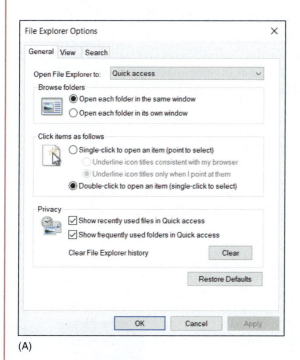
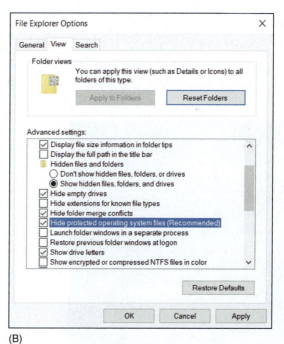

(A)   (B)

Figure 1-31 Use the File Explorer Options or Folder Options box to control how Explorer works and displays files and folders

3. To save your changes and close the File Explorer Options or Folder Options box, click **OK**.

> ★ **A+ Exam Tip** The A+ Core 2 exam expects you to know how to view hidden files and file extensions in File Explorer and Windows Explorer.

POWER OPTIONS

The **Power Options applet** of Control Panel can help you conserve power and increase the amount of time before a battery pack on a laptop needs recharging. Power is managed by putting the computer into varying degrees of suspend or sleep modes.

> ⭐ **A+ Exam Tip** The A+ Core 2 exam might give you a scenario and expect you to know which power options to change to solve a problem, including using power plans and sleep (suspend), hibernate, and standby modes.

Here are the different power-saving states:

▲ *Sleep mode*. Using Windows 10/8/7, you can put the computer into sleep mode, also called standby mode or suspend mode, to save power when you're not using the computer. If applications are open or other work is in progress, Windows first saves the current state, including open files, to memory and saves some of the work to the hard drive. Then everything is shut down except memory and enough of the system to respond to a wake-up. In sleep mode, the power light on the laptop might blink from time to time. (A laptop generally uses about 1 to 2 percent of battery power for each hour in sleep mode.) To wake up the computer, press the power button; for some computers, you press a key or touch the touch pad. Windows wakes up in about two seconds. When Windows is in sleep mode, it can still perform Windows updates and scheduled tasks. Windows can be configured to go to sleep after a period of inactivity, or you can manually put it to sleep.

To put the system to sleep manually in Windows 10, click **Start**, then click the power icon and select **Sleep**. In Windows 10/8, you can open the **Quick Launch** menu, point to **Shut down or sign out**, and click **Sleep** (see Figure 1-32A). In Windows 8, you can use the charms bar, as you learned earlier in the chapter. For Windows 7, click **Start**, click the arrow to the right of Shut down, and then click **Sleep** (see Figure 1-32B). A laptop might also be configured to go to sleep when you close the lid.

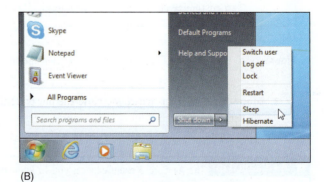

(A)   (B)

Figure 1-32 Put Windows to sleep using the (A) Windows 10/8 Quick Launch menu or (B) Windows 7 Start menu

▲ *Hibernation.* Hibernation saves all work to the hard drive and powers down the system. When you press the power button, Windows reloads its state, including all open applications and documents. When Windows is in sleep mode on a laptop and senses the battery is critically low, it will put the system into hibernation.

> ✎ **Notes** Hard drives are permanent or nonvolatile storage and memory is temporary or volatile storage. A hard drive does not require power to hold its contents, but memory, on the other hand, is volatile and loses its contents when it has no power. In hibernation, the computer has no power and everything must therefore be stored on the hard drive.

APPLYING | CONCEPTS   CONFIGURING WINDOWS POWER PLANS

Follow these steps to configure power plans in Windows 10:

1. Open Control Panel in Classic view and click **Power Options**. The Power Options window opens. Figure 1-33 shows the window for one laptop. The plans might be different for other laptops.

Figure 1-33   Power plans in Windows 10

2. You can customize each plan. For example, under Balanced (recommended), click **Change plan settings**. The Edit Plan Settings window appears (see the left side of Figure 1-34). Notice in the figure the various times of inactivity required before the computer goes into sleep mode; these are called sleep timers.

3. To see other changes you can make, click **Change advanced power settings**. Using the Power Options window (see the right side of Figure 1-34), you can control the number of minutes before the hard drive turns off; control what happens when you close the lid, press the sleep button, or press the power button; and set the brightness level of the LCD panel to conserve power. You can also use this box to set what happens when the battery gets low or critically low. Make your changes and click **OK** to close the box.

(continues)

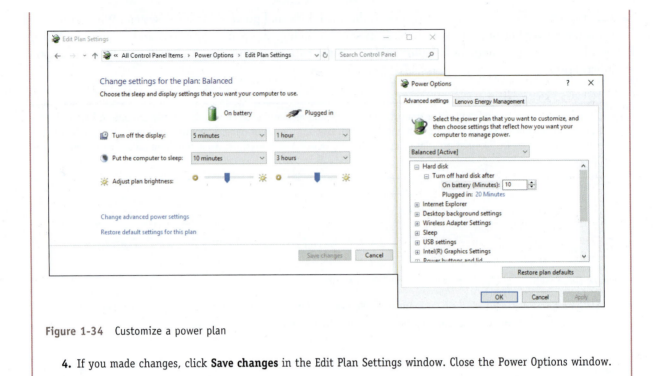

Figure 1-34   Customize a power plan

> **4.** If you made changes, click **Save changes** in the Edit Plan Settings window. Close the Power Options window.

As an IT support technician, you need to be able to sit down at a working computer and within 5 or 10 minutes find the details about what software and hardware are installed on the system and its general health. Within 20 minutes, you should be able to solve any minor problems the computer might have, such as a broken network connection. Some quick and easy support tools that can help you are the System window, System Information window, and Windows 10 Settings app. All these tools are discussed next.

> ★ **A+ Exam Tip**   The A+ Core 2 exam expects you to know how to use File Explorer, Windows Explorer, the System window, and the System Information window. If the utility can be accessed by more than one method, you are expected to know all of the methods.

SYSTEM WINDOW

A+ CORE 2 1.6

The System window is your friend. It can give you a quick look at what hardware and software are installed and can get you to other useful Windows tools. To open the System window in Windows 10, open **Control Panel** and click **System**. In Windows 8, open the Quick Launch menu (press **Win+X**) and click **System**. In Windows 7, click **Start**, right-click **Computer**, and select **Properties** from the shortcut menu. (Alternately, you can open **Control Panel** and click **System**.) Figure 1-35 shows the resulting System window for one Windows 10 laptop.

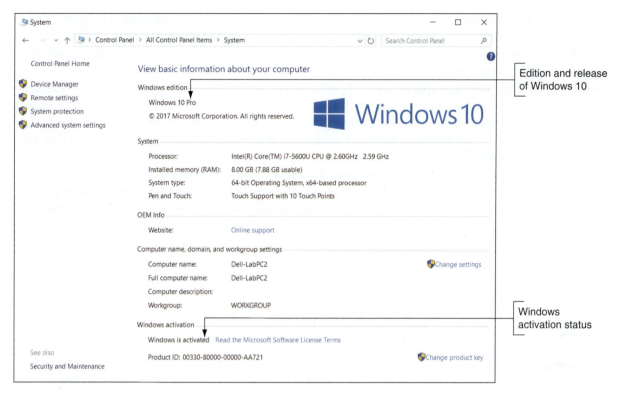

Figure 1-35 The System window reports Windows 10 Pro is installed

So what technical information are you looking at? Here is the rundown:

▲ Windows 10/8/7 comes in several editions; you can see this system has the Windows 10 Pro edition installed.

▲ The type of OS installed is a 64-bit OS. A **32-bit operating system** processes 32 bits at a time, and a **64-bit operating system** processes 64 bits at a time. Most editions of Windows 10/8/7 come in either 32-bit or 64-bit versions. A 64-bit OS performs better than a 32-bit OS, but requires more memory. A 32-bit OS can support up to 4 GB of memory, and a 64-bit OS can support much more. The details of how much memory each edition of Windows can support are covered in Chapter 2.

▲ The processor installed is the Intel Core i7-5600U, and 8 GB of RAM is installed.

▲ You can also see that Windows 10 is activated. (If it is not, refer to Chapter 2 to learn how to activate Windows.)

> ✏ **Notes** Windows 8/7 relies on the Control Panel applets to manage most settings. Windows 10 introduced the Settings app for settings a user might need to change, but settings a technician might change are still done with Control Panel applets. In Windows 10, you often find the same setting in both locations. For example, the About page (refer back to Figure 1-4) in the Settings app gives information similar to that shown in the System window in Control Panel.

That's a lot of useful information for a first look at a computer.

SYSTEM INFORMATION WINDOW

Turn to the **System Information** window (msinfo32.exe) for more details about a system, including installed hardware and software, the current system configuration, and currently running programs. For example, you can use the window to find out what BIOS/UEFI version is installed on the motherboard, how much RAM is installed, the directory where the OS is installed, the size of the hard drive, the names of currently running drivers, a list of startup programs, print jobs in progress, currently running tasks, and much more. Because the System Information window gives so much useful information, help-desk technicians often ask a user on the phone to open it and report information about the computer.

When strange error messages appear during startup, use the System Information window to get a report of drivers that loaded successfully. Device drivers are small programs stored on the hard drive that tell the computer how to communicate with a specific hardware device such as a printer, network card, or scanner. If you have saved the System Information report when the system was starting successfully, comparing the two reports can help identify the problem device.

To run System Information in Windows 10, enter **msinfo32** in the search box. For Windows 8, open the **Quick Launch** menu, click **Run**, and enter **msinfo32.exe** in the Run box. In Windows 7, click **Start** and enter **msinfo32.exe** in the search box. The System Information window for one computer is shown in Figure 1-36. To drill down to more information in the window, click items in the left pane.

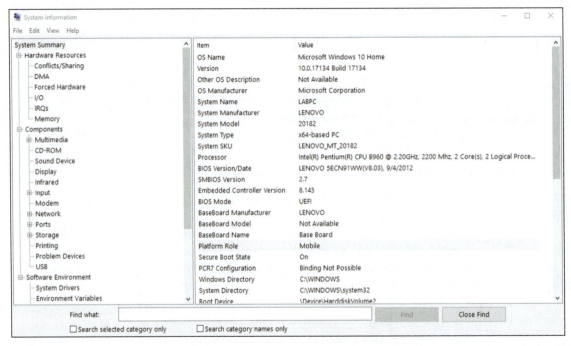

Figure 1-36 Use the System Information utility to examine details about a system

WINDOWS 10 SETTINGS APP

The Windows 10 Settings app is a user-friendly interface to access numerous Windows settings. You can open the Settings app from the Start menu, the Quick Launch menu, or by pressing the hotkeys **Win+I**. On the Start menu, click **Start** and then click the **Settings** icon on the far-left side of the menu (see Figure 1-37).

Click to open the Settings app

Figure 1-37 Access the Settings app from the Start menu

The Settings app includes links to Control Panel and has a search box near the top that makes it easy to jump straight to a setting you want to adjust (see Figure 1-38). For example, suppose you want to configure Windows to use a different language. When you type **language** in the search box, several actions appear in the drop-down list, including *Add a language to this device*. The primary menu includes settings for the following:

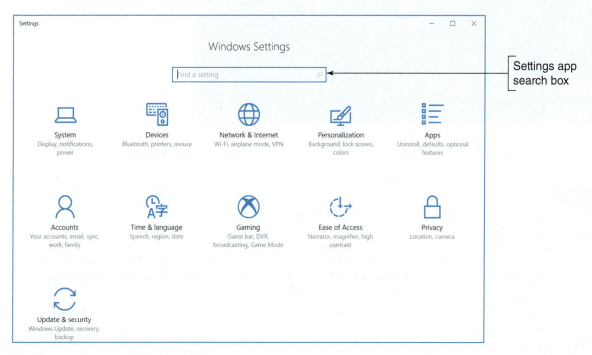

Settings app search box

Figure 1-38 The new Windows 10 Settings app

> **Notes** Some items in the Settings app may be unavailable if you are logged in with a Standard account. Use an account with administrative privileges to view all available settings.

▲ *System*. The catchall for information and settings that affect the function of your computer is the System group. Go here to adjust display, notification, power, sleep, storage, and tablet-mode settings.

▲ *Devices*. The Devices group includes settings for printers and scanners, connected devices, Bluetooth, mouse and touch pad devices, typing, AutoPlay, and USB.

◢ *Network & Internet*. The Network & Internet group provides network status, data usage information, and settings for different connections, including Wi-Fi, Ethernet, dial-up, VPN, and mobile hotspots. Go here to set up new connections. Airplane mode and proxy settings are also available for mobile devices. The link to the Network and Sharing Center takes you to more connection settings.

◢ *Personalization*. The Personalization group is where you find settings for the background, colors, lock screen, themes, Start menu, and taskbar. For example, to adjust your screen for working in low-light conditions, click **Personalization**, click **Colors** in the left pane, scroll down to **Choose your app mode**, and then click **Dark** (see Figure 1-39).

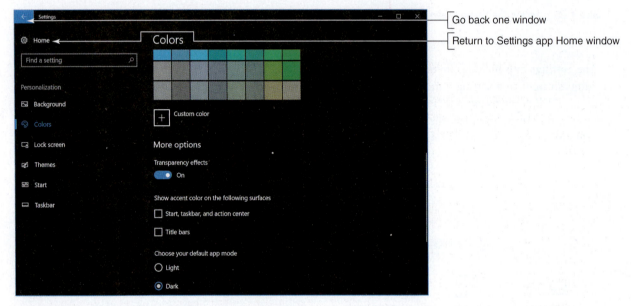

Figure 1-39   Dark app mode is ideal for low-light conditions

> ✎ **Notes**   To go back one window in the Settings app, click the left arrow in the upper-left corner of the Settings window. To return to the Settings app Home window, click **Home**, as shown in Figure 1-39.

◢ *Apps*. To uninstall applications, set default applications, and check other application settings, use the Apps group. For example, to make Outlook the default app for email, click **Apps**, click **Default apps**, and then change the setting from Mail to Outlook.

◢ *Accounts*. To find your Windows account information or link your account to a Microsoft account, use the Accounts group. The Accounts group also includes email and app accounts, sign-in options, Microsoft account sync settings, options to sign in to work or school networks, and options to add new user accounts to the computer. You will learn more about accounts later in this text.

◢ *Time & language*. The Time & language group provides settings for date and time, region and language, and speech.

◢ *Gaming*. The Gaming group contains settings for the Game bar, Game DVR, broadcasting, and Game Mode. When you turn on Game Mode, Windows improves the gaming experience by prioritizing system resources for the game being played on the computer.

◢ *Ease of Access*. This group provides all the standard access settings, such as narrator, magnifier, closed captions, and more.

◢ *Privacy*. Find the settings to restrict or allow app access to your information in the Privacy group. You can limit app access and use of your location, camera, microphone, notifications, speech, inking, typing, account information, contacts, calendar, call history, email, messaging, radios, and other devices. The

Privacy group is also where you adjust settings for feedback, diagnostic, and usage data that is sent to Microsoft. You can also choose which apps are allowed to run in the background.

▲ *Update & security*. The Windows update status and settings, as well as the Windows Defender settings, are found in the Update & security group. Here you also find settings for backups, recovery, and activation, and links to Find My Device if you lose your connected devices, such as a phone. Finally, you find settings for developers, such as device discovery, remote desktop, and PowerShell.

WINDOWS | 8   ACTION CENTER

The Windows 8/7 Action Center is the tool to use when you want to make a quick jab at solving a computer problem. If a hardware or application problem is easy to solve, the Action Center can probably do it in a matter of minutes because it lists errors and issues that need attention and proposed solutions. The Action Center flag appears in the notification area of the taskbar. If the flag has a red X beside it, as shown in Figure 1-40, Windows considers the system to have an important issue that needs resolving immediately. When you click the flag, you can see a brief report of issues, as shown in the figure.

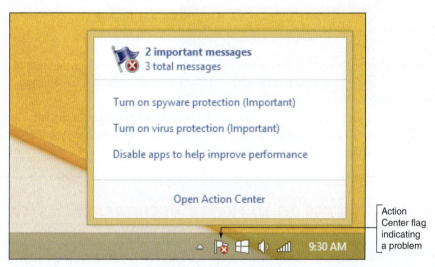

Figure 1-40   A red X on the Windows 8 Action Center flag in the taskbar indicates a critical issue needs resolving

To open the Action Center, you can click the red flag in the taskbar and then click **Open Action Center**. Alternately, you can open **Control Panel** and click **Action Center**. The Action Center window for one Windows 8 computer is shown in Figure 1-41. (The Windows 7 Action Center is similar.) Notice the colored bar to the left of a problem. A red bar indicates a critical problem that needs immediate attention. In this example, antivirus software is not running on the system. An orange bar indicates a less critical problem, such as apps running in the background that might be slowing down the system or no backups scheduled. Click the button to the right of a problem to find a recommended solution.

(continues)

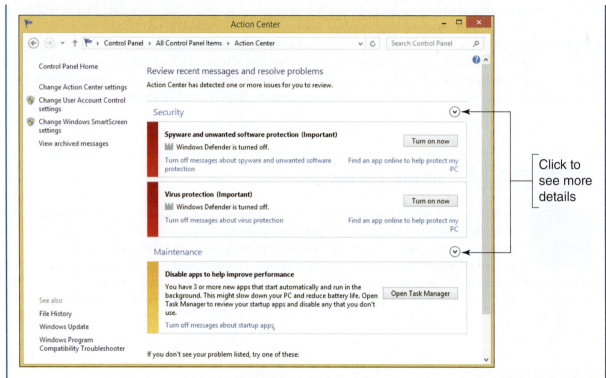

Figure 1-41 The Action Center shows a critical problem that needs a resolution

To see other information available under the Security or Maintenance group, click the down arrow to the right of a group. For example, when you click the arrow to the right of Security, detailed information appears for Windows Firewall, Windows Update, and other security settings.

To see a complete list of past and current problems on a computer, click **View archived messages** in the left pane of the Action Center. This report helps you understand the history of problems on a computer that you are troubleshooting. The problems in this list might or might not have a solution.

HOW WINDOWS CONTROLS ACCESS TO NETWORK RESOURCES

**A+
CORE 2
1.8**

An essential task of IT technicians is to connect computers to a wired or wireless network and support these connections, as you learned in Chapter 3. Once a computer is connected to a network, you need to look at the ways Windows accesses resources on the network. If a network is public, such as a public hotspot at a local coffee shop or airport, resources on the network aren't shared. However, private networks often share their data files, printers, and other resources. In this part of the chapter, you learn how Windows can access resources on a network using a Windows workgroup, homegroup, or domain, and you learn about options that Windows uses to secure a network connection.

WINDOWS WORKGROUP AND HOMEGROUP

**A+
CORE 2
1.8**

A network that doesn't have centralized control, such as one in a small office or home office (SOHO), is called a peer-to-peer (P2P) network. Windows can access resources on a P2P network by using file shares and/or a workgroup; Windows 8/7 can use a homegroup. (Windows 10 does not support homegroups.) Workgroups and homegroups can form a logical group of computers and users that share resources (see Figure 1-42), where administration, resources, and security on a workstation are controlled by that workstation.

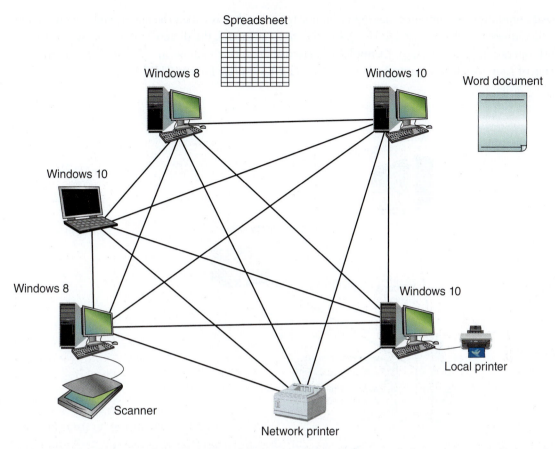

Figure 1-42 A Windows workgroup is a type of peer-to-peer network where no single computer controls the network and each computer controls its own resources

> **Notes** When looking at the diagrams in Figure 1-42 and later in Figure 1-43, know that the connecting lines describe the logical connections between computers and not the physical connections. Both networks might be physically connected the same way, but logically, resources are controlled by each computer on the network or by using a centralized database. In network terminology, the arrangement of physical connections between computers is called the **physical topology**. The logical way the computers connect on a network is called the **logical topology**.

In a Windows **workgroup**, each computer maintains a list of users and their rights on that particular computer. The computer allows a user on the network to access local resources based on the rights she has been given. In a **homegroup**, each computer shares files, folders, libraries, and printers with other computers in the homegroup. (In Windows 10/8/7, a **library** is a collection of folders.) A homegroup provides less security than a workgroup because any user of any computer in the homegroup can access homegroup resources. For this reason and others, the homegroup feature was removed from Windows 10 in the March 2018 update.

> ★ **A+ Exam Tip** The A+ Core 2 exam expects you to be able to contrast a workgroup, homegroup, and domain and know which to use in a given scenario. You also need to know that homegroups only apply to Windows 8/7, and no longer to Windows 10.

WINDOWS DOMAIN

A+ CORE 2 1.8

A Windows **domain** is implemented on a larger, private network, such as a corporate or college network. The domain forms a logical group of networked computers that share a centralized directory database of user account information and security (see Figure 1-43). A Windows domain is a type of **client/server** network, which is a network where resources are managed by centralized computers. A computer making a request from another is called the client, and the computer answering the request is called the server. Using the client/server model, the directory database is controlled by a network operating system (NOS). Examples of network operating systems are Windows Server and various forms of Linux such as Ubuntu Server and Red Hat Enterprise Linux (RHEL).

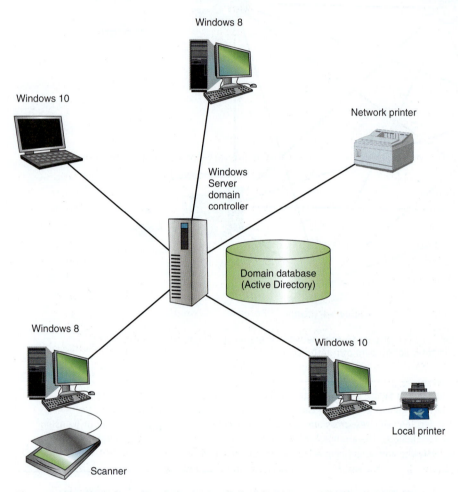

Figure 1-43   A Windows domain is a type of client/server network where security on each computer or other device is controlled by a centralized database on a domain controller

> **Notes**   Windows Home editions do not support joining a domain. If you plan to join a domain on your network, install Windows 10 Professional, Enterprise, or Education edition; Windows 8.1 Professional or Enterprise edition; or Windows 7 Professional, Enterprise, or Ultimate edition.

Windows 10/8 allows three types of accounts to sign in to Windows: a local account, which applies only to the local computer and is also called an offline account; a Microsoft account (always an email address); and a network ID. Windows 7 uses local accounts and network IDs but does not use Microsoft accounts. A Microsoft account signs you in to the local computer and to Microsoft resources in the cloud, such as OneDrive. A network ID signs you in to a Windows domain to which the local computer belongs.

Figure 1-44 Active Directory and Azure AD are two Microsoft options for managing a domain

Microsoft offers two options for managing a domain—Active Directory and Azure Active Directory (see Figure 1-44):

▲ *Active Directory.* Windows Server controls a network using the directory database called **Active Directory (AD)**. Each user on the network must have his own domain-level account, the most common of which is called a **domain user account** or network ID. These accounts are kept in AD and assigned by the network or system administrator. If you are connecting a computer to a domain, the administrator will tell you the network ID and password to the domain that you can use to sign in to the network. Active Directory normally manages a domain for users on company premises. Remote users can join the domain using a VPN or DirectAccess connection. A VPN is a security technique that encrypts data transmitted between a private network and a computer somewhere on the Internet. Windows DirectAccess was designed to eliminate the need for a VPN.

▲ *Azure Active Directory.* **Azure Active Directory (Azure AD)** manages users in the cloud and creates a virtual network of users connected through the Internet. Whereas AD is managed by Windows Server installed on private computers on company premises, Azure AD runs in the cloud from 28 Microsoft data centers around the world that offer Azure AD as a public service. Windows 10 professional and business editions allow work-owned devices and personal devices to join Azure AD. Windows 10 home editions and all editions of Windows 8/7 do not support Azure AD.

Windows 10 offers three ways to authenticate a user so that the computer can join a domain:

▲ *Domain join.* This method is used in Windows 10/8/7 to join an Active Directory domain maintained by a corporation or school. This is the traditional way employees on company premises access resources on the corporate network.

▲ *Azure AD join.* This method is primarily intended as a way for work-owned devices to access cloud resources, such as Office 365, from anywhere on the Internet. For example, a company might provide company-owned laptops to its sales force that work from many remote locations to access company resources in the cloud. Azure AD uses email addresses as account names.

▲ *Bring your own device (BYOD) experience.* Microsoft calls joining a personal device to Azure AD the **BYOD experience**. When a personal device joins Azure AD, you can access corporate resources, such as corporate databases, while still accessing personal resources, such as your personal OneDrive. The process works by using a personal account to sign in to Windows, followed by a secondary sign-in to authenticate to Azure AD. A school might use the BYOD experience to allow students to access school resources using their personal devices via the Internet.

Here is how to join a domain using each of the three methods:

1. Sign in to Windows using an administrator account. Open the **Settings** app. Click the **Accounts** group, and then click **Access work or school**.

2. Under *Connect to work or school*, click **Connect**. See Figure 1-45.

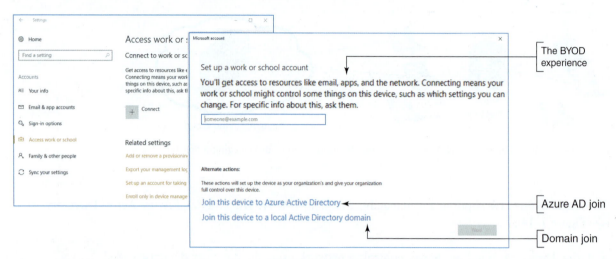

Figure 1-45 Three ways to join a domain

3. Do one of the following:

▲ For a domain join, click **Join this device to a local Active Directory domain**. Enter the domain name and click **Next**. Follow the on-screen directions. The next time you sign in to Windows, use your network ID on the domain.

▲ For an Azure AD join, click **Join this device to Azure Active Directory**. Enter the email address for the work or school account you are accessing and click **Next**. Follow the on-screen directions. The next time you sign in to Windows, use the same email address.

▲ For the BYOD experience, enter your Azure AD email address and click **Next**. Follow the on-screen directions. You will then have access to organizational resources using SSO (Single Sign On) as well as access to your personal resources, such as your personal OneDrive. The next time you sign in to Windows, use your personal account. You will automatically be signed in to Azure AD.

> 📝 **Notes** If your computer is part of a domain, press **Ctrl+Alt+Del** when Windows starts to display a sign-in screen, and then enter your network ID and password.

DOMAIN SETUP

A+
CORE 2
1.8

If a computer is already connected to a physical network, you have signed in to Windows with a local user account, and you want to access resources controlled by a Windows domain on the network, you'll need to change the way Windows connects to the network. To make the change, you'll need the network ID and password to the domain provided by the network administrator. Open the System window (see Figure 1-46). Under *Computer name, domain, and workgroup settings*, click **Change settings**. In the System Properties box that appears, click **Network ID** and follow the directions on screen. The next time you restart the computer, you can sign in with your network ID and password to authenticate to the domain.

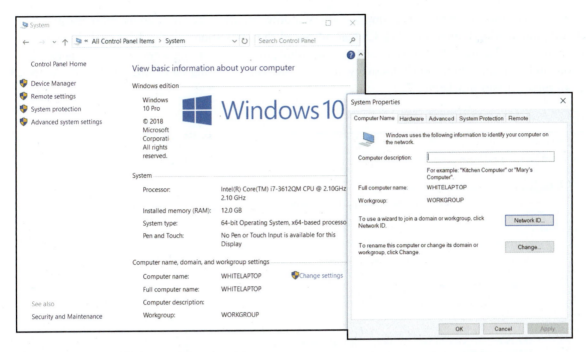

Figure 1-46   Set up Windows to join a domain

Now let's look at the different ways that Windows handles public and private network connections.

PUBLIC AND PRIVATE NETWORKS

A+ CORE 2 1.8   When you connect a Windows computer to a network the first time, Windows asks how you want to secure the network connection. When connecting to a public network, such as when you connect your laptop to a public wireless network at a local airport, you always want to ensure that your computer is protected from outside hackers and malware. Windows 10/8 offers three ways to secure a network connection:

▲ *Public network.* When using Public network security, Windows configures strong firewall settings, the computer is hidden from other devices on the network, and you can't share files or printers. This option is the most secure.

▲ *Private network.* When using Private network security, the computer is discoverable and you can share files and printers. In Windows 8/7, you can join a homegroup. Windows 10/8/7 computers can join a workgroup.

▲ *Domain network.* When the computer is set up to join a Windows domain, it yields control for authenticating users and sharing files, folders, and printers to settings in Active Directory or Azure Activity Directory managing the domain.

Windows 7 offers four network security options, which have different names and slightly different default settings:

▲ *Public network.* Network Discovery is turned off and you cannot join a homegroup or workgroup. This option is the most secure.

▲ *Home network.* Network Discovery is turned on and you can join a homegroup or workgroup.

▲ *Work network.* Network Discovery is turned on and you can join a workgroup, but you cannot join a homegroup.

▲ *Domain network.* When the computer is set up to join a Windows domain, it yields control for authenticating users and sharing its resources to Active Directory managing the domain.

If you want to change the setting that controls how Windows secures a network connection, open the **Network and Sharing Center** and click **Change advanced sharing settings**. In the Advanced sharing settings window (see Figure 1-47), you can change the public, private, home, or work status of a network connection, and you can turn network discovery and file and printer sharing on or off. You learn how to manage all these settings in Chapter 7.

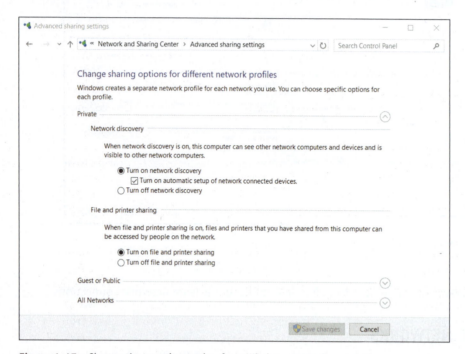

Figure 1-47   Change the security setting for a Windows network connection

WHAT CUSTOMERS WANT: BEYOND TECHNICAL KNOW-HOW

A+
CORE 2
4.7

Probably the most significant indication that an IT technician is doing a good job is that customers are consistently satisfied. In your career as an IT support technician, commit to providing excellent service and to treating customers as you would want to be treated in a similar situation. One of the most important ways to achieve customer satisfaction is to do your best by being prepared, both technically and personally. Being prepared includes knowing what customers want, what they don't like, and what they expect from an IT technician.

Equally important to being prepared technically is knowing how to work effectively with people in a technical world, which is one of the most sought-after skills in today's service-oriented work environments. An employer once told me, "It's not hard to find technically proficient people these days. But it's next to impossible to find people who know how to get along with others and can be counted on when managers are not looking over their shoulders." I could sense his frustration, but I also felt encouraged to know that good social skills and good work ethics can take you far in today's world. My advice to you is to take this part of the chapter seriously. It's important to be technically proficient, but the skills learned in this part of the chapter just might be the ones that make you stand out above the crowd to land that new job or promotion.

> ✏ **Notes** People respond in kind to the position of your facial muscles. Try smiling when you greet someone and see what happens.

BECOMING A COMPETENT AND HELPFUL SUPPORT TECHNICIAN

**A+
CORE 2
4.7**

The following traits distinguish a competent and helpful technician from a technician who is incompetent or unhelpful in the eyes of the customer:

◢ *Be dependable and reliable.* Customers appreciate and respect those who keep their word. If you promise to be back at 10:00 the next morning, be there on time. If you cannot keep your appointment, never ignore your promise. Call, apologize, let the customer know what happened, and reschedule your appointment. Also, do your best to return phone calls the same day and return email within two days.

> ✏ **Notes** Quote from R.C., an employer: "When I choose a person to work for me, in a lot of cases, I choose based on his or her past dependability or attendance. I am less concerned about a person's ability because I can train anyone to do a specific job. I cannot, however, train anyone to do anything if he or she is not present for me to train. Being dependable and reliable has a profound impact on customer relationships as well."

◢ *Keep a positive and helpful attitude.* This helps establish good customer relationships. You communicate your attitude in your tone of voice, the words you choose, how you use eye contact, your facial expressions, how you dress, and in many other subjective and subtle ways. Generally, your attitudes toward your customers stem from how you see people, how you see yourself, and how you see your job. Your attitude is a heart issue, not a head issue. To improve your attitude, you must do it from your heart. That's pretty subjective and cannot be defined with a set of rules, but it always begins with a decision to change. As you work with customers or users, make it a habit not to patronize or talk down to them. Don't make customers or users feel inferior. People appreciate it when they feel your respect for them, even when they have made a mistake or are not knowledgeable. If a problem is simple to solve, don't make other people feel they have wasted your time. Your customer or user should always be made to feel that the problem is important to you.

APPLYING | CONCEPTS   CUSTOMER SERVICE

Josie walked into a computer parts store and wandered over to the cleaning supplies looking for Ace monitor wipes. She saw another brand of wipes, but not the ones she wanted. Looking around for help, she noticed Mary stocking software on the shelves in the next aisle. She walked over to Mary and asked for help finding Ace monitor wipes. Mary put down her box, walked over to the cleaning supply aisle without speaking, picked up a can of wipes, and handed them to Josie, still without speaking a word. Josie explained she was looking for Ace wipes. Mary yelled over three aisles to a coworker in the back room, "Hey, Billy! This lady says she wants Ace monitor wipes. We got any?" Billy came from the back room and said, "No, we only carry those," pointing to the wipes in Mary's hand, and returned to the back room. Mary turned to Josie and said, "We only carry these," and then put the wipes back on the shelf. She turned to walk back to her aisle when Josie said to Mary, "Well, those Ace wipes are great wipes. You might want to consider carrying them." Mary said, "I'm only responsible for software." Josie left the store.

(continues)

Discuss this situation in a small group of students and answer the following questions:

1. If you were Josie, how would you feel about the service in this store?

2. What would you have expected to happen that did not happen?

3. If you were Mary, how could you have provided better service?

4. If you were Billy, is there anything more you could have done to help?

5. If you were the store manager, what principles of good customer service would you want Billy and Mary to know that would have helped them in this situation?

© iStockphoto.com/Sportstock

Figure 1-48 Learn to listen before you decide what a user needs or wants

▲ *Listen without interrupting your customer.* When you're working with or talking to a customer, focus on him or her. Don't assume you know what your customer is about to say. Let her say it, listen carefully, and don't interrupt (see Figure 1-48). Make it your job to satisfy this person, not just your organization, your boss, your bank account, or the customer's boss.

▲ *Use proper and polite language.* Speak politely and use language that won't confuse your customer. Avoid using slang or jargon, which is technical language that only technical people understand. Avoid acronyms (initial letters that stand for words). For example, don't say to a nontechnical customer, "I need to ditch your KVM switch," when you could explain yourself better by saying, "I need to replace that small switch box on your desk that controls your keyboard, monitor, and mouse."

▲ *Show sensitivity to cultural differences.* Cultural differences happen because we are from different countries and societies. Culture can cause us to differ in how we define or judge good service. For example, culture can affect our degree of tolerance for uncertainty. Some cultures are willing to embrace uncertainty, and others strive to avoid it. Those who tend to avoid uncertainty can easily get upset when the unexpected happens. For these people, you need to make special efforts to communicate early and often when things are not going as expected.

▲ *Express patience and honor to those with physical disabilities.* For the physically disabled, especially the hearing- or sight-impaired, communication can be more difficult. It's your responsibility in these situations to do whatever is necessary to find a way to communicate. It's especially important to have an attitude that expresses honor and patience, which you will unconsciously express in your tone of voice, your choice of words, and your actions.

✏ **Notes** Employers look for technicians with good social skills and work ethics because they realize that technicians with these skills are good for business.

▲ *Take ownership of the problem.* Taking ownership of the customer's problem means to accept the problem as your own. Doing that builds trust and loyalty because the customer knows you can be counted on. Taking ownership of a problem also increases your value in the eyes of your coworkers and boss. People who don't take ownership of the problem at hand are likely to be viewed as lazy, uncommitted, and uncaring. One way to take ownership of a problem is not to engage your boss in unproductive discussions about a situation he expects you to handle on your own.

APPLYING | CONCEPTS   SELF-CONTROL

Jack had a bad day on the phones at the networking help desk in Atlanta. An electrical outage coupled with a generator failure had caused servers in San Francisco to be down most of the day. The entire help-desk team had been fielding calls all day explaining to customers why they did not have service and giving expected recovery times. The servers were finally online, but it was taking hours to get everything reset and functioning. No one had taken a break all afternoon, but the call queue was still running about 20 minutes behind. Todd, the boss, had asked the team to work late until the queue was empty. It was Jack's son's birthday and his family was expecting Jack home on time. Jack moaned as he realized he might be late for Tyler's party. Everyone pushed hard to empty the queue. As Jack watched the last call leave the queue, he logged off, stood up, and reached for his coat.

And then another call comes. Jack is tempted to ignore it, but decides it has to be answered. It's Lacy, the executive assistant to the CEO (chief executive officer over the entire company). When Lacy calls, all priorities yield to her, and Lacy knows it. The CEO is having problems printing to the laser printer in his office. Would Jack please walk down to his office and fix the problem? Jack asks Lacy to check the simple things: "Is the printer turned on? Is it plugged in?" Lacy gets huffy and says, "Of course, I've checked that. Now come right now. I need to go." Jack walks down to the CEO's office, takes one look at the printer, and turns it on.

He turns to Lacy and says, "I suppose the on/off button was just too technical for you." Lacy glares at him in disbelief. Jack says, "I'll be leaving now." As he walks out, he begins to form a plan as to how he'll defend himself to his boss in the morning, knowing the inevitable call to Todd's office will come.

In a group of two or four students, one student should play the role of Jack and another the role of Todd. Discuss these questions:

1. Todd is informed the next morning of Jack's behavior, and calls Jack into his office. He likes Jack and wants him to be successful in the company. Jack is resistant and feels justified in what he did. As Todd, what do you think is important that Jack understand? How can you explain this to Jack so he can accept it? What would you advise Jack to do?

2. Switch roles or switch team members and replay the roles.

3. What are three principles of relating to people that would be helpful for Jack to keep in mind?

▲ *Portray credibility*. Convey confidence to your customers. Don't allow yourself to appear confused, afraid, or befuddled. Troubleshoot the problem in a systematic way that portrays confidence and credibility. Get the job done and do it with excellence. Credible technicians also know when the job is beyond their expertise and when to ask for help.

▲ *Work with integrity and honesty*. Don't try to hide your mistakes from your customer or your boss. Everyone makes mistakes, but don't compound them by a lack of integrity. Accept responsibility and do what you can to correct the error.

▲ *Know the law with respect to your work*. For instance, observe the laws concerning the use of software. Don't use or install pirated software.

▲ *Dress and behave professionally*. A professional at work knows not to allow his emotions to interfere with business relationships. If a customer is angry, allow the customer to vent, keeping your own professional distance. (You do, however, have the right to expect a customer not to talk to you in an abusive way.) Dress appropriately for the environment. Take a shower each day and brush your teeth after each meal. Use mouthwash. Iron your shirt. If you're not in good health, try as best you can to take care of the problem. Your appearance matters. And finally—don't use rough language; it is *never* appropriate.

> **Notes** Your customers might never remember what you said or did, but they will always remember how you made them feel.

PLANNING FOR GOOD SERVICE

**A+
CORE 2
4.7**

Your customers can be "internal," meaning you work for the same company and might consider the customers colleagues, or they can be "external" (they come to you or your company for service). Customers can be highly technical or technically naive, represent a large company or simply own a home computer, be prompt or slow at paying their bills, want only the best (and be willing to pay for it) or be searching for bargain service, be friendly and easy to work with or demanding and condescending. In each situation, the key to success is always the same: Don't allow circumstances or personalities to affect your commitment to excellence, and treat the customer as you would want to be treated.

> ⭐ **A+ Exam Tip** The A+ Core 2 exam expects you to know that when serving a customer, you should be on time, avoid distractions, set and meet expectations and timelines, communicate the status of the solution with the customer, and deal appropriately with customers' confidential materials.

Most good service for customers of IT support begins with entries in call tracking software, so let's start there.

CALL TRACKING SOFTWARE

Your organization is likely to use **call tracking software** to track support calls and give technicians a place to keep their call notes. Figure 1-49 shows a window in *everything HelpDesk* software, which is a popular call tracking application.

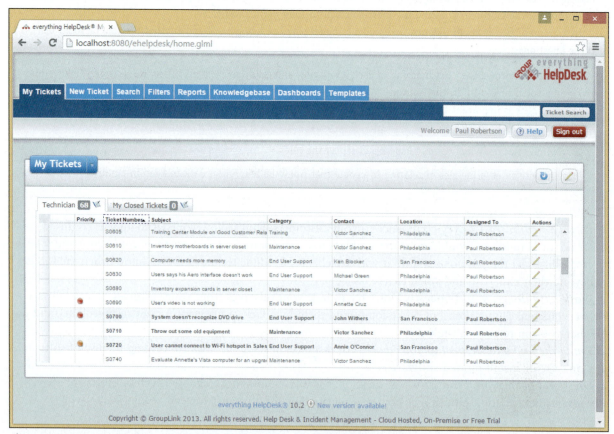

Figure 1-49 Call tracking software allows you to create, edit, and close tickets used by technicians

When someone initiates a call for help, whoever receives the call starts the process by creating a ticket (sometimes called an incident), which is a record of the request and what is happening to resolve it. The call tracking software might track: (1) the date, time, and length of help-desk or on-site calls, (2) causes of and solutions to problems already addressed, (3) who is currently assigned to the ticket and who has already worked on it, (4) who did what and when, and (5) how each call was officially resolved. The ticket is entered into the call tracking system and stays open until the issue is resolved. Support staff assigned to the ticket document their progress under this ticket in the call tracking system. As an open ticket ages, more attention and resources are assigned to it, and the ticket might be escalated (passed on to someone more experienced or who has more resources available) until the problem is finally resolved and the ticket closed. Help-desk personnel and managers acknowledge and sometimes even celebrate those who consistently close the most tickets!

As you support customers and solve computer problems, it's very important to include detailed information in your call notes so that you have the information as you solve the problem or when faced with a similar problem later. Sometimes another person must pick up your open ticket, and she should not have to waste time finding out information you already knew. Also, tracking-system notes are sometimes audited.

INITIAL CONTACT WITH A CUSTOMER

Your initial contact with a customer might be when the customer comes to you, such as in a retail setting, when you go to the customer's site, when the customer calls you on the phone, when the customer reaches you by chat or email, or when you are assigned a ticket already entered in a call tracking system. In each situation, always follow the specific guidelines of your employer. Let's look at some general guidelines for handling first contact with customers.

When you answer the phone, identify yourself and your organization. (Follow the guidelines of your employer on what to say.) Follow company policies to obtain specific information when answering an initial call, such as name (get the right spelling), phone number, and business name. For example, your company might require that you obtain a licensing or warranty number to determine whether the customer is entitled to receive your support. After you have obtained the information you need and confirmed you are authorized to help the customer, open up the conversation for the caller to describe the problem.

Prepare for on-site visits by reviewing information given to you by the person who took the call. Know the problem you are going to address, the urgency of the situation, and what computer, software, and hardware need servicing. Arrive with a complete set of equipment appropriate to the visit, which might include a toolkit, flashlight, multimeter, ESD strap and mat, and bootable media.

When you arrive at the customer's site, greet the customer in a friendly manner and shake his or her hand (see Figure 1-50). Use terms such as Mr. or Ms. and Sir or Ma'am when addressing the customer, unless you are certain the customer expects you to use his or her first name. If the site is a residence, you should *not* remain there when only a minor is present. If a minor

© iStockphoto.com/killerb10

Figure 1-50 If a customer permits it, begin each new relationship with a handshake

child answers the door, ask to speak with an adult and don't allow the adult to leave the house with only you and the child present.

After initial greetings, the first thing you should do is listen and ask questions. As you listen, it's fine to take notes, but don't start the visit by filling out your paperwork. Save the paperwork for later, or have the essentials already filled out before you reach the site.

INTERVIEW THE CUSTOMER

Troubleshooting begins by interviewing the user. As you ask the user questions, take notes and keep asking questions until you thoroughly understand the problem. Have the customer reproduce the problem, and carefully note each step taken and its results. This process gives you clues about the problem and the customer's technical proficiency, which helps you know how to communicate with the customer.

> ★ **A+ Exam Tip** The A+ Core 2 exam expects you to be able to clarify customer statements by asking open-ended questions to narrow the scope of the problem and by restating the issue or question.

Use diplomacy and good manners when you work with a user to solve a problem. For example, if you suspect that the user dropped the computer, don't ask, "Did you drop the laptop?" Put the question in a less accusatory manner: "Could the laptop have been dropped?"

SET AND MEET CUSTOMER EXPECTATIONS

A professional technician knows that it is her responsibility to set and meet expectations with a customer. It's important to create an expectation of certainty with customers so that they are not left hanging and don't know what will happen next.

Figure 1-51 Advise and then allow a customer to make repair or purchasing decisions

Part of setting expectations is to establish a timeline with your customer for the completion of a project. If you cannot solve the problem immediately, explain to the customer what needs to happen and the timeline that he should expect for a solution. Then keep the customer informed about the progress of the solution. For example, you can say to a customer, "I need to return to the office and research the cost of parts that need replacing. I'll call you tomorrow before 10:00 a.m. with an estimate." If you later find out you need more time, call the customer before 10:00 a.m., explain your problem, and give him a new time to expect your call. This kind of service is very much appreciated by customers and, if you are consistent, you will quickly gain their confidence.

Another way to set expectations is to give customers an opportunity to make decisions about repairs to their equipment. When explaining to the customer what needs to be done to fix a problem, offer repair or replacement options if they apply (see Figure 1-51). Don't make decisions for your customer. Explain the problem and what you must do to fix it, giving as many details as the customer wants. When a customer must make a choice, state the options in a way that does not unfairly favor the most lucrative solution for you as the technician or for your company. For example, if you must replace a motherboard (a costly repair in parts and labor), explain to the customer the total cost of repairs and then help him decide if it's better to purchase a new system or repair the existing one.

WORK WITH A CUSTOMER ON SITE

As you work with a customer on site, avoid distractions. Don't accept personal calls or texts on your cell phone, and definitely don't check social media sites when you're on the job. Most organizations require that you answer calls from work, but keep them to a minimum. Be aware that the customer might be listening, so be careful not to discuss problems with coworkers, the boss, or other situations that might put the company, its employees, or products in a bad light with the customer. If you absolutely must excuse yourself from the on-site visit for personal reasons, explain the situation to the customer and return as soon as possible.

When working at a user's desk, follow these general guidelines:

1. As you work, be as unobtrusive as possible. Consider yourself a guest in the customer's office or residence. Don't make a big mess. Keep your tools and papers out of the customer's way. Don't pile your belongings and tools on top of the user's papers, books, and so forth.

2. Protect the customer's confidential and private materials. For example, if you are working on the printer and discover a budget report in the out tray, quickly turn it over so you can't read it, and hand it to the customer. If you notice a financial spreadsheet is displayed on the customer's computer screen, step away and ask the user if she wants to first close the spreadsheet before you work with the computer. If sensitive documents are on the customer's desk, you might let him know and ask if he would like to put them out of your view or in a safe place.

3. Don't take over the mouse or keyboard from the user without permission.

4. Ask permission again before you use the printer or other equipment.

5. Don't use the phone without permission.

6. Accept personal inconvenience to accommodate the user's urgent business needs. For example, if the user gets an important call while you are working, don't allow your work to interfere. You might need to stop work and perhaps leave the room.

7. Also, if the user is present, ask permission before you make a software or hardware change, even if the user has just given you permission to interact with the computer.

8. Don't disclose information about a customer on social media sites, and don't use those public outlets to complain about difficulties with a customer.

In some IT support situations, it is appropriate to consider yourself a support to the user as well as to the computer. Your goals can include educating the user as well as repairing the computer. If you want users to learn something from a problem they caused, explain how to fix the problem and walk them through the process if necessary. Don't fix the problem yourself unless they ask you to do so. It takes a little longer to train the user, but it is more productive in the end because the user learns more and is less likely to repeat the mistake (see Figure 1-52).

© iStockphoto.com/Sportstock

Figure 1-52 Teaching a user how to fix her problem can prevent it from reoccurring

WORK WITH A CUSTOMER ON THE PHONE

Phone support requires more interaction with customers than any other type of IT support. To understand the problem and give clear instructions, you must be able to visualize what the customer sees at his or her computer. Patience is required if the customer must be told each key to press or command button to click. Help-desk support requires excellent communication skills, good phone manners, and lots of patience (see Figure 1-53). As your help-desk skills improve, you will learn to think through the process as though you were sitting in front of the computer yourself. Drawing diagrams and taking notes as you talk can be very helpful. In some cases, help-desk support personnel might have software that enables the remote control of customers' computers. Examples of this type of software are GoToAssist by Citrix at *netviewer.com* and LogMeIn Rescue by LogMeIn at *secure.logmeinrescue.com*. Always communicate clearly with customers when using this type of software, so that they understand what type of access they are allowing you to have on their computers.

© iStockphoto.com/mediaphotos

Figure 1-53   Learn to be patient and friendly when helping users

If your call is accidentally disconnected, call back immediately. Don't eat or drink while on the phone. If you must put callers on hold, tell them how long it will be before you get back to them. Speak clearly and don't talk too fast. Don't complain about your job, your boss, coworkers, your company, or other companies or products to your customers. A little small talk is okay and is sometimes beneficial in easing a tense situation, but keep it upbeat and positive.

DEAL WITH DIFFICULT CUSTOMERS

Most customers are polite and appreciate your help. If you make it a habit to treat others as you want to be treated, you'll find that most of your customers will tend to treat you well, too. However, occasionally you'll have to deal with a difficult customer. In this part of the chapter, you learn how to work with customers who are not knowledgeable, who are overly confident, and who complain.

WHEN THE CUSTOMER IS NOT KNOWLEDGEABLE

When on site, you can put a computer in good repair without depending on a customer to help you. But when you are trying to solve a problem over the phone, with a customer as your only eyes, ears, and hands, a computer-illiterate user can present a challenge. Here are some tips for handling this situation:

- Be specific with your instructions. For example, instead of saying, "Open File Explorer," say, "Using your mouse, right-click the Start button, and click File Explorer from the menu."
- Don't ask the customer to do something that might destroy settings or files without first having the customer back them up carefully. If you think the customer can't handle your request, ask for some on-site help.
- Frequently ask the customer what is displayed on the screen to help you track the keystrokes and action.

- Follow along at your own computer. It's easier to direct the customer keystroke by keystroke if you are doing the same things.
- Give the customer plenty of opportunity to ask questions.
- Genuinely compliment the customer whenever you can to help the customer gain confidence.
- If you determine that the customer cannot help you solve the problem without a lot of coaching, you might need to tactfully request that the caller have someone with more experience call you. The customer will most likely breathe a sigh of relief and have someone take over the problem.

> ✎ **Notes** When solving computer problems in an organization other than your own, check with technical support within that organization instead of working only with the user. The user might not be aware of policies that have been set on his computer to prevent changes to the OS, hardware, or applications.

WHEN THE CUSTOMER IS OVERLY CONFIDENT

Sometimes customers might want to give advice, take charge of a call, withhold information they think you don't need to know, or execute commands at the computer without letting you know, so that you don't have enough information to follow along. A situation like this must be handled with tact and respect for the customer. Here are a few tips:

- When you can, compliment the customer's knowledge, experience, or insight.
- Slow the conversation down. You can say, "Please slow down. You're moving too fast for me to follow. Help me catch up."
- Don't back off from using problem-solving skills. You must still have the customer check the simple things, but direct the conversation with tact. For example, you can say, "I know you've probably gone over these simple things already, but could we just do them again together?"
- Be careful not to accuse the customer of making a mistake.
- Even though the customer might be using technical jargon, keep to your policy of not using jargon back to the customer unless you're convinced he truly understands you.

> ★ **A+ Exam Tip** The A+ Core 2 exam expects you to know that it is important not to minimize a customer's problem and not to be judgmental toward a customer.

WHEN THE CUSTOMER COMPLAINS

When you are on site or on the phone, a customer might complain to you about your organization, products, or service or the service and product of another company. Consider the complaint to be helpful feedback that can lead to a better product or service and better customer relationships. Here are a few suggestions that can help you handle complaints and defuse customer anger:

- Be an active listener, and let customers know they are not being ignored. Look for the underlying problem. Don't take complaints or anger personally.
- Give the customer a little time to vent and apologize when you can. Then start the conversation by asking questions, taking notes, and solving problems. Unless you must have the information for problem solving, don't spend a lot of time finding out exactly who the customer dealt with and what happened to upset the customer.
- Don't be defensive. It's better to leave the customer with the impression that you and your company are listening and willing to admit mistakes. No matter how much anger is expressed, resist the temptation to argue or become defensive.
- Know how your employer wants you to handle a situation where you are verbally abused. For example, you might say something like this in a calm voice: "I'm sorry, but my employer does not require me to accept this kind of talk."

▲ If the customer is complaining about a product or service that is not from your company, don't start by saying, "That's not our problem." Instead, listen to the customer complain. Don't appear as though you don't care.

▲ If the complaint is against you or your product, identify the underlying problem if you can. Ask questions and take notes. Then pass these notes on to people in your organization who need to know.

▲ Sometimes simply making progress or reducing the problem to a manageable state reduces the customer's anxiety. As you are talking to a customer, summarize what you have both agreed on or observed so far in the conversation (see Figure 1-54).

© iStockphoto.com/Kameleon007

Figure 1-54 When a customer is upset, try to find a place of agreement

▲ Point out ways that *you* think communication could be improved. For example, you might say, "I'm sorry, but I'm having trouble understanding what you want. Could you please slow down, and let's take this one step at a time?"

APPLYING | CONCEPTS   CULTURE OF HONOR

Andy is one of the most intelligent and knowledgeable support technicians in his group at CloudPool, Inc. He is about to be promoted to software engineer and today is his last day on the help desk. Sarah, a potential customer with little computer experience, calls asking for help in accessing the company website. Andy says, "The URL is www dot cloud pool dot com." Sarah responds, "What's a URL?" Andy's patience grows thin. He's thinking to himself, "Oh, help! Just two more hours and I'm off these darn phones." He answers Sarah in a tone of voice that says, hey, I really think you're an idiot! He says to her, "You know, lady! That address box at the top of your browser. Now enter www dot cloud pool dot com!" Sarah gets flustered and intimidated and doesn't know what to say next. She really wants to know what a browser is, but instead she says, "Wait. I'll just ask someone in the office to help me," and hangs up the phone.

Discuss the situation with others in a small group and answer these questions:

1. If you were Andy's manager and overheard this call, how would you handle the situation?

2. What principles of working with customers does Andy need to keep in mind?

Two students sit back-to-back, one playing the role of Andy and the other playing the role of Sarah. Play out the entire conversation. Others in the group can offer suggestions and constructive criticism.

THE CUSTOMER DECIDES WHEN THE WORK IS DONE

When you think you've solved the problem, allow the customer to decide if the service is finished to his or her satisfaction. For remote support, the customer generally ends the call or chat session, not the technician. If you end the call too soon and the problem is not completely resolved, the customer can be frustrated, especially if it is difficult to contact you again.

For on-site work, after you have solved the problem, complete these tasks before you close the call:

1. If you changed anything on the computer after you booted it, reboot one more time to make sure you have not caused a problem with the boot.

2. Allow the customer enough time to be fully satisfied that all is working. Does the printer work? Print a test page. Does the network connection work? Can the customer sign in to the network and access data on it?

3. If you backed up data before working on the problem and then restored the data from backups, ask the user to verify that the data is fully restored.

4. Review the service call with the customer. Summarize the instructions and explanations you have given during the call. This is an appropriate time to fill out your paperwork and explain to the customer what you have written. Then ask if she has any questions.

5. Explain preventive maintenance to the customer, such as deleting temporary files from the hard drive or cleaning the mouse. Most customers don't have preventive maintenance contracts for their computers and appreciate the time you take to show them how to take better care of their equipment. One technician keeps a pack of monitor wipes in his toolkit and ends each call by cleaning the customer's monitor screen.

To demonstrate a sincere concern for your customer's business and that you have owned the problem, it's extremely important to follow up later with the customer, ask if he is still satisfied with your work, and ask if he has any more questions. For example, you can say to the customer, "I'll call you on Monday to make sure everything is working and you're still satisfied with the work." On Monday, make that call. As you do, you're building customer loyalty.

> ★ **A+ Exam Tip** The A+ Core 2 exam expects you to know to follow up with the customer at a later date to verify his or her satisfaction.

SOMETIMES YOU MUST ESCALATE A PROBLEM

You are not going to solve every computer problem you encounter. Knowing how to escalate a problem properly so it is assigned to people higher in the support chain is one of the first things you should learn on a new job. Know your company's policy for escalation. What documents or entries in the call tracking software do you use? Who do you contact? How do you pass the problem on—do you use email, a phone call, or an online entry in a database? Do you remain the responsible "support" party, or does the person now addressing the problem become the new contact? Are you expected to keep in touch with the customer and the problem, or are you totally out of the picture?

When you escalate, let the customer know. Tell the customer you are passing the problem on to someone who is more experienced or has access to more extensive resources. If you check back with the customer only to find out that the other support person has not called or followed through to the customer's satisfaction, don't lay blame or point fingers. Just do whatever you can to help within your company guidelines. Your call to the customer will go a long way toward helping the situation.

WORK WITH COWORKERS

Learn to be a professional when working with coworkers. A professional at work is someone who puts business matters above personal matters (see Figure 1-55). In big bold letters, I can say **the key to being professional is to learn not to be personally offended when someone lets you down or does not please you.** Remember, most people do the best they can considering the business and personal constraints they're up against. Getting offended leads to becoming bitter about others and about your job. Learn to keep negative opinions to yourself, and to expect the best of others. When a coworker starts to gossip, try to politely change the subject.

Know your limitations and be willing to admit when you can't do something. For example, Larry's boss stops by his desk and asks him to accept one more project. Larry already is working many hours overtime just to keep up. He needs to politely say to his boss, "I can accept this new project only if you relieve me of some of these tasks."

© iStockphoto.com/Chris Schmidt

Figure 1-55 Coworkers who act professionally are fun to work with

APPLYING │ CONCEPTS   ACTIVE LEARNING

Ray was new at a corporate help desk that supported hospitals across the nation. He had only had a couple of weeks of training before he was turned loose on the phones. He was a little nervous the first day he took calls without a mentor sitting beside him. His first call came from Fernanda, a radiology technician who was trying to sign in to the network to start the day. When Fernanda entered her network ID and passcode, an error message stated her user account was not valid. She told Ray she had tried signing in several times on two different computers. Ray checked his database and found her account, which appeared to be in good order. He asked her to try again. She did and got the same results. In his two weeks of training, this problem had never occurred. He told her, "I'm sorry, I don't know how to solve this problem." She said, "Okay, well, thank you anyway," and hung up. She immediately called the

(continues)

help-desk number back and the call was answered by Jackie, who sits across the room from Ray. Fernanda said, "The other guy couldn't fix my problem. Can you help me?"

"What other guy?" Jackie asked.

"I think his name was Ray."

"Oh, him! He's new and he doesn't know much, and besides that, he should have asked for help. Tell me the problem." Jackie reset the account and the problem was solved.

In a group of three or more students, discuss and answer the following questions:

1. What mistake did Ray make? What should he have done or said?

2. What mistake did Jackie make? What should she have done or said?

3. What three principles of relating to customers and coworkers would be helpful for Ray and Jackie to keep in mind?

>> CHAPTER SUMMARY

Windows Interfaces

- An operating system manages hardware, runs applications, provides an interface for users, and stores, retrieves, and manipulates files.

- Windows 10 offers two graphical user interfaces: the desktop and Tablet mode. Windows 8 offers two GUIs: the modern interface and the Windows 8 desktop. The Windows 7 desktop offers the Aero user interface.

- Ways to launch a program from the Windows 10 desktop include using the Start menu, the search box, the Quick Launch menu, an icon pinned to the taskbar, File Explorer, a shortcut on the desktop, and the Run option on the Quick Launch menu.

- Ways to launch a program from the Windows 8 desktop include using the Start screen, the Quick Launch menu, an icon pinned to the taskbar, File Explorer, a shortcut on the desktop, and the Run option on the Quick Launch menu.

- Ways to launch a program from the Windows 7 desktop include using the Start menu, the search box, an icon pinned to the taskbar, Windows Explorer, or a shortcut on the desktop.

Windows Tools for Users and Technicians

- Windows 10/8 File Explorer and Windows 7 Windows Explorer are used to manage files and folders on storage devices. Folders are organized in a top-down hierarchical structure of subfolders.

- The file extension indicates how file contents are organized and formatted and what program uses the file.

- Control Panel gives access to a group of utility programs used to manage the system. Technicians generally prefer the Classic view for Control Panel.

- The Windows 10 File Explorer Options and Windows 8/7 Folder Options applets in Control Panel change the way files and folders are displayed in Explorer.

- The Sound applet in Control Panel controls audio, including default speakers and microphones.

- The Power Options applet in Control Panel manages power settings on a computer.

- The System window gives a quick overview of the system, including which edition and version of Windows is installed and the amount of installed memory.

◢ The System Information window gives much more information about the computer than the System window, including information on hardware, device drivers, the OS, and applications.

◢ The Settings app is a centralized location for users to access common Windows 10 settings.

How Windows Controls Access to Network Resources

◢ Windows 10/8/7 supports workgroups and domains to manage resources on a private network. In addition, Windows 8/7 supports homegroups to manage resources on a private network. Workgroups are more secure than homegroups.

◢ Windows 10/8 supports public and private settings to secure a network connection, and Windows 7 supports public, home, and work settings to secure a network connection.

◢ Join a Windows computer to a domain using one of these methods: (1) use a network ID when you sign in to Windows to authenticate the user to Active Directory on the local network or through some type of VPN; (2) use an email address and password when you sign in to Windows to authenticate the user to Azure AD in the cloud; or (3) use an email address and password to authenticate to Azure AD in the cloud as a secondary login after you have already signed in to Windows with your personal user account.

◢ Use the Settings app to set up a computer to connect to a workgroup or to authenticate a user so that the computer can join a domain.

◢ Use the Network and Sharing Center to change the security settings for a Windows network connection.

What Customers Want: Beyond Technical Know-How

◢ Customers want more than just technical know-how. They want a positive and helpful attitude, respect, good communication, sensitivity to their needs, ownership of their problem, dependability, credibility, integrity, honesty, and professionalism.

◢ Customers expect their first contact with you to be professional and friendly, and expect that listening to their problem or request will be your first priority.

◢ Know how to ask penetrating questions when interviewing a customer about a problem or request.

◢ Set and meet customer expectations by using good communication about what you are doing or intending to do and allowing the customer to make decisions where appropriate.

◢ Deal confidently and gracefully with customers who are difficult, including those who are not knowledgeable, are overly confident, or complain.

◢ When you first start a new job, find out how to escalate a problem you cannot solve.

>> KEY TERMS

For explanations of key terms, see the Glossary for this text.

32-bit operating system	BYOD experience	compressed (zipped) folder	File Explorer Options
64-bit operating system	call tracking software	Control Panel	applet
Action Center	Category view	Cortana	file extension
Active Directory (AD)	charm	device drivers	file name
Aero user interface	charms bar	domain	Folder Options applet
Azure Active Directory	child directories	domain user account	folders
(Azure AD)	Classic view	escalate	gadgets
Branchcache	client/server	File Explorer	

graphical user interface (GUI)
hibernation
homegroup
library
live tiles
logical topology
Media Center
Metro UI
Metro User Interface
modern interface
navigation pane

Network and Sharing Center
Notepad
notification area
operating system (OS)
path
peer-to-peer (P2P)
physical topology
pinning
Power Options applet
Recycle Bin
root directory

service
Settings app
sleep mode
sleep timers
Sound applet
standby mode
Start screen
subdirectories
suspend mode
System Information
system tray

System window
systray
taskbar
Task View
ticket
volume
Windows 8.1
Windows 10
Windows Explorer
workgroup

>> THINKING CRITICALLY

These questions are designed to prepare you for the critical thinking required for the A+ exams and may use content from other chapters and the web.

1. When Kristy recently started a photography business, she downloaded Photoshop to her computer to edit her photos. She notices her computer freezes when she is using Photoshop, so she asks you to help her fix the problem. Your research discovers that Photoshop requires a lot of RAM to run smoothly, and you need to know how much RAM Kristy's computer has to see if that is the problem. Which Windows tools from the following list can you use to know how much RAM is installed on a system? Select all that apply.

   a. System window

   b. Power Options applet

   c. System Information window

   d. Network and Sharing Center

2. John is traveling for work and is spending a week at a new branch. He needs to print an email, but he isn't able to add the network printer to his computer. He is using a Windows 10 Pro laptop, is connected to the network, and can access the Internet. What is a likely and easy fix to John's problem?

   a. The computer is not set to find resources shared on the network; use the Settings app to fix the problem.

   b. The computer is not set to find resources shared on the network; use the Network and Sharing Center to fix the problem.

   c. John did not correctly authenticate to the Windows domain; use the Settings app to fix the problem.

   d. The drivers for the network printer need to be updated. Use Device Manager to fix the problem.

3. Mary wants her 32-bit installation of Windows 7 Professional to run faster. She has 4 GB of memory installed on the motherboard. She decides more memory will help. She installs an additional 2 GB of memory for a total of 6 GB, but does not see any performance improvement. What is the problem and what should you tell Mary?

   a. She should use Control Panel to install the memory in Windows 7. After it is installed, performance should improve. Tell Mary how to open Control Panel.

   b. A 32-bit OS cannot use more than 4 GB of memory. Tell Mary she has wasted her money.

   c. A 32-bit OS cannot use more than 4 GB of memory. Tell Mary to upgrade her system to the 64-bit version of Windows 7 Professional.

   d. A 32-bit OS cannot use more than 4 GB of memory. Explain the problem to Mary and discuss the possible solutions with her.

4. Jack needs to email two documents to a friend, but the files are so large his email server bounced them back as undeliverable. What is your advice?

   a. Tell Jack to open the documents, break each of them into two documents, and then email the four documents separately.

   b. Tell Jack to put the two documents in a compressed folder and email the folder.

   c. Tell Jack to put each document in a different compressed folder and email each folder separately.

   d. Tell Jack to put the documents on a USB drive and snail mail the drive to his friend.

5. Jawana has been working on a paper for her Anatomy class for weeks. One day her little brother was on her computer and accidentally deleted her paper from the Documents folder. How can Jawana recover her deleted paper?

6. A technician needs to be prepared to launch programs even when utility windows or the Windows desktop cannot load. What is the program name for the System Information utility? What is the program name for the Remote Desktop utility?

7. Suppose you are a customer who wants to have a computer repaired. List five main characteristics that you would want to see in your computer repair person.

8. When you receive a phone call requesting on-site support, what is one thing you should do before you make an appointment?

9. You make an appointment to do an on-site repair, but you are detained and find out that you will be late. What is the best thing to do?

10. When making an on-site service call, what should you do before making any changes to software or before taking the case cover off a computer?

11. What should you do after finishing your computer repair?

12. What is a good strategy to follow if a conflict arises between you and your customer?

13. You have exhausted your knowledge of a problem and it still is not solved. Before you escalate it, what else can you do?

14. If you need to make a phone call while on a customer's site and your cell phone is not working, what do you do?

15. What is one thing you can do to help a caller who needs phone support and is not a competent computer user?

16. Describe what you should do when a customer complains to you about a product or service that your company provides.

17. Robert works in a call center and receives a call from Kathy. Kathy says she can no longer access the online reporting application for her weekly reports through her web browser. You ask your boss, and he tells you that the server team changed the application's URL during an upgrade over the weekend. He asks you to make sure all the other technicians are aware of this change. What is the best way to share this information?

   a. Print a flyer with the new URL and post it on the wall in the call center.

   b. Send out a mass email with the new URL to all the technicians.

   c. Update the knowledge base article that contains the application's URL in the call tracking application.

   d. Yell the new URL to all technicians sitting in the call center.

>> HANDS-ON PROJECTS

Hands-On | Project 1-1   Practicing Using the Quick Launch Menu

Do the following to practice using the Quick Launch menu:

1. Click the **Power** icon on the Start menu. What are the options on the Power icon menu?

2. Open the **Quick Launch** menu, and practice using several options on the menu. What are the submenu items that appear when you point to *Shut down or sign out*?

3. Click **Power Options** on the Quick Launch menu. The Settings app opens to the Power & sleep page. Sometimes you need to use links in the Settings app to navigate to the control panel applets and find more options. Find the settings in the Power Options window that allow you to change the options available in the *Shut down or sign out* menu.

4. Go to the **Start** menu. Click your account icon on the left side of the Start menu. What options appear in the drop-down menu? Try the Lock and Sign out options, and describe what each option does.

Hands-On | Project 1-2   Creating Shortcuts

Do the following to practice creating shortcuts on the Windows desktop:

1. Open Windows 10/8 File Explorer or Windows 7 Windows Explorer and create a folder called **Temp** under the root directory of the hard drive. List the steps you took.

2. Add a subfolder to Temp called **MyFiles**. List the steps you took.

3. Create a text file named **Text1.txt** in the MyFiles folder. List the steps you took.

4. Create a shortcut to the Text1.txt file on the Windows desktop. List the steps you took.

5. In the MyFiles folder, rename the file **Text2.txt**.

6. Double-click the shortcut on the desktop. Did that cause an error? Did the shortcut name change when you changed the name of the original file? Did it open the correct file?

7. The program file for Microsoft Paint is mspaint.exe. Use Windows Explorer to locate the program file and launch the Microsoft Paint program.

8. Create a shortcut to Microsoft Paint on the Windows desktop. Launch Microsoft Paint using the shortcut.

9. To clean up after yourself, delete the Temp folder and the shortcuts. Close the two Paint windows.

Hands-On | Project 1-3   Using the System Information Utility

Do the following to run the System Information utility and gather information about your system:

1. Use the **msinfo32.exe** command to launch the System Information window.

2. Browse through the different levels of information in this window and answer the following questions:
   a. What OS and OS version are you using?
   b. What is your CPU speed?
   c. What is your BIOS manufacturer and version?
   d. How much video RAM is available to your video adapter card? Explain how you got this information.
   e. What is the name of the driver file that manages your network adapter? Your optical drive?

Hands-On | Project 1-4   Installing and Uninstalling Windows 10/8 Apps

Windows 10/8 apps are installed from the Windows Store. Follow these steps to install an app and then uninstall it:

1. Open the Start menu.

> **↻ OS Differences**   In Windows 8, you must have a Microsoft account to get apps from the Windows Store. If you don't already have an account, you can get one free at *live.com*.

2. To install an app, click the **Microsoft Store** tile. Next, scroll through the apps in the Store or use its search box to find an app (see Figure 1-56). Click a free one, such as Windows Help+Tips, and follow the directions on screen to install it. If you did not sign in to Windows using a Microsoft account, you are asked to sign in so that you can apply this app to all your devices using this Microsoft account; in Windows 10, you can decline and install this app only on the local machine.

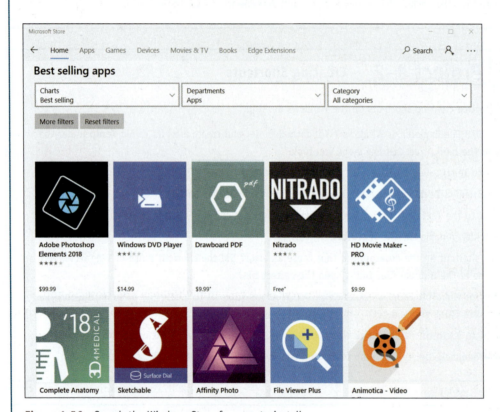

Figure 1-56   Search the Windows Store for apps to install

3. Launch the app and practice using it to make sure it works.

4. To uninstall the app, right-click the app tile on the Start menu. Click **Uninstall** and follow the directions on screen.

>> REAL PROBLEMS, REAL SOLUTIONS

REAL PROBLEM 1-1 Using Windows Help and Support

The best IT support technicians are the ones who continually teach themselves new skills. You can teach yourself to use and support Windows by using the web, a couple of apps in Windows 10 called Get Help and Tips, or the Windows Help and Support utility in Windows 8/7. To start the apps in Windows 10, type **get help** in the search box or type **tips** in the search box. In Windows 8, type **Help and Support** on the Start screen. In Windows 7, click **Start** and then click **Help and Support**. If you are connected to the Internet, clicking links can take you to the Microsoft website, where you can find information and watch videos about Windows.

Do the following to research a topic so you can become an independent learner about Windows:

1. The Windows 10/8/7 Snipping Tool can help you take screenshots of the Windows desktop. These screenshots are useful when documenting computer problems and solutions. Use Get Help or Windows Help and Support to find out how to use the Snipping Tool. Use it to take a screenshot of your Windows desktop. Save the screenshot into a file on a USB flash drive or on the hard drive. Print the file contents.

2. Access the *support.microsoft.com* website for Windows support. Save or print one article from the Knowledge Base that addresses a problem when installing Windows 10/8/7.

3. Search the web to learn the purpose of the pagefile.sys file. What website did you use to find your answer? Why is the Microsoft website considered the best source for information about the pagefile.sys file?

REAL PROBLEM 1-2 Documenting How to Use Windows

This problem requires a microphone, and a webcam would also be useful. Make a screen recording with a voiceover to teach end users how to use Windows. Do the following:

1. Screencast-O-Matic offers free software to make a screen recording with voice and video. Go to *screencast-o-matic.com* and launch the online video recording software. You might be required to download and install the software.

2. Select a Windows feature to explain. For example, you can explain how to open and close an app, install or uninstall an app, create a shortcut, empty the Recycle Bin, or use the Start menu. You or your instructor might have other ideas.

3. Use the Screencast-O-Matic software to make a screen recording that explains how to use the Windows feature you selected. The recording should be no longer than three minutes. Explain the steps as you go. The software records your screen movements, your voice if a microphone is detected, and video if a webcam is detected.

4. View the video. If you see a problem, record it again. When you're satisfied with your video, save it as an MP4 file.

REAL PROBLEM 1-3 Learning a New App Available in Windows 10

Sometimes you might encounter an application that you are not familiar with, yet you might be asked to help a user answer questions about the app. In that case, you can search for the information you need in the application's Help system. In this Real Problem, you use the Help system and online tutorials for Sway, a new app available for free in Windows 10. Perform the following steps, looking up Help information as necessary to learn how to proceed. If you are already familiar with Sway, pretend you are not and rely on Help information instead. To practice using Sway, complete the following tasks:

1. Create a new Sway story.

2. Choose a design and layout.

3. Add a title, photographs, and text.

4. Add focus points on photographs.

5. Share the URL to your Sway story with another person and have her watch what you created using a web browser.

REAL PROBLEM 1-4 Installing and Using the Mouse Without Borders App

This Real Problem requires two computers on the same network, both with Internet access. Install the free Microsoft app Mouse Without Borders on both computers. This app allows one computer's mouse and keyboard to control up to four computers. The app is very useful when you frequently switch between two different computers, even when you are using both Windows 10 and Windows 8. Complete the following tasks:

1. Open Edge and search for the Mouse Without Borders download. Make sure your system meets the minimum system requirements.

2. Download and install the app from the Microsoft Download Center webpage.

3. Use Mouse Without Borders to connect two computers on the same network.

4. On the first computer, use the mouse and keyboard to control the second computer by opening an app on it without touching its mouse or keyboard.

Installing Windows

Windows 10, 8, and 7 all share the same basic Windows architecture, and all have similar characteristics. Windows 10 includes free upgrades called builds. Windows 8 includes a free upgrade to Windows 8.1 via the Windows Store. Windows 10 is available for purchase directly from Microsoft, but you can no longer purchase Windows 8 or 7. (However, Windows 8.1 and 7 can be purchased from other vendors.)

This chapter discusses how to plan a Windows installation and the steps to perform a Windows 10, Windows 8.1, or Windows 7 installation in various scenarios, including what to do after the OS is installed. You also learn what to expect when installing Windows on computers in a large enterprise.

> ✎ **Notes** In the text, we use the term "Windows 8" to refer to Windows 8.0 and Windows 8.1.

HOW TO PLAN A WINDOWS INSTALLATION

As an IT support technician, you can expect to be called on to install Windows in a variety of situations. You might need to install Windows on a new hard drive, after an existing Windows installation has become corrupted, or to upgrade from one OS to another. Many decisions need to be made before the installation, and most of these decisions apply to any Windows operating system.

CHOOSING THE EDITION, LICENSE, AND VERSION OF WINDOWS

When buying a Windows operating system, know that the price is affected by the Windows edition and type of license you purchase. You learned about the different editions in Chapter 1. You also need to decide between 32-bit and 64-bit architecture. In this part of the chapter, you learn about your options when purchasing Windows and how to make sure your computer qualifies for the version and edition you've selected.

OEM OR RETAIL LICENSE

When buying Windows, you can purchase a retail license or an Original Equipment Manufacturer (OEM) license. Options for both types of licenses include 32-bit and 64-bit. Here are the key differences between an OEM license and a retail license:

◢ The OEM license is for builders and manufacturers of computers and can be installed only on a new computer. You can purchase and download a Windows 10 OEM license from a third party such as Amazon at *amazon.com* or Newegg at *newegg.com*.

◢ An OEM license allows all hardware upgrades except for an upgrade to a different model of motherboard.

◢ An OEM license costs less than a retail license. Microsoft generally refers technical support for an OEM license to the computer manufacturer or builder.

◢ Retail licenses can be purchased from the Microsoft online store at *microsoftstore.com*. Microsoft sells Windows 10 as either a download or on a boxed USB flash drive (sometimes called an Install Stick) that's shipped to you with the installation files. Whether you're doing a clean install of Windows 10 or an upgrade from Windows 8/7 to Windows 10, the retail license costs the same.

◢ The benefit of a retail license over an OEM license is that it can be transferred to a different computer, and you get Microsoft direct support from Microsoft support personnel.

When you download the Windows 10 setup files from Microsoft, you start by downloading the Media Creation Tool. After you install and launch the tool, you use it to download Windows setup files; you also have the option to create a bootable DVD or USB flash drive. You learn how to use the Media Creation Tool later in this chapter.

> ✎ **Notes** The Media Creation Tool and Windows setup files can be downloaded for free from Microsoft. Therefore, when you purchase Windows 10, you are really only purchasing a **product key**, which is required to activate a license to use Windows 10. The product key is emailed to your Microsoft account email address.

32-BIT OR 64-BIT ARCHITECTURE

Recall that an operating system can process 32 bits or 64 bits at a time. A 64-bit installation of Windows generally performs better than a 32-bit installation if you have enough RAM. (Table 2-1 shows how much RAM is supported by popular editions of Windows.) Also, 64-bit installations of Windows can support 64-bit applications, which run faster than 32-bit applications. Even though you can install 32-bit applications in a 64-bit OS, always choose 64-bit applications for best performance. Keep in mind that 64-bit installations of Windows require 64-bit device drivers.

Operating System	32-Bit Architecture	64-Bit Architecture
Windows 10 Home Windows 8.1	4 GB	128 GB
Windows 10 Pro Windows 10 Enterprise Windows 8.1 Pro Windows 8.1 Enterprise	4 GB	512 GB
Windows 7 Home Premium	4 GB	16 GB
Windows 7 Professional Windows 7 Enterprise Windows 7 Ultimate	4 GB	192 GB

Table 2-1   Maximum memory supported by Windows 10, 8.1, and 7 editions and versions

> ✎ **Notes** All processors (CPUs) used in personal computers today are hybrid processors and can handle a 32-bit or 64-bit OS. However, the Intel Itanium and Xeon processors used in high-end workstations and servers are true 64-bit processors and require a 64-bit OS.

> ✎ **Notes** How much memory or RAM you can install in a computer depends not only on the OS installed, but also on how much memory the motherboard can hold. To know how much RAM a motherboard can support, see the motherboard documentation.

VERIFYING THAT YOUR SYSTEM QUALIFIES FOR WINDOWS

**A+
CORE 2
1.1, 1.3**   The minimum hardware requirements for Windows 10/8/7 are listed in Table 2-2. (These minimum requirements are also the Microsoft recommended requirements.) Beginning with Windows 8, in addition to the requirements listed, Microsoft requires three technologies used by the processor (NX, PAE, and SSE2). All processors built in the last 10 years use these technologies, so the move was intended to prevent a new edition of Windows from being installed on a system that was more than 10 years old. Know, however, that Microsoft occasionally changes the minimum and recommended requirements for its OSs.

Hardware	For 32-Bit Windows	For 64-Bit Windows
Processor	1 GHz or faster; for Windows 10/8, must support NX, PAE, and SSE2	
Memory (RAM)	1 GB	2 GB
Free hard drive space	16 GB	20 GB
Video device and driver	DirectX 9 device with WDDM 1.0 or higher driver	

Table 2-2   Minimum and recommended hardware requirements for Windows 10/8/7

> ✎ **Notes** The three processor technologies are NX (Never Execute or No Execute), which prevents malware from hiding in the data storage area of another program; PAE (Physical Address Extension), which was originally intended to allow 32-bit processors to use more than 4 GB of RAM but is no longer used for that purpose because it gave device drivers a big headache; and SSE2 (Streaming SIMD Extensions 2), which allows a processor to execute a single instruction multiple times.

> ★ **A+ Exam Tip** The A+ Core 2 exam may give you a scenario and ask you to demonstrate hardware compatibility requirements for a Windows installation.

MBR OR GPT PARTITIONING SYSTEM

You need to be aware of the partitioning method you will use on the hard drive. A hard drive is divided into one or more partitions. Windows can use one of two methods to partition a hard drive: The **Master Boot Record (MBR)** method is older, allows for four partitions, and is limited to 2.2-TB drives. The **GUID Partition Table (GPT)** method is newer, allows for any size of hard drive, and for Windows can have up to 128 partitions on the drive. GPT is required for drives larger than 2.2 TB.

When an MBR or GPT partition is formatted with a file system and assigned a drive letter (such as drive C:), it is called a **volume**. A **file system** is the overall structure an OS uses to name, store, and organize files on a volume; Windows is always installed on a volume that uses the NTFS file system. For most installations, you install Windows on the only hard drive in the computer and allocate all the space on the drive to one partition that Windows setup calls drive C:. Windows is installed in the C:\Windows folder. You learn more about partitions and file systems in Chapter 4.

BIOS/UEFI FIRMWARE ON THE MOTHERBOARD

To understand if your system qualifies for Windows 10/8/7, it helps to understand how Windows relates to hardware by using device drivers and firmware on the motherboard, as shown in Figure 2-1. (In the figure, the kernel is the part of Windows responsible for relating to hardware.)

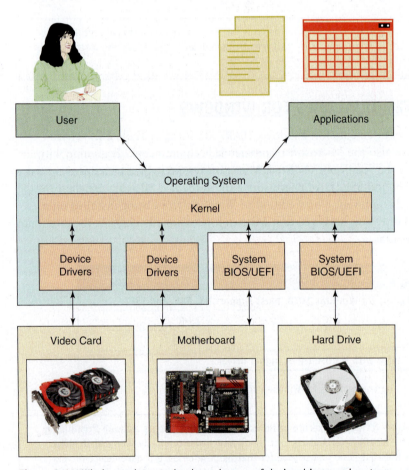

Figure 2-1 Windows relates to hardware by way of device drivers and system BIOS/UEFI

When a computer is first turned on, it uses some devices such as the keyboard, monitor, and hard drive before the OS starts up. The motherboard BIOS/UEFI is contained on a chip on the motherboard (see Figure 2-2) and manages these essential devices. This chip is called a firmware chip because it holds programs.

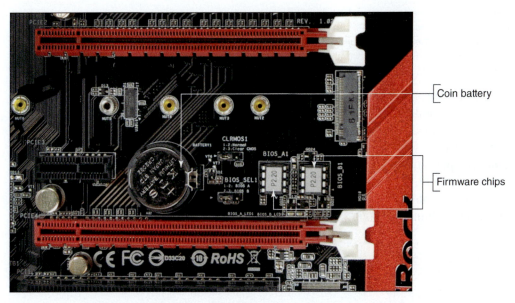

Figure 2-2 A chip on a motherboard contains BIOS/UEFI used to start the computer, hold motherboard settings, and run essential devices. The chip retains power from a nearby coin battery when the computer is turned off.

All modern motherboards use firmware called **UEFI (Unified Extensible Firmware Interface)**. UEFI is a much improved replacement for **BIOS (basic input/output system)** and offers legacy support for BIOS compatibility. BIOS stores its setup information on the motherboard, while UEFI stores its setup information and some drivers on the motherboard and the hard drive. The motherboard BIOS/UEFI provides three main functions:

◢ The **system BIOS/UEFI** contains instructions for running essential hardware devices before an operating system is started. After the OS is started, it might continue to use system BIOS/UEFI or use device drivers to communicate with these devices.

◢ The **startup BIOS/UEFI** starts the computer and finds a boot device that contains an operating system. Boot devices that a system might support include an internal or external hard drive, CD or DVD drive, bootable USB flash drive, and the network. After it finds a boot device, the firmware turns the startup process over to the OS.

> ✎ **Notes** When choosing a boot device, consider that **solid-state drives** are faster than magnetic hard drives because they have no moving parts. USB flash drives are also solid-state devices. Some hard drives might be **hot-swappable**, which means they are inserted into an easily accessible hot-swap bay and can be exchanged without powering down the system.

◢ The **setup BIOS/UEFI** is used to change motherboard settings. You can use it to enable or disable a device on the motherboard (for example, the network port, video port, or USB ports), change the date and time that is later passed to the OS, and select the order of boot devices for startup BIOS/UEFI to search when looking for an operating system to load. This order of boot devices is called the **boot priority order**.

Most computers today give you the option of booting the system in UEFI mode or the legacy BIOS mode, which is called **UEFI CSM (Compatibility Support Module) mode**. You must select which firmware mode you will use *before* you install Windows. Here are points to help you decide:

◢ UEFI mode is required if the hard drive is larger than 2.2 TB or is using the GPT partitioning system. (However, a hard drive manufacturer might provide device drivers to allow a drive larger than 2.2 TB to use the MBR partitioning system and legacy BIOS.)

> ✏ **Notes** Seagate offers its DiscWizard device drivers that you can install on Seagate's 3-TB hard drive so you can install the hard drive in a system that only has legacy BIOS. DiscWizard creates two MBR virtual hard drives and presents them to BIOS; they appear to BIOS to be two physical MBR hard drives.

◢ UEFI and the GPT partitioning system for the hard drive work only with 64-bit versions of Windows 10/8/7. A 32-bit version of Windows 10/8/7 can read and write to a GPT disk but not boot from it.

◢ UEFI has a security system called Secure boot, which helps to prevent malware from hijacking a system during or before the operating system load. UEFI mode and Windows work together to ensure that no unsecured device driver, application, or OS component is loaded during startup. If you want to enable Secure boot, you must use UEFI, GPT, and a 64-bit edition of Windows.

◢ Ultimately, the only times you might select the CSM mode are when you use a legacy MBR hard drive or install a 32-bit version of Windows 10/8/7.

APPLYING | CONCEPTS   SELECTING THE FIRMWARE MODE AND BOOT PRIORITY ORDER

You can use BIOS/UEFI setup to change the firmware mode and boot priority order. See the motherboard documentation to find out how to access and use BIOS/UEFI setup. Here are steps for one system:

1. To access BIOS/UEFI setup, press a key such as **Del** or **F2** early in the boot process before Windows starts to load. When the BIOS/UEFI setup screen appears, look for a screen to manage the boot. For example, the Boot screen for one motherboard's firmware is shown in Figure 2-3.

Source: American Megatrends, Inc.

Figure 2-3 The Boot screen for BIOS/UEFI setup

2. To use CSM mode, which requires the MBR partitioning system:
   a. Click **CSM (Compatibility Support Module)** and make sure that CSM is enabled (see Figure 2-4).

(continues)

Source: American Megatrends, Inc.

Figure 2-4 Enable or disable CSM mode

    b. On the Boot screen (see Figure 2-3), click **Secure Boot**. In the Secure Boot menu, select **Other OS** for the OS Type (see Figure 2-5).

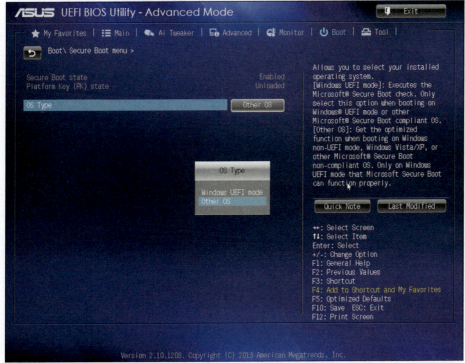

Source: American Megatrends, Inc.

Figure 2-5 Select Other OS to allow Windows to install on an MBR hard drive

(continues)

3. To use UEFI mode and the GPT partitioning system, use the same screens from the previous step to disable **CSM** (see Figure 2-4) and set the OS Type to **Windows UEFI mode** (see Figure 2-5).

4. Normally, BIOS/UEFI is set to boot first from the internal hard drive. If you plan to install Windows by booting from a DVD, USB flash drive, or external hard drive connected to a USB port, you need to change the boot priority order. To make the change, look for a Boot screen or menu. For the system shown in Figure 2-6, boot options are the DVD drive, hard drive, and network port. Also, know that sometimes the DVD drive is labeled CD-ROM in BIOS/UEFI setup.

Source: American Megatrends, Inc.

Figure 2-6 Set the boot order in BIOS/UEFI setup

In a corporate or enterprise environment, automated methods might be in place to install a fresh copy of Windows on a workstation from deployment servers on the network. To use this method, you configure BIOS/UEFI setup to boot from the network and locate a deployment server to install Windows. How to do that is covered later in this chapter.

APPLICATION AND HARDWARE COMPATIBILITY

Verify that the applications you already have installed will work in a new OS you are about to install. You can go to the application manufacturer's website to check for compatibility with the new OS.

Device drivers are small programs stored on the hard drive that tell the computer how to communicate with a specific hardware device such as a printer, network card, or scanner. These drivers are installed on the hard drive when the OS is first installed or when new hardware is added to the system. A device driver is written to work for a specific OS, such as Windows 10, 8.1, or 7. In addition, a 32-bit OS requires 32-bit drivers and a 64-bit OS requires 64-bit drivers.

Windows provides some device drivers and the manufacturer of the hardware device provides others. When you purchase a printer, video card, digital camera, scanner, or other hardware device, a CD that

2

contains the device drivers is usually bundled with the device along with a user manual (see Figure 2-7). You can also download the drivers for a device from the manufacturer's website. Be sure you have the correct Windows device drivers for all your critical devices, such as your network card or motherboard.

Figure 2-7   A device such as this video card comes packaged with its device drivers stored on a CD

If you are not sure your devices will work with Windows 10/8/7, one solution is to set up a dual boot. A dual boot, also called a multiboot, allows you to install the new OS without disturbing the old one so you can boot to either OS. After the installation, you can test your software or hardware. If they work under the new OS, you can delete the old one. If they don't work, you can still boot to the old OS and use it. How to set up a dual boot is covered later in this chapter.

CHOOSING THE TYPE OF INSTALLATION: IN-PLACE UPGRADE, CLEAN INSTALL, OR DUAL BOOT

A+ CORE 2 1.3

If you are installing Windows on a new hard drive, you must perform a clean install. If an OS is already installed on the hard drive, you have three choices:

▲ *Clean install*. You can perform a clean install, overwriting the existing operating system and applications. In the Windows setup program, a clean install is called a custom installation. The main advantage of a clean install is that problems with the old OS are not carried forward and you get a fresh start. During the installation, you will have the option to reformat the hard drive, erasing everything on it. If you don't format the drive, data will still be on it. The previous operating system settings and user profiles are collectively stored in the Windows.old folder that setup creates on the hard drive. After Windows is installed, you will need to install the applications. After you're sure the new installation is working as expected, you can delete the Windows.old folder to save space on the drive. Windows 10 automatically deletes most of the content of this folder 28 days after the installation.

▲ *In-place upgrade*. If the upgrade path allows it, you can perform an in-place upgrade installation. An in-place upgrade is a Windows installation that is launched from the Windows desktop and carries forward user settings and installed applications from the old OS to the new one. A Windows OS is already *in place* before you begin the new installation. An in-place upgrade is faster than a clean install and is appropriate if the system is generally healthy and does not have problems. To perform an in-place upgrade, Microsoft requires that certain editions and versions of Windows be installed already and running the latest version of either Windows 8.1 or Windows 7 with Service Pack 1 installed. These qualifying OSs are called **upgrade paths**. Table 2-3 outlines the acceptable upgrade paths for Windows 10 compatibility.

Windows 8		Windows 7	
From OS	To OS	From OS	To OS
Windows 8.1	Windows 10 Home	Windows 7 Starter	Windows 10 Home
		Windows 7 Home Basic	
		Windows 7 Home Premium	
Windows 8.1 Pro	Windows 10 Pro	Windows 7 Professional	Windows 10 Pro
Windows 8.1 Pro for Students		Windows 7 Ultimate	

Table 2-3 In-place upgrade paths to Windows 10

> ✎ **Notes** You can upgrade from Windows 10 Home to Windows 10 Pro by using the Settings app within Windows. If you have already purchased a Windows 10 Pro product key, simply change the product key on the Activation page in the Settings app and then follow the on-screen instructions. Alternately, you can go to the Microsoft Store app, purchase Windows 10 Pro, then follow the on-screen instructions. The upgrade is easy and does not require going through the entire upgrade process.

◢ *Multiboot.* You can install Windows in a second partition on the hard drive and create a dual-boot situation with the other OS, or even install three OSs, each in its own partition in a multiboot environment. Don't create a dual boot unless you need two operating systems, such as when you need to verify that applications and hardware work under Windows 10 before you delete the old OS. Windows 10/8/7 all require that they be the only operating system installed on a partition, so to set up a dual boot, you'll need at least two partitions on the hard drive or a second hard drive.

In addition to the information in Table 2-3, keep these tips in mind:

◢ A 64-bit version of Windows can only be upgraded to a 64-bit OS. A 32-bit OS can only be upgraded to a 32-bit OS.

◢ If you want to install a 64-bit version of Windows on a computer that already has a 32-bit OS installed, you must perform a clean install.

> ✎ **Notes** If your current installation of Windows is corrupted, you might be able to repair the installation rather than reinstalling Windows. Chapter 6 covers how to fix a corrupted Windows installation.

UNDERSTANDING THE CHOICES YOU'LL MAKE DURING THE INSTALLATION

A+
CORE 2
1.3

While Windows is installing, you must choose which drive and partition to install Windows in, the size of a new partition, and how Windows will connect to the network. Next, you'll learn how to decide on the size of the Windows partition and how Windows will connect to the network.

THE SIZE OF THE WINDOWS PARTITION

For a clean install or dual boot, you can decide not to use all the available space on the drive for the Windows partition. Here are reasons not to use all the available space:

▲ *You plan to install more than one OS on the hard drive, creating a dual-boot system.* For example, you might want to install Windows 8 on one partition and leave room for another partition where you intend to install Windows 10, so you can test software under both operating systems. (When setting up a dual boot, always install the older OS first.)

▲ *Some people prefer to use more than one partition or volume to organize data on their hard drives.* For example, you might want to install Windows and all your applications on one partition and your data on another. Having your data on a separate partition makes backing up easier. In another situation, you might want to set up a volume on the drive that is used exclusively to hold data backups on another computer on the network. The size of the partition that will hold Windows 10/8/7 and its applications should be at least 16 GB for a 32-bit install and 20 GB for the 64-bit install, but a larger volume is nearly always preferred.

> ⚡ **Caution** It's convenient to back up one volume to another volume on a different hard drive. However, *don't* back up one volume to another volume on the same hard drive; if the drive fails, all volumes on the drive might be damaged and you could lose both your data and your backup.

In Chapter 4, you learn to use the Disk Management utility after Windows is installed to create partitions from unallocated space and to resize, delete, and split existing partitions.

NETWORK CONFIGURATION

Recall from Chapter 1 that all editions of Windows 10/8/7 can join a workgroup, Windows 8/7 computers can join a homegroup, and professional editions of Windows 10/8/7 can join a Windows domain. (Windows 10 does not support homegroups.) To join a domain, you'll need the name of the domain and the network ID and password assigned to you by the private network's administrator. To join a homegroup, you'll need its password. To use a workgroup, you configure each computer to share its folders and files to specific people on the local network. You can connect to a homegroup or domain during the installation, or you can wait and make the connection after the installation is complete. How to share folders and files on a local network is covered in Chapter 7.

You also need to know that the Windows installation process usually has no problems connecting to the network and the Internet without your help. However, you might need to know how the IP address is assigned. An IP address uniquely identifies a computer on the network, and it might be assigned dynamically (by a server each time the workstation connects to the network) or statically (permanently assigned to the workstation). If the network is using static IP addressing, you need the IP address for the workstation. How to change IP address assignments is covered in Chapter 3.

FINAL CHECKLIST BEFORE BEGINNING THE INSTALLATION

Before you begin the installation, complete the final checklist shown in Table 2-4 to verify that you are ready.

Questions to Answer	Further Information
Does the computer meet the minimum or recommended hardware requirement?	CPU: RAM: Hard drive partition size: Free space on the partition:
Do you have the Windows device drivers for your hardware devices and application setup CDs?	List hardware and software that need to be upgraded:
Do you have the product key available? (It might not be required if you are reinstalling Windows 10.)	Product key:
How will users be recognized on the network?	Homegroup password (for Windows 8/7): Domain name: Computer name: Network ID: Network password:
How will the computer be recognized on the network?	Static or dynamic IP addressing: IP address (for static addressing):
Will you do an upgrade or a clean install?	Current operating system: Does the old OS qualify for an upgrade?
For a clean install, will you set up a dual boot?	List reasons for a dual boot: Size of the second partition: Free space on the second partition:
Have you backed up important data on your hard drive?	Location of backup:

Table 2-4 Checklist to complete before installing Windows

Before getting into the step-by-step instructions for installing an OS, here are some general tips for installing Windows:

- Verify that you have all application software CDs or DVDs available and all device drivers.
- Back up all important data on the drive. How to perform backups is covered in Chapter 4.
- For upgrade installations and clean installs in which you do not plan to reformat the hard drive, run antivirus/anti-malware software to make sure the drive is free from malware. If Windows will not start or you suspect malware is present, perform a clean installation of Windows. If you suspect the hard drive is damaged, you can use the format command to scan the drive for bad sectors before you begin the installation. This process is discussed later in the chapter and in Chapter 4.
- If you want to begin the installation by booting from the Windows USB flash drive or DVD, use BIOS/UEFI setup to verify that the boot sequence is first USB or the optical drive, and then the hard drive.
- In BIOS/UEFI setup, disable any virus protection setting that prevents the boot area of the hard drive from being altered.
- Set BIOS/UEFI to use UEFI mode (which uses GPT and possibly Secure boot) or UEFI CSM mode (which uses MBR partitions on the hard drive). Know that Windows will install on a GPT drive only when CSM mode is disabled and will install on an MBR drive only when CSM mode is enabled.
- For a laptop computer, connect the AC adapter and use this power source for the complete OS installation, updates, and installation of hardware and applications. You don't want the battery to fail in the middle of the installation.

> **Notes** In general, it's best not to upgrade an OS on a laptop unless you want to use some feature the new OS offers. For laptops, follow the general rule, "If it ain't broke, don't fix it." Many hardware components in a laptop are proprietary, and the laptop manufacturer is the only source for these drivers. If you are considering upgrading a laptop to Windows 10, check the laptop manufacturer's website for advice and to download Windows 10 drivers, which are called **third-party drivers** because they are not included in BIOS/UEFI or Windows. It's very important to have a Windows 10 driver for your network port without having to depend on the network or Internet to get one after Windows 10 is installed. Also know that many Windows 8/7 drivers work with Windows 10.

VERIFY THAT YOU HAVE THE WINDOWS 10 PRODUCT KEY

Typically, you'll purchase Windows 10 online, with the product key emailed to the Microsoft account used to make the purchase. If you purchased Windows 10 on a USB flash drive, look for the product key printed on the cover of the flash drive case, on a card inside the case, or affixed to the back of the Windows documentation booklet.

However, keep in mind that the product key might not be required to reinstall Windows. After Windows 10 is activated the first time with a valid product key, Windows assigns a digital license to the machine and stores it along with information about the computer's physical hardware (called the hardware signature) on Microsoft activation servers. If Windows is installed later, it can retrieve this information from Microsoft servers rather than requesting that you re-enter the product key.

In addition, for a laptop, all-in-one, or other brand-name computer, the computer manufacturer might have stored the Windows product key on motherboard firmware. When reinstalling Windows, setup can retrieve this product key from firmware. Either way, the new Windows installation is assigned a digital license and you don't have to enter the product key during the installation.

> **Notes** To determine if Windows was activated using a product key or digital license, open the Settings app, click **Update & security**, and click **Activation** (see Figure 2-8).

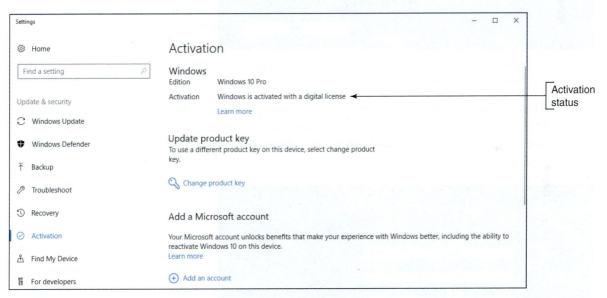

Figure 2-8 This installation of Windows was activated using a digital license stored on Microsoft activation servers

APPLYING | CONCEPTS — USING THE MEDIA CREATION TOOL TO CREATE A BOOTABLE WINDOWS SETUP DVD OR FLASH DRIVE

To create the installation media, you'll need a blank DVD, 4-GB or larger USB flash drive, or at least 4 GB of free space on your hard drive. Use a blank flash drive because any data on it will be lost. To use the Media Creation Tool to download Windows setup files and create a bootable DVD or USB flash drive, follow these steps:

1. To download and install the Media Creation Tool, use a working computer, go to the website *microsoft.com/en-us/software-download/windows10*, and click **Download tool now**. Save the file and then run **MediaCreationTool1803.exe**.

(continues)

2. Accept the license terms. On the next window shown in Figure 2-9, select **Create installation media (USB flash drive, DVD, or ISO file) for another PC** and click **Next**.

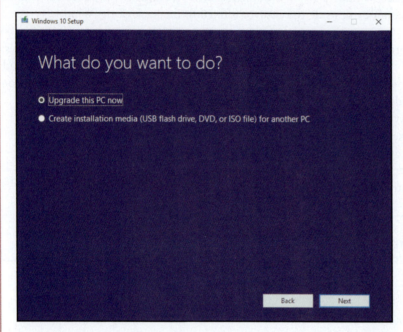

Figure 2-9   The Media Creation Tool can be used to upgrade a computer or to create installation media

3. Select a language and architecture (64-bit or 32-bit), as shown in Figure 2-10. (The only edition available to select is Windows 10.) Alternatively, if you're creating installation media as a troubleshooting tool for the computer you're using, check **Use the recommended options for this PC**. Click **Next**.

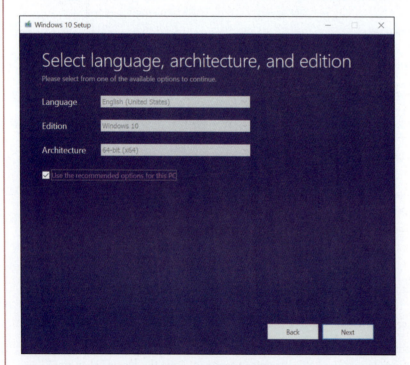

Figure 2-10   The installation medium is bit specific: Choose 32-bit for a 32-bit computer and 64-bit for a 64-bit computer

(continues)

> **✎ Notes** The best practice is to save the Windows setup files to a USB flash drive or ISO image. You never know when you'll need the files later to repair a corrupted Windows installation.

4. On the next screen, select **USB flash drive** or **ISO file**, which you can later burn to a DVD. If you choose *USB flash drive*, the tool searches for the drive. If you choose *ISO file*, the tool asks for the location to save the file (see Figure 2-11). Navigate to the location, click **Save**, and follow the on-screen instructions. After the download completes, if you chose to save an ISO file, you will be given the opportunity to insert a DVD in the disk drive, right-click the ISO file, and click **Burn disc image**.

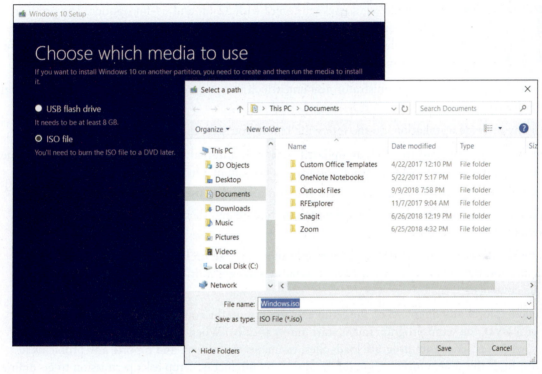

Figure 2-11 Select a location to save the ISO file

Here's some useful information about an ISO file:

⊿ An ISO file, also called an ISO image or disc image, is an image of an optical disc, including its file system and all its files and folders. An ISO (International Organization for Standardization) file has an .iso file extension.

⊿ To see the contents of an ISO file, open File Explorer or Windows Explorer, right-click the file, and click **Mount**. The ISO file is assigned a drive letter and you can drill down into its contents.

⊿ If you have an optical drive that can write to DVDs and you want to burn a DVD from an ISO file, insert a blank DVD in your optical drive and double-click the ISO file. Follow the on-screen directions and Windows does the rest.

⊿ Later in the chapter, you learn how to mount an ISO file to a virtual DVD drive in a virtual machine and use it to install Windows in the VM, as you would with a physical DVD installed in a physical computer.

INSTALLING WINDOWS 10, WINDOWS 8.1, AND WINDOWS 7

In this part of the chapter, you learn the steps to install Windows as an in-place upgrade, clean install, and dual boot. You also learn how to handle the special situation of using a Windows upgrade product key to install Windows on a new hard drive. Later in the chapter, you learn to install Windows 10 on a virtual machine. As you install and configure software, be sure to document what you do. This documentation will be helpful for future maintenance and troubleshooting. In a project at the end of this chapter, you will develop a documentation template.

Let's begin with how to perform an in-place upgrade of Windows 10.

WINDOWS 10 IN-PLACE UPGRADE

The Windows 10 upgrade retail package comes with 32-bit and 64-bit options. The product key is found in a slip pocket inside the box or is included in the emailed receipt. Here are the steps to perform an in-place upgrade from Windows 8.1 to Windows 10 when you're working with a Windows 10 setup DVD or USB flash drive:

1. Sign in to Windows using an administrator account, which is a user account that has the right to install system software.

2. As with any upgrade installation, do the following before you start the upgrade:

   ◢ Scan the system for malware using an updated version of anti-malware software. When you're done, be sure to close the anti-malware application so it's not running in the background.

   ◢ Uninstall any applications or device drivers you don't intend to use in the new installation.

   ◢ Make sure your backups of important data are up to date and then close any backup software running in the background.

3. Insert the Windows 10 setup DVD or flash drive or mount the setup ISO file. Recall that to mount an ISO file, you right-click it and click **Mount**. Windows assigns a drive letter to the file and you can access its contents.

4. Open **File Explorer** and double-click the **setup.exe** program in the root of the device or mounted ISO file. (For a DVD, the setup program might start automatically.) When the User Account Control box appears, click **Yes**. The setup program loads files, examines the system, and reports any problems it finds. If it finds the system meets minimum hardware requirements, setup asks permission to go online for updates (see Figure 2-12). Make your selection and click **Next**.

5. The next window requests the product key (see Figure 2-13). Enter the product key; Windows verifies that the key is valid. If the computer is connected to the Internet, setup will automatically activate Windows during the installation. Click **Next**.

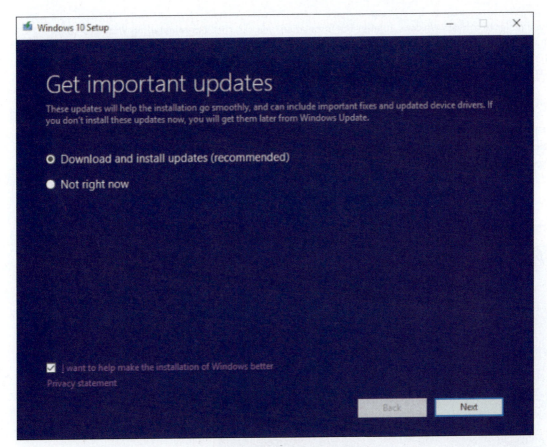

Figure 2-12 Decide how you will handle updates during the setup process

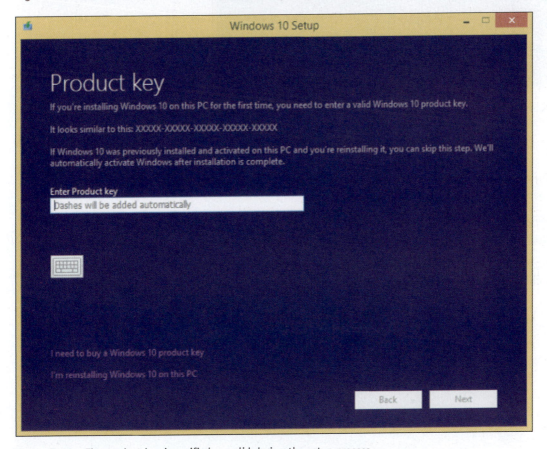

Figure 2-13 The product key is verified as valid during the setup process

> 📝 **Notes** If you prefer to activate Windows 10 after the installation, you can click **I'm reinstalling Windows 10 on this PC**, which allows you to proceed without a product key and install Windows 10 although it's not yet activated. This is a good way to practice Windows installations.

6. The *License terms* window appears. Click **Accept**.

7. Wait for updates to download. Then, in the *Ready to install* window, verify that **Keep personal files and apps** is selected. To specify what you want to retain from the previous installation, click **Change what to keep** (see Figure 2-14).

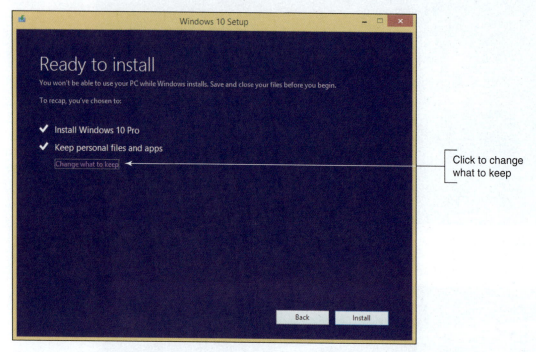

Figure 2-14 Windows is ready to install as an upgrade, but you can still change what to keep

8. In the *Choose what to keep* window (see Figure 2-15), decide what you want to do with Windows settings, personal files, and apps:

   ◢ The first two options perform upgrades to Windows 10.

   ◢ The Nothing option performs a clean install of Windows 10.

   In this example, you are doing an in-place upgrade installation, so select **Keep personal files and apps**, and then click **Next**. The *Ready to install* window appears again.

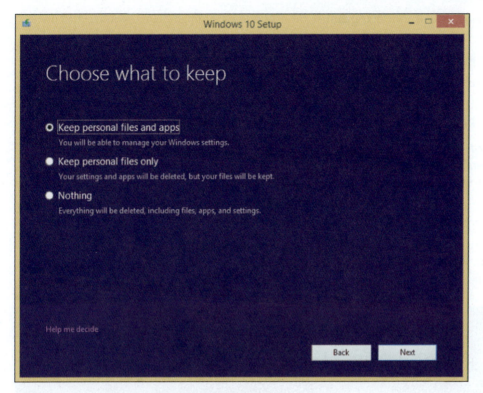

Figure 2-15 Decide what to keep of the old installation

9. On the *Ready to install* window, verify the choices listed and click **Install** to begin the installation.

10. During the installation, setup might restart the system several times. When the *Welcome to Windows 10!* screen appears showing your user name, click **Next**.

11. On the *Choose privacy settings for your device* screen, select the privacy settings for location, speech recognition, diagnostics, tailored experiences with diagnostic data, and relevant ads, and then click **Accept**.

> 📝 **Notes** You might need to scroll down to view all the privacy settings on this screen.

12. On the *Meet Cortana* screen, you can decide to give Microsoft permission to use your information to personalize your experience with Cortana. To read more about the type of information Microsoft collects for Cortana, click **Learn more**. Click **Not now** or **Use Cortana** to move to the next screen.

13. The *New apps for the new Windows* screen appears. Review the new apps built into Windows 10. Click **Next**.

14. Settings are applied and the Windows 10 sign-on screen appears. You can now use the new upgrade to Windows 10.

WINDOWS 10 CLEAN INSTALL

Recall that a clean install is the best option to use if the current installation is sluggish or causing problems, the currently installed OS does not allow for an in-place upgrade, or you're installing Windows 10 on a new hard drive or new desktop computer you're building.

If you have a Windows 8/7 installation that qualifies for a Windows 10 upgrade and you need to do a clean install, follow these steps:

1. Begin by starting the installation from the Windows desktop as you would for an upgrade.

2. Follow the previous steps for an in-place upgrade to enter the product key, accept license terms, and download updates.

3. When you get to the *Ready to install* window (refer back to Figure 2-14), click **Change what to keep**.

4. On the *Choose what to keep* window (refer back to Figure 2-15), click **Nothing** and click **Next**. Then continue with the installation. The contents of the volume holding the previous version of Windows is deleted. If the hard drive has other volumes, they are left unchanged.

Use the following steps to perform a clean install on a newly installed hard drive, on a new computer you're building, or on a computer that has a corrupted Windows installation that refuses to start:

1. Boot from the Windows setup DVD or USB flash drive. Recall that you first might need to change the boot priority order in BIOS/UEFI. In the Windows Setup screen (see Figure 2-16), select the language and regional preferences and click **Next**. On the next screen, click **Install now**.

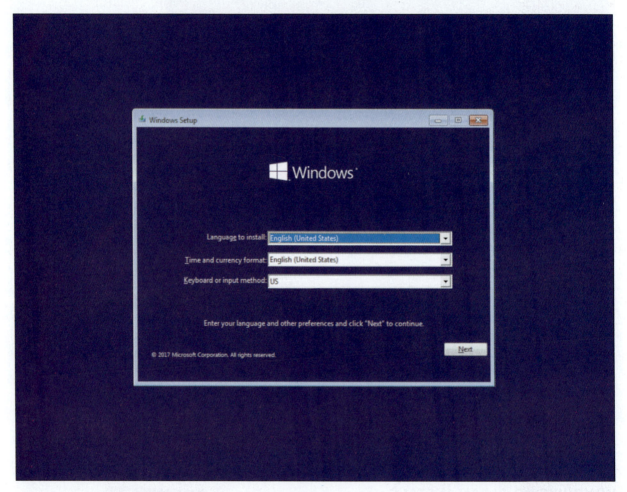

Figure 2-16 Decide on language and keyboard preferences

2. Enter your product key on the next screen (see Figure 2-17). Click **Next**. Setup verifies that the key is a valid product key, which then determines the version of Windows to install.

> ✎ **Notes** If you prefer to enter the product key after you have installed Windows, click **I don't have a product key**. On the next screen, select the version of Windows you want to install.

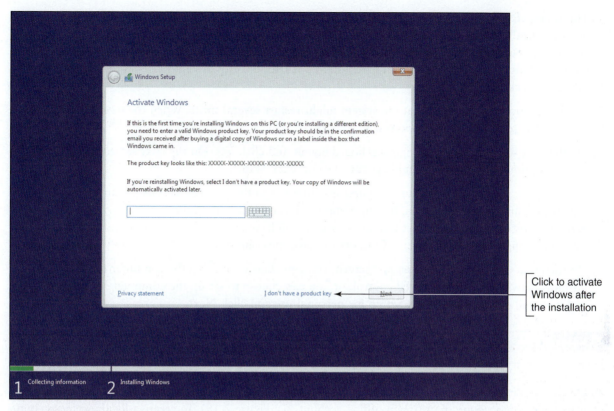

Figure 2-17 Enter a valid product key

3. Accept the license agreement on the next screen and click **Next.** On the next screen (see Figure 2-18), click **Custom: Install Windows only (advanced).**

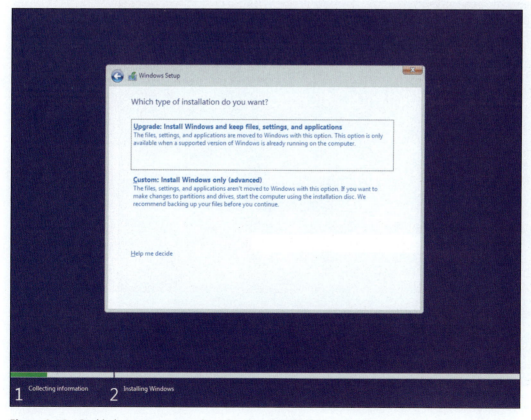

Figure 2-18 Decide between an upgrade and a clean installation

4. The *Where do you want to install Windows?* screen appears. Select the drive and volume where you want to install Windows. By default, setup will use the entire unallocated space for the Windows volume. If you want to use only a portion of the space, click **New** and enter the size of the volume. (Setup will also create a small system partition that it later uses for system files and the startup process.) Click **Next** to continue.

5. The installation begins. Note that the system might restart several times. When the next screen appears, choose your region and then click **Yes**.

6. On the next screen, choose the right keyboard layout and click **Yes**. On the next screen, which gives you the option of adding a second keyboard layout, click **Skip**.

7. The setup program detects if your computer is connected to the Internet, checks for updates, and then moves on to the next screen. If your computer has no connection, the *Let's connect you to a network* screen appears. The next few steps assume you have an Internet connection; if you don't, your experience might be different. Click **Ethernet** to make the connection.

8. On the *How would you like to set up?* screen, you can choose to set up the computer on a school or business network and have limited control, or you can choose to set up the computer for personal use and have full control of it. Select **Set up for personal use** and click **Next**.

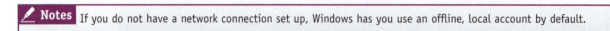

Notes If you do not have a network connection set up, Windows has you use an offline, local account by default.

9. On the *Sign in with Microsoft* screen, you can choose to use an existing Microsoft account, create a new Microsoft account, or create an offline account (see Figure 2-19). To create a local, offline account, click **Offline account**.

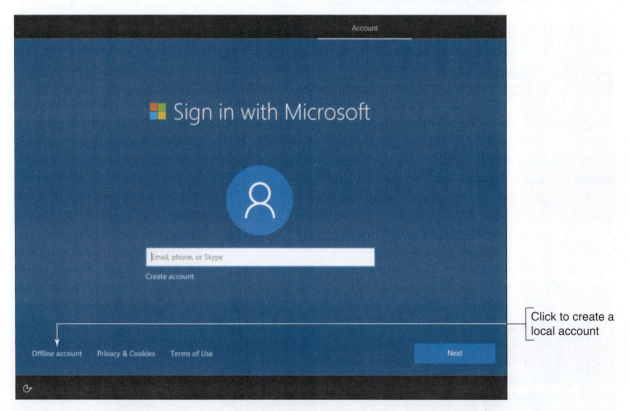

Figure 2-19 Choose the type of account to set up

10. On the *Sign in with Microsoft Instead?* screen, Microsoft again encourages you to use a Microsoft account instead of an offline account (see Figure 2-20). To continue creating an offline account, click **No**.

Click to create a local account

Click to use a Microsoft account

Figure 2-20 During setup, Microsoft strongly encourages the use of a Microsoft account and not a local account

11. On the next screen, enter the name for the user of the local account. (Again you see at the bottom of the screen that Microsoft is still encouraging you to use a Microsoft account.) Click **Next**, enter a password for the offline account, click **Next**, confirm the password, click **Next**, create a password hint, and then click **Next**.

12. On the *Make Cortana your personal assistant?* screen, you can give Microsoft permission to use your information to personalize your experience with Cortana. To read more about the type of information Microsoft collects for Cortana, click **Learn more**. To accept Cortana, click **Yes**.

13. On the next screen, select the device's privacy settings for location, speech recognition, diagnostics, tailored experiences with diagnostic data, and relevant ads, and then click **Accept**.

14. The installation continues, settings are applied, and the Windows desktop appears. You can now use the new installation of Windows 10.

WINDOWS | 8   STEPS TO PERFORM A WINDOWS 8.1 CLEAN INSTALL

**A+
CORE 2
1.3**

Recall that a clean install is the best option to use if the current installation is sluggish or giving problems, the currently installed OS does not allow for an in-place upgrade, or you're installing Windows 8.1 on a new hard drive.

If you have a Windows 7 installation that qualifies for a Windows 8.1 upgrade and you need to do a clean install, begin by starting the installation from the Windows desktop as you would for an upgrade. When

(continues)

you get to the window shown earlier in Figure 2-15, click **Nothing** and continue with the installation. The volume holding the old Windows installation is formatted and everything on the volume is lost. If the hard drive has other volumes, they are left unchanged.

> **◇ OS Differences** The steps and screenshots for a clean install in this section are for Windows 8.1. The steps for Windows 8.0 work about the same way.

To perform a clean install of Windows 8.1, you can begin the installation from the Windows 8.1 DVD or USB flash drive:

- ◢ *If no operating system is installed on the PC, begin the installation by booting from the Windows 8.1 setup DVD or USB flash drive*. Using this method, you will not be using the upgrade option, but will be required to do a Custom installation, also called a clean install.
- ◢ *If an operating system is already installed on the PC, you can begin the installation from the* Windows *desktop or by booting from the Windows 8.1 setup DVD or USB flash drive*. Either way, you can perform a Custom installation.

Follow these steps to begin the installation by booting from the Windows 8.1 setup DVD or USB flash drive:

1. Boot from the Windows setup DVD or USB flash drive. In the Windows Setup screen, select the language and regional preferences and click **Next**. On the next screen, click **Install now**.

2. Enter your product key on the next screen. Setup verifies that the key is a valid product key. Click **Next**.

3. Accept the license agreement on the next screen and click **Next**. On the next screen, click **Custom: Install Windows only (advanced)**.

4. On the next screen, select the drive and volume where you want to install Windows. By default, setup will use the entire unallocated space for the Windows volume. If you want to use only a portion of the space, click **New** and enter the size of the volume. (Setup will also create a small reserved partition that it later uses for system files and the startup process.) Click **Next** to continue.

> **✎ Notes** If you don't see the *New* link on the *Where do you want to install Windows?* screen, click **Drive options (advanced)** to see it and other links you can use to manage the space on the hard drive.

5. The installation begins, and the system might restart several times. You can select a screen color and enter the PC name. Next, the Settings screen appears.

6. After you have made your choices on the Settings screen, the *Sign in to your Microsoft account* screen appears. (Microsoft *really* encourages you to use a Microsoft account.) As with an in-place upgrade, you can sign in using an existing Microsoft account or create a new Microsoft account. In addition, you can create a new local account.

   If you want to create a new local account, click **Create a new account**. On the next screen, click **Sign in without a Microsoft account**. On the Your account screen, enter the local account name, password, and password hint, and then click **Finish**.

7. The installation continues, settings are applied, and the Start screen appears. You can now use the new installation of Windows 8.1.

> **◇ OS Differences** A clean install of Windows 7 works about the same as a Windows 8.1 installation. Boot from the Windows 7 setup DVD and follow the on-screen instructions.

MULTIBOOT INSTALLATIONS

**A+
CORE 2
1.3**

You can install two or more operating systems on the same computer in a multiboot situation—for example, Windows 10 and Ubuntu Desktop. Each OS must have its own hard drive partition and each partition must have enough free space to hold the OS, with room for applications, data, and OS working space. Recall that Windows 10/8/7 needs *at least* 16 GB (32-bit) or 20 GB (64-bit) of free space for the OS. Also know you cannot boot more than one OS at a time. To create a multiboot environment, always install Windows operating systems in order from older to newer.

> **Notes** If an OS is already installed, you might need to shrink a partition to make room for a second partition to hold the next OS. For Windows, use Disk Management to shrink a partition, create a new partition, or format a partition. Windows requires the NTFS file system. How to use Disk Management is covered in Chapter 4.

Here are the steps to set up a dual-boot system with two operating systems (using Windows 8.1 and 10 as examples):

1. Install Windows 8.1. If you plan to install Windows 10 on the same hard drive as Windows 8.1, leave some unallocated space for the Windows 10 partition. (See the setup screen in Figure 2-21, which works the same in Windows 8.1 as in Windows 10.) On this screen, click **New**. You can then specify how much of the total unallocated space you want to use for the Windows 8.1 installation.

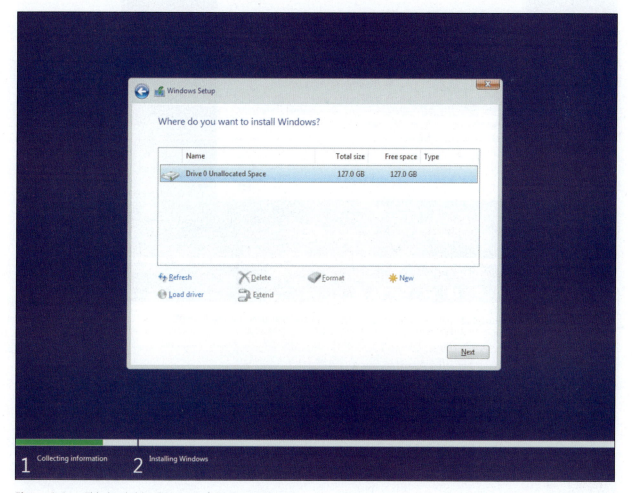

Figure 2-21 This hard drive has not yet been partitioned

2. To install Windows 10, first make sure you have (a) a second partition with enough free space to hold the Windows 10 installation, (b) enough unallocated space on the drive to create a new partition while installing Windows 10, or (c) a second hard drive to hold the Windows 10 installation.

3. Start the Windows 10 installation by booting from the Windows 10 setup DVD or USB flash drive. The Windows Setup screen appears. Follow the steps given earlier in this chapter to perform a clean install.

4. When you're asked where to install Windows, select the partition or unallocated space to hold the installation. For example, select **Unallocated Space** to hold the Windows 10 installation, as shown in Figure 2-22. Don't select the partition where the older operating system is already installed; doing so causes the setup program to install Windows 10 in place of the older OS. Continue on to complete the clean install.

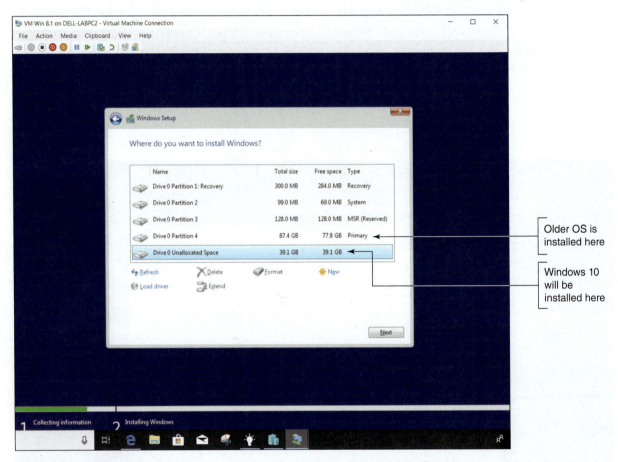

Figure 2-22 Select unallocated space or a partition other than the one used by the first OS installation

After the installation, when you boot with a dual boot, the boot loader menu automatically appears and asks you to select an operating system, as shown in Figure 2-23.

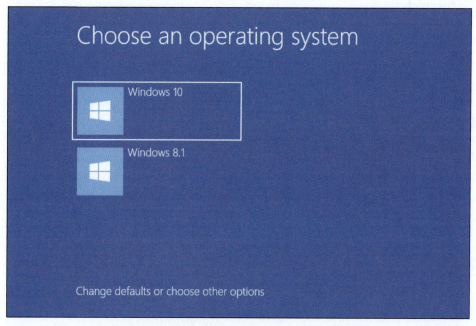

Figure 2-23 The boot loader menu in a dual-boot environment

When using a dual boot, you can execute an application while one OS is loaded even if the application is installed under the other OS, as long as each OS is using the same architecture (32-bit or 64-bit). If the application is not listed on the Windows 10 Start menu or the Windows 8.1 Start screen, locate the program file in File Explorer. Double-click the application to run it.

SOLVING PROBLEMS WITH INSTALLATIONS

In this part of the chapter, we look at a few special situations you might encounter when installing Windows and what to do about them, including how to use an upgrade product key with a new hard drive and problems that require preparing a hard drive before the installation.

USE AN UPGRADE PRODUCT KEY ON A NEW HARD DRIVE

Suppose a Windows upgrade license has been used to install Windows on a computer and later the hard drive fails. You replace the hard drive with a new one, and now you need to reinstall and activate Windows. Microsoft doesn't sell a Windows 10 upgrade product key, but it did offer a free upgrade to Windows 10 from Windows 8.1 or 7 for a short time. These first free releases of Windows 10 can be activated using Windows 8.1, 8, or 7 product keys. Starting with the 1607 release of Windows 10, Windows began to use digital licenses that are linked to a Microsoft account. If you do not have a valid product key or did not link your Windows activation to a Microsoft account, you must buy a new Windows license with a product key. If you used a Microsoft account and Version 1607 or later, you can reinstall Windows 10 by simply logging in with your Microsoft account and activating Windows using the Activation troubleshooter in the Settings app. When you launch the Activation troubleshooter, click **I changed hardware on this device recently**. You will be required to use a Microsoft account to proceed.

In a situation where a Windows 7 system was upgraded to Windows 8.0 and then updated to Windows 8.1:

1. Reinstall Windows 7. You don't need to enter the product key during the installation or to activate Windows 7.

2. Reinstall Windows 8.0 using the upgrade product key and make sure Windows 8 is activated after the installation.

3. Download and install the free Windows 8.1 upgrade from the Windows Store.

APPLYING | CONCEPTS   CONVERTING AN MBR DRIVE TO GPT

Suppose you want to use a 64-bit version of Windows and UEFI firmware mode, thus requiring you to use the GPT partitioning system. However, your hard drive has already been partitioned with the MBR system. The error won't show up until you get to the step in the installation where you select the partition or unallocated space on the hard drive to hold the Windows installation (see Figure 2-24).

Follow these steps to use the **diskpart** command to wipe the partition system off the hard drive. All data on the drive will be destroyed and then you can convert the drive to GPT:

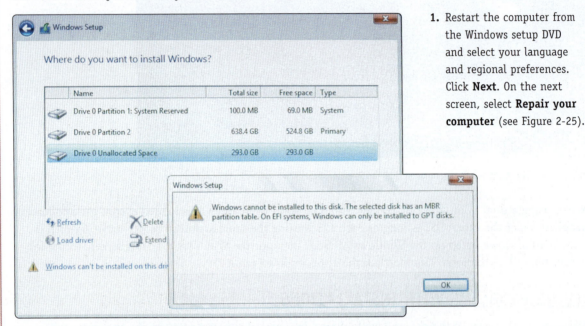

1. Restart the computer from the Windows setup DVD and select your language and regional preferences. Click **Next**. On the next screen, select **Repair your computer** (see Figure 2-25).

Figure 2-24   An error appears when Windows is in UEFI mode and requires the GPT partitioning system

Figure 2-25   Use the Windows setup DVD to launch a command prompt

(continues)

2. On the next screen, click **Troubleshoot**. On the Advanced options screen, click **Command Prompt**. A command prompt window appears. Type **diskpart** and press **Enter**. The DISKPART> prompt appears, as shown in Figure 2-26.

3. At the DISKPART> prompt, use the commands shown in Table 2-5 and Figure 2-26 to select the hard drive, clean it, and convert it to a GPT drive:

Command	Description
list disk	**List the hard drives installed. If you have more than one hard drive, use the size of the drive to determine which one you want to clean. Most likely, you will have one hard drive identified as Disk 0.**
select disk 0	**Make Disk 0 the selected hard drive.**
clean	**Clean the partition table and all partitions from the drive.**
convert gpt	**Convert the partitioning system to GPT.**
exit	**Exit the diskpart utility.**

Table 2-5 Diskpart commands to convert an MBR drive to GPT

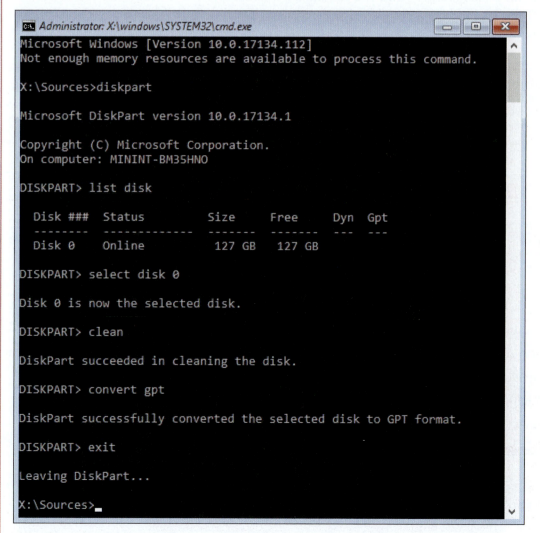

Figure 2-26 The command prompt window with diskpart running

(continues)

4. Enter one more **exit** command to close the command prompt window. On the setup screen that appears, click **Turn off your PC**.

5. You can now restart the system and install Windows in UEFI mode, which uses the GPT partitioning system.

REPAIR A DAMAGED HARD DRIVE

Besides diskpart, you can also use the format command in the command prompt window available from Windows setup media. Two types of formats are:

▲ Quick format, which creates an empty root directory for a volume, effectively resulting in all data being deleted from the volume. When Windows installs and formats the hard drive, it uses a quick format to save time.
▲ Full format, which creates an empty root directory, checks each sector on the volume for errors, and marks bad sectors so they will not be used by the file system.

If you suspect the hard drive is damaged and Windows will not start, launch the command prompt window from the Windows setup media and perform a full format. How to use the format command is covered in Chapter 4. In addition, the diskpart commands include the format command, with options for a quick or full format.

> ⚡ **Caution** If sensitive data is on the hard drive, know that a quick or full format will not actually erase this data from the drive; hackers have been known to be able to read such data even after the volume is formatted. To actually erase the data, you can use a zero-fill utility available from hard drive manufacturers. This software overwrites everything on the drive with zeroes. You learn more about zero-fill utilities in Chapter 8.

WHAT TO DO AFTER A WINDOWS INSTALLATION

A+
CORE 2
1.3, 1.5,
1.6, 1.7,
2.6, 2.7

After you have installed Windows, you need to do the following:

1. Verify that you have network access.

2. Activate Windows.

3. Install updates for Windows and verify update settings and anti-malware settings.

4. Install hardware.

5. Set up user accounts and transfer or restore user data and preferences from backups to the new system.

6. Install applications.

7. Turn Windows features on or off.

8. For laptops, use Control Panel to configure power-management settings. Power management was covered in Chapter 1.

> ⚡ **Caution** To protect your computer from malware, don't surf the web for drivers or applications until you have updated Windows and verified that anti-malware software is providing real-time protection from malware.

VERIFYING NETWORK ACCESS

A+
CORE 2
1.5

Do the following to verify network and Internet access:

1. To make a wired connection to a network when using Windows, simply plug in the network cable and let Windows do the rest. To create a wireless connection, click the network icon in the taskbar and select the wireless network. You might need to enter a password to the Wi-Fi network.

2. To verify access to the local network, open File Explorer or Windows Explorer and verify that you can see other computers on the network (see Figure 2-27). Try to drill down to see shared resources on these computers.

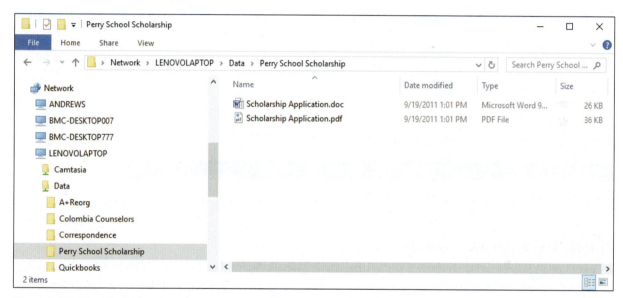

Figure 2-27   Use File Explorer to access resources on your network

3. To verify Internet access, open Internet Explorer and try to navigate to a couple of websites.

If a problem arises, the problem might be that you need to install the drivers for the motherboard, including the drivers for the onboard network port. Also, the IP address, wireless network, or network security settings might be wrong. How to configure network settings and troubleshoot network connections is covered in Chapter 3.

ACTIVATING WINDOWS

A+
CORE 2
1.3

To make sure a valid Windows license has been purchased for each installation of Windows, Microsoft requires product activation. If you entered a product key during the installation, Windows is already activated.

To view the activation status, open the **Settings** app, select the **Update & security** group, and then select **Activation**. Figure 2-28 shows the Activation window for a system that is not activated. To activate, you have a couple of options. First, make sure you're connected to the Internet. If you need to purchase Windows 10, click **Go to Store**. If you already have a product key, click **Change product key**.

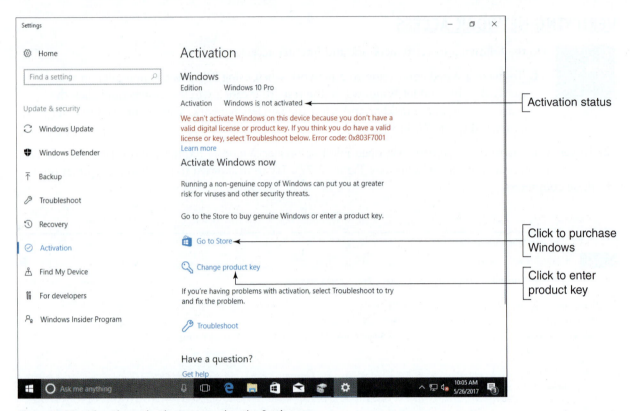

Figure 2-28 View the activation status using the Settings app

PROBLEMS WITH ACTIVATION

As explained earlier in this chapter, if the system already has a digital license or the product key is stored on the motherboard firmware, an upgrade or clean install will activate itself; you don't need to enter a product key. Here are some situations that might cause trouble when activating Windows:

▲ *Replacing a failed hard drive.* If you replace a failed hard drive with a new drive, you should still be able to perform a clean install of Windows 10 on the new hard drive and rely on the digital license, with no need to enter the product key. During setup, don't enter a product key. After Windows is installed, open the **Settings** app, select the **Activation** group, and verify that Windows is activated. If it is not, click **Troubleshoot** in the Activation window. Windows troubleshoots the problem and offers solutions. For example, when you click **I changed hardware on this device recently** in Figure 2-29, the troubleshooter gives you the opportunity to communicate with Microsoft and verify that the computer has a license to use Windows.

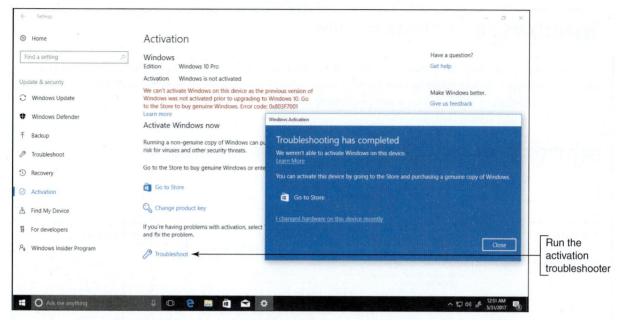

Figure 2-29 The activation troubleshooter resolves activation problems and might lead you to a chat window with Microsoft support

▲ *Upgrading the motherboard.* If the system is working, be sure to associate your Microsoft account with the Windows installation before you upgrade the motherboard. To do so, add the account and sign in to Windows using it. This will associate the digital license and hardware signature stored on Microsoft activation servers with your Microsoft account.

Later, after you upgrade the motherboard, start Windows and sign in using your Microsoft account. The system should be activated when Microsoft servers recognize your Microsoft account and the machine. If the installation is not activated, open the **Settings** app, select the **Activation** group, and then click **Troubleshoot**.

▲ *Replacing a failed motherboard.* Suppose the motherboard fails and you replace it, but you have never signed in to Windows using the Microsoft account that purchased the product key. In that case, Windows might not activate automatically and the Activation troubleshooter might not be able to resolve the problem. In this situation, you most likely will need to talk with Microsoft support staff and explain the problem.

▲ *Upgrading from Windows 8 Home to Windows 10 Pro.* When upgrading from Windows 8 Home to Windows 10 Pro, the installation may automatically upgrade to Windows 10 Home without giving you the option to choose Pro. If this happens, go to the Activation window after the installation is complete and enter your new product key for Windows 10 Pro. The system should reactivate with Windows 10 Pro.

▲ *Reinstalling Windows 10 Pro.* Suppose Windows 10 Pro is activated on a system and then gets corrupted. You perform a clean install to fix the problem, but setup automatically installs and activates Windows 10 Home without asking for a product key. You can fix the problem by going to the Activation window and changing the product key to the **default product key** for Pro: VK7JG-NPHTM-C97JM-9MPGT-3V66T. The system should reactivate with Windows 10 Pro.

WINDOWS | 8 ACTIVATE WINDOWS

To view the activation status for Windows 8/7, go to the System window. Figure 2-30 shows the window for a system that is not activated. To activate, make sure you're connected to the Internet and click **Activate Windows**. On the next screen, if necessary, you can enter a new product key and then activate Windows.

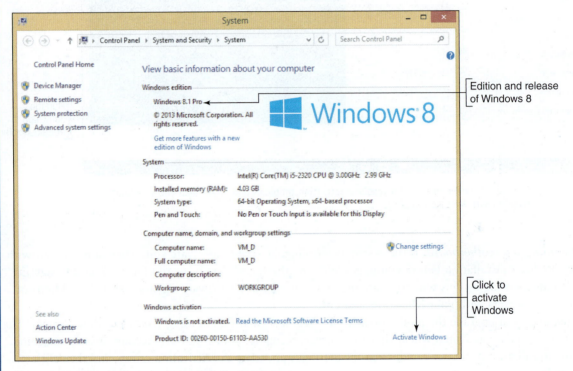

Figure 2-30 Use the System window to activate Windows

INSTALLING WINDOWS UPDATES

A+
CORE 2
1.3, 1.5,
2.7

The Microsoft websites offer patches, fixes, and updates for known problems and have an extensive knowledge base that documents problems and their solutions. It's important to keep these updates current on your system to fix known problems and plug up security holes that might allow malware. Be sure to install updates before you attempt to install software or hardware.

Windows 10 updates automatically by default on a regular basis. To apply any pending Windows 10 updates, open the **Settings** app and click the **Update & security** group. In the Windows Update window (see Figure 2-31), you can view the update status and install any available updates. Depending on the situation, you might click **Restart now** to finish installing updates, click **Install now** to install available updates, or click **Check for updates** if no updates are available. Keep installing important updates and checking for more updates until no more are available. You might need to restart the system after certain updates are installed.

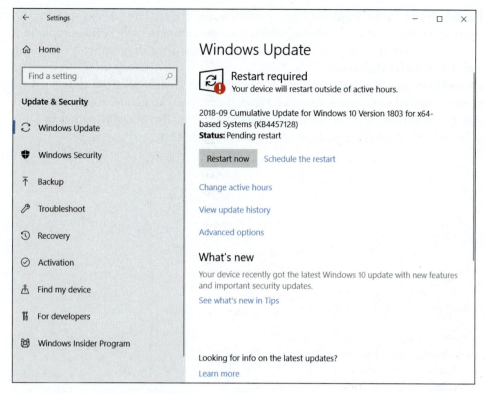

Figure 2-31 View and manage Windows 10 updates

Tools you can use to manage update settings include the Settings app, Group Policy, and the Registry Editor. Here's a brief list of your options for managing updates from the Settings app:

▲ **View or uninstall an update.** In the Settings app, click **Update & security** and then click **Windows Update** in the left pane. Click **View update history** to review recent updates and to uninstall updates that are available for uninstallation (see Figure 2-32).

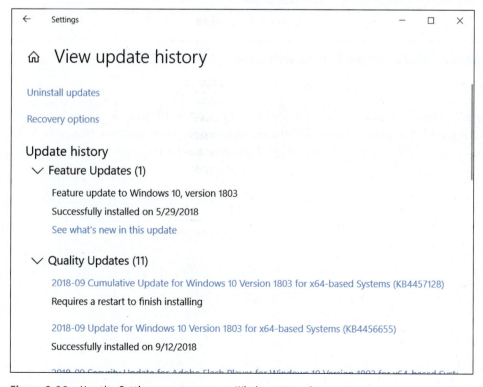

Figure 2-32 Use the Settings app to manage Windows 10 updates

▲ *Schedule restarts and active hours.* In the Windows Update window, use the Update settings section to schedule a pending restart or to set active hours, during which time the computer will avoid automatic restarts. Note that if a scheduled restart occurs outside of active hours but when the computer is in use, you will have an opportunity to delay the restart.

▲ *Update other Microsoft products and Windows features.* In the Windows Update window, click **Advanced options**. On the Advanced options window (see Figure 2-33), you can choose to receive updates to other Microsoft products along with Windows updates. You can also allow Windows to automatically sign you in and finish installing updates after a Windows restart.

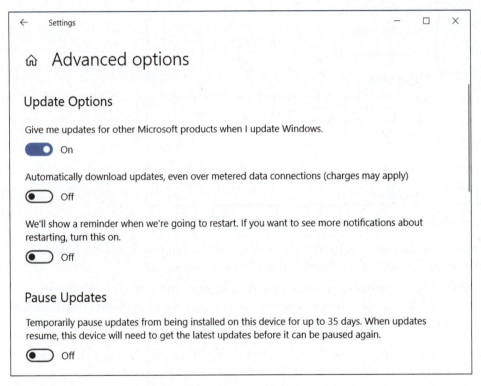

Figure 2-33 Control how updates to Windows and Microsoft apps are installed

▲ *Defer or pause updates.* For business and professional editions of Windows 10, you can open the Advanced options window and then choose when updates are installed or pause updates. Notice in Figure 2-33 that updates can be deferred for up to 35 days. You cannot defer or pause security updates in this window.

2

WINDOWS | 8 UPDATE WINDOWS 8

To view and manage Windows 8/7 update settings, open the **System** window and click **Windows Update** in the left pane. In the Windows Update window (see Figure 2-34), click **Check for updates** in the left pane. Don't forget to keep checking for and installing updates until there are no more to install. To change Windows Update settings, click **Change settings** in the Windows Update window and use the Change settings window.

Figure 2-34   View and manage Windows 8 updates

   If Windows 8.0 is installed, you can update it to Windows 8.1 for free. Open the Windows Store app on the Start screen, select the Windows 8.1 update, and follow the on-screen directions to download and install it.

✷ OS Differences Recall that Windows 7 releases major updates as a service pack. On a Windows 7 system, if you see a service pack listed in the updates, install all the updates listed above it. Then install the service pack as the only update to install. It takes about 30 minutes and a reboot to download and install a service pack. Only the latest OS service pack will install because it includes all the content from previous service packs.

MALWARE PROTECTION

Windows includes its own preinstalled, anti-malware software called Windows Defender Antivirus in Windows 10 and Windows Defender in Windows 8/7. To verify that the utility is running in Windows 10, open **Control Panel,** click **Security and Maintenance,** and expand the Security group (see Figure 2-35).

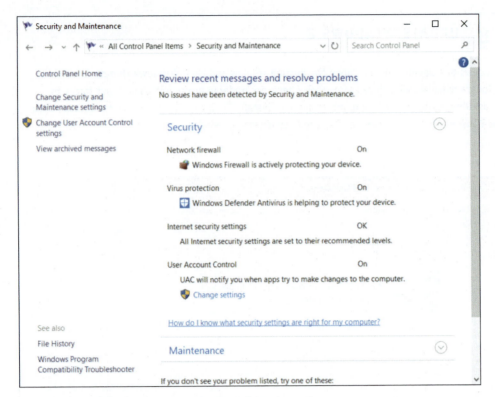

Figure 2-35 Verify that Windows Defender Antivirus is running

To verify protection in Windows 8, launch **Windows Defender** from the Start screen or menu. On the Settings tab, verify that **Real-time protection** is turned on.

> **OS Differences** In Windows 7, Windows Defender is not considered adequate protection against malware. For Windows 7, it's best to install third-party anti-malware software.

INSTALLING HARDWARE

A+ CORE 2 1.3, 1.5, 1.6

You're now ready to install the hardware devices that were not automatically installed during the Windows installation. Be sure to install 32-bit drivers for a 32-bit OS and 64-bit drivers for a 64-bit OS. Also, as much as possible, install drivers designed for the specific OS: Windows 10, Windows 8.1, or Windows 7. Sometimes drivers designed for an older OS will still work in the newer one. As you install each device, reboot and verify that the software or device is working before you move on to the next item. Most likely, you will need to do the following:

▲ *Install the drivers for the motherboard.* Motherboard drivers might come on a CD or DVD bundled with the motherboard, or you can download them from the motherboard manufacturer's website. To start the installation, double-click a setup program on the disc or that you downloaded and follow the on-screen directions.

▲ *Even though Windows has embedded video drivers, install the drivers that came with the video card so you can use all the features the card offers.* These drivers are on disc or are downloaded from the video card manufacturer's website.

▲ *Install printers.* To install a local USB printer, all you have to do is plug it in and Windows will install it automatically. For a network printer, you can run the setup program that came with the printer and the program will find and install the printer. Alternately, open Control Panel in Classic view and open the **Devices and Printers** window. Then click **Add a printer** and follow the on-screen directions.

⏴ *For other hardware devices, always read and follow the manufacturer's directions for the installation.* Sometimes you are directed to install the drivers before you connect the device, and sometimes you will first need to connect the device.

If a problem arises while installing hardware in Windows 10, open Control Panel and click **Troubleshooting**. In the Troubleshooting app (see Figure 2-36), click **Hardware and Sound**. Windows will search for hardware installation problems and suggest solutions. If the problem persists, turn to Device Manager.

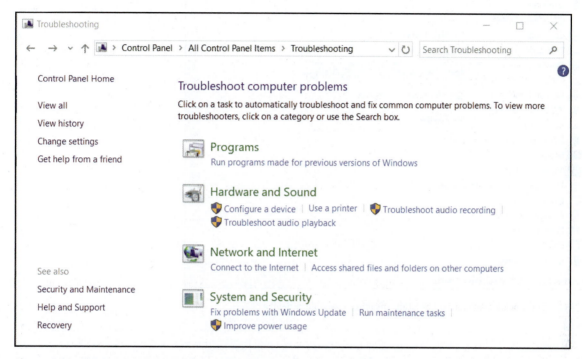

Figure 2-36 Use the Troubleshooting app in Control Panel to resolve hardware installation problems

> ◇ **OS Differences** If a problem occurs while Windows 8/7 is installing a device, it automatically launches the Action Center to help find a solution. Follow the on-screen directions to allow Windows to help you resolve the problem.

USE DEVICE MANAGER

Device Manager is your primary Windows tool for managing hardware. (Its program file is named devmgmt.msc.) It lists all installed hardware devices and the drivers they use. Using Device Manager, you can disable or enable a device, update its drivers, uninstall a device, and undo a driver update (called a **driver rollback**).

> ★ **A+ Exam Tip** The A+ Core 2 exam expects you to know which scenarios are appropriate for using Device Manager. You also need to know how to use the utility and how to evaluate its results.

To access Device Manager, use one of these methods:

⏴ For Windows 10/8, right-click **Start** and select **Device Manager**.
⏴ Open the System window and click **Device Manager**.
⏴ Enter the **devmgmt.msc** command in the Windows 10/7 search box or the Windows 8 Run box.

A Device Manager window is shown in Figure 2-37.

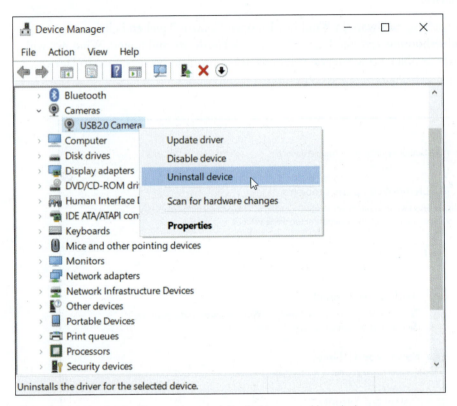

Figure 2-37 Use Device Manager to uninstall, disable, or enable a device

Click an arrow to expand the view of an item or to collapse the view. Here are ways to use Device Manager to solve problems with a device:

▲ *Uninstall and reinstall the device.* To uninstall the device, right-click it and click **Uninstall device** on the shortcut menu, as shown in Figure 2-37. (Alternately, you can click **Properties** in the shortcut menu to open the Properties box and then click **Uninstall Device** on the Driver tab, as shown in Figure 2-38A.) Then reboot the system. Windows will recognize that the device is not installed and attempt to install the appropriate driver. Look for issues during the installation that point to the source of the problem. Sometimes, though, reinstalling a device is all you need to do. Notice in Figure 2-38B that the selected Device type is Cameras, and that the camera is connected through a USB interface. Sometimes USB devices are listed in Device Manager and sometimes they are not.

▲ *Look for error messages offered by Device Manager.* To get more information about a device, look for error messages that show up on the General tab of the Properties box (see Figure 2-38B). Some messages might suggest a solution.

▲ *Update or roll back the drivers.* Click the **Driver** tab (see Figure 2-38A) to update the drivers and roll back (undo) a driver update.

2

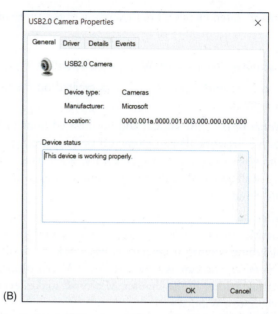

(A)

(B)

Figure 2-38 (A) Use the device's Properties box to uninstall a device and (B) solve problems with device drivers

---

APPLYING | CONCEPTS UPDATING DEVICE DRIVERS

Follow these steps to use Device Manager to update device drivers:

1. For best results, locate and download the latest driver files from the manufacturer's website to your hard drive. Be sure to use 64-bit drivers for a 64-bit OS and 32-bit drivers for a 32-bit OS. If possible, use drivers specifically designed for Windows 10, Windows 8.1, or Windows 7.

2. Using Device Manager, right-click the device and select **Properties** from the shortcut menu. The Properties box for that device appears. Select the **Driver** tab and click **Update Driver**. The Update Driver Software box opens.

3. To search the Internet for drivers, click **Search automatically for updated driver software**. If you have already downloaded drivers to your computer, click **Browse my computer for driver software** and point to the downloaded files. Note that Windows is looking for an .inf file to identify the drivers. Continue to follow the on-screen directions to complete the installation.

 Notes By default, Device Manager hides legacy devices that are not Plug and Play. To view installed legacy devices, click the **View** menu of Device Manager and check **Show hidden devices**.

SETTING UP USER ACCOUNTS

**A+
CORE 2
1.7, 2.6**

As you know, a user must sign in to Windows with a valid user account to gain access to the OS. When you install Windows as a clean installation, you create a user account and you can create others later. Here's a brief overview of the types of user accounts and the privileges associated with them:

▲ *The scope of the account.* Windows offers three types of user accounts, each with a different scope:

    ▲ *Local account.* A local account is created on the local computer and is recognized only on the local computer.

    ▲ *Network ID.* Professional and business editions of Windows allow a user to sign in to Windows with a network ID and password that are created and maintained on a Windows domain in Active Directory or Azure Active Directory. When you sign in to Windows using this type of account, you are authenticated to the local computer and to the Windows domain on a corporate network or in the cloud.

    ▲ *Microsoft account.* For Windows 10/8, a Microsoft account is an email address initially set up at the Microsoft website, *live.com*. The account gives you access to several types of online accounts, including Microsoft OneDrive, Facebook, LinkedIn, Twitter, Skype, and *Outlook.com*. On a Windows computer, you can associate or link a Microsoft account to a local account or a network ID. As you learned earlier in the chapter, Microsoft makes every effort to encourage you to use a Microsoft account in Windows.

> **✎ Notes**   A Microsoft account is an example of a **single sign-on (SSO)** account, which accesses multiple, independent resources, systems, or applications after you sign in one time to one account.

▲ *Privileges for the account.* In Windows, there are two types of privileges assigned to a user account: those for an administrator account and for a standard account. An administrator account has more privileges than a standard account and is used by people responsible for maintaining and securing the system.

APPLYING | CONCEPTS   CREATING A LOCAL ACCOUNT

To create a new account, you can use the Windows 10 Settings app, the Windows 8 Settings charm, the Windows 7 User Accounts applet in Control Panel, or, for all editions of Windows, the Computer Management console in Control Panel. You have more control over creating and setting up an account when you use the Computer Management console, as you learn in Chapter 7. For now, let's use one of the other methods; follow these steps to create a local account:

1. Sign in to Windows with an administrator account.

2. Do one of the following to create an account:

    ▲ *Windows 10.* Open the **Settings** app. Click **Accounts**. Click **Family & other people** and click **Add someone else to this PC**. See Figure 2-39. Click **I don't have this person's sign-in information** and click **Add a user without a Microsoft account** (see the right side of Figure 2-39). Enter a user name, enter the password twice, and click **Next**.

(continues)

2

Figure 2-39 Bypass the Microsoft account and create a local account

▲ *Windows 8*. Open the **Settings** charm and click **Change PC settings**. On the PC settings screen, click **Accounts**. On the Accounts screen, click **Other accounts** (see Figure 2-40). Click **Sign in without a Microsoft account (not recommended)**, and click **Next**. Follow the on-screen directions to set up the account.

Figure 2-40 Set up a new user account

3. In Windows 10/8, the account created is a standard account. To change the account type to administrator, click the account and click **Change account type**. Then select **Administrator** and click **OK**. To remove the account, select it and click **Remove**.

The first time a user signs in to Windows with the account, user files and folders (called the user profile) are created in the C:\Users folder.

> **◔ OS Differences** You create an account in Windows 7 by signing in to it using an administrator account. Open Control Panel in Classic view and click **User Accounts**. Click **Manage another account**. Click **Create a new account**. Enter the user name and select **Standard user** or **Administrator**. Click **Create Account**.

After you have created user accounts in a new installation of Windows, you might want to transfer user data files from the C:\Users folder or other folders on the hard drive to the new computer. How to share files and folders on a network is covered in Chapter 7.

> **✎ Notes** After moving user data from one computer to another, the best practice is to leave the user data on the original computer untouched for at least two months. This practice gives the user plenty of time to make sure everything has been moved over.

USE A MICROSOFT ACCOUNT WITH WINDOWS 10/8

You might want to associate your local account with your Microsoft account, or set up Windows to sign in with your Microsoft account so that you can get easy access to Microsoft resources in the cloud, such as OneDrive. However, know that anyone with administrative rights to the computer can access your Microsoft private settings, apps, online accounts, and OneDrive stored on the local computer. Therefore, you would only want to set up your Microsoft account on a computer where you trust people with administrative access to the computer. Here are the details of making the switch:

▲ *For Windows 10.* To connect an existing local account or network ID to a Microsoft account, open the **Settings** app, click **Users**, and then click **Sign in with a Microsoft account instead**. See Figure 2-41. Follow the on-screen directions, which include entering your current Windows password.

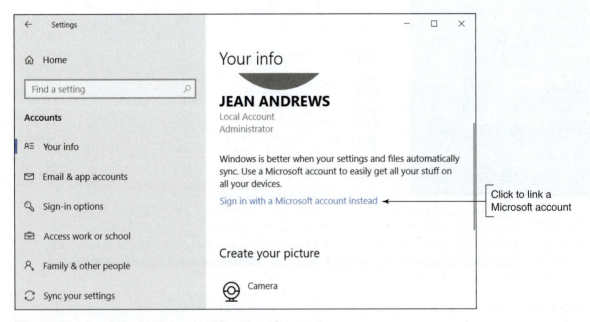

Figure 2-41 Associate a local account with a Microsoft account

▲ *For Windows 8.* Open the **charms** bar, select the **Settings** charm, select **Change PC settings**, and click **Accounts**. Select **Your account** and then click **Connect to a Microsoft account**. Follow the on-screen directions.

If you want to switch the user account back to the local account, go back to your account settings, click **Your info**, and click **Sign in with a local account instead**. On a Windows 8 computer, go back to your account settings and click **Disconnect**.

Recall that you can sign in to Windows using a local account, network ID, or Microsoft account. As you ponder the differences among these accounts, consider where the account is authenticated:

- A local account is authenticated on the local computer and gives access to the local computer. An administrator local account has more access than a standard local account.
- A network ID is authenticated by a computer on the network, which gives you access to the local computer and other resources on the Windows domain.
- A Microsoft account is authenticated on the *live.com* website, which gives access to the local computer and online resources, such as OneDrive and *Facebook.com*. A Microsoft account can be a standard account or an administrator account. It can also be associated with a network ID so that you can sign in with the Microsoft account and be authenticated to the Windows network as well as to *live.com*.

USER ACCOUNT CONTROL DIALOG BOX

At some point while you are working with a computer to maintain or troubleshoot it, the User Account Control (UAC) dialog box will pop up (see Figure 2-42). If the UAC box appears and you are signed in as an administrator, all you have to do is click Yes to close the box and move on, as shown in Figure 2-42A. If the user account does not have administrative privileges, you'll have to enter the password of an administrative account to continue, as shown in Figure 2-42B.

Figure 2-42 (A) The User Account Control box of an administrator does not require an administrative password; (B) the UAC box of a standard user requires an administrative password

The purposes of the UAC box are: (1) to prevent malicious background tasks from gaining administrative privileges when the administrator is signed in, and (2) to make it easier for an administrator to sign in using a less powerful user account for normal desktop activities, but still be able to perform administrative tasks while signed in as a regular user. The UAC box stands as a gatekeeper to malware installing behind your back because someone has to click the UAC box before the installation can proceed.

You can control how the UAC box works. In Control Panel, click **User Accounts** and click **Change User Account Control settings**. The User Account Control Settings window appears (see Figure 2-43). In the figure, the recommended setting is selected.

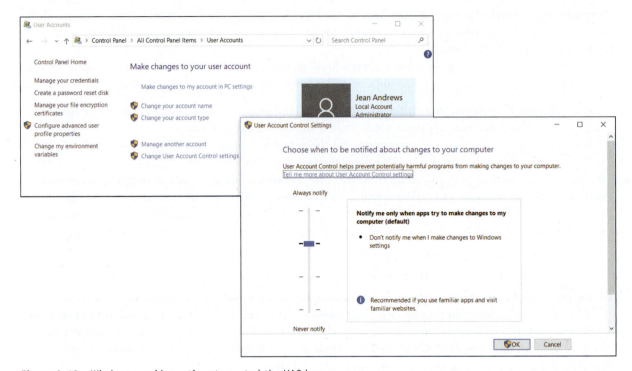

Figure 2-43   Windows provides options to control the UAC box

INSTALLING APPLICATIONS

A+
CORE 2
1.6, 1.7

Before installing an application, consider:

▲ *System requirements*. How much free space on the hard drive does the app need for the installation and how much RAM will the app use when running?

▲ *Compatibility with the OS*. If at all possible, install applications designed for the specific OS: Windows 10, Windows 8.1, or Windows 7. For best performance, install 64-bit apps in a 64-bit OS. It's possible to install 32-bit apps in a 64-bit OS, but you cannot install 64-bit apps in a 32-bit OS.

▲ *Impact to network performance*. Before installing software, research how much network activity the software produces. You might want to set its priority as high or low on the network to control its performance or to keep it from hogging network resources. How to prioritize applications on the network is covered in Chapter 3.

▲ *Impact to device security*. For an application that uses the Internet, consider if it will make the computer vulnerable to attack. Read manufacturer documentation and reviews about how to secure the application and the system, such as making changes to Windows Firewall or installing each app in its own secured virtual machine on the host computer.

▲ *Local user permissions*. Here are the situations you need to know when dealing with local user permissions:

　　▲ A user account with administrator privileges has permission to install software for all users; this software is normally installed in the C:\Program Files folder or the C:\Program Files (x86) folder.

2

Both folders require administrator permissions to edit the folder's contents. For these installations, expect a UAC box to appear to verify the installation (refer back to Figure 2-42A).

▲ A user with standard privileges can install software that is designed to install in his C:/Users profile folder and does not make changes to protected areas of the Windows registry. (The registry is a database of Windows settings.) The software can only be used by this one user account.

▲ If a user signed in with a standard account attempts to install software, such as anti-malware software, that is designed to run under all user accounts, a UAC box appears (see Figure 2-42B). To continue with the installation, the user must enter the password for an administrator user account.

Applications can be installed in Windows 10/8/7 from CD, DVD, or USB flash drive, from a downloaded application file, directly from the web, from the Windows 10/8 Windows Store, or from a folder shared by another computer on the network.

To install applications from a disc, USB flash drive, or software downloaded from the Internet, open File Explorer or Windows Explorer, locate and double-click the setup program file, and follow the on-screen directions to launch the installation routine.

When installing a program directly from the web, click the link on the website to install the software and follow the on-screen directions. To install apps in the Windows Store, use the Store app on the Windows 10 taskbar or the Windows 8 Start screen. After an application is installed, you might also need to install any updates available for the application on the manufacturer's website.

> **✎ Notes** In Chapter 7, you learn that you can map a network drive to a folder that is shared by another computer on the network. For example, this shared folder can appear as drive Z: in your File Explorer window. It's common for administrators to put application setup programs in a shared folder for users on the network to install on their local computers. However, the setup program might give errors when you attempt to run it from the mapped network drive. The solution is to copy the setup program and other setup files to your computer and run it locally. In Chapter 5, you learn about other tasks you can try when an application fails to install.

UNINSTALL APPLICATIONS

If you need to uninstall an application, do one of the following:

▲ For Windows 10/8/7, open **Control Panel** and click **Programs and Features**.
▲ For Windows 10, right-click **Start** or press **Win+X**, and click **Apps and Features**.
▲ For Windows 8, right-click **Start** or press **Win+X**, and click **Programs and Features**.

Figure 2-44 shows the Programs and Features window. Using either the Programs and Features window or the Apps and Features window, select an app and click **Uninstall**. When you select an app in the Programs and Features window, the buttons at the top of the list will change based on the software. For example, in Figure 2-44, the Bonjour software offers the options to Uninstall and Repair the software. (Bonjour by Apple allows Windows to find resources on a network offered by Apple devices.)

> **✎ Notes** The new Windows Store apps can be uninstalled only in the Apps and Features window and not in the Programs and Features window. In Chapter 4, you learn how to use PowerShell to uninstall apps.

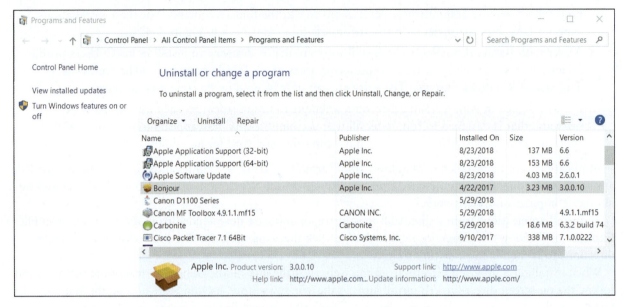

Figure 2-44   Select a program from the list to view your options to manage the software

Recall that you can also uninstall a Windows 10/8 app that provides a tile on the Start menu or Start screen. Right-click the app tile and then click **Uninstall**.

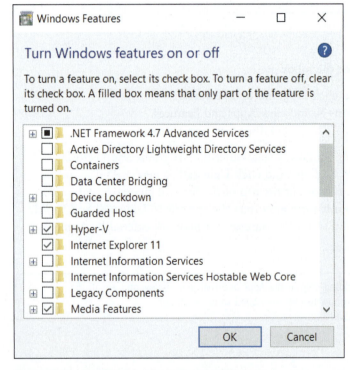

Figure 2-45   Turn Windows features on or off

TURNING WINDOWS FEATURES ON OR OFF

**A+
CORE 2
1.5, 1.6**

You can save on system resources by turning off Windows features you will not use, and you might need to turn on some features that are turned off by default. To control Windows features, open the Programs and Features window and click **Turn Windows features on or off** in the left pane (refer to Figure 2-44). The Windows Features box opens (see Figure 2-45). Check or uncheck the features you want or don't want and then click **OK**. Sometimes a restart is necessary for the changes to take effect.

The Windows installation, devices, user accounts, and applications should now be good to go. Restart the computer and make one last check that all is well. Now would be a good time to document what you did after the installation. A project at the end of this chapter will help you organize your documentation for each computer you support. Also consider making a backup of the entire Windows volume in the event of a hard drive failure or corrupted installation. How to make backups is covered in Chapter 4.

INSTALLATIONS IN A VIRTUAL MACHINE

**A+
CORE 2
1.3**
Another type of Windows installation is when you install Windows in a virtual computer. A virtual computer or **virtual machine (VM)** is software that simulates the hardware of a physical computer. Using this software, you can install and run multiple operating systems at the same time on a single computer, which is called the host machine. These multiple instances of operating systems can be used to train users, run legacy software, and support multiple operating systems. For example, help-desk technicians can run a virtual machine for each OS they support on a single computer and quickly switch from one OS to another by clicking a window. Another reason to use a virtual machine is that you can capture screenshots of the boot process in a virtual machine, which is how some screenshots were made for this text.

Software used to manage VMs installed on a workstation is called a **hypervisor**. Some popular hypervisors for Windows are Client Hyper-V and Virtual PC by Microsoft (*microsoft.com*), VirtualBox by Oracle (*virtualbox.org*), and VMware Player by VMware, Inc. (*vmware.com*). Client Hyper-V is embedded in Windows 10/8 Pro or Enterprise, but is not available for other Windows releases. Virtual PC is free for download in all other editions of Windows 10/8/7 except Windows 7 Starter. VirtualBox and VMware Player are freeware. Be aware that virtual machine programs require a lot of memory and might slow down your system. Figure 2-46 shows two virtual machines running under VirtualBox.

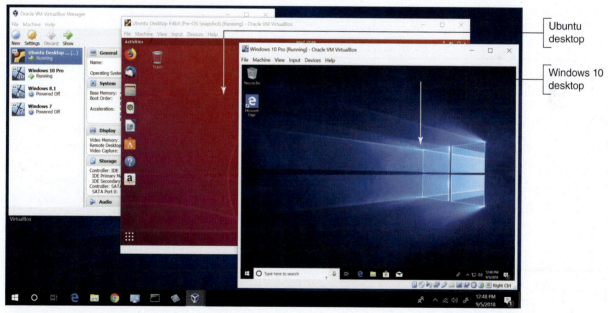

Figure 2-46   Two virtual machines running under VirtualBox

Source: VirtualBox (Oracle)

INSTALL WINDOWS IN A CLIENT HYPER-V VM

Client Hyper-V is the virtual machine (VM) manager that is part of 64-bit Windows 10 Pro. If your processor and motherboard support hardware-assisted virtualization (HAV), you can use Client Hyper-V to install and manage virtual machines on the desktop. Generation 1 VMs allow either a 32-bit or 64-bit installation of an OS in a VM. Generation 2 VMs require a 64-bit guest operating system. Hyper-V can connect a VM to the local network. Client Hyper-V supports dynamically expanding virtual hard drives and dynamically allocated memory. When using dynamically expanding virtual hard drives, the VM ties up only the portion of the host's hard drive that the VM's hard drive is actually using. When using dynamic memory, the VM ties up only the portion of allocated memory that it is actually using.

APPLYING │ CONCEPTS   SETTING UP A VM

Here are the steps to set up a VM using Windows 10 Pro:

1. Go into BIOS/UEFI setup on your computer and make sure virtualization is enabled.

2. Hyper-V is disabled in Windows 10 Pro by default. To turn it on, open the **Settings** app, select the **Apps** group, select **Apps and features**, and click **Programs and Features**. In the Programs and Features window, click **Turn Windows features on or off**. Place a check mark by **Hyper-V** and click **OK**. You'll need to restart the system for the change to take effect.

3. To launch the Hyper-V Manager, open the search box, type **Hyper-V**, and then click **Hyper-V Manager**. The Hyper-V Manager window appears on the desktop. In the Hyper-V Manager pane on the left, select the host computer (see Figure 2-47).

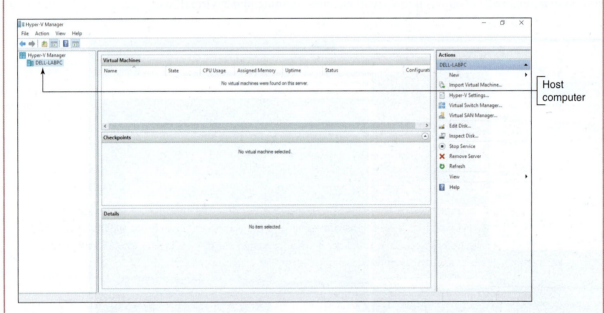

Figure 2-47   Select the host computer for managing Hyper-V virtual machines

4. To give your VMs access to the network or the Internet, you first need to install a virtual switch. To create a virtual switch, click **Virtual Switch Manager** in the Actions pane on the right side of the Hyper-V Manager window.

5. The Virtual Switch Manager window appears (see Figure 2-48). In the left pane, make sure **New virtual network switch** is selected. To bind the virtual switch to the physical network adapter so the VMs can access the physical network, click **External** in the right pane. Click **Create Virtual Switch**.

(continues)

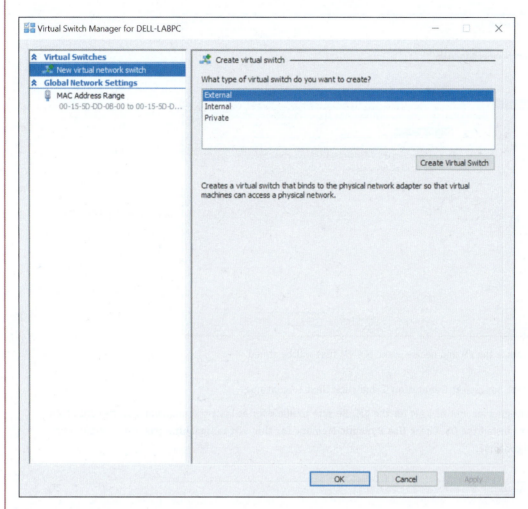

Figure 2-48 Create a virtual switch

6. The Virtual Switch Properties box appears; the new switch is shown in the right pane. In this pane, you can name the virtual switch or leave the default name. You can also select the network adapter to use for the switch. For most situations, that would be the wired Ethernet adapter. Make sure **Allow management operating system to share this network adapter** is checked, and then click **Apply**. Click **Yes** to create the virtual switch. Click **OK** to close the window.

7. You're now ready to create a VM. In the Actions pane, click **New**, and then click **Virtual Machine**. This opens the New Virtual Machine Wizard, where you can set the name and location of the VM files and configure memory and the virtual hard drive. Click **Next**. (Notice you can click **Finish** to accept default settings for the VM.)

8. Assign a name to the VM. If you want the VM files to be stored in a different location than the default, check **Store the virtual machine in a different location**, and browse to that location (see Figure 2-49). After you've selected the location, click **Next**.

(continues)

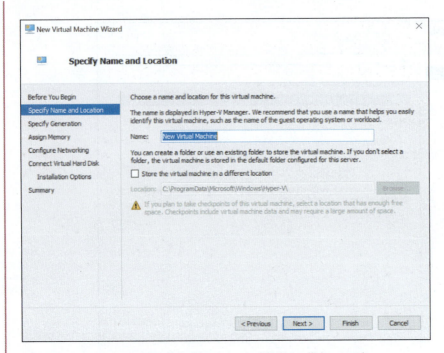

Figure 2-49 Name the VM and decide where the VM files will be stored

9. In the next box, select **Generation 1** and click **Next** to continue.

10. Set the desired amount of RAM for the VM. Be sure to allow for at least the minimum requirement of RAM needed to install the OS. Check **Use Dynamic Memory for this virtual machine** (see Figure 2-50). Click **Next** to continue.

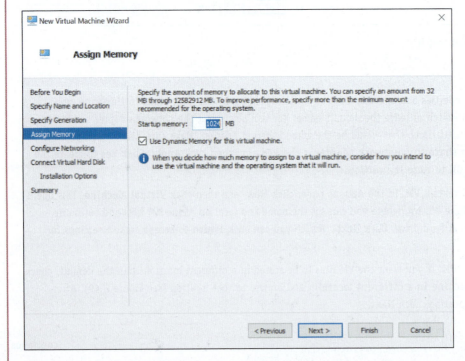

Figure 2-50 Use dynamic memory to conserve memory on the host computer

11. In the Configure Networking dialog box, select the virtual switch you created earlier and click **Next**.

12. In the Connect Virtual Hard Disk dialog box, select **Create a virtual hard disk** and click **Next**.

13. The Installation Options dialog box appears (see Figure 2-51). To install Windows from the ISO file you downloaded earlier using the Media Creation Tool, select **Install an operating system from a bootable CD/DVD-ROM**. Select **Image file (.iso)**. Click **Browse** and select the ISO file for the Windows installation. Click **Next** to continue. The last dialog box in the New Virtual Machine Wizard shows a summary of your selections. Click **Finish** to create the VM. The new VM is listed in the Virtual Machines pane in the Hyper-V Manager window.

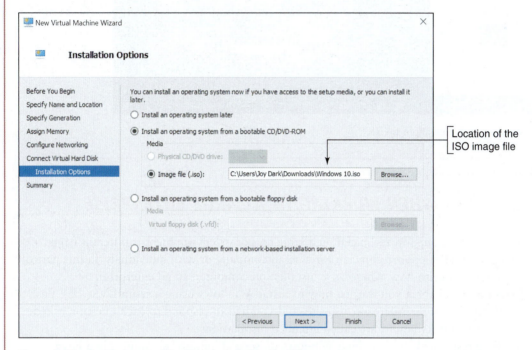

Figure 2-51   Decide how an OS will be installed in the VM

14. To manage the VM's virtual hardware, select the VM in Hyper-V Manager and click **Settings** near the bottom of the Actions pane. The Settings dialog box for the VM appears. Select the hardware in the left pane and apply your settings in the right pane.

15. To install Windows, you need to boot from the virtual DVD drive. Click **BIOS** in the left pane and select **Boot from CD** in the right pane.

16. Close the **Settings** box. To start the VM, select it and click **Start** in the Actions pane. The VM boots up and Windows setup starts. A thumbnail of the VM appears in the bottom-middle pane of the Hyper-V Manager window. To see the VM in a separate window, double-click the thumbnail. Figure 2-52 shows the VM window at the beginning of the OS installation. Notice in the figure that several VMs have been created, and three of them are currently running.

> ✎ **Notes** If you are trying to install an OS in a new VM and you get an error after the Product Key screen, try shutting down and restarting the VM. Then start the install again.

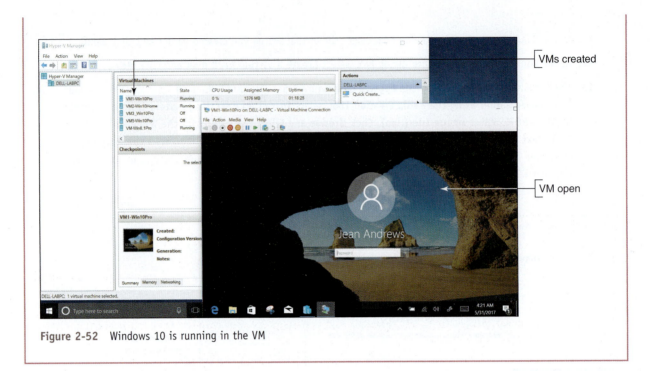

Figure 2-52 Windows 10 is running in the VM

SPECIAL CONCERNS WHEN WORKING IN A LARGE ENTERPRISE

**A+
CORE 2
1.3, 1.4**

Working as an IT support technician in a large corporate environment is different from working as an IT support technician for a small company or with individuals. In this part of the chapter, you learn how Windows is installed on computers in an enterprise.

Earlier in the chapter, you learned how to install Windows using a setup DVD, USB flash drive, or files downloaded from the Microsoft website, and you had to respond to each question asked during setup. These types of installations are called attended installations.

If, however, you were responsible for installing Windows on several hundred computers in a large corporation, you might want a less time-consuming method. These methods are called deployment strategies. As an IT support technician in a large corporation, most likely you would not be involved in choosing or setting up the deployment strategy. However, you need to be aware of the different strategies so you have a general idea of what will be expected when you are asked to provide desk-side or help-desk support as Windows is being deployed in your organization or a desktop OS that has failed needs to be refreshed.

Beginning with Windows 10, Microsoft expanded the methods it offers to deploy Windows in an enterprise. These methods are listed in Table 2-6. Some methods were designed to work with on-premises domains controlled by Active Directory (AD) and others work with Azure Active Directory (AAD) in the cloud.

Category	Method	Description
Modern deployments: Use these methods with AD or AAD domains.		
	Windows Autopilot	Streamlines the OOBE (out-of-box experiences) for devices preregistered with the enterprise. When a user receives a new device, turns it on, connects to the Internet, and enters his user name and password, the device is automatically joined to AAD and configured with settings and content specific for the organization without further user input.

Table 2-6 Deployment strategies for Windows 10 (continues)

Category	Method	Description
	In-place upgrade	Automates an in-place upgrade from Windows 8/7 to Windows 10 using a setup created by a system administrator with tools in the Microsoft Deployment Toolkit (MDT).
Dynamic deployments: Use these methods with AAD domains.		
	Subscription activation	Used to upgrade Windows 10 Pro to Windows 10 Enterprise. When a user signs in to AAD, the Windows upgrade happens automatically without user input or a restart. Product keys and Windows licensing information are kept in AAD, not on the local computer. This method creates a Windows subscription.
	Azure Active Directory join with MDM	MDM (Mobile Device Management) is software that forces devices to comply with corporate policies when they join an AAD domain.
	Provisioning packages	When a device joins AAD and MDM is not implemented, a provisioning package containing settings, apps, and data specific for the enterprise is downloaded to the device and applied with minimal input from the user. This package is easier to set up than an image, which is used in traditional deployments.
Traditional image deployments: Use these methods for on-premises AD domains when older deployment strategies are already established in the enterprise.		
	Bare metal	Also called wipe and load deployment, a standard image is created that contains the OS, drivers, applications, settings, and data specific for the enterprise. The image can be deployed on a new, empty hard drive or the drive can first be wiped clean.
	Refresh	Also called wipe and load deployment, user settings and data are saved and the hard drive is wiped clean before the standard image is applied. Then the image is applied and the user state is reinstalled.
	Replace	Used to replace an old device with a new one. After the standard image is applied to the new computer, the user state is copied from the old computer and applied to the new one.

Table 2-6 Deployment strategies for Windows 10 (continued)

METHODS TO DEPLOY A STANDARD IMAGE

A standard image contains the entire Windows volume in a single Windows Imaging (WIM) file, which has a .wim file extension. Installing Windows on a computer via a standard image is called image deployment. Here are a few details about image deployments:

◢ A standard image is hardware independent, meaning it can be installed on any computer. (In Chapter 4, you learn to create other types of images that can only be used on the computer that created them.)
◢ A standard image is created in a process called drive imaging. Microsoft provides several tools you can use to image a drive; many are included in the MDT.
◢ Deploying a standard image always results in a clean install rather than an upgrade.

Image deployment can be started using one of these methods:

◢ *Local installation.* Your company might provide you with a bootable flash drive or DVD that contains the image. When you boot from the device, Windows Preinstallation Environment (Windows PE) is launched; this is a minimum operating system used to start the installation. Follow the on-screen instructions.

◢ *Network installation.* To boot to the network and deploy the image from a server, first go to BIOS/ UEFI setup and configure it to boot from a network device. You might need to search the motherboard documentation for help; in general, you'll need to change the following or similar settings, which are likely to be on an Advanced screen or Boot screen:

◢ Enable the Network Stack (see Figure 2-53). For the LAN controller, enable the PXE option.

◢ Disable Secure boot, Fast boot, and Quiet mode.

◢ Enable CSM support. In the CSM group, enable Boot from network devices.

◢ Change the boot priority so that an IPv4 Network boot is listed first. If you don't see it as an option, reboot after making the changes in the previous three bullets. The Network boot option should then be available.

◢ Select the Network boot option to have the computer launch the Preboot eXecution Environment or Pre-Execution Environment (PXE). The identification for the Network boot option might include IPv4 and the name of the network adapter, as shown in Figure 2-54. PXE searches for a server on the network to provide a bootable operating system (Windows PE on the deployment server).

◢ *Push automation.* A technician does not start the image deployment; rather, the installation uses push automation when a user is not likely to be sitting at the computer. The entire remote network installation is automated and no user intervention is required. The process can turn on a computer that is turned off and even works when no OS is installed on the computer or the current OS is corrupted.

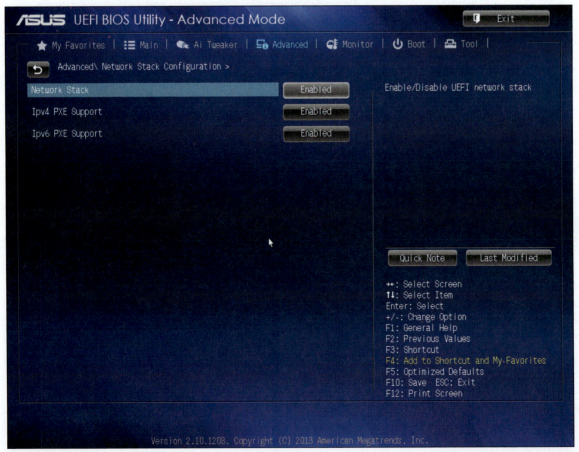

Source: American Megatrends, Inc.

Figure 2-53 Configure BIOS/UEFI setup to boot to the network

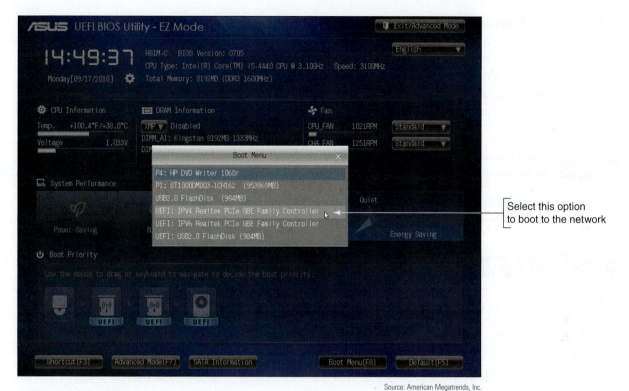

Source: American Megatrends, Inc.

Figure 2-54 When you click IPV4 Realtek PCIe GBE Family Controller, this system reboots to the network

Depending on how the system administrator has set up the deployment, you might be required to respond to questions as the installation progresses. An **unattended installation** does not require any responses, such as the administrator password or domain name, because these responses are stored in an **answer file**. After the installation completes, the User State Migration Tool might be used to transfer user settings, user data files, and application settings to the new installation.

The degree of work required by a technician to deploy an image is called high-touch, lite-touch, or zero-touch. The less involved the technician or user is, the more work is required by the system administrator to set up the deployment. For this reason, lite-touch or zero-touch deployments are only used in very large organizations.

> **✏ Notes** IT support technicians find that large enterprises appreciate quick and easy solutions to desktop or laptop computer problems. Technicians quickly learn that their marching orders are almost always "replace or reimage." Little time is spent trying to solve the underlying problem when hardware can quickly be replaced or a Windows installation can quickly be reimaged.

USING USMT SOFTWARE

**A+
CORE 2
1.3, 1.4**

The **User State Migration Tool (USMT)** can be used when deploying Windows in a Windows domain to copy user files and settings from one computer to another. Let's look briefly at what to expect when using the following three commands, which are part of the USMT software:

▲ **scanstate** copies user settings and files from the source computer to a safe location.
▲ **loadstate** applies these settings and files to the destination computer.
▲ **usmtutils** provides encryption options and hard drive management.

The scanstate, loadstate, and usmtutils command lines can be lengthy and include references to .xml files along with other parameters. The details of these command lines are not covered in this text. Most likely, the commands are stored in batch files provided by the system administrator. A **batch file** has a .bat file extension and contains a list or batch of OS commands that are executed as a group. These batch files might be automatically executed as part of a zero-touch installation or manually executed in a lite-touch or high-touch installation. To manually execute a batch file, you type the name of the file at a command prompt.

> ✎ **Notes** A system administrator uses the **DISM (Deployment Image Servicing and Management)** commands to initially capture (create) and manage a standard image. The DISM command also comes with Windows 10; you can use it to repair a corrupted Windows installation. You learn to use some DISM commands in Chapter 5.

>> CHAPTER SUMMARY

How to Plan a Windows Installation

◢ Windows can be purchased as a less expensive OEM version or a more expensive retail version. The OEM version can only be installed on a new computer.

◢ Each edition of Windows 10, Windows 8, and Windows 7 (except Windows 7 Starter) is available in either 32- or 64-bit versions. A 32-bit OS cannot address as much memory as a 64-bit OS. A 64-bit OS performs better and requires more memory than a 32-bit OS.

◢ Before purchasing Windows, make sure your system meets the minimum hardware requirements and that all the hardware and applications will work under the OS. A 64-bit OS requires 64-bit drivers.

◢ A hard drive contains one or more partitions or volumes and can use the MBR or GPT partitioning system. To use UEFI Secure boot, the partitioning system must be GPT and the Windows installation must be 64-bit.

◢ Normally, Windows is installed on the C: volume in the C:\Windows folder. The volume in which Windows is installed must use the NTFS file system.

◢ A computer might have legacy BIOS installed on the motherboard or have the newer UEFI firmware installed. Most UEFI firmware offers the option to support legacy BIOS when in UEFI CSM mode.

◢ Windows can be installed as an in-place upgrade, a clean installation, or in a multiboot environment with another OS.

◢ Windows can be installed from the setup DVD, a USB flash drive, files downloaded from the Internet via the Media Creation Tool, or in a virtual machine.

Installing Windows 10, Windows 8.1, and Windows 7

◢ A technician needs to know how to perform an in-place upgrade, a clean install, or a multiboot with Windows.

◢ The steps for installing or upgrading Windows 8.1 are about the same as those for Windows 10.

◢ A clean install is the best option to use if the current installation is sluggish or giving problems, or if you're installing Windows on a new desktop computer that you're building.

◢ In a multiboot, each OS must be installed on its own partition. Make sure you have enough free space on a partition before installing Windows on it, and make sure it doesn't currently hold an OS.

What to Do After a Windows Installation

◢ After a Windows installation, verify network access, activate Windows, install any Windows updates or Windows 7 service packs, verify that automatic updates are configured correctly, install hardware and applications, create user accounts and transfer or restore user data and preferences from backups, and turn Windows features on or off.

◢ Virtual machine software can provide multiple instances of operating systems for training users, running legacy software, and supporting multiple operating systems.

Special Concerns When Working in a Large Enterprise

◢ Three types of deployments for installing Windows in a large enterprise are modern deployments, dynamic deployments, and traditional image deployments. Modern deployments are done using Active Directory or Azure Active Directory, dynamic deployments use AAD, and traditional deployments use AD.

◢ Zero-touch deployments require the most time to set up, but do not require a technician to be at the computer when the installation happens.

>> KEY TERMS

For explanations of key terms, see the Glossary for this text.

active hours
administrator account
answer file
batch file
BIOS (basic input/output system)
boot loader menu
boot priority order
clean install
custom installation
default product key
device drivers
Device Manager
digital license
diskpart
DISM (Deployment Image Servicing and Management)
drive imaging
driver rollback
dual boot
file system

full format
GUID Partition Table (GPT)
hardware signature
hot-swappable
hypervisor
image deployment
in-place upgrade
ISO file
ISO image
loadstate
local account
Master Boot Record (MBR)
Media Creation Tool
Microsoft account
Microsoft Deployment Toolkit (MDT)
multiboot
Original Equipment Manufacturer (OEM) license

Preboot eXecution Environment
Pre-Execution Environment (PXE)
product activation
product key
Programs and Features
provisioning package
push automation
quick format
remote network installation
scanstate
Secure boot
service pack
setup BIOS/UEFI
single sign-on (SSO)
solid-state drive
standard account
standard image
startup BIOS/UEFI
system BIOS/UEFI

third-party drivers
UEFI (Unified Extensible Firmware Interface)
UEFI CSM (Compatibility Support Module) mode
unattended installation
upgrade paths
User Account Control (UAC) dialog box
User State Migration Tool (USMT)
usmtutils
virtual machine (VM)
volume
Windows Defender Antivirus
Windows.old folder
Windows Preinstallation Environment (Windows PE)

>> THINKING CRITICALLY

These questions are designed to prepare you for the critical thinking required for the A+ exams and may use content from other chapters and the web.

1. You are planning an upgrade from Windows 8.1 to Windows 10. Your system uses a network card that you don't find on the Microsoft Windows 10 list of compatible devices. What do you do next?

a. Abandon the upgrade and continue to use Windows 8.1.

b. Check the website of the network card manufacturer for a Windows 10 driver.

c. Buy a new network card.

d. Install a dual boot for Windows 8.1 and Windows 10 and only use the network when you have Windows 8.1 loaded.

2. You have just installed Windows 10 and now want to install your favorite game that worked fine under Windows 8.1. When you attempt the installation, you get an error. What is your best next step?

a. Purchase a new version of your game—one that is compatible with Windows 10.

b. Download any updates to Windows 10.

c. Reinstall Windows 8.1.

d. Install a VM running Windows 8.1.

3. You have 32-bit Windows 8.1 installed on your computer, and you purchase a license for Windows 10 Pro. You want to install Windows 10 using the 64-bit architecture. In which way(s) can you install Windows 10?

a. You can perform an upgrade, but not a clean install.

b. You can perform an upgrade or a clean install.

c. You can perform a clean install, but not an upgrade.

d. None of the above

4. A laptop reports that it has made a wireless network connection but cannot access the network or the Internet. Arrange the following steps in the best order to troubleshoot the problem:

a. Use Device Manager to uninstall the wireless adapter and install it again.

b. Disable and enable the wireless network adapter.

c. Disconnect the connection and connect again to the wireless network.

d. Use Device Manager to update the wireless adapter drivers.

5. Which installation of Windows 10 requires you to enter a product key during the install process?

a. You are replacing a failed hard drive that already had Windows 10 installed.

b. You are replacing a failed motherboard on a system with Windows 10 installed and a Microsoft account was not used to sign in to Windows.

c. You are replacing a failed motherboard on a system with Windows 10 installed and a Microsoft account had been used to sign in to Windows.

d. Windows 10 has become corrupted and you decide to perform a clean install to recover the OS.

6. Which of the following methods can you use to install Windows 10 in a VM? Select all that apply.

a. Clean install from an ISO image

b. Clean install from a USB flash drive

c. Upgrade from Windows 8 using an ISO image

d. Clean install from a setup DVD

7. Suppose you want to boot a VM from its virtual DVD drive, but it boots to the VM's hard drive. Which of the following could be the source of this problem? Select all that apply.

2

a. There is no DVD or ISO file mounted to the virtual DVD drive.

b. The virtual DVD drive is not enabled.

c. The boot sequence is not correct in the VM's BIOS/UEFI settings.

d. The hard drive does not have an OS installed.

8. You are setting up a Windows 10 desktop computer that requires 4 TB of storage. Which options work (select all that apply)? Which option is the recommended best practice?

a. Install one 3-TB hard drive with the MBR partitioning system and 64-bit Windows 10.

b. Install two 1.5-TB hard drives with the GPT partitioning systems and 32-bit Windows 10.

c. Install two 1.5-TB hard drives with the MBR partitioning systems and 64-bit Windows 10.

d. Install two 1.5-TB hard drives with the GPT partitioning systems and 64-bit Windows 10.

9. If you suspect a computer is infected with a virus and you are ready to upgrade from Windows 8 to Windows 10, what is your best practice?

a. Perform a clean install of Windows 10 rather than an upgrade.

b. Scan the system for malware before you perform the Windows 10 upgrade.

c. Install Windows 8 as an in-place upgrade to remediate the system and then upgrade to Windows 10.

d. Completely erase the hard drive with a full format and then install Windows 10.

10. After setting up a dual-boot installation with Windows 8 and Windows 10, how do you boot the system into Windows 8?

a. Start the system as normal; the oldest OS automatically loads.

b. Start the system as normal; the newest OS automatically loads.

c. Start the system and select the OS in the boot loader menu.

d. Go into BIOS/UEFI setup and set the boot priority order to start with Windows 8.

11. After a Windows installation, what is the easiest way to determine that you have Internet access?

a. Open the Network and Sharing Center and verify that Wi-Fi is turned on and shows no errors.

b. Open Internet Explorer and browse to a website.

c. Open Device Manager and check the network adapter for errors.

d. Verify that the local router has lights blinking to indicate connectivity.

12. After installing the device drivers for a video adapter, you still are not able to use the special features of the adapter. What is your next step?

a. Open Device Manager and check for errors.

b. Uninstall the adapter and try the installation again.

c. Update Windows.

d. Check the website of the video adapter's manufacturer for guidance.

13. The PXE programming code is used to boot a computer when it is searching for an OS on the network. Where is this code stored?

a. On the deployment server

b. On the motherboard

    c. On the Windows volume of the local hard drive

    d. In the cloud in Azure Active Directory

14. What is an advantage of using a dynamic hard drive in a VM?

15. Ming is building an inexpensive computer to use for her online classes, and needs to purchase Windows. What is the most cost-effective way Ming can purchase and activate a selected version of Windows?

>> HANDS-ON PROJECTS

Hands-On | Project 2-1   Installing 64-Bit Windows 10 Pro

Use the Media Creation Tool to download Windows 10 setup files, and then install 64-bit Windows 10 Pro on your lab computer. If you need help with the installation, see the directions in the chapter. Set up Windows to use a local account to sign in to Windows. Write down each decision you have to make as you perform the installation. If you get any error messages during the installation, write them down and list the steps you took to recover from them. How long did the installation take?

Hands-On | Project 2-2   Using the Internet for Problem Solving

Access the *support.microsoft.com* website for Windows 10 support. Print one article from the Knowledge Base that addresses a problem when installing Windows 10. In your own words, write a paragraph describing the problem and a paragraph explaining the solution. If you don't understand the problem or the solution from this article, do a search online for additional information so that you can give a well-rounded description of both the problem and the solution.

Hands-On | Project 2-3   Installing Windows 8.1 in a VM

This project assumes you already have 64-bit Windows 10 Pro installed on a computer. Do the following:

1. Enable Client Hyper-V and set up a VM in it.

2. Using the Media Creation Tool, create an ISO file to install Windows 8.1 in the VM.

3. Verify that you can use Internet Explorer in the VM to surf the web.

Hands-On | Project 2-4 Installing Windows 10 in a VM as a Dual Boot

This project assumes you already have 64-bit Windows 10 Pro installed and a VM with Windows 8.1 installed on a computer. Do the following:

1. Using the Media Creation Tool, create an ISO file to install Windows 10 in the VM.
2. Open the VM you already created with Windows 8.1 installed and create a second partition with at least 16 GB.
3. Mount the Windows 10 ISO file to the VM. In the Settings app for the Windows 8.1 VM, change the firmware settings to boot from a file. Restart the Windows 8.1 VM and install Windows 10 as a dual boot on the partition you just created.
4. Verify that you can use Microsoft Edge in the VM to surf the web.

Hands-On | Project 2-5 Recommended Updates

On a Windows 10 system connected to the Internet, open the **Settings** app and click the **Update & security** group. Under *Looking for info on the latest updates?*, click **Learn more**. Windows Update opens the Microsoft website and recommends Windows updates. Print the webpage showing a list of recommended updates. Then, on a Windows 8.1 system connected to the Internet, open the System window and click **Windows Update**. Windows Update searches the Microsoft website and recommends Windows updates. Print the webpage showing a list of recommended updates. For a lab computer, don't perform the updates unless you have your instructor's permission.

Hands-On | Project 2-6 Creating a Documentation Form

Support technicians are expected to maintain documentation for each computer for which they are responsible. Create a document that a technician can use when installing Windows and performing all the chores mentioned in the chapter that are needed before and after the installation. The document needs a checklist of what to do before the installation and a checklist of what to do after the installation. It also needs a place to record decisions made during the installation, the applications and hardware devices installed, user accounts created, and any other important information that might be useful for future maintenance or troubleshooting. Don't forget to include a way to identify the computer, the name of the technician doing the work, and when the work was done.

>> REAL PROBLEMS, REAL SOLUTIONS

REAL PROBLEM 2-1 Recovering Data from a Corrupted Windows Installation

As an IT support technician for a small organization, it's your job to support the computers, the small network, and the users. One of your coworkers, Jason, comes to you in a panic. His Windows 10 system won't boot, and he has lots of important data files in several locations on the drive. He has no idea which folders hold the files. Besides the application data he's currently working on, he's especially concerned about losing email addresses, email, and his Internet Explorer Favorites links.

After trying everything you know about recovering Windows 10, you conclude the OS is corrupted beyond repair. You decide there might be a way to remove the hard drive from Jason's computer and connect it to another computer so that you can recover the data. Search the Internet and find a device that you can use to connect Jason's hard drive to another computer through one of its USB ports. The hard drive uses a SATA hard drive interface. Print the webpage showing the device and its price.

REAL PROBLEM 2-2 Troubleshooting an Upgrade

Your friend, Thomas, has upgraded his Windows 8.1 desktop to Windows 10. After the installation, he discovers his media card reader does not work. He calls you on the phone and asks you what to do. Do the following to plan your troubleshooting approach:

1. List the questions you should ask Thomas to help diagnose the problem.

2. List the steps you would take if you were sitting at the computer solving the problem.

3. What do you think is the source of the problem? Explain your answer.

Setting Up a Local Network

After completing this chapter, you will be able to:

- Describe network types and the Internet connections they use
- Connect a computer to a wired or wireless network
- Configure and secure a multifunction router on a local network
- Troubleshoot network connections using the command line

In this chapter, you learn about the types of networks and the technologies used to build networks. You also learn to connect a computer to a network and how to set up and secure a small wired or wireless network.

This chapter prepares you to assume responsibility for supporting both wired and wireless networks in a small office/home office (SOHO) environment. In later networking courses, you'll learn more about the hardware used in networking, including network devices, connectors, cabling, networking tools, and the types of networks used for Internet connections. Let's get started by looking at the types of networks you might encounter as an IT support technician and the types of connections they might use to connect to the Internet.

> ★ **A+ Exam Tip** Much of the content in this chapter applies to both the A+ Core 1 220-1001 exam and the A+ Core 2 220-1002 exam.

TYPES OF NETWORKS AND NETWORK CONNECTIONS

**A+
CORE 1
2.2, 2.3,
2.4, 2.7**

A computer network is created when two or more computers can communicate with each other. Networks can be categorized by several methods, including the technology used and the size of the network. When networks are categorized by their size or physical area they cover, these are the categories used, listed from smallest to largest:

**A+
CORE 2
1.8**

▶ *PAN.* A **PAN (personal area network)** consists of personal devices such as cell phones and laptop computers communicating at close range. PANs can use wired connections (such as USB or Lightning) or wireless connections (such as Bluetooth or Wi-Fi, also called 802.11).

▶ *LAN.* A **LAN (local area network)** covers a small local area, such as a home, office, or a small group of buildings. LANs can use wired (most likely Ethernet) or wireless technologies (most likely Wi-Fi). A LAN allows workstations, servers, printers, and other devices to communicate and share resources.

▲ *WMN.* A **WMN (wireless mesh network)** consists of many wireless devices communicating directly with each other rather than through a single, central device. Some or all of the devices on the WMN can serve as connection points for other devices to communicate across longer distances. This technology is commonly used in IoT (Internet of Things) wireless networks, where many types of devices, such as thermostats, light switches, door locks, and security cameras, are connected to the network and on to the Internet.

▲ *MAN.* A **MAN (metropolitan area network)** covers multiple buildings in a large campus or a portion of a city, such as a downtown area. It's usually the result of a cooperative effort to improve service to its users. Network technologies used can be wireless (most likely LTE) and/or wired (for example, Ethernet with fiber-optic cabling).

▲ *WAN.* A **WAN (wide area network)** covers a large geographical area and is made up of many smaller networks. The best-known WAN is the Internet. Some technologies that connect a single computer or LAN to the Internet include DSL, cable Internet, satellite, cellular WAN, and fiber optic.

> ★ **A+ Exam Tip** The A+ Core 1 exam expects you to be able to compare LAN, WAN, PAN, MAN, and WMN networks.

Now let's look at network technologies used for Internet connections.

INTERNET CONNECTION TECHNOLOGIES

**A+
CORE 1
2.2, 2.3,
2.4, 2.7**

**A+
CORE 2
1.8**

To connect to the Internet, a device or a network first connects to an **Internet service provider (ISP)**, such as Xfinity or Spectrum. The most common types of connections for SOHO networks are DSL and cable Internet (commonly called cable or cable modem). See Figure 3-1. When connecting to an ISP, know that upload speeds are generally slower than download speeds. These rates differ because users typically download more data than they upload. Therefore, an ISP devotes more of the available bandwidth to downloading and less of it to uploading.

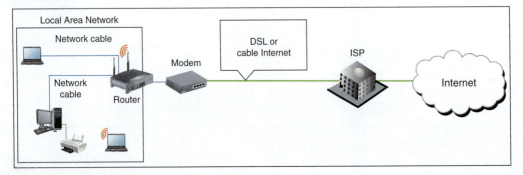

Figure 3-1 An ISP stands between a LAN and the Internet

Networks are built using one or more technologies that provide varying degrees of bandwidth. **Bandwidth** is the theoretical number of bits that can be transmitted over a network connection at one time, similar to the number of lanes on a highway. The networking industry refers to bandwidth as a measure of the maximum rate of data transmission in bits per second (bps), thousands of bits per second (Kbps), millions of bits per second (Mbps), or billions of bits per second (Gbps). Bandwidth is the theoretical or potential speed of a network, whereas **data throughput** is the average of the actual speed. In practice, network transmissions experience delays, called **latency**, that result in slower network performance. For example, wired signals traveling across long cables or wireless signals crossing long distances through the air can cause signal strength degradation, resulting in latency. Latency is measured by the round-trip time it takes for a message to travel from source to destination and back to source.

Table 3-1 lists network technologies used by local networks to connect to the Internet. The table is more or less ordered from slowest to fastest maximum bandwidth within each category, although latency can affect the actual bandwidth of any particular network. We'll explore each of these technologies in more depth throughout this chapter.

Technology (Wireless or Wired)	Maximum Speed	Description
Wireless Internet connection: Satellite and WiMAX		
Satellite	Up to 15 Mbps	Requires a dish to send to and receive from a satellite, which is in a relative fixed position with the Earth.
WiMAX	Up to 30 Mbps	Requires a transmitter to send to and receive from a WiMAX tower up to 30 miles away. WiMAX was once popular in rural areas for wireless Internet connections, but it is losing this market space to cellular solutions such as LTE.
Wireless Internet connection: Cellular		
3G cellular (third-generation cellular)	At least 200 Kbps, but can be up to 4 Mbps	Improved over earlier technologies and allows for transmitting data and video. Uses either CDMA or GSM mobile phone services. Speeds vary widely according to the revision standards used.
4G cellular (fourth-generation cellular)	100 Mbps to 1 Gbps	Higher speeds are achieved when the mobile device stays in a fixed position. A 4G network typically uses LTE (Long Term Evolution) technology.
5G cellular (fifth-generation cellular)	10–50 Gbps and beyond	At the time of this writing, 5G devices are expected on the market as soon as 2019 with more widespread use beginning in 2020, and additional improvements to the technology in later years.
Wired Internet connection: Telephone		
Dial-up or regular telephone (POTS, for plain old telephone service)	Up to 56 Kbps	Slow access to an ISP using a modem and dial-up connection over phone lines.
ISDN	64 Kbps or 128 Kbps	**ISDN (Integrated Services Digital Network)** is an outdated business-use connection to an ISP over dial-up phone lines.
SDSL (Symmetric Digital Subscriber Line)	Up to 22 Mbps	Equal bandwidth in both directions. SDSL is a type of broadband technology. (**Broadband** refers to a networking technology that carries more than one type of signal on the same cabling infrastructure, such as DSL and telephone or cable Internet and TV.) DSL uses regular phone lines and is an always-up or always-on connection that does not require a dial-up.
ADSL (Asymmetric DSL)	640 Kbps upstream and up to 24 Mbps downstream	Most bandwidth is allocated for data coming from the ISP to the user. Slower versions of ADSL are called ADSL Lite or DSL Lite. ISP customers pay according to a bandwidth scale.
VDSL (very-high-bit-rate DSL)	Up to 70 Mbps	A type of asymmetric DSL that works only over a short distance.

Table 3-1 Networking technologies (continues)

Technology (Wireless or Wired)	Maximum Speed	Description
Other wired Internet connections		
Cable Internet	Up to 160 Mbps, depending on the type of cable	Connects a home or small business to an ISP, usually comes with a cable television subscription, and shares cable TV lines. If available, fiber-optic cable gives highest speeds.
Dedicated line using fiber optic	Up to 43 Tbps	Dedicated fiber-optic line from ISP to business or home. Speeds vary widely with price.
Wired local network: Ethernet		
Fast Ethernet (100BaseT)	100 Mbps	Used for local networks.
Gigabit Ethernet (1000BaseT)	1000 Mbps or 1 Gbps	Fastest Ethernet standard for small, local networks.
10-Gigabit Ethernet (10GBaseT)	10 Gbps	Typically requires fiber media, is mostly used on the backbone of larger enterprise networks, and can also be used on WAN connections.
Wireless local network: Wi-Fi		
802.11a	Up to 54 Mbps	No longer used.
802.11b	Up to 11 Mbps	Experiences interference from cordless phones and microwaves.
802.11g	Up to 54 Mbps	Compatible with and has replaced 802.11b.
802.11n	Up to 600 Mbps	Uses **multiple input/multiple output (MIMO)**, which means an access point can have up to four antennas to improve performance.
802.11ac	Theoretically up to 7 Gbps, but currently at 1.3 Gbps	Supports up to eight antennas and supports **beamforming**, which detects the locations of connected devices and increases signal strength in those directions.
802.11ad	Up to 7 Gbps	This throughput can only be achieved when the device is within 3.3 m of the access point.

Table 3-1 Networking technologies (continued)

> **Notes** Pending Wi-Fi standards include 802.11 ax, which is designed to improve performance in highly populated areas, and 802.11 ay, which is expected to achieve maximum throughput of 20 Gbps and extend the range of 802.11 ad. Approval of both standards is expected in 2019.

Currently, cable Internet and DSL are the two most popular ways to make an Internet connection for a home network. Let's first compare these two technologies and then we'll look at fiber-optic dedicated lines, satellite, dial-up, and cellular WAN connections.

> ★ **A+ Exam Tip** The A+ Core 1 exam expects you to be able to compare these network types used for Internet connections: cable, DSL, dial-up, fiber, satellite, ISDN, and cellular (tethering and mobile hotspot).

COMPARE CABLE INTERNET AND DSL

Here are the important facts about cable Internet and DSL:

▲ **Cable Internet** is a broadband technology that uses cable TV lines and is always connected (always up). With cable Internet, the TV signal to your television and the data signals to your computer or LAN share the same **coaxial (coax) cable**, an older cable form that is rarely used today in a local area network. The **cable modem** converts a computer's digital signals to analog when sending them and converts incoming analog data to digital.

▲ **DSL (Digital Subscriber Line)** is a group of broadband technologies that covers a wide range of speeds. DSL uses ordinary copper phone lines and a range of frequencies on the copper wire that are not used by voice, making it possible for you to use the same phone line for voice and DSL at the same time. When you make a regular phone call, you dial in as usual. However, the DSL part of the line is always connected (always up) for most DSL services.

When deciding between cable Internet and DSL, consider these points:

▲ Both cable Internet and DSL can sometimes be purchased on a sliding scale, depending on the bandwidth you want to buy. Subscriptions offer residential and more expensive business plans. Business plans are likely to have increased bandwidth and better support when problems arise.

▲ With cable Internet, you share the TV cable infrastructure with your neighbors, which can result in service becoming degraded if many people in your neighborhood are using cable Internet at the same time. With DSL, you're using a dedicated phone line, so your neighbors' surfing habits are not important.

▲ With DSL, static over phone lines in your house can be a problem. The DSL company provides filters to install at each phone jack (see Figure 3-2), but still the problem might not be fully solved. Also, your phone line must qualify for DSL; some lines are too dirty (too much static or noise) to support DSL. Figure 3-3 shows a **DSL modem** that can connect directly to a computer or to a router on your network.

Figure 3-2 When DSL is used in your home, filters are needed on every phone jack except the one used by the DSL modem

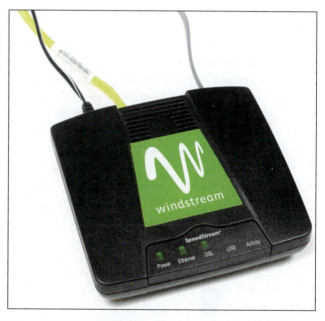

Figure 3-3 This DSL modem connects to a phone jack and a computer or router to provide a broadband connection to an ISP

▲ Both cable and DSL connections typically require a modem device at the entry to your SOHO network. Although you might be able to find the modem's default login instructions online, you'll likely never have to change any settings on the modem itself. Configuring a DSL or cable modem consists of plugging the correct cables into the correct ports. For example, Figure 3-4 shows a cable modem with the ISP cable connected on the right. The yellow Ethernet cable connects to the local network, and a phone line is plugged into the Voice-over-IP (VoIP) phone service provided by the ISP over the Internet. Also notice the Reset button in the figure, which you can use to reset a modem to its factory default settings. When troubleshooting a modem, try rebooting it first, and only use the reset as a last resort.

Figure 3-4   Use a cable modem to connect the ISP's coaxial cable to the LAN's Ethernet cable

DEDICATED LINE USING FIBER OPTIC

Another broadband technology used for Internet access is fiber optic. The technology connects a dedicated line from your ISP to your place of business or residence. This dedicated line is called a point-to-point (PTP) connection because no other business or residence shares the line with you. Television, Internet data, and voice communication all share the broadband fiber-optic cable, which reaches all the way from the ISP to your home. Alternatively, the provider might install fiber-optic cabling up to your neighborhood and then run coaxial cable (similar to that used in cable Internet connections) for the last leg of the connection to your business or residence. Upstream and downstream speeds and prices vary.

SATELLITE

People who live in remote areas and want high-speed Internet connections often have limited choices. DSL and cable options might not be available where they live, but satellite access is available from pretty much anywhere. Internet access by satellite is available even on airplanes. Passengers can connect to the Internet using a wireless hotspot and satellite dish on the plane. A satellite dish mounted on top of your house or office building communicates with a satellite used by an ISP offering the satellite service (see Figure 3-5). One disadvantage of satellite is that it requires line-of-sight wireless connectivity without obstruction from mountains, trees, and tall buildings. Another disadvantage is that it experiences higher delays in transmission (called latency), especially when uploading, and is therefore not a good solution for an Internet connection that will be used for videoconferencing or voice over Internet.

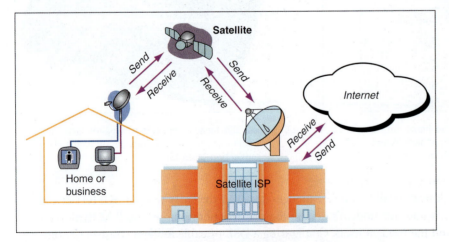

Figure 3-5   Communication by satellite can include television and Internet access

DIAL-UP

Of all the types of networking connections, dial-up or POTS (plain old telephone service) is the least expensive and slowest connection to the Internet. Dial-up connections are painfully slow, but you might still need them when traveling, and they're good at home when your broadband connection is down.

CELLULAR WAN

A **wireless wide area network (WWAN)**, also called a **cellular network** or cellular WAN because it consists of cells, is provided by companies such as Verizon and AT&T. Each cell is controlled by a base station (see Figure 3-6), which might include more than one transceiver and antenna on the same tower to support various technologies for both voice and data transmission. Two established cellular technologies are GSM (Global System for Mobile Communications) and CDMA (Code Division Multiple Access). In the United States, Sprint and Verizon use CDMA, while AT&T and T-Mobile—along with most of the rest of the world—use GSM. **Long Term Evolution (LTE)** and Voice over LTE (VoLTE) provide both data and voice transmissions and are expected to ultimately replace both GSM and CDMA.

Cellular devices that use GSM or LTE require a **SIM (Subscriber Identification Module) card** to be installed in the device; the card contains the information that identifies your device to the carrier (see Figure 3-7). CDMA networks don't require SIM cards unless they also use LTE. Most carriers today use a combination of GSM and LTE or CDMA and LTE.

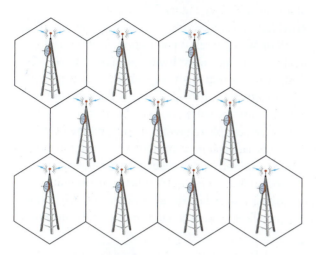

Figure 3-6 A cellular WAN is made up of many cells that provide coverage over a wide area

Figure 3-7 A SIM card contains proof that your device can use a cellular network

Most smartphones are linked by the manufacturer to a specific cellular provider and will need to be validated on that provider's network to connect to it. To connect a computer using mobile broadband to a cellular network, you need the hardware and software to connect and, for most networks, a SIM card. Here are your options for software and hardware devices that can connect to a cellular network, and general steps for how to create each connection. Keep in mind that when you purchase any of these devices from a carrier or manufacturer, detailed instructions are most likely included for connecting to the cellular network.

▲ *Embedded mobile broadband modem.* A laptop or other mobile device might have an embedded broadband modem. In this situation, you still need to subscribe to a carrier. If a SIM card is required, insert the card in the device. For some laptops, the card slot might be in the battery bay, and you must remove the battery to find the slot. Then use a setting or application installed on the device to connect to the cellular network.

Figure 3-8 Tether your laptop to your cell phone using a USB cable

▲ ***Cell phone tethering.*** You can tether your computer or another device to your cell phone. The cell phone connects to the cellular network and provides communication to the tethered device. To use your phone for tethering, your carrier contract must allow it. The phone and other device can connect by way of a USB cable (see Figure 3-8), a proprietary cable provided by your cell phone manufacturer, or a Bluetooth or Wi-Fi wireless connection. Your carrier is likely to provide you software to make the connection, or the setting might be embedded in the phone's OS. If software is provided, install the software first and then use the software to make the connection. Otherwise, enable the tether in your phone's OS.

▲ ***USB broadband modem.*** For any computer, you can use a USB broadband modem (sometimes called an air card), such as the one shown in Figure 3-9. The device requires a contract with a cellular carrier. If needed when using a USB broadband modem, insert the SIM card in the modem (see Figure 3-10). When you insert the modem into a USB port, Windows finds the device, and the software stored on the device automatically installs and runs. A window provided by the software then appears and allows you to connect to the cellular network.

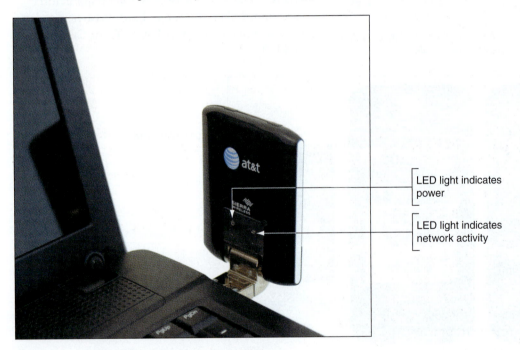

LED light indicates power

LED light indicates network activity

Figure 3-9 A USB broadband modem by Sierra Wireless

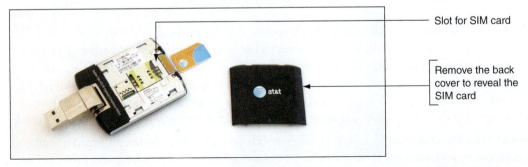

Slot for SIM card

Remove the back cover to reveal the SIM card

Figure 3-10 A SIM card with subscription information on it might be required to use a cellular network

▲ *LTE installed Internet.* Some cellular companies offer home Internet service through their cellular WAN infrastructure. Verizon calls its service LTE Internet Installed, and AT&T calls its service FWI (Fixed Wireless Internet). The ISP installs an LTE router at the home, possibly with an external antenna, which then connects wirelessly to the ISP's cellular network. The router provides a Wi-Fi hotspot as well as a few Ethernet ports for wired devices. Typically, the router can't be moved to other locations like a smartphone can—it's designed to be used only at the location where the subscription is established. Data usage caps also may apply.

▲ *Mobile hotspot.* Some mobile devices can create a mobile hotspot that computers and other mobile devices can connect by Wi-Fi to your device and on to the Internet. Some cellular ISPs, such as AT&T, also offer devices dedicated to this purpose.

Now that you understand some basics about the different types of networks and methods of connecting those networks to the Internet, you're ready to learn about different ways to connect computers to local networks.

CONNECTING A COMPUTER TO A LOCAL NETWORK

**A+
CORE 1
2.2, 2.3,
2.6, 3.2**

Connecting a laptop or desktop computer to a network is quick and easy in most situations. Here, we begin with a summary of how to connect to a wired or wireless network, and then you learn how to connect to a VPN. (In Chapter 9, you learn how to connect smartphones and tablets to networks.)

**A+
CORE 2
1.8**

> ★ **A+ Exam Tip** The A+ Core 2 exam expects you to know which type of network connection (VPN, wired, wireless, cellular, or dial-up) is appropriate for a given scenario and to know how to make the connection.

CONNECTING TO AN ETHERNET WIRED OR WI-FI WIRELESS LOCAL NETWORK

**A+
CORE 1
2.3, 3.2**

To connect a computer to a network using an Ethernet wired or Wi-Fi wireless connection, follow these steps:

1. In general, before you connect to any network, the network adapter and its drivers must be installed and Device Manager should report no errors.

**A+
CORE 2
1.8**

2. Do one of the following to connect to the network:

   ▲ For a wired network, plug in the network cable to the Ethernet port. The port is also called an RJ-45 port and looks like a large phone jack. An RJ-45 connector looks similar to an RJ-11 connector, only larger (see Figure 3-11). Indicator lights near the network port should light up to indicate connectivity and activity. For Ethernet, Windows should automatically configure the connection.

   ▲ For a wireless network, click the **Network** icon in the taskbar on the desktop and select a wireless network. Click **Connect**. If the network is secured, you must enter the security key to the wireless network to connect.

3. If this is the first time you've connected to a local network, you'll be asked if you want to make the PC discoverable. For private networks (such as your home or business), click **Yes**, and for public networks (such as a coffee shop hotspot), click **No**.

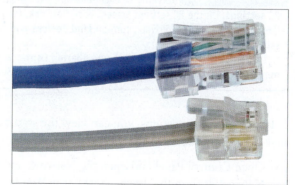

Figure 3-11 RJ-45 and RJ-11 connectors

> ✏️ **Notes** For a private corporate or enterprise network, Windows Server or Microsoft Azure is likely to manage access to the network using a Windows domain. You must sign in to the Windows domain with a user name and password. Press **Ctrl+Alt+Del** to access the sign-on screen. The user name might be text such as Jane Smith or an email address such as *JSmith@mycompany.com*. You learn more about private networks, public networks, and Windows domains in Chapter 1.

4. Open your browser and make sure you can access the web. For wireless connections, some hotspots provide an initial page called a captive portal, where you must enter a code or agree to the terms of use before you can use the network. On a private network, open File Explorer or Windows Explorer and drill down into the Network group to verify that network resources are available (see Figure 3-12).

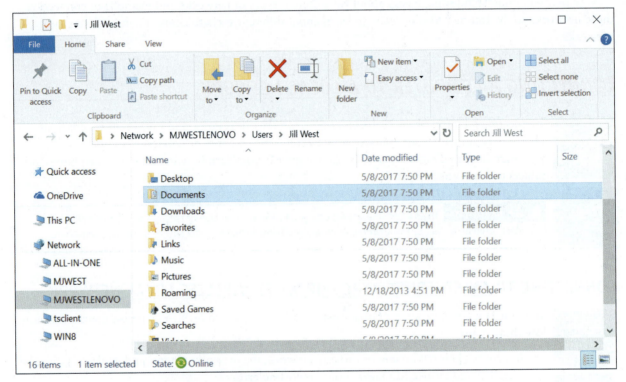

Figure 3-12 File Explorer shows resources on the network

To view and change network security settings in Windows 10, open the Settings app and click **Network & Internet**. Click **Change connection properties**, and then select either **Public** or **Private**.

> ○ **OS Differences** To verify or change security settings in Windows 8, click the **Settings** charm and click **Change PC settings**. On the PC settings screen, click **Network**. On the Network screen, if necessary, click **Connections**. To set the network security to Private, turn on **Find devices and content**. To set the network security to Public, turn this setting off.
> In Windows 7, open the **Network and Sharing Center** window. If the network location is **Home network** or **Work network**, click it. The Set Network Location box appears. Select a network type and click **Close**.

For wireless connections, you can view the status of the connection, including the security key used to make the connection. Do the following:

1. Open **Control Panel** and open the **Network and Sharing Center**. Alternately, you can right-click the **Network** icon in the desktop taskbar in Windows 10 and click **Open Network & Internet settings**, which opens the Network & Internet group in the Settings app. In Windows 8/7, click **Open Network**

and Sharing Center. In the Network and Sharing Center (see Figure 3-13), click **Change adapter settings**, or in the Network & Internet window, click **Change adapter options**. The Network Connections window appears (see Figure 3-14).

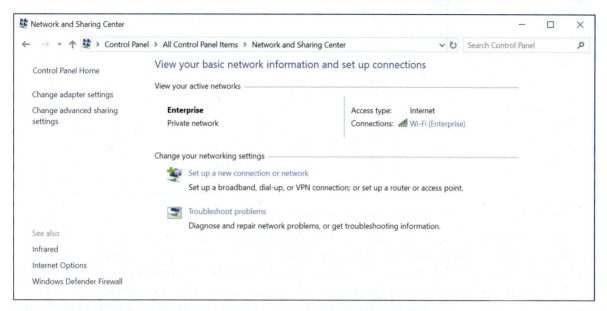

Figure 3-13 The Network and Sharing Center reports a healthy wireless network connection

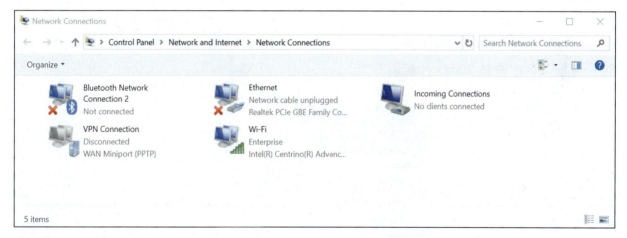

Figure 3-14 The Network Connections window can be used to repair broken connections

Notes For Windows 10, a shortcut to open the Network & Internet window in the Settings app is to press **Win+X** and click **Network Connections**. For Windows 8, the same shortcut will open the Network Connections window.

2. In the Network Connections window, right-click the **Wi-Fi** connection and click **Status**. In the Wi-Fi Status box (see Figure 3-15), click **Wireless Properties**. In the Wireless Network Properties box, select the **Security** tab. To view the security key, check **Show characters**. You can also see the security and encryption types that Windows automatically detected and applied when it made the connection.

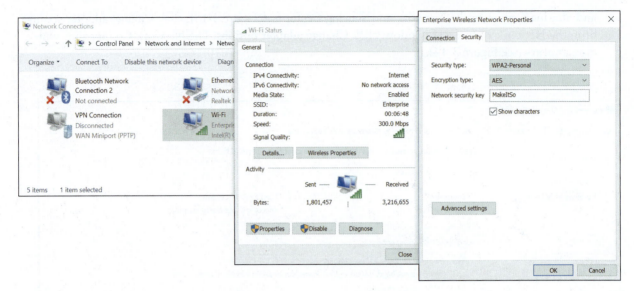

Figure 3-15   Verify that the Network security key for the wireless network is correct

If you have a problem making a network connection, you can reset the connection. Open the Network Connections window and right-click the network connection. Select **Disable** from the shortcut menu, as shown in Figure 3-16. Right-click the connection again and select **Enable**. The connection is reset. Try again to browse the web or access resources on the network. If you still don't have local or Internet access, it's time to dig a little deeper into the source of the problem. More network troubleshooting tools and solutions are covered later in this chapter.

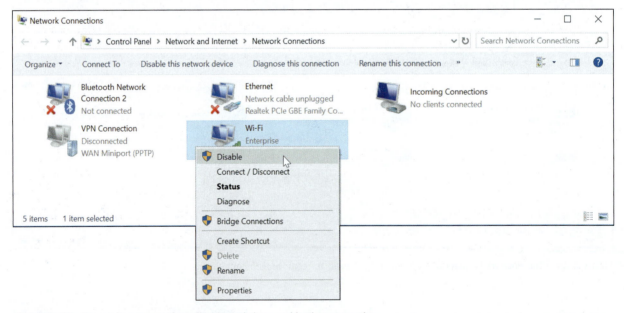

Figure 3-16   To repair a connection, disable and then enable the connection

CREATING A VPN CONNECTION

A+
CORE 1
2.3, 2.6

A+
CORE 2
1.8

A **virtual private network (VPN)** is often used by telecommuting employees to connect to the corporate network by way of the Internet. A VPN protects data by encrypting it from the time it leaves the remote computer until it reaches a server on the corporate network, and vice versa. The encryption technique is called a tunnel or tunneling (see Figure 3-17).

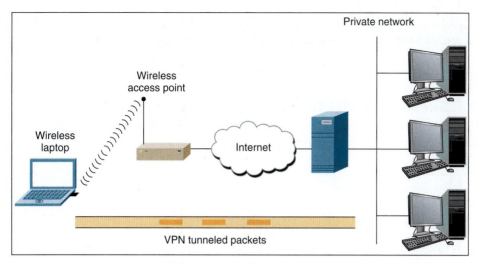

Figure 3-17   With a VPN, tunneling is used to send encrypted data over wired and wireless networks and the Internet

A VPN can be managed by operating systems, routers, or third-party software such as OpenVPN (*openvpn.net*). A VPN connection is a virtual connection, which means you are setting up the tunnel over an existing connection to the Internet. When creating a VPN connection on a personal computer, always follow directions given by the network administrator who hosts the VPN. The company website might provide VPN client software to download and install on your computer. Then you might be expected to double-click a configuration file to complete the VPN connection. OpenVPN uses an .ovpn file for this purpose.

Here are the general steps using Windows to connect to a VPN:

1. In the Network and Sharing Center (refer back to Figure 3-13), click **Set up a new connection or network**. Then select **Connect to a workplace - Set up a dial-up or VPN connection to your workplace** (see Figure 3-18) and click **Next**.

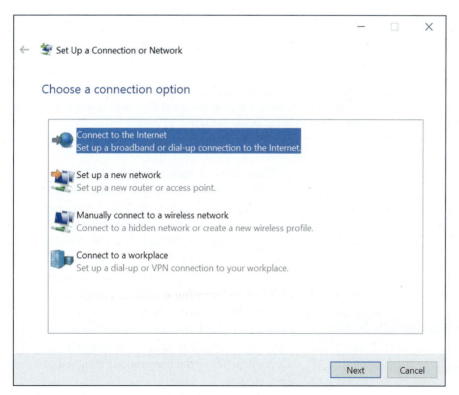

Figure 3-18   Create a dial-up connection to an ISP

> ✎ **Notes**   In Windows 10, you can accomplish the first part of this step in the Settings app. Open the Network & Internet group in the Settings app, click **Dial-up**, and then click **Set up a new connection**. The dialog box shown in Figure 3-18 appears.

2. In the Connect to a Workplace dialog box, click **Use my Internet connection (VPN)**. In the next dialog box, enter the IP address or domain name of the network (see Figure 3-19). Your network administrator can provide this information. Name the VPN connection and click **Create**.

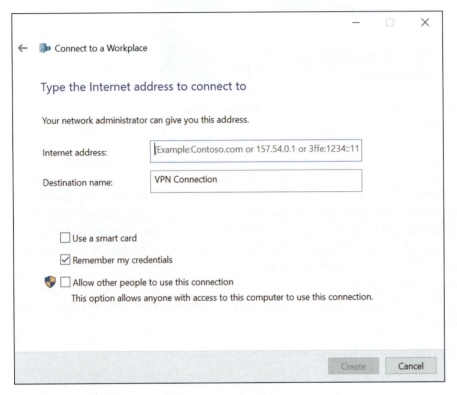

Figure 3-19   Enter connection information to the VPN

> ↻ **OS Differences**   Windows 10/8 requires you to enter your user name and password at the time you connect to a VPN. Windows 7 gives you the option to enter this information when you set up the VPN or as you connect to it.

Figure 3-20   Enter your user name and password to connect to your VPN

Whenever you want to use the VPN connection, click the **Network** icon in the taskbar. In the list of available networks, click the **VPN connection** and click **Connect**. Enter your user name and password (see Figure 3-20) and click **OK**. Your user name and password are likely to be the same network ID and password to your user account on the Windows domain on the corporate network.

After the connection is made, you can use your browser to access the corporate secured intranet websites or other resources. The resources you can access depend on the permissions assigned to your user account.

Problems connecting to a VPN can be caused by the wrong authentication protocols used when passing the user name and password to the VPN. To configure these settings, return to the Network and Sharing Center and click **Change adapter settings**. In the Network Connections window, right-click **VPN Connection** and click **Properties**. In the Properties box, select the **Security** tab (see Figure 3-21). Here you can select security settings for the type of VPN, encryption requirements, and authentication protocols given to you by the network administrator.

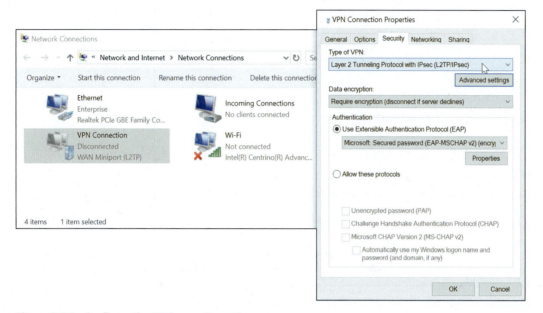

Figure 3-21   Configure the VPN's security settings

CREATING A DIAL-UP CONNECTION

Here are the bare-bones steps you need to set up and support a dial-up connection:

1. Install an internal or external dial-up modem in your computer. Make sure Device Manager recognizes the card without errors.

2. Plug the phone line into the dial-up modem port on your computer and into the wall jack. Phone lines use **RJ-11** connectors (RJ stands for registered jack), which are the same connectors used for wired telephones.

3. Open the **Network and Sharing Center** window. In Windows 10/8/7, open the Control Panel and click **Network and Sharing Center**.

> ⭐ **A+ Exam Tip**   Windows 10 includes many options for accessing the Network and Sharing Center, and the A+ Core 2 exam expects you to be familiar with multiple methods for accessing any of the common utilities. One of the quickest ways to get to the Network and Sharing Center is to right-click **Start**, click **Network Connections**, then click **Network and Sharing Center**.

4. In the Network and Sharing Center window, click **Set up a new connection or network**. In the dialog box that appears (refer back to Figure 3-18), select **Connect to the Internet - Set up a broadband or dial-up connection to the Internet** and click **Next**.

5. In the next dialog box, click **Dial-up**. In the next box (see Figure 3-22), enter the phone number to your ISP, your ISP user name and password, and the name you decide to give the dial-up connection. Then click **Create**.

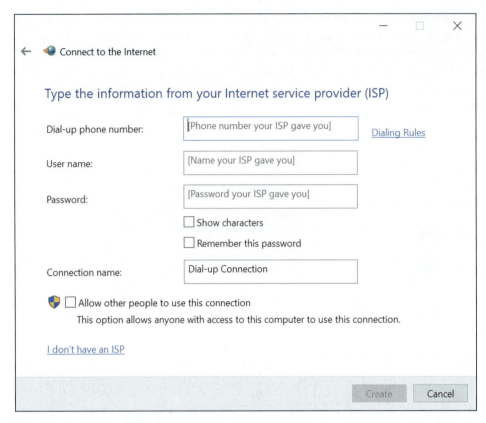

Figure 3-22   Enter a phone number and account information to your ISP

To use the connection, click your **Network** icon in the taskbar. In the list of available connections, select your dial-up connection (see Figure 3-23A). In Windows 10, this opens the Dial-up page in the Settings app, where you click the dial-up connection again and click **Connect**. In Windows 8/7, click **Connect**. The Connect dialog box appears, where you can enter your password (see Figure 3-23B). Click **Dial**. You will hear the modem dial the ISP and make the connection.

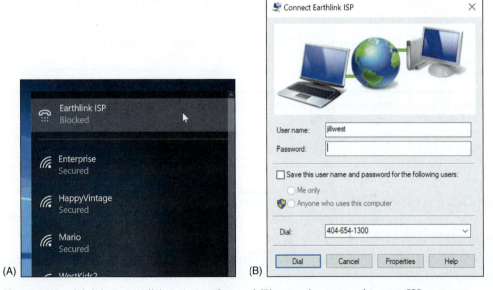

Figure 3-23   (A) Select your dial-up connection, and (B) enter the password to your ISP

If the dial-up connection won't work, here are some things you can try:

◢ Is the phone line working? Plug in a regular phone and check for a dial tone. Is the phone cord securely connected to the computer and the wall jack?

◢ Does the modem work? Check Device Manager for reported errors about the modem. Does the modem work when making a call to another phone number (not your ISP)?

◢ Check the Dial-up Connection Properties box for errors. To do so, click **Change adapter settings** in the Network and Sharing Center, and then right-click the dial-up connection and select **Properties** from the shortcut menu. Is the phone number correct? Has a 1 been added in front of the number by mistake? Does the number need to start with a 9 to get an outside line? If you need to add a 9, you can put a comma in the field (for example, "9,4045661200"), which causes a slight pause after the 9 is dialed.

◢ Try dialing the number manually from a phone. Do you hear beeps on the other end? Try another phone number.

◢ When you try to connect, do you hear the number being dialed? If so, the problem is most likely with the phone number, the phone line, or the user name and password.

◢ Try removing and reinstalling the dial-up connection.

Now let's turn our attention to how to configure settings for a network connection, including dynamic, static, and alternate address configurations.

DYNAMIC AND STATIC IP CONFIGURATIONS

A+ CORE 1 2.3

A+ CORE 2 1.8

Computers use IP addresses to find each other on a network. An **IP address** is assigned to a network connection when the connection is first made and can be:

◢ A 32-bit string, written as four decimal numbers called octets and separated by periods, such as 192.168.100.4

◢ A 128-bit string, written as eight hexadecimal numbers separated by colons, such as 2001:0000:B80:0000:0000:D3:9C5A:CC

Most networks use 32-bit IP addresses, which are defined by **IPv4 (Internet Protocol version 4)**. Some networks use both 32-bit addresses and 128-bit addresses, which are defined by **IPv6 (Internet Protocol version 6)**.

> ✎ **Notes** The suite of rules that define network communication is called **TCP/IP (Transmission Control Protocol/Internet Protocol)**. IP (Internet Protocol) is a set of rules for IP addressing. IPv4 is an earlier version of IP, and IPv6 is the latest version. A **protocol** is a set of rules computers must follow in order to communicate.

A **host** is any device, such as a desktop computer, laptop, or printer, on a network that requests or serves up data or services to other devices. To communicate on a network or the Internet, a host needs this TCP/IP information:

◢ Its own IP address—for example, 192.168.100.4.

◢ A **subnet mask**, which is four decimal numbers separated by periods—for example, 255.255.255.0. When a computer wants to send a message to a destination computer, it uses its subnet mask to decide whether the destination computer is on its own network or another network.

◢ The IP address of a **default gateway**. Computers can communicate directly with each other on the same network. However, when a computer sends a message to a computer on a different network, it sends the message to its default gateway, which is connected to the local network and at least one other network. The gateway sends the message on its way to other networks. For small businesses and homes, the default gateway is a router.

◢ The IP addresses of one or more **DNS (Domain Name System** or **Domain Name Service) servers**. Computers use IP addresses to communicate, but people use computer names, such as *www.cengage.com*, to address a computer. When you enter *www.cengage.com* in your browser address box, your computer must find the IP address of the *www.cengage.com* web server and does so by querying a DNS server. DNS servers can access databases spread all over the Internet that maintain lists of computer names (such as *www.cengage.com*) and their IP address assignments. This group of databases is called the Internet namespace and finding the IP address for a computer name is called **name resolution**. In the Internet namespace, *cengage.com* is the name of the Cengage domain and *www.cengage.com* is the name of a web server in that domain.

The IP address, subnet mask, default gateway, and DNS server addresses can be manually assigned to a computer's network connection; the computer's IP address is called a **static IP address**. Alternately, all of this information can be requested from a server on the network when a computer first connects to the network. The IP address it receives is called a **dynamic IP address**, and the server that assigns the address from a pool of addresses it maintains is called a **DHCP (Dynamic Host Configuration Protocol) server**. A computer or other device (such as a network printer) that requests address information from a DHCP server is called a **DHCP client**. It is said that the client is leasing an IP address. A DHCP server that serves up IPv6 addresses is often called a **DHCPv6 server**.

> ★ **A+ Exam Tip** The A+ Core 1 exam expects you to know what a DHCP server is and may give you a scenario that requires you to use static and dynamic IP addressing.

Most networks use dynamic IP addressing. By default, Windows requests dynamic IP configuration from the DHCP server and there is nothing for you to configure. In some situations, however, a computer must have a static IP address, so as an IT support technician, you need to know how to configure static IP addressing.

Follow these steps to configure static IP addressing:

1. Open the **Network Connections** window. Right-click the network connection and click **Properties**. In the Properties box on the **Networking** tab (as shown in the middle box of Figure 3-24), select **Internet Protocol Version 4 (TCP/IPv4)** and click **Properties**. The TCP/IPv4 Properties box appears (see the right side of Figure 3-24).

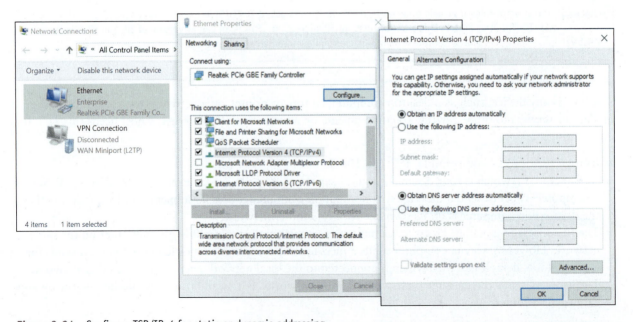

Figure 3-24 Configure TCP/IPv4 for static or dynamic addressing

2. By default, dynamic IP addressing is used, which selects *Obtain an IP address automatically* and *Obtain DNS server address automatically*. To change the settings to static IP addressing, select **Use the following IP address**. Then enter the IP address, subnet mask, and default gateway.

3. If your network administrator has given you the IP addresses of DNS servers, select **Use the following DNS server addresses** and enter up to two IP addresses. If you have additional DNS IP addresses, click **Advanced** and enter them on the **DNS** tab of the Advanced TCP/IP Settings box.

> **Notes** As an IT support technician, it's unlikely you'll ever be called on to configure static IPv6 addressing. However, to do so, use the Ethernet Properties box in the middle of Figure 3-24. Select **Internet Protocol Version 6 (TCP/IPv6)** and click **Properties**.
>
> You can also uncheck **Internet Protocol Version 6 (TCP/IPv6)** to disable it. For most situations, you need to leave it enabled. A bug in Windows 7 might prevent you from joining a homegroup if IPv6 is disabled.

> **Notes** In Windows 10, you can use the Settings app to configure static IP addressing. On the Status page in the Network & Internet group, click **Change connection properties**. Scroll down and click **Edit** under *IP settings*. Automatic (DHCP) is the default setting (see Figure 3-25A). To enter static IP address information, click **Manual**. In the Edit IP settings box (see Figure 3-25B), turn on IPv4 and enter the information.

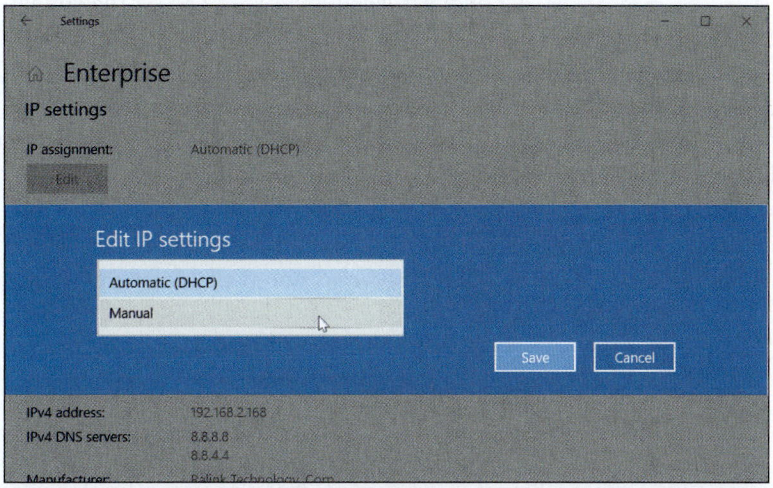

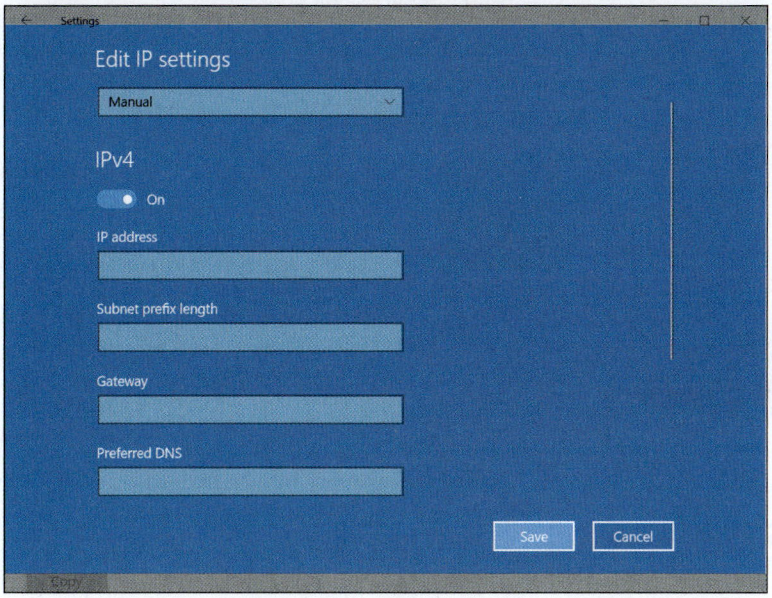

Figure 3-25 Set static IP addressing information in the Settings app

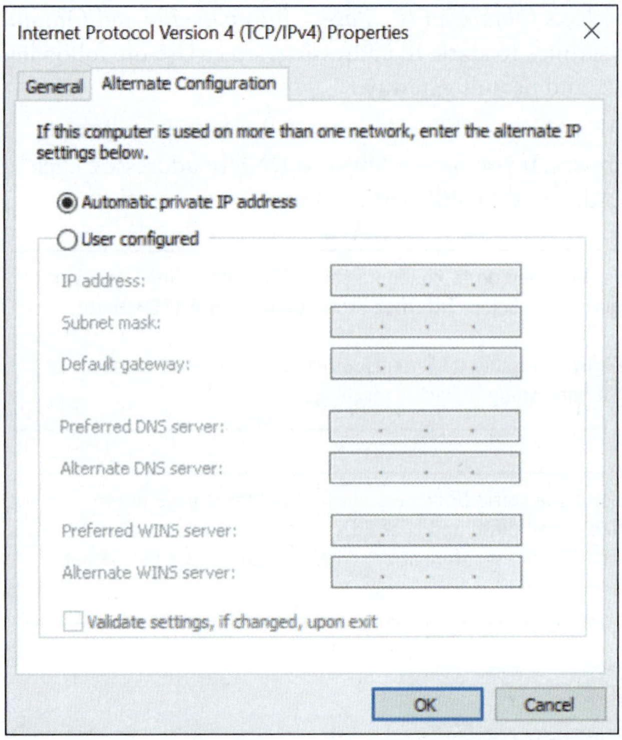

Internet Protocol Version 4 (TCP/IPv4) Properties   ✕

General | Alternate Configuration

If this computer is used on more than one network, enter the alternate IP settings below.

◉ Automatic private IP address

○ User configured

IP address:

Subnet mask:

Default gateway:

Preferred DNS server:

Alternate DNS server:

Preferred WINS server:

Alternate WINS server:

☐ Validate settings, if changed, upon exit

OK   Cancel

Figure 3-26   Create an alternate static IP address configuration

ALTERNATE IP ADDRESS CONFIGURATION

> **A+**
> **CORE 1**
> **2.3**

> **A+**
> **CORE 2**
> **1.8**

Suppose an employee with a laptop often travels, and her work network uses static IP addressing, even though most public networks use dynamic IP addressing. How do you configure her computer's network connection settings? For travel, you would configure the computer to use dynamic IP addressing in order to connect to public networks. However, when the computer attempts to connect to the corporate network, it needs a static IP address. The solution is to create an alternate configuration that the computer will use only if needed.

To create an alternate configuration, first use the General tab of the TCP/IPv4 Properties box shown earlier in Figure 3-24 to set the configuration for dynamic IP addressing. Then click the **Alternate Configuration** tab. As you can see in Figure 3-26, by default Windows sets an **Automatic private IP address (APIPA)**, which is an IP address beginning with 169.254, when it cannot find a DHCP server. Select **User configured**. Then enter a static IP address, subnet mask, default gateway, and DNS server addresses for the alternate configuration to be used on the company network. Click **OK** and close all boxes. Now the computer will first attempt to gather network connection settings from a DHCP server. If a DHCP server is not available on the network, the computer will instead use the new static IP settings you just entered.

> ★ **A+ Exam Tip**   The A+ Core 2 exam expects you to know in a scenario when it is appropriate to configure an alternate IP address, including setting the static IP address, subnet mask, DNS addresses, and gateway address.

Figure 3-27   USB devices provide wired and wireless network connections

MANAGING NETWORK ADAPTERS

> **A+**
> **CORE 1**
> **2.2, 2.3**

> **A+**
> **CORE 2**
> **1.8**

A computer makes a wired or wireless connection to a local network by way of a network adapter, which might be a network port embedded on the motherboard or a **network interface card (NIC)** installed in an expansion slot on the motherboard. In addition, the adapter might be an external device plugged into a USB port (see Figure 3-27). A network adapter is often called a network interface card or NIC even when it's not really a card but a USB device or a device embedded on the motherboard. It might also be called a network controller or network adapter.

3

Here are a network adapter's features you need to be aware of:

◢ *The drivers a NIC uses.* A NIC usually comes bundled with drivers on CD or the drivers can be downloaded from the web. Windows has several embedded NIC drivers. After you install a NIC, you install its drivers. Problems with the network adapter can sometimes be solved by using Device Manager to update the drivers or uninstall the drivers and then reinstall them.

◢ *Ethernet speeds.* For wired networks, the four speeds for Ethernet are 10 Mbps, 100 Mbps (Fast Ethernet), 1 Gbps (Gigabit Ethernet), and 10 Gbps (10-gigabit Ethernet). Most network adapters sold today for local networks use Gigabit Ethernet and support the two slower speeds. To see the speeds a NIC supports, open its Properties box in **Device Manager**. Select the **Advanced** tab. In the list of properties, select **Speed & Duplex**. You can then see available speeds in the Value drop-down list (see the right side of Figure 3-28). If the adapter connects with slower network devices on the network, the adapter works at the slower speed. Notice that the drop-down list has options for half duplex or full duplex. Full duplex sends and receives transmissions at the same time. Half duplex works in only one direction at a time. Select **Auto Negotiation** for Windows to use the best possible speed and duplex for a particular connection.

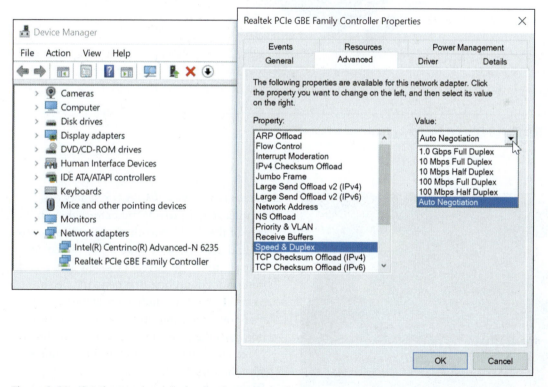

Figure 3-28 Set the speed and duplex for the network adapter

▲ *MAC address.* Every NIC (wired or wireless) has a 48-bit (6-byte) identification number, called the MAC address or physical address, hard-coded on the card by its manufacturer. The MAC address is unique for that adapter and is used to identify the adapter on the local network. An example of a MAC address is 00-0C-6E-4E-AB-A5. Most likely, the MAC address is printed on the device (see Figure 3-29).

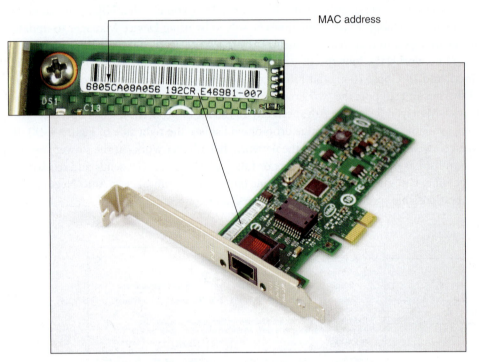

MAC address

Figure 3-29 This Gigabit Ethernet adapter by Intel uses a PCIe ×1 slot

Figure 3-30 Status indicator lights for the onboard network port

▲ *Status indicator lights.* A wired network adapter might provide indicator lights on the side of the RJ-45 port that indicate connectivity and activity (see Figure 3-30). When you first discover you have a problem with a computer not connecting to a network, be sure to check the status indicator lights to verify that you have connectivity and activity. If not, then the problem is related to hardware. Next, check the cable connections to make sure they are solid.

▲ *Wake-on-LAN.* A NIC might support Wake-on-LAN, which allows it to wake up the computer when it receives certain communication on the network. To use the feature, it must be enabled on the NIC. Open the NIC's Properties box in Device Manager and click the **Advanced** tab. Make sure **Wake on Magic Packet** and **Wake on pattern match** are both enabled (see Figure 3-31A).

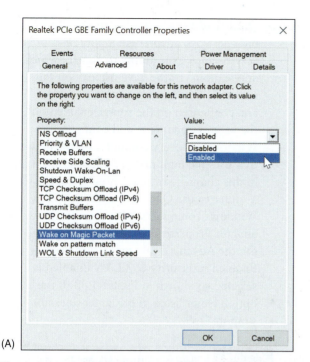
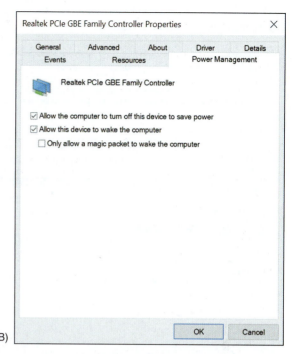

(A)   (B)

Figure 3-31 Enable Wake-on-LAN (A) using the Advanced tab, or (B) using the Power Management tab of the network adapter's Properties box

> ✏️ **Notes** Some NICs provide a Power Management tab in the Properties box. To use the Power Management tab to enable Wake-on-LAN, check **Allow this device to wake the computer** (see Figure 3-31B).

For an onboard NIC, you must also enable Wake-on-LAN in BIOS/UEFI setup. Reboot the computer, enter BIOS/UEFI setup, and look for the option on a power-management screen. Figure 3-32 shows the BIOS/UEFI screen for one onboard NIC. It is not recommended that you enable Wake-on-LAN for a wireless network adapter.

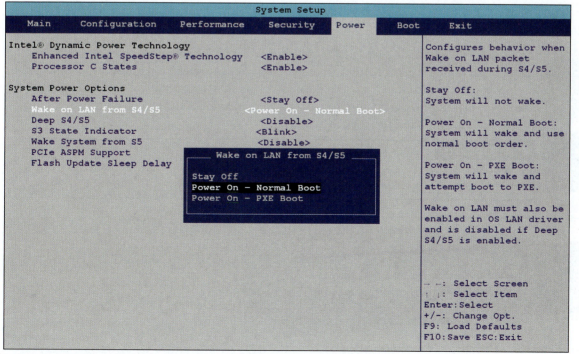

Figure 3-32 Use the Power screen in the BIOS/UEFI setup to enable Wake-on-LAN

Source: Intel

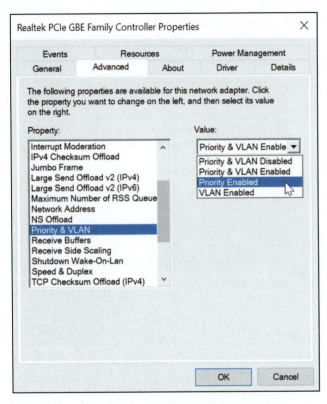

Figure 3-33   Select Priority Enabled to allow the network adapter to support QoS on the network

◢ *Quality of Service (QoS).* Another feature on a network adapter is Quality of Service (QoS), the ability to control which applications' traffic have priority on the network. The feature must be enabled and configured on the router, enabled on the network adapters, and configured in Windows for every computer on the network that uses the high-priority applications. Later in this chapter, you learn how to configure a router to use QoS. To enable QoS on a Windows computer's NIC, open the network adapter Properties box in Device Manager. On the Advanced tab, make sure **Priority Enabled** or **Priority & VLAN Enabled** is selected, as shown in Figure 3-33. If the option is not listed, the adapter does not support QoS.

> **✎ Notes** A VLAN is a virtual LAN, and QoS is sometimes implemented using VLAN technology. You'll learn more about VLANs when you study virtualization.

Now that you know how to connect a computer to a network, let's look at how to set up the network itself. The process of building and maintaining a large, corporate network is outside the scope of this text. However, working with smaller networks, such as those used in homes and small businesses, helps prepare you to work in larger network environments.

SETTING UP A MULTIFUNCTION ROUTER FOR A SOHO NETWORK

A+ CORE 1 2.2, 2.3, 2.4, 2.6

A+ CORE 2 2.2, 2.3, 2.6, 2.10

An IT support technician is likely to be called on to set up a small office or home office (SOHO) network. As part of setting up a small network, you need to know how to configure a multipurpose router to stand between the network and the Internet. A router (see Figure 3-34) is a device that manages traffic between two or more networks and can help find the best path for traffic to get from one network to another.

> **★ A+ Exam Tip** The A+ Core 1 and A+ Core 2 exams may require you to evaluate the needs of a business or residence in a given scenario and to install, configure, and secure a SOHO wired and wireless router based on these needs.

Figure 3-34   A router connects the local network to the Internet

FUNCTIONS OF A SOHO ROUTER

Routers can range from small ones designed to manage a SOHO network that connects to an ISP (costing around $50 to $300) to those that manage multiple networks and extensive traffic (costing several thousand dollars). On a small office or home network, a router stands between the ISP network and the local network (see Figure 3-35), and the router is the local network's gateway to the Internet.

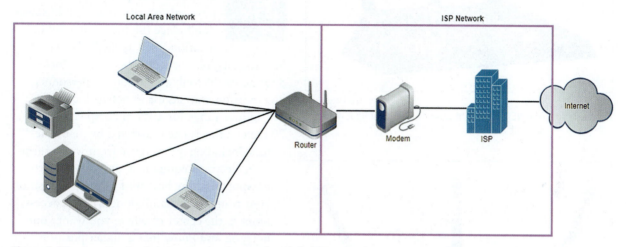

Figure 3-35 A router stands between a local network and the ISP network and manages traffic between them

Note in the figure that computers can connect to this router using wired or wireless connections. This is because a SOHO router often serves different functions in a single device. A typical SOHO router usually combines these functions:

◢ As a router, it stands between two networks—the ISP network and the local network—and routes traffic between the two networks.

◢ As a switch, it manages several network ports that can be connected to wired computers on the local network or to a dedicated switch that provides even more ports for locally networked computers.

◢ As a DHCP server, it can provide IP addresses to computers and other devices on the local network.

◢ As a wireless access point (WAP), it enables wireless devices to connect to the network. These wireless connections can be secured using wireless security features.

◢ As a firewall, it blocks unwanted traffic from the Internet and can restrict Internet access for local devices behind the firewall. Restrictions on local devices can apply to days of the week, time of day, keywords used, certain websites, and specific applications. It can also limit network and Internet access to specified computers, based on their MAC addresses.

◢ If the router is used as an FTP (File Transfer Protocol) server, you can connect an external hard drive to the router, and the FTP firmware on the router can be used to share files with network users.

An example of a multifunction router is the Nighthawk AC1900 by NETGEAR, shown in Figures 3-36 and 3-37. It has one Internet port for the broadband modem (cable modem or DSL modem) and four ports for devices on the network. The USB port can be used to plug in a USB external hard drive for file sharing on the network. The router is also a wireless access point with multiple antennas to increase speed and range.

Source: Amazon.com

Figure 3-36   The NETGEAR Nighthawk AC1900 dual band Wi-Fi Gigabit router

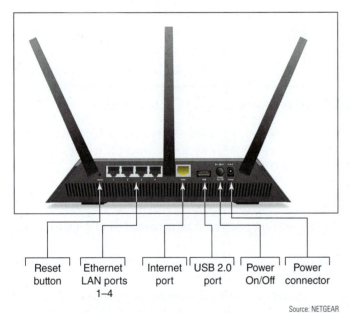

| Reset button | Ethernet LAN ports 1–4 | Internet port | USB 2.0 port | Power On/Off | Power connector |

Source: NETGEAR

Figure 3-37   Connections and ports on the back of the NETGEAR router

INSTALLING AND CONFIGURING A ROUTER ON THE LOCAL NETWORK

A+ CORE 1 2.3, 2.6

A+ CORE 2 2.2, 2.6, 2.10

When deciding where to physically place a router, consider its physical security. If the router will be used as a wireless access point, make sure it is centrally located to create the best Wi-Fi hotspot for users. For physical security in a small business, don't place the router in a public location, such as the lobby. For best security, place the router behind a locked door accessible only to authorized personnel in a location with access to network cabling. The indoor range for a Wi-Fi hotspot is up to 70 meters; this range is affected by many factors, including interference from walls, furniture, electrical equipment, and other nearby hotspots. For the best Wi-Fi strength, position your router or a stand-alone wireless access point in the center of where you want your hotspot, and know that a higher position (near the ceiling) works better than a lower position (on the floor).

For routers that have external antennas, raise the antennas to vertical positions. Plug in the router and connect network cables to devices on the local network. Connect the network cable from the ISP modem or other device to the uplink port on the router.

To configure a router for the first time or change its configuration, always follow the directions of the manufacturer. You can use any computer on the network that uses a wired connection (it doesn't matter which computer) to configure the firmware on the router. You'll need the IP address of the router and the default user name and password to the router setup. To find this information, look in the router documentation or search online for your model and brand of router.

Here are the general steps for one router, the Nighthawk AC1900 by NETGEAR, although the setup screens for your router may be different:

1. Open your browser and enter the IP address of the router in the address box. In our example, the address is 192.168.1.1. The Windows Security box appears (see Figure 3-38). For our router, the default user name and password are both **admin**, although yours might be different.

Figure 3-38 Enter the user name and password to the router firmware utility

2. The main setup page of the router firmware appears in your browser window. Figure 3-39 shows the main page for a router that has already been configured. Notice the BASIC tab is selected. Most of the settings you'll need are on the ADVANCED tab. Begin by poking around to see what's available and to find the settings you need. If you make changes, be sure to save them. When finished, click **Logout** and close the browser window.

Figure 3-39 The main screen for router firmware setup

Source: NETGEAR

Following are some changes you might need to make to the router's configuration. To secure your router, always change the router password, which is described next.

CHANGE THE ROUTER PASSWORD

It's extremely important to protect access to your network and prevent others from hijacking your router. If you have not already done so, change the router's default administrative password. For our router, click the **ADVANCED** tab, click **Administration**, and click **Set Password** (see Figure 3-40). Change the password and click **Apply**. If the firmware offers the option, disable the ability to configure the router over the wireless network. Know that this password to configure the router firmware is different from the password needed to access the router's wireless network.

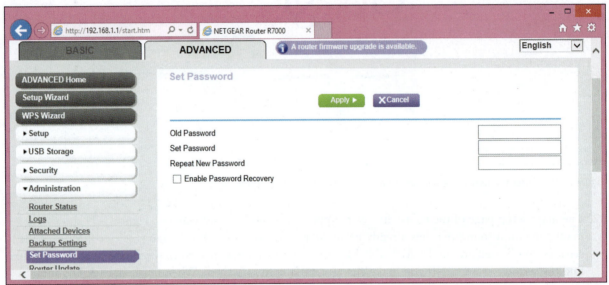

Source: NETGEAR

Figure 3-40   Change the router firmware password

> ⚡ **Caution**   Changing the router password is especially important if the router is a wireless router. Unless you have disabled or secured the wireless access point, anyone within its range—even outside your building—can use your wireless network. If they guess the default password to the router, they can change the password to hijack your router. Also, your wireless network can be used for criminal activity. After you first install a router and before you do anything else, change your router password and disable the wireless network until you have time to set up and test the wireless security. To give even more security, change the default user name if the router utility allows that option.
>
> For best security, get in the habit of always changing the default administrative password for any wireless device, such as a Roku or security camera, that you might connect to a wireless network.

CONFIGURE THE DHCP SERVER

To configure the DHCP server for our sample router, click the **ADVANCED** tab and then click **LAN Setup** in the Setup group (see Figure 3-41). On this page, you can enable or disable the DHCP server and set the IP address of the router and subnet mask for the network. For the DHCP server, set the starting and ending IP addresses, which determines the range of IP addresses DHCP can serve up. After making changes on this page, click **Apply** to save your changes.

Figure 3-41 Configure the DHCP server in the router firmware

Source: NETGEAR

> ✎ **Notes** As you advance in your networking skills, you'll learn how to choose subnet masks and ranges of IP addresses to divide a large network into more manageable subnets. For now, know that if your range of IP addresses varies only in the last octet, the subnet mask is 255.255.255.0. If the range of IP addresses varies in the last two octets, the subnet mask is 255.255.0.0.

RESERVE IP ADDRESSES

A network device such as a printer needs a consistent IP address at all times so computers that access the printer don't need to be told its new IP address each time it reconnects to the network. In addition, a computer that is running a service, such as a web server for other computers on the network, needs a consistent IP address so that other computers can consistently find the web server. You could assign the printer and web server IP addresses by configuring the device or computer for static IP addressing. Alternately, you can assign static IP addresses to a device or computer by creating an address reservation on the DHCP server so that the DHCP client receives the same IP address from the server every time it connects to the network. Do the following to reserve an IP address:

1. To identify the computer or printer, you'll need its MAC address. When the client is connected to the network, click the **ADVANCED** tab and click **Attached Devices** in the Administration group (see Figure 3-42). Copy the MAC address (select it and press **CTRL+C**) or write it down.

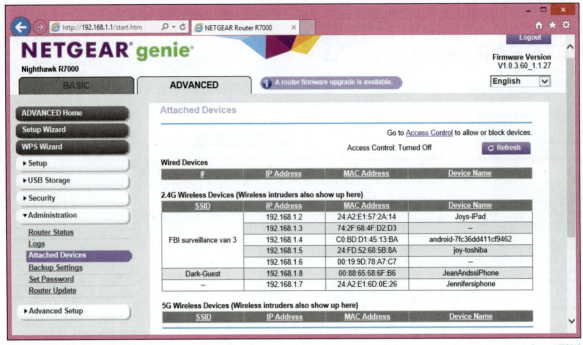

Figure 3-42   View the MAC addresses of devices connected to the network

Source: NETGEAR

2. To assign a reserved IP address to the client, go to the LAN Setup page shown in Figure 3-41 and click **Add** under **Address Reservation**. In the IP address field, enter the IP address to assign to the computer or printer. Be sure to use an IP address in the range of IP addresses assigned by the DHCP server. Select the MAC address from the list of attached devices or copy or type the MAC address in the field. Click **Apply** to save your changes. In Figure 3-43, a Canon network printer is set to receive the IP address 192.168.1.200 each time it connects to the network. It's helpful to network users to write this IP address on a label taped in plain sight on the printer or web server.

Figure 3-43   Use address reservation to assign a reserved IP address to a computer or other device

Source: NETGEAR

MAC ADDRESS FILTERING

MAC address filtering allows you to restrict access to your network to certain computers or devices. If a MAC address is not entered in the table of MAC addresses, the device is not allowed to connect to the network. For our sample router, the MAC address table can be viewed and edited on the ADVANCED tab of the Access Control page in the Security group (see Figure 3-44). To turn on Access Control, check the **Turn on Access Control** check box and then allow or block each MAC address in the table.

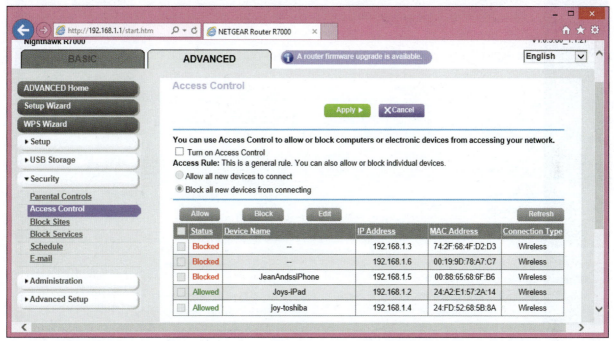

Figure 3-44   Use MAC address filtering to allow and block devices on the network

Source: NETGEAR

> **Notes** It's fairly easy to fake a MAC address when attacking a network. Therefore, MAC address filtering is not considered an effective security measure.

QOS FOR AN APPLICATION OR DEVICE

As you use your network and notice that one application or device is not getting the best service, you can improve its network performance using the Quality of Service (QoS) feature discussed earlier in this chapter. Wireless devices used for streaming multimedia (for example, a Roku) and applications used for video conferencing (for example, Skype) might need a high priority. For one sample router, do the following:

1. Sign in to the router firmware and go to the **Media Prioritization** page (see Figure 3-45). Turn on **Prioritization**. Then you can drag a device into the High Priority list. You can also select an application or online game from one of the two drop-down lists on the right and drag it to the High Priority list.

2. Notice in the figure that a Roku device is listed for the highest priority, followed by the Skype application. Click **OK** to save your changes.

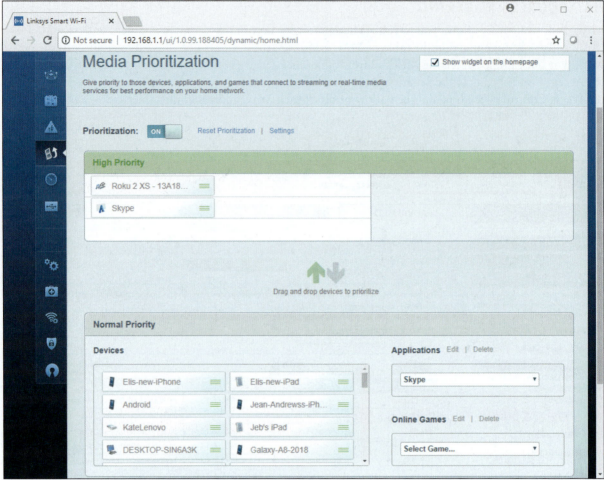

Figure 3-45 High priority is given to a device or app for best QoS

UNIVERSAL PLUG AND PLAY

Universal Plug and Play (UPnP) helps computers on the local network automatically discover and communicate with services provided by other computers on the local network. Enable UPnP if computers on the network use applications, such as messaging, gaming, or Windows Remote Assistance, which run on other local computers and there is a problem establishing communication. Basically, a computer can use the router to advertise its service and automatically communicate with other computers on the network. UPnP is considered a security risk because shields between computers are dropped, which hackers might exploit. Therefore, use UPnP with caution.

For our sample router, UPnP is enabled on the UPnP page in the Advanced Setup group on the ADVANCED tab (see Figure 3-46). Any computers and their ports that are currently using UPnP are listed.

UPDATE ROUTER FIRMWARE

As part of maintaining a router, know that router manufacturers occasionally release updates to the router firmware. The router setup utility can be used to download and apply these updates. For our sample router, you can click **A router firmware upgrade is available** on any of the setup screens (for example, see Figure 3-46) to see the Firmware Upgrade Assistant page (see Figure 3-47). Use this page to perform the upgrade.

Source: NETGEAR

Figure 3-46   Turn on UPnP

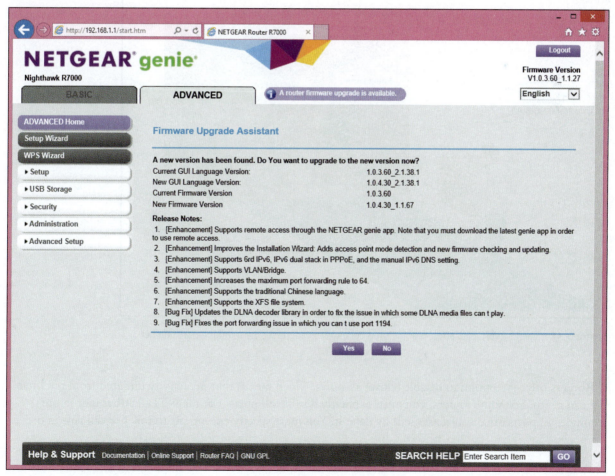

Source: NETGEAR

Figure 3-47   Update router firmware

Now let's look at the concepts and steps to put up a firewall to control traffic to and from your network and the Internet. Then we'll look at how to set up a wireless network.

LIMITING INTERNET TRAFFIC ON YOUR NETWORK

<table>
<tr><td>A+
CORE 1
2.2, 2.3</td></tr>
<tr><td>A+
CORE 2
2.10</td></tr>
</table>

To protect resources on the network, a router's firewall can examine each message coming from the Internet and decide if the message is allowed onto the local network. A message is directed to a particular computer (identified by its IP address) and to a particular application running on that computer. The application is identified by a port number, also called a port or **port address**.

Most applications used on the Internet or a local network are **client/server applications**. Client applications, such as Internet Explorer, Google Chrome, or Outlook, communicate with server applications such as a web server or email server. Each client and server application installed on a computer listens at a predetermined port that uniquely identifies the application on the computer.

Suppose a computer with an IP address of 138.60.30.5 is running an email server listening at port 25 and a web server application listening at port 80. If a client computer sends a request to 138.60.30.5:25 (IP address and port 25), the email server listening at that port responds. On the other hand, if a request is sent to 138.60.30.5:80 (IP address and port 80), the web server listening at port 80 responds (see Figure 3-48).

Figure 3-48   Each server application running on a computer is addressed by a unique port number

Routers offer the option to disable (close) all ports, which means that no activity initiated from the Internet can get in. For some routers, you must explicitly disable all ports. For the NETGEAR router in our example, all ports are disabled (closed) by default. You must specify exceptions to this firewall rule in order to allow unsolicited traffic from the Internet. Exceptions are allowed using port forwarding or a DMZ. In addition to managing ports, you can also limit Internet traffic by filtering content. All these techniques are discussed next.

> ⭐ **A+ Exam Tip** The A+ Core 1 and A+ Core 2 exams may give a scenario that expects you to resolve a problem by implementing port forwarding/mapping, whitelists, blacklists, content filtering, parental controls, and a DMZ.

PORT FORWARDING

Suppose you're hosting an Internet game or website or want to use Remote Desktop to access your home computer from the Internet. In these situations, you need to enable (open) certain ports to certain computers so that activity initiated from the Internet can get past your firewall. This technique, called **port forwarding** or port mapping, means that when the firewall receives a request for communication from the Internet to the specific computer and port, the request will be allowed and forwarded to that computer on the network. The computer is defined to the router by its static IP address. For example, in Figure 3-49, port 80 is open and requests to port 80 are forwarded to the web server listening at that port. This one computer on the network is the only one allowed to receive requests at port 80.

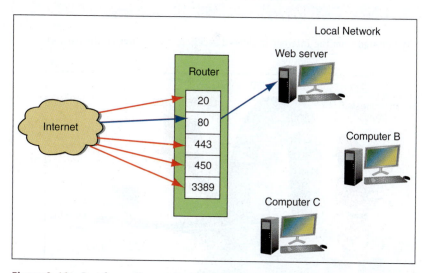

Figure 3-49 Port forwarding on a network

To configure port forwarding for our sample router, click the **ADVANCED** tab, click **Port Forwarding/ Port Triggering** in the Advanced Setup group (see Figure 3-50), and verify that **Port Forwarding** is selected. Select the **Service Name**, enter the static IP address of the computer providing the service in the Server IP Address field, and click **Add**. Notice in the figure that the Remote Desktop application on a device outside the network can use port forwarding to communicate with the computer whose IP address is 192.168.1.90 using port 3389. The situation is illustrated in Figure 3-51. This computer is set to support the Remote Desktop server application.

> ✎ **Notes** If you want to use a domain name rather than an IP address to access a computer on your network from the Internet, you'll need to purchase the domain name and register it in the Internet namespace to associate it with your static IP address assigned by your ISP. Several websites on the Internet let you do both; one site is by Network Solutions at *networksolutions.com*.

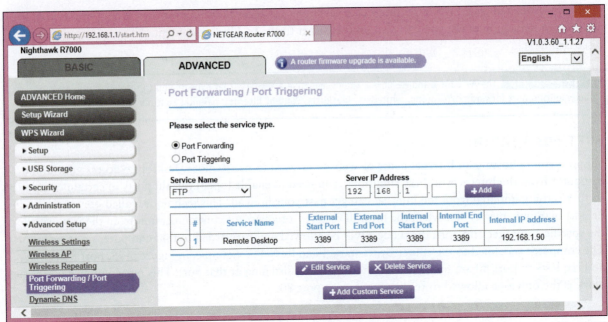

Figure 3-50 Using port forwarding, activity initiated from the Internet is allowed access to a computer on the network

Figure 3-51 With port forwarding, a router allows messages past the firewall that are initiated outside the network

Also notice the IP address for the message in Figure 3-51 is directed to the router's IP address. With port forwarding, the router forwards all traffic to port 3389 to the one computer with this open port, even through traffic is directed to the router's IP address. Here are some tips to keep in mind when using port forwarding:

▲ You must lease a static IP address for your router from your ISP so that people on the Internet can find you. Most ISPs will provide you a static IP address for an additional monthly fee.

▲ For port forwarding to work, the computer on your network must have a static IP address so that the router knows where to send the communication.

▲ Using port forwarding, your computer and network are more vulnerable because you are allowing external users directly into your private network. For better security, turn on port forwarding only when you know it's being used.

DMZ

A DMZ (demilitarized zone) in networking is a computer or network that is not protected by a firewall or has limited protection. You can drop all your shields protecting a computer by putting it in a DMZ, and the firewall no longer protects it. If you are having problems getting port forwarding to work, putting a computer in a DMZ can free it to receive any communication from the Internet. All unsolicited traffic from the Internet that the router would normally drop is forwarded to the computer designated as the DMZ server.

> ⚡ **Caution** If a DMZ computer is compromised, it can be used to attack other computers on the network. Use it only as a last resort when you cannot get port forwarding to work. It goes without saying you should not leave the DMZ enabled unless you are using it.

To set up a DMZ server for our sample router, click the **ADVANCED** tab and select **WAN Setup** in the Setup group (see Figure 3-52). Check **Default DMZ Server** and enter the static IP address of the computer.

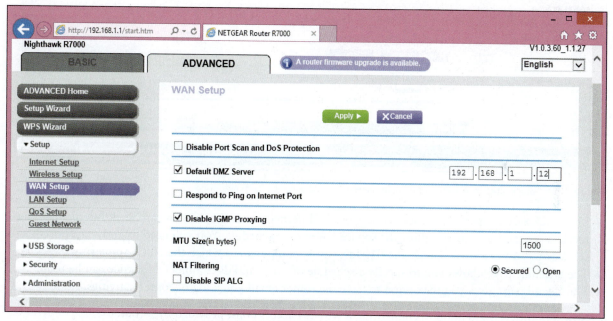

Figure 3-52   Set up an unprotected DMZ server for the network   Source: NETGEAR

CONTENT FILTERING AND PARENTAL CONTROLS

Routers normally provide a way for employers or parents to limit the content that computers on the local network can access on the Internet. Filtering can apply to specific computers, users, websites, categories of websites, keywords, services, time of day, and day of the week. Criteria for filtering can draw from blacklists (lists of what cannot be accessed) or whitelists (lists of what can be accessed).

For our sample router, content filtering and parental controls are managed in the Security group on the ADVANCED tab. Here are the options:

▲ The Parental Controls page provides access to the Live Parental Controls application and website at *netgear.com/lpc*, where parents can manage content allowed from the Internet and monitor websites and content accessed.

▲ The Block Sites page (see Figure 3-53) allows you to create a blacklist of keywords or websites to block. Notice you can also specify a trusted IP address of a computer on the network that is allowed access to this content.

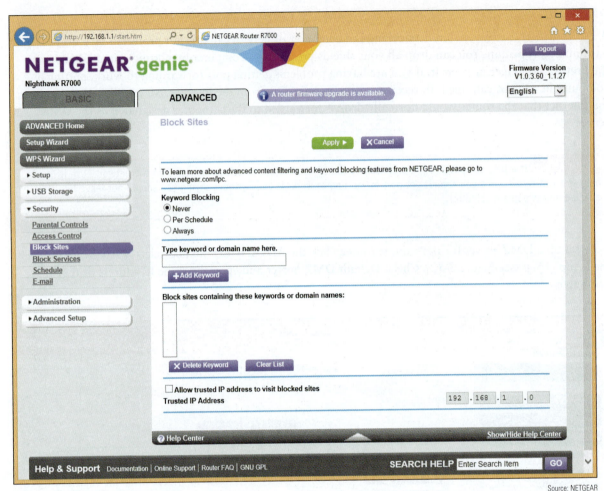

Figure 3-53   Block sites by keyword or domain names

Source: NETGEAR

- ▲ The Block Services page can block services on the Internet. For example, you can block Internet gaming services or email services, or allow the service based on a schedule. You will need to know the ports these services use. You can also specify the IP addresses of computers to which the block applies.
- ▲ The Schedule page allows you to specify a schedule of times and days a blocked service can be used.
- ▲ The E-mail page gives you the option to have the router email you a log of router activities.

Now let's turn our attention to configuring a wireless access point provided by a router.

SETTING UP A WIRELESS NETWORK

> **A+**
> **CORE 1**
> **2.3, 2.4**

A wireless network is created by a wireless access point. The standards for a local wireless network are called **Wi-Fi (Wireless Fidelity)**, and their technical name is IEEE 802.11. The IEEE 802.11 standards, collectively known as the 802.11 a/b/g/n/ac standards, have evolved over the years. This list details the progression of ranges and frequencies for each standard:

> **A+**
> **CORE 2**
> **2.3, 2.10**

- ▲ *802.11a.* Short range up to 50 meters with radio frequency of 5.0 GHz
- ▲ *802.11b.* Longer range of 100 meters (indoor ranges are less than outdoor ranges) and radio frequency of 2.4 GHz
- ▲ *802.11g.* Same range and frequency as 802.11b but with faster speeds up to 54 Mbps
- ▲ *802.11n.* Can use either 5.0-GHz or 2.4-GHz radio frequency with an indoor range up to 70 meters and an outdoor range up to 250 meters
- ▲ *802.11ac.* Uses the 5.0-GHz radio frequency and has the same ranges as 802.11n, except performance stays stronger at the edges of its reach

Figure 3-54 A wireless network adapter with two antennas supports 802.11a/b/g/n/ac Wi-Fi standards

Wireless computers and other devices on the **wireless LAN (WLAN)** must support the latest wireless standard for it to be used. If not, the connection uses the latest standard both the WAP and client support. Figure 3-54 shows a wireless adapter that has two antennas and supports the 802.11ac standard. Most new adapters, wireless computers, and mobile devices support 802.11ac and are backward compatible with older standards.

Now let's look at the various features and settings of a wireless access point and how to configure them.

📝 **Notes** When configuring your wireless access point, it's important you are connected to the router using a wired connection. If you change a wireless setting and you are connected wirelessly, your wireless connection will be dropped immediately and you cannot continue configuring the router until you connect again.

SECURITY KEY

The most common and effective method of securing a wireless network is to require a security key before a client can connect to the network. By default, a network that uses a security key encrypts data traversing the network. Use the router firmware to set the security key. For best security, enter a security key that is different from the password for the router's configuration utility.

📝 **Notes** When it comes to making secure passwords and passphrases, longer is better and randomness is crucial. To make the strongest passphrase or security key, use a random group of numbers, uppercase and lowercase letters, and, if allowed, at least one symbol. At the bare minimum, use at least eight characters in the passphrase.

For our sample router, the security key can be set on the ADVANCED tab of the Wireless Setup page in the Setup group (see Figure 3-55). Here, the security key is called the Password or Network Key. Click **Apply** to save your changes.

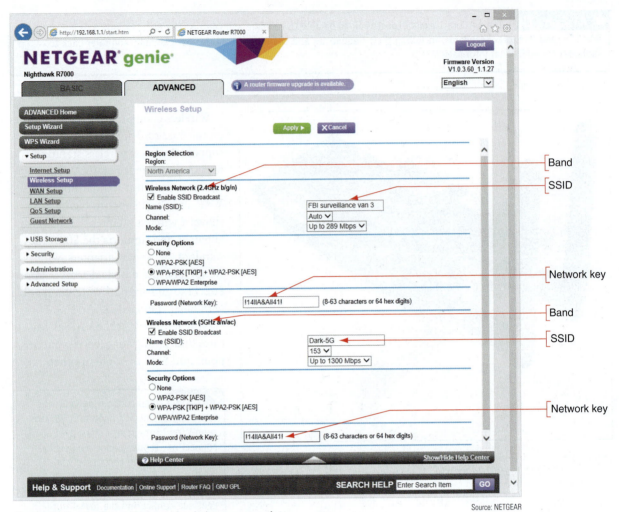

Figure 3-55   Configure the router's wireless access point

Source: NETGEAR

SET ENCRYPTION

When you set a security key, routers by default encrypt wireless transmissions. You can change the encryption protocols used or disable encryption. (Encrypting transmissions increases security but slows down the network; disabling encryption can improve performance and might be appropriate when you are not concerned about transmissions being hacked.) The three main security standards for 802.11 wireless networks are:

▲ *WEP.* WEP (Wired Equivalent Privacy) is no longer considered secure because the key used for encryption is static (it doesn't change).

▲ *WPA.* WPA (Wi-Fi Protected Access) is stronger than WEP and was designed to replace it. WPA typically uses TKIP (Temporal Key Integrity Protocol, pronounced *tee-kip*) for encryption. TKIP generates a different key for every transmission; however, the encryption algorithm used for its calculations is no longer considered secure.

▲ *WPA2.* WPA2 (Wi-Fi Protected Access 2), also called the 802.11i standard, is the current wireless security standard. WPA2 typically uses AES (Advanced Encryption Standard) for encryption, which provides faster and more secure encryption than TKIP. All wireless devices sold today support the WPA2 standard.

▲ *WPA3.* WPA3 (Wi-Fi Protected Access 3) offers better encryption and additional features over WPA2. For example, you can securely configure a nearby wireless device, such as a wireless webcam or motion sensor, over the wireless network, eliminating the need to connect the device with a wired connection to configure it. Another feature is Individual Data Encryption, which allows a secure connection for your laptop or other wireless device over a public, unsecured Wi-Fi network.

To configure Wi-Fi encryption for our sample router, first notice in Figure 3-55 that this router supports two wireless frequencies or bands: 2.4 GHz used by 802.11 b/g/n standards and 5 GHz used by 802.11 a/n/ac. Each band can have its own encryption type and security key. For the most flexibility, set both bands to allow any encryption standard the router supports. For our router, that's **WPA-PSK [TKIP] + WPA2-PSK [AES]** encryption. This setting means a wireless connection will use WPA2 encryption unless an older device does not support it, in which case the connection reverts to WPA encryption. Alternately, for best security, set both bands to require the highest standard the router supports. For our router, that's **WPA2-PSK [AES]**. Using this setting, the router will reject any older devices not capable of supporting this encryption standard. Click **Apply** to save your changes.

> ✎ **Notes** WPA/WPA2 Enterprise is more secure than WPA/WPA2 PSK, also known as WPA/WPA2 Personal. PSK (pre-shared key) relies on a passphrase shared with all network users, which could be compromised. Enterprise relies on a secure authentication server to manage all users on the network. However, very few SOHO networks have the resources to set up and host an authentication service. In most cases, when setting up a SOHO network, your most secure option is WPA2-PSK or, better yet, WPA2 Personal with AES encryption.

CHANGE THE DEFAULT SSID AND DISABLE SSID BROADCASTING

The Service Set Identifier (SSID) is the name of a wireless network. When you look at Figure 3-55, you can see that each frequency band has its own SSID and you can change that name. Each band is its own wireless network, which the access point (router) connects to the local wired network. When you give each band its own SSID and connect a wireless computer to your network, you can select the band by selecting the appropriate SSID. If your computer supports 802.11ac, you would want to select the SSID for the 5-GHz band in order to get the faster speeds of the 802.11ac standard. If you selected the SSID for the 2.4-GHz band, the connection would revert to the slower 802.11n standard.

Also notice in Figure 3-55 the option to Enable SSID Broadcast. When you disable SSID broadcasting, the wireless network will appear as Unnamed or Unknown Network on an end user's device. When a client selects this network, she is given the opportunity to enter the SSID. If she doesn't enter the name correctly, she will not be able to connect. This security method is not considered strong because software can be used to discover an SSID that is not being broadcast.

SELECT CHANNELS FOR THE WLAN

A channel is a specific radio frequency within a broader frequency. For example, two channels in the 2.4-GHz band are 2.412 GHz and 2.437 GHz. In the United States, eleven channels are available for wireless communication in the 2.4-GHz band. In order to avoid channel overlap, however, devices in the 2.4-GHz band select channels 1, 6, or 11, resulting in three nonoverlapping channels available for use. The 5-GHz band offers up to 24 nonoverlapping channels in the United States, although some of those channels are restricted in certain areas, such as near an airport. For most networks, you can allow auto channel selection so the device scans for the least busy channel. However, if you are trying to solve a problem with interference from a nearby wireless network, you can manually set each network to a different channel and make the channels far apart to reduce interference. For example, in the 2.4-GHz band, set the network on one WAP to channel 1 and set a nearby WAP's network to channel 11. For one router, the Wi-Fi Settings page provides a drop-down menu to select a specific channel or allow the router to automatically select the least busy channel (see Figure 3-56).

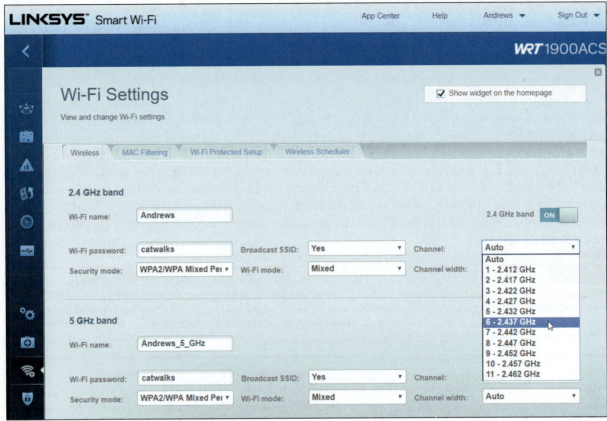

Figure 3-56 Select a channel in the 2.4-GHz band

RADIO POWER LEVELS AND WAP PLACEMENT

You've already learned that an access point should be placed in a central location to maximize its range in the target area. This also minimizes the signal's reach outside of the target area, which increases security. A wireless signal that reaches to public areas, such as a parking lot or the street, invites unauthorized users to park nearby and take their time attempting to crack your wireless security measures. Some high-end access points allow you to adjust the radio power levels the wireless network can use. To reduce interference, save on electricity, or limit the range of the network to your own property, reduce the power level.

WIRELESS QOS

Earlier, you learned you can improve QoS for a device, online game, or other application by assigning it to a high-priority list. In addition, for wireless devices, you can further improve QoS by enabling WMM (Wi-Fi Multimedia). When WMM is enabled, the wireless access point will prioritize wireless traffic for audio, video, and voice over other types of wireless network traffic. For one sample router, look back at Figure 3-45. When you click **Settings** on this router firmware page, the Settings box shown in Figure 3-57 appears. Turn on **WMM Support** and click **OK**. The Roku shown in Figure 3-45 is already prioritized as a device. Now multimedia traffic on the Wi-Fi network has priority.

Source: Linksys

Figure 3-57 Prioritize multimedia traffic over the wireless portion of the network

WI-FI PROTECTED SETUP (WPS)

You also need to know about **Wi-Fi Protected Setup (WPS)**, which is designed to make it easier for users to connect their computers to a wireless network when a hard-to-remember SSID and security key are used. WPS generates the SSID and security key using a random string of hard-to-guess letters and numbers. The SSID is not broadcast, so both the SSID and security key must be entered correctly to connect. Rather than having to enter these difficult strings, a user presses a button on a wireless computer or on the router, or enters an eight-digit PIN assigned to the router (see Figure 3-58). All computers on the wireless network must support WPS for it to be used, and you must enable WPS on the router, as shown in the figure.

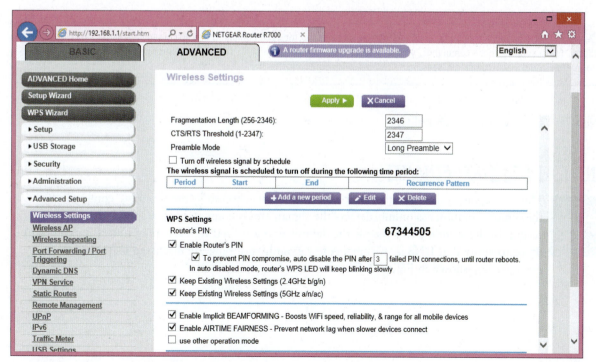

Figure 3-58 Enable WPS and decide how the router's PIN is used

Source: NETGEAR

WPS might be a security risk if it's not managed well. To improve WPS security, turn on auto disable so that WPS will be disabled after a few failed PIN entries. If the router doesn't have the auto disable feature, don't use WPS—an eight-digit PIN is easy to hack with repeated attempts. In addition, if the router has a WPS button to push, don't use WPS unless the router is in a secured physical location. For improved security, turn on WPS only when you are working with a user to connect to the wireless network, and then turn it off.

> ⭐ **A+ Exam Tip** The A+ Core 1 exam may give you a scenario that requires you to install and configure a wireless network, including Wi-Fi 802.11 standards, frequencies, channels (1–11), and encryption.

> ⭐ **A+ Exam Tip** The A+ Core 2 exam expects you to compare and contrast wireless security protocols (including WEP, WPA, WPA2, TKIP encryption, and AES encryption). Also, given a scenario, you are expected to know when it is appropriate to use SOHO router features, including changing the default SSID and password, setting encryption, disabling SSID broadcasting, antenna and access point placements, radio power levels, and WPS.

TROUBLESHOOTING NETWORK CONNECTIONS

Windows includes several utilities you can use to troubleshoot networking problems. In this part of the chapter, you learn to use ping, ipconfig, nslookup, tracert, two net commands, and netstat. Most of these program files are found in the \Windows\System32 folder.

> ⭐ **A+ Exam Tip** The A+ Core 2 exam expects you, when given a scenario, to know when and how to use these network utilities: ping, ipconfig, ifconfig, tracert, netstat, net use, net user, and nslookup. You should know when and how to use each utility and how to interpret results.

> 🖉 **Notes** Only the more commonly used parameters or switches for each command are discussed in this part of the chapter. For several of these commands, you can use the /? or /help parameter to get more information. For even more information about each command, search the *technet.microsoft.com* site.

Now let's see how to use each utility.

PING [-A] [-T] [*TARGETNAME*]

The ping command tests connectivity by sending an echo request to a remote computer. If the remote computer is online, detects the signal, and is configured to respond to a ping, it responds. (Responding to a ping is the default Windows setting.) Use ping to test for connectivity or to verify that DNS is working. A few examples of ping are discussed in Table 3-2. Two examples are shown in Figure 3-59.

Ping Command	Description
ping 69.32.208.75	Ping tests for connectivity using an IP address. If the remote computer responds, the round-trip times are displayed.
ping –a 69.32.208.75	The –a parameter tests for name resolution. Use it to display the host name and verify that DNS is working.
ping –t 69.32.208.75	The –t parameter causes pinging to continue until interrupted. To display statistics, press Ctrl+Break. To stop pinging, press Ctrl+C.
ping 127.0.0.1	This is called a loopback address test. The IP address 127.0.0.1 always refers to the local computer. If the local computer does not respond, you can assume there is a problem with the network connection's configuration.
ping cengage.com	Use a host name to find out the IP address of a remote computer. If the computer does not respond, suspect there is a problem with DNS. On the other hand, some computers are not configured to respond to pings.

Table 3-2   Examples of the ping command

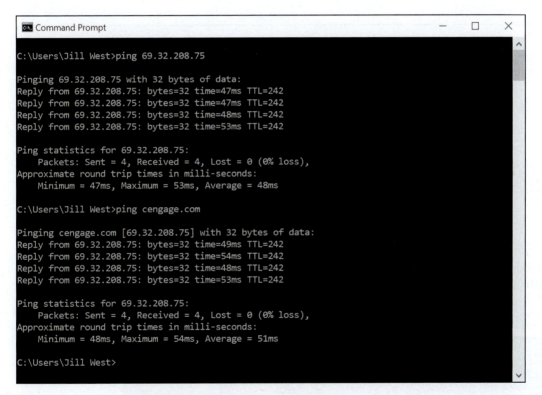

Figure 3-59   Use ping to test for connectivity and name resolution

IPCONFIG [/ALL] [/RELEASE] [/RENEW] [/DISPLAYDNS] [/FLUSHDNS]

A+
CORE 2
1.4

The ipconfig (IP configuration) command can display network configuration information and refresh the TCP/IP assignments for a connection, including its IP address. Some examples of the command are listed in Table 3-3.

Ipconfig Command	Description
ipconfig /all	Displays a network connection's configuration information, including the MAC address.
ipconfig /release	Releases the IP address and other TCP/IP assignments when dynamic IP addressing is being used.
ipconfig /release6	Releases an IPv6 address and other TCP/IP assignments.
ipconfig /renew	Leases a new IP address from a DHCP server. Make sure you release the IP address before you renew it.
ipconfig /renew6	Leases a new IPv6 address from a DHCP IPv6 server. Make sure you release the IPv6 address before you renew it.
ipconfig /displaydns	Displays information about name resolutions that Windows currently holds in the DNS resolver cache.
ipconfig /flushdns	Flushes the name resolver cache, which might solve a problem when the browser cannot find a host on the Internet.

Table 3-3 Examples of the ipconfig command

> ✏ **Notes** The **ifconfig (interface configuration)** command is similar to ipconfig, and is used on UNIX, Linux, and macOS operating systems. You'll learn more about how to use Linux and macOS in Chapter 10.

NSLOOKUP [*COMPUTERNAME*]

The **nslookup (namespace lookup** or **name server lookup)** command is used to test name resolution problems with DNS servers by allowing you to request information from a DNS server's zone data. Zone data is the portion of the DNS namespace that the server knows about. For example, to find out what your DNS server knows about the domain name *microsoft.com*, use this command:

```
nslookup microsoft.com
```

Figure 3-60 shows the results. Notice in the figure that the DNS server reports five different IPv4 addresses assigned to *microsoft.com*. It also reports that this information is nonauthoritative, meaning that it is not the authoritative, or final, name server for the *microsoft.com* domain name.

```
Command Prompt                                          —   □   ×
C:\Users\Jill West>nslookup microsoft.com
Server:  google-public-dns-a.google.com
Address:  8.8.8.8

Non-authoritative answer:
Name:    microsoft.com
Addresses:  104.43.195.251
         23.96.52.53
         23.100.122.175
         191.239.213.197
         104.40.211.35


C:\Users\Jill West>_
```

Figure 3-60 The nslookup command reports information about the Internet namespace

A **reverse lookup** is when you use the nslookup command to find the host name when you know a computer's IP address, such as:

```
nslookup 69.32.208.75
```

To find out the default DNS server for a network, enter the nslookup command with no parameters.

TRACERT [*TARGETNAME*]

A+
CORE 2
1.4

The **tracert (trace route)** command can be useful when you're trying to resolve a problem reaching a destination host such as an FTP site or website. The command sends a series of requests to the destination computer and displays each hop to the destination. (A hop happens when a message moves from one router to another.) For example, to trace the route to the *cengage.com* web server, enter this command in a command prompt window:

```
tracert cengage.com
```

The results of this command for one location are shown in Figure 3-61; your results will be different. A message is assigned a Time to Live (TTL), which is the number of hops it can make before a router drops the message and sends an error message back to the host that sent the original message (see Figure 3-62). The tracert command creates its report from these messages. If a router doesn't respond, the *Request timed out* message appears.

```
Command Prompt                                                  —    □    ×

C:\Users\Jill West>tracert cengage.com

Tracing route to cengage.com [69.32.208.75]
over a maximum of 30 hops:

  1     2 ms     2 ms     2 ms  192.168.2.1
  2      *        *        *     Request timed out.
  3    11 ms    11 ms    12 ms  96-34-119-245.static.unas.tx.charter.com [96.34.119.245]
  4    14 ms    15 ms    53 ms  96-34-119-135.static.unas.tx.charter.com [96.34.119.135]
  5    17 ms    19 ms    16 ms  96-34-119-144.static.unas.tx.charter.com [96.34.119.144]
  6    21 ms    21 ms    21 ms  crr02spbgsc-bue-401.spbg.sc.charter.com [96.34.69.254]
  7    22 ms    29 ms    36 ms  bbr01spbgsc-bue-4.spbg.sc.charter.com [96.34.2.50]
  8    38 ms    50 ms    38 ms  bbr01gnvlsc-bue-800.gnvl.sc.charter.com [96.34.0.134]
  9      *        *        *     Request timed out.
 10    52 ms    54 ms    49 ms  4.69.216.229
 11    50 ms    48 ms    47 ms  CINCINNATI.bar1.Cincinnati1.Level3.net [4.59.40.178]
 12    53 ms    50 ms    58 ms  69.32.128.159
 13      *        *        *     Request timed out.
 14    51 ms    49 ms    49 ms  us-store.cengage.com [69.32.208.75]

Trace complete.

C:\Users\Jill West>_
```

Figure 3-61   The tracert command traces a path to a destination computer

Figure 3-62 A router eliminates a message that has exceeded its TTL

THE NET COMMANDS

A+
CORE 2
1.4

The net command is several commands in one, and most of the net commands require an elevated command prompt window, which allows commands that require administrator privileges in Windows. In this section, you learn about the net use and net user commands. The net use command connects or disconnects a computer from a shared resource or can display information about connections.

> ✎ **Notes** One way to get an elevated command prompt window is to open **Task Manager**, click **File**, click **Run new task**, type **cmd**, check **Create this task with administrative privileges**, and click **OK**. See Figure 3-63. The command prompt window that appears has Administrator in the title bar.

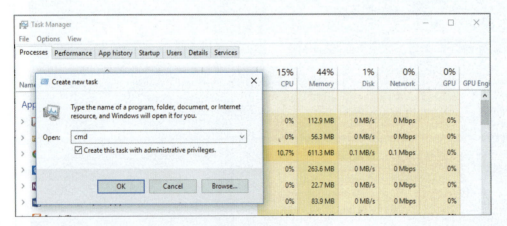

Figure 3-63 Open an elevated command prompt window

Use the following commands to pass a user name and password to the \\bluelight remote computer, and then map a network drive to the \Medical folder on that computer:

```
net use \\bluelight\Medical /user:"Jean Andrews" mypassword
net use z: \\bluelight\Medical
```

The double quotation marks are needed in the first command above because the user name has a space in it.

A persistent network connection is one that happens at each logon. To make the two commands persistent, add the /persistent parameter like this:

```
net use \\bluelight\Medical /user:"Jean Andrews" mypassword /persistent:yes
net use z: \\bluelight\Medical /persistent:yes
```

The **net user** command manages user accounts. For example, the built-in administrator account is disabled by default. To activate the account, use this net user command:

```
net user administrator /active:yes
```

> ✎ **Notes** Other important net commands are net localgroup, net accounts, net config, net print, net share, and net view. Consider doing a Google search on these commands to find out how they work.

NETSTAT [-A] [-B] [-O]

The **netstat (network statistics)** command gives statistics about network activity and includes several parameters. Table 3-4 lists a few netstat commands.

Netstat Command	Description
`netstat`	Lists statistics about the network connection, including the IP addresses of active connections.
`netstat >>netlog.txt`	Directs output to a text file.
`netstat -b`	Lists programs that are using the connection (see Figure 3-64) and is useful for finding malware that might be using the network. The −b switch requires an elevated command prompt.
`netstat -b -o`	Includes the process ID of each program listed. When you know the process ID, you can use the taskkill command to kill the process.
`netstat -a`	Lists statistics about all active connections and the ports the computer is listening on.

Table 3-4 Netstat commands

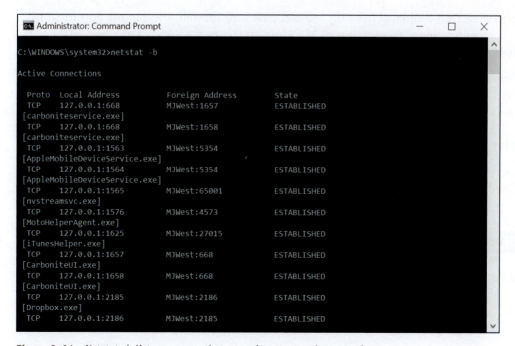

Figure 3-64 Netstat -b lists programs that are using a network connection

> **✎ Notes** Many commands other than netstat can use the >> parameter to redirect output to a text file. For example, try the ping or tracert command with this parameter:
>
> ```
> tracert cengage.com >>C:\Users\"Jill West"\Documents\testfile.txt
> ```

>> CHAPTER SUMMARY

Types of Networks and Network Connections

◢ Networks are categorized by size as a PAN, LAN, WMN, MAN, or WAN.

◢ Performance of a network technology is measured in bandwidth and latency.

◢ The two most popular ways to connect to the Internet are cable Internet and DSL. Other methods used include dedicated fiber optic, satellite, dial-up, and cellular wireless technologies (3G, 4G, 5G, and/or LTE).

Connecting a Computer to a Local Network

◢ A VPN protects data by encrypting it from the time it leaves the remote computer until it reaches a server on the corporate network, and vice versa.

◢ A host needs an IP address, subnet mask, default gateway, and IP addresses for DNS servers to communicate with other hosts on the local or remote networks.

◢ Network adapters, commonly called NICs, are rated by speed and each has a MAC address. Some NICs have status indicator lights and wake-on-LAN and QoS features.

Setting Up a Multifunction Router for a SOHO Network

◢ A multifunction router for a small office/home office network might serve several functions, including router, switch, DHCP server, wireless access point, firewall, and FTP server.

◢ It's extremely important to change the administrative password on a router as soon as you install it, especially if the router also serves as a wireless access point.

◢ To allow certain network traffic initiated from the Internet past your firewall, you can use port forwarding, a DMZ, and content filtering with whitelists or blacklists. Access to the network can be controlled by MAC address filtering.

◢ To secure a wireless access point, you can require a security key, enable encryption (WEP, WPA, WPA2, or WPA3), disable SSID broadcasting, and adjust radio power levels. You can also set wireless channels and wireless QoS to maximize the efficiency of a wireless network.

Troubleshooting Network Connections

◢ Useful Windows command-line utilities for network troubleshooting are ping, ipconfig, nslookup, tracert, net use, net user, and netstat. The Linux ifconfig command is similar to the Windows ipconfig command.

>> KEY TERMS

For explanations of key terms, see the Glossary for this text.

3G	802.11a	802.11g	AES (Advanced Encryption Standard)
4G	802.11ac	802.11n	
5G	802.11b	address reservation	

APIPA (Automatic private IP address)
bandwidth
beamforming
blacklist
broadband
cable Internet
cable modem
cellular network
channel
client/server application
coaxial (coax) cable
data throughput
default gateway
DHCP (Dynamic Host Configuration Protocol)
DHCP client
DHCP server
DHCPv6 server
DMZ (demilitarized zone)
DNS (Domain Name System or Domain Name Service)
DNS server
DSL (Digital Subscriber Line)
DSL modem
dynamic IP address
elevated command prompt window

fiber optic
fiber-optic cable
firewall
FTP (File Transfer Protocol)
FTP server
full duplex
half duplex
host
ifconfig (interface configuration)
IP address
ipconfig (IP configuration)
IPv4 (Internet Protocol version 4)
IPv6 (Internet Protocol version 6)
ISDN (Integrated Services Digital Network)
ISP (Internet service provider)
LAN (local area network)
latency
line-of-sight wireless connectivity
LTE (Long Term Evolution)
MAC address
MAC address filtering
MAN (metropolitan area network)

MIMO (multiple input/multiple output)
mobile hotspot
name resolution
net use
net user
netstat (network statistics)
NIC (network interface card)
nslookup (namespace lookup or name server lookup)
PAN (personal area network)
physical address
ping
port address
port forwarding
protocol
QoS (Quality of Service)
reverse lookup
RJ-11
RJ-45
router
SIM (Subscriber Identification Module) card
SSID (Service Set Identifier)
static IP address
subnet mask
switch

TCP/IP (Transmission Control Protocol/Internet Protocol)
tether
TKIP (Temporal Key Integrity Protocol)
tracert (trace route)
UPnP (Universal Plug and Play)
VPN (virtual private network)
Wake-on-LAN
WAN (wide area network)
WAP (wireless access point)
WEP (Wired Equivalent Privacy)
whitelist
Wi-Fi (Wireless Fidelity)
WLAN (wireless LAN)
WMN (wireless mesh network)
WPA (Wi-Fi Protected Access)
WPA2 (Wi-Fi Protected Access 2)
WPA3 (Wi-Fi Protected Access 3)
WPS (Wi-Fi Protected Setup)
WWAN (wireless wide area network)

>> THINKING CRITICALLY

These questions are designed to prepare you for the critical thinking required for the A+ exams and may use content from other chapters and the web.

1. You have just finished installing a network adapter and booted up the system, installing the drivers. You open File Explorer on a remote computer and don't see the computer on which you installed the new NIC. What is the first thing you check? The second thing?

   a. Has IPv6 addressing been enabled?

   b. Is the computer using dynamic or static IP addressing?

   c. Do the lights on the adapter indicate it's functioning correctly?

   d. Has the computer been assigned a computer name?

2. As an IT technician, you arrive at a customer's home office to troubleshoot problems he's experiencing with his printer. While questioning the customer to get an understanding of his network, you find that he has a new Wi-Fi router that connects wirelessly to a new desktop and two new laptops, in addition to multiple smartphones, tablets, and the network printer. He also has several smart home devices, including security cameras, light switches, door locks, and a thermostat supported by an IoT controller hub. To work on the printer, which type of network will you be interacting with?

    a. PAN

    b. WAN

    c. WMN

    d. LAN

3. While you work on the customer's printer, he continues chatting about his network and problems he's been experiencing. One complaint is that his Internet service slows down considerably in the evening. You suspect you know the cause of this problem: His neighbors arrive home in the evening and bog down the ISP's local infrastructure. To be sure, you take a quick look at the back of his modem. What type of cable connected to the WAN port would confirm your suspicions and why?

4. Your customer then asks you if it would be worth the investment for him to have Ethernet cabling installed to reach each of his workstations, instead of connecting them by Wi-Fi to his network. Specifically, he wants to know if that would speed up communications for the workstations. You examine his router and find that it's using 802.11ac Wi-Fi. Would you advise him to upgrade to Ethernet? Why or why not?

    a. Yes, because Ethernet is faster than 802.11ac.

    b. Yes, because wired connections are always faster than wireless connections.

    c. No, because installing Ethernet cabling is more expensive than the increased speed is worth.

    d. No, because 802.11ac speeds are faster than Ethernet.

5. You run the ipconfig command on your computer, and it reports an IP address of 169.254.75.10 on the Ethernet interface. Which device assigned this IP address to the interface?

    a. The ISP's DNS server

    b. The local network's DHCP server on the SOHO router

    c. The cable modem

    d. The local computer

6. A friend of yours is having trouble getting good Internet service. He says his house is too remote for cable TV—he doesn't even have a telephone line to his house. He's also really frustrated with satellite service because cloudy skies or storms often disrupt the signal. You ask him what provider he uses for his cell phone. He says he has Verizon for his cell, which gets a good signal at his house. What Internet service will you recommend he look into getting for his home network?

    a. Dial-up

    b. LTE installed Internet

    c. DSL

    d. Cable Internet

7. You've just received a call from Human Resources asking for assistance with a problem. One of your company's employees, Renee, has recently undergone extensive surgery and will be homebound for 3–5 months. She plans on working from home and needs a solution to enable frequent and extended access to the company network's resources. Which WAN technology will you need to configure for Renee and which tool will you use to configure it?

    a. WWAN using the Network Connections window

    b. Dial-up using the Network and Sharing Center

    c. Ethernet using the Network Connections window

    d. VPN using the Network and Sharing Center

8. Describe two different methods of opening the Network and Sharing Center in Windows 10.

9. In this chapter, you learned how to set a static IP address in Windows. Most Linux OSs allow these settings to be changed from the command line. Search online to see how to do this. What Linux command is used to set the interface to a static IP address?

10. Your boss has asked you to configure a DHCP reservation on the network for a Windows computer that is used to configure other devices on a network. To do this, you need the computer's MAC address. What command can you enter at the command line to access this information?

11. You're setting up a Minecraft gaming server so that you and several of your friends can share a realm during your gameplay. To do this, your friends will need to access your server over the Internet, which means you must configure your router to send this traffic to your game server. Which router feature will you use and which port must you open?

12. While troubleshooting an Internet connection problem for your network, you restarted the modem and then the router. The router is now communicating with the Internet, which you can confirm by observing the blinking light on the router's WAN indicator. However, now your laptop is not communicating with the router. Order the commands below to fix the problem and confirm connectivity.

    a. ping

    b. ipconfig /renew

    c. nslookup microsoft.com

    d. ipconfig /release

13. You have just installed a SOHO router in a customer's home and the owner has called to say his son is complaining that Internet gaming is too slow. His son is using a wireless laptop. Which possibilities should you consider to speed up the son's gaming experience? Select all that apply.

    a. Verify that the wireless connection is using the fastest wireless standard the router supports.

    b. Disable encryption on the wireless network to speed up transmissions.

    c. Suggest the son use a wired Gigabit Ethernet connection to the network.

    d. Enable QoS for the gaming applications on the router and on the son's computer.

14. You need a VPN to connect to a private, remote network in order to access some files. You click the network icon in your taskbar to establish the connection, and realize there is no VPN option available on the menu. What tool do you need to use to fix this problem?

    a. net command

    b. netstat command

    c. Network and Sharing Center

    d. Network Connections window

15. You're troubleshooting a network connection for a client at her home office. After pinging the network's default gateway, you discovered that the cable connecting the desktop to the router had been damaged by foot traffic and was no longer providing a reliable signal. You replaced the cable, this time running the cable along the wall so it won't be stepped on. What do you do next?

>> HANDS-ON PROJECTS

Hands-On | Project 3-1 Investigating Verizon FiOS

Verizon (*verizon.com*) offers FiOS, an alternative to DSL and cable for wired broadband Internet access to a residence or small business. FiOS is a fiber-optic Internet service that uses fiber-optic cable all the way to your house or business to provide both telephone service and Internet access. Search the web for answers to these questions about FiOS:

1. Give a brief description of FiOS and how it is used for Internet access.
2. What downstream and upstream speeds can FiOS support?
3. When using FiOS, does your telephone voice communication share the fiber-optic cable with Internet data?
4. Is FiOS available in your area?

Hands-On | Project 3-2 Investigating Network Connection Settings

Using a computer connected to a network, answer these questions:

1. What is the hardware device used to make this connection (network card, onboard port, wireless)? List the device's name as Windows sees it in the Device Manager window.
2. What is the MAC address of the wired or wireless network adapter? What command or window did you use to get your answer?
3. For a wireless connection, is the network secured? If so, what is the security type?
4. What is the IPv4 address of the network connection?
5. Are your TCP/IP version 4 settings using static or dynamic IP addressing?
6. What is the IPv6 address of your network connection?
7. Disable and enable your network connection. Now what is your IPv4 address?

Hands-On | Project 3-3 Researching a Wireless LAN

Suppose you have a DSL connection to the Internet in your home and you want to connect two laptops and a desktop computer in a wireless network to the Internet. You need to purchase a multifunction wireless router like the ones you learned to configure in this chapter. You also need a wireless adapter for the desktop computer. (The two laptops have built-in wireless networking.) Use the web to research the equipment needed to create the wireless LAN and answer the following:

1. Save or print two webpages showing two different multifunctional wireless routers. What is the brand, model, and price of each router?
2. Save or print two webpages showing two different wireless adapters a desktop computer can use to connect to the wireless network. Include one external device that uses a USB port and one internal device. What is the brand, model, and price of each device?
3. Which router and wireless adapter would you select for your home network? What is the total cost of both devices?

Hands-On | Project 3-4 Viewing and Clearing the DNS Cache

Open a command prompt window and use the ipconfig /displaydns command to view the DNS cache on your computer. Then use the ipconfig /flushdns command to clear the DNS cache.

>> REAL PROBLEMS, REAL SOLUTIONS

REAL PROBLEM 3-1 Setting Up a Small Network

The simplest possible wired network is two computers connected together using a crossover cable. In a crossover cable, the send and receive wires are crossed so that one computer can send and the other computer receives on the same wire. At first glance, a crossover cable looks just like a regular network cable (also called a patch cable) except for the labeling, as shown in Figure 3-65.

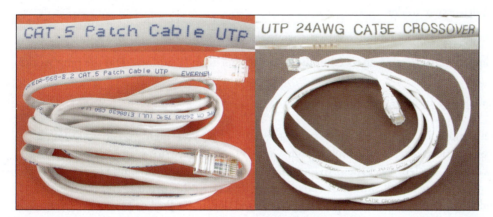

Figure 3-65   A patch cable and crossover cable look the same but are labeled differently

Do the following to set up and test a small network:

1. Connect two computers using a crossover cable. Using the Network and Sharing Center, verify that your network is up. Using ipconfig, determine each computer's IP address. What is the IPv4 address of Computer A? Of Computer B?

2. On each computer, try to ping the other computer. Does it work? Why or why not? What specific output do you get?

3. Convert the TCP/IP configuration to static IP addressing. Assign 192.168.10.4 to one computer and 192.168.10.5 to the other computer. The subnet mask for both computers is 255.255.255.0.

4. Ping each computer from the other computer. Does it work? Why or why not?

5. Without changing the subnet masks, change the IP address of one computer to 192.168.90.1. Can you still ping each computer? What specific output do you get?

6. Return the computers to the same subnet and IP addresses you used in step 3. Verify that each computer can ping the other.

REAL PROBLEM 3-2 Using the Hosts File

The hosts file in the C:\Windows\System32\drivers\etc folder has no file extension and contains computer names and their associated IP addresses on the local network. An IT support technician can manually edit the hosts file when the association is needed for address resolution on the local network and a DNS server is not available on the local network.

> ✎ **Notes** For an entry in the hosts file to work, the remote computer must always have the same IP address.

Using your small network you set up in Real Problem 3-1, do the following to use the hosts file:

1. Verify that each computer can ping the other.

2. What is the name of each computer? For Windows 10/8, press **Win+X** and click **System** to find out.

3. Try to ping each computer using its computer name rather than its IP address. Did the ping work?

4. On Computer A, copy the hosts file to a new location and edit it using Notepad. Add the entry that associates the IP address of Computer B with its computer name. As you save the file, be sure not to assign it a file extension. Rename the original hosts file and then copy the edited hosts file to the C:\Windows\System32\drivers\etc folder.

5. Repeat step 4 for the hosts file on Computer B to associate the name and IP address of Computer A.

6. Try to ping each computer, this time using its computer name rather than IP address. Did the ping work?

REAL PROBLEM 3-3 Installing and Using Packet Tracer

If you plan to pursue networking or security as your area of specialty in IT, you might consider earning a few Cisco networking certifications after you complete your CompTIA A+, Network+, and Security+ certifications. The Cisco Networking Academy website provides many useful tools for advancing your networking education. One of those tools is a network simulator called Packet Tracer. In this project, you download and install Packet Tracer, and create a very basic network using simulated devices in Packet Tracer. This version of Packet Tracer is free to the public, and your school does not have to be a member of Cisco's Networking Academy for you to download and use it.

To get the Packet Tracer download, you must first sign up for the free Introduction to Packet Tracer online course on the Cisco Networking Academy website. Complete the following steps to create your account:

1. In your browser, navigate to **netacad.com/courses/packet-tracer**. Enroll in the course.

2. Open the confirmation email and confirm your email address. Configure your account and save this information in a safe place. You will need this information again.

3. Click Courses and select the Introduction to Packet Tracer course.

   Now you are ready to download and install Packet Tracer. If you need help with the download and installation process, launch the course and navigate to Chapter 1, Section 1.1, Topic 1.1.2 for additional guidance. Complete the following steps:

4. Inside the course, click **Student Resources**, and then click **Download and install the latest version of Packet Tracer**. Download the latest version for your computer, and then install Packet Tracer. Note that the download might not complete in the MS Edge browser; if you encounter a problem, try Google Chrome instead. When the installation is complete, run **Cisco Packet Tracer**.

5. When Packet Tracer opens, sign in with your Networking Academy account that you created earlier. If you see a Windows Security Alert, allow access through your firewall. Cisco Packet Tracer opens. The interface window is shown in Figure 3-66.

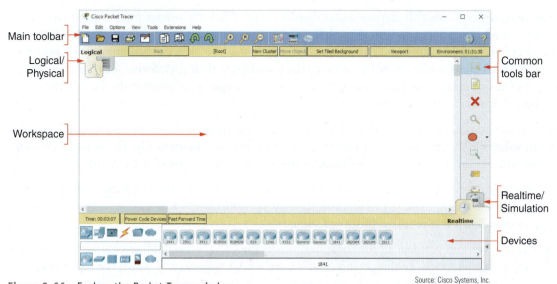

Figure 3-66 Explore the Packet Tracer window

Source: Cisco Systems, Inc.

The Introduction to Packet Tracer course presents an excellent introduction to Packet Tracer and provides lab activities. Let's build a very simple network in Packet Tracer so you can get familiar with the user interface.

6. First you need a router. In Packet Tracer (and in most network diagrams), routers look like a hockey puck with four arrows on top. In the Devices pane, make sure the **Network Devices** group is selected and the **Routers** subgroup, is selected. Drag a **2901** router from the selection pane into the workspace.

7. Next, add a switch. In network diagrams, switches look like rectangular boxes with four arrows on top. Click to select the **Switches** subgroup, then drag a **2960-24TT** switch to the workspace.

8. Now you're ready to add a couple of computers. Select the **End Devices** group. Drag a **Generic PC** and a **Generic Laptop** to the workspace. Arrange all the devices as shown in Figure 3-67.

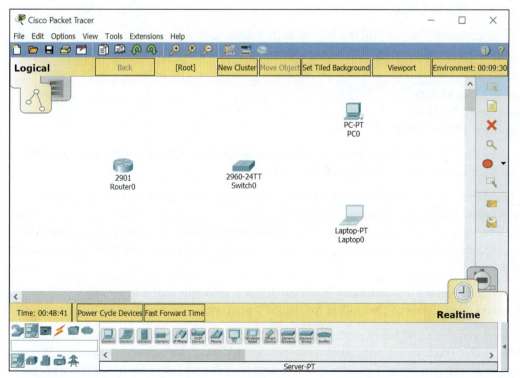

Figure 3-67 Arrange the devices on your network diagram

Source: Cisco Systems, Inc.

9. Now you're ready to connect the devices with Ethernet cables. Click the orange lightning icon to select the **Connections** group. Use the lightning icon from the selection pane to automatically select the correct connection type for each connection you make. After you click the **Automatically Choose Connection Type** lightning icon, click **PC0** to start the connection, then click **Switch0** to complete the connection. The link starts as orange, and as the connection is negotiated between the PC and the switch, the link turns to green on both ends.

10. Create an automatic connection from **Laptop0** to **Switch0**, and another automatic connection from **Switch0** to **Router0**. The laptop-to-switch connection will come up automatically. The switch-to-router connection will remain red because it requires additional configuration before it will work.

11. Click **Router0** to see its configuration window. On the Physical tab, you can see a picture of the device itself, both front and back. Explore this window to see what information is available to you, but don't change anything. When you're ready, click the **Config** tab.

    In Packet Tracer, you can perform all the configurations at the CLI (command line interface) or through a GUI (graphic user interface). In this project, you'll use the GUI options, and watch the *Equivalent IOS Commands* pane at the bottom of the window to see what commands you're executing.

12. To activate the router's interface, click the **GigabitEthernet0/0** interface in the left pane. Position the configuration window off to the side of the workspace so you can see Router0 and monitor any changes to the connection. Change the Port Status to **On**. What happens to the connection in the workspace?

13. Let's add IP configuration information. Give the connection the IP Address of **192.168.43.1** and a Subnet Mask of **255.255.255.0**. Then close Router0's configuration window.

14. Next, add IP address configuration information to the endpoint devices. Click **PC0** to open its configuration window. Here, you could use the Config tab or tools from the Desktop tab. Click **Desktop**, then click **IP Configuration**. You have two options: DHCP or Static. For now, you'll have to use Static. Why?

15. Make sure **Static** is selected, then give the PC the following IP configuration:
    ◢ IP Address: **192.168.43.100**
    ◢ Subnet Mask: **255.255.255.0**
    ◢ Default Gateway: **192.168.43.1**

    With this configuration, what device will the PC use as its default gateway?

16. Close PC0's configuration window, then use the same steps to give Laptop0 the following IP configuration:
    ◢ IP Address: **192.168.43.200**
    ◢ Subnet Mask: **255.255.255.0**
    ◢ Default Gateway: **192.168.43.1**

17. On Laptop0, close the IP Configuration pane. On the Desktop tab, click **Command Prompt**. Ping PC0 from Laptop0. What command did you use? Did it work?

18. You can use Simulation mode to watch the ping messages travel over the network. Close Laptop0's configuration window, then click the **Simulation mode** tab in the bottom right of the Packet Tracer window (refer back to Figure 3-66). Open Laptop0's **Command Prompt** window again, and position this window off to the side of the workspace so you can see the devices. Ping the router. What command did you use? Did it work?

19. This network is not connected to a simulated WAN connection, although it could be. Which device in this network would you connect to the modem for the ISP's network?

20. Packet Tracer gives you a safe and fun environment to explore networking concepts. Take a few minutes to look around the Packet Tracer menus and options, and perhaps add more devices to your network. When you're ready, close all open windows. You do not need to save your Packet Tracer file unless you want to.

Maintaining Windows

After completing this chapter, you will be able to:

- Set up and perform scheduled preventive maintenance tasks to keep Windows healthy

- Prepare for disaster by keeping good backups of user data, the Windows volume, and Windows system files

- Use Windows tools, including Disk Management, to manage hard drives

- Use commands to manage files, folders, and hard drives

- Connect to remote computers for screen and file sharing

Earlier in the text, you learned how to install Windows. This chapter takes you to the next step in learning how to support a Windows operating system: maintaining the OS after it is installed. Most Windows problems stem from poor maintenance. If you are an IT support technician responsible for the ongoing support of several computers, you can make your work easier and your users happier by setting up and executing a good maintenance plan for each computer you support. A well-maintained computer gives fewer problems and performs better than one that is not maintained. In this chapter, you learn how to schedule regular maintenance tasks, prepare for disaster by setting up backup routines for user data and system files, use Windows tools and commands to manage files, folders, and hard drives, and remotely access computers so that you can share screens and files.

This text covers Windows 10, 8.1, 8.0, and 7. As you read, you might consider following the steps in the chapter using a Windows 10 system, and then going through the steps again using a Windows 8 or Windows 7 system.

SCHEDULING PREVENTIVE MAINTENANCE

Regular preventive maintenance can keep a Windows computer performing well for years. At least once a month, you need to verify critical Windows settings and clean up the hard drive. These skills are covered in this part of the chapter. If you notice the system is slow as you do this maintenance, you need to dig deeper to improve Windows performance, which is covered in Chapter 5.

> 🖉 **Notes** When you're responsible for a computer, be sure to keep good records of all that you do to maintain, upgrade, or fix it. When performing preventive maintenance, take notes and include them in your documentation. The Computer Inventory and Maintenance document available at *cengage.com* can help you organize your notes.

VERIFYING CRITICAL WINDOWS SETTINGS

The Windows settings discussed here are critical for keeping the system protected from malware and hackers. Users sometimes change these settings without realizing their importance. Check the following settings; if you find they are incorrect, take time to explain to the computer's primary user how important they are. Here are the critical Windows settings you need to verify:

▲ *Windows updates.* Install any important Windows updates or Windows 7 service packs that are waiting to be installed and verify that Windows Update is configured to automatically allow updating. These updates may include updates to Windows, applications, device drivers, and firmware. You learned how to configure Windows Update in Chapter 2.

▲ *Antivirus/anti-malware software.* To protect a system against a malicious attack, you need to verify that anti-malware software is configured to scan the system regularly and that it is up to date. If you discover it is not scanning regularly, take the time to do a thorough scan for viruses. For Windows 10/8, Windows Defender is running in the background. To verify this, follow the directions in Chapter 2.

▲ *Network security setting.* To secure the computer against attack from the network, use the Network and Sharing Center to check that the network security type is set correctly for the optimum firewall settings. The network types are public and private in Windows 10/8, and public, work, and home in Windows 7. How to verify the network type was covered in Chapter 1. Further details of configuring network security in Windows are discussed in Chapter 7.

▲ *Backups of user data, the Windows volume, and system files.* Following directions given later in the chapter, verify that backup routines are running as expected to protect data and software from loss or corruption.

To keep Windows performing well, do the following:

▲ *Uninstall software you no longer need.* This helps overall performance by reducing the number of startup processes running in the background. To uninstall software, use the Windows 10/8 Apps & Features window or the Windows 10/8/7 Programs and Features window. Also, for Windows 10/8, turn off live tiles you don't watch.

▲ *Clean up the hard drive.* A hard drive needs at least 15 percent free space on drive C:, where Windows is installed. Later in the chapter, you learn how to use Disk Cleanup to erase unnecessary files on drive C:. You can also move data on the drive to other media.

> 🖉 **Notes** Don't forget that what you learn about maintaining Windows also applies to Windows in a VM. When maintaining a VM, make sure Windows in a VM is updated, anti-malware software is installed and running, and network settings are secure.

PATCH MANAGEMENT

When researching a problem, suppose you discover that Microsoft or a manufacturer's website offers a fix or patch for Windows, a device driver, or an application. To download and apply compatible software, you need to make sure you get a 32-bit patch for a 32-bit installation of Windows, a device driver, or an application. For a 64-bit installation of Windows, make sure you get a 64-bit device driver. An application installed in a 64-bit OS might be a 32-bit application or a 64-bit application.

The documentation on the Microsoft website or other sites might be cryptic about the type of patch. Follow these guidelines when reading error messages or documentation:

◢ The term *x86* refers to 32-bit CPUs or processors and to 32-bit operating systems. For example, the Microsoft website might say a patch to fix a problem with a USB device applies to a Windows 10, x86-based version. This means the patch is for a 32-bit version of Windows 10.

◢ The term *x64* refers to 64-bit operating systems. For example, Microsoft offers two versions of Windows 10: the x86 version and the x64 version.

◢ All CPUs installed in personal computers today are hybrid processors that can process either 32 bits or 64 bits. The term *x86-64* refers to these processors, such as the Intel Core i5 or an AMD Ryzen processor. (AMD64 refers specifically to these hybrid AMD processors.) The term x86-64 can also refer to a 64-bit OS. For example, a Windows message might read, "You are attempting to load an x86-64 operating system." Take that to mean you are attempting to load a 64-bit OS on a computer that has a hybrid 32-bit/64-bit processor installed, such as the Ryzen 5 1500x or Intel Core i5-7500.

◢ The term *IA64* refers specifically to 64-bit Intel processors such as the Xeon or Itanium, which is used in servers or high-end workstations.

> ★ **A+ Exam Tip** The A+ Core 2 exam expects you to know the difference between 32-bit and 64-bit operating systems and, when given a scenario, to select compatible software for patch management.

Now let's look at how to perform on-demand backups and how to schedule routine backups.

BACKUP PROCEDURES

A backup is an extra copy of a data file or software file that you can use if the original file is damaged or destroyed. Losing data due to system failure, a virus, file corruption, or some other problem really makes you appreciate the importance of having backups.

> ✎ **Notes** With data and software, here's a good rule of thumb: If you can't get along without it, back it up.

APPLYING | CONCEPTS   BACKUPS PAY OFF

Dave was well on his way to building a successful career as an IT support technician. His IT tech support shop was doing well, and he was excited about his future. But one bad decision changed everything. He was called to repair a server at a small accounting firm. The call was on the weekend when he was normally off, so he was in a hurry to get the job done. He arrived at the accounting firm and saw that the problem was an easy one to fix, so he decided not to do a backup before working on the system. During his repairs, the hard drive crashed and all data on the drive was lost—four million dollars' worth! The firm sued, Dave's business license was stripped, and he was ordered to pay the money the company lost. A little extra time to back up the system would have saved his whole future. True story!

Because most of us routinely write data to the hard drive, this section focuses on backing up from the hard drive to other media. However, when you store important data on any medium—such as a flash drive, external hard drive, CD, or in the cloud—always keep a copy of the data on another device or in the cloud. Never trust important data to only one location.

In this part of the chapter, you learn how to make a disaster recovery plan and then learn how to use Windows to back up user data, entire volumes, and critical Windows system files.

PLANNING FOR DISASTER RECOVERY

A+
CORE 2
4.3

The time to prepare for disaster is before it occurs. If you have not prepared, the damage from a disaster will most likely be greater than if you had made and followed disaster recovery plans. Suppose the hard drive on your computer stopped working and you lost all its data. What would be the impact? Are you prepared for this to happen? Here are decisions you need to make for your backup and recovery plans:

▲ *Decide on the type of backup.* Different backup types include different kinds of data:

  ▲ You might back up single files or folders, in which case you might also have access to previous versions of a file; this is called a file-level backup and allows granular control over which content is included in the backup and which content can be recovered on a file-by-file basis. File-level backups are appropriate for backing up user data, but generally are not considered good options for backing up applications and Windows.

  ▲ You might back up an entire volume of a drive, called an image-level backup. Restoring from an image-level backup would also restore your OS installation, applications, user account settings, and user data. However, the process restores the entire backup image and does not allow selecting portions of the backup separately.

  ▲ You might need a separate backup plan for critical applications, which are any applications required to keep a business functioning while other backup solutions are being used to recover from any data loss. Consider cloud solutions or virtualization options as backups for critical applications such as email, databases, or office productivity software.

▲ *Decide on the backup destination.* For example, for a personal computer or small network, options include backup to a cloud, network drive, CD, DVD, Blu-ray, SD card, USB flash drive, external hard drive, or other media. Here are points to keep in mind:

  ▲ A cloud storage backup service such as Carbonite (*carbonite.com*), Backblaze (*backblaze.com*), Amazon Drive (*amazon.com/amazondrive*), Google Drive (*drive.google.com*), or iCloud Drive (*icloud.com*) is the easiest, most reliable, and most expensive solution. You pay a yearly subscription for the service, and it guarantees your backups, which are automatically done when your computer is connected to the Internet. If you decide to use one of these services, be sure to restore files from backup occasionally to make sure your backups are happening as you expect and that you can recover a lost file.

  ▲ Local storage backups are relatively inexpensive and convenient, in that data is easily accessible at your location. This method might present a problem, however, if a catastrophic event, such as a fire or flood, destroys the building where your original data and backups are all located. For this reason, always keep backups at an off-site location.

  ▲ Even though it's easy to do, don't make the mistake of backing up your data to another volume or folder on the same hard drive. When a hard drive crashes, most likely all volumes go down together and you will lose your data and your backup. Back up to another device and, for extra safety, store it at an off-site location.

> ✎ **Notes** For individuals or small networks, backups to the cloud are generally more expensive than backing up to a local server or external hard drive. For large networks, storing data in the cloud, such as Google Cloud or Amazon Web Services, can save money over buying and maintaining backup storage solutions on location.

▲ *Decide on the backup software.* Windows offers one or more backup utilities. However, you can purchase third-party backup software that might offer more features. Read reviews about the software and consider:

  ▲ Hard drive manufacturers often bundle backup software with a new hard drive or you can download the software from the manufacturer's website.

  ▲ What does the software back up? Files or the entire image of a volume?

  ▲ Does the software provide a way to boot from backup media so you can easily access the backups when the hard drive crashes?

  ▲ Can you schedule when backups occur?

  ▲ Does the software support backing up to a remote location, such as a different branch office where you can easily access the backups?

▲ *Decide how simple or complex your backup strategy needs to be.* A backup and recovery plan for individuals or small organizations might be very simple. However, large organizations might require that backups be documented each day and scheduled at certain times of the day or night, and recovery plans might have to be tested on a regular basis. Know the requirements of your organization when creating a backup and recovery plan. As a general rule of thumb, back up data for at least every 4 to 6 hours of data entry. This might mean a backup needs to occur twice a day, daily, weekly, or monthly. Find out the data entry habits of workers before making your backup schedule and deciding on the folders or volumes to back up.

▲ *Consider ways of ensuring business continuity.* Not all disasters are directly related to data loss. A loss of power or Internet connection can also interfere with business productivity, and physical or electrical damage to computer or network hardware is another significant concern. Plugging a computer's power cord into a **surge protector** can protect against voltage spikes by blocking or grounding excessive voltage. An **uninterruptible power supply (UPS)** can be strategically placed on the network to supply power when voltage drops during brownouts or short-term blackouts and ensure that routers, switches, and servers keep running during a power outage. See Figure 4-1. Also consider physical security to protect against theft or vandalism. You can learn more about surge protectors and UPS devices in Appendix A, and you'll learn more about physical security in Chapter 8.

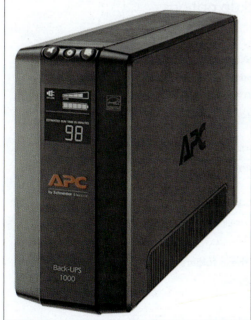

Source: amazon.com

Figure 4-1 A UPS protects a desktop computer, server, or network devices from low voltages and blackouts

After you have a backup plan working, test the recovery plan. In addition, you need to occasionally retest the recovery plan to make sure all is still working as you expect. Do the following:

▲ *Test the recovery process.* Erase a file on the hard drive, and use the recovery procedures to verify that you can re-create the file from the backup. This test also verifies that the backup medium works, that the recovery software is effective, and that you know how to use it. After you are convinced that the recovery works, document how to perform it.

▲ *Keep backups in a safe place and routinely test them.* Don't leave a backup DVD or other media lying around for someone to steal. Backups of important and sensitive data should be kept under lock and key at an off-site location. In case of fire, keep enough backups off-site so that you can recover data even if the entire building is destroyed. Routinely verify that your backups are good by performing a test recovery of a backed-up file or folder. Backups are useless if the data on the backup is corrupted.

📝 **Notes** One reason that organizations use cloud solutions, such as Microsoft Azure, Google Cloud, and Amazon Web Services, is that work can be done from any location by signing in to the online service where applications and data are kept in the cloud. Cloud computing greatly eliminates the need for an organization to maintain its own backups and still be protected against local catastrophic events.

Now let's see how to back up user data, the entire Windows volume, and important Windows system files.

BACKING UP USER DATA AND THE SYSTEM IMAGE

**A+
CORE 2
4.3**

Here are the tools offered by Windows 10/8/7 for backups:

▲ Windows 10 offers File History or Backup and Restore to back up user data and create a system image.

▲ Windows 8 uses File History but not Backup and Restore. In addition, Windows 8 offers the recimg command to create a custom refresh image, which is a type of system image.

▲ Windows 7 offers Backup and Restore to back up user data and to create a system image.

A system image is a backup of the entire Windows volume, including the Windows installation, applications, user settings, and data. The best time to create the image is right after you've installed Windows, hardware, applications, and user accounts and customized Windows settings. The image is stored in a single file with a .wim file extension. The WIM file uses the Windows Imaging File (WIM) format and is a compressed file that contains many related files.

Next, let's see how these backup tools work.

WINDOWS 10/8 FILE HISTORY

Windows 10/8 File History backs up user data stored in the Documents, Music, Pictures, Videos, and Desktop folders, as well as offline OneDrive files (for Microsoft accounts) and other folders as determined by the user. When the backup is enabled, it first makes a full backup to another medium. By default, it scans for file and folder changes every hour and keeps as many generations of backups as free space allows on the storage device.

Follow these steps to use File History on a Windows 10 computer:

1. First connect your backup device. In the Settings app, click **Update & Security**, then click **Backup**. When you click **Add a drive**, Windows searches for a usable drive. Select the drive or click **Show all network locations** to find and select a drive on the network. File History connects to the drive and turns on.

2. To manage these backups, click **More options**. On the Backup options window shown in Figure 4-2, you can set how often backups are made (every 10 minutes up to daily), how long old backups should be kept (forever, until space is needed, 1 month, 1 year, and so forth), and which folders to back up.

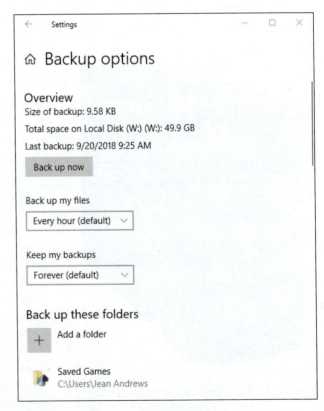

Figure 4-2   Backup options for File History

File History can also be accessed through Control Panel (see Figure 4-3). Click items in the left pane to turn File History on or off, change File History settings, and restore files from backup. Using the File History window in Control Panel, you can click System Image Backup (see Figure 4-3) to start the process of creating a system image.

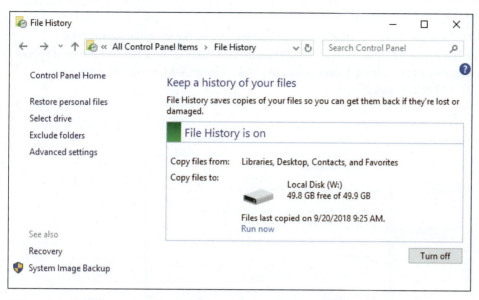

Figure 4-3 Control File History settings and restore files from backup

⭐ **A+ Exam Tip** The A+ Core 2 exam might give you a scenario that expects you to create, use, and test backups.

RESTORE FILES AND FOLDERS IN FILE HISTORY

To restore a file or folder from backup, open the **File History** window from Control Panel and click **Restore personal files**. You can view and recover items from the backups (see Figure 4-4). Use the left and right arrow keys on either side of the green **Restore** button at the bottom of the window to select a backup, and then drill down into the backup to find the file or folder you need. Select an item to see a preview, and then click the **Restore** button to restore the item. If you prefer to save the previous version in a different location so as not to overwrite the newest version of the file, right-click the **Restore** button and click **Restore to**. Navigate to the location where you want to save the previous version and then click **Select Folder**.

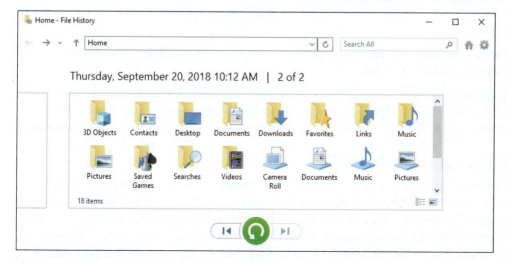

Figure 4-4 Drill down into backups to find what you want to restore

Another way to restore a file or folder from backup is to use File Explorer or Windows Explorer. Follow these steps:

1. When you restore a file or folder to a previous version, the current file or folder can be overwritten by the previous version. To keep the original, first copy—not move—the folder or file to a new location so that you can revert to the copy if necessary.

2. Right-click the file or folder and select **Restore previous versions** from the shortcut menu. The Properties box for the file or folder appears with the Previous Versions tab selected. Windows displays a list of all previous versions of the file or folder it has kept (see Figure 4-5); these versions were created by File History or Backup and Restore.

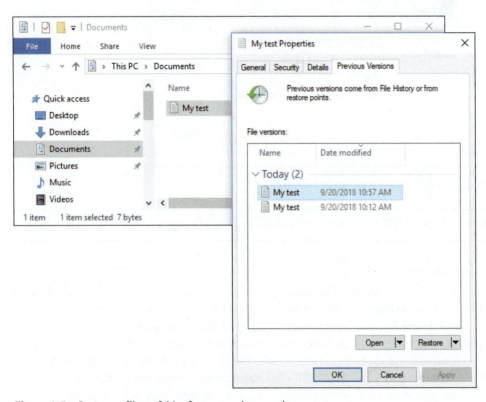

Figure 4-5 Restore a file or folder from a previous version

3. Select the version you want and click **Restore**. A message box asks if you are sure you want to continue. Click **Restore** and then click **OK**.

4. Open the restored file or folder and verify that it is the version you want. If you decide you need another version, delete the file or folder, and copy the file or folder you saved in Step 1 back into the original location. Then return to Step 2 and try again, this time selecting a different previous version.

WINDOWS 10/7 BACKUP AND RESTORE

Windows 10 and Windows 7 offer Backup and Restore to back up any folder on the hard drive and create a system image. Generally, File History is designed to be an easy tool for users to manage their own backups, and Backup and Restore is designed for technicians who prefer more granular control of backups.

The folders and volume are first backed up entirely; this is called a full backup. Then, on the schedule you set, any file or folder is backed up if it has changed or been created since the last backup. This is called an incremental backup. Occasionally, Windows does another full backup. If you've established a backup schedule in File History on a Windows 10 machine, those settings will appear in the Backup and Restore window.

Follow these steps to save a backup and set up an ongoing backup schedule using Backup and Restore in Windows 10:

1. Open Control Panel in Classic view, and click **Backup and Restore**. If no backup has ever been scheduled on the system, the window will look like the one shown in Figure 4-6. Click **Set up backup**.

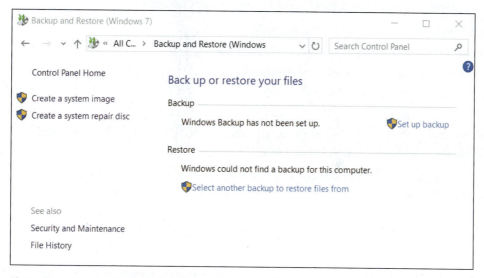

Figure 4-6 Use the Backup and Restore window to schedule backups

2. In the next dialog box, select the device or location to hold the backup. All Windows 10 editions and Windows 7 Professional, Ultimate, and Enterprise editions allow you to save the backup to a network location. To use a shared folder on the network for the backup destination, click **Save on a network**. In the resulting box, click **Browse** and point to the folder. See Figure 4-7. Also enter the user name and password on the remote computer that the backup utility will use to authenticate to that computer when it makes the backup. You cannot save to a network location when using Windows 7 Home editions. For these editions, the *Save on a network* button is missing in the window where you select the backup destination.

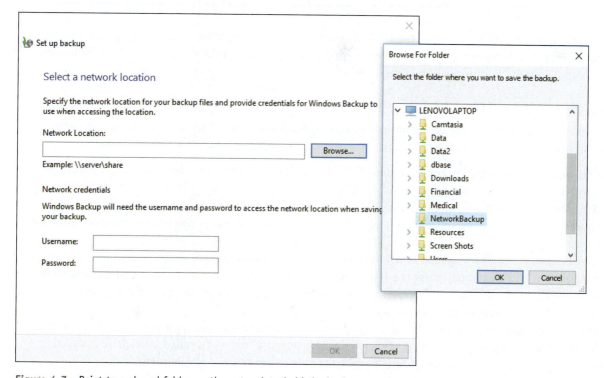

Figure 4-7 Point to a shared folder on the network to hold the backups

3. In the next box, you can allow Windows to decide what to back up or choose for yourself. Select **Let me choose** so that you can select the folders to back up. Click **Next**.

4. In the next box, make your selections. If the backup medium can hold the system image, the option to include the image is selected by default. If you don't want to include the image, uncheck the option. Click **Next** to continue. Here are folders that might contain important user data:

   ◢ Application data is usually found in C:\Users*username*\AppData.

   ◢ Internet Explorer favorites are in C:\Users*username*\Favorites.

   ◢ Better still, back up the entire user profile at C:\Users*username*.

   ◢ Even better, back up all user profiles at C:\Users.

5. In the next box, you can verify that the correct items are selected. To change the default schedule, click **Change schedule**. In the next box, you can choose to run the backup daily, weekly, or monthly and select the time of day. Make your selections and click **OK**.

6. Review your backup settings, and click **Save settings and run backup**. The backup proceeds. A shadow copy is made of any open files so that they are included in the backup.

Later, you can return to the Backup and Restore window to change the backup settings or to turn off the backup.

> 🖉 **Notes** One limitation of Windows File History and Backup and Restore is that you can have only one scheduled backup routine.

> 🖉 **Notes** After Windows does a full backup, it only backs up files that have changed since the last full backup. Occasionally, it does another full backup. Each full backup is called a backup period. Windows keeps as many backup periods as it has space on the backup device. As free space fills, it deletes the oldest backup periods. To see how space is used on your backup media, click **Manage space** in the Backup and Restore window. In the Manage Windows Backup disk space, you can click **View backups** to delete a backup period, but be sure to keep the most recent backup periods.

To recover backed-up items, open the Backup and Restore window, scroll down to the bottom of the window, and click **Restore my files**. Locate and select multiple files or folders to restore. Then follow the on-screen directions to restore all the selected items.

MAINTAIN A SYSTEM IMAGE

As you've already learned, the backup of a Windows volume is called a system image. Here are points to keep in mind when creating a system image and using it to recover a failed Windows volume:

◢ *Creating a system image takes some time.* Before creating a system image on a laptop, plug the laptop into an AC outlet so that a failed battery will not interrupt the process.

◢ *A system image includes the entire drive C: or other drive on which Windows is installed.* When you restore a hard drive using the system image, everything on the volume is deleted and replaced with the system image.

◢ *Don't depend just on the system image as your backup.* You should back up individual folders that contain user data separately from the system image. If only individual data files or folders need to be recovered, you would not want to use the system image for the recovery because it would totally replace the entire Windows volume.

◢ *You can create a system image any time after Windows is installed, and then you can use this image to recover from a failed hard drive.* Using the system image to recover a failed hard drive is called reimaging the drive. The details of how to reimage a drive are covered in Chapter 6.

WINDOWS | 8 CUSTOM REFRESH IMAGE

A **custom refresh image** was intended to replace the Windows 7 system image. However, it was not as popular, so the recimg command used to create a custom refresh image is not included in Windows 10.

Here are the steps to create a Windows 8 custom refresh image:

1. Open an elevated command prompt window. One way to do so is to press **Win+X** and click **Command Prompt (Admin)**. Respond to the UAC box. The Administrator: Command Prompt window opens.

2. Enter the following command, substituting a drive and folder for the sample path shown:

   ```
   recimg /createimage D:\MyImage
   ```

Creating the image takes some time, and then the image and its location are registered as the **active recovery image**. The image is stored in a large .wim file that you can view using File Explorer. You can create as many refresh images as you like, but only one is designated as the active recovery image, and it's the one that will be used when you refresh the Windows 8 installation. How to perform a Windows 8 refresh is covered in Chapter 6.

The recimg command can also be used to manage refresh images. The parameters for the command are listed in Table 4-1.

Command	Result
`recimg /createimage <path>`	**Creates the refresh image and registers its location as the active refresh image**
`recimg /showcurrent`	**Displays the location of the active refresh image**
`recimg /deregister`	**Deregisters the active recovery image; during the refresh process, Windows will not find an image and will revert to a hidden recovery partition on the hard drive or the Windows 8 setup files for the refresh**
`recimg /setcurrent <path>`	**Registers a refresh image in the path given; the image at this location is now the active refresh image**

Table 4-1   The recimg command and parameters

Suppose you've created multiple refresh images and you want to select a particular image for a refresh. Figure 4-8 shows the commands you can use to change the active refresh image from the one stored in the D:\MyImage folder to one stored in the D:\MyImage2 folder.

Notes Because a refresh image must be named CustomRefresh.wim, you must store each image in a separate folder.

(continues)

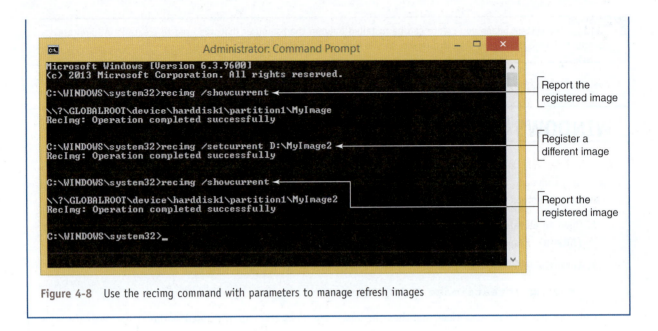

Figure 4-8 Use the recimg command with parameters to manage refresh images

BACKING UP WINDOWS SYSTEM FILES WITH SYSTEM PROTECTION

**A+
CORE 2
4.3**

When the System Protection utility is turned on, it automatically backs up system files and stores them on the hard drive at regular intervals and just before you install software or hardware. These snapshots of the system are called restore points and include Windows system files that have changed since the last restore point was made. A restore point does not contain all user data, and you can manually create a restore point at any time. System Restore (rstrui.exe) restores the system to its condition at the time a restore point was made. If you restore the system to a previous restore point, user data on the hard drive will not be altered, but you can affect installed software and hardware, user settings and passwords, and OS configuration settings. You'll learn how to use System Restore in Chapter 5.

ENABLE SYSTEM PROTECTION

System Protection is turned off by default in Windows 10. To enable System Protection, open **Control Panel** and open the **System** window. In the System window, click **System protection**. The System Protection tab of the System Properties box appears (see the left side of Figure 4-9). Make sure protection is turned on for the drive containing Windows, which indicates that restore points are created automatically. In Figure 4-9, protection for drive C: is on and other drives are not being protected. To make a change, click **Configure**. The System Protection box appears, as shown on the right side of the figure. If you make a change to this box, click **Apply** and then click **OK**.

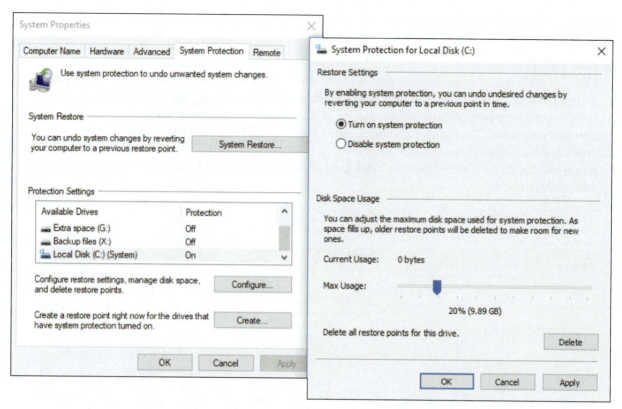

Figure 4-9   Make sure System Protection is turned on for the volume on which Windows is installed

Restore points are normally kept in a folder named C:\System Volume Information, which is not accessible to the user. Restore points are taken at least every 24 hours, and they can use up to 15 percent of disk space. If disk space gets very low, restore points are no longer made, which is one more good reason to keep at least 15 percent or more of the hard drive free.

MANUALLY CREATE A RESTORE POINT

To manually create a restore point, use the System Protection tab of the System Properties box, as shown on the left side of Figure 4-9. Click **Create**. In the System Protection box, enter a name for the restore point, such as "Before I tested software," and click **Create**. The restore point is created.

MANAGING FILES, FOLDERS, AND STORAGE DEVICES

In this part of the chapter, you learn how files, folders, and volumes on a hard drive are organized, how to manage hard drive partitions and volumes using the Disk Management utility, and how to improve hard drive performance. Let's begin the discussion with how partitions and file systems work in Windows.

HOW PARTITIONS AND FILE SYSTEMS WORK

Recall that a hard drive is organized into partitions, volumes, and file systems. Total capacities for today's drives are measured in GB (gigabytes, roughly one million bytes) or TB (terabytes, roughly one trillion bytes). Before a hard drive leaves the factory, a process called low-level formatting organizes the space in a long series of logical blocks; this is called Logical Block

Addressing (LBA). When you first prepare a new hard drive for use, the drive is further organized into one or more partitions using one of two partitioning systems:

▲ *MBR partitions*. The Master Boot Record (MBR) partitioning system keeps a map of partitions in a partition table stored at the beginning of the hard drive called the MBR. Recall that the MBR system is required when a computer is using a 32-bit operating system or legacy BIOS. The MBR partition table can track up to four partitions on a drive. A drive can have one, two, or three primary partitions, also called volumes. The fourth partition is called an extended partition and can hold one or more volumes called logical drives, which are tracked in their own partition table separately from the primary partitions. Figure 4-10 shows how an MBR hard drive is divided into three primary partitions and one extended partition.

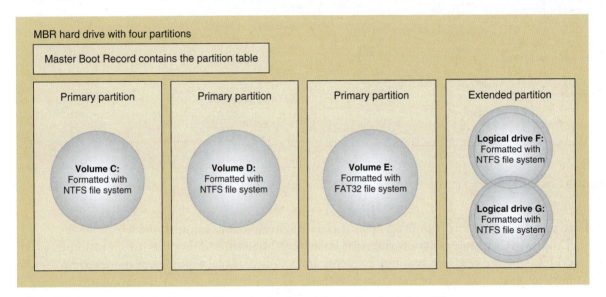

Figure 4-10   A hard drive with four partitions; the fourth partition is an extended partition

> ★ **A+ Exam Tip**   The A+ Core 2 exam expects you to know the difference between a primary and extended partition and between a volume and logical drive on an MBR hard drive.

▲ *GPT partitions*. The Globally Unique Identifier Partition Table (GUID or GPT) system can support up to 128 partitions and is required for drives larger than 2.2 TB. Recall that GPT requires a 64-bit operating system and UEFI firmware and is needed to use Secure boot, a feature of UEFI and the OS. Most new computers sold today use the GPT system.

The first sector in a GPT system contains the protective MBR, which provides information to legacy software that doesn't recognize GPT systems so that the legacy software will not attempt to repair or install an MBR system on the drive. GPT tracks all partitions in a single partition table, which it stores in the GPT header immediately following the protective MBR. GPT systems also back up the partition table at the end of the disk (see Figure 4-11).

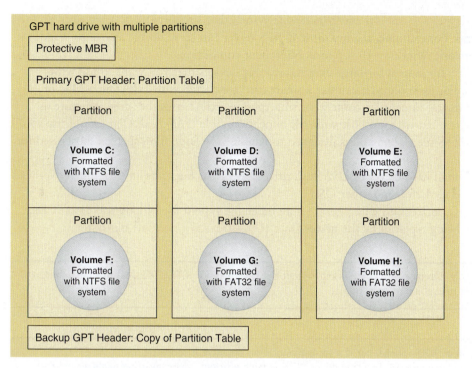

GPT hard drive with multiple partitions

Protective MBR

Primary GPT Header: Partition Table

Partition

Volume C:
Formatted
with NTFS file
system

Partition

Volume D:
Formatted
with NTFS file
system

Partition

Volume E:
Formatted
with NTFS file
system

Partition

Volume F:
Formatted
with NTFS file
system

Partition

Volume G:
Formatted
with FAT32 file
system

Partition

Volume H:
Formatted
with FAT32 file
system

Backup GPT Header: Copy of Partition Table

Figure 4-11   A hard drive using GPT partitioning

WINDOWS FILE SYSTEMS

Before a partition or drive can be accessed, it must be assigned a drive letter such as C: or D: and formatted using a file system. Recall that the file system is the overall structure an OS uses to name, store, and organize files and folders on a drive. Installing a drive letter, file system, and root directory on a volume is called **formatting** the drive or **high-level formatting**. This formatting can happen during the Windows installation.

> ✎ **Notes**   In most Microsoft documentation, a partition is called a partition until it is formatted with a file system and assigned a drive letter. Then it is called a volume.

Here is a list of file systems supported by Windows:

▲ *NTFS.* For most editions of Windows, **NTFS (New Technology file system)** is required for the volume on which Windows is installed. NTFS was designed to replace the older FAT32 file system; it is more reliable, efficient, and secure than FAT32. NTFS supports encryption, disk quotas (limiting the hard drive space available to a user), and file and folder compression. If you boot the system from another boot medium such as a DVD, you can access a volume using a FAT file system. If the volume uses NTFS, an administrator password is required to gain access.

▲ *ReFS.* The latest file system by Microsoft is the **Resilient File System (ReFS)**, which is designed to improve on the NTFS file system by offering better performance. ReFS also offers **fault tolerance**, which protects data when sectors on the hard drive fail, eliminating the need for repairs using chkdsk, and it offers compatibility with virtualization and data redundancy in a RAID system. (RAID joins multiple hard drives into one virtual hard drive space.) ReFS is included in Windows 10 Pro for Workstations, but not with Windows 10 Pro or other editions of Windows 10.

- *NFS*. The NFS (Network File System) is a client/server file system that supports file sharing over a network across platforms. For example, a Linux-hosted NFS server can serve up file shares to Windows workstations on the network. Windows 10 supports NFS client connections.
- *exFAT*. Choose the exFAT file system for large external storage devices that you want to use with other operating systems. For example, you can use a smart card formatted with exFAT in a Mac or Linux computer or in a digital camcorder, camera, or smartphone. exFAT uses the same structure as the older FAT32 file system, but with a 64-bit-wide file allocation table (FAT). exFAT does not use as much overhead as the NTFS file system and is designed to handle very large files, such as those used for multimedia storage.
- *FAT32*. Use FAT32 for small hard drives or USB flash drives because it does not have as much overhead as NTFS and is supported by Linux and other OSs.
- *CDFS and UDF*. CDFS (Compact Disc File System) is an older file system used by optical discs (CDs, DVDs, and BDs), and is being replaced by the newer UDF (Universal Disk Format) file system.

> ★ **A+ Exam Tip** The A+ Core 2 exam expects you to know about the FAT32, exFAT, NTFS, CDFS, and NFS file systems, including which is appropriate to use in a given scenario.

> ✏ **Notes** Windows installs on an NTFS volume, but if a second volume on the drive is formatted using the FAT32 file system, you can convert that volume to NTFS. For large drives, NTFS is more efficient, and converting might improve performance.

HOW PARTITIONS ARE USED DURING THE BOOT

With MBR hard drives, one of the primary partitions is designated the active partition, which is the bootable partition that startup BIOS/UEFI turns to when searching for an operating system to load. In GPT systems, this bootable partition is called the EFI System Partition (ESP); UEFI turns to it to find and start the operating system. The OS program it looks for in this partition is called the boot loader or boot manager.

In Windows, the MBR active partition or the GPT EFI System Partition is called the system partition. For Windows 10/8/7, the boot manager program is named BootMgr (with no file extension). The boot manager turns to the volume that is designated the boot partition, where the Windows operating system is stored, and continues the process of starting Windows.

> ✏ **Notes** Don't be confused by the terminology here. It is really true that, according to Windows terminology, the Windows OS is on the boot partition and the boot manager is on the system partition, although that might seem backward. The computer starts or boots from the system partition and loads the Windows operating system from the boot partition. Typically, the boot partition and folder where Windows is stored is C:\Windows.

USING DISK MANAGEMENT TO MANAGE HARD DRIVES

A+ CORE 2 1.3, 1.5

The primary tool for managing hard drives is Disk Management. In Chapter 2, you learned how to install Windows on a new hard drive. This installation process initializes, partitions, and formats the drive. After Windows is installed, you can use Disk Management to install and manage drives. In this part of the chapter, you learn to use Disk Management to manage partitions on a drive, prepare a new drive for first use, mount a drive, use Windows dynamic disks, and troubleshoot problems with the hard drive.

4

APPLYING | CONCEPTS   EXAMINING HARD DRIVES USING DISK MANAGEMENT

Let's use Disk Management (diskmgmt.msc) to view the hard drives in two systems:

1. To open the Disk Management window, use one of these methods:

   ▲ For Windows 10/8, right-click **Start** and click **Disk Management**. You can find Disk Management in the Windows 7 Start menu.

   ▲ Press **Win+R** and enter **diskmgmt.msc** in the Windows 10/7 search box or the Windows 8 Run box.

   In Figure 4-12, you can see an example of the Disk Management window showing three MBR hard drives in a system. In this computer, Windows is installed on Disk 0; Disk 1 is an unformatted drive, and Disk 2 is formatted using the NTFS file system. On Disk 0, the first partition is the System Reserved partition, which is designated the active partition and the Windows system partition. The boot partition is drive C:, where Windows is stored.

2. To see the Disk 0 Properties box, right-click **Disk 0** on the left side of the Disk Management window and click **Properties**. The Properties box appears, as shown in Figure 4-12. Select the **Volumes** tab to find out the partitioning system for the disk.

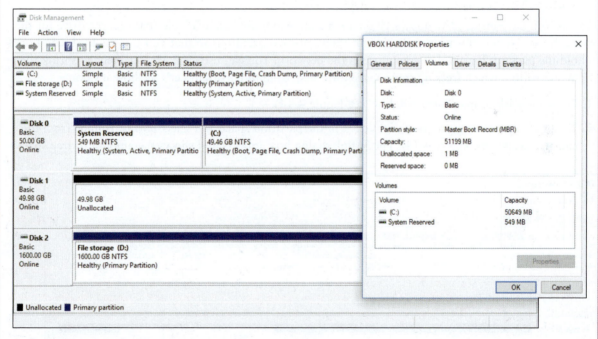

Figure 4-12   Three MBR disks with Windows 10 installed on Disk 0

Figure 4-13 shows another computer that has a single GPT hard drive installed. Among other partitions, it contains an OEM recovery partition, the EFI System Partition, and drive C:, which is designated the boot partition and holds the Windows 10 installation.

(continues)

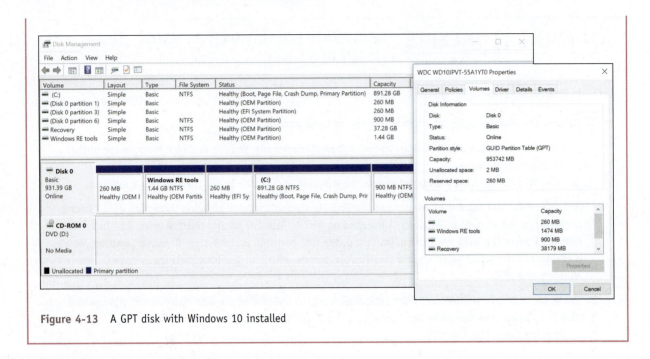

Figure 4-13   A GPT disk with Windows 10 installed

RESIZE, CREATE, AND DELETE PARTITIONS

Suppose you have installed Windows 10 on a hard drive and used all available space on the drive for the one partition. Now you want to split the partition into two partitions so that you can use the second one to hold the backups for another computer on the network. You can use Disk Management to shrink the original partition, which frees up some space for a new Ubuntu partition. Let's see how it's done:

1. Open the Disk Management window (see Figure 4-14).

2. To shrink the existing partition, right-click in the partition space and select **Shrink Volume** from the shortcut menu (see Figure 4-14). The Shrink dialog box appears and shows the amount of free space

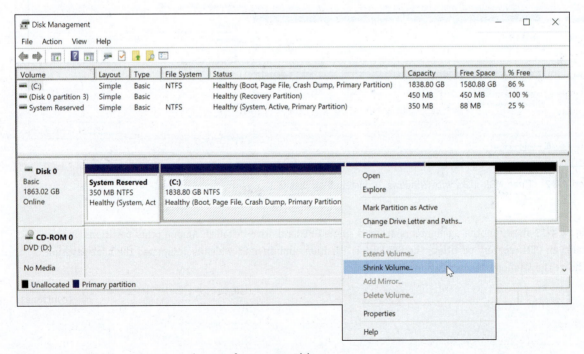

Figure 4-14   Shrink a volume to make room for a new partition

on the partition. Enter the amount in MB to shrink the partition; this amount cannot be more than the available amount of free space so that no data on the partition will be lost. (For best performance, be sure to leave at least 20 percent free space on the existing partition.) Click **Shrink**. The disk now shows unallocated space.

3. To create a new partition in the unallocated space, right-click in that space and select **New Simple Volume** from the shortcut menu (see Figure 4-15). The New Simple Volume Wizard opens.

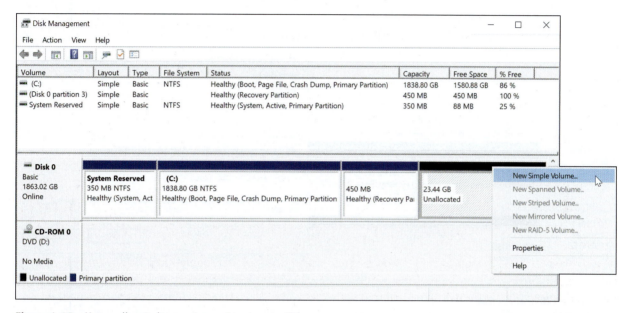

Figure 4-15 Use unallocated space to create a new partition

4. Follow the on-screen directions to enter the size of the volume in MB, select a drive letter for the volume, and select a file system. Leave the Allocation unit size at Default. You can also enter a Volume label and decide to do a quick format. (A quick format does not check the volume for bad sectors.) The partition is then created and formatted with the file system you chose. When you open Explorer, you should see the new volume listed.

Notice in Figure 4-14 the options on the shortcut menu for this MBR system, where you can make the partition the active partition (the one BIOS/UEFI looks to for an OS), change the drive letter for a volume, format the volume (which erases all data on it), extend the volume (increase its size), and shrink or delete the volume. An option that is not available for the particular volume and situation is grayed out.

> ★ **A+ Exam Tip** The A+ Core 2 exam expects you to know how to use Disk Management to extend, split, and shrink partitions and configure a new hard drive in a system.

PREPARE A DRIVE FOR FIRST USE

When you install a new, second hard drive in a computer, use Disk Management to prepare the drive for use. This happens in a two-step process:

1. *Initialize the disk.* When the disk is initialized, Windows identifies it as a basic disk. A basic disk is a single hard drive that works independently of other hard drives. When you first open Disk Management after you have installed a new hard drive, the Initialize Disk box automatically appears (see Figure 4-16). Select the partitioning system (MBR or GPT) and click **OK**. Disk Management now reports the hard drive as a Basic disk.

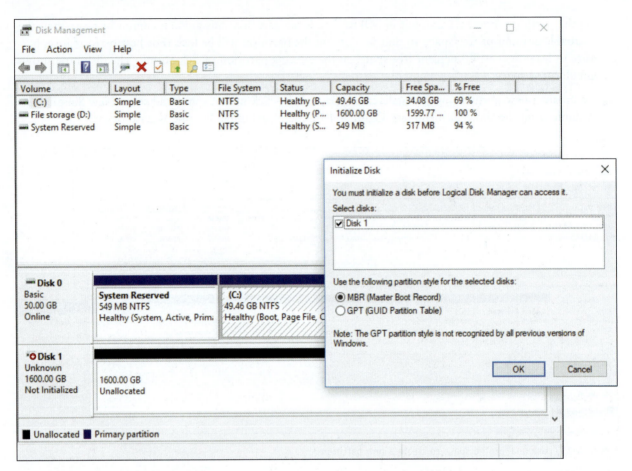

Figure 4-16 Use the Initialize Disk box to set up a partitioning system on new hard drives

> **Notes** After installing a new hard drive, if you don't see the Initialize Disk box when you first open Disk Management, right-click in the Disk area and select **Initialize Disk** from the shortcut menu. The Initialize Disk box will appear.

2. ***Create a volume and format it with a file system.*** As you learned to do earlier, you can now create a New Simple Volume in unallocated space on the disk.

HOW TO MOUNT A DRIVE

A mounted drive is a volume that can be accessed by way of a folder on another volume so that the folder has more available space. A mounted drive is useful when a folder is on a volume that is too small to hold all the data you want in the folder. In Figure 4-17, the mounted drive gives the C:\Projects folder a capacity of 20 GB. The C:\Projects folder is called the mount point for the mounted drive.

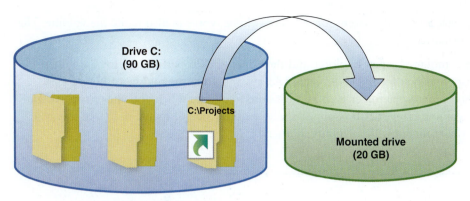

Figure 4-17 The C:\Projects folder is the mount point for the mounted drive

Follow these steps to mount a drive:

1. Make sure the volume that will host the mounted drive uses the NTFS file system. The folder on this volume, called the mount point, must be empty. You can also create the folder during the mount process. In this example, we are mounting a drive to the C:\Projects folder.

2. Using Disk Management, right-click in the unallocated space of a disk. In our example, we're using Disk 3 (the fourth hard drive). Select **New Simple Volume** from the shortcut menu. The New Simple Volume Wizard launches. Using the wizard, specify the amount of unallocated space you want to devote to the volume. Our example uses 20 GB, although the resulting size of the C:\Projects folder will only show about 19 GB because of overhead.

3. As you follow the wizard, the box shown on the left side of Figure 4-18 appears. Select **Mount in the following empty NTFS folder**, and then click **Browse**. In the Browse for Drive Path box that appears (see the right side of Figure 4-18), you can drill down to an existing folder or click **New Folder** to create a new folder on drive C:.

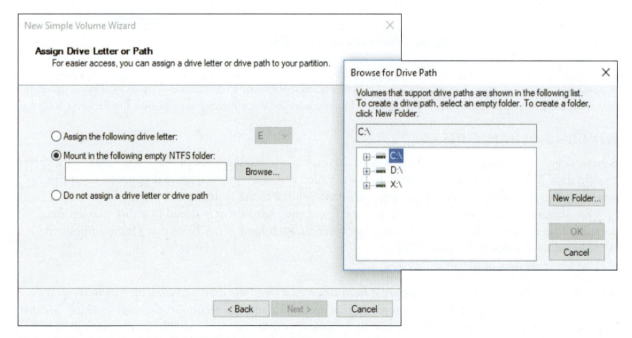

Figure 4-18 Select the folder that will be the mount point for the new volume

4. Complete the wizard by selecting a file system for the new volume; you can also name the volume. The volume is created and formatted.

5. To verify that the drive is mounted, open Explorer and then open the Properties box for the folder. In our example, the Properties box for the C:\Projects folder is shown in the middle of Figure 4-19. Notice the Properties box reports the folder type as a Mounted Volume. When you click **Properties** in the Properties box, the volume Properties box appears (see the right side of Figure 4-19). In this box, you can see the size of the mounted volume minus overhead.

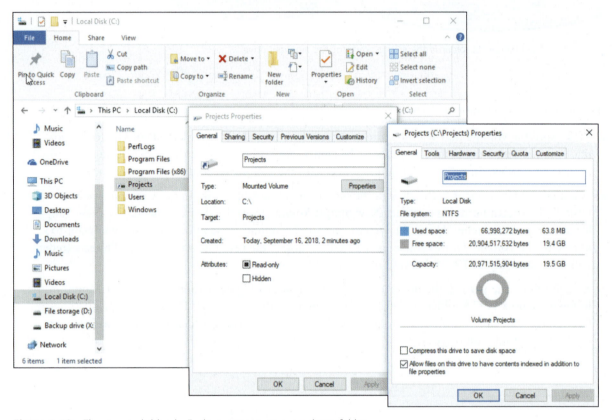

Figure 4-19 The mounted drive in Explorer appears as a very large folder

You can think of a mount point, such as C:\Projects, as a shortcut to a volume on a second hard drive. If you look closely at the left window in Figure 4-19, you can see the shortcut icon beside the Projects folder.

WINDOWS DYNAMIC DISKS

A basic disk works independently of other hard drives, but a dynamic disk can work with other hard drives to hold data. Volumes stored on dynamic disks are called dynamic volumes. Several dynamic disks can work together to collectively present a single dynamic volume to the system.

When dynamic disks work together, data to configure each hard drive is stored in a disk management database that resides in the last 1 MB of storage space on each hard drive. Note that Home editions of Windows do not support dynamic disks.

Here are three uses of dynamic disks:

▲ *For better reliability, you can configure a hard drive as a dynamic disk and allocate the space as a simple volume.* This is the best reason to use dynamic disks and is a recommended best practice. Because of the way a dynamic disk works, the simple volume is considered more reliable than when it is stored on a basic disk. A volume that is stored on only one hard drive is called a simple volume.

▲ *You can implement dynamic disks on multiple hard drives to extend a volume across these drives (called spanning).* This volume is called a spanned volume.

▲ *Dynamic disks can be used to piece data across multiple hard drives to improve performance and/or provide fault tolerance (protecting data against loss).* The technology to configure two or more hard drives to work together as an array of drives is called RAID (redundant array of inexpensive disks or redundant array of independent disks).

　▲ Joining hard drives together to improve performance is called striping or RAID 0. The volume is called a striped volume (see Figure 4-20). RAID 0 can improve performance because the work is shared between two hard drives. However, RAID 0 does not provide fault tolerance (if one drive fails, the data is lost).

　▲ Copying one hard drive to another as a backup is called mirroring or RAID 1. The volume is called a mirrored volume. RAID 1 improves fault tolerance because if one drive fails, you have another copy of the data. RAID 1 can reduce performance because the drives operate at the speed of the slowest drive.

When RAID is implemented in this way using Disk Management, it is called software RAID. A more reliable way of configuring RAID is to use BIOS/UEFI setup on a motherboard that supports RAID, which is called hardware RAID.

Figure 4-20 A simple volume is stored on a single disk, but a striped volume or a mirrored volume is stored on an array of dynamic disks

> ★ **A+ Exam Tip** The A+ Core 2 exam expects you to select which RAID type is appropriate to use in a given scenario.

　You can use Disk Management to convert two or more basic disks to dynamic disks. Then you can use unallocated space on these disks to create a simple volume or a Windows array of disks using a spanned, striped, or mirrored volume. To convert a basic disk to dynamic, right-click the Disk area and select **Convert to Dynamic Disk** from the shortcut menu (see Figure 4-21). Then right-click free space on the disk and select **New Simple Volume**, **New Spanned Volume**, **New Striped Volume**, or **New Mirrored Volume** from the shortcut menu. If you were to select spanning or striping in Figure 4-21, you could make Disk 1 and Disk 2 dynamic disks that hold a single volume. The size of the volume would be the sum of the space on both hard drives. If you were instead using mirroring in Figure 4-21, you could make Disk 2 mirror the volume on Disk 1 as a backup copy. The size of the volume would be the space both hard drives have in common—which means it would be the size of the smaller of the two disks.

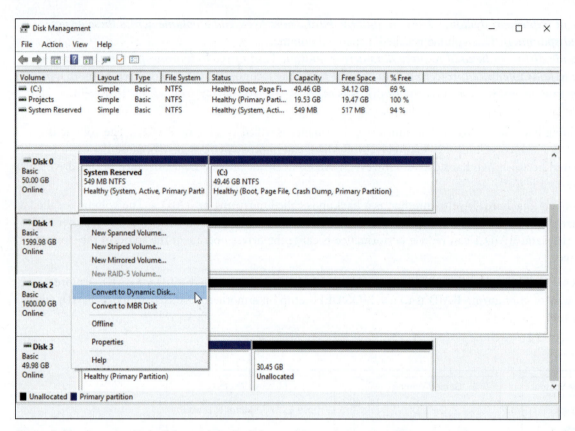

Figure 4-21   Convert a basic disk to a dynamic disk

> 📝 **Notes**   When Windows implements RAID, know that you cannot install an OS on a spanned or striped volume that uses software RAID. You can, however, install Windows on a hardware RAID drive.
>
> Also, after you have converted a basic disk to a dynamic disk, you cannot revert it to a basic disk without losing all data on the drive.

Now for some serious cautions about software RAID where you use Windows for spanning, striping, and mirroring: Microsoft warns that when Windows is used for software RAID, the risk of catastrophic failure increases and can lead to data loss. Microsoft suggests you only use Windows spanning, striping, or mirroring when you have no other option. In other words, spanning, striping, and mirroring in Windows aren't very safe. Instead, use a mounted drive or use hardware RAID to expand the size of a volume or to copy a volume to another drive.

WINDOWS STORAGE SPACES

Storage Spaces in Windows 10/8 is a potential replacement for traditional Windows software RAID. With Storage Spaces, you can create a storage pool using any number of internal or external backup drives that use interfaces such as SATA (Serial ATA), SAS (Serial Attached SCSI), or even USB. Then you create one or more virtual drives, called spaces, from this pool, which appear as normal drives in File Explorer. Drives used for Storage Spaces can be formatted with the NTFS or ReFS file system.

Storage Spaces is designed for resiliency, which resists data loss in the event of drive failure. The following storage options offer varying degrees of resiliency in Storage Spaces:

▲ *Simple.* A simple storage space combines multiple physical drives into a single logical drive with no built-in data backup. This option offers no resiliency.

▲ *Two-way mirroring.* A logical drive can be mirrored, which means the data is duplicated across multiple physical drives used to create the space.

▲ *Three-way mirroring*. In three-way mirroring, data is stored in triplicate to provide additional resiliency against data loss, although this feature requires that at least five physical drives be used to create the storage pool.

▲ *Parity*. To provide even greater resiliency, parity spaces maintain multiple copies of data (depending on the configuration) plus parity checking, which is a way to check backed-up data for any loss and re-create compromised data through parity calculations.

A single storage pool can be divided into multiple spaces, and each space can be configured with different resiliency settings. As pool capacity is depleted, more drives can be added to increase the available space without reconfiguring the space. In fact, the space can be configured as if it has more virtual storage than the physical drives actually offer by using a feature called thin provisioning. For example, in Figure 4-22, you can see the total of storage spaces presented to users is 12 TB; however, the physical hard drive capacities add up to only 8 TB. As the space actually used approaches 8 TB, the administrator is prompted to add more physical storage to the pool, which can eventually meet the 12-TB maximum capacity.

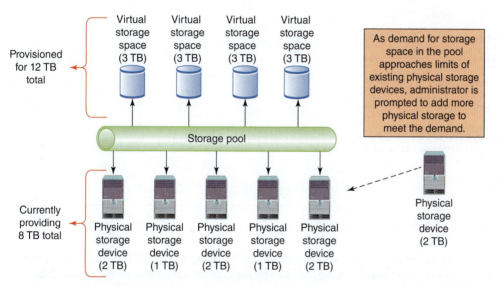

Figure 4-22 Thin provisioning allows for additional physical devices as needed without reconfiguring space available to users

To set up a system to use Storage Spaces, do the following:

1. Attach any drives to the computer that you intend to use for your storage pool. These can include SATA, SAS, or certain USB devices, and they do not have to match in capacity. Make sure the drives are identified as basic disks. All data on the storage drives will be lost during formatting, so be sure to back up anything important first.

2. In Classic view of Control Panel, click **Storage Spaces**. Click **Create a new pool and storage space**. Respond to the UAC box.

3. Any drives that are compatible with Storage Spaces will be listed. Select the drives to format. All data on the selected drives will be lost. Click **Create pool** to prepare the drives.

4. After the drives are ready, use the Create a storage space window (see Figure 4-23) to assign a name and drive letter for the storage space and select a file system. File system options include NTFS; for Windows 10 Pro Workstation, ReFS is an option.

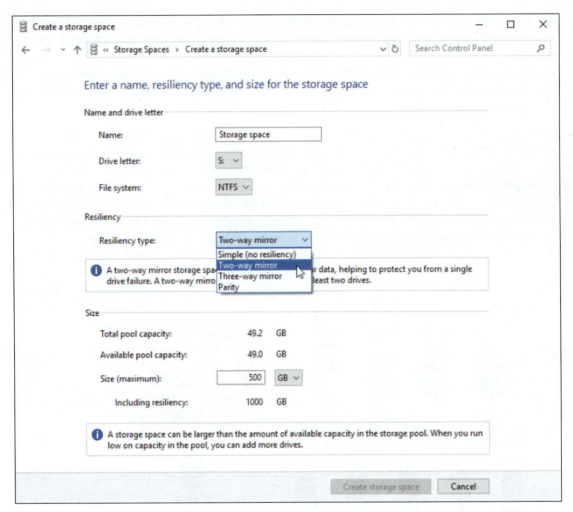

Figure 4-23 Define the resiliency type for the new storage space

5. Select a resiliency type. Options include simple (no resiliency), two-way mirror, three-way mirror, and parity. Then, if you plan to use thin provisioning, adjust the maximum size of the storage pool. Sizes can be set in GB or TB. Notice that you can set a maximum size well beyond the actual sizes of the disks in the pool, and you'll be notified when you need to add more drives to provide that space. Click **Create storage space**. The storage space is created and formatted.

6. After the storage space is created, you can return to the Storage Spaces window to change the name, drive letter, and size of an existing storage space.

USE DISK MANAGEMENT TO TROUBLESHOOT HARD DRIVE PROBLEMS

Notice in Figure 4-21 that the system has four hard drives (Disk 0, Disk 1, Disk 2, and Disk 3), and information about the disks and volumes is shown in the Disk Management window. When you are having a problem with a hard drive, it helps to know what the information in the window means. Here are the disk and volume statuses you might see in this window:

▲ *Healthy*. The healthy volume status shown in Figure 4-21 indicates that the volume is formatted with a file system and that the file system is working without errors.

▲ *Failed*. A failed volume status indicates a problem with the hard drive or that the file system has become corrupted. To try to fix the problem, make sure the hard drive data cable and power cable are secure. Data on a failed volume is likely to be lost. For dynamic disks, if the disk status is Offline, try bringing the disk back online. (Details are covered later in this list.)

▲ *Online*. An online disk status indicates the disk has been sensed by Windows and can be accessed by either reading or writing to the disk.

▲ *Active*. One volume on an MBR system will be marked as Active. This is the volume that startup BIOS/UEFI looks to for an OS boot manager to load.

▲ *EFI System Partition*. In GPT systems, one volume will be marked as the EFI System Partition. BIOS/UEFI looks to this volume to find an OS boot manager to load an OS.

▲ *Unallocated*. Space on the disk is marked as unallocated if it has not yet been partitioned.

▲ *Formatting*. This volume status appears while a volume is being formatted.

▲ *Basic*. When a hard drive is first sensed by Windows, it is assigned the Basic disk status. A basic disk can be partitioned and formatted as a stand-alone hard drive.

▲ *Dynamic*. The following status indicators apply only to dynamic disks:

   ▲ *Offline*. An offline disk status indicates a dynamic disk has become corrupted or is unavailable. The problem can be caused by a corrupted file system, loose drive cables, a failed hard drive, or another hardware problem. If you believe the problem is corrected, right-click the disk and select **Reactivate Disk** from the shortcut menu to bring the disk back online.

   ▲ *Foreign drive*. If you move a hard drive that has been configured as a dynamic disk on one computer to another computer, it will report the disk as a foreign drive. To fix the problem, you need to import the foreign drive. Right-click the disk and select **Import Foreign Disks** from the shortcut menu. You should then be able to see the volumes on the disk.

   ▲ *Healthy (At Risk)*. The dynamic disk can be accessed, but I/O errors have occurred. Try returning the disk to online status. If the volume status does not return to healthy, back up all data and replace the drive.

If you are still having problems with a hard drive, volume, or mounted drive, check Event Viewer for events about the drive that might have been recorded there. These events might help you understand the nature of the problem and what to do about it. How to use Event Viewer is covered in Chapter 5.

IMPROVING HARD DRIVE PERFORMANCE

A+ CORE 2 1.5, 3.1

For best performance, Windows needs at least 15 percent free space on the hard drive that it uses as working space, so it's important to uninstall software you no longer need and delete unneeded files occasionally. Disk Management includes a Disk Cleanup (cleanmgr.exe) utility that deletes temporary files on the drive. In addition, a hard drive can be optimized to improve performance; how that's done depends on the type of hard drive.

Two types of hard drives are magnetic hard disk drives (HDDs), which contain spinning platters, and solid-state drives (SSDs), which contain flash memory. For magnetic hard drives, Windows automatically defragments the drive once a week, and for SSDs, Windows automatically trims the drive weekly. Let's look at what each of these operations accomplishes:

▲ *Magnetic hard drives*. To defragment is to rearrange fragments or parts of files on the drive so each file is stored on the drive in contiguous clusters. Each platter on a magnetic hard drive is divided into tracks, which are divided into sectors (see Figure 4-24). In a file system, a cluster, also called a file allocation unit, is a group of whole sectors. The number of sectors in a cluster is fixed and is determined when the file system is first installed. A file is stored in whole clusters, and the unused space at the end of the last cluster, called slack, is wasted free space. As files are written and deleted from an HDD, clusters are used,

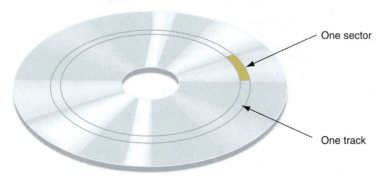

One sector

One track

Figure 4-24 A magnetic hard drive is divided into concentric circles called tracks, and tracks are divided into sectors

released, and used again. New files written on the drive can be put in available clusters spread over the drive. Over time, drive performance is affected when the moving read/write arm of a magnetic drive must move over many areas of the drive to collect all the fragments of a file. Defragmenting a drive rewrites files in contiguous clusters and improves drive performance.

▲ *Solid-state drives*. Defragmenting an SSD can reduce the life of the drive and is not recommended—Windows disables defragmenting for solid-state drives. However, data on an SSD still needs trimming. To trim an SSD is to erase a block on the drive that is filled with unused data. SSDs are organized in blocks, and each block contains many pages. A file can spread over several pages in various blocks. Each time a new page is written to the drive, the entire block to which it belongs must be read into a buffer, erased, and then rewritten with the new page included. When a file is deleted, information about the file is deleted, but the actual data in the file is not erased. This can slow down SSD performance because the unused data must still be read and rewritten in its block. To improve performance, Windows sends the trim command to an SSD drive to erase a block that no longer contains useful data so that a write operation does not have to manage the data.

> **⟨⟩ OS Differences** Windows 7 does not support optimizing an SSD.

APPLYING | CONCEPTS   CLEANING AND OPTIMIZING HARD DRIVES

To delete unneeded files on a drive and verify that the drive is being automatically defragged or trimmed, use the **Disk Cleanup** utility (cleanmgr.exe) and the **Defragment and Optimize Drives** (dfrgui.exe) utility. Do the following when starting the utilities from Explorer:

1. To delete unneeded files, open Explorer, right-click drive **C:**, and click **Properties**. On the General tab of the drive Properties box, click **Disk Cleanup** to calculate how much space can be cleaned up. Select the file types to delete (see Figure 4-25) and click **OK**.

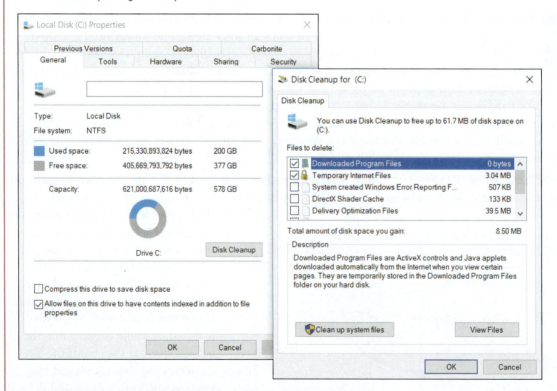

Figure 4-25   Delete unneeded files on a hard drive to free up space

(continues)

> ✏️ **Notes** When Windows installs, it stores the old installation in the Windows.old folder. Windows 10 deletes the folder 28 days after the installation. If you see the Windows.old folder in Windows 8/7 systems, include it in the list to be deleted to free up disk space.

2. To optimize the hard drive, select the **Tools** tab in the drive Properties box and click **Optimize**. The Optimize Drives box appears (see Figure 4-26). This system has two hard drives installed. Drive C: is an SSD and drive F: is a magnetic HDD.

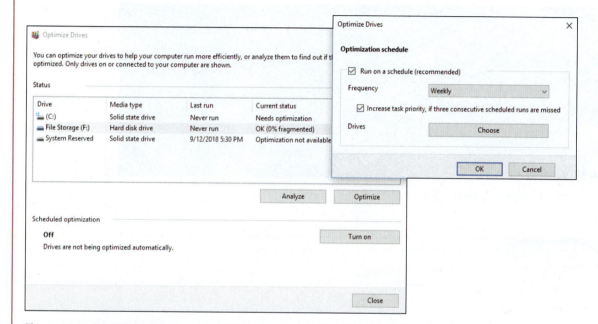

Figure 4-26   Windows is set to automatically defragment a magnetic hard drive once a week

3. Here are tasks you can do:

▲ For a magnetic drive, click **Analyze** for Windows to tell you if a drive needs defragmenting. To defrag the drive, click **Optimize**. The process can take a few minutes to several hours. If errors occur while the drive is defragmenting, check the hard drive for errors and try to defragment again.

▲ For a solid-state drive, click **Optimize** to trim the SSD.

▲ Near the bottom of Figure 4-26, you can see optimization is turned off. To turn it on, click **Turn on**. In the box that appears (see the right side of the figure), check **Run on a schedule (recommended)** and select **Weekly** for the Frequency. Click **OK**.

Throughout this chapter, you've learned a lot about Windows maintenance tasks, backup procedures, and how to manage hard drives. The next part of this chapter discusses ways to perform many related tasks from a command-line interface.

USING A COMMAND-LINE INTERFACE (CLI)

**A+
CORE 2
1.3, 1.4**

IT support technicians find it is much faster to manipulate files and folders and perform other tasks by using commands in a command prompt window than by using Explorer and other graphical tools. In some troubleshooting situations, you have no other option but to use a command prompt window.

Windows has two levels of command prompt windows: a standard window and an elevated window. In a standard window, the default directory is the currently signed-in user's folder and commands have the same permissions as that user. Commands issued in an elevated command prompt window have administrative privileges and the default directory is C:\Windows\System32.

To open a standard command prompt window (see Figure 4-27), enter **command** or **cmd** in the Windows 10/7 search box or the Windows 8 Run box, and then click **Command Prompt**.

Figure 4-27 A command prompt window

> **⟨⟩ OS Differences** For Windows 8, Command Prompt is listed in the Quick Launch menu. Press **Win+X** and click **Command Prompt**.

To open an elevated command prompt window, type **cmd** or **command** in the Windows 10/7 search box or the Windows 8 Run box, right-click **Command Prompt**, and click **Run as administrator**. Then respond to the UAC box. The Administrator: Command Prompt window is shown in Figure 4-28. Notice the word *Administrator* in the title bar, which indicates the elevated window, and the default directory, which is the C:\WINDOWS\system32 folder.

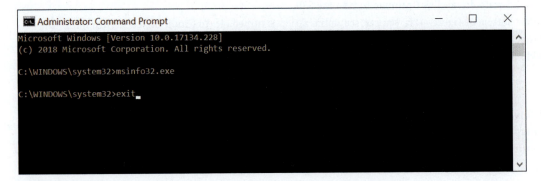

Figure 4-28 An elevated command prompt window has administrative privileges

> **⟨⟩ OS Differences** To get an elevated command prompt window in Windows 8, press **Win+X**, click **Command Prompt (Admin)**, and respond to the UAC box. In Windows 7, click **Start**, **All Programs**, **Accessories**, and right-click **Command Prompt**. Then select **Run as administrator** from the shortcut window and respond to the UAC box.

Here are some tips for working in a command prompt window:

⊿ Type **cls** and press **Enter** to clear the window.

⊿ To retrieve the last command you entered, press the up arrow. To retrieve the last command line one character at a time, press the right arrow.

⊿ To terminate a command before it is finished, press **Ctrl+C**, **Ctrl+Break**, or **Ctrl+Pause**.

⊿ To access settings for the command prompt window, right-click the title bar and click **Properties**. You can change the background color, font, font color, and font size so you can better read the text in the window, adjust opacity so you can see what's behind the window as you work, and access Ctrl key shortcuts.

⊿ To close the window, type **exit** (see Figure 4-28) and press **Enter**.

> ✎ **Notes** Many of the commands you learn about in this section can also be used in the Windows Recovery Environment (Windows RE), which can be loaded from within Windows during troubleshooting. When Windows refuses to start, you can load Windows RE from Windows setup media or a USB or DVD recovery drive. How to use the Recovery Environment is covered in Chapters 5 and 6.

COMMANDS TO MANAGE FILES AND FOLDERS

If the command you are using applies to files or folders, the path to these files or folders is assumed to be the default drive and directory. The default drive and directory, also called the current drive and directory, shows in the command prompt. For example, in Figure 4-27, the default drive is C: and the default path is C:\Users\Jill West. If you use a different path in the command line, the path you use overrides the default path. Also know that Windows makes no distinction between uppercase and lowercase in command lines (however, Linux does).

Now let's look at the file-naming conventions you will need to follow when creating files, wildcard characters you can use in command lines, and several commands useful for managing files and folders.

FILE-NAMING CONVENTIONS

When using the command prompt window to create a file, keep in mind that file name and file extension characters can be the letters *a* through *z*, the numbers *0* through *9*, and the following characters:

_ ^ $ ~ ! # % & – { } ( ) @ ' `

In a command prompt window, if a path or file name has spaces in it, it is sometimes necessary to enclose the path or file name in double quotation marks.

WILDCARD CHARACTERS IN COMMAND LINES

As you work at the command prompt, you can use wildcard characters in a file name to apply the command to a group of files or to abbreviate a file name if you do not know the entire name. The question mark (?) is a wildcard for one character, and the asterisk (*) is a wildcard for one or more characters. For example, if you want to find all file names in a directory that start with *A* and have a three-letter file extension, you would use the following command:

```
dir a*.???
```

> ★ **A+ Exam Tip** The A+ Core 2 exam expects you to know how to use the dir, cd, copy, xcopy, robocopy, chkdsk, format, /?, and shutdown commands, which are all covered in this chapter. Other commands also required for the A+ Core 2 exam are covered in other chapters.

> ✎ **Notes** Many commands can use parameters in the command line to affect how the command will work. Parameters (also called options, arguments, or switches) often begin with a slash or a hyphen followed by a single character. In this chapter, you learn about the basic parameters used by a command for the most common tasks. For a full listing of the parameters available for a command, use the help command. Another way to learn about commands is to follow this link on the Microsoft website: *docs.microsoft.com/en-us/windows-server/administration/windows-commands/windows-commands*.

HELP OR *<COMMAND NAME>* /?

Use the help command to get help about any command. You can enter help followed by the command name or enter the command name followed by /?. Table 4-2 lists some sample applications of this command.

Command	Result
help xcopy xcopy /?	**Gets help information about the xcopy command**
help	**Lists all commands**
help xcopy | more	**Lists information about the xcopy command one screen at a time; press Space to see the next screen, or Enter to advance one line at a time**

Table 4-2   Sample help commands

> ✎ **Notes** Windows commands are not case sensitive. You can type help, Help, or HELP and you'll get the same result.

> ★ **A+ Exam Tip** The A+ Core 2 exam does not give you access to /? or the help command and expects you to know how to structure each command and its parameters covered in this and other chapters.

DIR [*<FILENAME>*] [/P] [/S] [/W]

Use the dir command to list files and directories. In Microsoft documentation about a command (also called the command syntax), the brackets [ ] in a command line indicate the parameter is optional. In addition, the parameter included in < >, such as *<filename>*, indicates that you can substitute any file name in the command. This file name can include a path or file extension. Table 4-3 lists some examples of the dir command.

Command	Result
dir /p	**Lists one screen at a time**
dir /w	**Presents information using wide format, where details are omitted and files and folders are listed in columns on the screen**
dir *.txt	**Lists all files with a .txt file extension in the default path**
dir d:\data*.txt	**Lists all files with a .txt file extension in the D:\data\ folder**
dir myfile.txt	**Checks that a single file, such as myfile.txt, is present**
dir /s	**Includes subdirectory entries**

Table 4-3   Sample dir commands

CD [<DRIVE>:\[<PATH>]] OR CD..

The cd (change directory) command changes the current default directory. You enter cd followed by the drive (a volume letter, such as C:) and the entire path that you want to be current, like so:

```
C:\> cd C:\game\chess
```

The command prompt now looks like this:

```
C:\game\chess>
```

To move up from a child directory to its parent directory, use the .. (dot, dot) variation of the command:

```
C:\game\chess> cd..
```

The command prompt now looks like this:

```
C:\game>
```

Remember that .. (dot, dot) always indicates the parent directory. You can move from a parent directory to one of its child directories simply by stating the name of the child directory:

```
C:\game> cd chess
```

The command prompt now looks like this:

```
C:\game\chess>
```

Remember not to put a backslash in front of the child directory name; doing so tells the OS to go to a directory named chess that is directly under the root directory.

> **Notes** Two commands closely related to cd are md (make directory), which creates a subdirectory under a directory, and rd (remove directory), which removes an empty directory.

COPY [/V] [/Y] <SOURCE> [<DESTINATION>]

The copy command copies a single file or group of files. The original files are not altered. To copy a file from one drive to another, use a command similar to this one:

```
E:\> copy C:\Data\Myfile.txt E:\mydata\Newfile.txt
```

The drive, path, and file name of the source file follow the copy command. The drive, path, and file name of the destination file follow the source file name. If you don't specify the file name of the destination file, the OS assigns the file's original name to this copy. If you omit the drive or path of the source or the destination, then the OS uses the current default drive and path.

To copy the file myfile.txt from the root directory of drive C: to drive E:, use the following command:

```
C:\> copy myfile.txt E:
```

Because the command does not include a drive or path before the file name myfile.txt, the OS assumes that the file is in the default drive and path. Also, because there is no destination file name specified, the file written to drive E: will be named myfile.txt.

To copy all files in the C:\Docs directory to the USB flash drive designated drive E:, use the following command:

```
C:\> copy c:\docs\*.* E:
```

To make a backup file named system.bak of the SYSTEM registry hive file in the \Windows\System32\config directory of the hard drive, use the following command:

```
C:\Windows\system32\config> copy system system.bak
```

If you use the copy command to duplicate multiple files, the files are assigned the names of the original files. When you duplicate multiple files, the destination portion of the command line cannot include a file name.

Here are two parameters that are useful with the copy command:

▲ */v.* When the /v switch is used, the size of each new file is compared with the size of the original file. This slows down the copying but verifies that the copy is done without errors.

▲ */y.* When the /y switch is used, a confirmation message does not ask you to confirm before overwriting a file.

> **✎ Notes**   When trying to recover a corrupted file, you can sometimes use the copy command to copy the file to new media, such as from the hard drive to a USB drive. If the copy command reports a bad or missing sector during the copying process, choose the option to ignore that sector. The copying process then continues to the next sector. The corrupted sector will be lost, but others can likely be recovered. The recover command can be used to accomplish the same thing.

XCOPY *<SOURCE>* [*<DESTINATION>*] [/S] [/E] [/C] [/Y] [/D:[*DATE*]]

The xcopy command is more powerful than the copy command. It follows the same general command-source-destination format as the copy command, but it offers several more options. Table 4-4 shows some of these options.

Command	Result
xcopy C:\docs*.* E: /s	Uses the /s parameter to include subdirectories in the copy; this command copies all files in the directory C:\docs, as well as all subdirectories under \ docs and their files, to drive E:, unless the subdirectory is empty
xcopy C:\docs*.* E: /e	Works the same as /s but empty subdirectories are included in the copy
xcopy C:\docs*.* E: /d: 03-14-19	Uses the /d switch to examine the date; this command copies all files from the directory C:\docs created or modified on or after March 14, 2019
xcopy C:\docs*.* E: /y	Uses the /y switch to overwrite existing files without prompting
xcopy C:\docs*.* E: /c	Uses the /c switch to keep copying even when an error occurs

Table 4-4   Sample xcopy commands

ROBOCOPY *<SOURCE>* *<DESTINATION>* [/S] [/E] [/LOG:*<LOGFILE>*] [/LOG+:*<LOGFILE>*] [/MOVE] [/PURGE]

The robocopy (robust file copy) command is similar to the xcopy command. It offers more options than xcopy and is intended to replace xcopy. A few options for robocopy are listed in Table 4-5.

Command	Result
robocopy C:\docs*.* E: /s	Uses the /s switch to include subdirectories in the copy but does not include empty directories
robocopy C:\docs*.* E: /e	Uses the /e switch to include subdirectories, even the empty ones
robocopy C:\docs*.* E: /log:Mylog.txt	Records activity to a log file and overwrites the current log file
robocopy C:\docs*.* E: /log+:Mylog.txt	Appends a record of all activity to an existing log file
robocopy C:\docs*.* E: /move	Moves files and directories, deleting them from the source
robocopy C:\docs*.* E: /purge	Deletes files and directories at the destination that no longer exist at the source

Table 4-5   Sample robocopy commands

COMMANDS TO MANAGE HARD DRIVES

Several commands can be used to manage hard drives either when setting up a new hard drive, refreshing a hard drive, or during troubleshooting. Sometimes these commands are easier than digging through menus for a needed utility. If you're restricted to the Windows Recovery Environment during troubleshooting, these commands might be your only means of accessing some of these tools.

CHKDSK [<VOLUME>:] [/F] [/R]

The chkdsk (check disk) command fixes file system errors and recovers data from bad sectors. Recall that a file is stored on the hard drive as a group of clusters. The FAT32 and exFAT file systems use a FAT (file allocation table) to keep a record of each cluster that belongs to a file. In Figure 4-29, you can see that each cell in the FAT represents one cluster and contains a pointer to the next cluster in a file. The NTFS file system uses a database called the master file table (MFT) to hold similar information.

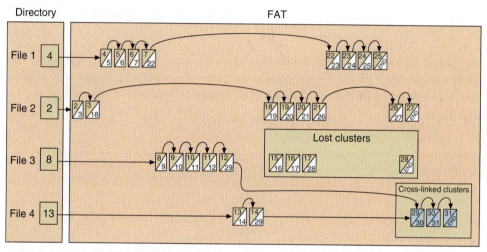

Figure 4-29 Lost and cross-linked clusters

> ✎ **Notes** For an interesting discussion of how the FAT works, see the document FAT Details.pdf on the companion website for this text at *cengage.com*. See the Preface for more information.

Used with the /f parameter, chkdsk searches for and fixes two types of file system errors made by the FAT or MFT:

▲ *Lost clusters (also called lost allocation units).* Lost clusters are clusters that are marked as used in the FAT or MFT, but they do not belong to any file. In effect, the data in these clusters is lost.

▲ *Cross-linked clusters.* Cross-linked clusters are marked in the FAT or MFT as belonging to more than one file.

Used with the /r parameter, chkdsk checks for lost clusters, cross-linked clusters, and bad sectors on the drive. The FAT and MFT keep a table of bad sectors that they normally do not use. However, over time, a sector might become unreliable. If chkdsk determines that a sector is unreliable, it attempts to recover the data from the sector and marks the sector as bad so that the FAT or MFT will not use it again.

Used without any parameters, the chkdsk command only reports information about a drive and does not make any repairs.

An elevated command prompt is required to use the chkdsk command. In the following sample commands, the command prompt is not shown because the default drive and directory are not important. To check the hard drive for file system errors and repair them, use this command:

```
chkdsk C:/f
```

To redirect a report of the findings of the chkdsk command to a file that you can later print, use this command:

```
chkdsk C:>Myfile.txt
```

Use the /r parameter of the chkdsk command to fix file system errors and examine each sector of the drive for bad sectors, like so:

```
chkdsk C:/r
```

If chkdsk finds data that it can recover, it asks you for permission to do so. If you give permission, it saves the recovered data in files that it stores in the root directory of the drive.

> **✎ Notes** Use either the /f or /r parameter with chkdsk, but not both. Using both parameters is redundant. For the most thorough check of a drive, use /r.

The chkdsk command will not fix anything unless the drive is locked, which means the drive has no open files. If you attempt to use chkdsk with the /f or /r parameter when files are open, chkdsk tells you of the problem and asks permission to schedule the run the next time Windows is restarted. Know that the process will take plenty of time.

> **✎ Notes** The chkdsk command is also available from the Windows Recovery Environment.

DEFRAG [<VOLUME>:] [/C]

The Disk Defragmenter defrag command examines a magnetic hard drive for fragmented files and rewrites these files to the drive in contiguous clusters. Use this command to optimize a magnetic hard drive's performance. Table 4-6 shows two examples of the command. Recall that it's not a good idea to defrag solid-state storage devices such as an SSD, flash drive, or smart card. Doing so can shorten the life of the drive.

Command	Result
defrag C:	**Defrags volume C:**
defrag /C	**Defrags all volumes on the computer, including volume C:**

Table 4-6   Sample defrag commands

The defrag command requires an elevated command prompt window in Windows. It is not available under the Windows Recovery Environment.

FORMAT <VOLUME:>[/Q] [FS:<FILESYSTEM>]

You can format a hard drive or other storage device using Disk Management. In addition, you can use the format command from a command prompt window and from the Windows Recovery Environment. This high-level format installs a file system on the device and *erases all data on the volume*. Table 4-7 lists various sample uses of the format command.

Command	Result
`format D:`	**Performs a full format of volume D: using the default file system for the volume type**
`format D: /q`	**Performs a quick format of volume D: by re-creating an empty root directory; use it to quickly format a previously formatted disk that is in good condition; /q does not read or write to any other part of the disk**
`format D: /fs:NTFS`	**Formats volume D: using the NTFS file system**
`format D: /fs:FAT32`	**Formats volume D: using the FAT32 file system**
`format D: /fs:EXFAT`	**Formats volume D: using the extended FAT file system**

Table 4-7   Sample format commands

SHUTDOWN [/I] [/R] [/S] [/M \\<COMPUTERNAME>] [/T XX]

Use the shutdown command to shut down the local computer or a remote computer. You must be signed in with an administrator account to use this command. By default, the command gives users a 30-second warning before shutdown. To shut down a remote computer on the network, you must have an administrator account on that computer and be signed on the local computer with that same account and password. Table 4-8 lists some shutdown commands.

Command	Result
`shutdown /r`	**Restarts the local computer**
`shutdown /s /m \\bluelight`	**Shuts down the remote computer named \\bluelight**
`shutdown /s /m \\bluelight /t 60`	**Shuts down the \\bluelight computer after a 60-second delay**
`shutdown /i`	**Displays the Remote Shutdown dialog box so you can choose computers on the network to shut down**

Table 4-8   Sample shutdown commands

WINDOWS 10 POWERSHELL AND UBUNTU BASH INTERFACES

**A+
CORE 2
1.3, 1.4,
4.8**

As you become more comfortable with command-line interfaces, you'll find they can be more flexible and convenient than a graphical interface, especially for commands you use frequently. Microsoft continues to make significant improvements to command-line options in Windows, including increased emphasis on PowerShell and the addition of a Linux shell. The three command-line interfaces (CLI) offered by Windows 10 are the Command Prompt, PowerShell, and Linux shell interfaces. First, let's explore PowerShell cmdlets, and then we'll see how the Linux shell works in Windows 10.

POWERSHELL

Windows PowerShell is designed to replace the command prompt utility for providing a command-line interface. Windows PowerShell processes objects called cmdlets (pronounced "command-lets") that essentially run prebuilt programs, similar to batch files. Windows PowerShell contains thousands of cmdlets so that users don't have to build their own. Technicians or programmers who program their own cmdlets can build customized objects using existing cmdlets as building blocks.

PowerShell skills are becoming increasingly important for all IT technicians. In this part of the chapter, we look at some basic PowerShell cmdlets as a starting point to help you warm up to PowerShell.

POWERSHELL CMDLET SYNTAX

Native PowerShell cmdlet syntax almost always starts with a verb followed by a noun and connected with a hyphen, as in *verb-noun*. For example, consider the cmdlet Get-ChildItem. The *Get* verb defines the action and the *ChildItem* noun defines the object of that action. "Get" simply means to retrieve something; an item is a file or folder, and "ChildItem" is any item within another item. So, the cmdlet Get-ChildItem retrieves items in one or more specified locations, similar to how dir works at the command prompt.

Some cmdlets have parameters, such as the -Depth parameter in the Get-ChildItem cmdlet. This parameter allows you to specify how many layers to search in the targeted location to retrieve child items. To use this parameter, you must also use the -Recurse parameter, which instructs PowerShell to retrieve items within child items (such as files within folders) at the targeted location. For example, Get-ChildItem -Recurse -Depth 2 delivers a list of items in the current folder, that folder's child folders, and folders within those child folders, but the list goes no deeper than two child layers of folders. In a project at the end of this chapter, you get some practice using the Get-ChildItem cmdlet with parameters.

Set, Copy, and Remove are other verb options for cmdlets. Other noun options include Help, Location, Content, Process, and Service. With this information, you can deduce the names of several helpful cmdlets, as shown in Table 4-9.

Cmdlet	Description
Get-Item	Retrieves files and folders
Get-Process	Retrieves the processes running on a computer
Set-Location	Changes the current working location to a specified location
Copy-Item	Copies an item to a specified location
Remove-Item	Deletes an item
Get-Verb	Shows a list of all cmdlet verbs
Get-Verb *-Location	Shows a list of all cmdlet verbs available for a specific noun, where the asterisk is a wildcard in place of any verb attached to the noun *Location*
Get-Command	Shows a list of all available cmdlets

Table 4-9   Common PowerShell cmdlets

> ✎ **Notes**   PowerShell cmdlets are not case sensitive. You can type Get-Item or get-item and you'll get the same result.

APPLYING | CONCEPTS   USING POWERSHELL

Let's learn to use PowerShell by looking at an example of how helpful and powerful it can be. Even a clean copy of Windows comes with several apps that you might not want and that cannot be removed through the Apps & features window or the Programs and Features window. For example, you might not want Xbox installed on a computer you use for work. You can use PowerShell to uninstall unwanted apps.

Complete the following steps to install an app from the Windows Store and then remove it using PowerShell:

1. Open the **Windows Store** and find a simple app to install, such as Dropbox. Click **Get** to download and install the app. Close the Windows Store.

2. Open the **Settings** app and click **Apps**.

3. Scroll down to the app you just installed. In most cases, you can use this window to remove the app, but some apps can't be uninstalled from here. For example, as shown in Figure 4-30, the Uninstall button is grayed out for the Maps app.

(continues)

4

Figure 4-30 Some apps cannot be uninstalled through the Apps & features window

4. Let's use PowerShell to uninstall an app. PowerShell offers a standard PowerShell window and an elevated PowerShell window. Use one of these methods to open an elevated PowerShell window:

   ◢ For Windows 10, press **Win+X** and click **Windows PowerShell (Admin)**.
   ◢ For Windows 8, open the Start screen and type **powershell**. Right-click **Windows PowerShell** and click **Run as administrator**.
   ◢ For Windows 7, click **Start**, **All Programs**, **Accessories**, and **Windows PowerShell**. In the folder, right-click **Windows PowerShell** and click **Run as administrator**.

5. If needed, click **Yes** in the UAC dialog box.

6. Enter **Get-AppxPackage** to see a list of all apps installed for the current user. Wade through and find the entry for the app you just installed. (It's most likely at the bottom of the list because you just installed it.) For example, Figure 4-31 shows Dropbox installed on the system.

```
Administrator: Windows PowerShell                                    —   □   ×

Name               : C27EB4BA.Dropbox
Publisher          : CN=852D08DC-3DFB-4331-AD77-990D03FE9E36
Architecture       : X64
ResourceId         :
Version            : 4.5.3.0
PackageFullName    : C27EB4BA.Dropbox_4.5.3.0_x64__xbfy0k16fey96
InstallLocation    : C:\Program Files\WindowsApps\C27EB4BA.Dropbox_4.5.3.0_x64__xbfy0k16fey96
IsFramework        : False
PackageFamilyName  : C27EB4BA.Dropbox_xbfy0k16fey96
PublisherId        : xbfy0k16fey96
IsResourcePackage  : False
IsBundle           : False
IsDevelopmentMode  : False
Dependencies       : {Microsoft.VCLibs.140.00_14.0.24123.0_x64__8wekyb3d8bbwe,
                     Microsoft.NET.Native.Framework.1.3_1.3.24201.0_x64__8wekyb3d8bbwe,
                     Microsoft.NET.Native.Runtime.1.4_1.4.24201.0_x64__8wekyb3d8bbwe,
                     C27EB4BA.Dropbox_4.5.3.0_neutral_split.scale-150_xbfy0k16fey96}


PS C:\WINDOWS\system32>
```

Figure 4-31 Find the app you just installed

7. Select and copy the text for the PackageFullName field of the app to be removed. Enter the command **Remove-AppxPackage** <*PackageFullName*>, as shown in Figure 4-32.

(continues)

Figure 4-32 The text for the PackageFullName field must be typed exactly; therefore, it's easiest to copy and paste

8. Enter the command **Get-AppxPackage** to confirm the app was removed. Also check the Settings app to make sure the app is no longer listed there.

9. Enter **exit** to close the PowerShell session.

> **Notes** By default, Windows 10 lists Windows PowerShell in the Quick Launch menu. You can change this setting so Command Prompt is listed. Open the **Settings** app, click **Personalization,** and click **Taskbar**. Scroll down and turn the slider button to **Off** under *Replace Command Prompt with Windows PowerShell in the menu when I right-click the start button or press Windows key+X.*

Here are some other basic cmdlet features you should know:

▲ *Aliases for command prompt commands.* An alias is a nickname or shortcut for a cmdlet. For convenience, many of the commands you're accustomed to using in a command prompt window also work in PowerShell. These commands are defined as aliases for native PowerShell cmdlets. For example, one default alias for Get-ChildItem is dir. Therefore, you can enter dir in PowerShell to execute the Get-ChildItem cmdlet. Note that an alias applies only to the referenced command and does not include parameters or values (such as a file name) that might be used by the command.

> **Notes** You can create your own aliases using the Set-Alias and New-Alias cmdlets. For example, **Set-Alias show Get-ChildItem** assigns the alias *show* to the cmdlet *Get-ChildItem.*

▲ *List of aliases.* The cmdlet **Get-Alias** shows all the available aliases in the current session, including the default aliases and other aliases you created during the session.
▲ *Help.* To find the cmdlet assigned to a specific alias, use the Help cmdlet (also called Get-Help). For example, enter **help dir** to see the output shown in Figure 4-33. Here you can see that dir is an alias for Get-ChildItem.

> **Notes** At the bottom of Figure 4-33, a message informs the user that the Help files for the cmdlet are not available on the computer. You must install the PowerShell help files to access them; open an elevated PowerShell window, type **Update-Help**, and press **Enter**. The process will take a few minutes. When you return to the PowerShell prompt, enter **help dir** again to see how much additional information you can access.

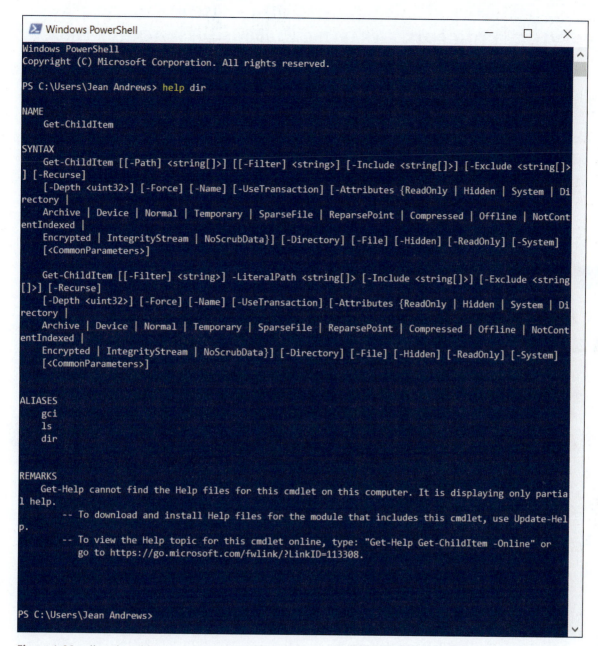

Figure 4-33 dir, gci, and ls are all aliases for Get-ChildItem

UBUNTU BASH ON WINDOWS

In response to customer feedback, Microsoft built a Linux shell into Windows 10 that provides a shell prompt to enter Linux commands. Note that this shell is not a VM, and it's not a fully separate operating system; rather, it's a shell that allows users to interact with underlying Windows functions and system files. The new shell requires a Windows component, **Windows Subsystem for Linux (WSL)**, to support it. WSL installs a subset of the Ubuntu distribution of Linux, which is one of the most popular distributions. By default, Ubuntu provides Bash, which is its most popular shell. This shell is called **Bash on Ubuntu on Windows**, Bash on Windows, or Ubuntu Bash. (It's possible to install other Ubuntu shells by using switcher software in PowerShell.) Many Linux commands work in WSL running Ubuntu Bash.

WSL runs on any 64-bit Windows 10 system with the Anniversary Update build 14393 or later. You must first turn on Developer Mode and then enable the Windows Subsystem for Linux (Beta) feature. As its name suggests, this feature is still in beta as Microsoft continues to resolve many bugs and gaps in compatibility.

APPLYING | CONCEPTS   ENABLING WINDOWS SUBSYSTEM FOR LINUX (WSL) AND INSTALLING UBUNTU BASH

Complete the following steps to enable Windows Subsystem for Linux and install Ubuntu Bash on a Windows 10 system:

1. First, turn on Developer Mode.
   a. Open the **Settings** app and click **Update & Security**. In the left pane, scroll down and click **For developers**.
   b. Select **Developer mode**, as shown in Figure 4-34. Click **Yes** to turn on Developer Mode and close the Settings app.

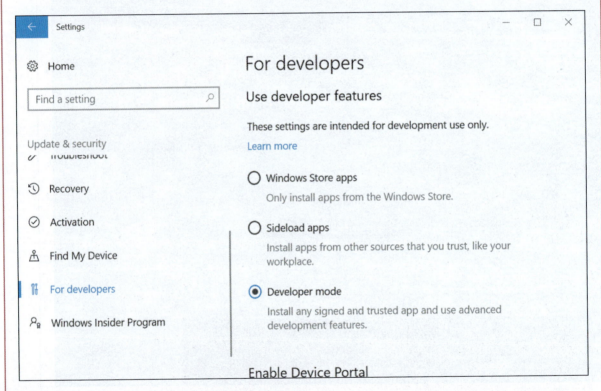

Figure 4-34   Turn on Developer Mode from the Settings app

2. Enable Windows Subsystem for Linux.
   a. Open **Control Panel** and click **Programs and Features**. In the left pane, click **Turn Windows features on or off**.
   b. Scroll down and click **Windows Subsystem for Linux (Beta)**, as shown in Figure 4-35. Click **OK**.

(continues)

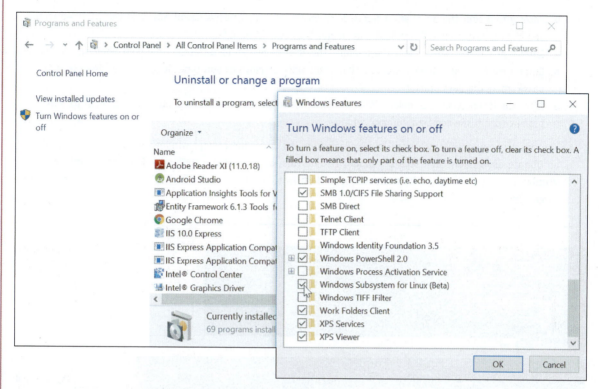

Figure 4-35 Turn on the Windows Subsystem for Linux (Beta) feature

    c. Restart the computer when the changes are complete to finish enabling Windows Subsystem for Linux.

3. Install and run Bash on Ubuntu on Windows from the command prompt.

    a. Open a command prompt window and enter **bash** (see Figure 4-36). Note that the first time you enter the bash command, Windows downloads and installs Ubuntu on Windows.

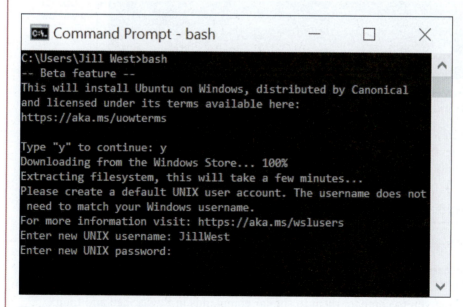

Figure 4-36 The first time you enter the bash command, Windows will download and install Ubuntu on Windows

(continues)

   b. Enter **y** to accept the installation terms. Bash on Ubuntu on Windows downloads from the Windows Store, and then is extracted and installed. This might take several minutes.

   c. Enter a new UNIX user name at the prompt. This user name can be different from your Windows user name.

   d. Enter a password at the next prompt. The cursor will not move as you type the password. Re-enter the password at the next prompt.

   e. After the installation is complete, Windows switches to the Bash on Ubuntu environment with its shell prompt within the command prompt window.

4. You can continue to interact with Ubuntu Bash from the command prompt window, or you can open Bash on Ubuntu on Windows in a separate window. To do this, click **Start** and then click **Bash on Ubuntu on Windows** in the Start menu. You can also open Bash from within PowerShell. See Figure 4-37 to compare the three windows.

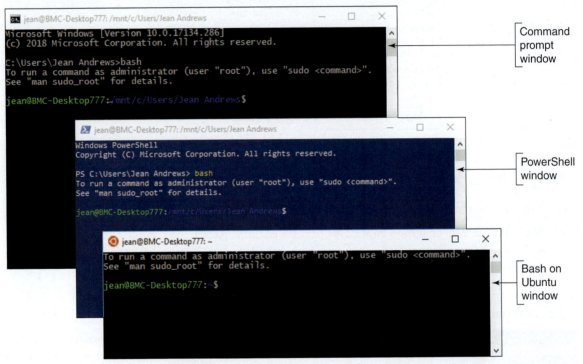

Figure 4-37   Bash on Ubuntu can be accessed from the command prompt, PowerShell, or its own app, Bash on Ubuntu on Windows

At this point, most commonly used Linux commands will work as usual at the Ubuntu shell prompt. The commands interact with the underlying Windows system files, and changes to those files can be monitored through other Windows tools. You'll learn more about Linux commands in Chapter 10.

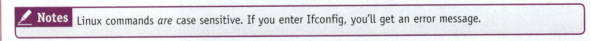

> 🖉 **Notes**   Linux commands *are* case sensitive. If you enter Ifconfig, you'll get an error message.

It might seem like you're learning three different languages when you try switching among Command Prompt, PowerShell, and Linux. Table 4-10 provides a quick look at some of the most familiar commands in Command Prompt, allowing you to compare them to similar commands in PowerShell and Linux. Keep in mind that each command will function differently in its respective environment and will also offer various options and limitations. What's really interesting is to explore the extent of these differences and learn how a command in one environment might offer options that another environment does not. What other commands would you add to this list?

Command Prompt	PowerShell	Ubuntu Bash
dir	Get-ChildItem	ls
ipconfig	Get-NetIPConfiguration Get-NetIPAddress	ifconfig iwconfig
ping	Test-NetConnection	ping
cd	Set-Location	cd
tasklist	Get-Process	ps
help *command* *command* /?	Get-Help *command*	*command* -help
exit	Exit	exit

Table 4-10 Common commands in three CLIs

REMOTE CONNECTIONS

A+
CORE 2
1.5, 1.6,
1.8, 4.9

You might find it handy to access your Windows desktop from a remote location, and technicians are sometimes called upon to assist users remotely. Windows 10/8/7 offers Remote Desktop Connection (RDC) for screen and file sharing and Remote Assistance to assist users by screen sharing. In Windows 10, you have a new option to remotely assist a user: Quick Assist. Finally, if using a Windows feature isn't your preferred method, you can also use third-party software for a remote connection.

REMOTE DESKTOP CONNECTION (RDC)

A+
CORE 2
1.5, 1.6,
1.8, 4.9

Remote Desktop Connection (RDC), commonly called Remote Desktop, gives a user access to a Windows desktop from anywhere on the Internet. As a software developer, I find Remote Desktop extremely useful when I work from a remote location (my home office) and need to access a corporate network to support software on that network. Using the Internet, I can access a file server on these secured networks to make my software changes. Remote Desktop is easy to use and relatively safe for the corporate network. To use Remote Desktop, the computer you want to remotely access (the server) must be running business or professional editions of Windows 10/8/7, but the computer you're using to access it (the client) can be running any version of Windows.

> 🖉 **Notes** Remote Desktop Protocol (RDP) is used by the Windows Remote Desktop and Remote Assistance services and these services listen at port 3389.

> ⭐ **A+ Exam Tip** The A+ Core 2 exam expects you to know how to use Remote Desktop and Remote Assistance and to know which is appropriate in a given scenario.

APPLYING │ CONCEPTS CONFIGURING REMOTE DESKTOP ON TWO COMPUTERS

**A+
CORE 2
1.5, 1.6,
1.8, 4.9**

In this section, you see how to set up Remote Desktop for first use, and then you learn how to use it.

How to Set Up Remote Desktop for First Use

The host or server computer is the computer that serves up Remote Desktop to client computers that can "remote in to" (remotely access) the server. To prepare your host computer, you need to configure it for static IP addressing and configure the Remote Desktop service. Here are the steps needed:

1. Configure the computer for static IP addressing. How to assign a static IP address is covered in Chapter 3.

2. If your computer is behind a firewall, configure the router for port forwarding and allow incoming traffic on port 3389. Forward that traffic to the IP address of your desktop computer. You learned how to set up port forwarding in Chapter 3.

3. To turn on the Remote Desktop service, open the **System** window in Control Panel and click **Remote settings** in the left pane. The System Properties box appears with the Remote tab selected (see Figure 4-38). In this window, you can control settings for Remote Assistance and Remote Desktop. In the Remote Desktop area, check **Allow remote connections to this computer**. Leave the box checked for *Allow connections only from computers running Remote Desktop with Network Level Authentication (recommended)*.

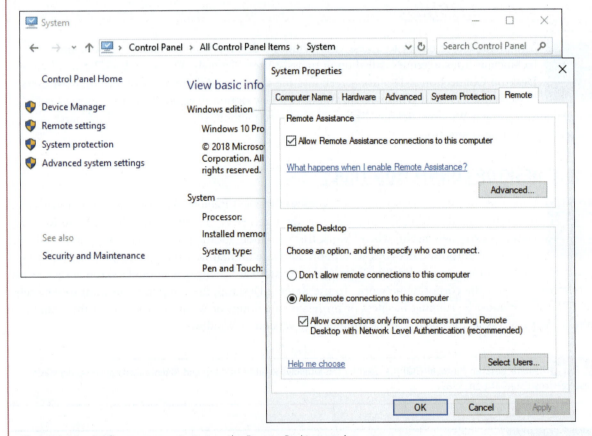

Figure 4-38   Configure a computer to run the Remote Desktop service

◇ **OS Differences**   To enable Remote Desktop on a Windows 7 computer, go to the Remote Desktop area on the Remote tab in the System Properties box, and check **Allow connections from computers running any version of Remote Desktop (less secure)**.

(continues)

> ✎ **Notes** Server applications such as Remote Desktop listen for network activity from clients. If you want these server applications to be available at all times, you can set your network adapter properties to Wake-on-LAN, which you learned about in Chapter 3.

4. Users who have administrative privileges are allowed to use Remote Desktop by default, but other users need to be added. If you need to add a user, click **Select Users** and follow the on-screen directions. Then close all windows.

5. To verify that Windows Firewall is set to allow Remote Desktop activity on this computer, open **Control Panel** and click **Windows Defender Firewall**. (Click **Windows Firewall** in Windows 8.) The Windows Defender Firewall window appears (see Figure 4-39). In the left pane, click **Allow an app or feature through Windows Defender Firewall**.

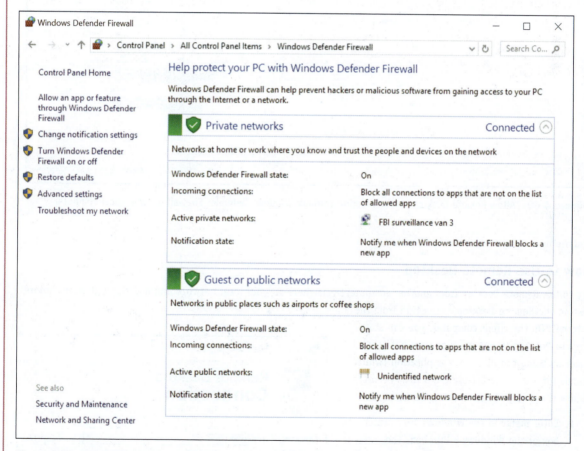

Figure 4-39 Windows Defender Firewall can block or allow activity on the network to your computer

> ◊ **OS Differences** To allow Remote Desktop activity on a Windows 7 computer, open the Windows Firewall window and click **Allow a program or feature through Windows Firewall**.

6. The Allowed apps window appears. Scroll down to Remote Desktop and adjust the settings as needed (see Figure 4-40). Click **OK** to apply any changes.

(continues)

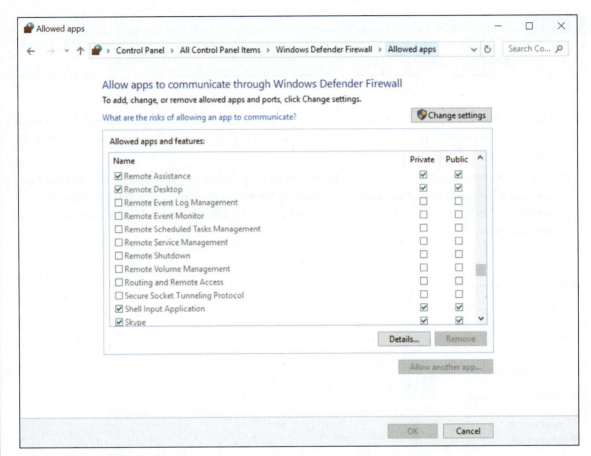

Figure 4-40 Allow Remote Desktop communication through Windows Defender Firewall on your local computer

You are now ready to test Remote Desktop.

How to Use Remote Desktop

Try to use Remote Desktop from another computer somewhere on your local network and make sure it works before testing the Remote Desktop connection from the Internet. On the client computer, you can start Remote Desktop to remote in to your host computer by using the **mstsc.exe** application (which stands for **Microsoft Terminal Services Client**). Follow these steps to use Remote Desktop:

1. Enter **mstsc** in the Windows 10/7 search box or the Windows 8 Run box. The Remote Desktop Connection box opens (see Figure 4-41).

2. Enter the IP address or the host name of the computer to which you want to connect. If you decide to use a host name, begin the name with two backslashes, as in \\CompanyFileServer.

Figure 4-41 The IP address of the remote computer can be used to connect to it

(continues)

Notes If you have trouble using the host name to make a Remote Desktop connection on a local network, try entering the host name and IP address of the remote computer in the hosts file in the C:\Windows\System32\ drivers\etc folder of the client computer.

3. If you plan to transfer files from one computer to the other, click **Show Options** for Windows 10/8 or **Options** for Windows 7, and then click the **Local Resources** tab, as shown on the left side of Figure 4-42. Click **More** to see the box on the right side of the figure. Check **Drives** and click **OK**. Click **Connect** to make the connection. If a warning box appears, click **Connect** again. If another warning box appears, click **Yes**.

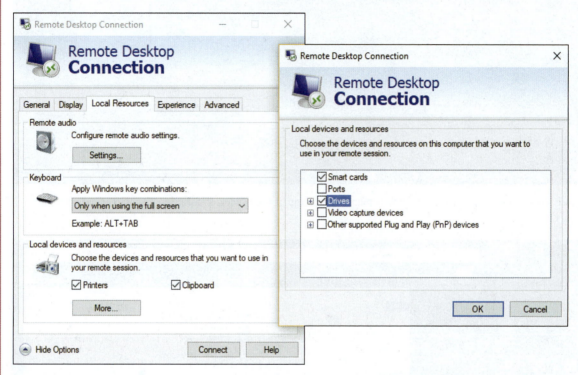

Figure 4-42 Allow drives and other devices to be shared using the Remote Desktop Connection

4. A Windows security box is displayed by the remote computer (see Figure 4-43). Sign in with a user name and password for the remote computer. If a warning box reports that the remote computer might not be secure, click **Yes** to continue the connection.

5. The desktop of the remote computer appears with a toolbar at the top of the screen, as shown in Figure 4-44. Click **Restore Down** to show both the remote desktop and the local desktop on the same screen, as shown in Figure 4-45.

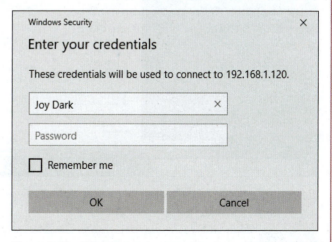

Figure 4-43 Enter your user name and password on the remote computer

(continues)

Figure 4-44   The RDC connection toolbar is pinned to the top of the window showing the remote computer's screen

Figure 4-45   The desktop of the remote computer is available on your local computer

> ✎ **Notes**   When a remote desktop connection is made, the user sitting at the remote computer will see it return to the sign-on screen.

(continues)

6. When you click in the remote desktop's window, you can work with the remote computer just as if you were sitting in front of it, except response time is slower. To move files back and forth between computers, use File Explorer or Windows Explorer on the remote computer. Files on your local computer and on the remote computer will appear in the Explorer window on the remote computer. Specifically, the files will appear in the This PC group in Windows 10/8 or the Windows 7 Computer group. For example, you can see drive C: on each computer labeled in Figure 4-45. To close the connection to the remote computer, sign out from the remote computer or close the desktop window.

> ✎ **Notes** Even though Windows normally allows more than one user to be signed in at the same time, this is not the case with Remote Desktop. When a Remote Desktop session is opened, all local users on the remote computer must sign out after receiving a warning, as shown in Figure 4-46.

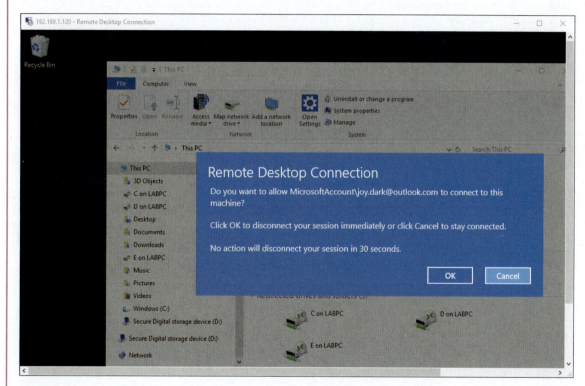

Figure 4-46 Local users must sign out before a Remote Desktop Connection can happen

Is your host computer as safe as it was before you set it to serve up Remote Desktop and enabled port forwarding to it? Actually, no, because a port has been opened, so take this into account when you decide to use Remote Desktop.

REMOTE ASSISTANCE

**A+
CORE 2
1.5, 1.6**

Remote Assistance differs from Remote Desktop in that a user on the server computer can remain signed in during the remote session, retains control of the session, and can see the screen. This is helpful when troubleshooting problems on a computer. The user who needs your help sends you an invitation by email or chat to connect to her computer using Remote Assistance. When you respond to the invitation, you can see the user's desktop just as she sees it; if the user gives you permission, you can take control of her computer to change settings or do whatever else is needed to fix her problem or show her how to perform a task. Think of Remote Assistance as a way to provide virtual desk-side support.

There are several ways to initiate a Remote Assistance session. The first method listed is the most reliable:

▲ The user saves an invitation file and then sends that file to the technician. The file can be sent by any method, including email, chat, or posting to a shared folder on the network.

▲ The user can send an automated email through the Remote Assistance app. This option only works if the system is configured with a compatible email program.

▲ The user can use Easy Connect, which is the easiest method to start a Remote Assistance connection but only works if both computers used for the connection are using Windows. Also know that some routers don't support the Peer Name Resolution Protocol (PNRP), which is the protocol Easy Connect uses to establish a Remote Assistance connection.

▲ The technician can initiate a session. This method is the most difficult to use; it requires that Group Policies be applied on the technician's computer. You learn more about Group Policy later in the text.

> **✎ Notes** Easy Connect is the easiest method for the user when initiating a Remote Assistance connection but it can be the most difficult for the technician to set up. If Easy Connect is grayed out when starting a session, chances are that the PNRP service might be down. To start the service, enter the **services.msc** command to open the Services console (see Figure 4-47). Select **Peer Name Resolution Protocol** and click **Start**. You learn more about services and the Services console in Chapter 5.

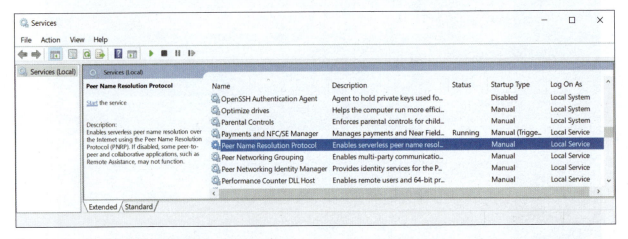

Figure 4-47 Use the Services console to start a service

To initiate a Remote Assistance connection when the user sends an invitation to the technician, follow these steps:

1. To allow Remote Assistance sessions on the user's computer, called the host computer, open the **System** window in Control Panel and click **Remote settings** in the left pane. If the user does not have administrative permissions, he must respond to the UAC box by entering an administrator password. The System Properties box appears with the Remote tab selected (refer back to Figure 4-38).

2. In the Remote Assistance area, check **Allow Remote Assistance connections to this computer**, and then click **OK**.

3. In the search box, type **remote assistance**, then click **Invite someone to connect to your PC and help you, or offer to help someone else**. The Windows Remote Assistance box appears, as shown in Figure 4-48.

> **↻ OS Differences** To launch Remote Assistance in Windows 8, open **Control Panel** in Category view. Click **System and Security**. Under System, click **Launch remote assistance**. (Alternately, you can press **Win+S** to open the search box and type **Invite**, then click **Invite someone to connect to your PC and help you**.)
>
> To launch Remote Assistance in Windows 7, click **Start**, type **Remote Assistance** in the search box, and then click **Windows Remote Assistance**.

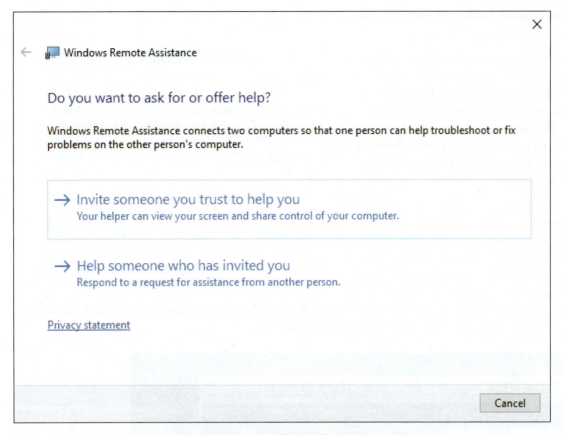

Figure 4-48   Create or respond to an invitation to connect

4. Click **Invite someone you trust to help you,** then click **Save this invitation as a file.** Point to a location to save the file and click **Save.** Remote Assistance provides a password for the user to give the technician in order to create the connection (see the left side of Figure 4-49). The user can send the invitation file to the technician as an email attachment or by other means.

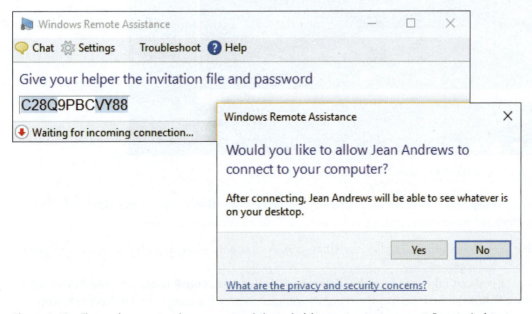

Figure 4-49   The user's computer shows a password the technician must enter to connect Remote Assistance

The technician can respond to the invitation into Remote Assistance as follows:

1. On the technician's computer, the technician double-clicks the invitation file she has received from the user. In the box that appears (see Figure 4-50), the technician enters the password that appeared on the user's screen and clicks **OK**. (Most often, the user reads the password to the technician over the phone.)

2. The user's computer generates a warning box requesting permission for the technician's computer to connect (see the right side of Figure 4-49). The user clicks **Yes** to allow the connection. The user's desktop turns black and the Remote Assistance management window appears. The technician's computer opens the Windows Remote Assistance window, as shown in Figure 4-51, with a live feed from the user's computer.

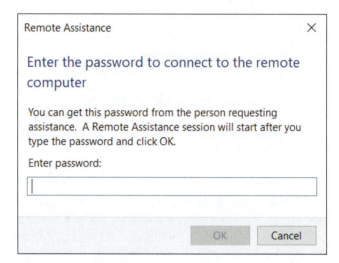

Figure 4-50   The technician enters the password to start a Remote Assistance session

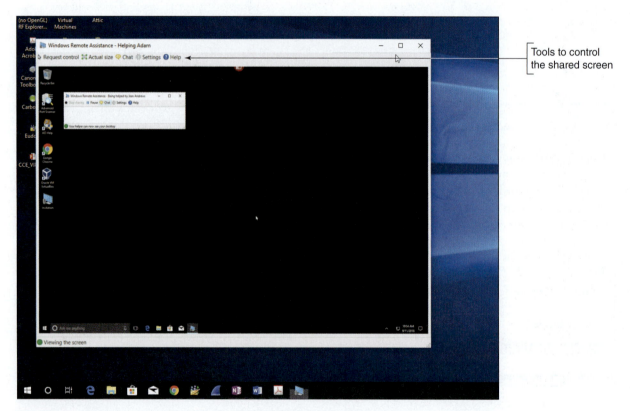

Figure 4-51   Control the shared screen using the toolbar options at the top

Using Remote Desktop, you can share files between computers, but Remote Assistance does not allow for file sharing. Here are some things you can do during a Remote Assistance session:

▲ To open a chat session with the user, click the **Chat** icon. A chat pane appears in the Remote Assistance window on both desktops.

▲ To ask the user if you can take control of his desktop, click **Request control** in the Remote Assistance control window. When the user accepts the request, you can control his computer. The user can stop sharing control by clicking **Stop sharing**.

◢ The user can hide his desktop from you at any time by clicking **Pause** in the control window.

◢ Either of you can disconnect the session by closing the control window.

◢ A log file is kept of every Remote Assistance session in the C:\Users*username*\Documents\Remote Assistance Logs folder. The file includes the chat session. If you type instructions during the chat session that will later help the user, he can use the log file to remind him of what was said and done.

◢ If an invitation created by a user is not used within six hours, the invitation expires. This time frame can be changed by clicking **Advanced** in the Remote Assistance section on the Remote tab of the System Properties dialog box.

If you have problems making the connection, do the following:

1. Windows Firewall on the user's computer might be blocking Remote Assistance. Verify that Remote Assistance is checked as an exception to blocked apps in the Windows Firewall window.

2. If you are outside the user's local network, the hardware firewall protecting his network might be blocking Remote Assistance. Verify that port forwarding on that hardware firewall is enabled for Remote Assistance. Remote Assistance uses port 3389, the same RDP port used by Remote Desktop.

> 🖉 **Notes** Because Remote Assistance can be difficult to set up, Windows 10 offers Quick Assist, which is more universally compatible with existing network hardware configurations. For Quick Assist to work, both computers must be running Windows 10, the technician providing assistance must have a Microsoft account, and the person receiving the connection must agree to it by entering a code generated by the technician's client computer.

THIRD-PARTY REMOTE ACCESS

Remote Desktop and Remote Assistance require you to open a port to your network, which is a security risk. Third-party remote access software executed from a browser window is more secure because the browser initiates communication outside the protected network and open listening ports are not required. Examples of this type of software, some of which are free, are TeamViewer (*teamviewer.com*), GoToMyPC by Citrix (*gotomypc.com*), LogMeIn (*logmein.com*), and Zoom (*zoom.us*). When evaluating third-party remote access applications, consider the following:

◢ Where is software installed? On the host, on the client, or on both computers?

◢ How secure is the connection? Are you required to open incoming ports?

◢ How are live screens shared? For example, is a live screen shared only by the host computer or can it be shifted to another computer in the same screen sharing session?

◢ Can files be shared in one or both directions during the same screen sharing session?

>> CHAPTER SUMMARY

Scheduling Preventive Maintenance

◢ Regular preventive maintenance includes verifying Windows Update, anti-malware, and network security settings, uninstalling software you no longer need, and cleaning up and optimizing the hard drive.

◢ Apply 32-bit patches to 32-bit applications and OSs. Apply 64-bit patches to 64-bit applications and OSs.

Backup Procedures

◢ You need a plan for disaster recovery in the event the hard drive fails. This plan needs to include routine backups of data files, the entire Windows volume, critical applications, and system files.

◢ You can back up to local storage or to the cloud. Test your backups to make sure you can restore from them.

◢ Windows 10/8 File History and Windows 10/7 Backup and Restore can be used to schedule routine backups of user data files. Both tools can back up a system image.

◢ The best time to create a system image is right after you've installed Windows, hardware, applications, and user accounts and customized Windows settings.

◢ A Windows 8 custom refresh image backs up the entire Windows volume.

◢ System Protection creates restore points, which include Windows system files that have changed since the last restore point was made.

Managing Files, Folders, and Storage Devices

◢ The MBR partitioning system can support only three primary partitions and one extended partition.

◢ The GPT partitioning system can support up to 128 partitions and hard drives larger than 2.2 TB. A GPT hard drive contains a protective MBR for compatibility with legacy software.

◢ Windows file systems include NTFS, ReFS, NFS, exFAT, FAT32, CDFS, and UDF.

◢ An MBR hard drive has a designated active partition and GPT drives have a designated EFI System Partition that contains the Windows boot manager program that starts Windows. In Windows, this partition is called the system partition.

◢ Use Disk Management to manage hard drives and partitions. Use it to create, delete, and resize partitions, mount a drive, manage dynamic disks, and solve problems with hard drives.

◢ Windows Storage Spaces is expected to replace the Windows solution for software RAID and can support thin provisioning, which allows for physical hard drives to be added to the storage pool as need demands.

◢ To improve hard drive performance, use the Disk Cleanup tool and the Defragment and Optimize Drives tool to clean and optimize the drive.

Using a Command-Line Interface (CLI)

◢ Commands used to manage files, folders, and storage media include help, dir, cd, copy, xcopy, robocopy, chkdsk, defrag, format, and shutdown.

◢ The PowerShell command-line interface uses cmdlets with parameters and is intended to ultimately replace the command prompt window.

◢ Using the Ubuntu Bash interface, you can enter Linux commands in a Windows shell and interact with the Windows system.

Remote Connections

◢ Remote Desktop gives you access to your Windows desktop and file sharing from anywhere on the Internet. Remote Assistance lets you provide remote support to users but does not allow file sharing.

◢ When using Remote Assistance, the user on the host computer can remain signed in during the remote session, retains control of the session, and can see the screen.

◢ When evaluating third-party remote access applications, consider how screens and files are shared and the security of the connection.

Windows interface, it appears as a second hard drive. You can store data in folders and files on the VHD and even install Windows in the VHD. Follow these steps to create a VHD:

1. In Disk Management, click **Action** in the menu bar and click **Create VHD**. Follow the on-screen directions to create the VHD, specifying its location on the hard drive and its size. You can make the size dynamically expanding. The VHD is listed as a Disk in the Disk Management window.

2. Right-click the new disk and click **Initialize Disk**. Use the GPT partitioning system for the disk.

3. To format the disk, right-click the unallocated space on the disk and click **New Simple Volume**. The VHD is now ready for use and appears in File Explorer or Windows Explorer as a new volume.

Discuss in your class and research online how a VHD might be useful. What are two uses of a VHD in which it offers advantages over using a physical hard drive?

4

Troubleshooting Windows After Startup

After completing this chapter, you will be able to:

- Explain the concepts and describe Windows tools used to solve problems with Windows, applications, and hardware

- Apply recommended best practices to troubleshoot Windows-related problems

- Troubleshoot problems with slow startup and slow performance

- Troubleshoot application errors and crashes

- Manually remove software when an application fails to uninstall

- Troubleshoot hardware problems in Windows

In previous chapters, you learned about the tools and strategies to install and maintain Windows and about the importance of keeping good backups. This chapter takes you one step further as an IT support technician so that you can solve problems with Windows, applications, and hardware using Windows tools and methods. This chapter is about problems that occur after startup. Troubleshooting Windows startup is covered in Chapter 6. We begin the chapter by learning about the Windows concepts and tools you'll need to optimize and troubleshoot Windows. Then we turn our attention to general steps you can follow when solving Windows, applications, and hardware problems, and finally move on to specific problems you might encounter and how to solve them. As you read the chapter, you might consider following along using a Windows 10/8/7 system.

> ✎ **Notes** Windows installed in a virtual machine is an excellent environment to use when practicing the skills in this chapter.

CONCEPTS AND WINDOWS TOOLS FOR SOLVING PROBLEMS WITH WINDOWS, APPLICATIONS, AND HARDWARE

Knowledge is power when it comes to supporting Windows. In this part of the chapter, you learn more about how Windows works and how it is structured. We also survey several Windows tools that are useful when solving a problem with Windows, applications, Windows users, networks, and hardware. In later parts of the chapter, you learn to use these tools to solve typical problems you might encounter as an IT technician supporting Windows.

WHAT ARE THE SHELL AND THE KERNEL?

It might sound like we're talking about a grain of wheat, but Windows has a shell and a kernel, and you need to understand what they are and how they work so you can solve problems with each. A shell is the portion of an OS that relates to the user and to applications. The kernel is responsible for interacting with hardware. Figure 5-1 shows how the shell and kernel relate to users, applications, and hardware. In addition, the figure shows a third component of an OS, the configuration data. For Windows, this data is primarily contained in the registry.

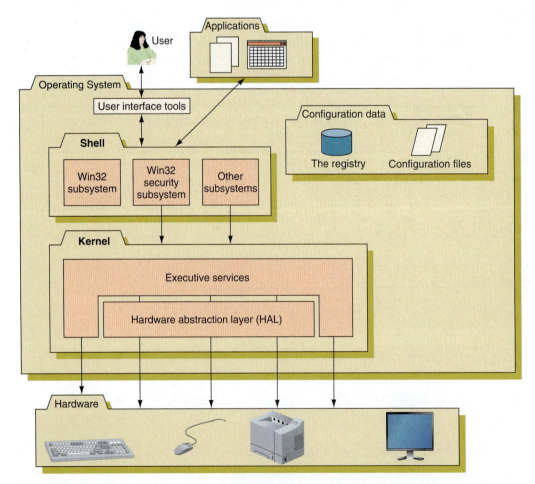

Figure 5-1   Inside an operating system, different components perform various functions

THE WINDOWS SHELL

The shell provides tools such as File Explorer or the Windows desktop as a way for the user to do such things as select music to burn to a CD or launch an application. For applications, the shell provides commands and procedures that applications can call on to do such things as print a document, read from a storage device, or display a photograph on the screen.

The shell is made up of several subsystems that all operate in **user mode**, which means these subsystems have only limited access to system information and can access hardware only through other OS services. One of these subsystems, the Win32 security subsystem, provides sign-in to the system and other security functions, including privileges for file access. All applications relate to Windows by way of the Win32 subsystem.

THE WINDOWS KERNEL

The kernel, or core, of the OS is responsible for interacting with hardware. Because the kernel operates in **kernel mode**, it has more power to communicate with hardware devices than the shell has. Applications operating under the OS cannot get to hardware devices without the shell passing those requests to the kernel. This separation of tasks provides for a more stable system and helps to prevent a wayward application from destabilizing the system.

The kernel has two main components: (1) the **HAL (hardware abstraction layer)**, which is the layer closest to the hardware, and (2) the **executive services** interface, which is a group of services that operate in kernel mode between the user mode subsystems and the HAL. Executive services contained in the ntoskrnl.exe program file manage memory, I/O devices, file systems, some security, and other key components directly or by way of device drivers.

> ✎ **Notes** In Task Manager, the Windows processes group on the Processes tab shows that the Windows kernel process ntoskrnl.exe appears as System.

When Windows is first installed, it builds the HAL based on the type of CPU installed. The HAL cannot be moved from one computer to another, which is one reason you cannot copy a Windows installation from one computer to another.

DIRECTORY STRUCTURES

A+
CORE 2
1.4, 1.5,
1.6

Folder or directory locations you need to be aware of include those for user files, program files, and Windows data. In the folder locations given in this discussion, we assume Windows is installed on drive C:.

USER PROFILE NAMESPACE

When a user first signs in to Windows, a **user profile** is created. This collection of user data and settings consists of two general items:

▲ *A user folder together with its subfolders.* These items are created under the C:\Users folder—for example, C:\Users\Jean Andrews. This folder contains a group of subfolders collectively called the **user profile namespace.** (In general, a namespace is a container to hold data—for example, a folder.)

▲ *NTUSER.DAT.* NTUSER.DAT is a hidden file stored in the C:\Users*username* folder that contains user settings. Each time the user signs in, the contents of this file are copied to a location in the registry.

5

PROGRAM FILES

Here is where Windows stores program files unless you select a different location when a program is installed:

◢ Program files are stored in C:\Program Files for 32-bit versions of Windows. Only 32-bit applications can be installed in a 32-bit installation of Windows.

◢ In 64-bit versions of Windows, 64-bit programs are stored in the C:\Program Files folder, and 32-bit programs are stored in the C:\Program Files (x86) folder. (For best performance, when you have the option, install 64-bit applications in a 64-bit installation of Windows.)

Here are folders that applications and some utilities use to launch programs at startup:

◢ A program file or shortcut to a program file stored in the C:\Users*username*\AppData\Roaming\Microsoft\Windows\Start Menu\Programs\Startup folder launches at startup for an individual user.

◢ A program file or shortcut to a program file stored in the C:\ProgramData\Microsoft\Windows\Start Menu\Programs\Startup folder launches at startup for all users.

FOLDERS FOR WINDOWS DATA

An operating system needs a place to keep hardware and software configuration information, user preferences, and application settings. This information is used when the OS is first loaded and when needed by hardware, applications, and users. Windows uses a database called the registry for most of this information. In addition, Windows keeps some data in text files called initialization files, which often have an .ini or .inf file extension.

Here are some important folder locations used for the registry and other Windows data:

◢ *Registry location.* The Windows registry is stored in the C:\Windows\System32\config folder.
◢ *Backup of the registry.* A backup of the registry is stored in the C:\Windows\System32\config\RegBack folder.
◢ *Fonts.* Fonts are stored in the C:\Windows\Fonts folder.
◢ *Temporary files.* These files, which are used by Windows when it is installing software and performing other maintenance tasks, are stored in the C:\Windows\Temp folder.
◢ *Offline files.* Offline files are stored in the CSC (client-side caching) folder, which is C:\Windows\CSC. The folder is managed by Sync Center, an applet in Control Panel, which syncs files in a shared folder on the network with the \CSC folder on the local computer. Users can work with the \CSC folder when the computer is offline; later, when the computer is connected to the network, Sync Center can sync up the files with those on the network share. How to use Sync Center is covered in Chapter 7.

> ✎ **Notes** Most often, Windows is installed on drive C:, although in a dual-boot environment, one OS might be installed on C: and another on a different drive. For example, Windows 8 can be installed on C: and Windows 10 installed on E:. Also, drive C: for one OS in a dual-boot system is likely to have a different drive letter in the other OS.
>
> If the drive letter of the Windows volume is not known, it is written in Microsoft documentation as *%SystemDrive%*. For example, the location of the Program Files folder is written as *%SystemDrive%*\Program Files.

HOW WINDOWS MANAGES APPLICATIONS

> **A+**
> **CORE 2**
> **1.4, 1.5,**
> **1.6**

When an application is first installed, its program files are normally stored on the hard drive. When the application is launched, the program is copied from the hard drive into memory and there it is called a process. A process is a program that is running under the authority of the shell, together with the system resources assigned to it. System resources might include other programs the process has started and memory addresses to hold its data. When the process makes a request for resources, this request is made to the Win32 subsystem and is called a thread. A thread is a single task, such as the task of printing a file that the process requests from the kernel. Figure 5-2 shows two threads in action, which is possible because the process and Windows support multithreading. Sometimes a process is called an instance, such as when you say to a user, "Open two instances of Internet Explorer." Technically, you are saying to open two Internet Explorer processes.

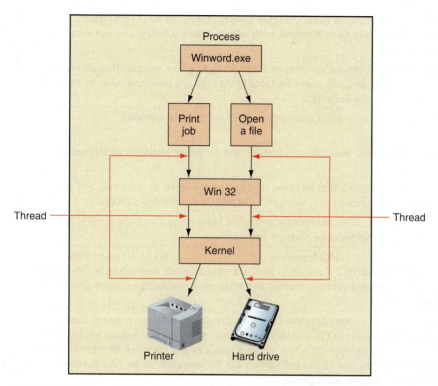

Figure 5-2   A process with more than one thread is called multithreading

SURVEY OF WINDOWS TOOLS AND TECHNIQUES

A+
CORE 2
1.4, 1.5,
1.6
With an understanding of how Windows is structured, let's turn our attention to useful tools and techniques for managing and troubleshooting Windows, applications, users, hardware, and networks. Table 5-1 lists many of these tools. As you read through the list, try to form a context for how you might use a tool to help you solve a Windows-related problem. To get started, launch each tool and take a look at how its window is organized, the basic functions available, and what is on each tab in a window. Later in the chapter, you learn how to apply each tool as you address many typical Windows problems.

> ⭐ **A+ Exam Tip**   The A+ Core 2 exam gives you a scenario with possible alternatives toward a solution. It expects you to know which Windows tool to use and how to use it to resolve a problem. These Windows tools include Computer Management, Performance Monitor, the Services console, System Configuration, Data Sources, Print Management, Event Viewer, Task Manager, the Registry Editor, MMC, and DxDiag. All of these tools are discussed in this chapter.

> ⭐ **A+ Exam Tip**   In performance-based questions on the A+ Core 2 exam, you are expected to know how to access a Windows tool using more than one method. It's a good idea to know the command that launches a given tool.

Tool	Description
Use these tools to conveniently access and manage other Windows tools:	
Control Panel	Control Panel is a collection of small programs, called applets, that are used to manage many Windows settings. To open Control Panel in Windows 10/7, enter Control Panel in the search box. For Windows 8, right-click Start and click Control Panel.
Administrative Tools	This applet in Control Panel contains several tools used by IT technicians. You need to be signed in to Windows with administrator privileges to use many of these tools.
Computer Management (compmgmt.msc)	This console in the Administrative Tools group is where you can find several Windows tools and add your own tools to manage the local computer or other computers on the network.
Microsoft Management Console (MMC, mmc.exe)	Use this console to build your own customized console windows.
Use these tools to observe Windows, Windows user, network, application, and hardware activities as tracked and logged by Windows:	
Event Viewer (eventvwr.msc)	Just about anything that happens in Windows is logged by Windows, and these logs can be viewed using Event Viewer in the Administrative Tools group.
Performance Monitor (perfmon.msc)	Performance Monitor in the Administrative Tools group can track activity by hardware and software to measure performance.
Reliability Monitor	Reliability Monitor, also known as reliability history, can be accessed from Control Panel or Task Manager to find out what changes were made to the system around the time a problem started and what other problems occurred about that same time.
Resource Monitor (resmon.exe)	Resource Monitor monitors the CPU, hard drive, network, and memory in real time. If you suspect CPU, memory, hard drive, or network resources are being used excessively by an application or malware, you can use Resource Monitor to identify the process. You can access the tool on the Performance tab of Task Manager or in the Administrative Tools group.
Solve Windows, application, networking, and Windows user problems with these tools:	
Task Manager (taskmgr.exe)	Task Manager lets you view the applications and processes running on your computer as well as information about process and memory performance, network activity, and user activity. Use Task Manager to end a process causing trouble and to enable or disable programs that launch at Windows startup. One way to access Task Manager is to press Ctrl+Alt+Del and click Task Manager.
System Configuration (msconfig.exe)	Use the System Configuration utility (commonly called "*M-S-config*") in the Administrative Tools group to temporarily disable programs from launching at startup in order to troubleshoot a startup problem.
Services console (services.msc)	Use the Services console in the Administrative Tools group to control Windows and third-party services installed on a system.
Troubleshooting	Use the Troubleshooting applet in Control Panel to automatically troubleshoot and fix many common Windows problems involving applications, hardware, sound, networking, Windows updates, and maintenance tasks.
Group Policy (gpedit.msc)	Group Policy is used on a Windows domain to secure and manage the domain; it can control what users can do and how Windows clients in the domain can be used.
Local Group Policy (gpedit.msc)	Local Group Policy is a limited version of Group Policy included in business and professional editions of Windows (not home editions) and applies to the local computer. Use it to control a variety of application, user, and Windows settings.
Registry Editor (regedit.exe)	Use the Registry Editor to back up and edit the Windows registry.

Table 5-1 Tools and techniques to solve Windows-related problems (continues)

Tool	Description
Solve Windows problems using these tools:	
System File Checker (sfc.exe)	Use System File Checker (SFC) to verify and replace Windows system files. It keeps a cache of current system files in case it needs to refresh a damaged file.
DISM (dism.exe)	Use DISM (Deployment Image Servicing and Management) to repair corrupted Windows system files when SFC cannot do the job or Windows Update is corrupted.
Windows Updates	Use Windows Updates to download and apply the latest Windows updates to solve problems with Windows, applications, and hardware. In Windows 10, open Windows Updates in the Settings app. For Windows 8/7, use the System window to find Windows Updates.
Clean boot	A clean boot disables all third-party software that has been added to the Windows startup process. To clean boot, use System Configuration and Task Manager to disable all but Microsoft services launched at startup. You learn how to do this later in the chapter.
Safe Mode, aka Safe boot	Safe Mode goes beyond a clean boot; it not only eliminates third-party software from Windows startup, it also reduces startup to only the Windows minimum configuration necessary to start the OS. It can create a stable environment when the Windows system or device drivers become corrupted. First try a clean boot. If that doesn't resolve a problem, try Safe Mode. To do so, use System Configuration to restart the computer in Safe boot.
System Restore (rstrui.exe)	Use System Restore to revert the system back to a previously saved restore point before a problem started.
Solve application errors or crashes with these tools:	
Programs and Features (appwiz.cpl)	Use the Programs and Features tool in Control Panel to repair and uninstall applications and enable and disable Windows features.
tasklist	The tasklist command reports the process identifier (PID), which is a number that identifies each running process.
taskkill	The taskkill command uses the process ID to kill the task or process. Use taskkill to end a process when Task Manager is unable to do so.
Component Services	Use Component Services (also called COM+) in the Administrative Tools group to register components in the Windows registry so that an application can access the component. This resolves a problem that happens when a component is not correctly registered to the application when it is first installed or the connection between the two gets broken.
Secondary logon	Use a secondary logon to run an application using administrator privileges that refused to run under the authority of a standard user. Use the Properties dialog box of the application program file to perform a secondary logon.
Compatibility mode	To solve an incompatibility problem with the OS, try running the application in compatibility mode by using the Properties dialog box of the application program file.
Digital signature	A digital signature verifies that the application is not a rogue application and that it is certified as Windows-compatible by Microsoft. Verify a digital signature using the Properties dialog box of the application program file.
Data Sources	Use Data Sources, also called ODBC Data Sources (Open Database Connectivity Data Sources), to create a connection between a local application and a remote database so that the application can manage the database. Data Sources can be accessed in the Administrative Tools group.
Task Scheduler (taskschd.msc)	Use Task Scheduler in the Administrative Tools group to schedule a program to run at a future time, including at startup.

Table 5-1 Tools and techniques to solve Windows-related problems (continues)

Tool	Description
Manage and solve problems with hardware using these tools:	
Device Manager (devmgmt.msc)	Recall Device Manager in Control Panel is the go-to tool to make sure Windows has correctly installed a hardware device and to solve problems with a device.
Print Management (printmanagement.msc)	Use Print Management in the Administrative Tools group to monitor and manage printer queues for all printers on the network.
Display applet (desk.cpl)	Use the Display applet to manage display settings. In Windows 10, access Display settings in the Settings app. For Windows 8/7, use Control Panel.
DxDiag (dxdiag.exe)	Use the DxDiag (DirectX Diagnostic Tool) command to diagnose problems with DirectX. DirectX is Microsoft's interface between video and sound hardware and the applications that use these devices. Some gaming applications or other apps that rely heavily on graphics and sound require the latest version of DirectX. DxDiag can tell you which version of DirectX is installed; you can download the latest version from *Microsoft.com*.
Memory Diagnostics (mdsched.exe)	Use Memory Diagnostics in Administrative Tools to test memory before or after Windows is launched.
chkdsk	The chkdsk command checks the hard drive for a corrupted file system and bad sectors on the drive. Use this command to check drive C: and recover data: `chkdsk c: /r`
Disk Defragmenter (defrag.exe)	Defrag a magnetic hard drive to improve drive performance.

Table 5-1 Tools and techniques to solve Windows-related problems (continued)

> 🖉 **Notes** If you have not already used a tool listed in Table 5-1, open the tool's window and take a good look at its features and menus before you continue with the chapter. If you can, open each tool using more than one method. Try to remember at least one way to open it. Don't worry if you don't know how to use the tool—that's coming up.

> ★ **A+ Exam Tip** If an often-used Windows utility can be launched from a command prompt, the A+ Core 2 exam expects you to know the program name of that utility.

APPLYING | CONCEPTS USING WINDOWS TOOLS TO MANAGE TOOLS

Windows offers several windows and consoles to help access and organize Windows tools. Take a quick look at each to get familiar with how a window or console works and the tools each one contains:

▲ *Control Panel*. Control Panel is a collection of applets used to manage most Windows settings. By default, Control Panel opens in Category view, but applets are easier to find in Classic view, also called icon view. To switch to Classic view, click **Category** and select either Large icons or Small icons. Also, the search box in the upper-left corner of Control Panel can help you quickly find an applet.

▲ *Administrative Tools*. In Classic view of Control Panel, click **Administrative Tools** to see a group of tools used by technicians and developers to support Windows. Figure 5-3 shows the Administrative Tools window for Windows 10 Pro. The Home editions of Windows don't include several of these tools.

▲ *Computer Management*. **Computer Management** (compmgmt.msc) contains several tools that can be used to manage the local computer or other computers on the network. The window is called a **console** because it consolidates several Windows administrative tools. To use most of these tools, you must be signed in as an administrator, although you can view certain settings in Computer Management if you are signed in with lesser privileges. The Computer Management window is shown in Figure 5-4.

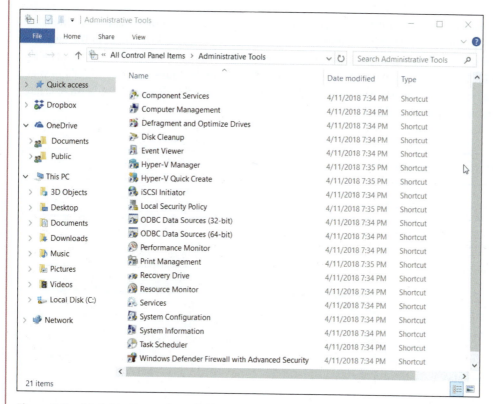

Figure 5-3 Administrative tools available in Windows 10 Pro

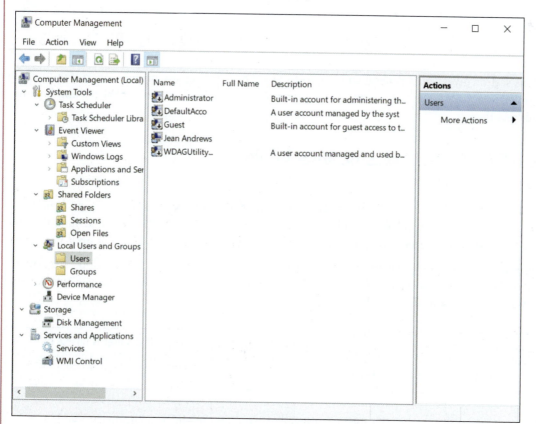

Figure 5-4 Windows Computer Management combines several administrative tools into a single, easy-to-access window

(continues)

▲ ***Microsoft Management Console (MMC).*** You can build your own console to hold the tools you use often, and you can copy this console to any computer you support. To build a console, first sign in to Windows using an account with administrator privileges and then open the **Microsoft Management Console** (**MMC**; the program file is mmc.exe). A new empty console is created, as shown in Figure 5-5. Tools you add to your console are called **snap-ins** and the console is saved in a file with an .msc file extension. You learn to create your own console in a project at the end of this chapter.

> 🖊 **Notes** A program that can work as a snap-in under the MMC has an .msc file extension.

Figure 5-5 An empty console

BEST PRACTICES TO TROUBLESHOOT WINDOWS-RELATED PROBLEMS

**A+
CORE 2
1.4, 1.5,
1.6, 3.1**

This section gives you a general strategy to follow when solving any problem with Windows, an application, or hardware. Later in the chapter, you'll learn about specific problems and how to address them.

STEP 1: INTERVIEW THE USER AND BACK UP DATA

**A+
CORE 2
3.1**

When the user is available, always start troubleshooting by interviewing the user:

1. ***Interview the user and back up data.*** Find out as much information as you can from the user about the problem, when it started, and what happened to the system around the time the problem started. Also ask if valuable data is on the system, and back it up if necessary.

2. ***Ask the user to reproduce the problem while you watch.*** Many problems with applications are caused by user error. Watch carefully as the user shows you the problem. If you see him making a mistake, be tactful as you explain the problem and its solution.

> 🖊 **Notes** A problem might be caused by an underlying intermittent conflict or other issue. If the user is unable to reproduce the problem, don't dismiss the user's ability to help you understand the nature of the problem. Continue asking the user questions as you investigate the problem.

3. ***Try a reboot.*** Reboots solve a lot of application problems and one might be a shortcut to your solution. If it doesn't work, no harm is done and you're ready to begin investigating the system. (Before you restart the system, be sure to ask the user if she needs to save her work.)

STEP 2: ERROR MESSAGES, THE WEB, COWORKERS, AND LOGS MIGHT HELP

**A+
CORE 2
3.1**

Windows might display an error message and offer a solution. Logs kept by Windows can offer clues. Following are a few examples of how to get help from Windows, the web, and coworkers.

USE EVENT VIEWER AND RELIABILITY MONITOR TO LOOK FOR CLUES

The Event Viewer logs might give clues about hardware or network failure, OS error messages, a device or service that has failed to start, or general protection faults, which can cause Windows to lock up or hang. Use Reliability Monitor to look for errors with applications or with key hardware components such as the hard drive.

Here are general steps to use Event Viewer:

1. Open Event Viewer in the Administrative Tools group or by using the command **eventvwr.msc.** To see events, select a log in the left pane and then drill down into subcategories of these logs. For example, Figure 5-6 shows events in the Administrative Events log. Select an event to see more about it. In the figure, the selected event is that the computer was not able to lease an IP address from the DHCP server.

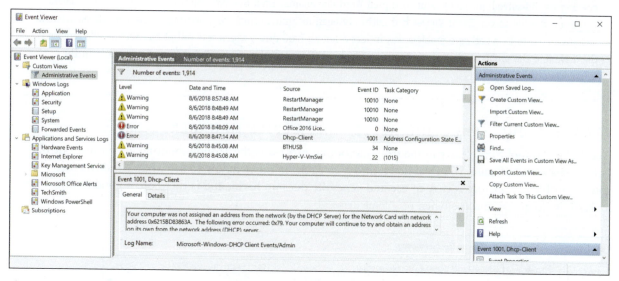

Figure 5-6 Use Event Viewer to see logs about hardware, Windows, security, and application events

2. To sort a list of events, click a column heading in the middle pane. After you have selected an event, click the Details tab to show more information about the event.

The types of events are Critical, Error, Warning, Information, and Audit Success. Error events are the most important and indicate something went wrong with the system, such as a scheduled backup failing to work. Warning events indicate failure might occur in the future, and Critical events indicate a problem occurred with a critical Windows process.

Here are the logs that are the most useful:

▲ *Administrative Events log.* This filtered log shows only Critical, Error, and Warning events intended for the administrator. This log is in the Custom Views category and is selected in Figure 5-6.
▲ *Application log.* In the Windows Logs group, look in the Application log for events recorded by an application. This log might help you identify why an application is causing problems.
▲ *Security log.* Events in the Security log are called audits and include successful and unsuccessful sign-ins to a user account and attempts from another computer on the network to access shared resources on this computer.
▲ *Setup log.* Look in the Setup log for events recorded at the time applications are installed.

▲ *System log.* Look in the System log to find events triggered by Windows components, such as a device driver failing to load or a problem with hardware.

▲ *Forwarded Events log.* This log receives events that were recorded on other computers and sent to this computer.

When you first encounter a Windows, hardware, application, or security problem, get in the habit of checking Event Viewer as one of your first steps toward investigating the problem. To save time, first check the Administrative Events log because it filters out all events except Critical, Error, and Warning events.

APPLYING | CONCEPTS   EVENT VIEWER SOLVES A MYSTERY

Event Viewer can be useful in solving intermittent hardware problems. For example, I once worked in an office where several people updated Microsoft Word documents stored on a file server. For weeks, people complained about these Word documents getting corrupted. We downloaded the latest patches for Windows and Microsoft Office and scanned for viruses, thinking that the problem might be with Windows or the application. Then we suspected a corrupted template file for building the Word documents. But nothing we did solved our problem of corrupted Word documents. Then one day someone thought to check Event Viewer on the file server. Event Viewer had faithfully been recording errors when writing to the hard drive. What we had suspected to be a software problem was in fact a failing hard drive, which was full of bad sectors. We replaced the drive and the problem went away. That day I learned the value of checking Event Viewer very early in the troubleshooting process.

TRY THE TROUBLESHOOTING APPLET AND DEVICE MANAGER

Another go-to tool to use early in the troubleshooting process is the Troubleshooting applet in Control Panel, as shown in Figure 5-7. Drill down into a category in this window to see what Windows offers to solve a problem. This tool is easy to use and generally does no harm, and is therefore a good tool to show a user how to access and use when problems arise.

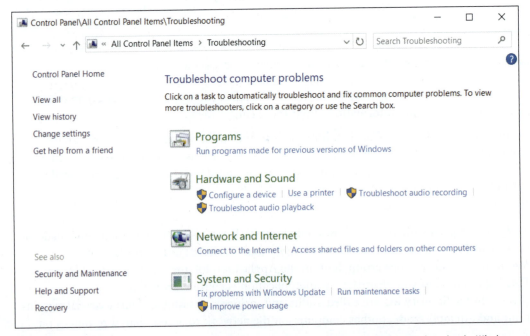

Figure 5-7   Use the Troubleshooting applet early in the troubleshooting process to solve simple Windows, application, hardware, network, and security problems

When the problem is hardware-related, check Device Manager. Sometimes using Device Manager to uninstall a device and then reinstalling the device solves the problem.

FIND AND ASK FOR HELP

For Windows problems, search for the error message or description of the problem on the web. When you perform a Google search, add **site:microsoft.com** to the end of the search text to target your search to Microsoft websites. For problems with hardware and applications, try searching the website of the manufacturer for support and help. Also, search the web on the error message, application, or description of the problem. Look for forums where others have posted the same problem with the same app or device. Someone else has likely posted a solution. However, be careful and don't take the advice unless you trust the website. After you've made a reasonable effort to find help on your own, ask for help from coworkers who are more experienced.

> ✎ **Notes** Working while a customer looks over your shoulder can be awkward. A customer needs her IT support technician to appear confident and in charge. To maintain your customer's confidence in your technical abilities, you might want to find privacy when searching the web or talking with coworkers.

STEP 3: CONSIDER THAT THE DATA OR THE APPLICATION MIGHT BE CORRUPTED

> **A+**
> **CORE 2**
> **3.1**

Now that you've interviewed the user, backed up important data, examined the system, and investigated the problem, it's time to come up with a theory as to the cause of the problem. For general problems with applications, consider and do these things:

▲ *Consider data corruption.* For applications such as Microsoft Office that use data files, it might appear that the application, Windows, or hardware has a problem when the problem is really a corrupted data file. Try creating an entirely new data file. If that works, then suspect that previous errors might be caused by corrupted data. You might be able to recover part of a corrupted file by changing its file extension to .txt and importing it into the application as a text file.

▲ *Check application settings and logs for errors.* Maybe a user has made one too many changes to the application settings, which can cause a problem with missing toolbars and other functions. Write down each setting the user has changed and then restore all settings back to their default values. If the problem is solved, restore each setting to the way the user had it until you find the one causing the problem. The process will take some time, but users can get upset if you change their application settings without justification.

▲ *Repair the application.* The application setup might have the option to repair the installation. Look for it in the Programs and Features window, on the setup disc for the application, or on the manufacturer's website.

▲ *Uninstall and reinstall the application.* Do so with caution because you might lose any customized settings, macros, or scripts. Also know this still might not solve a problem with a corrupted application because registry entries might not be properly reset during the uninstall process.

> ⚡ **Caution** When researching a problem, suppose you discover that Microsoft or a manufacturer's website offers a fix or patch you can download and apply. To get the right patch, recall you need to make sure you get a 32-bit patch for a 32-bit installation of Windows, a device driver, or an application. For a 64-bit installation of Windows, make sure you get a 64-bit device driver. An application installed in a 64-bit OS might be a 32-bit application or a 64-bit application.

STEP 4: CONSIDER OUTSIDE INTERFERENCE

The problem could be caused by a virus, Windows, applications other than the one that presented the initial symptoms, or hardware.

MALWARE IS AT WORK

Scan the system for malware using up-to-date anti-malware software. In Chapter 8, you learn more about symptoms that indicate malware is at work and how to scan for and remove malware.

FAULTY MEMORY

Errors with memory are often difficult to diagnose because they can appear intermittently and might be mistaken as application errors, user errors, or other hardware component errors. Sometimes these errors cause the system to hang, a BSOD (blue screen of death) error might occur, or the system continues to function with applications giving errors or data being corrupted. You can quickly identify a problem with memory or eliminate memory as the source of a problem by using the Windows Memory Diagnostics (mdsched.exe) tool. It works before Windows is loaded to test memory for errors and can be used on computers that don't have Windows installed. Use one of these two methods to start the utility:

▲ *Use the mdsched.exe command*. After Windows has started, enter the **mdsched.exe** command. A dialog box appears and asks if you want the tool to immediately restart the system and run the test or wait until the next restart.

▲ *Boot from Windows setup media*. If Windows is not the installed operating system or you cannot boot from the hard drive, boot the computer from the Windows setup USB drive or DVD to test memory for errors. Follow these steps:

1. If necessary, change the boot priority order in BIOS/UEFI setup to boot first from the optical drive or USB drive. Boot from the Windows setup DVD or USB drive.

2. On the opening screen for Windows 10/8, select your language and click **Next**. On the next screen (see Figure 5-8), click **Repair your computer**. Next choose **Troubleshoot**. For Windows 10, the Advanced options screen appears; for Windows 8, you must click **Advanced options** to see this screen.

Figure 5-8   The opening menu when you boot from Windows 10 setup media

3. On the Advanced options screen (see Figure 5-9), choose **Command Prompt**. In the command prompt window, enter the **mdsched.exe** command.

> **◇ OS Differences**   For Windows 7, after booting from the Windows 7 setup DVD, select the Windows installation to repair. On the System Recovery Options screen, click **Windows Memory Diagnostic**. For Windows 7, it is not necessary to open a command prompt window to test memory.

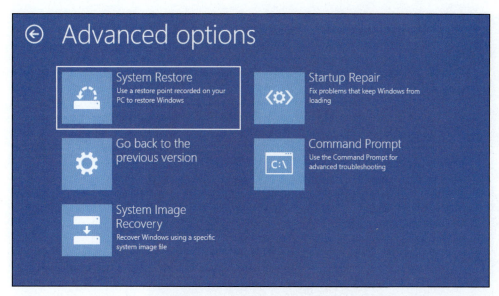

Figure 5-9 The Windows 10 Advanced options screen launched from Windows 10 setup media

If the tool reports memory errors, replace all memory modules installed on the motherboard.

CORRUPTED HARD DRIVE

To eliminate the hard drive as the source of a Windows or application error, use the **chkdsk c: /r** command to check the drive. The error-checking utility searches for bad sectors on a volume and recovers the data from them if possible. It then marks the sector as bad so that it will not be reused. Also check Event Viewer for warnings or errors regarding the hard drive.

LOW ON SYSTEM RESOURCES

Malware, applications, background services, device drivers, or Windows might be hogging system resources to slow down the system and/or prevent an application from working or cause Windows errors.

Use Task Manager to verify that a process is not using excessive system resources. Several ways to access Task Manager are:

▲ Press **Ctrl+Alt+Del**. Depending on your system, the security screen (see Figure 5-10) or Task Manager appears. If the security screen appears, click **Task Manager**. This method works well when the system has a problem and is frozen.
▲ Press **Ctrl+Shift+Esc**.
▲ For Windows 10/8, press **Win+X** and click **Task Manager** in the Quick Launch menu. For Windows 7, click **Start**, enter **taskmgr.exe** in the search box, and press **Enter**.

✎ Notes When working with a virtual machine, you cannot send the Ctrl+Alt+Del keystrokes to the guest operating system in the VM because these keystrokes are always sent to the host operating system. To send the Ctrl+Alt+Del keystrokes to a VM in Windows Client Hyper-V, click the **Action** menu in the VM window and click **Ctrl+Alt+Delete** (see Figure 5-11).

To send the Ctrl+Alt+Del keystrokes to a VM in Oracle VirtualBox, click **Input** in the menu bar at the top of the VM window. For the system shown in Figure 5-12A, you can see the keystrokes to press for Ctrl+Alt+Del are Host+Del. By default, the Host key in VirtualBox is the right Ctrl key. To verify the Host key for your installation of VirtualBox, look in the bottom-right corner of the VM window (see Figure 5-12B).

Figure 5-10   Use the security screen to launch Task Manager

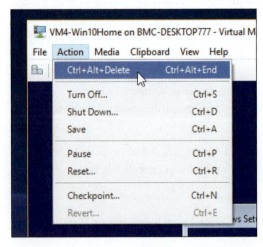

Figure 5-11   Send the Ctrl+Alt+Del keystrokes to a VM managed by Windows 10 Pro Client Hyper-V

The Windows 10 Task Manager window is shown in Figure 5-13. If you see very limited information in the window, click **More details** to see the details shown in the figure.

Here are important details about each tab in Task Manager:

▲ *Processes tab and Details tab.* The Processes tab shows running processes organized by Apps, Background processes, and Windows processes. Right-click a process and click **Go to details** (see Figure 5-13) to jump to the Details tab, where you see the name of the program file and other details about the running program. On the Details tab (see Figure 5-14), a hung process is reported as Not Responding. To end the task, select it and click **End task**. The application will attempt a normal shutdown; if data has not been saved, you are given the opportunity to save it.

> ✎ **Notes**   If your desktop locks up, you can use Task Manager to refresh it. To do so, press **Ctrl+Alt+Del** and open **Task Manager**. Click the **Processes** tab. In the Windows processes group, select **Windows Explorer** and click **Restart**. (Yes, Windows 10/8 Task Manager really does call Explorer "Windows Explorer.")
>
> In Windows 7, click the Processes tab and select and end the **explorer.exe** process. Then click **File** in the menu bar and click **New Task (Run)**. Enter **explorer.exe** in the Create New Task box, and click **OK**. Your desktop will be refreshed and any running programs will still be open.

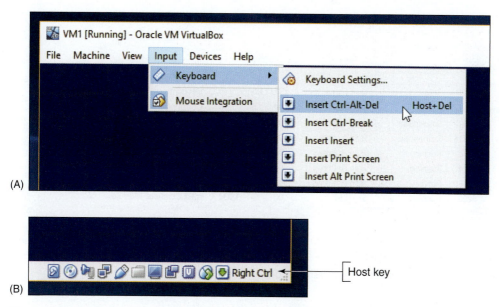

(A)

(B)

Figure 5-12 For Oracle VirtualBox, (A) send the Ctrl+Alt+Del keystrokes to a VM, and (B) verify the Host key for the VM

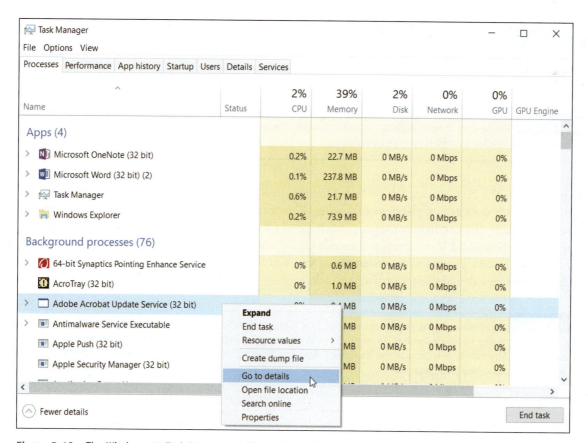

Figure 5-13 The Windows 10 Task Manager window with the Processes tab selected

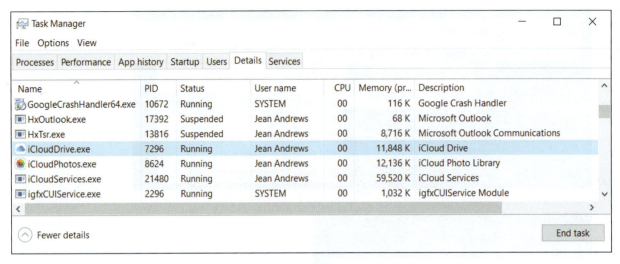

Figure 5-14 Use the Details tab to end a task that is not responding

If you want to end a process and all related processes, click the **Details** tab, right-click the process, and select **End Process Tree** from the shortcut menu. Be careful not to end critical Windows processes; ending these might crash your system.

♦ OS Differences The Windows 7 Task Manager window has six tabs: Applications, Processes, Services, Performance, Networking, and Users. The Applications tab of Task Manager is used to view a list of running processes. You can end a process that is not responding on this tab or end it on the Processes tab.

★ A+ Exam Tip The A+ Core 2 exam expects you to understand the purposes of each tab in Task Manager and know when to use a tab to resolve a problem in a given scenario.

▲ *Performance tab.* The Performance tab of Task Manager (see Figure 5-15) allows you to monitor performance of key devices in the system and network connections. For example, Figure 5-15 shows the CPU selected, where you can monitor what percentage of CPU resources are in use. You can also see whether Hardware-assisted Virtualization is enabled. Also notice the link to open the Resource Monitor, which can identify each process using system resources. Check for such a process if you suspect malware might be at work in a denial-of-service (DoS) attack.

♦ OS Differences In Windows 7, the Performance tab of Task Manager monitors performance of the CPU and memory and gives you access to the Resource Monitor. To monitor the performance of network connections, see the Networking tab of Task Manager. Alternately, you can use the Windows 7 Resource Monitor to monitor the performance of the CPU, memory, hard drive, and network connections.

5

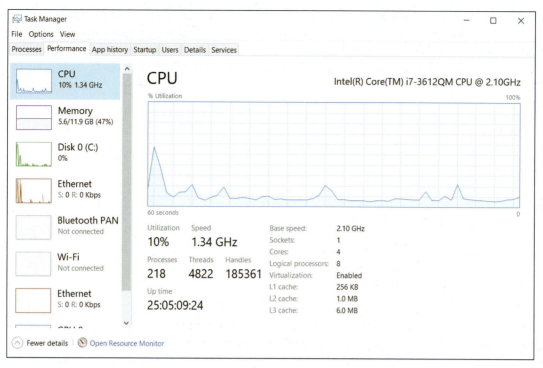

Figure 5-15   Use the Performance tab to view system resource usage

▲ *App history tab.* The App history tab (see Figure 5-16) shows the resources that a program is using. For example, it's useful when deciding if a live tile or other app is using too much CPU time or network resources.

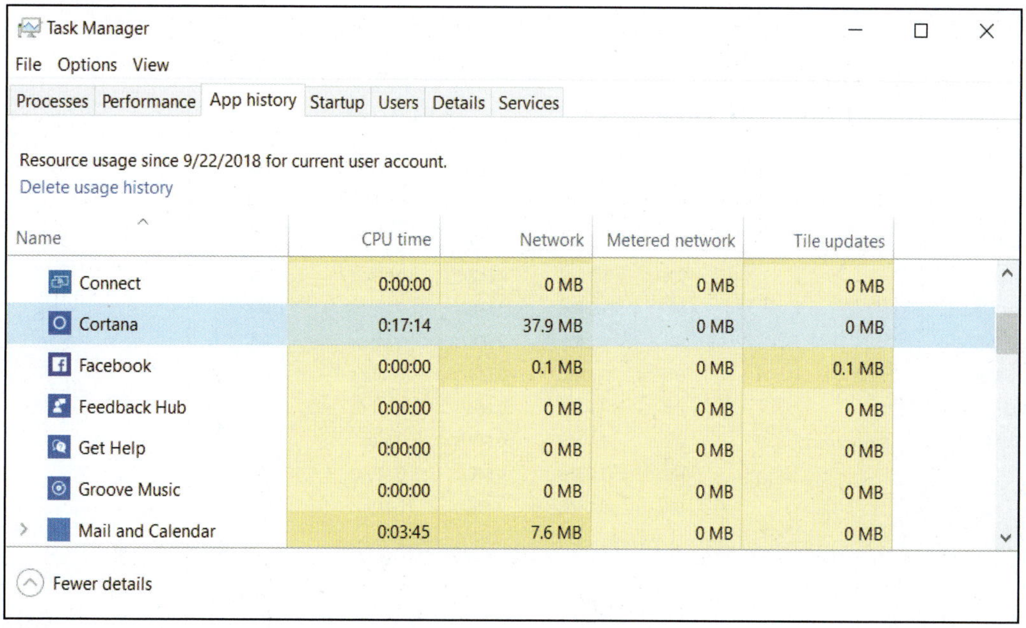

Figure 5-16   The App history tab can help you decide if a background program is hogging system resources

> ✎ **Notes**   To conserve resources, you can disable a live tile on the Windows 10 Start menu or Windows 8 Start screen from updating itself. Go to the **Start** menu or screen, right-click the tile, and click **Turn live tile off** in the shortcut menu.

▲ *Startup tab.* The Startup tab of Task Manager in Windows 10/8 is used to manage startup items (see Figure 5-17). Click a white arrow to expand the items in a group. To disable a program from launching at startup, select it and click **Disable** at the bottom of the window or in the shortcut menu. To see the program file location, right-click it and click **Open file location**, as shown in the figure.

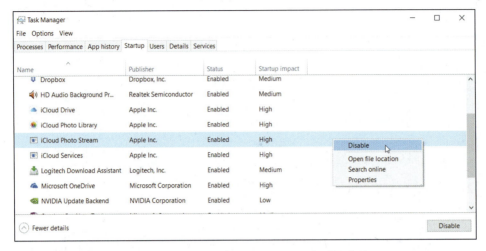

Figure 5-17 Startup processes are managed on the Startup tab of Task Manager

▲ *Users tab.* The Users tab (see Figure 5-18) lists currently signed-in users. Expand the list for a user to show processes started by the user that might be affecting overall system performance. Notice that the statuses of some programs on this tab are listed as Suspended. If certain apps remain idle for a short time, they're suspended so they don't require the attention of the CPU. When the app is used again, it automatically comes out of suspension, and the CPU once again begins servicing it. To disconnect a remote user or sign out a local user from the system, select the user and click **Disconnect** or **Sign out** at the bottom of the screen.

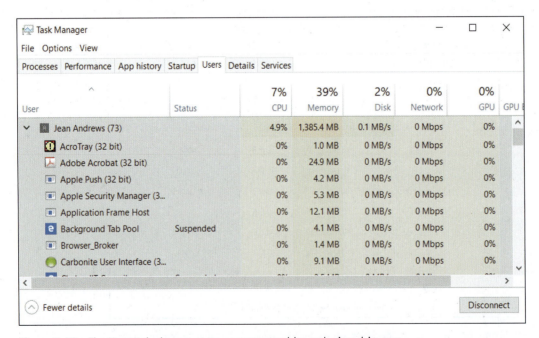

Figure 5-18 The Users tab shows system resources used by each signed-in user

▲ *Services tab.* The Services tab (see Figure 5-19) lists the services currently installed along with the status of each service. You can stop, start, or restart a service by right-clicking it and selecting the action in the shortcut menu. Services can also be managed from the Services console, as discussed later in this chapter.

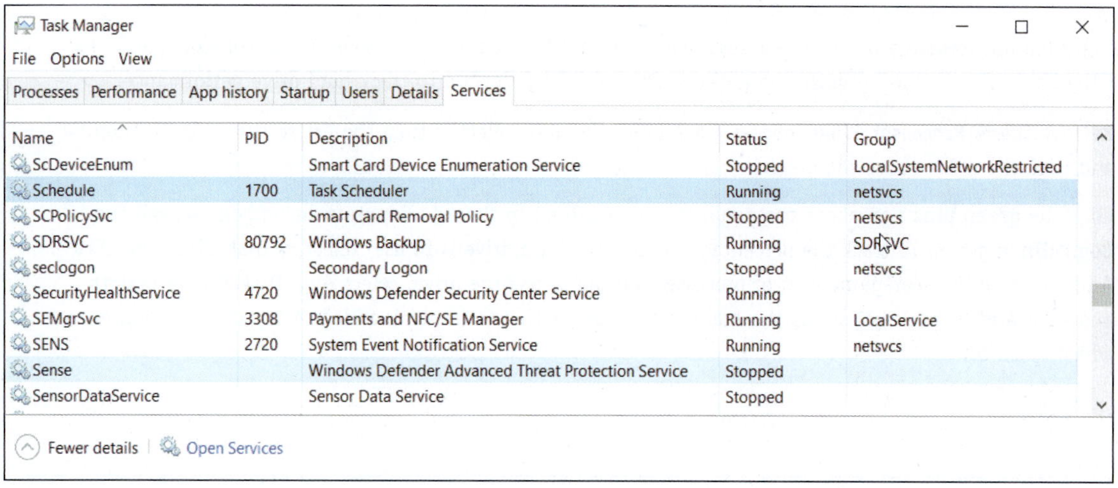

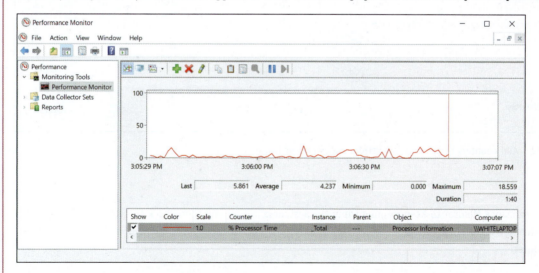

Figure 5-19 The Services tab of Task Manager gives the current status of all installed services

The system might be slow because the OS does not have the hardware resources it needs. Use System Information (msinfo32.exe) to find the model and speed of the installed processor and hard drive and the amount of memory installed. Compare all these values with the minimum and recommended requirements for Windows listed in Chapter 2. If you suspect that the processor, hard drive, or memory is a bottleneck, use Performance Monitor to get more information. If the bottleneck appears to be graphics, the problem might be solved by updating the graphics drivers or video adapter.

APPLYING | CONCEPTS   OBSERVING HARDWARE ACTIVITY USING PERFORMANCE MONITOR

Performance Monitor (perfmon.msc) tracks activity by hardware and software to measure performance. It can monitor in real time and can save collected data in logs for future use. Software developers might use this tool to evaluate how well their software is performing and to identify software and hardware bottlenecks.

To open Performance Monitor, enter the **perfmon.msc** command or open it from the Administrative Tools group in Control Panel. Performance Monitor offers hundreds of counters used to examine many aspects of the system related to performance. The Windows default setting is to show the % Processor Time counter the first time you open the window (see Figure 5-20). This counter appears as a red line in the graph and tracks activity of the processor.

Figure 5-20 Performance Monitor uses counters to monitor various activities of hardware and software

(continues)

To keep from unnecessarily using system resources, only use the counters you really need. For example, if you suspect the hard drive is slowing down the entire system, do the following to track hard drive performance:

1. Remove the **% Processor Time** counter. To delete a counter, select it from the list so that it is highlighted and click the red **X** above the graph.

2. Click the **green plus** sign above the graph to add counters. In the Add Counters dialog box, expand the **LogicalDisk** group. To track the percentage of time the hard drive is in use, select **% Disk Time** and click **Add**. To track the average number of processes waiting to use the drive, select **Avg. Disk Queue Length** and click **Add**. Figure 5-21 shows the Add Counters box with two counters added. After all your counters are added, click **OK**.

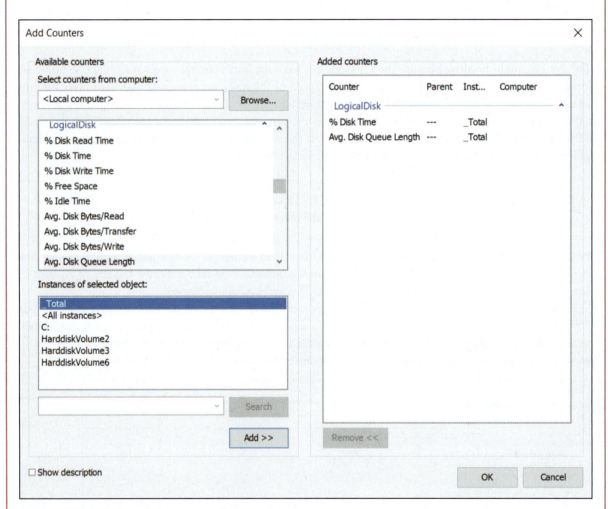

Figure 5-21   Add counters to set up what Performance Monitor tracks

Allow Performance Monitor to keep running while the system is in use, and then check the counters. The results for one system are shown in Figure 5-22. Select each counter and note the average, minimum, and maximum values for the counter.

(continues)

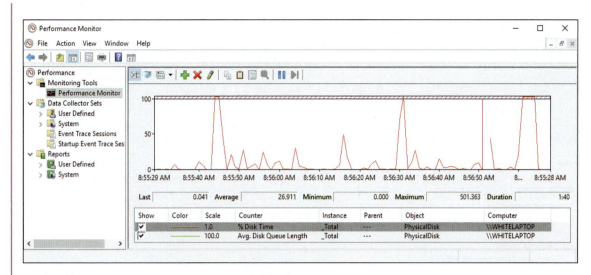

Figure 5-22 Two counters can measure hard drive performance

If the % Disk Time is more than 80 percent and the Avg. Disk Queue Length is above two, you can conclude that the hard drive is working excessively hard and processes are slowed down waiting on the drive. Anytime a process must wait to access the hard drive, you are likely to see degradation in overall system performance.

> **✎ Notes** To find out which counters to use to measure specific performances, search the Microsoft website or perform a general web search.

If you find that the system is slow because of a hardware component, discuss the situation with the user. You might be able to upgrade the hardware or OS or remove background processes drawing on hardware resources.

> **↻ OS Differences** The Windows 7 **Aero interface** might be slowing down the system as it uses computing power. If disabling it improves performance, you can keep it disabled or upgrade memory and/or the video card to support it. To disable the Aero interface, right-click the desktop, select **Personalize** from the shortcut menu, and click **Windows 7 Basic**.

INCOMPATIBLE APPLICATIONS OR THIRD-PARTY SERVICES

Sometimes you can't install or run an application without errors because there is a conflict or compatibility issue with other software. To eliminate these conflicts, run the application causing problems after a clean boot. A clean boot eliminates third-party software from starting during the boot and is done using System Configuration and Task Manager. If a clean boot allows the application to run without errors, you need to methodically zero in on the third-party program until you discover the one in conflict. Try disabling half of these programs. If the problem persists, disable the other half. Continue disabling half of the half until you find the program in conflict.

> **⚡ Caution** Don't depend on System Configuration or Task Manager to be a permanent fix to disable a startup program or service. Once you've decided you want to make the change permanent, use other methods to permanently remove that process from Windows startup. For example, you might uninstall a program, remove it from a startup folder, or use the Services console to disable a service.

APPLYING | CONCEPTS   PERFORMING A CLEAN BOOT

Let's see how to perform a clean boot to disable all third-party software during Windows startup:

1. To open System Configuration, enter the **msconfig.exe** command. The Windows 10 System Configuration box is shown in Figure 5-23 with the General tab selected.

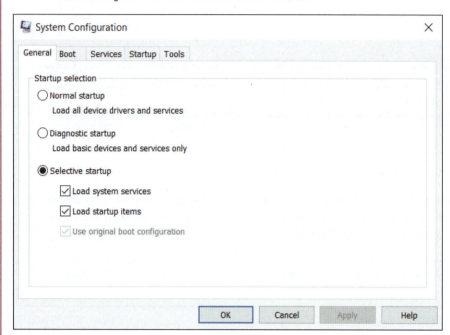

Figure 5-23   Use the General tab to control how Windows starts

2. Click the **Services** tab and check **Hide all Microsoft services**. The list now shows only services put there by third-party software (see Figure 5-24). Click **Disable all**.

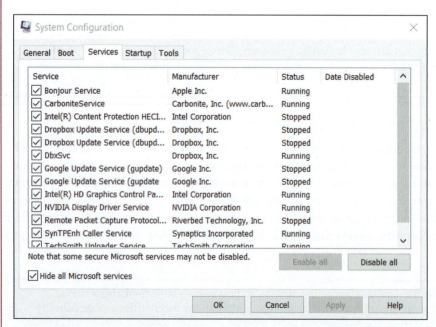

Figure 5-24   Use the Services tab of System Configuration to view and control services launched at startup

3. Click the **General** tab and notice that Selective startup is now selected. Click **Apply** and close the System Configuration box.

4. Open **Task Manager** and select the **Startup** tab (refer back to Figure 5-17). For each startup item, select it and click **Disable**. Close the Task Manager window and restart Windows.

Verify that the problem is solved in a clean boot environment. If the problem involves an application that will not install, install it now; then you can return the system to a normal startup. If the problem involves an application giving errors, you need to disable half the startup items and continue to disable half until you discover the startup program that is in conflict.

Here's how to return to a normal Windows startup:

1. Open the **System Configuration** box. On the General tab, click **Normal startup**. On the Services tab, uncheck **Hide all Microsoft services**. Verify that all services are now checked.

2. Open **Task Manager**. In the Task Manager window, select each startup item and enable it. Close all windows and restart the system.

> **↻ OS Differences** In Windows 10/8, the Startup tab in System Configuration is used only to open Task Manager, where startup items can be enabled and disabled. However, in Windows 7, startup items are managed on the Startup tab in System Configuration.

The Tools tab in the System Configuration box gives you quick access to other Windows tools you might need during a troubleshooting session (see Figure 5-25).

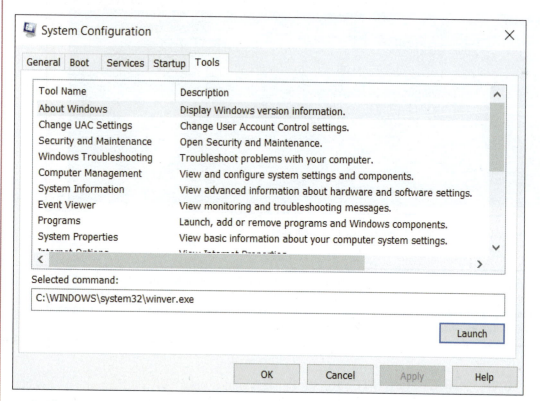

Figure 5-25 The Tools tab makes it easy to find troubleshooting tools

> **✎ Notes** System Configuration reports only what it is programmed to look for when listing startup programs and services. It looks only in certain registry keys and startup folders, and sometimes does not report a startup process. Therefore, don't consider its list of startup processes to be complete.

STEP 5: CONSIDER THAT WINDOWS MIGHT BE THE PROBLEM

An application or device might be giving problems because Windows system files are missing or corrupted. Here's what to do.

UPDATE WINDOWS

Make sure all critical and important Windows updates are installed. Microsoft Office and other Microsoft application updates are included in Windows updates.

USE SYSTEM FILE CHECKER

For essential hardware devices, use the System File Checker (SFC) to verify and replace system files, which include device drivers for many hardware devices. To run SFC, close all applications, open an elevated command prompt window, and enter the **sfc /scannow** command (see Figure 5-26). If corrupted system files are found, you might need to use Windows setup media to restore the files.

If you have problems running the SFC utility, boot the computer into Safe boot and run the sfc /scannow command again in Safe Mode. If you still have problems, know that you will learn more about repairing system files in Chapter 6.

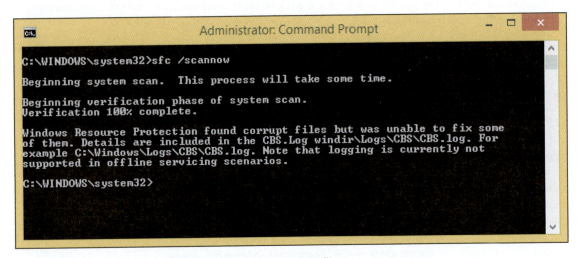

Figure 5-26 Use System File Checker to verify Windows system files

> **Notes** Recall from Chapter 4 that to get an elevated command prompt window in Windows 10, type **cmd** in the search box, right-click **Command Prompt**, and click **Run as administrator**. In Windows 8, right-click **Start** and click **Command Prompt (Admin)**. In Windows 7, click **Start**, **All Programs**, and **Accessories**. Then right-click **Command Prompt** and select **Run as administrator** from the shortcut menu.

USE DISM TO REPAIR SYSTEM FILES

In Chapter 2, you learned that DISM commands are used to create, manage, and deploy standard system images. You can also use the commands to repair an existing Windows installation, which sometimes works when SFC does not work. SFC depends on Windows Update to download the system files it needs to replace corrupted ones, but if Windows Update is not working, SFC cannot complete the repairs. DISM, on the other hand, gets new copies of system files from a Windows standard image available on the local machine or network. When troubleshooting a corrupted Windows installation, first try SFC; if that doesn't work, turn to DISM.

When using the DISM commands, know that a standard image is normally stored in the install.wim file and is called an offline image, and a running installation of Windows is called an online image. In addition, a virtual hard drive with a .vhd file extension that contains an installation of Windows is considered an offline image. Let's look at a few DISM commands, listed in the most likely order that you will use them:

1. To scan the current Windows installation for corrupted system files, use this command, which takes some time:

```
dism /online /cleanup-image /scanhealth
```

2. To report if system files in the Windows image have been flagged as corrupted, use this command:

```
dism /online /cleanup-image /checkhealth
```

3. Use this command to search for and replace corrupted system files, using Windows Update to find new system files:

```
dism /online /cleanup-image /restorehealth
```

4. If Windows Update is not working, you can use the system files stored in a standard image to replace corrupted files. Use the DISM command with the /source parameter to point to the image and the /limitaccess parameter to not use Windows Update to find replacement files:

```
dism /online /cleanup-image /restorehealth /source:install.wim /limitaccess
```

This last DISM command assumes the install.wim file is in the C:\Windows\System32 folder. You can add a path to a different location in the command line. If you don't have a standard image available, you can extract one from the Windows setup files, as you'll see in a project at the end of this chapter. Also know that DISM keeps a log file of what it did at C:\Windows\Logs\DISM\dism.log.

BOOT WINDOWS IN SAFE MODE

Safe Mode, also called Safe boot, loads Windows with a minimum configuration and can create a stable environment when Windows gets corrupted. There are several ways to start Safe Mode, which you learn about in Chapter 6. One way is to open System Configuration, click the **Boot** tab, and check **Safe boot** (see Figure 5-27). If the application in question needs the Internet to work, select **Network**. Click **OK** and restart the system.

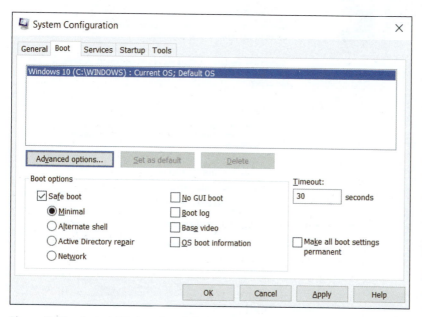

If the application works in Safe Mode, you can assume the problem is not with the application but with the operating system or device drivers. Try System Restore, which is discussed next, to repair the system. To return the system to a normal startup, open System Configuration again and click **Normal startup** on the General tab.

USE SYSTEM RESTORE

If you know the approximate date the error started and that date is in the recent past, use System Restore (rstrui.exe)

Figure 5-27 Restart Windows in a Safe boot with minimal Windows configuration

to restore the system to a point just before the problem started. Reverting to a restore point can solve problems with corrupted registry entries used by applications, device driver updates, or other Windows problems. However, System Restore can cause problems of its own, so use it with caution. Keep these points in mind:

◢ System Restore might make many changes to a system. If you know which change caused a problem, try to undo that particular change first. The idea is to use the least invasive solution first. For example, if updating a driver has caused a problem, first use Device Manager to perform a driver rollback and undo that change.

◢ System Restore won't help you if you don't have restore points to use. System Protection must be turned on so that restore points are automatically created.

◢ Restore points replace certain keys in the registry but cannot completely rebuild a totally corrupted registry. Therefore, System Restore can recover from errors only if the registry is somewhat intact.

◢ The restore process cannot remove a virus or worm infection. However, it might help you start a system that is infected with a virus that launches at startup. After Windows has started, you can then use anti-malware software to remove the infection.

◢ System Restore might create a new problem. Often when using a restore point, anti-malware software gets out of whack and sometimes even needs reinstalling. Therefore, use restore points sparingly.

◢ Restore points are kept in a hidden folder on the hard drive. If that area of the drive is corrupted, the restore points are lost. Also, if a user turns System Protection off, all restore points are lost.

◢ Viruses and other malware sometimes hide in restore points. To completely clean an infected system, you need to delete all restore points by turning System Protection off and back on.

◢ If Windows will not start, you can launch System Restore using startup recovery tools, which are covered in Chapter 6.

> ★ **A+ Exam Tip** The A+ Core 2 exam gives you a scenario and expects you to know when and how to use System Restore to solve a Windows, hardware, or application problem within that scenario.

Here's how to use System Restore:

1. Enter the **rstrui.exe** command. The System Restore box appears and shows the most recent restore point selected (see Figure 5-28).

2. Do one of the following:

   ◢ For most situations, select the most recent restore point to make the least possible changes to your system, and then click **Next**.

   ◢ To see other restore points, select **Choose a different restore point** and click **Next**. Select a restore point and click **Next**.

3. Click **Finish**. The system restarts and the restore point is applied.

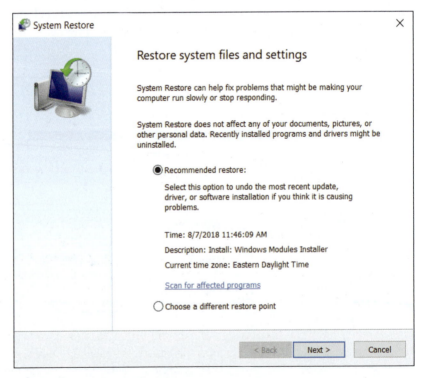

Figure 5-28 Select a restore point

Now that you understand the general approach to take when troubleshooting problems with Windows, applications, and hardware, let's look at some specific problems you might face and what to do about them.

SLOW STARTUP AND SLOW PERFORMANCE

A+ CORE 2 1.4, 1.5, 1.6, 3.1 If Windows starts slowly (sometimes called a slow startup or slow boot) or performs slowly, use the following steps to clean up the startup process and improve performance. We're assuming Windows starts with no errors. If Windows refuses to start or starts with errors, use the tools and techniques described in Chapter 6.

> ★ **A+ Exam Tip** The A+ Core 2 exam expects you to know how to troubleshoot and solve problems with slow system performance.

STEP 1: OBSERVE STARTUP

A+ CORE 2 3.1 To get a benchmark of how fast Windows starts and see what might be causing the problem of a slow startup, do the following:

1. Use a stopwatch or a watch with a second hand to time a normal startup from the moment you press the power button until the wait icon on the Windows desktop disappears.

2. Follow the steps given earlier in the chapter to set up a clean boot. Time the boot again, this time using a clean boot. Note the differences.

If there is no difference, you can assume startup processes are not the source of the problem. If the difference is significant, follow the steps in this part of the chapter to reduce Windows startup to essentials. If the performance problem still exists after a clean boot, you can assume that the problem is with hardware or Windows settings. You can then look for bottlenecks with hardware and consider that Windows might be corrupted, using the tools presented earlier in the chapter.

STEP 2: BACK UP USER DATA

A+ CORE 2 3.1 As always, if valuable data is not backed up, back it up before you apply any of the fixes in this chapter. You don't want to risk losing the user's data.

> 🖊 **Notes** If you are able to interview the user to find out when slow performance began, use Reliability Monitor (called reliability history in Windows 10) to discover what changes were made to the system around that time and what other problems occurred.

STEP 3: PERFORM ROUTINE MAINTENANCE

A+ CORE 2 1.4, 1.5, 1.6, 3.1 It might seem pretty mundane, but the first things you need to do to improve Windows performance are the routine maintenance tasks that you learned in Chapter 4. These tasks are summarized here:

◄ *Verify critical Windows settings.* Make sure Windows updates are current. Verify that antivirus software is updated and set to routinely scan for viruses. Make sure the network connection is secured and backups are happening as you expect. If the system is experiencing a marked decrease in performance, suspect a virus and use up-to-date antivirus software to perform a full scan of the system.

▲ *Uninstall software you no longer need and optimize the hard drive.* Make sure drive C: has at least 15 percent free space and the hard drive is being defragged or optimized weekly. If you suspect hard drive problems, use chkdsk to check the hard drive for errors and recover data.

STEP 4: INVESTIGATE AND ELIMINATE STARTUP PROGRAMS

**A+
CORE 2
1.4, 1.5,
1.6, 3.1**

To speed up startup, search for unnecessary startup programs you can eliminate. Tools that can help are System Configuration (msconfig.exe), startup folders, and Task Manager. Follow these steps to investigate startup:

1. Open the **Startup** tab in Windows 10/8 Task Manager or the **Startup** tab in Windows 7 System Configuration. In the list of startup items, look for a specific startup program you don't want. If you're not sure of the purpose of a program, right-click it in Windows 10/8 and click **Search online** in the shortcut menu. (For Windows 7, scroll to the right in the Command column to see the location and name of the startup program file, and use that information for a web search.) Then search the web for information on this program. Be careful to use only reliable sites for credible information.

⚡ **Caution** A word of caution is important here: Many websites will tell you a legitimate process is malicious so that you will download and use their software to get rid of the process. However, their software is likely to be adware or spyware that you don't want. Make sure you can trust a site before you download from it or take its advice.

2. If you want to find out whether disabling a startup entry gives problems or improves performance, temporarily disable it using Windows 10/8 Task Manager or Windows 7 System Configuration. To permanently disable a startup item, it's best to uninstall the software or remove the entry from a startup folder. See Appendix B for a list of startup folders.

✎ **Notes** The startup folder for all users is hidden by default. In Chapter 1, you learned how to "unhide" folders that are hidden.

3. As you research startup processes, Task Manager can tell you what processes are currently running. Open Task Manager and select the **Processes** tab. If you see a process and want to know its program file location, right-click the process in Windows 10/8 and click **Open file location**. File Explorer opens at the program file's location.

◇ **OS Differences** For Windows 7, you can find out the file location by clicking **View** and clicking **Select Columns**. In the Select Process Page Columns box, check **Image Path Name** and click **OK**. The Image Path Name column is added to the Processes tab.

For extremely slow systems that need a more drastic fix, set Windows for a clean boot. Then restart the system and see what problems you have if a program you really need is disabled. Enable just the services and programs you decide you need.

Regardless of the method you use, be sure to restart the system after each change and note what happens. Do you get an error message? Does a device or application not work? If so, you have probably disabled a service or program you need.

Has performance improved? If performance does not improve by disabling services or startup programs, go back and enable them again. If a non-Microsoft service or startup program didn't cause the problem, turn your attention to Microsoft services or startup programs. Start disabling them one at a time.

> ★ **Caution** You might be tempted to disable all Microsoft services. If you do, however, you are disabling Networking, Event Logging, Error Reporting, Windows Firewall, Windows Installer, Windows Backup, Print Spooler, Windows Update, System Protection, and other important services. These services should be disabled only when testing for performance problems and then immediately enabled when the test is finished. Also, know that if you disable the Volume Shadow Copy service, all restore points kept on the system will be lost. If you intend to use System Restore to fix a problem with the system, don't disable this service. If you are not sure what a service does, read its description in the Services console before you change its status.

Remember that you don't want to permanently leave System Configuration or Task Manager in control of startup. After you have used these tools to identify the problem, use other tools to permanently remove the problem service or program from startup. Use the Services console to disable a service, use the Programs and Features window to uninstall software, and remove program files from startup folders. After the problem is fixed, return System Configuration and/or Task Manager to a normal startup.

Don't forget to restart the computer after making a change to verify that all is well.

STEP 5: CHECK FOR UNWANTED SCHEDULED TASKS

A+ CORE 2 1.5, 3.1

When applications install, they often schedule tasks to check for and download their program updates, and malware sometimes hides as a scheduled task. Scheduled tasks might be unnecessary and can slow a system down. The best way to uninstall a scheduled task is to uninstall the software that is responsible for the task. Open the Task Scheduler window and search through tasks to find those you think are unnecessary or causing trouble. Research the software the task works with and then decide if you want to uninstall the software or disable the task.

APPLYING | CONCEPTS USING TASK SCHEDULER TO MANAGE STARTUP PROGRAMS

To get familiar with Task Scheduler and use it to remove unnecessarily scheduled tasks from Windows startup, do the following:

1. Task Scheduler stores tasks in files and subfolders in the C:\Windows\System32\Tasks folder. Open Windows 10/8 **File Explorer** or Windows 7 **Windows Explorer** and drill down into this folder to see the list of scheduled task files. One example is shown in Figure 5-29.

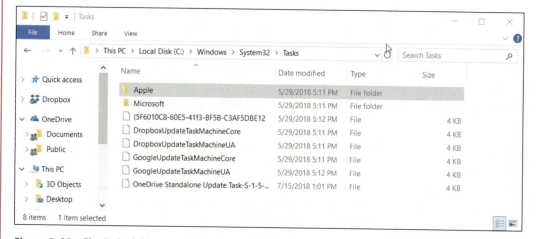

Figure 5-29 The Tasks folder contains tasks managed by Task Scheduler

(continues)

2. To open Task Scheduler, enter the **taskschd.msc** command or double-click **Task Scheduler** in the Administrative Tools group. The Task Scheduler window is shown in Figure 5-30.

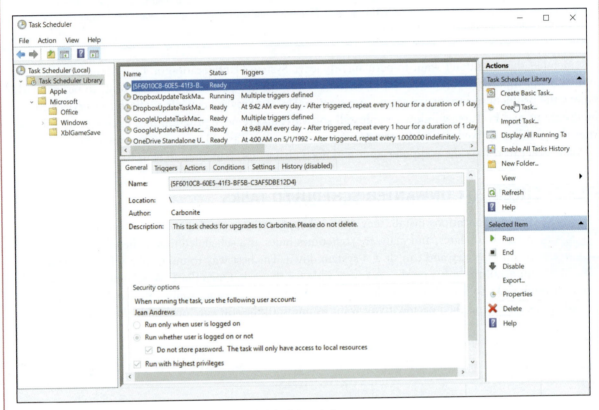

Figure 5-30 View and manage tasks from the Task Scheduler window

3. To explore tasks, drill down into groups and subgroups in the left pane. Notice in the left pane of Figure 5-30 that the groups and subgroups match up with the folder structure in the Tasks folder of Explorer. Tasks in a group are listed in the middle pane.

4. To see details about a task, including what triggers it, what actions it performs, the conditions and settings related to the task, and the history of past actions, select the task and then click the tabs in the lower-middle pane. For example, in the list of tasks shown in Figure 5-30, you can see that the Carbonite program task runs under the Jean Andrews account even when the user is not logged on.

5. To delete, disable, or run a task, select it, and in the Actions pane, click Delete, Disable, or Run. You can also create your own tasks. To do so, click **Create Basic Task** in the Actions pane and follow the wizard to create the task.

6. When you're finished, close **Task Scheduler**. If you made changes in Task Scheduler, don't forget to restart the system to make sure all is well before you move on.

> ✎ **Notes** Tasks can be hidden in the Task Scheduler window. To be certain you're viewing all scheduled tasks, unhide them. In the menu bar, click **View** and make sure **Show Hidden Tasks** is checked.

STEP 6: CHECK FOR LOW SYSTEM RESOURCES

**A+
CORE 2
1.4, 1.5,
1.6, 3.1**

Follow directions in the "Low on System Resources" section earlier in this chapter to check a hardware component that might be a bottleneck. Also, you might be able to improve performance by moving the virtual memory file, pagefile.sys; Windows uses this file in the same way it uses memory to enhance the amount of RAM in a system. Normally, pagefile.sys is a hidden file stored in the root directory of drive C:. To save space on drive C:, you can move pagefile.sys to another volume on the same hard drive or to a different hard drive, but don't move it to a different hard drive unless you know that drive is at least as fast as the current one. If the drive is as fast as the one on which Windows is installed, performance should improve. Also, make sure the new volume has plenty of free space to hold the file—at least three times the amount of installed RAM.

> ★ **A+ Exam Tip** The A+ Core 2 exam expects you to know how to configure virtual memory for optimal performance.

APPLYING | CONCEPTS   CHANGING THE LOCATION OF PAGEFILE.SYS

To change the location of pagefile.sys, follow these steps:

1. Open the System window and click **Advanced system settings** in the left pane. The System Properties box appears with the Advanced tab selected (see Figure 5-31).

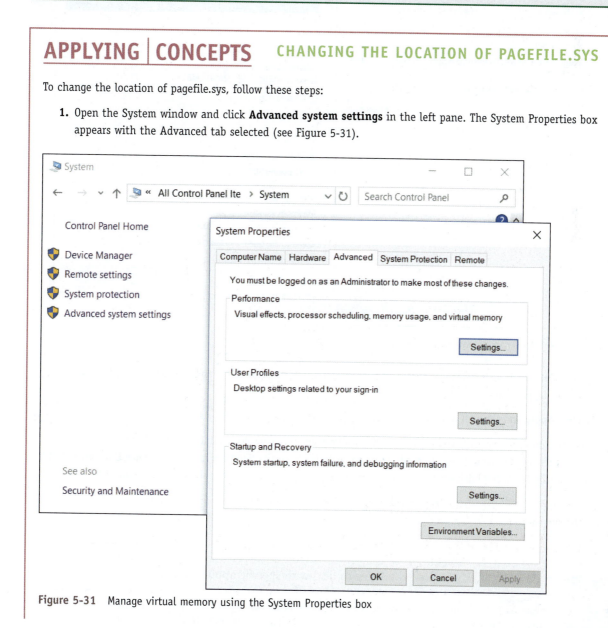

Figure 5-31   Manage virtual memory using the System Properties box

(continues)

5

2. In the Performance section, click **Settings**. In the Performance Options box, select the **Advanced** tab and click **Change**. The Virtual Memory dialog box appears.

3. Uncheck **Automatically manage paging file size for all drives** (see Figure 5-32). Select the drive where you want to move the paging file. For best performance, allow Windows to manage the size of the paging file. If necessary, select **System managed size** and click **Set**.

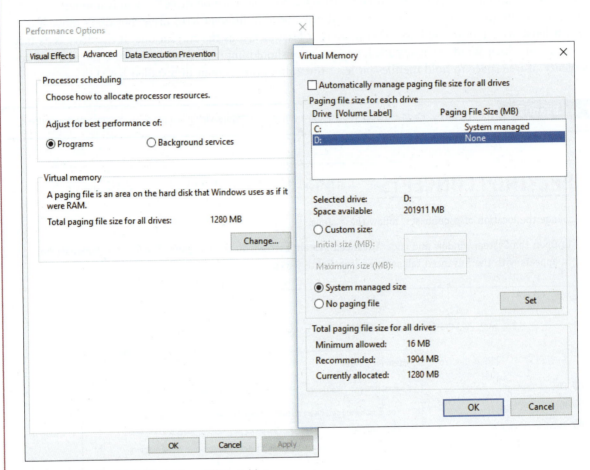

Figure 5-32 Move pagefile.sys to a different drive

4. Click **OK**. Windows informs you that you must restart the system for the change to take effect. Click **OK** to close the warning box.

5. Click **Apply** and close all boxes. Then restart the system.

If you still don't have enough free space on the Windows volume, consider adding a second hard drive to the system. In fact, if you install a second hard drive that is faster than the Windows hard drive, know that reinstalling Windows on the faster hard drive will improve performance. You can then use the slower, older hard drive for data.

APPLICATION ERRORS AND CRASHES

**A+
CORE 2
1.4, 1.5,
1.6, 3.1**

In this part of the chapter, you learn to deal with specific application errors and crashes.

✎ Notes If you are troubleshooting a problem and make a change to the system, be sure to restart Windows and check to see if the problem is resolved before you move on to the next fix.

APPLICATION HANGS

If an application is locked up and not responding, use Task Manager to end it. If Task Manager can't end a process, use the tasklist and taskkill commands. The tasklist command returns the process identifier (PID), which is a number that identifies each running process. The taskkill command uses the process ID to kill the process. Here's how to use the commands, using Notepad as our sample application:

1. Open a command prompt window and start Notepad with the **notepad.exe** command. Be sure the Notepad window and the command prompt window are positioned so both are visible on your screen.

2. Use the **tasklist | more** command to see a list of processes currently running (press the Spacebar to scroll to the next page). Note the PID of the Notepad process—for example, 7132. (You can also view PIDs on the Details tab of Task Manager.)

3. Enter the command **taskkill /f /pid:7132**, substituting the PID you noted in Step 2. The /f parameter forcefully kills the process. Be careful using this command; it is so powerful that you can end critical system processes that will cause the system to shut down.

SLOW-PERFORMING APPLICATION

Each application running on your computer is assigned a priority level, which determines its position in the queue for CPU resources. You can use Task Manager to change the priority level for an application that is already open. If an application performs slowly, increase its priority. You should only do this with very important applications because giving an application higher priority than certain background system processes can sometimes interfere with the operating system.

To use Task Manager to change the priority level of an open application, do the following:

1. In Task Manager, click the **Processes** tab, right-click the application, and click **Go to details**.

2. On the Details tab, right-click the selected program and point to **Set priority**. Set the new priority to **Above normal** (see Figure 5-33). If that doesn't give satisfactory performance, try **High**.

Remember that any changes you make to an application's priority level affect only the current session.

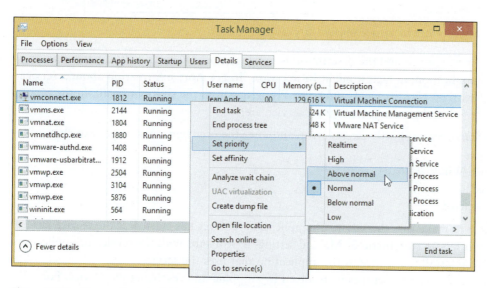

Figure 5-33   Change the priority level of a running application

> ↻ **OS Differences** For Windows 7, you can set the priority for a process in Task Manager by beginning with the **Applications** tab. Right-click the application and select **Go To Process**. On the Processes tab, right-click the selected process and point to **Set Priority**. You can then set the new priority.

SERVICE FAILS TO START

A+ CORE 2 1.5, 3.1

An error results when an application expects a background service to be running but it failed to start. Research the application documentation and find out if the app relies on a service to work. To manage services, enter the **services.msc** command to open the Services console. If the Extended tab at the bottom of the window is not selected, click it (see Figure 5-34). This tab gives a description of a selected service.

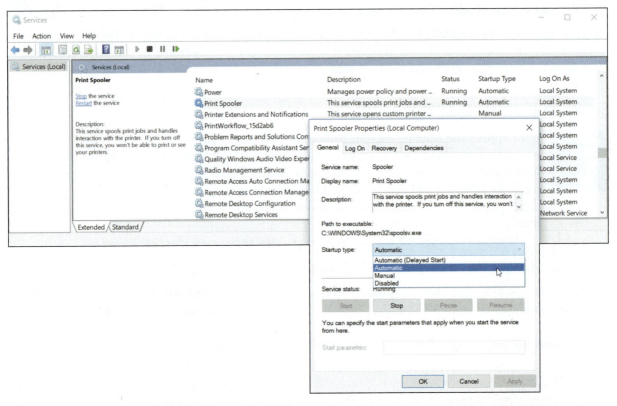

Figure 5-34 The Services console is used to manage Windows services

When you click a service to select it and the description is missing, most likely it's a third-party service put there by an installed application; in fact, it might be malware. To get more information about a service or to stop or start a service, right-click its name and select **Properties** from the shortcut menu. In the Properties box (see Figure 5-34), the startup types for a service are:

◢ *Automatic (Delayed Start).* Starts shortly after startup and after the user signs in, so as not to slow down the startup process

◢ *Automatic.* Starts when Windows loads

◢ *Manual.* Starts as needed

◢ *Disabled.* Cannot be started

Use the Services console to make sure the service an application requires has started. If the service has failed to start, make sure it has an Automatic or Manual setting. If problems with the service or application persist, you might need to reinstall the service or the application that uses the service.

Other problems with a service can sometimes be resolved by stopping and restarting the service. For example, stopping and restarting the Spooler service might solve a problem with print jobs not moving on to the printer. To stop or restart, right-click the service and use the shortcut menu.

📝 **Notes** If you suspect a Windows system service is causing a problem, you can use System Configuration to disable the service. If this works, try replacing the service file with a fresh copy from Windows setup media.

FILE FAILS TO OPEN

A+ CORE 2 3.1

Windows depends on the file extension to associate a data file with an application used to open it; this is called the file association. An application associated with a file extension is called its default program. When you double-click a data file and Windows examines the file extension but doesn't know which application to call on to open the file, it displays an error message. The solution to this problem is to change the file association for the file extension.

APPLYING | CONCEPTS SOLVING FILE ASSOCIATION PROBLEMS

A+ CORE 2 3.1

In our example, the Transact.dbf file shown in Figure 5-35A is a legacy database file created by dBASE, and the error box in Figure 5-35A appeared when the user double-clicked the file.

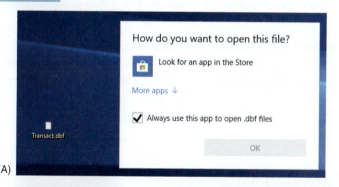

(A)

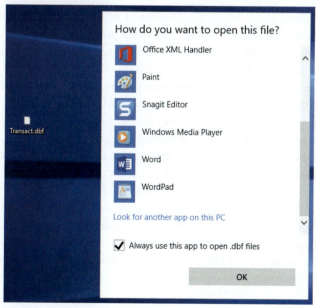

(B)

Figure 5-35 Windows does not know which application to use to open the data file

Follow these steps to instruct Windows to use Microsoft Excel to open files with a .dbf file extension:

1. When Windows displays an error message asking which application it should use to open a file, click **More apps**, as shown in Figure 5-35A. (For Windows 8/7, click **More Options**.) At the bottom of the box (see Figure 5-35B), click **Look for another app on this PC**. (For Windows 7, click **Select a program from a list of installed programs**.)

2. The *Open with* window appears. Locate the program file for Microsoft Excel, as shown in Figure 5-36, and click **Open**. (If you don't know an application's program file and location, launch the application and then open Task Manager. On the Processes tab of Task Manager, right-click the application and click **Open file location**. File Explorer or Windows Explorer opens and highlights the program file. You can see the path to the program file at the top of the Explorer window.)

(continues)

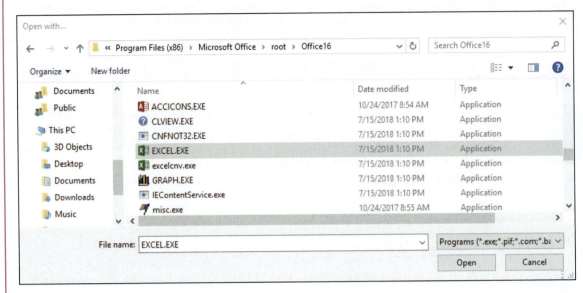

Figure 5-36   Locate and select the EXCEL.EXE application program file

3. When you double-click the **Transact.dbf** file, the file opens in an Excel window. Also, the icon used for the file on the desktop is now the Excel icon.

You might need to change the program associated with a file extension. For example, suppose you tried to associate the Transact.dbf file with Microsoft Access, and when you opened the file, Access gave an error. To change a file association, right-click the file in Explorer and click **Open with**. Next, for Windows 10, click **Choose another app**, check **Always use this app to open files**, and then find and select the new application. (For Windows 8/7, click **Choose default program** and find the new application to associate with the file extension.)

MISSING DLL OR COMPONENT NOT REGISTERED

A+
CORE 2
1.5, 1.6,
3.1

Most applications have a main program file that uses a collection of many smaller programs called components or objects that serve the main program. The main program for an application has an .exe file extension and relies on several component services that often have .dll file extensions. (DLL stands for Dynamic Link Library.) Problems with applications can be caused by a missing DLL program or a broken association between the main program and a component.

If you get an error message about a missing DLL, the easiest way to solve the problem might be to reinstall the application. However, if that is not advisable, you can identify the path and name of the missing DLL file and recover it from backup or from the application installation files.

On the other hand, the file might be present and undamaged, but the application cannot find it because the relationship between the two is broken. Relationships between a main program and its components are normally established by entries in the registry when the application is installed. The process is called registering a component. In addition, you can use Component Services (also called COM+) in the Administrative Tools group to register components. The tool is often used by application developers and system administrators when developing and deploying an application. For example, a system administrator might use COM+ when installing an application on servers or client computers where an application on one computer calls an application on another computer on the network.

★ **A+ Exam Tip**   The A+ 220-902 exam expects you to know how to handle missing DLL errors and to know when it's appropriate to use the Component Services tool.

As an IT support technician, you might be asked by a system administrator or software provider to use the COM+ tool to help solve a problem with an application giving errors. Suppose you get this error when installing an application:

Error 1928 "Error registering COM+ application."

When you contact the help desk of the application provider, you might be instructed to use the COM+ tool to solve the problem. To open the tool, open Control Panel and click **Administrative Tools**, then double-click **Component Services**. The Component Services window is shown in Figure 5-37. To learn how to use the tool, click **Help** in the menu bar. The application provider should be able to step you through the process of registering one of their components.

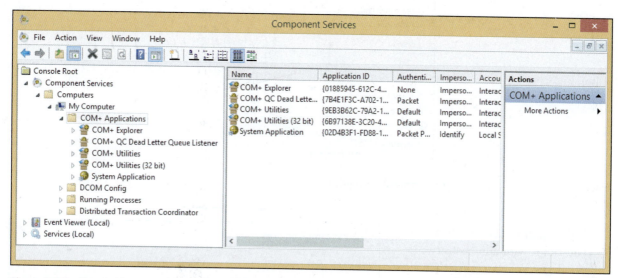

Figure 5-37 Use the Component Services window to register components used by an application

APPLICATION HAS NEVER WORKED

**A+
CORE 2
1.5, 1.6,
3.1**

If an application has never worked or stops working after the OS has been upgraded, follow these steps:

1. *Update Windows and search the web.* Installing all important and critical Windows updates can sometimes solve a problem with an application that won't install. Also check the website of the software manufacturer and the Microsoft support site (*support.microsoft.com*) for solutions. Search on the application name or the error message you get when you try to run it. Verify that the application is approved by its manufacturer to work in the installed OS.

2. *Run the installation program or application as an administrator.* The program might require that the user have privileges not assigned to the current user account. Try running the application with administrator privileges, which Windows calls a secondary logon. Use Explorer to locate the executable program file in a subfolder of the Program Files or Program Files (x86) folder. Right-click the file and select **Run as administrator** from the shortcut menu (see Figure 5-38).

> ✎ **Notes** To run a program from a user account other than administrator, hold down the Shift key and right-click the program file. Then select **Run as different user** from the shortcut menu. You must then enter the user name and password of another user account in the Windows Security box.

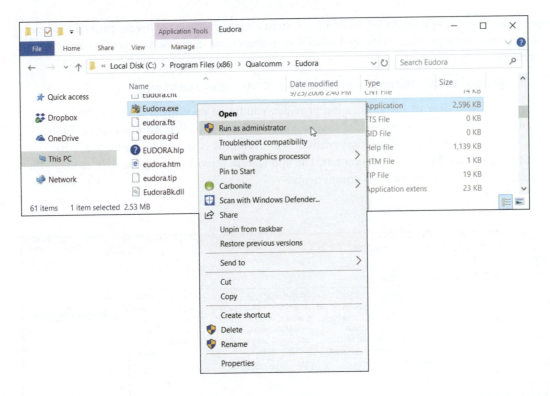

Figure 5-38 Execute a program using administrative privileges

If the program works when you run it with administrative privileges, you can make that setting permanent. To do so, right-click the program and select **Properties** from the shortcut menu. Then click the **Compatibility** tab and check **Run this program as an administrator** (see Figure 5-39). Click **Apply** and then close the Properties box.

3. *Consider whether an older application is having compatibility problems with Windows.* Some older applications cannot run under Windows 10/8 or they run with errors. In the Properties box shown in Figure 5-39, click **Run compatibility troubleshooter**. Windows makes its recommendations, such as enabling Compatibility mode for Windows XP programs. Test the program and click **OK** to make the change permanent.

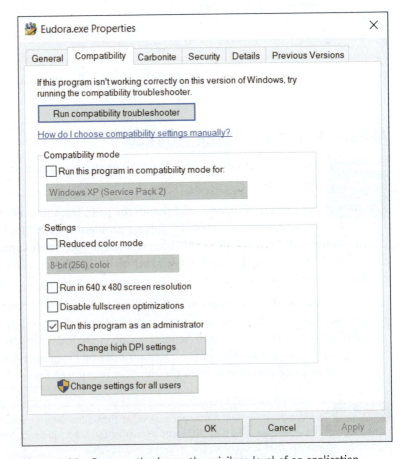

Figure 5-39 Permanently change the privilege level of an application

4. *Verify that the application is digitally signed*. Although applications that are not digitally signed can still run on Windows, a digital signature does verify that the application is not a rogue application and that it is certified as Windows-compatible by Microsoft. To view the digital signature, select the **Digital Signatures** tab of the program file's Properties box. Select a signer in the list and click **Details** (see Figure 5-40). If the Digital Signatures tab is missing, the program is not digitally signed.

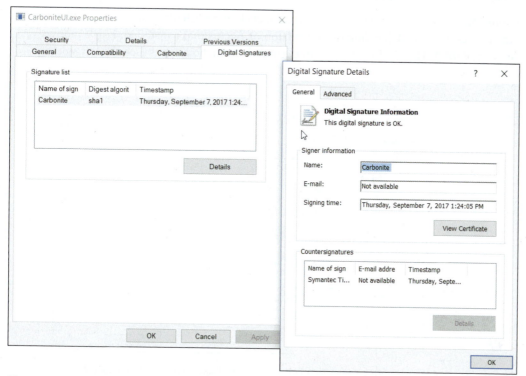

Figure 5-40 This program is digitally signed

ODBC DATA SOURCES

As an IT technician, you might be called on to help set up a local computer on a corporate network to connect to a remote database stored on a company database server. For example, suppose Microsoft Access is installed on the local computer and you want to configure it to connect to a Microsoft SQL Server database on a server. Open Database Connectivity (ODBC) is the technology used to create the data source, which provides access to the database and includes the drivers required to interface between Access and the data (see Figure 5-41). Drivers for Microsoft SQL Server must be installed on the local computer (Windows has SQL drivers installed by default). Then you can use the ODBC Data Sources tool in the Administrative Tools group of Control Panel to configure the data source.

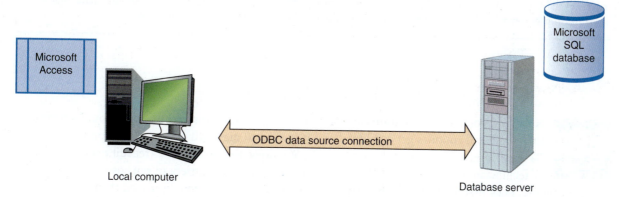

Figure 5-41 Microsoft Access connects to an ODBC data source on a corporate network

Do the following to create a new data source for Microsoft Access so that it can work with a remote Microsoft SQL Server database:

1. For Windows 10/8, you need to know whether Access is installed as a 32-bit or 64-bit application. One easy way to find out is to look on the Processes tab of Task Manager when the application is open. You'll see "32 bit" or "64 bit" listed in the application name.

2. Open the **Administrative Tools** group. For Windows 10/8, click either **ODBC Data Sources (32-bit)** or **ODBC Data Sources (64-bit)**, depending on the version of Access that's installed. For Windows 7, click **Data Sources (ODBC)**. The ODBC Data Source Administrator box opens (see the left side of Figure 5-42).

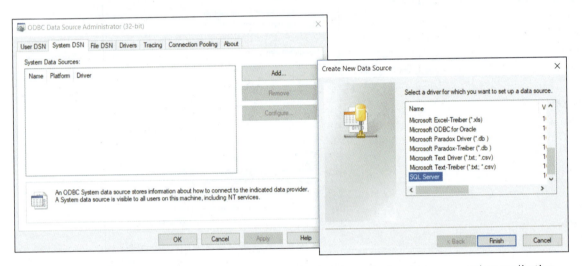

Figure 5-42 Use the Data Sources tool to create a connection between a foreign data source and an application

3. To make the data source apply to all users of the system, click the **System DSN** tab. (DSN stands for Data Source Name; the **User DSN** tab applies only to the current user.) Click **Add**. The Create New Data Source box appears (see the right side of Figure 5-42). Scroll down, select **SQL Server**, and click **Finish**. Follow the on-screen directions to enter the name of the SQL Server computer on the network and the sign-in ID and password to SQL Server. The database administrator in your organization can supply this information.

> ✎ **Notes** If you don't see the driver you need in the Create New Data Source box, close all windows and use Explorer to locate the C:\Windows\SysWOW64\Odbcad32.exe program file. When you double-click this file, the ODBC Data Source Administrator box appears and you can then access all ODBC drivers installed on the local computer.

AN APPLICATION FAILS TO UNINSTALL

A+ CORE 2 1.5, 1.6, 3.1

Normally, you use the Programs and Features window to uninstall an application. However, some uninstall routines get corrupted and you need to manually uninstall the application. To do so, you need to know how to use the Windows Registry Editor (regedit.exe). As an IT technician, you will be called on to edit the registry for a variety of purposes, not just to remove software. Let's first look at how the registry is organized and how to edit it, and then we'll explore the details of manually removing software.

REGISTRY EDITOR

Many actions, such as installing application software or hardware, can result in changes to items in the registry, called keys, which are assigned values. Changes to the registry can include adding or removing keys and their values or editing the values assigned to existing keys. For a few difficult problems, you might need to edit the values assigned to a key or remove a registry key. This part of the chapter looks at how the registry is organized, which keys might hold entries causing problems, and how to back up and edit the registry using the Registry Editor. Let's first look at how the registry is organized.

HOW THE REGISTRY IS ORGANIZED

The registry is the most important Windows component that holds information for Windows. The registry is a database designed with a treelike structure (called a hierarchical database) that contains configuration information for Windows, users, software applications, and installed hardware devices. During startup, Windows builds the registry in memory and keeps it there until Windows shuts down. During startup, after the registry is built, Windows reads from it to obtain information to complete the startup process. After Windows is loaded, it continually reads from many of the subkeys in the registry.

Windows builds the registry from the current hardware configuration and from information it takes from the following files:

▲ Five files stored in the C:\Windows\System32\config folder; these files are called hives, and they are named the SAM (Security Accounts Manager), SECURITY, SOFTWARE, SYSTEM, and DEFAULT hives. (Each hive is backed up with a log file and a backup file, which are also stored in the C:\Windows\System32\config folder.)

▲ C:\Users*username*\Ntuser.dat file, which holds the preferences and settings of the currently signed-in user.

After the registry is built in memory, it is organized into five high-level keys (see Figure 5-43). Each key can have subkeys, and subkeys can have more subkeys and can be assigned one or more values. The way data is organized in the hive files is different from the way it is organized in registry keys. Figure 5-44 shows the relationship between registry keys and hives. For example, notice that the HKEY_CLASSES_ROOT key contains data that comes from the SOFTWARE and DEFAULT hives, and some of this data is also stored in the larger HKEY_LOCAL_MACHINE key.

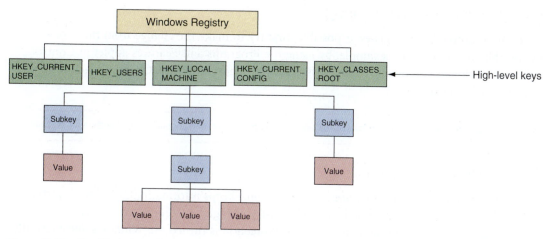

Figure 5-43 The Windows registry is logically organized in five keys with subkeys

Here are the five keys, including where they get their data and their purposes:

▲ **HKEY_LOCAL_MACHINE (HKLM)** is the most important key and contains hardware, software, and security data. The data is taken from four hives: the SAM hive, the SECURITY hive, the SOFTWARE hive, and the SYSTEM hive. In addition, the HARDWARE subkey of HKLM is built when the registry is first loaded, based on data collected about the current hardware configuration.

▲ **HKEY_CURRENT_CONFIG (HKCC)** contains information that identifies each hardware device installed on the computer. Some of the data is gathered from the current hardware

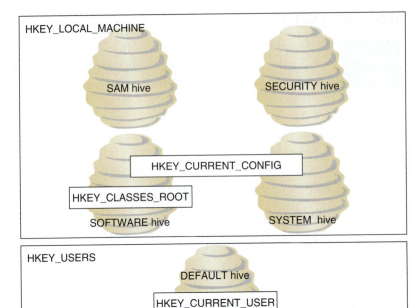

Figure 5-44   The relationship between registry keys and hives

configuration when the registry is first loaded into memory. Other data is taken from the HKLM key, which got its data primarily from the SYSTEM hive.

▲ **HKEY_CLASSES_ROOT (HKCR)** stores information that determines which application to open when the user double-clicks a file. This file association relies on the file's extension. Data for this key is gathered from the HKLM key and the HKCU key.

▲ **HKEY_USERS (HKU)** contains data about all users and is taken from the DEFAULT hive.

▲ **HKEY_CURRENT_USER (HKCU)** contains data about the current user. The key is built when a user signs in using data kept in the HKEY_USERS key and in the Ntuser.dat file of the current user.

> ✏ **Notes** Device Manager reads data from the HKLM\HARDWARE key to build the information it displays about hardware configurations. You can consider Device Manager to be an easy-to-view presentation of this HARDWARE key data.

BEFORE YOU EDIT THE REGISTRY, BACK IT UP!

When you think you need to edit the registry, if possible, first try to make the change from the Windows tool that is responsible for the key—for example, by using the Programs and Features applet in Control Panel. If that doesn't work and you must edit the registry, always back it up first. Changes made to the registry are implemented immediately.

> ⚡ **Caution** There is no undo feature in the Registry Editor, and no opportunity to change your mind once the edit is made.

Here are the ways to back up the registry:

▲ *Use System Protection to create a restore point.* A restore point keeps information about the registry. You can restore the system to a restore point to undo registry changes, as long as the registry is basically intact and not too corrupted. Also know that, if System Protection is turned on, Windows automatically makes a daily backup of the registry hive files to the C:\Windows\System32\Config\RegBack folder.

▲ *Back up a single registry key just before you edit the key.* This method, called exporting a key, should always be used before you edit the registry. How to export a key is explained in the following steps.

▲ *Make an extra copy of the C:\Windows\System32\config folder.* This is what I call the old-fashioned shotgun approach to backing up the registry. This backup will help if the registry gets totally trashed. You can boot from Windows setup media and use the Windows Recovery Environment to get a command prompt window that you can use to restore the folder from your extra copy. This method is drastic and not recommended except in severe cases. Still, just to be on the safe side, you can make an extra copy of this folder just before you start any serious digging into the registry.

In some situations, such as when you're going to make drastic changes to the registry, you'll want to play it safe and use more than one backup method. Extra registry backups are always a good thing! Now let's look at how to back up an individual key in the registry, and then you'll learn how to edit the registry.

BACK UP, EDIT, AND RESTORE INDIVIDUAL KEYS

A less time-consuming method of backing up the registry is to back up a particular key that you plan to edit. However, know that if the registry gets corrupted, having a backup of only a particular key most likely will not help you much when trying a recovery. Also, although you could use this technique to back up the entire registry or an entire tree within the registry, it is not recommended.

To back up a registry key along with its subkeys, follow these steps:

1. To open the Registry Editor, enter the **regedit** command and respond to the UAC box. Figure 5-45 shows the Registry Editor with the five main keys and several subkeys listed. Click the triangles on the left to see subkeys. When you select a subkey, such as KeyboardClass in the figure, the names of the values in that subkey are displayed in the right pane along with the data assigned to each value.

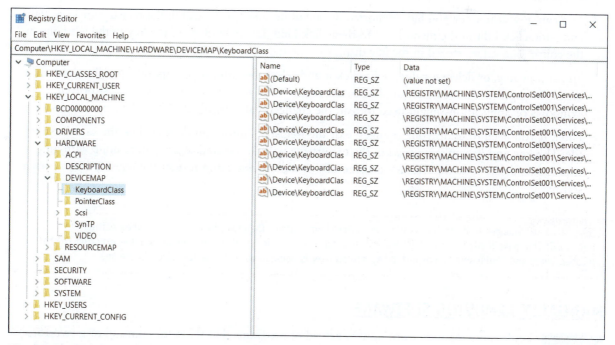

Figure 5-45   The Registry Editor showing the five main keys, subkeys, values, and data

> **Notes** The full path to a selected key displays in the bar at the top of the Windows 10 editor window and at the bottom of the Windows 8/7 editor window. If the bar is missing, click **View** in the menu bar. For Windows 10, make sure **Address Bar** is checked. For Windows 8/7, make sure **Status Bar** is checked.

2. Suppose we want to back up the registry key that contains a list of installed software, which is HKLM\ SOFTWARE\Microsoft\Windows\CurrentVersion\Uninstall. (HKLM stands for HKEY_LOCAL_ MACHINE.) First click the appropriate triangles to navigate to the key. Next, right-click the key and select **Export** from the shortcut menu, as shown in Figure 5-46. The Export Registry File dialog box appears.

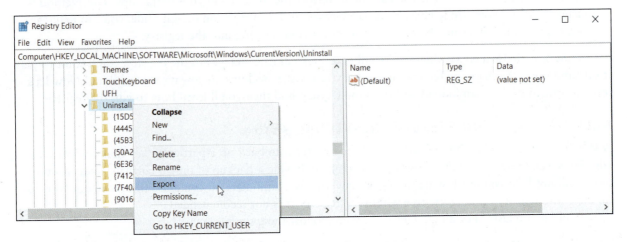

Figure 5-46   Using the Registry Editor, you can back up a key and its subkeys with the Export command

3. Select the location to save the export file and name the file. The desktop is a convenient place to store an export file while you edit the registry. Click **Save** when done. The saved file will have a .reg file extension.

4. You can now edit a key you have exported or one of its subkeys. To search the registry for keys, values, and data, click **Edit** in the menu bar and then click **Find**. Locate and select the key in the left pane of the editor. The values stored in the key display in the right pane.

5. To edit, rename, or delete a value, right-click it and select the appropriate option from the shortcut menu. Changes are immediately applied to the registry and there is no undo feature. (However, Windows or applications might need to read the changed value before it affects their operations.)

6. Later, if you need to undo your changes, exit the Registry Editor and double-click the saved export file. The key and its subkeys saved in the export file will be restored. After you're done with an export file, delete it so that no one accidentally double-clicks it and reverts the registry to an earlier setting.

> ⚡ **Caution**   Changes made to the registry take effect immediately. Therefore, take extra care when editing the registry. If you make a mistake and don't know how to correct a problem you create, double-click the exported key to recover. When you double-click an exported key, the registry is updated with the values stored in the key.

MANUALLY REMOVING SOFTWARE

A+
CORE 2
1.5, 1.6,
3.1

You're now ready to learn how to get rid of programs that refuse to uninstall or give errors when uninstalling. Doing so often causes problems later, so use the methods discussed in this section only as a last resort after normal uninstall methods have failed.

Here are the high-level steps:

1. First try to locate and use an uninstall routine provided by the software. If this works, you are done and can skip the next steps.

2. Delete the program folders and files that hold the software.

3. Delete the registry entries used by the software.

4. Remove the entries in the Start menu and delete any shortcuts on the desktop.

5. Remove any entries that launch processes at startup.

> ✎ **Notes** Before uninstalling software, make sure it's not running in the background. For example, antivirus software cannot be uninstalled if it's still running. You can use Task Manager to end all processes related to the software, and you can use the Services console to stop services related to the software. Then remove the software.

Now let's step through the process of manually removing software.

STEP 1: FIRST TRY THE UNINSTALL ROUTINE

Most programs written for Windows have an uninstall routine that can be accessed from the Programs and Features window or launched from the Windows 10/7 Start menu or Windows 8 Start screen. First, try one of these methods before moving on to Step 2.

STEP 2: DELETE PROGRAM FILES

If the uninstall routine is missing or does not work, the next step is to delete the program folders and files that contain the software. In our example, we'll delete the RegServe software without using its uninstall routine. (RegServe is utility software that can clean the registry of unused keys.) Follow these steps:

1. If you have not already done so, close the application.

2. Look for the program folder in the C:\Program Files or C:\Program Files (x86) folder. In Figure 5-47, you can see the RegServe folder under the C:\Program Files (x86) folder. Keep in mind, however, the program files might be in another location that was set by the user when the software was installed.

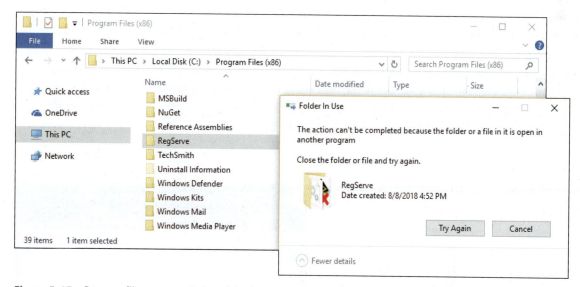

Figure 5-47 Program files are usually found in the Program Files or Program Files (x86) folder

3. Delete the **RegServe** folder and all its contents. As you do, the *Folder In Use* box shown on the right side of Figure 5-47 might report the program is in use. In this situation, do the following:

   a. Look for the program file reported on the **Processes** tab of Task Manager. If you see it listed, end the process (see Figure 5-48).

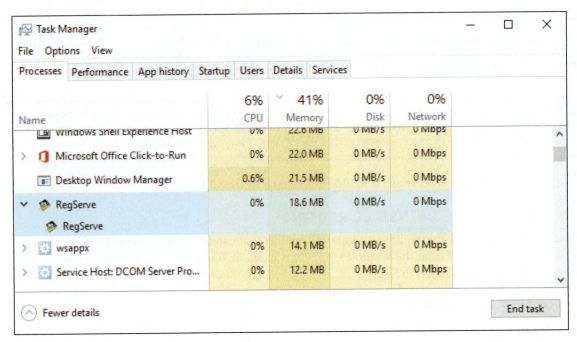

Figure 5-48 Task Manager shows a process is running and needs to be stopped before the program files can be deleted

b. If you don't find the program on the Processes tab, check the **Services** tab. If you find it there, select it and stop the service.

c. After the program or service is stopped, try to delete the program folder again. If you still cannot delete the folder, look for other running programs or services associated with the software. Look for a program or service that has a program file location in the RegServe folder or its subfolders.

d. Try deleting all the subfolders and files in the RegServe folder until you find a particular file that you cannot delete. This program file is the process you must first stop before you can delete it. In our example, the program file that could not be deleted was RSListener.exe. See Figure 5-49. After it was stopped, the RegServe folder could be deleted.

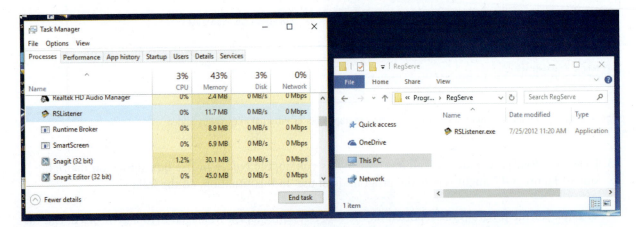

Figure 5-49 A running process prevents the RegServe folder and its running process from being deleted

STEP 3: DELETE REGISTRY ENTRIES

Editing the registry can be dangerous, so do it with caution and be sure to back up first! Do the following to delete registry entries that cause a program to be listed as installed software in the Programs and Features window of Control Panel:

1. To be on the safe side, back up the entire registry using one or more of the methods discussed earlier in the chapter.

2. Open the Registry Editor by entering the **regedit** command.

3. Locate a key that contains the entries that make up the list of installed software. Use the following criteria to decide which key to locate:

   ▲ For a 32-bit program installed in a 32-bit OS or for a 64-bit program installed in a 64-bit OS, locate this key:

   HKEY_LOCAL_MACHINE\Software\Microsoft\Windows\CurrentVersion\Uninstall

   ▲ For a 32-bit program installed in a 64-bit OS, locate this key:

   HKEY_LOCAL_MACHINE\SOFTWARE\Wow6432Node\Microsoft\Windows\CurrentVersion\Uninstall

> ✎ **Notes** Recall that 32-bit programs normally install in the \Program Files (x86) folder on a 64-bit system. These 32-bit programs normally use the Wow6432Node subkey in the registry of a 64-bit OS. However, occasionally you'll see a 32-bit app in the Uninstall key tree for 64-bit apps.

4. Back up the Uninstall key to the Windows desktop so that you can backtrack, if necessary. To do that, right-click the **Uninstall** key and select **Export** from the shortcut menu (see Figure 5-46 earlier in the chapter).

5. In the Export Registry File dialog box, select **Desktop**. Enter the file name as **Save Uninstall Key**, and click **Save**. You should see a new file icon named Save Uninstall Key.reg on your desktop.

6. The Uninstall key can be a daunting list of all the programs installed on your computer. When you expand the key, the left pane shows a long list of subkeys, which might have meaningless names that won't help you find the program you're looking for. Select the first subkey in the Uninstall key and watch as its values and data are displayed in the right pane. Step down through each key, watching for a meaningful name of a subkey in the left pane or meaningful details in the right pane until you find the program you want to delete. If you don't find the application in the Uninstall key for 32-bit apps, check the Uninstall key for 64-bit apps. Occasionally you'll see a 32-bit app in the 64-bit Uninstall key tree.

7. To delete the key, right-click it and select **Delete** from the shortcut menu. Confirm the deletion, as shown in Figure 5-50. Be sure to search through all the keys in this list because the software might have more than one key. Delete them all and exit the Registry Editor.

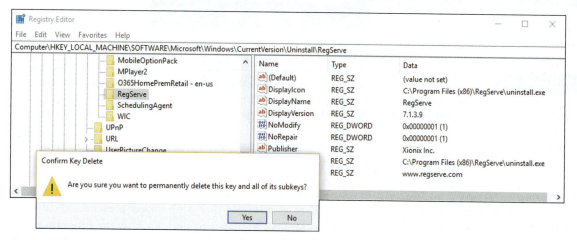

Figure 5-50 Select a subkey under the Uninstall key to display its values and data in the right pane and to delete the subkey

8. Open the Programs and Features window and verify that the list of installed software is correct and the software you are uninstalling is no longer listed.

9. If the list of installed software is not correct, restore the Uninstall registry key by double-clicking the **Save Uninstall Key.reg** icon on your desktop.

10. As a last step when editing the registry, clean up after yourself by deleting the Save Uninstall Key.reg file on your desktop. Right-click the icon and select **Delete** from the shortcut menu.

STEP 4: REMOVE PROGRAM SHORTCUTS

For Windows 10, you can remove the app from the **Start** menu by opening the menu, right-clicking the app, and clicking **More**. Then click **Remove from this list**. See Figure 5-51. If the program has shortcuts on the desktop, delete them.

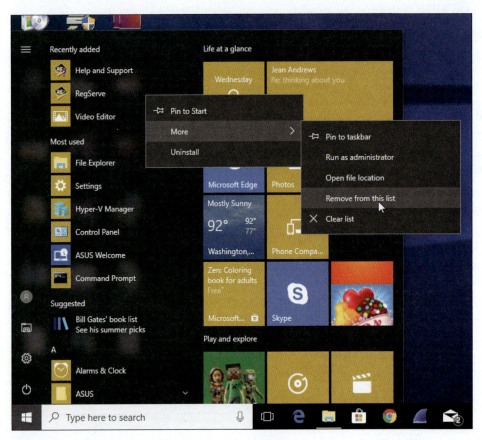

Figure 5-51   Remove an app from the Windows Start menu

> **◊ OS Differences** For Windows 8, go to the Start screen and type the name of the program. The Problem with Shortcut box appears. When you click **Yes**, the program will no longer be listed on the Start screen or Apps screen. For Windows 7, you can remove the program from the All Programs menu by right-clicking the program and selecting **Delete** from the shortcut menu.

STEP 5: REMOVE STARTUP PROCESSES

Restart the system and watch for any startup errors about a missing program file. The software might have stored startup entries in the registry, in startup folders, or as a service that is no longer present and causing an error. If you see an error, use System Configuration or Task Manager to find out how the program is set to start. This entry point is called an orphaned entry. You'll then need to delete this startup entry by editing the registry, deleting a shortcut in a startup folder, or disabling a service using the Services console.

It's unlikely you will be able to completely remove all keys in the registry that the software put there. A registry cleaner can help you find these orphaned keys, but if no errors appear at startup, you can just leave these keys untouched. Also, an installation might put program files in the C:\Program Files\Common Files folder or the C:\Program Files (x86)\Common Files folder. Most likely you can just leave these untouched as well. Address all error messages you encounter and stop there.

TROUBLESHOOTING HARDWARE PROBLEMS IN WINDOWS

A+
CORE 2
1.4, 1.5,
1.6, 3.1

Now we're ready to discuss dealing with display problems, network printing problems, and limited network connectivity.

DISPLAY SETTINGS AND GRAPHICS SOFTWARE

A+
CORE 2
1.5, 1.6,
3.1

For Windows 10, you can access the display settings by right-clicking the desktop and clicking **Display settings**. Alternately, you can click **Display** in the Settings window. The Display window is shown in Figure 5-52. For a dual-monitor setup, select the display you want to adjust, as shown in the figure.

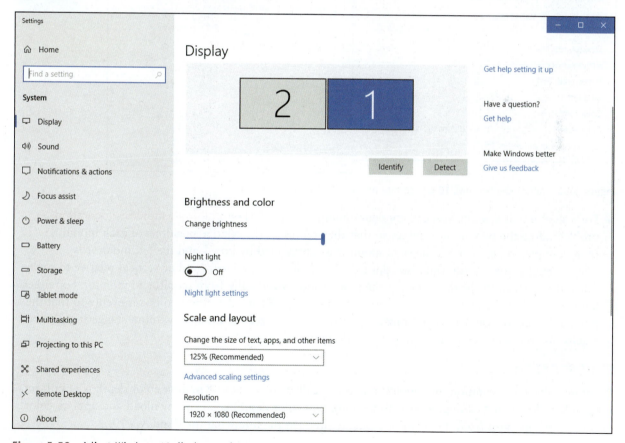

Figure 5-52 Adjust Windows 10 display settings

Here are a few basic display settings:

▲ To adjust **resolution** (the number of horizontal and vertical pixels used to build one screen), click the Resolution drop-down menu and select the highest or recommended resolution. The recommended resolution is usually the **native resolution**, which is the optimal resolution the monitor was designed to support.

▲ The refresh rate is the number of times the monitor refreshes the screen in one second. To set the rate, scroll down and click **Advanced display settings**. Click **Display adapter properties for Display** for the display device you want to configure. The video adapter properties box for that display appears. Click the **Monitor** tab and select the highest value available under Screen refresh rate (see Figure 5-53).

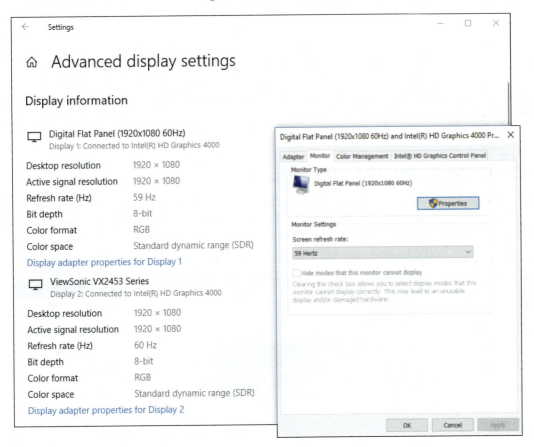

Figure 5-53 Adjust the Windows 10 refresh rate on the monitor properties box

▲ For a dual-monitor setup, you can configure multiple displays. For a multiple monitor orientation problem, drag the two monitor boxes so that they represent the relative positions of each monitor. (For example, in Figure 5-52, the right monitor is represented by box 1 and the left monitor is represented by box 2.) You can also adjust the boxes so they are horizontal or vertical relative to each other. If you stack the boxes vertically, the pointer moves vertically from monitor to monitor. For either a horizontal or vertical multiple monitor misalignment problem, align the two boxes evenly so that the pointer moves straight across or straight up or down to the second monitor without staggering. For best results, use the same screen resolution for both monitors.

COLOR DEPTH

Accurate color representation on a monitor screen is called color depth. The best color depth is important for graphics design and editing photos. To get optimum color depth, you can download and apply a color profile for the monitor from the monitor manufacturer. Do the following for Windows 10:

1. Look on the front or rear of the monitor for its brand and model.

2. Go to the monitor manufacturer's website and download the latest drivers for the monitor model (not the video adapter) and the version of Windows installed. The color profile file, which has an .icm file extension, should be in the downloaded package. To find the file, you might need to unzip a downloaded zipped folder or execute a downloaded executable file.

3. Open the video adapter properties box shown earlier in Figure 5-53 and select the **Color Management** tab. Then click **Color Management**. The Color Management box appears. See Figure 5-54.

4. In the drop-down menu, select the monitor and check **Use my settings for this device**. To add a new profile, click **Add** and click **Browse**. Then point to the .icm file you downloaded. Click **Add**.

5. In the Color Management box, select the added profile and click **Set as Default Profile**. You should notice colors on the screen change slightly after applying a new color profile.

6. There's one more color adjustment you can make. On the Color Management box, click the **Advanced** tab, click **Calibrate display**, and follow the on-screen directions to calibrate brightness and contrast settings.

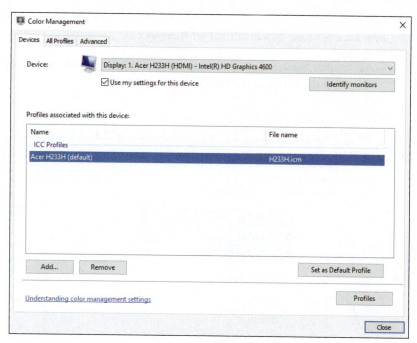

Figure 5-54 Use the Color Management box to apply a color profile

WINDOWS | 8   DISPLAY SETTINGS FOR WINDOWS 8

**A+
CORE 2
1.5, 1.6, 3.1**

For Windows 8/7, use the Display applet in Control Panel to manage display settings. The Display window for Windows 8 is shown in Figure 5-55.

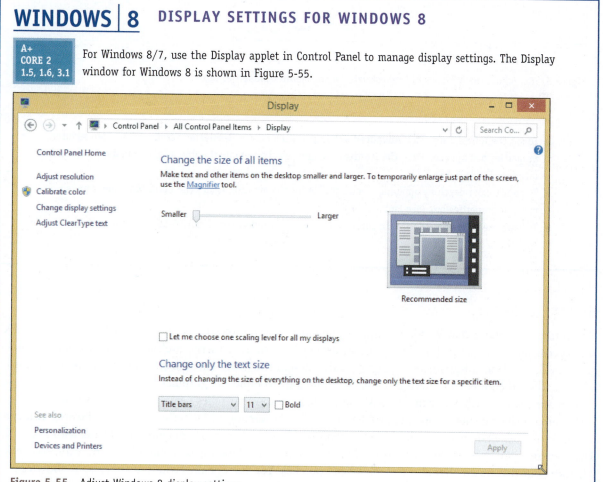

Figure 5-55 Adjust Windows 8 display settings

(continues)

Here are a few basic display settings for Windows 8/7:

▲ To adjust resolution, click **Adjust resolution**. The Screen Resolution window shown in Figure 5-56 appears. Select the highest or recommended resolution.

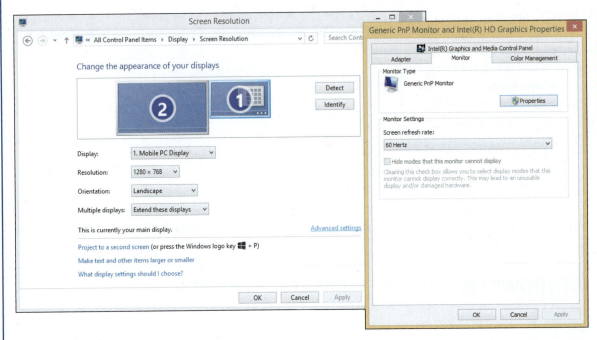

Figure 5-56   Adjust the Windows 8/7 refresh rate on the monitor properties box

▲ To set the refresh rate, click **Advanced settings** on the Screen Resolution window. The video adapter properties box appears. Click the **Monitor** tab and select the highest value available under Screen refresh rate (see Figure 5-56).

▲ To adjust color depth by applying a color profile for the monitor, select the **Color Management** tab on the monitor properties box (see Figure 5-56).

▲ To calibrate color, click **Calibrate color** on the Display window (see Figure 5-55) and follow the on-screen directions.

UPDATE DIRECTX

Recall from Chapter 2 that Windows requires the video adapter and drivers to support DirectX 9. DirectX is a Microsoft software development tool that developers can use to write multimedia applications, such as games, video-editing software, and computer-aided design software. The video firmware on the video card or motherboard chipset can interpret DirectX commands to build 3D graphics.

If an application such as a game or desktop publishing app that relies heavily on graphics is not performing well or giving errors, the problem might be the version of DirectX the system is using. You can use the dxdiag.exe command to display information about hardware and diagnose problems with DirectX. The first time you execute the **dxdiag.exe** command, a message box appears and asks if you want to check whether your drivers are digitally signed. When you click **Yes**, the opening window appears, as shown in Figure 5-57. Look for the version of DirectX that's installed (version 12 in the figure).

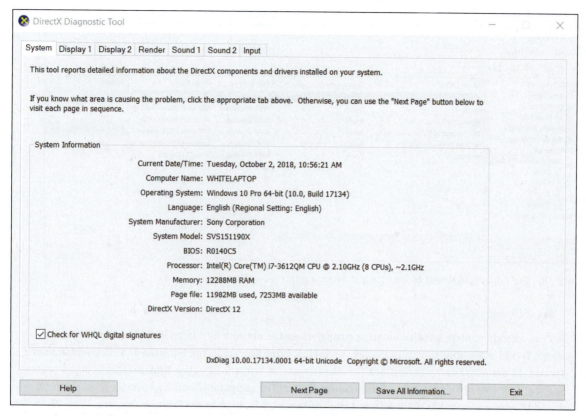

Figure 5-57 The DirectX Diagnostic tool reports information about DirectX components

To find out the latest version of DirectX published by Microsoft, go to *microsoft.com* and search on "DirectX End-User Runtime Web Installer." You can use a link on the page to download and install a new version of DirectX.

PRINT MANAGEMENT

A+ CORE 2 1.5, 1.6, 3.1

Windows professional and business editions offer the Print Management (printmanagement.msc) console in the Administrative Tools group of Control Panel. (Home editions don't provide the Print Management tool.) It comes in handy when you're responsible for managing several printers and users. Rather than having to walk over to a computer that has an installed printer with a problem, you can manage the computer's printer queue and other print issues while sitting at your own workstation. In Print Management, each computer on the network that has installed printers is considered a print server.

APPLYING | CONCEPTS   **LEARNING TO USE PRINT MANAGEMENT**

A+ CORE 2 1.5, 1.6, 3.1

Follow these steps to learn to use Print Management:

1. Open **Control Panel** and **Administrative Tools**. Double-click **Print Management**. The Print Management window appears.

2. In the Print Servers group, drill down to your local computer and click **Printers**. The list of printers installed on your computer appears, as shown in Figure 5-58.

(continues)

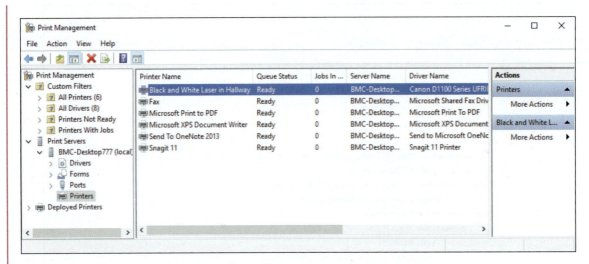

Figure 5-58   Use Print Management to monitor and manage printers on the network

3. You can manage printers installed on other computers on the network by adding each computer as a print server. To add other print servers to the list, right-click **Print Servers** in the left pane and click **Add/Remove Servers**. In the Add/Remove Servers box (see the left side of Figure 5-59), click **Browse**. Locate the computer (see the right side of Figure 5-59) and click **Select Server**. The computer is now listed under Add servers in the Add/Remove Servers box. Click **Add to List**. The computer is listed in the Print servers area. Click **OK** to close the Add/Remove Servers box.

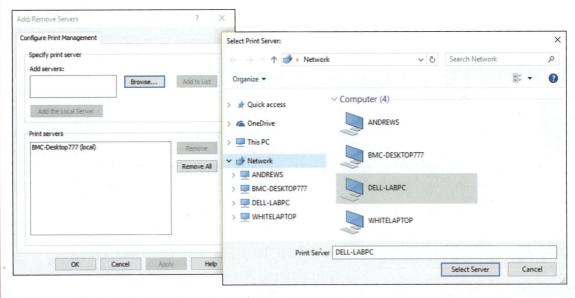

Figure 5-59   Select a print server to monitor and manage

4. The computer is now listed as a print server in the left pane of the Print Management window. Notice in Figure 5-60 that you can view a computer on the network that has its printer offline. Right-click this printer to see a menu with options that you can use to manage the printer and its printer queue.

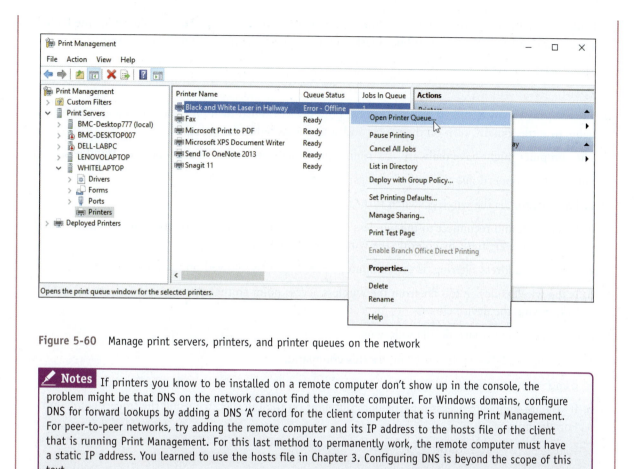

Figure 5-60 Manage print servers, printers, and printer queues on the network

> **✎ Notes** If printers you know to be installed on a remote computer don't show up in the console, the problem might be that DNS on the network cannot find the remote computer. For Windows domains, configure DNS for forward lookups by adding a DNS 'A' record for the client computer that is running Print Management. For peer-to-peer networks, try adding the remote computer and its IP address to the hosts file of the client that is running Print Management. For this last method to permanently work, the remote computer must have a static IP address. You learned to use the hosts file in Chapter 3. Configuring DNS is beyond the scope of this text.

LIMITED CONNECTIVITY

IT technicians are often asked to help when the local network has no connectivity or limited connectivity. Here is a brief list of what to do to solve these types of problems:

1. Verify that the network cable between the computer and the router or wall jack is not damaged and is securely connected at both ends.

2. For SOHO routers, connect the cable to a different port on the router. You know you have connectivity when the port LED lights are blinking. If the power LED light on the router is blinking, the problem is with the router and the router firmware might be corrupted. If LED lights don't indicate connectivity, consider the problem is hardware-related. You might need to replace the network adapter.

3. Go to Device Manager on the computer and disable then enable the network adapter. Update the device drivers.

4. As you learned to do in Chapter 3, go to the TCP/IP Properties box and verify the TCP/IP configuration for the connection. Most likely the correct option is *Obtain an IP address automatically*. Verify that the computer is getting a unique IP address from the router. When two computers on the network have the same IP address, connectivity errors occur. Have two computers been assigned the same static IP address? An administrator needs to check all static IP address assignments for duplicated addresses.

5. Update the network settings. Try using the following two commands to release and renew the DHCP assignments for the IP address, subnet mask, default gateway, and DNS server addresses:

```
ipconfig /release
```

```
ipconfig /renew
```

6. Try resetting the modem and router. Turn off both devices. Then turn on the modem and wait for the lights to settle. Finally, turn on the router and wait for its lights to settle.

7. The computer might have malware. Try running anti-malware software and updating Windows.

8. For wireless connections, check these things:

   a. For a laptop, is the wireless switch turned on?

   b. Disconnect and reconnect to the wireless network. Try removing or forgetting the wireless network profile and start fresh by entering the wireless security key.

   c. For MAC address filtering, is the computer's MAC address allowed on the network?

   d. Is the wireless device too far from the wireless access point so that the signal is too weak? Try moving the device closer.

9. For Internet connectivity, do the following:

   a. To eliminate DNS as the problem, try this command:

   ```
   ping www.cengage.com
   ```

   b. If you are unable to access a particular computer on the Internet, try using the tracert command. For example:

   ```
   tracert www.cengage.com
   ```

   c. If you can access resources on the local network but don't have Internet connectivity, contact your ISP and ask them to reset the connection at their end.

   For more information about troubleshooting network connectivity problems, see Chapter 3.

>> CHAPTER SUMMARY

Concepts and Windows Tools for Solving Problems with Windows, Applications, and Hardware

▲ The Windows OS is made up of two main components: the shell and the kernel. The shell provides an interface for users and applications. The kernel is responsible for interacting with hardware.

▲ A process is a program running under the shell, together with all the resources assigned to it. A thread is a single task that a process requests from the kernel.

▲ Windows tools that conveniently access and manage other Windows tools are Control Panel, Administrative Tools, Computer Management, and Microsoft Management Console (MMC).

▲ Tools to observe, track, and log Windows, user, network, application, and hardware activities are Event Viewer, Performance Monitor, Reliability Monitor, and Resource Monitor.

▲ Tools for solving Windows, application, networking, and Windows user problems are Task Manager, System Configuration, the Services console, the Troubleshooting applet, Group Policy, Local Group Policy, and the Registry Editor.

- ▲ Other tools for solving Windows problems are System File Checker, DISM, Windows Updates, a clean boot, Safe Mode (Safe boot), and System Restore.

- ▲ Tools for solving application errors and crashes are Programs and Features, tasklist, taskkill, Component Services, secondary logons, Compatibility mode, digital signatures, Data Sources, and Task Scheduler.

- ▲ Tools for solving problems with hardware are Device Manager, Print Management, the Display applet, DxDiag, Memory Diagnostics, chkdsk, and Disk Defragmenter.

Best Practices to Troubleshoot Windows-Related Problems

- ▲ General steps to solve Windows-related problems are to (1) interview the user and back up data, (2) get help from error messages, the web, coworkers, and event logs, (3) consider that the data or the application might be corrupted, (4) consider outside interference such as malware, faulty memory, a corrupted hard drive, low system resources, and incompatible applications or third-party services, and (5) consider that Windows might be corrupted.

Slow Startup and Slow Performance

- ▲ General steps to solve problems with slow performance or slow startup are to (1) get a benchmark by using a stopwatch or watch to time startup to the point the Windows desktop loads and observe any errors that appear in the startup process, (2) back up user data, (3) perform routine maintenance, (4) investigate and eliminate unwanted startup programs, (5) eliminate unwanted scheduled tasks, and (6) check for low system resources.

Application Errors and Crashes

- ▲ The commands taskkill and tasklist can be used to forcefully end an application that is hung.

- ▲ Task Manager can change the priority level to improve performance of an application.

- ▲ The Services console is used to change the way a background service is started.

- ▲ In Explorer, use the shortcut menu for a data file to create a file association so that Windows knows which application is associated with the given data file. This solves the problem of a file that fails to open.

- ▲ Use Component Services to solve the problem that causes an error message to appear for an unregistered component or missing DLL. The tool creates the association between the DLL or component and its application in the Windows registry.

- ▲ When an application has never worked, update Windows, search the web for help, try running the application in compatibility mode or as an administrator using a secondary logon, and verify that the application is legitimate with a digital signature.

- ▲ To solve a problem when connecting a local database application to a database source online, use ODBC Data Sources to connect the application with the database server.

An Application Fails to Uninstall

- ▲ When an application fails to uninstall, you might need to manually edit the Windows registry using the Registry Editor.

- ▲ Always back up registry keys before editing them.

- ▲ To manually remove software, (1) try the uninstall routine, (2) delete program files, (3) delete registry entries, (4) remove program shortcuts, and (5) remove startup processes.

Troubleshooting Hardware Problems in Windows

◢ Use Display settings to adjust the resolution, refresh rate, multiple monitor orientation, and color depth for monitors.

◢ Use the dxdiag command to determine which version of DirectX is installed. DirectX is Microsoft software that works with graphics software and graphics adapter video drivers.

◢ Print Management makes it easy to manage network printers and their connections with workstations on the network.

◢ Limited network connectivity problems can be solved by verifying network cable connections, network port activity, NIC device drivers, TCP/IP configuration (network settings), cable or DSL modem connectivity to the ISP, wireless connectivity and access, and DNS name resolution.

>> KEY TERMS

For explanations of key terms, see the Glossary for this text.

Administrative Tools
Aero interface
chkdsk
clean boot
color depth
compatibility mode
Component Services (COM+)
Computer Management
console
data source
Data Sources
default program
digital signature
DirectX
DISM (Deployment Image Servicing and Management)
DxDiag (DirectX Diagnostic Tool)

dxdiag.exe
Event Viewer
executive services
file association
Group Policy
HAL (hardware abstraction layer)
HKEY_CLASSES_ROOT (HKCR)
HKEY_CURRENT_ CONFIG (HKCC)
HKEY_CURRENT_USER (HKCU)
HKEY_LOCAL_ MACHINE (HKLM)
HKEY_USERS (HKU)
initialization files
kernel
kernel mode
Local Group Policy
Memory Diagnostics

Microsoft Management Console (MMC)
multiple monitor misalignment
multiple monitor orientation
native resolution
Open Database Connectivity (ODBC)
pagefile.sys
Performance Monitor
Print Management
process
Programs and Features
refresh rate
registry
Registry Editor
reliability history
Reliability Monitor
resolution
Resource Monitor

Safe Mode
secondary logon
Services console
shell
snap-in
System Configuration
System File Checker (SFC)
System Restore
taskkill
tasklist
Task Manager
Task Scheduler
thread
Troubleshooting applet
user mode
user profile
user profile namespace
virtual memory

>> THINKING CRITICALLY

These questions are designed to prepare you for the critical thinking required for the A+ Core 2 exam and may use information from other chapters or from the web.

1. A user complains that her computer is performing slowly. She tells you the problem started about a week ago when new database software was installed. The software runs in the background to update a database synced between the user's workstation and database server. Which is the best tool or method to use to determine if the new software is hogging computer resources?

   a. Uninstall the database software and see if performance improves.

   b. Use Performance Monitor and Process counters to observe performance.

    c. Use the Performance tab of Task Manager to observe database software activity.

    d. Install more memory to improve system resources to handle the new software.

2. You have exhausted your knowledge of a problem and it still is not solved. Before you escalate it, what else can you do?

    a. Go back through the problem one more time, looking for what you overlooked.

    b. Explain to the user that you cannot solve his problem but you will find someone who can.

    c. Ask a knowledgeable coworker for help.

    d. Interview the user one more time to make sure you correctly understand the problem.

3. You are having difficulty uninstalling freeware a user accidentally installed while surfing the web. You look online and see the software is designed to work in an x86-based version of Windows. In which folder should you expect to find the program files for the software?

    a. C:\Windows

    b. C:\Program Files (x86)

    c. C:\Program Files

    d. It depends on the version of Windows installed.

4. You are troubleshooting an application problem and want to eliminate faulty memory as a source of the problem. Which command do you use?

    a. Mdsched.exe

    b. Taskmgr.exe

    c. Msconfig.exe

    d. Sfc /scannow

5. When a user, Belinda Lim, signs in to Windows, she cannot see her Documents folder in File Explorer and some of her Windows user settings are lost. You suspect her user profile is corrupted. Which tool or method should you use first to investigate and/or solve the problem? Second?

    a. Check the C:\User\Belinda Lim\Documents folder.

    b. Check the C:\Users\Belinda Lim\Documents folder.

    c. Use the chkdsk command.

    d. Use the sfc command.

6. An application is frozen and you cannot close its application window. What is the first thing you should do to end the process? Second thing?

    a. Use the tasklist command.

    b. Use Task Manager.

    c. Reboot the system.

    d. Use the taskkill command.

7. How can you eliminate the possibility that an application error is caused by another application or service running in the background?

8. How does Windows know which application to use to open a file when you double-click the file in File Explorer or Windows Explorer?

9. When Windows first starts and the user signs in, a message about a missing DLL appears. Which tool or method should you use first to solve the problem? Second?

a. Use Task Manager to identify the startup process.

b. Use the Services console to stop the process that needed the DLL.

c. Search the web on the error message to better understand the problem.

d. Use Component Services to register the DLL.

10. If an application works when the system is loaded in Safe Mode, but does not work when Windows is loaded normally, what can you assume?

11. A user tells you that Microsoft Word gives errors when saving a file. What should you do next?

a. Install Windows updates that also include patches for Microsoft Word.

b. Ask the user when the problem first started.

c. Ask the user to save the error message as a screenshot the next time the error occurs and email it to you.

d. Use Task Manager to end the Microsoft Word program.

12. When trying to improve performance of a slow system, you notice in Task Manager that the superfetch service is using a high percentage of CPU time. What is your next best step?

a. Disable superfetch to improve performance.

b. Update Windows to improve superfetch performance.

c. Superfetch is an essential Windows process and should not be disabled. Move on to other solutions to improve performance.

d. Ask the user if he uses the superfetch service. If he doesn't, uninstall it.

13. You need to install a customized console on 10 computers. What is the best way to do that?

a. When installing the console on the first computer, write down each step to make it easier to do the same chore on the other nine.

b. Create the console on one computer and copy the .mmc file to the other nine.

c. Create the console on one computer and copy the .msc file to the other nine.

14. What is the name of the program file that you can enter in the Windows search or Run box to execute Event Viewer? What process is running when Event Viewer is displayed on the screen? Why do you think the running process is different from the program file name?

15. When cleaning up the startup process, which of these should you do first?

a. Use the Registry Editor to look for keys that hold startup processes.

b. Run System Configuration to see what processes are started.

c. After you have launched several applications, use Task Manager to view a list of running tasks.

d. Run the Defrag utility to optimize the hard drive.

16. Using the Internet, investigate each of the following startup processes. Identify the process and write a one-sentence description.

a. Acrotray.exe

b. Ieuser.exe

17. Using Task Manager, you discover an unwanted program that is launched at startup. Of the items listed below, which ones might lead you to the permanent solution to the problem? Which ones would not be an appropriate solution to the problem? Explain why they are not appropriate.

a. Look at the registry key that launched the program to help determine where in Windows the program was initiated.

b. Use Task Manager to disable the program.

c. Search Task Scheduler for the source of the program being launched.

d. Use System Configuration to disable the program.

e. Search the startup folders for the source of the program.

18. List the program file name and path for the following utilities. (*Hint*: You can use Explorer or a Windows search to locate files.)

a. Task Manager

b. System Configuration

c. Services Console

d. Microsoft Management Console

e. Registry Editor

19. A customer reports that his recently purchased computer does not consistently run his old applications. Application errors occur intermittently, and data files get corrupted. He has tried uninstalling and reinstalling the apps, and the problems persist. As you troubleshoot the problem, you reboot the system and get a BSOD error. The customer tells you the BSOD has occasionally appeared. Which subsystem is most likely causing the problem? What is the next best step?

a. Windows is corrupted; reinstall Windows.

b. Windows Update is not working; use System Restore.

c. Memory is faulty; run Memory Diagnostics.

d. Applications are faulty; uninstall and reinstall the applications causing errors.

>> HANDS-ON PROJECTS

Hands-On | Project 5-1   Using the Microsoft Management Console

Using the Microsoft Management Console, create a customized console. Put two snap-ins in the console: Device Manager and Event Viewer. Store your console on the Windows desktop. Copy the console to another computer and install it on the Windows desktop.

Hands-On | Project 5-2   Using Event Viewer

Event Viewer can be intimidating to use but is really nothing more than a bunch of logs to search and manipulate. If you have Microsoft Office installed, open a Word document, make some changes in it, and close it without saving your changes. Now open Event Viewer and look in **Applications and Services Logs** and **Microsoft Office Alerts**. What event is recorded about your actions?

Hands-On | Project 5-3   Launching Programs at Startup

Do the following to practice launching programs at startup, listing the steps you took for each activity:

1. Configure Scheduled Tasks to launch Notepad each time the computer starts and any user signs in. List the steps you took.

2. Put a shortcut in a startup folder so that any user launches a command prompt window at startup. See Appendix B for a list of startup folders.

3. Restart the system and verify that both programs are launched. Did you receive any errors?

4. Remove the two programs from the startup process.

Hands-On | Project 5-4   Editing and Restoring the Registry

When you install Windows on a new computer, Windows setup gives you the opportunity to enter the computer's registered owner and registered organization. Practice editing and restoring the registry by doing the following to change the registered owner name:

1. Enter the command **winver.exe**, which displays the About Windows box. Who is the registered owner and registered organization of the computer?

2. Using the Registry Editor, export the registry key HKEY_LOCAL_MACHINE\SOFTWARE\Microsoft\Windows NT\CurrentVersion to an export file stored on the desktop.

3. With the HKEY_LOCAL_MACHINE\SOFTWARE\Microsoft\Windows NT\CurrentVersion key selected in the left pane, double-click the **RegisteredOwner** value in the right pane. The Edit String box appears (see Figure 5-61). Change the Value data, which is highlighted in the box, and click **OK**.

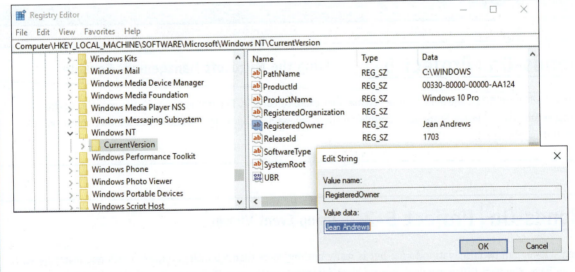

Figure 5-61   Change the name of the registered owner of Windows

4. Use the **winver** command again to display the About Windows box. Did the new name appear as the registered owner? Close the box.

5. Close the Registry Editor window. To restore the Value data to its original name, double-click the exported key on your desktop. Once again, use the **winver** command to display the About Windows box and verify that the original name is restored. Close the box.

6. Delete the exported registry key stored on the desktop.

Hands-On | Project 5-5   Finding Lost Downloaded Files

Your friend is using Internet Explorer to send and receive email using her Hotmail account. She received a Word document attached to an email message from a business associate. She double-clicked the Word attachment and spent a couple of hours editing it, saving the document as she worked. Then she closed the document. But where's the document now? When she later needed it, she searched her email account online and the Documents folder on her hard drive, but she could not find the document. She called you in a panic asking you to help her find her lost document.

Hint: In what folders does Internet Explorer store its temporary files? What are the paths to these folders on the hard drive?

> ✏️ **Notes** As an IT technician, it's helpful to be familiar with the locations of temporary folders that might contain lost files. However, a shortcut to finding a lost Word document is to open Word, click **File**, click **Open**, and then search through the Recent Documents list.

>> REAL PROBLEMS, REAL SOLUTIONS

REAL PROBLEM 5-1 Cleaning Up Startup

Using a computer that has a problem with a sluggish startup, apply the tools and procedures you learned in this chapter to clean up the startup process. Take detailed notes of each step you take and its results. (If you are having a problem finding a computer with a sluggish startup, consider offering your help to a friend, a family member, or a nonprofit organization.)

REAL PROBLEM 5-2 Manually Removing Software

To practice manually removing software, install WinPatrol from *winpatrol.com*. (WinPatrol monitors Windows and alerts you when an application attempts to add a startup process.) Following the directions in the chapter, manually remove the software, listing the steps you used. (Do not use the uninstall routine provided by WinPatrol.) After you have manually removed the software, reboot the system. Did you get any error messages?

REAL PROBLEM 5-3 Using DISM to Repair Windows

When SFC cannot fix a problem with a corrupted Windows 10 installation, you can use DISM commands to repair system files. The following steps extract a standard image from the Windows setup files and use the image to repair a Windows installation. Follow these steps:

1. Follow directions in Chapter 2 to download the Windows setup ISO file from the Microsoft website.

2. In File Explorer, right-click the ISO file and click **Mount**. The ISO file is mounted and assigned a drive letter. You can now drill down into the file.

3. Copy the **install.esd** file in the \sources folder of the ISO drive to the root of drive C:.

4. Use this command to examine the install.esd file and to see the images in it.

   ```
   dism /get-wiminfo /wimfile:C:\install.esd
   ```

   What is the index number for Windows 10 Pro? In our example in Figure 5-62, the number is 6.

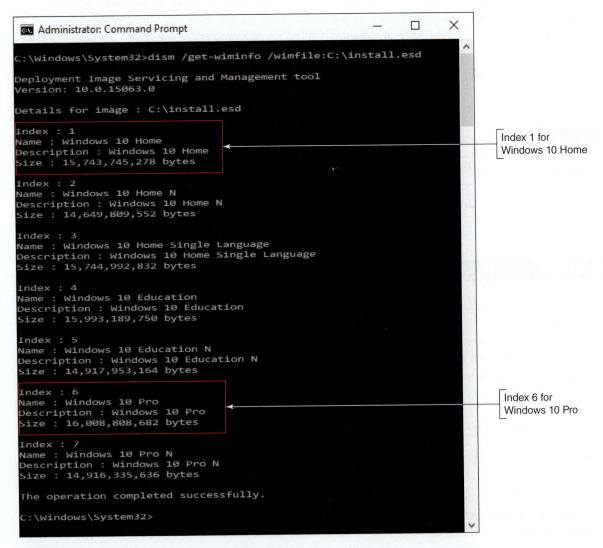

Figure 5-62 Examine the install.esd file for image indexes

5. Extract the install.wim file from install.esd for Windows 10 Pro. The install.wim file will be stored in the C:\Windows\System32 folder. Use the index number from Step 4 in this command:

```
dism /export-image /sourceimagefile:C:\install.esd /sourceindex:6 /
destinationimagefile:install.wim /compress:max /checkintegrity
```

6. Use this command to repair Windows system files using the files from the install.wim image you just extracted:

```
dism /online /cleanup-image /restorehealth /source:install.wim /
limitaccess
```

7. To save space on your hard drive, you can delete the C:\install.esd file. However, you might want to leave install.wim in the C:\Windows\System32 folder in case you need it to later repair the Windows installation.

Troubleshooting Windows Startup

After completing this chapter, you will be able to:

- Describe the boot process from the time you press the power button until the Windows desktop or Start screen loads

- Create bootable media and backups to prepare for Windows startup problems

- Implement appropriate Windows tools to solve Windows startup problems

- Implement appropriate Windows tools to reimage or reload Windows

- Troubleshoot Windows startup problems

You've already learned how to deal with application and hardware problems, and Windows problems after the OS has started. In this chapter, you take your troubleshooting skills one step further by learning to deal with startup problems caused by Windows. When Windows fails to start, it can be stressful if important data has not been backed up or the user has pressing work to do with the computer. What helps more than anything else is to have a good understanding of Windows startup and a good plan for approaching startup problems.

We begin the chapter with a discussion of what happens when you first turn on a computer and Windows starts. The more you understand about startup, the better your chances of fixing startup problems. Then you learn about Windows tools specifically designed to handle startup problems. Finally, you learn about strategies for solving startup problems.

UNDERSTANDING THE BOOT PROCESS

Knowledge is power. The better you understand what happens when you first turn on a computer until Windows is loaded and the Windows desktop or Start screen appears, the more likely you will be able to solve a problem when Windows cannot start. Let's begin by noting the differences between a hard boot and a soft boot.

> ✎ **Notes** Most techies use the terms *boot* and *startup* interchangeably. However, in general, the term *boot* refers to the hardware phase of starting up a computer. Microsoft consistently uses the term *startup* to refer to how its operating systems are booted—I mean, started.

DIFFERENT WAYS TO BOOT

The term booting comes from the phrase "lifting yourself up by your bootstraps" and refers to the computer bringing itself up to a working state without the user having to do anything but press the On button. Two fundamental ways to boot a computer are:

▲ A hard boot, or cold boot, involves turning on the power with the on/off switch.
▲ A soft boot, or warm boot, involves using the operating system to reboot. In Windows, a soft boot is called a restart.

A hard boot takes more time than a soft boot because a hard boot requires the initial steps performed by BIOS/UEFI. Most desktop cases have three power buttons, which for one system are shown in Figure 6-1.

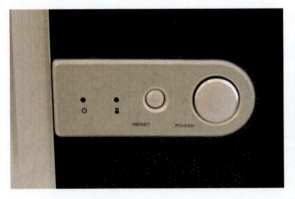

Figure 6-1 This computer case has two power buttons on the front and one power switch on the rear

Here's how the buttons work:

▲ The power button in front can be configured as a "soft" power button, causing a Windows restart.
▲ The reset button initializes the CPU so that it restarts at the beginning of the BIOS/UEFI startup program. The computer behaves as though the power were turned off and back on and then goes through the entire boot process.

◂ The switch on the rear of the case simply turns off the power abruptly and is a "hard" power button. If you use this switch, wait 30 seconds before you press the power button on the front of the case to boot the system. This method gives you the greatest assurance that memory will clear. However, if Windows is abruptly stopped, it might give an error message when you reboot.

How the front two buttons work can be controlled in BIOS/UEFI setup. Know, however, that different cases offer different options.

When Windows hangs, first try a restart. If that doesn't work, try a shutdown and then power the system back up. Windows shutdown closes all open applications, user sessions, services, devices, and system processes and then powers down the computer. If a shutdown does not work, press the reset button on the front of the case. If that doesn't work, turn off the power switch on the rear of the case, wait 30 seconds, turn it back on, and then press the power button on the front of the case.

STEPS TO BOOT THE COMPUTER AND START WINDOWS

A+ CORE 2 3.1

Recall that BIOS/UEFI is responsible for getting a system up and going and finding an OS to load. Table 6-1 lists the components and files stored on the hard drive that are necessary to start Windows. The table can serve as a guide as you study the steps to see what happens from the time power is turned on until Windows is started. In these steps, we assume the OS is loaded from the hard drive.

Component or File	Partition and Path*	Description
BIOS systems using MBR partitioning		
MBR	The first sector of the hard drive is called the Master Boot Record (MBR)	BIOS looks to the partition table in the MBR to locate the active partition.
System partition	Also called the active partition or System Reserved partition	The system partition holds the Boot Manager, Boot Configuration Data (BCD) store, and other files and folders needed to begin Windows startup. For Windows, these files are stored in the root and \Boot directory of the hidden system partition.
Boot Manager	In the root of the system partition	Windows Boot Manager, bootmgr (with no file extension), accesses the BCD store and locates the Windows Boot Loader.
BCD store	\Boot directory on the system partition	The Boot Configuration Data (BCD) store is a database file named BCD (no file extension) and is organized the same as a registry hive. It contains boot settings that control the Boot Manager and can be viewed and edited with the bcdedit command.
UEFI systems using GPT partitioning		
GPT partition table	At the beginning of the hard drive and a backup copy at the end of the drive	UEFI looks to the GPT partition table to locate the EFI System Partition.
System partition	The EFI System Partition (ESP) is normally 100 MB to 200 MB in size.	The system partition holds the Windows Boot Manager, BCD, and other supporting files. For Windows, the Boot Manager is bootmgfw.efi and is stored in \EFI\Microsoft\Boot. A backup copy of bootmgfw.efi is at \EFI\Boot\bootx64.efi.

Table 6-1 Software components and files needed to start Windows (continues)

Component or File	Partition and Path*	Description
Boot Manager	For Windows, \EFI\Microsoft\Boot on the ESP	Bootmgfw.efi loads EFI applications based on variables stored in onboard RAM and reads the BCD store to find out other boot parameters (such as a dual boot).
BCD store	\EFI\Microsoft\Boot on the ESP	Entries in the BCD store point the Windows Boot Manager to the location of the Windows Boot Loader program.
All Windows BIOS and UEFI systems		
Windows Boot Loader	C:\Windows\System32*	Windows Boot Manager turns control over to the Windows Boot Loader, which loads and starts essential Windows processes. Two versions of the program file are: winload.exe (BIOS) winload.efi (UEFI)
Resume from hibernation	C:\Windows\System32	This Windows Boot Loader is used when Windows resumes from hibernation: winresume.exe (BIOS) winresume.efi (UEFI)
Ntoskrnl.exe	C:\Windows\System32	Windows kernel
Hal.dll	C:\Windows\System32	Dynamic Link Library handles low-level hardware details
Smss.exe	C:\Windows\System32	Sessions Manager program responsible for starting user sessions
Csrss.exe	C:\Windows\System32	Win32 subsystem manages graphical components and threads
Winlogon.exe	C:\Windows\System32	Logon process
Services.exe	C:\Windows\System32	Service Control Manager starts and stops services
Lsass.exe	C:\Windows\System32	Authenticates users
System registry hive	C:\Windows\System32\Config	Holds data for the **HKEY_LOCAL_MACHINE** key of the registry
Device drivers	C:\Windows\System32\Drivers	Drivers for required hardware

*It is assumed that Windows is installed in C:\Windows.

Table 6-1   Software Components and Files Needed to Start Windows (continued)

A successful boot depends on essential hardware devices, BIOS/UEFI, and the operating system all performing without errors. Let's look at the steps to start a Windows computer. Several of these steps are diagrammed in Figures 6-2 and 6-3 to help you visually understand how the steps work.

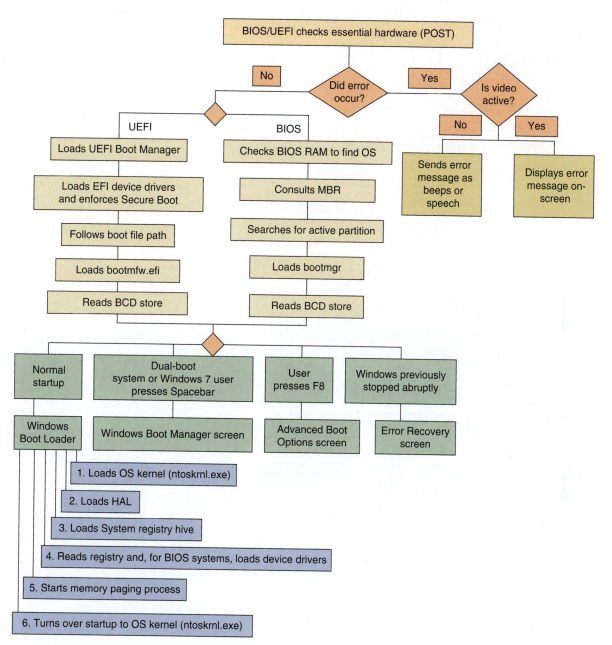

Figure 6-2 Steps to booting the computer and loading Windows

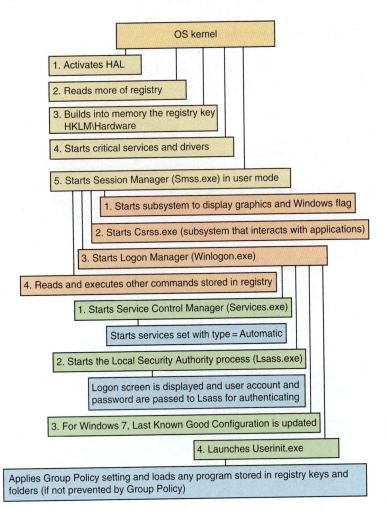

Figure 6-3 Steps to complete loading Windows

Study these steps carefully because the better you understand startup, the more likely you'll be able to solve startup problems:

1. Startup BIOS/UEFI is responsible for the early steps in the boot process. Onboard RAM accessible to BIOS/UEFI holds an inventory of hardware devices, hardware settings, security passwords, date and time, and startup settings. Startup BIOS/UEFI reads this information and then surveys the hardware devices it finds present, comparing it with the list kept in its RAM.

> ✎ **Notes** Onboard RAM, also called onboard memory, nonvolatile RAM, or NVRAM, is used by BIOS/UEFI to hold configuration data and keeps its data even when power is turned off. Onboard RAM is different from system memory or RAM, which holds programs and data only while the system is turned on.

2. Startup BIOS/UEFI runs POST (power-on self test), which is a series of tests to find out if the firmware can communicate correctly with essential hardware components required for a successful boot. Any errors are indicated as a series of beeps, recorded speech, or error messages on the screen (after video is checked). If the key is pressed to request BIOS/UEFI setup, the BIOS/UEFI setup program runs.

3. Based on information kept in onboard RAM, startup UEFI loads the UEFI boot manager and device drivers. BIOS/UEFI then turns to the hard drive or other boot device to locate and launch the Windows Boot Manager. If BIOS/UEFI cannot find a Windows Boot Manager or cannot turn over operation to it, one of these error messages appears:

```
Missing operating system
Error loading operating system
Windows failed to load
Invalid partition table
```

4. The Windows Boot Manager does the following:

   a. It reads the settings in the BCD.

   b. The next step depends on entries in the BCD and these other factors:

      ▲ *Option 1.* For normal startups that are not dual booting, no menu appears and Boot Manager finds and launches the Windows Boot Loader program.

      ▲ *Option 2.* If the computer is set up for a dual-boot environment, Boot Manager displays the *Choose an operating system* screen, as shown in Figure 6-4.

      ▲ *Option 3.* If Windows was previously stopped abruptly or another error occurs, the Windows Startup Menu appears (see Figure 6-5) to give you the option to troubleshoot the problem.

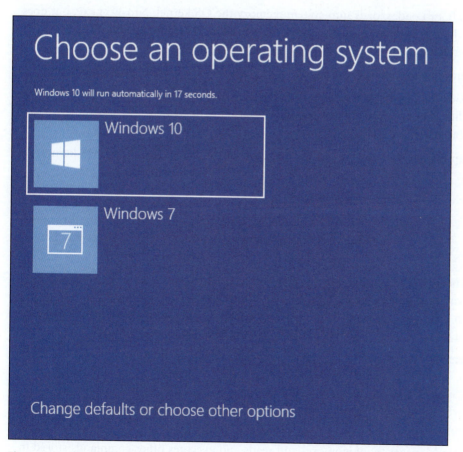

Figure 6-4 In a dual-boot setup, Windows Boot Manager provides a choice of operating systems

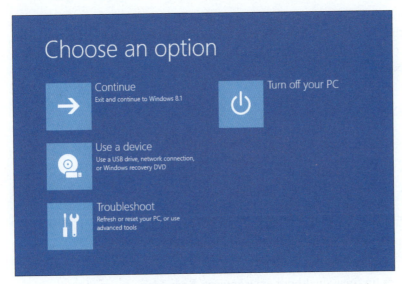

Figure 6-5   The Windows Startup Menu offers the opportunity to troubleshoot
a problem with startup

5. Windows Boot Loader (winload.exe or winload.efi) is responsible for loading Windows components. It does the following:

   a. For normal startups, Boot Loader loads into system memory the OS kernel, Ntoskrnl.exe, but does not yet start it. Boot Loader also loads into memory the hardware abstraction layer (Hal.dll), which will later be used by the kernel.

   b. Boot Loader loads into memory the system registry hive (C:\Windows\System32\Config\System).

   c. Boot Loader then reads the registry key just created, HKEY_LOCAL_ MACHINE\SYSTEM\Services, looking for and loading into memory the device drivers that must be launched at startup. The drivers are not yet started.

   d. Boot Loader starts up the memory paging process and then turns over startup to the OS kernel (Ntoskrnl.exe).

6. The kernel (Ntoskrnl.exe) does the following:

   a. It activates the HAL, reads more information from the registry, and builds into memory the registry key HKEY_LOCAL_ MACHINE\HARDWARE, using information that has been collected about the hardware.

   b. The kernel then starts critical services and drivers that are configured to be started by the kernel during the boot. Recall that drivers interact directly with hardware and run in kernel mode, while services interact with drivers. Most services and drivers are stored in C:\Windows\System32 or C:\Windows\System32\Drivers and have an .exe, .dll, or .sys file extension.

   c. After the kernel starts all services and drivers configured to load during the boot, it starts the Session Manager (Smss.exe), which runs in user mode.

7. The Session Manager (Smss.exe) loads the graphical interface and starts the client/server run-time subsystem (csrss.exe), which also runs in user mode. Csrss.exe is the Win32 subsystem component that interacts with applications.

8. Smss.exe starts the Logon Manager (winlogon.exe) and reads and executes other commands stored in the registry, such as a command to replace system files placed there by Windows Update.

9. Winlogon.exe does the following:

   a. It starts the Service Control Manager (services.exe). Services.exe starts all services listed with the startup type of Automatic in the Services console.

   b. Winlogon.exe starts the Local Security Authority process (lsass.exe). The sign-in screen appears (see Figure 6-6), and the user account and password are passed to the lsass.exe process for authenticating.

   c. Winlogon.exe launches userinit.exe. For Windows 10/7, the desktop is launched. For Windows 8, the Start screen is launched.

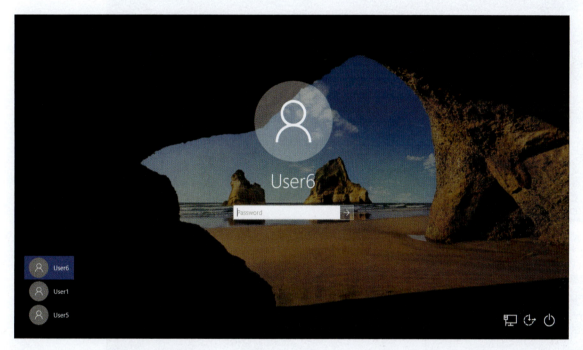

Figure 6-6   The Windows sign-in screen

10. Userinit.exe applies Group Policy settings and any programs not trumped by Group Policy that are stored in startup folders and startup registry keys. See Appendix B for a list of these folders and registry keys.

The Windows startup is officially completed when the Windows desktop or Start screen appears and the pinwheel wait icon disappears.

> **⟳ OS Differences**   For Windows 7, if the OS encounters an error during startup, the Windows 7 Error Recovery screen appears (see Figure 6-7). Also, Windows 7 can be controlled by keystrokes entered during startup: If the user presses the Spacebar near the beginning of startup, the Windows 7 Boot Manager screen appears, which allows the user to run Windows Memory Diagnostics. If the user presses F8 at startup, the Windows 7 Advanced Boot Options screen appears (see Figure 6-8).

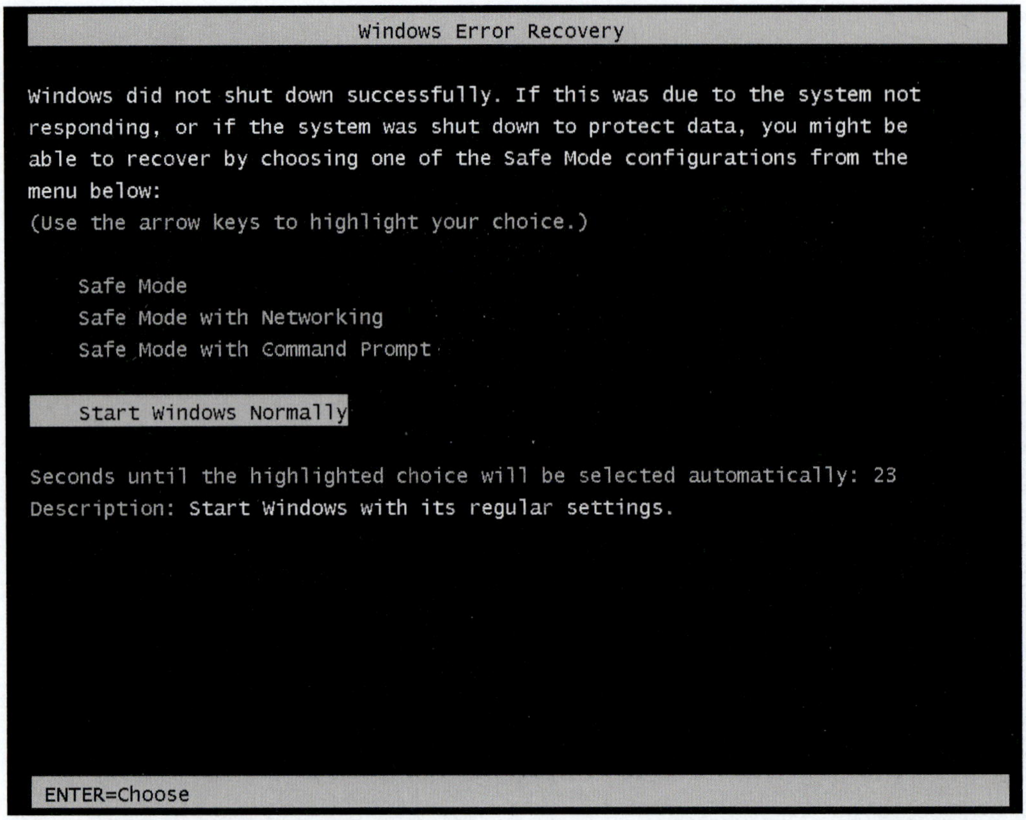

```
                        Windows Error Recovery

Windows did not shut down successfully. If this was due to the system not
responding, or if the system was shut down to protect data, you might be
able to recover by choosing one of the Safe Mode configurations from the
menu below:
(Use the arrow keys to highlight your choice.)


    Safe Mode
    Safe Mode with Networking
    Safe Mode with Command Prompt


    Start Windows Normally


Seconds until the highlighted choice will be selected automatically: 23
Description: Start Windows with its regular settings.
```

```
ENTER=Choose
```

Figure 6-7   The Windows Error Recovery screen appears if Windows 7 has been abruptly stopped

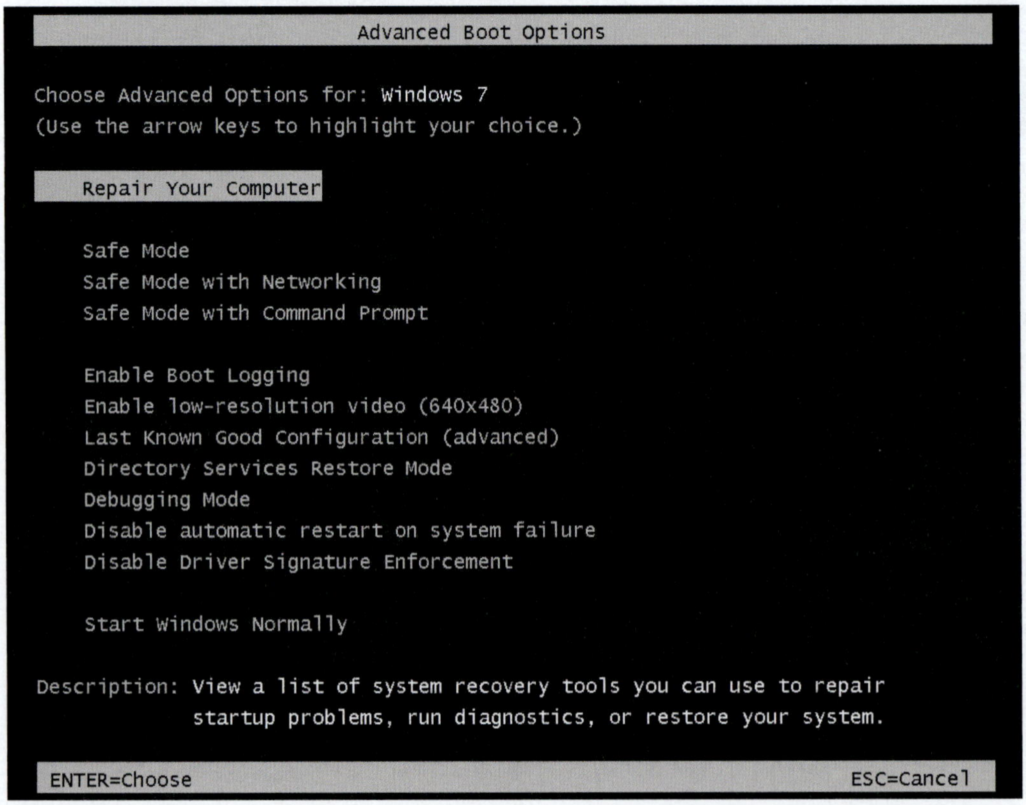

```
                        Advanced Boot Options

Choose Advanced Options for: Windows 7
(Use the arrow keys to highlight your choice.)

    Repair Your Computer

    Safe Mode
    Safe Mode with Networking
    Safe Mode with Command Prompt

    Enable Boot Logging
    Enable low-resolution video (640x480)
    Last Known Good Configuration (advanced)
    Directory Services Restore Mode
    Debugging Mode
    Disable automatic restart on system failure
    Disable Driver Signature Enforcement

    Start Windows Normally

Description: View a list of system recovery tools you can use to repair
            startup problems, run diagnostics, or restore your system.
```

```
ENTER=Choose                                                    ESC=Cancel
```

Figure 6-8   Press F8 during the boot to launch the Windows 7 Advanced Boot Options menu

With this basic knowledge of the boot in hand, let's turn our attention to what you can do to prepare for problems when Windows refuses to load.

WHAT TO DO BEFORE A PROBLEM OCCURS

**A+
CORE 2
3.1**

When troubleshooting startup, it helps to have a road map, which is the purpose of the diagram in Figure 6-9. It can help you organize in your mind the various ways to boot the system and the menus and procedures available to you depending on how the boot happens.

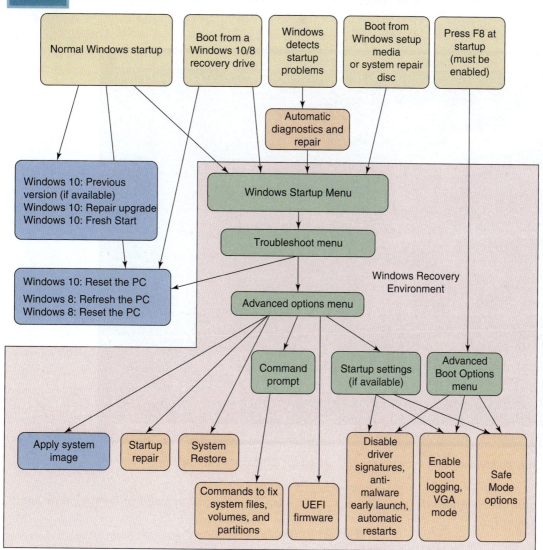

Figure 6-9 Methods to boot the system, menus that appear, and tools available on menus used to troubleshoot startup problems

As you learn to use each tool, keep in mind that you want to use the tool that makes as few changes to the system as possible to fix the problem. Good preparation will make troubleshooting startup problems much simpler and more successful. When you are responsible for a computer and while the computer is still healthy, be sure to complete the following tasks:

▲ *Keep good backups*. Chapter 4 covers methods to back up data, applications, and user settings.
▲ *Create a system image*. Recall that a Windows 10/7 system image or a Windows 8 custom refresh image should be created right after you've installed Windows, hardware, applications, and user accounts, and

customized Windows settings. The image can be updated periodically. You learned to create a Windows 10/7 system image and Windows 8 custom refresh image in Chapter 4.

▲ *Configure Windows 10/8 to use the F8 key at startup.* The F8 key gives you access to the Advanced Boot Options menu in Windows, which you'll learn about later in this chapter. Windows 10/8 has the feature disabled by default, and Windows 7 has it enabled. To enable the F8 key at startup, open an elevated command prompt window and enter this command:

```
bcdedit /set {default} bootmenupolicy legacy
```

Figure 6-10 shows the Advanced Boot Options screen that appears when you press F8 during Windows 10 startup.

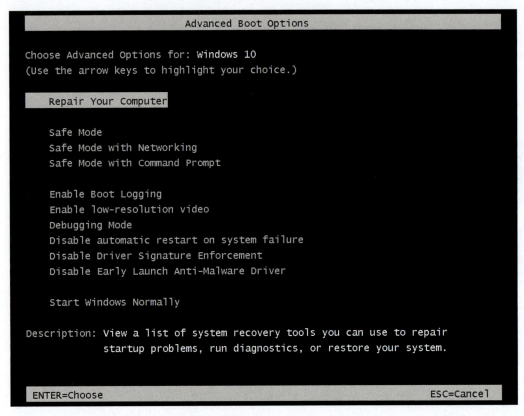

```
                        Advanced Boot Options

Choose Advanced Options for: Windows 10
(Use the arrow keys to highlight your choice.)

     Repair Your Computer

     Safe Mode
     Safe Mode with Networking
     Safe Mode with Command Prompt

     Enable Boot Logging
     Enable low-resolution video
     Debugging Mode
     Disable automatic restart on system failure
     Disable Driver Signature Enforcement
     Disable Early Launch Anti-Malware Driver

     Start Windows Normally

Description: View a list of system recovery tools you can use to repair
            startup problems, run diagnostics, or restore your system.


ENTER=Choose                                              ESC=Cancel
```

Figure 6-10   Use the Advanced Boot Options menu to troubleshoot difficult startup problems

Later, if you want to disable the use of F8 at startup, open an elevated command prompt window and enter this command:

```
bcdedit /set {default} bootmenupolicy standard
```

> **⚡ Caution**   As you learn to troubleshoot Windows 10/8 startup, don't depend on the F8 key to work during the boot because you never know when you'll work on a computer that has it disabled. All the tools available on the Advanced Boot Options screen are also available on the Startup Settings screen, which you can access without using F8. You learn about the Startup Settings screen later in this chapter.

▲ *Create recovery boot media.* If Windows can't boot from the hard drive, you may be able to repair the Windows installation using tools available in the **Windows Recovery Environment (Windows RE)**. Windows RE is normally stored on a hidden partition on the hard drive and is a lean operating system that can be launched to solve Windows startup problems. It provides both a graphical and command-line interface. Figure 6-9 shows Windows RE as a pink background. Menus in Windows RE are in green, tools are in blue and purple, and ways to launch Windows RE are in yellow boxes. Notice in the figure you can launch Windows RE after a normal Windows startup. However, if Windows won't start, you'll need other recovery boot media to launch it. Although it's possible to use recovery media created on a different computer than the one you are troubleshooting, the process is simplified if you already have these tools on hand. Figure 6-9 shows the three types of recovery boot media:

- ◢ Windows 10/7 DVD system repair disc
- ◢ Windows 10/8 USB recovery drive
- ◢ Windows 10 setup media created by the Media Creation Tool

The key to using a system repair disc or recovery drive is to create the disc or drive *before* it is needed. Let's look at each of the three recovery boot media.

> ✎ **Notes** All boot media are bit-specific. Use 32-bit media to repair a 32-bit Windows installation and 64-bit media to repair a 64-bit installation. Also, use Windows 10 recovery boot media to repair Windows 10 systems. Use Windows 8 recovery boot media for Windows 8 installations, and Windows 7 recovery boot media to repair Windows 7 installations.

WINDOWS 10/7 SYSTEM REPAIR DISC

A **system repair disc** is a bootable DVD with Windows repair tools that can start the system and fix problems. Using the DVD requires an optical drive. For Windows 10/7, open Control Panel and go to the **Backup and Restore (Windows 7)** window (see Figure 6-11). Click **Create a system repair disc**. A 32-bit Windows installation will create a 32-bit version of the repair disc, and a 64-bit Windows installation will create a 64-bit version of the repair disc. Windows 8 has the option to create a system repair disc, but it is hidden. To use a system repair disc, boot the system from the disc and select your keyboard layout. Then Windows RE is launched.

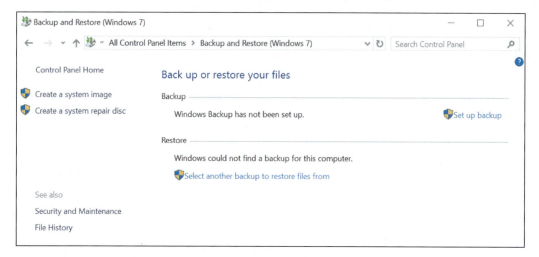

Figure 6-11 Create a system image or a system repair disc from Control Panel

WINDOWS 10/8 RECOVERY DRIVE

Suppose the hard drive in a laptop completely fails. You can purchase a new hard drive for the system, but a problem might arise when you install Windows on the new drive. Most laptops, all-in-one, and other brand-name computers include an OEM recovery partition on the hard drive that contains the drivers specific for the computer. Before a problem occurs, you can back up this OEM recovery partition to a Windows recovery drive. A recovery drive is a bootable USB flash drive that can access Windows 10/8 repair tools; in addition to holding an OEM recovery partition, it is handy when you need to repair a computer that doesn't have an optical drive.

> ✎ **Notes** A recovery drive is bit-specific: Use a 32-bit recovery drive to repair a 32-bit Windows installation and a 64-bit recovery drive to repair a 64-bit installation.

If you include the system files on the recovery drive, you have the option of reinstalling Windows from the recovery drive. As you can see in Figure 6-9, a recovery drive can be used to perform a Windows 10 reset or a Windows 8 refresh or reset. You learn to use these tools later in the chapter. You can use a recovery drive to repair a computer other than the one on which it was created. However, system files included on a recovery drive may not be compatible with all computers.

Do the following to create a recovery drive:

1. Open **Control Panel** in Classic view and click **Recovery**. Click **Create a recovery drive**, and respond to the UAC dialog box.

2. Choose whether to include system files (see Figure 6-12), which will copy the OEM recovery partition to the recovery drive. If the computer doesn't have an OEM recovery partition, the check box on this dialog box is gray and not available. Click **Next** to continue.

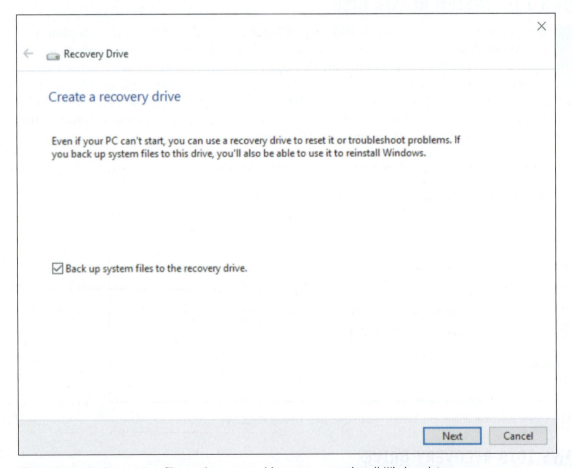

Figure 6-12   Back up system files to the recovery drive so you can reinstall Windows later

3. Windows reports the size of the USB flash drive needed (see Figure 6-13.) Plug in a USB flash drive that is large enough. Know that the entire USB flash drive will be formatted and everything on the drive will be lost.

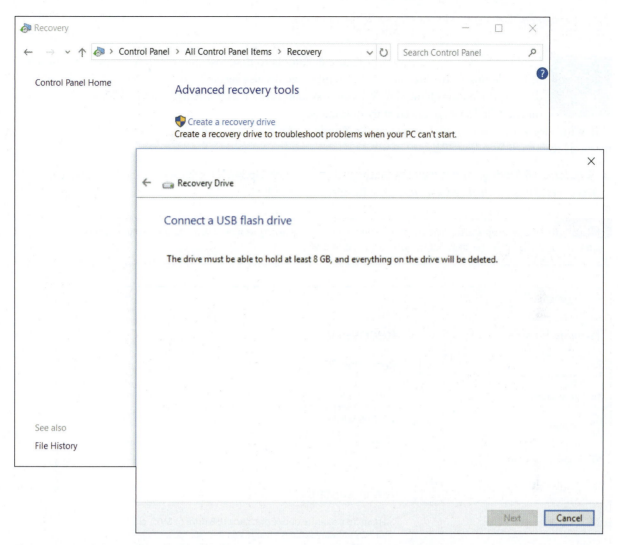

Figure 6-13 Windows reports the size of the USB flash drive needed to hold the recovery drive

4. Windows inspects the size of the drive; if it is large enough, you see it listed among available devices. Be careful to select the USB flash drive because everything on the drive will be lost. Click **Next**. Click **Create** to begin the process. It will take a while to complete. Then click **Finish**.

Be sure to label the flash drive well and put it in a safe place. For example, you can put it in an envelope, label it "Recovery drive for John Hawkins 64-bit Windows 10 Sony laptop," and store it in the computer's documentation file.

> **✎ Notes** If you copied the OEM recovery partition to the USB flash drive and are short on hard drive space on the computer, you can use Disk Management to delete the recovery partition and free up some space, and then expand the Windows volume.

WINDOWS 10 MEDIA CREATION TOOL

A+
CORE 2
3.1

You can launch Windows RE from a Windows setup DVD or flash drive. For Windows 10, recall you can use the Media Creation Tool on a working computer to create a bootable Windows setup ISO file, DVD, or flash drive. You learned how to use the Media Creation Tool in Chapter 2.

TOOLS FOR LEAST INVASIVE SOLUTIONS

Looking back at the diagram in Figure 6-9, tools to diagnose and repair Windows are shown in purple boxes. In this part of the chapter, we discuss several tools that are easy to use and don't make major changes to Windows system files or user settings, including several options on the Windows advanced startup screens.

If Windows works well enough to get to the Windows desktop, you can use one of the following methods to launch Windows RE:

▲ **Windows 10 Settings app.** Open the **Settings** app and click **Update & security**. In the left pane, click **Recovery**. Under *Advanced startup*, click **Restart now**. See Figure 6-14.

> ✎ **Notes** The Advanced startup option is not available on the Recovery window when you are using a remote connection to the computer or Windows 10 is installed in a VM.

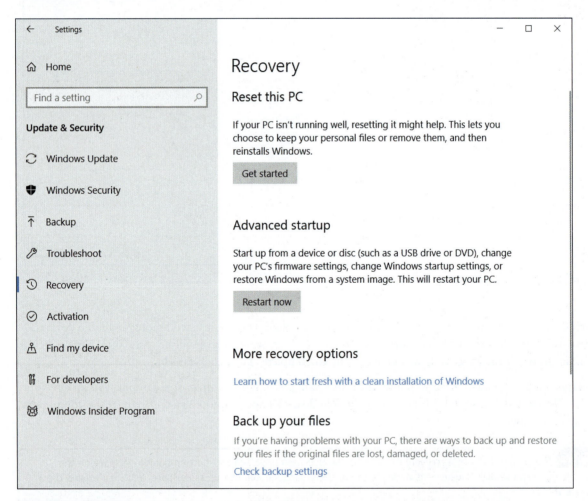

Figure 6-14   The Windows 10 Recovery page in the Settings app

> ↻ **OS Differences**   For Windows 8, you can launch Windows RE after a normal startup by opening the charms bar and clicking **Settings**. In the Settings pane, click **Change PC settings**. In the left pane of the PC settings window, click **Update and recovery**. In the Update and recovery pane, click **Recovery** and click **Restart now** (see Figure 6-15).
>   For Windows 7, press **F8** at startup and click **Repair Your Computer** on the Advanced Boot Options screen (refer back to Figure 6-10).

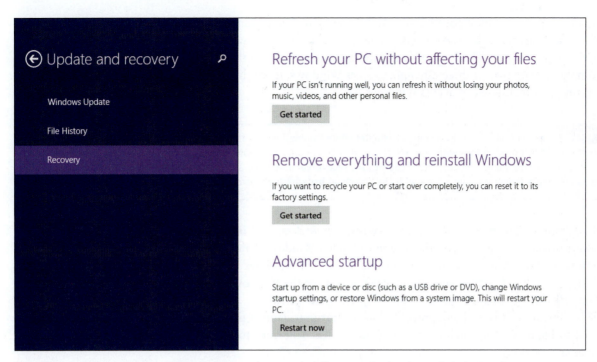

Figure 6-15   Refresh or reset a Windows 8 computer or restart the computer in advanced startup mode

▲ *Shift + Restart.* From the Windows 10/8 Start menu, click the **Power** icon. Press and hold the **Shift** key and click **Restart**.

▲ *Command prompt.* In a Windows 10/8/7 command prompt window, enter **shutdown /r /o**. The /r parameter instructs the computer to restart, and the /o parameter opens Windows RE after the restart.

> ✎ **Notes**   You can also use the shutdown command to remotely shut down computers over the network.

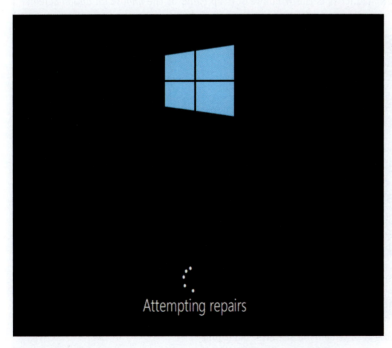

Figure 6-16   Windows automatically launches diagnostic and repair procedures after several restarts within a few minutes

Here are the methods to launch Windows RE when Windows cannot start normally:

▲ *Windows detects startup problems and launches automatic diagnostics and repairs.* If you restart the computer several times within a few minutes or Windows detects errors during startup, it automatically launches diagnostics (see Figure 6-16) and takes you through steps to attempt to repair the system. The process, called Automatic Repair or Startup Repair, includes running both Check Disk and System File Checker.

If Automatic Repair fails, you're given the option to boot into Windows RE, where you have access to other troubleshooting tools. Also know that if you cannot launch Windows RE after a normal Windows startup, which can sometimes happen when working with a Windows 10 installation in a VM, you can restart Windows several times. Each time you see the Windows flag appear, turn off the computer. After two or three attempts to start Windows, it will launch Automatic Repair on the next startup, and then you can access Windows RE.

> ✎ **Notes**   When you are trying to restart a computer while troubleshooting it yourself, you might find that Automatic Repair slows down or interferes with your efforts. In this case, you can disable Automatic Repair as follows: Open an elevated command prompt window, enter **bcdedit /set recoveryenabled no**, and then perform your own repair steps. You can reenable Automatic Repair later with the command **bcdedit /set recoveryenabled yes**.

▲ *Boot from a USB recovery drive, DVD system repair disc, or Windows setup DVD or USB drive.* These boot recovery media give you the option to launch Windows RE. You might have to adjust BIOS/UEFI settings to boot from these alternate media. To launch Windows RE from a Windows setup DVD or flash drive, click **Repair your computer** when you see the Windows Setup screen.

▲ *Press F8 during startup.* Earlier in the chapter, you learned how to configure Windows 10/8 to enable F8 at startup. If it is enabled, press **F8** during startup to launch the Advanced Boot Options menu (refer back to Figure 6-10), which is part of Windows RE. You learn to use the tools on this menu later in the chapter.

APPLYING | CONCEPTS   EXPLORING WINDOWS RE MENUS AND OPTIONS

Let's explore the menu screens in Windows RE, which are shown in green boxes in Figure 6-9. Follow these steps to explore Windows RE menus:

1. Start Windows and use one of the methods listed earlier to launch Windows RE. The first screen you see after Windows RE launches is the Windows Startup Menu or the *Choose an option* screen (see Figure 6-17).

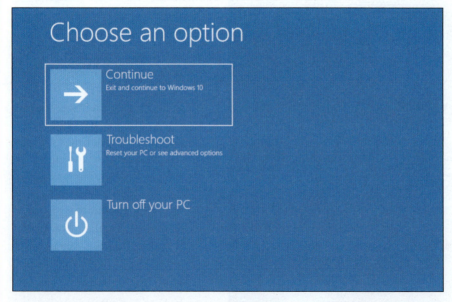

Figure 6-17   The Windows Startup Menu is the first screen you see after launching Windows RE

(continues)

2. Click **Troubleshoot** to see the **Troubleshoot** menu screen. Figure 6-18A shows the Windows 10 Troubleshoot screen, and Figure 6-18B shows the Windows 8 Troubleshoot screen.

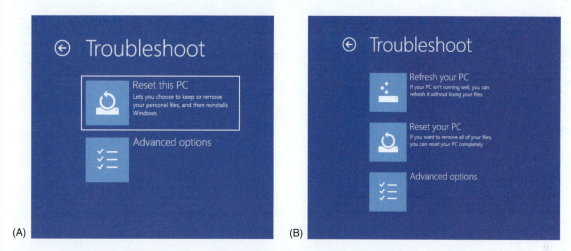

(A)　　　　　　　　　　　　　　　　　　　　　(B)

Figure 6-18　(A) Windows 10 reset or (B) Windows 8 refresh and reset are available on the Troubleshoot screen

3. Click **Advanced options** to see the Advanced options screen in Figure 6-19.

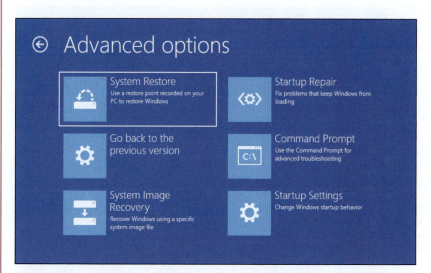

Figure 6-19　The option to go back to a previous version is available because this computer recently received a major Windows update

> ✎ **Notes**　Depending on the situation, you might see a seventh option on the Advanced options screen, which is UEFI Firmware Settings. Use this option to change settings in a computer's UEFI firmware.

4. To get a command prompt, click **Command Prompt**. Here you can enter various commands to troubleshoot and solve problems. To exit the command prompt, enter the **exit** command. You are returned to the Advanced options screen.

5. The Startup Settings option is available on the Advanced options screen shown in Figure 6-19 because Windows RE was launched after a normal Windows startup. Click **Startup Settings** to see the startup options shown in Figure 6-20.

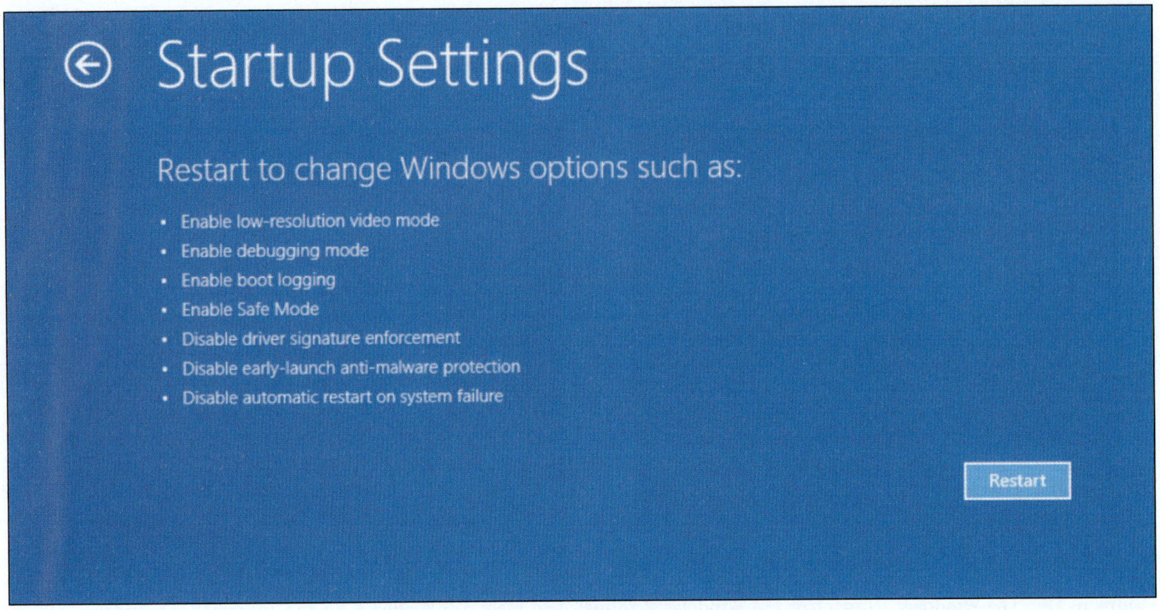

Figure 6-20 The Startup Settings menu gives options for how Windows starts up

6. Click **Restart**. After the restart, another Startup Settings screen appears (see Figure 6-21), which has more options than the first one. Press numbers or function keys F1 through F9 to launch the tools on this screen. The tools listed on this screen are the same as those listed on the Advanced Boot Options screen (refer back to Figure 6-10) that appears when you press F8 at startup.

7. To return to the Windows Startup Menu shown earlier in Figure 6-17, press **F10**. On the *Choose an option* screen, click **Continue** to reload Windows 10.

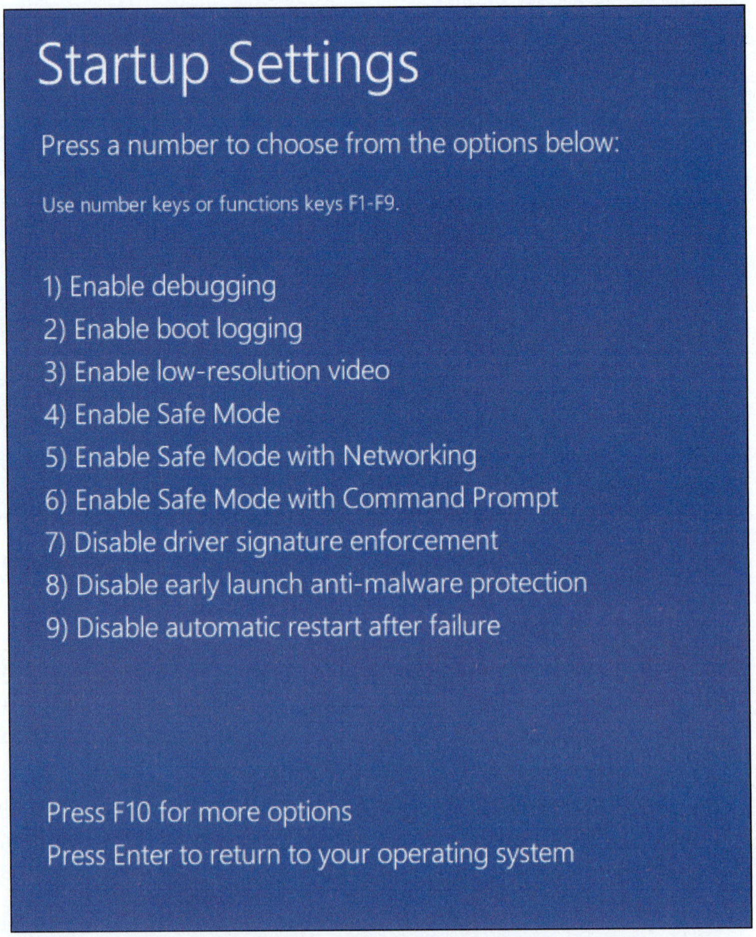

Figure 6-21 Press a function key or number to restart the system in a given mode

Next, we discuss some tools to repair Windows, including Startup Repair, Startup Settings, System Restore, and commands entered in a command prompt window.

STARTUP REPAIR

When addressing startup problems, the first tool to try is startup repair, which is a built-in diagnostic and repair tool. It can fix Windows system files without changing Windows settings, user data, or applications. You can't cause additional problems with the tool and it's easy to use.

To run startup repair in Windows RE, drill down to the Advanced options screen (refer back to Figure 6-19) and click **Startup Repair**. Windows RE examines the system, fixes problems, reports what it did, and might offer suggestions for further fixes. A log file of the process can be found at C:\Windows\System32\LogFiles\SRT\SRTTrail.txt.

> **OS Differences** For Windows 7, after you launch Windows RE, the Advanced Boot Options screen appears (refer back to Figure 6-8). Click **Repair Your Computer** and enter an administrator password. The System Recovery Options box appears (see Figure 6-22). Click **Startup Repair** to launch the startup repair process.

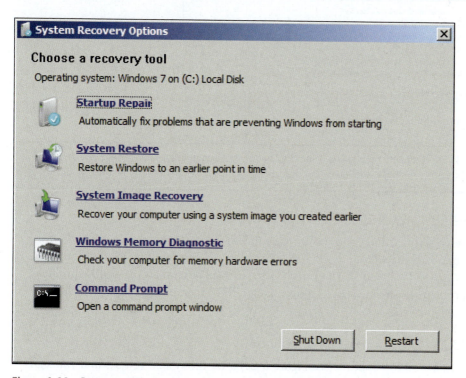

Figure 6-22 Recovery tools in Windows RE for a Windows 7 installation

CHANGING STARTUP SETTINGS

The Startup Settings option on the Advanced options screen shown in Figure 6-19 is available only when Windows RE is launched from the hard drive rather than other media. Following directions given earlier, launch Windows RE and drill down to the Startup Settings screen shown earlier in Figure 6-21. Here's a quick rundown of what these tools can do.

PRESS 1 OR F1: ENABLE DEBUGGING

This tool moves system boot logs from the failing computer to another computer for evaluation. The computers must be connected by way of a serial port.

PRESS 2 OR F2: ENABLE BOOT LOGGING

Windows loads normally and all files used during the load process are recorded in a log file, C:\Windows\Ntbtlog.txt (see Figure 6-23). Use this option to see what did and did not load during the boot. For instance, if you have a problem getting a device to work, check Ntbtlog.txt to see what driver files loaded. Boot logging is much more effective if you have a copy of Ntbtlog.txt that was made when everything worked as it should. Then you can compare the good load with the bad load, looking for differences.

> 📝 **Notes**   The Ntbtlog.txt file is also generated when you boot into Safe Mode.

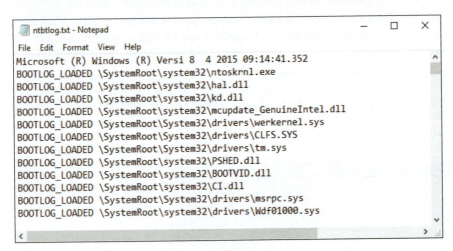

Figure 6-23   A sample C:\Windows\Ntbtlog.txt log file

> 📝 **Notes**   If Windows hangs during the boot, try booting using the Enable Boot Logging option. Then look at the last entry in the Ntbtlog.txt file. This entry might be the name of a device driver causing the system to hang.

PRESS 3 OR F3: ENABLE LOW-RESOLUTION VIDEO (640 × 480)

Use this option when the video settings don't allow you to see the screen well enough to fix a bad setting (for example, black fonts on a black background or a corrupted video driver). Booting in this mode gives you a very plain, standard video in VGA mode. You can then go to **Display settings**, correct the problem, and reboot normally. For problems with video drivers, open Device Manager and update, roll back, or uninstall and reinstall the video drivers.

PRESS 4 OR F4: ENABLE SAFE MODE

With this option, the Safe Mode desktop appears (see Figure 6-24) after the system restarts and you sign in to Windows. Launching Safe Mode and then restarting the system again can sometimes solve a startup problem. You can also go to the Windows desktop in Safe Mode and launch anti-malware software to scan the system for malware. You can open Event Viewer to find events that are helpful in troubleshooting the system, run the System File Checker command (**sfc /scannow**) to restore system files, use Device Manager to roll back a driver, use Memory Diagnostics (**mdsched.exe**) to verify memory, use the **chkdsk /r** command to check for file system errors, configure Windows for a clean boot on the next restart, and perform other troubleshooting tasks. Recall from Chapter 5 that you can also launch Safe Mode from the Boot tab on the System Configuration window, where Safe Mode is called Safe boot.

> ⭐ **A+ Exam Tip**   The A+ Core 2 exam gives you a scenario and expects you to know when and how to use Safe Mode to help resolve a Windows startup problem.

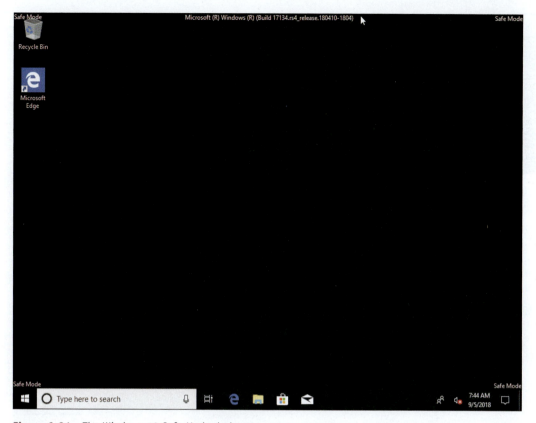

Figure 6-24 The Windows 10 Safe Mode desktop

PRESS 5 OR F5: ENABLE SAFE MODE WITH NETWORKING

Use this option when you need access to the network to solve the problem. For example, you might need to download updates to your anti-malware software. Also use this mode when the Windows installation files are available on the network, rather than Windows setup media, and you need to access those files.

PRESS 6 OR F6: ENABLE SAFE MODE WITH COMMAND PROMPT

If Safe Mode can't start, try Safe Mode with Command Prompt, which doesn't attempt to load the graphical interface. At the command prompt, use the **sfc /scannow** command to verify system files (see Figure 6-25). If the problem is still not solved, you can use the **rstrui** command to launch System Restore and then follow the on-screen directions to select a restore point. However, as Figure 6-26 shows, if restore points have not been previously made, System Restore cannot help. As you learn later in the chapter, you can also use this command prompt to restore a corrupted Windows registry from backups.

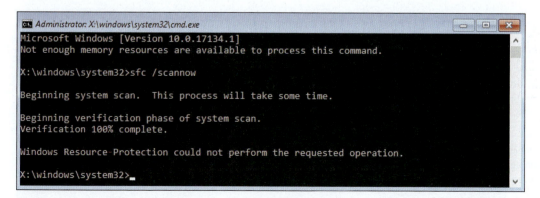

Figure 6-25 SFC finds and attempts to repair corrupted system files

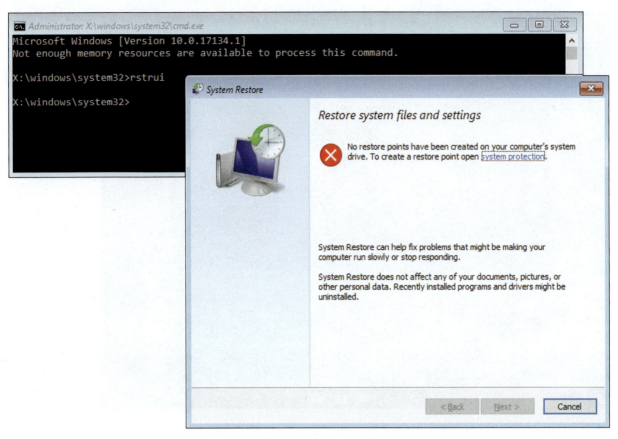

Figure 6-26 Use System Restore after booting to Safe Mode with Command Prompt

PRESS 7 OR F7: DISABLE DRIVER SIGNATURE ENFORCEMENT

All 64-bit editions of Windows require that kernel-mode drivers be digitally signed. Developers disable driver signature enforcement when they test kernel-mode device drivers that are not yet digitally signed. Don't use this option for troubleshooting Windows startup because doing so might allow malware drivers to load.

PRESS 8 OR F8: DISABLE EARLY LAUNCH ANTI-MALWARE DRIVER

Windows 10/8 allows anti-malware software to launch a driver before any third-party drivers are launched so it can scan these drivers for malware. Unless you're sure a driver is the problem, don't disable this security feature. (Windows 7 doesn't offer this option on its Advanced Boot Options screen.)

PRESS 9 OR F9: DISABLE AUTOMATIC RESTART ON SYSTEM FAILURE

By default, Windows automatically restarts immediately after a blue screen of death (BSOD) stop error, which is described in more detail later in this chapter. The error can cause the system to continually reboot rather than shut down. Press **F9** to disable automatic restarts and stop the rebooting.

> ✎ **Notes** To permanently disable automatic restarts, go to **Control Panel**, open the **System** window, and click **Advanced system settings**. In the Startup and Recovery group of the System Properties box, click **Settings**. In the Startup and Recovery box, uncheck **Automatically restart** (see Figure 6-27). Click **OK** twice and close the System window.

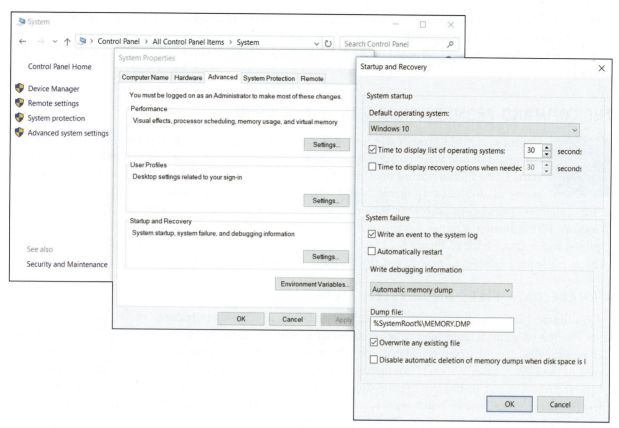

Figure 6-27 Permanently disable automatic restarts

PRESS F10: RETURN TO THE STARTUP SETTINGS SCREEN

Press F10 to return to the Windows Startup Menu screen shown previously in Figure 6-17.

> ✎ **Notes** As you use these startup settings tools, be sure to reboot after each attempt to fix the problem to make sure it has not been resolved before you try another tool. To exit Windows RE and relaunch Windows, press **Enter** on the Startup Settings screen.

> ⟳ **OS Differences** Windows 7 offers an option on the Advanced Boot Options menu called the Last Known Good Configuration, which is not available in Windows 10/8. The Windows 7 **Last Known Good Configuration** settings are saved in the registry each time the user successfully logs on to the system. If your problem is caused by a bad hardware or software installation, using the Last Known Good can, in effect, undo the bad installation. Try the Last Known Good option early in the troubleshooting session before a bad Last Known Good overwrites a good one. (However, know that if you sign in to Safe Mode, the Last Known Good is not saved.)

SYSTEM RESTORE

A+ CORE 2 3.1

Windows gives you several opportunities during the startup troubleshooting process to use System Restore to restore the system to an earlier point in time when a restore point was made. You can select System Restore from the Windows RE Advanced options screen (refer back to Figure 6-19) or the Windows 7 System Recovery Options screen (refer back to Figure 6-22). You can also perform System Restore in Safe Mode or from a command prompt with the **rstrui** command.

System Restore can cause problems of its own because Windows updates and updates to anti-malware software can be lost, and hardware devices and applications might need to be reinstalled. System Restore won't help if the file system is corrupted or the registry is trashed. In these situations, the command prompt might help.

THE COMMAND PROMPT WINDOW IN WINDOWS RE

**A+
CORE 2
3.1**

Use the command prompt window in Windows RE when the graphical interface is missing or corrupted or you want to use a specific command to fix a problem when Windows refuses to start. Using this command prompt, you have administrator privileges and full read and write access to all files on all drives. Many commands you learned about in Chapter 4 can be used at this command prompt. To access the Windows RE command prompt, click **Command Prompt** on the Windows 10/8 Advanced options screen (refer back to Figure 6-19) or the Windows 7 System Recovery Options screen (refer back to Figure 6-22).

Next are some examples of how to use the Windows RE command prompt to repair a system.

MANAGE DATA FILES AND SYSTEM FILES

As you learned in Chapter 5, you can use the SFC or DISM commands to restore critical Windows system files. Use the cd, copy, rename, and delete commands to manage data files and system files. For example, if key registry files are corrupted or deleted, the system will not start. You can restore registry files using files saved in the C:\Windows\System32\config\RegBack folder. This RegBack folder contains partial backups of the registry files put there after a successful boot. Use the commands in Table 6-2 to restore the registry files. In the table, we assume Windows is installed on drive C:. However, know that Windows RE is likely to assign a different drive letter to the Windows volume.

Command Line	Description
1. `c:`	Makes drive C: the current drive. The default directory is root.
2. `dir`	Examines the contents of drive C:. If this is not your Windows volume, try a different drive letter.
3. `cd \windows\system32\config`	Makes the Windows registry folder the current folder.
4. `ren default default.save` 5. `ren sam sam.save` 6. `ren security security.save` 7. `ren software software.save` 8. `ren system system.save`	Renames the five registry files.
9. `cd regback`	Makes the registry backup folder the current folder.
10. `copy system c:\windows\system32\config`	For hardware problems, first try copying just the System hive from the backup folder to the registry folder and then reboot.
11. `copy software c:\windows\system32\config`	For software problems, first try copying just the Software hive to the registry folder and then reboot.
12. `copy system c:\windows\system32\config` 13. `copy software c:\windows\system32\config` 14. `copy default c:\windows\system32\config` 15. `copy sam c:\windows\system32\config` 16. `copy security c:\windows\system32\config`	If the problem is still not solved, try copying all five hives to the registry folder and reboot.

Table 6-2   Steps to restore the registry files

After you try each fix, reboot the system to see if the problem is solved before you try the next fix.

REPAIR THE HARD DRIVE FILE SYSTEMS AND PARTITIONS

A corrupted file system or partition can cause a failure to boot. To repair the file system, first try the chkdsk /r command. If you decide the hard drive is so corrupted you must start over with a fresh installation of Windows, you can use the diskpart command to totally wipe the hard drive clean of everything, including the partitioning system, before you install Windows again using Windows setup media. You learned to use diskpart in Chapter 2; a project at the end of this chapter gives you more practice with diskpart. Diskpart and chkdsk can also be used in a normal command prompt window.

ENABLE NETWORKING

Networking is not normally available from the Windows RE command prompt. Use the wpeinit command to enable networking. The wpeinit command initializes Windows PE. Recall from Chapter 2 that Windows PE is the preinstallation-environment operating system that is launched prior to installing Windows in a clean install and includes networking components.

USE BOOTREC AND BCDEDIT TO REPAIR THE FILE SYSTEM AND KEY BOOT FILES

A failure to boot can be caused by a corrupted BCD. If startup repair does not fix the problem, you can use the bootrec command to repair the BCD and boot sectors. Use the bcdedit command to manually edit the BCD. (Be sure to make a copy of the BCD before you edit it.) Use the bootsect command to repair a dual-boot system. To get helpful information about these commands, enter the command followed by /?, such as bcdedit /?. Some examples of the bootrec and bcdedit commands are listed in Table 6-3.

Command Line	Description
bootrec /scanOS	Scans the hard drive for Windows installations not stored in the BCD
bootrec /rebuildBCD	Scans for Windows installations and rebuilds the BCD
bootrec /fixboot	Repairs the boot sector of the system partition
bootrec /fixmbr	Repairs the MBR for hard drives using the MBR partitioning system
bcdedit /enum	Displays the contents of the BCD

Table 6-3   Bootrec and bcdedit commands to repair system files and the file system

Although a startup repair should solve the problem when you get an error message at startup that "Bootmgr is missing," rebuilding the BCD store should also be able to resolve the same problem on a legacy BIOS and MBR system.

OPTIONS TO REINSTALL WINDOWS

After you have made reasonable efforts to repair a Windows installation, your next option is to reinstall Windows. The startup troubleshooting tools discussed in this part of the chapter affect the entire Windows installation on a computer rather than a few files or settings. Look back at Figure 6-9 and notice that these tools to reinstall Windows are shown in blue boxes; you can also see how to reach each tool. Some of these options allow you to keep personal data, and other options remove that data; the tools are listed here starting with the least intrusive solution:

1. *Windows 10/8 previous version*. Undo a recent Windows 10/8 update.

2. *Windows 10 repair upgrade*. Install Windows 10 as an upgrade over the existing installation, keeping personal data, apps, and Windows settings.

3. *Windows 10 Fresh Start.* Do a clean installation of the most recent version of Windows 10. User data, some Windows settings, and a few apps can be kept.

4. *Windows 10 reset.* Do a clean Windows 10 installation from recovery media or the recovery partition on the hard drive. User data, some Windows settings, and a few apps can be kept.

5. *Windows 8 refresh.* Restore Windows 8 from a custom refresh image with the option to keep user data and some apps.

6. *Apply a Windows 10/7 system image.* Use a system image to replace everything on the Windows volume. Current user data, Windows settings, and apps are lost.

7. *Windows 8 reset.* The hard drive is reformatted and a clean installation of Windows is done. If an OEM recovery partition is available, it is used for the Windows installation.

8. *Install Windows 10/8/7 from the OEM recovery partition.* Laptops and brand-name computers may have an OEM recovery partition on the hard drive that can be used to restore the system to factory state. Some manufacturer procedures allow user data to be kept.

9. *Windows 10/8/7 clean install from setup media.* This method is covered in Chapter 2 and may allow you to keep user data on the hard drive.

Let's see how the Windows previous version, repair upgrade, Fresh Start, reset, and refresh work.

WINDOWS 10 PREVIOUS VERSION

A+ CORE 2 3.1

Minor updates to Windows are distributed on the second Tuesday of each month (called "Patch Tuesday"). Major updates, called versions, come along once or twice a year. Recall that you can look up your computer's current Windows 10 version by opening the **Settings** app, clicking **System**, and then clicking **About**. For Windows 10/8/7, you can also enter the **winver** command in the Windows search box or Run box. The About Windows box that appears reports the current version and build of Windows. See Figure 6-28.

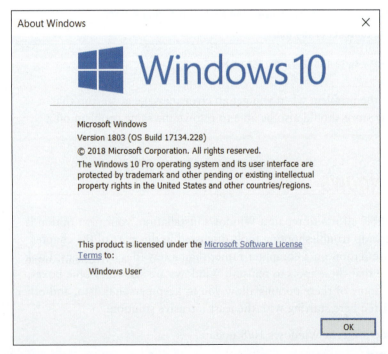

Figure 6-28 Version and build numbers can identify the major and minor Windows updates installed

Notes A Windows 10 version, such as the April 2018 Update, is assigned a version number, which appears as Version 1803 in Figure 6-28. A build number identifies updates to the current version. The major portion of the build number (such as 17134 for build 17134.228, shown in Figure 6-28) appears to be somewhat arbitrary and is notoriously unpredictable for future releases. However, the minor portion of the build number is more specific, in that these decimal places increment with each minor update.

A version includes all previous updates, so even minor updates are reinstalled when you install the next version. If a new version is giving problems, you can revert your system back to the earlier version as long as (1) the version was installed within the last 10 days; (2) you have not reset your computer during this time; and (3) the Windows.old folder has not been deleted.

To roll back Windows updates, including device drivers that come with Windows updates, do one of the following to revert your system to a previous version:

▲ *From the Windows desktop*. Open the **Settings** app, click **Update & security**, and then click **Recovery**. Under *Go back to the previous version of Windows 10*, click **Get started**. If this button is grayed out, the time limit for reverting to the previous version has already passed or the Windows.old folder is missing.

▲ *From Windows RE*. If the option is available, you can see it on the Advanced options screen in Windows RE, shown earlier in Figure 6-19. Use this method when a new version has caused the system to fail to start, such as when a critical driver is corrupted.

WINDOWS 10 REPAIR UPGRADE

If you're having problems with Windows updates or basic Windows functionality but you can still boot into Windows, you might consider performing a repair upgrade, also known as a repair install or an in-place upgrade. A repair upgrade is a nondestructive installation of Windows 10 over an existing Windows installation. This is not the same as a full reinstall because the Windows volume will not be reformatted. Just as with an upgrade from Windows 8 to Windows 10, you can keep personal files, apps, and Windows settings. Essentially, you trick the machine into thinking it's being upgraded while potentially repairing the Windows installation.

Keep these points in mind when doing a repair upgrade:

▲ Create Windows setup media, either on DVD or USB, or save an ISO file on the local hard drive.

▲ Make sure that you can fully boot into Windows 10. If you can't, you'll have to use a different troubleshooting tool.

▲ Even though all data, apps, and settings should be protected in a repair upgrade, make a backup just in case.

▲ Gather all product keys for all installed apps to make reinstallation of these apps easier should it become necessary.

> ✎ **Notes** Belarc Advisor (*belarc.com*) is a free tool that is quick and easy to use. It will produce a list of all installed apps along with their product keys if that information is available. Print a copy of the report and keep it in a safe place.

APPLYING | CONCEPTS   PERFORMING A REPAIR UPGRADE

The easiest way to perform a repair upgrade is to start with an ISO file created by the Media Creation Tool, as described in Chapter 2. Complete the following steps:

1. Sign in to Windows using an administrator account. Back up all personal data using one of the methods you learned about in Chapter 4.

2. Following steps in Chapter 2, download the correct ISO file for the Windows installation you're currently using on the computer to be repaired.

3. In File Explorer, double-click the ISO file that you created with the Media Creation Tool. This mounts the image and shows the included files.

4. Double-click **setup.exe**, as shown in Figure 6-29. Click **Yes** in response to the UAC dialog box.

(continues)

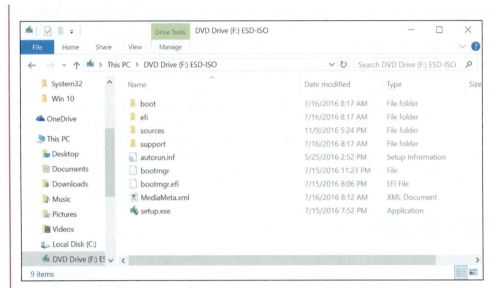

Figure 6-29 To begin the repair upgrade, double-click setup.exe on the virtual DVD in Explorer

5. On the first Windows 10 Setup window, make sure **Download and install updates (recommended)** is selected, and then click **Next**. Setup examines the system.

6. Click **Accept** on the Applicable notices and license terms window. Windows 10 Setup checks for and downloads updates.

7. If the *Choose what to keep* window appears, decide whether to keep personal files and apps, personal files only, or nothing. Sometimes setup makes these decisions for you and skips directly to the *Ready to install* window.

8. On the *Ready to install* window, make sure **Keep personal files and apps** appears and is checked, as shown in Figure 6-30. If not, click **Change what to keep** and select **Keep personal files and apps**, and then click **Next** to return to the *Ready to install* window. Click **Install** to begin the installation process, which will take a while and require several restarts. Enjoy a cup of tea or coffee while you wait.

9. When the lock screen appears, sign in to Windows. Once you see the desktop, all your files, apps, and settings should still be in place.

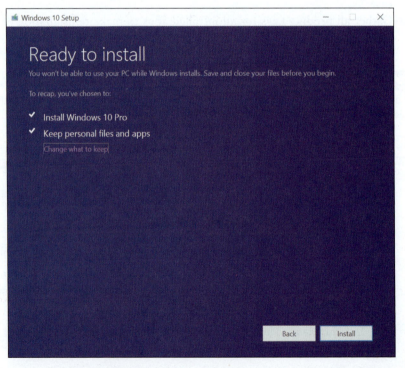

Figure 6-30 You can keep user data and settings and third-party apps during a repair upgrade

WINDOWS 10 FRESH START

A **Fresh Start** performs a clean installation of the most recent version of Windows 10 and is often used to remove manufacturer bloatware. Here's what is installed, kept, and not kept with a Fresh Start:

▲ *Installed*. The latest generic copy of Windows, free from manufacturer bloatware, is downloaded directly from the Microsoft website.

▲ *Kept*. User accounts, their settings, and personal data are kept as well as some Windows settings. Microsoft apps that are natively integrated in Windows and Microsoft store apps installed by the computer manufacturer are also kept.

▲ *Not kept*. All apps are removed, except as stated above. A list of removed apps is displayed on the desktop after the Fresh Start completes. Be aware that you also lose any manufacturer drivers or OEM system files.

To install a fresh copy of Windows 10, first make sure you're connected to the Internet and that you have sufficient storage space for the Windows image (about 3 GB). Open the Settings app, click **Update & security**, and then click **Recovery**. Under *More recovery options* (see Figure 6-31), click **Learn how to start fresh with a clean installation of Windows**. Then click **Yes** to switch to the Fresh start page, which is shown on the right side of Figure 6-31. Click **Get started** to begin the process. The tool downloads and performs a clean installation of Windows 10. Sign in to complete setup.

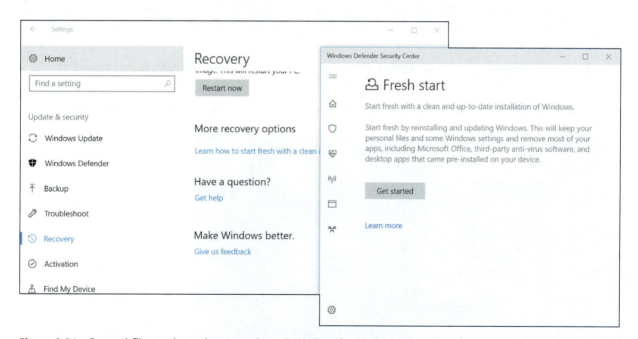

Figure 6-31 Personal files are kept when executing a Fresh Start for Windows 10

WINDOWS 10 RESET

A Windows 10 reset reinstalls Windows with the option of keeping user accounts, some Windows settings, and all personal data files. If you decide to remove data files, you can also choose to clean the drive. During a reset, any apps or drivers that were installed from third-party providers will be removed, and some changes made to Windows settings will be lost. Also, if your computer has received a major update within the past 10 days, you will lose the ability to revert to a previous version of Windows. If you're using a Microsoft account, you can choose to have many Windows settings automatically resynced to the device.

> **✎ Notes** The basic difference between a Windows 10 reset and Fresh Start is the source of the Windows installation files. A reset uses files taken from recovery media or the recovery partition on the hard drive, whereas a Fresh Start downloads a pristine, up-to-date copy of Windows from the Microsoft website. Fresh Start therefore gives you a cleaner reinstall or fresher start than a reset. On the other hand, a reset installs original manufacturer drivers and OEM system files, which may be needed for a customized system. Both methods are capable of retaining personal files.

> **✎ Notes** Before performing a reset, you might want to back up any desktop apps that you've customized or use frequently. Then you can restore the backed-up versions rather than installing fresh copies. To do this, store a copy of selected apps on a flash drive using a third-party app such as CloneApp (*Mirinsoft.com*), and then restore the apps along with their customized settings after the Windows reset is complete.

APPLYING | CONCEPTS   RESETTING A WINDOWS 10 COMPUTER

**A+
CORE 2
3.1**

If you are not able to start Windows, you can use Windows 10 setup media or a recovery drive to launch Windows RE. Drill down to the Troubleshoot screen (refer back to Figure 6-18) and click **Reset this PC** to start the reset.

Here are the steps in Windows 10 to reset a computer using the Settings app:

1. Sign in to Windows using an administrator account. If possible, first back up all personal files.

2. If a recovery partition is present, it will be used for the reset. If there's no recovery partition, insert bootable Windows media such as a recovery drive, system repair disc, or Windows setup media. The reset process will then use the media to install Windows.

3. Open the **Settings** app and click **Update & security**. In the left pane, click **Recovery**, as shown earlier in Figure 6-14. Under *Reset this PC*, click **Get started**.

4. In the *Choose an option* box, shown in Figure 6-32, decide whether to keep your files or to remove everything.

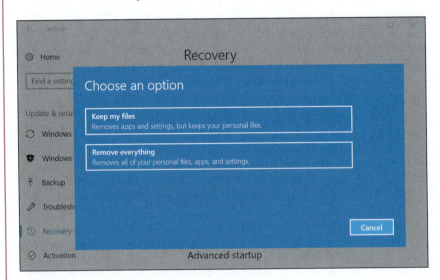

Figure 6-32 Keep your files or remove everything

> **✎ Notes** For a laptop, all-in-one, or other brand-name computer with a recovery partition present, you might see a third option on the *Choose an option* box: Restore factory settings. This option reinstalls the version of Windows that your computer came with (for example, Windows 8.1) and removes your personal files.

(continues)

5. If you click **Keep my files**, you're given a list of all apps that will be removed. If you've recently updated your computer, you might see a warning that you will not be able to undo the update. Click **Next** and then click **Reset** to begin.

6. If you click **Remove everything**, you're given the option to clean only the Windows volume or all volumes on the hard drive. Make your selections and click **Reset** to begin.

APPLYING A WINDOWS 10/7 SYSTEM IMAGE

You learned how to create a system image in Chapter 4. System image recovery tends to be an all-or-nothing recovery option where you replace the entire contents of a hard drive with whatever operating system state and personal data are saved in the system image. It recovers all personal files, system files, and installed apps that were in place at the time the system image was most recently created or updated. If your system image is updated regularly, this option could work very well for you when repairing or replacing hardware, such as a failed hard drive. However, if a software-related problem has been building for a while, a recently updated system image won't necessarily fix the root of the problem.

To recover Windows 10/8 using a system image file, reboot the computer into Windows RE, drill down to the **Advanced options** screen (refer back to Figure 6-19), and select **System Image Recovery**. For Windows 7, select **System Image Recovery** on the **System Recovery Options** screen shown earlier in Figure 6-22.

WINDOWS | 8 REFRESHING AND RESETTING A WINDOWS 8 COMPUTER

Windows 8 offers a refresh process that's not available in Windows 10 or Windows 7. In addition, a Windows 8 reset works differently than a Windows 10 reset. Let's see how to perform a Windows 8 refresh and then a reset.

REFRESH A WINDOWS 8 COMPUTER

In Chapter 4, you learned that Windows 8 prefers to use a custom refresh image of the Windows volume rather than the traditional system image. To solve a problem with a corrupted Windows 8 installation, you can perform a refresh in Windows 8. The refresh can use a custom refresh image that has been designated as the active recovery image, a hidden OEM recovery partition on the hard drive, or the Windows 8 setup DVD.

When you refresh a computer, the refresh saves installed apps that use the Windows 8 interface and current user settings and data. Unless you're working with a custom refresh image, Windows settings and desktop applications are lost during a refresh. Here's how to perform a refresh:

1. Because the system will restart a couple of times during the refresh, remove any discs in the optical drive and unplug any bootable external hard drives or USB flash drives. For a laptop, plug in the AC adapter so you don't lose battery power during the refresh. If the computer doesn't have a recovery partition and you haven't made a custom refresh image, insert the Windows setup DVD in the optical drive, which the refresh will use to perform a partial in-place upgrade of Windows 8.

2. Do one of the following, depending on the health of the Windows installation:

   ◢ If you can launch Windows, open the **charms bar**, click **Settings**, click **Change PC settings**, click **Update and recovery**, and click **Recovery**. Click **Get started** under *Refresh your PC without affecting your files* (refer back to Figure 6-15). A warning message appears (see Figure 6-33). Click **Next**. Click **Refresh**.

(continues)

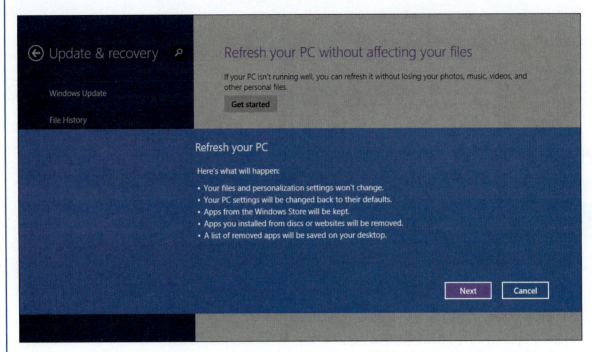

Figure 6-33 Windows lists what to expect from a refresh

◢ If you cannot launch Windows, boot from the Windows 8 setup DVD or a recovery drive to launch Windows RE. Drill down to the **Troubleshoot** screen (refer back to Figure 6-18B) and click **Refresh your PC**.

3. Windows verifies there's enough free space on the hard drive to perform the refresh. A lot of space is needed (as much as half the space on the Windows volume) because Windows will store the old Windows installation in a Windows.old folder and will also need space to back up apps and data. If there's not enough space, an error occurs, and you'll need to delete files or folders or move them to a different location to free up enough space, and then start the refresh again.

4. Another warning message appears. Click **Refresh** to continue. Next, user settings, user data, and Windows 8 apps are backed up, and Windows searches for media or an image to use to reinstall Windows. It uses this order for the search:

   a. *It checks for a custom refresh image.* If a custom refresh image was previously made and registered with the system, this image is used to refresh the system. (If desktop applications were included in the image, they are included in the refresh. Any desktop applications that were installed after the refresh image was created are lost and must be manually reinstalled.)

   b. *If no custom refresh image is found, Windows checks for an OEM recovery partition.* If it finds an OEM recovery partition, the image on the partition is used to refresh the computer to its factory state.

   c. *If no image or recovery partition is found, Windows requests the Windows setup DVD if it's not already available.* The refresh process will use the Windows setup DVD to perform a partial in-place upgrade of Windows 8.

5. The system restarts and the refresh begins. Progress is reported as a percentage of completion. The Windows volume is formatted, and Windows is reinstalled from an image or from the Windows setup files. User settings, data, and Windows 8 apps are restored from backup, and the system restarts.

(continues)

6. The names of desktop applications lost during the refresh are stored in a file named *Removed Apps.html* on the Windows desktop (see Figure 6-34). Open the file to see the list of applications. You'll need to reinstall these applications.

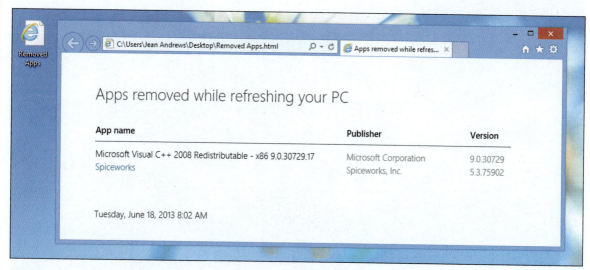

Figure 6-34 View a list of desktop applications lost during the refresh

7. The refresh created a Windows.old folder containing the old Windows installation. After you're sure you don't need anything in it, you can delete the folder to free up the disk space.

RESET A WINDOWS 8 COMPUTER

You might want to perform a **Windows 8 reset** when you're about to give away a computer, recycle it, or totally want to start over. The Windows volume is formatted and Windows is reinstalled. If an OEM recovery partition is present, the system is reset to its factory state. If there's no recovery partition, the process requests the Windows 8 setup DVD, which it uses to reinstall Windows. All user data and settings and installed apps are lost. You can use the recovery methods provided by the manufacturer (for example, press F12 or F10 at startup) or you can use Windows 8 to reset the system.

Here are the steps to reset a computer in Windows 8:

1. If a recovery partition is present, it will be used for the reset. If there's no recovery partition, insert the Windows setup DVD in the optical drive, which the reset process uses to perform a clean install of Windows.

2. Do one of the following:

   ◢ If you can launch Windows, go to the **Update and recovery** screen and click **Get started** under *Remove everything and reinstall Windows* (refer back to Figure 6-15). A warning message appears. Click **Next**.
   ◢ If you cannot launch Windows, boot from the Windows setup DVD or a recovery drive and make your way to the Troubleshoot screen shown earlier in Figure 6-18B. Click **Reset your PC**.

3. If the system contains more than one volume or hard drive, Windows asks if you want to format all drives or just the Windows volume. Click a box to make your selection.

(continues)

4. On the next screen (see Figure 6-35), you're asked to decide between a quick format and a thorough format. A thorough format makes it less likely someone can recover data on the drive. Make your selection by clicking a box.

Figure 6-35   Decide what type of format the reset will use

5. On the next screen, another warning appears. Click **Reset** to start the process. The system restarts and resetting begins. After another restart, you can step through the process of preparing Windows for first use.

OEM FACTORY RECOVERY PARTITION

Laptops, all-in-one computers, and brand-name desktops come with the OS preinstalled at the factory. This OEM (original equipment manufacturer) build of the OS is likely to be customized, and for laptops, the drivers might be specific to proprietary devices installed in the laptops.

The laptop or brand-name computer is likely to have a recovery partition on the hard drive that contains a copy of the OS build, device drivers, diagnostics programs, and preinstalled applications needed to restore the system to its factory state. This partition might or might not be hidden. For example, Figure 6-36 shows the Disk Management information for a hard drive on one laptop that has a 16.38-GB recovery partition.

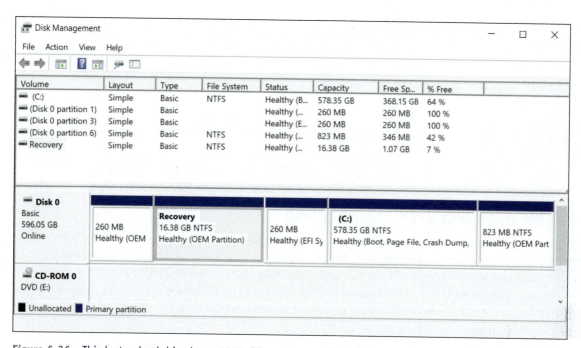

Figure 6-36 This laptop hard drive has a 16.38-GB recovery partition that can be used to recover the system

To know how to access the recovery tools stored on a recovery partition, see the manufacturer's website or look for a message at the beginning of the boot, such as "Press ESC for diagnostics" or "Press F12 to recover the system." For one Sony laptop, you press the red **Assist** button during the boot (see Figure 6-37). When you press the key or button, a menu appears with options to diagnose the problem, to repair the current OS installation, or to completely rebuild the entire hard drive to its factory state.

Figure 6-37 For this laptop, press the Assist button during the boot to launch programs on the recovery partition

If the laptop doesn't have a recovery partition or the partition is corrupted, look for the option to download recovery media from the manufacturer's website and use it to create a bootable USB flash drive or DVD. You can then use the media to install Windows to its factory state.

> ✏️ **Notes** When you first become responsible for a laptop, use a USB flash drive to make a Windows 10/8 recovery drive that includes the OEM recovery partition in case you must replace the laptop's hard drive. Know that if the laptop is more than three years old, the manufacturer might no longer provide the recovery media.

> ⚡ **Caution** Before upgrading a laptop to Windows 10, make sure the laptop manufacturer provides Windows 10 drivers for laptop components.

INSTALLING WINDOWS OVER THE NETWORK

Recall from Chapter 2 that in an enterprise environment, you can install Windows from a deployment image on the network. You must boot the computer to the network where it finds and loads Windows PE on the deployment server. Go into BIOS/UEFI setup and look for an advanced setup screen to enable PXE Support. The computer then boots to the Preboot eXecution Environment (PXE) and PXE then searches for a server on the network to provide Windows PE and the deployment image.

> ★ **A+ Exam Tip** The A+ Core 2 exam expects you to know how to use a preinstallation environment and a recovery image to help resolve a Windows startup problem.

TROUBLESHOOTING SPECIFIC WINDOWS STARTUP PROBLEMS

And now the fun begins! With your understanding of the boot process and Windows tools for troubleshooting startup in hand, let's work through a bunch of errors and problems that can affect Windows startup and see what can be done about them. When troubleshooting a startup problem, follow procedures to interview the user, back up important data or verify that you have current backups, research and identify any error messages, and determine what has just changed that might be the source of the problem.

When you know the source of the problem, decide which tool will be the least invasive to use yet still fix the problem. If that doesn't work, move on to the next tool. Remember that tools are described earlier in the chapter from least to most invasive.

IMPORTANT DATA ON THE HARD DRIVE

Troubleshooting a computer problem should always start with the most important question: Is there important data on the hard drive that's not backed up? Even if data is lost or corrupted, you might be able to recover it using Windows tools, third-party file recovery software, or commercial data recovery services. One good product is GetDataBack by Runtime Software (*runtime.org*), which can recover data and program files even when Windows cannot recognize the drive.

For less than $30, you can purchase a SATA-to-USB converter kit (see Figure 6-38) that includes a data cable and power adapter. You can use one of these kits to temporarily connect a desktop or laptop hard drive to a USB port on a working computer. Set the drive beside your computer and plug one end of the data cable into the drive and the other into the USB port. The AC adapter supplies power to the drive. While power is getting to the drive, be careful not to touch the circuit board on the drive.

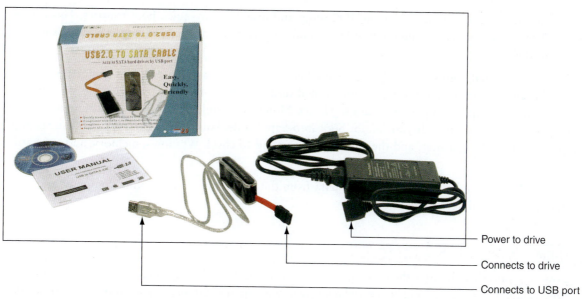

Figure 6-38 Use a SATA-to-USB converter to recover data from a drive using a SATA connector

Using File Explorer or Windows Explorer, you can browse the drive and copy data to other media. After you have saved the data, you can use diagnostic software from the hard drive manufacturer to examine the drive and possibly repair it or return the drive to its own computer and start troubleshooting there.

ERROR MESSAGES AND PROBLEMS

Problems that prevent Windows from booting can be caused by hardware, device drivers, services, applications, or Windows. This section covers what to do when error messages appear on a black or blue screen or when Windows gets corrupted.

STARTUP ERROR MESSAGES ON A BLACK SCREEN

Generally, problems that present as white text on a black screen are caused by hardware. Here are some possible error messages:

- No OS found
- A disk read error occurred
- Invalid boot disk
- Hard drive not found
- Disk boot failure
- No boot device found

Here is what's happening and what to do about it:

1. Start with the error message. Research the text shown on the screen so that you understand the problem and get solutions from trusted websites.

2. If you see spinning white dots on a black screen, Windows may be installing updates before it launches. Wait. It may take some time for the update installations to complete. If the system hangs indefinitely, the updates might be causing a problem. If a reboot doesn't solve the problem, boot into Windows RE and return to a previous version of Windows.

3. Consider that startup BIOS/UEFI might not be able to communicate with the hard drive. Check BIOS/UEFI setup for the boot sequence. Update the boot order so that you can try booting from another device.

4. For Windows 10/8, try going into BIOS/UEFI setup and disabling any quick boot features. This causes BIOS/UEFI to do a more thorough job of POST and reports more information on the screen as it performs POST.

5. Windows might halt and show a black screen when it encounters a video problem at startup. Try restarting the system in Safe Mode, as you learned to do earlier in the chapter. Then check Event Viewer for clues, update Windows, and use Device Manager to roll back drivers or disable or uninstall the video adapter. If you cannot boot into Safe Mode, launch Windows RE and use Startup Repair, Memory Diagnostics, and the chkdsk /r command to check Windows, memory, and the hard drive.

6. The hard drive might be failing. To recover data from the drive, move it to another computer and install it as a second hard drive.

PROBLEMS WITH USER PROFILES

If Windows bogs down right after the user signs in, the problem might be with loading the user profile. For a slow profile load, the user might see a black screen with spinning dots for several minutes. To fix the problem, try these tasks listed in the least invasive order:

1. Try the Windows Troubleshooting applet that you learned about in Chapter 5. Go to **Control Panel** and click **Troubleshooting**. On the Troubleshooting page, click **Run maintenance tasks** and follow the on-screen directions.

2. Make sure Windows updates are applied.

3. Run **sfc /scannow** to fix problems with system files.

4. Reduce startup items. Compare the time to load a user profile when starting Windows normally and during a clean boot.

5. Apply a restore point that was created before the problem started.

6. For Windows 10, try a repair upgrade.

7. Create a new user profile. You can copy user data files from the old profile into the new user profile namespace. (Locations of these files are given in Chapter 5.)

If the user profile gets corrupted, it might not load at all and you might see the error message, "The User Profile Service failed the logon." To rebuild the user profiles, do the following to repair Windows system files that affect the corrupted profiles:

◢ Do as many of the above steps as you can do when a single user profile is slow to load.

◢ Following directions given in Chapter 5, use the DISM commands to repair corrupted Windows system files.

◢ For Windows 10, perform a reset. Be sure to back up data before you do a reset.

Sometimes you can recover a user account by deleting it without deleting its files and then creating a new one with the same name.

To delete the account and keep its files, open Control Panel, click **User Accounts**, select the account, and click **Delete the account**. In the Delete Account window (see Figure 6-39), click **Keep Files** and then click **Delete Account**. The files are stored in a folder on your desktop and the account and its settings are deleted. Create a new account with the same name. Then you can copy the files saved to your desktop folder to the new user profile namespace.

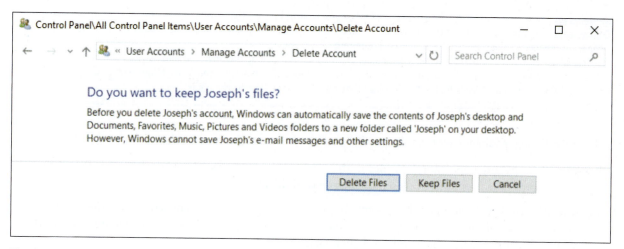

Figure 6-39 Delete a user account and its settings and keep the files in the user profile

If this doesn't work, you can edit the registry to delete an old profile or repair a corrupted one:

1. Launch the Registry Editor and back up this registry key:

   HKEY_LOCAL_MACHINE\SOFTWARE\Microsoft\Windows NT\CurrentVersion\ProfileList

2. Drill down into each S-1-5 folder in the above key until you find the correct user profile in the ProfileImagePath subkey (see Figure 6-40).

3. If the profile has a State subkey, set it to 0, as shown in the figure. If the profile has a RefCount subkey, set it to 0.

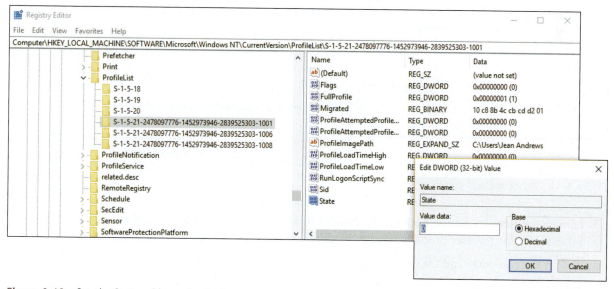

Figure 6-40 Set the State subkey value to 0

4. Close the Registry Editor and restart the computer.

> ✏ **Notes**   If you're searching for the correct S-1-5 folder and it has .bak in the name, remove .bak from the folder name. To rename a folder, right-click it and click **Rename**.
>
>   If you see two S-1-5 folders with the same name, except one has .bak at the end, you must switch the names: First rename the folder that does not contain .bak to .hold. Then remove the .bak from the other folder name. Next, rename the .hold folder to .bak. Then edit the S-1-5 folder that does not have .bak in the name.

If you still have problems with a user profile, you can follow these steps to delete the profile:

1. Manually copy any important data files in the user profile namespace to a new location. Recall that you can find these files in the C:\Users*username* subfolders.

2. Go to **Control Panel** and open the **System** window. Click **Advanced system settings**. In the System Properties box, select the **Advanced** tab and click **Settings** under User Profiles. See Figure 6-41. In the list of user profiles, select the profile and click **Delete**.

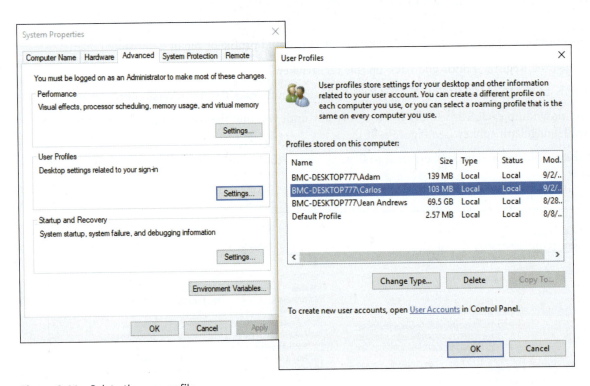

Figure 6-41   Delete the user profile

3. Launch the Registry Editor, back up the **ProfileList** key as you learned to do earlier, and locate the **S-1-5** folder for the user profile you want to delete. Right-click the **Sid** key and click **Delete**.

4. Restart the computer and create a new profile.

ERROR MESSAGES ON A BLUE SCREEN

Hardware and software errors can present as error messages on a Windows blue screen of death (BSOD) and are called stop errors. Also, sometimes Windows hangs with the pinwheel spinning, continuously restarts, or does an abrupt and improper shutdown. A BSOD, or stop error, happens when processes running in kernel mode encounter a problem and Windows must stop the system. Figure 6-42 shows an example of a Windows 8 blue screen with the stop error at the top and the specific number of the error near the bottom of the screen. Windows 10 blue screens may be much simpler, such as the one shown in Figure 6-43.

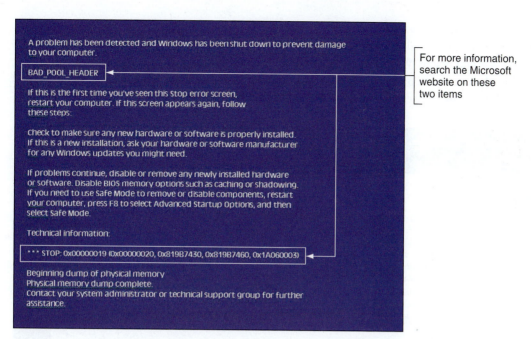

Figure 6-42 A blue screen of death (BSOD) is definitively not a good sign; time to start troubleshooting

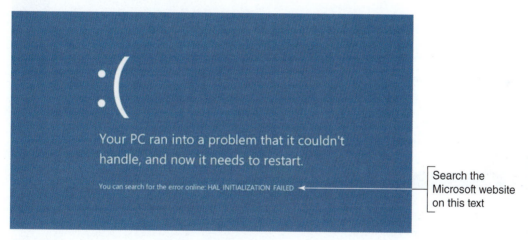

Figure 6-43 The Windows 10 stop error screen

A stop error can be caused by a corrupted Windows update, a corrupted registry, a system file that is missing or damaged, a device driver that is missing or damaged, bad memory, or a corrupted or failing hard drive. Stop errors can occur during or after startup. Here's what to do when you get a stop error:

1. As for the tools that are useful in solving stop errors, put the web at the top of your list! (But don't forget that some sites are unreliable and others mean you harm.) Search the Microsoft websites on the items labeled in Figure 6-42 or Figure 6-43.

2. Disconnect any peripheral devices that might be causing trouble, such as a docking station, USB device, projector, or extra monitor.

3. Reboot the system. Immediately after a reboot following a stop error, Windows displays an error message box or bubble with useful information. Follow the links in the box.

4. If possible, restart the system and enable boot logging. Check the C:\Windows\Ntbtlog.txt file to see if the correct driver files loaded.

5. Restart the computer a couple of times. Sometimes that's all you need to do to solve a problem. If Windows encounters errors, it will launch an automatic repair. If that doesn't fix the problem, you can launch Windows RE and restart Windows in **Safe Mode with Networking**. In Safe Mode, examine the log file created by Automatic Repair at C:\Windows\System32\LogFiles\Srt\SrtTrail.txt. See Figure 6-44. Also, recall that Safe Mode creates its own log file at C:\Windows\Ntbtlog.txt.

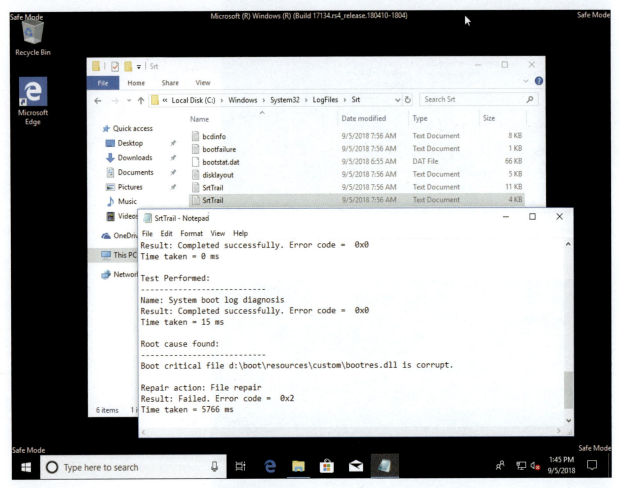

Figure 6-44   Examine the log file left by Automatic Repair

> 📝 **Notes**   If the stop error prevents Windows from loading the desktop and F8 has not yet been enabled at startup, you can force automatic repair by turning off the computer a couple of times as Windows launches.

ERRORS WITH HARDWARE AND DEVICE DRIVERS

If the blue screen names a device or device driver that caused the problem, do the following:

1. If the driver has been recently updated and the Safe Mode desktop is loaded, open **Device Manager** and roll back the driver.

2. Consider that the device driver might have been updated along with a Windows update. For recent Windows updates, try to return to a previous version of Windows.

3. A Windows update might fix the problem. Open the Settings app and update Windows.

4. Use Device Manager to uninstall the device. When given the option, select **Delete the driver software for this device**. Then reboot the system.

5. If the stop error does not identify the device but names a program file, open File Explorer or Windows Explorer on a working computer to locate the program file. Driver files are stored in the C:\Windows\System32\drivers folder. Right-click the file and select **Properties** from the shortcut menu. The Details tab of the Properties box tells you the purpose of the file (see Figure 6-45). You can then reinstall the device or program that caused the problem.

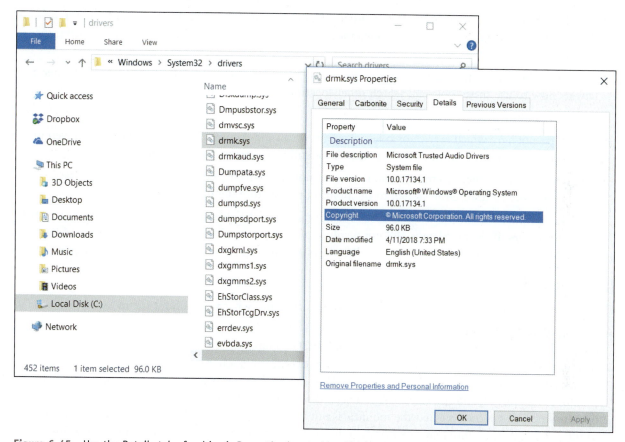

Figure 6-45 Use the Details tab of a driver's Properties box to identify the purpose of the driver

6. If you cannot start Windows in Safe Mode, use Windows RE to open a command prompt window. Then back up the registry and open the Registry Editor using the **regedit** command. Drill down to the service or device key. The key that loads services and drivers can be found in this location:

HKEY_LOCAL_MACHINE\System\CurrentControlSet\Services

Disable the service or driver by changing the Start value to 0x4. Close the Registry Editor and reboot. If the problem goes away, use the copy command to replace the service or driver program file, and restart the service or driver.

> ⚡ **Caution** Consider that the device might be physically damaged. If you feel excessive heat coming from the computer case or a peripheral device, immediately unplug the device or power down the system. Don't turn the device or system back on until the problem is solved; you don't want to start a fire! Other symptoms that indicate potential danger are strong electrical odors, unusual noises, no noise (such as when the fan is not working to keep the system cool), liquid spills on a device, and visible damage such as a frayed cable, melted plastic, or smoke. In these situations, turn off the equipment immediately.

ERRORS WITH SERVICES OR OTHER PROGRAMS

Applications don't generally cause stop errors because they all run in user mode rather than kernel mode. When a blue screen with a stop error identifies a service or other program that failed to start or is causing problems, do the following:

1. Check Event Viewer, which might provide events it has logged. Recall that critical errors and warnings are recorded in the Administrative Events log.

2. Use Task Manager to stop the service or other program causing the error. If you cannot end the process using Task Manager, use the taskkill command, as you learned to do in Chapter 5. Try restarting the program.

3. Use Task Manager or the Services console to disable the service from launching at startup. Chapter 5 covers how to use these tools and search other locations for startup programs.

4. Update Windows.

5. If you are not sure which service or other program is causing the problem, follow directions given in Chapter 5 to perform a clean boot. If a clean boot still gives errors, try a Safe boot.

6. Undo any recent changes to the system. If you are not sure which changes to undo, consider using System Restore to restore the system to the point in time before the problem started.

7. Use the Memory Diagnostics tool to check memory and use the **chkdsk /r** command to check the hard drive for errors. If the problem is still not resolved, you might need to repair Windows system files by using SFC and DISM commands or other Windows startup repair tools discussed in this chapter.

WINDOWS IS CORRUPTED

Here are some possible problems with Windows system files and what to do about them:

▲ *Missing Boot Configuration Data*. If the BCD store is corrupted or missing and Automatic Repair did not fix the problem, try using the **bootrec /rebuildBCD** command.

▲ *Improper shutdown*. The problem can be caused by overheating, a hardware problem, or the Windows kernel. After a restart, check Event Viewer for clues, apply Windows updates, verify memory with Memory Diagnostics, and use **chkdsk /r** to check the hard drive for errors.

▲ *No graphics appear*. Suspect that the monitor is not turned on, not getting power, or not connected to the computer. Try a different monitor or onboard video port. Try launching a command prompt in Windows RE and use it to perform a System Restore.

After you have done your best to back up user data and troubleshoot problems with hardware and applications, you may decide the Windows installation is beyond repair and it's time to reimage or reload Windows. As you learned in this chapter, the tools to use to reimage or reload Windows, listed in the least intrusive order, are the Windows 10 previous version (if available), a Windows 10 repair upgrade, Windows 10 Fresh Start, a Windows 10 reset, and applying a system image. For Windows 8, your options are a refresh and a reset. For Windows 7, your option is applying a system image. As a last resort, you can perform a clean installation of Windows 10/8/7, as you learned in Chapter 2. After you have Windows up and running again, you can restore the user data from backups.

>> CHAPTER SUMMARY

Understanding the Boot Process

▲ When you first turn on a system, startup BIOS/UEFI on the motherboard takes control and performs POST to examine hardware components and then find an operating system to load.

▲ Windows startup is managed by the Windows Boot Manager. For a BIOS system, the program is bootmgr. For a UEFI system, the program is bootmgfw.efi. The Windows Boot Loader is winload.exe or winload.efi. The Boot Configuration Data (BCD) store contains Windows startup settings.

What to Do Before a Problem Occurs

▲ Before a startup problem occurs, you can keep good backups, create a system image, configure the F8 key at startup, and create recovery boot media.

Tools for Least Invasive Solutions

▲ The Windows Recovery Environment (Windows RE) can be started from within Windows, from the Windows setup DVD or flash drive, from a recovery drive, or from a system repair disc. For Windows 7, press F8 at startup to launch Windows RE.

▲ Tools for startup troubleshooting include startup repair, startup settings, System Restore, Safe Mode, enabling boot logging, SFC, and the chkdsk, diskpart, bootrec, and bootsect commands.

Options to Reinstall Windows

▲ Tools that can be used to reinstall Windows are the Windows 10 previous version, a repair upgrade, Fresh Start, and a reset. Windows 8 tools are a refresh and a reset. With Windows 10/7, you can apply a system image. Some manufacturers offer a recovery partition on the hard drive to restore a computer to factory state. You can also reinstall Windows from Windows setup media.

Troubleshooting Specific Windows Startup Problems

▲ If a hard drive contains valuable data but will not boot, you might be able to recover the data by installing the drive in another system as the second, nonbooting hard drive.

▲ Use the web to research stop errors by the error title and error number listed on a black or blue screen.

▲ Improper shutdowns are most likely hardware related. Event Viewer might record failures. Use Memory Diagnostics and chkdsk to check memory and the hard drive. Consider overheating as a source of the problem.

▲ When a device or service causes the system to hang during a normal boot, boot into Safe Mode or perform a clean boot and disable the device or service. System Restore can return the system to a previously saved restore point before the problem occurred.

>> KEY TERMS

For explanations of key terms, see the Glossary for this text.

bcdedit	bootsect	recovery drive	warm boot
blue screen of death (BSOD)	cold boot	recovery partition	Windows 8 reset
Boot Configuration Data (BCD) store	Fresh Start	refresh	Windows Boot Loader
	hard boot	repair upgrade	Windows Recovery
booting	Last Known Good	soft boot	Environment (Windows
bootrec	Configuration	startup repair	RE)
	POST (power-on self test)	system repair disc	wpeinit

>> THINKING CRITICALLY

These questions are designed to prepare you for the critical thinking required for the A+ exams and may use content from other chapters and the web.

1. As a computer starts up, you see an error message about the HAL. At what point in startup does this error occur?

   a. When BIOS/UEFI is searching for an OS using devices listed in the boot priority order

   b. When Windows attempts to load the user profile

    c. When Windows attempts to launch critical device drivers

    d. When Windows attempts to launch the Windows kernel

2. Which Windows program must be running before a user can sign in to Windows?

    a. Kernel.exe

    b. Userinit.exe

    c. Explorer.exe

    d. Lsass.exe

    e. All of the above

3. As a computer starts up, you see an error message about a missing operating system. At what point in startup does this error occur?

    a. When BIOS/UEFI is searching for an OS using devices listed in the boot priority order

    b. When Windows attempts to load the user profile

    c. When Windows attempts to launch critical device drivers

    d. When Windows attempts to launch the Windows kernel

4. Your friend sees an error message during Windows startup about a corrupted bootmgr file. He has another computer with a matching configuration and decides to copy the bootmgr file from the working computer to the computer with the problem. Where can he locate the bootmgr file?

    a. C:\Boot\bootmgr

    b. System Reserved\Boot\bootmgr

    c. System Reserved\bootmgr

    d. All of the above

5. In question 4 above, your friend is having problems finding the bootmgr file and asks for your help. What is your best response?

    a. Use diskpart commands to "unhide" and locate the file.

    b. Use the File Explorer options applet to unhide the hidden bootmgr file.

    c. Explain to your friend that performing a startup repair is a better option.

    d. Explain to your friend that he can use the bootrec command to fix the bootmgr file without having to copy another file to the computer.

6. You are seeing multiple errors about device drivers failing to launch at startup. Of the following, which is the best option to try first? Second?

    a. Restore the SYSTEM hive from backup.

    b. Restore the SAM hive from backup.

    c. Perform a startup repair.

    d. Perform a Windows 10 reset.

7. A stop error halts the Windows 10 system while it is booting, and the booting starts over in an endless loop of restarts. How can you solve this problem?

    a. Use the Windows Startup Settings screen to disable automatic restarts.

    b. Press F8 at startup and then disable automatic restarts.

    c. Launch Windows 10 from setup media and perform a Windows 10 reset.

    d. Press F9 at startup and then disable automatic restarts.

8. If you are having a problem with a driver, which of the following should you try first? Second?

   a. Update the driver.

   b. Use System Restore to apply a restore point.

   c. Update Windows.

   d. Perform a clean boot.

9. When error messages indicate that the Windows registry is corrupted and you cannot boot from the hard drive, what tool or method is the first best option to fix the problem? The second best option?

   a. Use bootable media to launch Windows RE and use System Restore to apply a restore point.

   b. Use bootable media to launch Windows RE and perform a startup repair.

   c. Use bootable media to launch Windows RE and then use commands to recover the registry from backup.

   d. Refresh Windows using a system image or custom refresh image.

10. Your Windows system boots to a blue screen stop error and no Start screen or desktop. What do you do first?

   a. Reinstall Windows.

   b. Use the web to research the stop error messages and numbers.

   c. Attempt to boot into Windows RE using the Windows setup DVD or a recovery drive.

   d. Verify that the system is getting power.

11. You have important data on your hard drive that is not backed up and your Windows installation is so corrupted you know that you must refresh the entire installation. What do you do first?

   a. Use System Restore to apply a restore point.

   b. Make every attempt to recover the data.

   c. Perform an in-place upgrade of Windows.

   d. Reformat the hard drive and reinstall Windows.

12. Your computer displays the error message "A disk read error occurred." You try to boot from the Windows setup DVD and you get the same error. What is most likely the problem?

   a. The Windows setup DVD is scratched or damaged in some way.

   b. The hard drive is so damaged the system cannot read from the DVD.

   c. Both the optical drive and the hard drive have failed.

   d. The boot device order is set to boot from the hard drive before the optical drive.

13. When a driver is giving problems in Windows 10, which tool offers the least intrusive solution?

   a. Device Manager

   b. Windows Update

   c. System Restore

   d. Registry Editor

14. An error message is displayed during Windows startup about a service that has failed to start, and then the system locks up. You try to boot into Safe Mode, but get the same error message. What do you try next?

   a. Use the command prompt to edit the registry.

   b. Boot to Windows RE and enable boot logging.

   c. Perform an upgrade repair of Windows 10.

   d. Boot to Windows RE and perform a startup repair.

15. Stop errors happen when which type of processes encounter an error?

    a. Processes created by applications

    b. Processes created by Windows components running in user mode

    c. Processes created by Windows components running in kernel mode

    d. Processes created by anti-malware software

16. What is the command to use the System File Checker to immediately verify and repair system files?

17. What is the path and name of the log file created when you enable boot logging on the Windows 10/8 Startup Settings menu?

18. What information is contained in the C:\Windows\System32\LogFiles\SRT\SRTTrail.txt file?

>> HANDS-ON PROJECTS

Hands-On | Project 6-1   Using Boot Logs and System Information to Research Startup

Boot logs can be used to generate a list of drivers that were loaded during a normal startup and during a Safe Mode startup. Do the following to use boot logs to research startup:

1. Boot to the normal Windows desktop with boot logging enabled. Save the boot log just created to a different name or location so it will not be overwritten on the next boot.

2. Reboot the system in Safe Mode, which also creates a boot log. Compare the two logs, identifying differences in drivers loaded during the two boots. You can print both files and lay them side by side for comparison. An easier method is to compare the files using the Compare tool in Microsoft Word.

3. Use the System Information utility or other methods to identify the hardware devices loaded during normal startup but not loaded in Safe Mode. Which devices on your system did not load in Safe Mode?

As you identify the drivers not loaded during Safe Mode, these registry keys might help with your research:

   ▲ Lists drivers and services loaded during Safe Mode: HKLM\System\CurrentControlSet\Control\SafeBoot\ Minimal

   ▲ Lists drivers and services loaded during Safe Mode with Networking: HKLM\System\CurrentControlSet\ Control\SafeBoot\Network

Hands-On | Project 6-2   Taking Ownership and Replacing a Windows System File

In Chapter 5, you learned to use SFC and DISM commands to find and replace corrupted Windows system files. SFC keeps a log of its actions at C:\Windows\Logs\CBS\CBS.log, and DISM keeps a log at C:\Windows\Logs\DISM\dism. log. Sometimes these logs or BSOD error screens reveal the name and location of corrupted system or device driver files that Windows tools cannot replace. In this situation, you can manually replace the file. To do so, you can use the takeown command to take ownership of a file and the icacls command to get full access to the file. The Microsoft Knowledge Base Article 929833 at *support.microsoft.com* explains how to use these two commands.

(continues)

Do the following to practice manually replacing a system file:

1. Boot the computer into Safe Mode with Command Prompt.

2. Take ownership and gain full access to the C:\Windows\System32\jscript.dll file. What commands did you use?

3. Rename the jscript.dll file to jscript.dll.hold. Run the **sfc /scannow** command. Did SFC restore the jscript.dll file? What is the path and file name of the log file that lists repairs?

4. SFC restores a file using files accessed from Windows Update or stored on the Windows setup DVD or other folders on the hard drive. If SFC cannot restore a file, you might find a fresh copy in the C:\Windows\winsxs folder or its subfolders. Search these folders. Did you find a version of jscript.dll that is the same file size as the one in C:\Windows\System32? Other than the C:\Windows\winsxs folder, where else can you find a known good copy of a corrupted system file or device driver file?

> ✎ **Notes** To use a command prompt window to search for a file in a folder and its subfolders, use the **dir /s** command.

Hands-On | Project 6-3   Viewing the BCD Store

On two or more computers, open an elevated command prompt window and use the bcdedit /enum command to view the BCD store. One BCD store is shown in Figure 6-46.

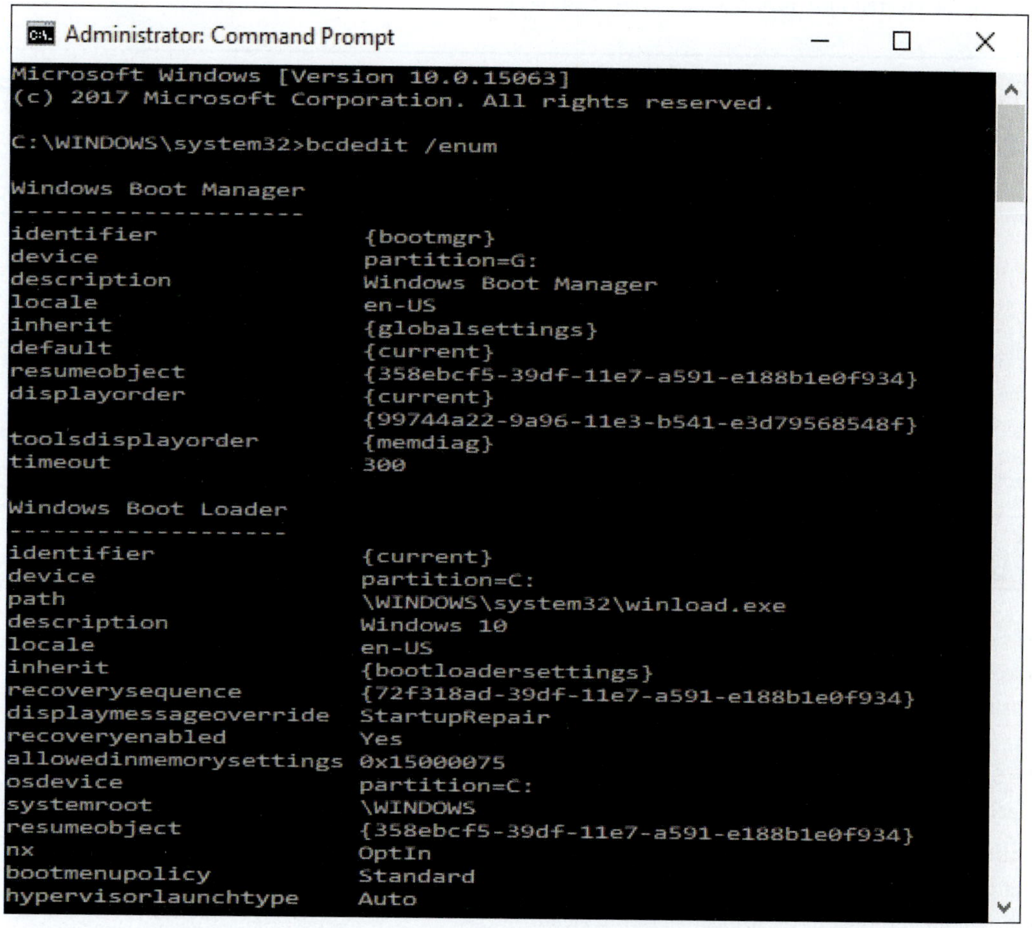

```
Administrator: Command Prompt                          —    □    ✕

Microsoft Windows [Version 10.0.15063]
(c) 2017 Microsoft Corporation. All rights reserved.

C:\WINDOWS\system32>bcdedit /enum

Windows Boot Manager
--------------------
identifier              {bootmgr}
device                  partition=G:
description             Windows Boot Manager
locale                  en-US
inherit                 {globalsettings}
default                 {current}
resumeobject            {358ebcf5-39df-11e7-a591-e188b1e0f934}
displayorder            {current}
                        {99744a22-9a96-11e3-b541-e3d79568548f}
toolsdisplayorder       {memdiag}
timeout                 300

Windows Boot Loader
--------------------
identifier              {current}
device                  partition=C:
path                    \WINDOWS\system32\winload.exe
description             Windows 10
locale                  en-US
inherit                 {bootloadersettings}
recoverysequence        {72f318ad-39df-11e7-a591-e188b1e0f934}
displaymessageoverride  StartupRepair
recoveryenabled         Yes
allowedinmemorysettings 0x15000075
osdevice                partition=C:
systemroot              \WINDOWS
resumeobject            {358ebcf5-39df-11e7-a591-e188b1e0f934}
nx                      OptIn
bootmenupolicy          Standard
hypervisorlaunchtype    Auto
```

Figure 6-46   A BCD store on a computer that uses the GPT partitioning system

(continues)

Answer the following questions:

1. Can you view the BCD store and determine if the system is using the MBR or GPT partitioning system? Why or why not?
2. Explain how you can look at the BCD store and tell if the system is a single boot or multiboot system.

Hands-On | Project 6-4   Researching Laptop Online Resources

Suppose the hard drive in a laptop has failed and you must replace the hard drive with a new one and then install Windows on the new drive. What online resources can help you? Do the following to find a service manual and recovery files for a laptop to which you have access, such as one you or a friend owns:

1. What are the brand, model, and serial number of the laptop?
2. What is the website of the laptop manufacturer? Print a webpage on that site that shows you what recovery files you can download to install Windows on a new hard drive for the laptop.
3. If the website provides a service manual, download the manual and print the pages that show how to replace the hard drive.
4. Based on what you have learned about online support for this laptop, what backups or recovery media do you think need to be created now, before a hard drive crash occurs?

Hands-On | Project 6-5   Practicing Using System Recovery Options

Launch Windows RE and do the following:

1. Execute the startup repair process. What were the results?
2. Launch System Restore. What is the most recent restore point? (Do not apply the restore point.)
3. Using the command prompt window, open the Registry Editor. What command did you use? Close the editor.
4. Using the command prompt window, copy a file from your Documents folder to a flash drive. Were you able to copy the file successfully? If not, what error message(s) did you receive?

Hands-On | Project 6-6   Using Startup Repair

When Startup Repair attempts to fix a system, it creates a log file with information about the steps taken during the repair process. If Startup Repair doesn't fix the system, you can use the log file to investigate the problem and perhaps manually fix it. Do the following to practice using Startup Repair and examine its log file:

1. Use the Settings app in Windows to launch Windows RE. From the initial Windows Startup Menu, click **Troubleshoot**, **Advanced options**, and then **Startup Repair**.
2. Diagnostics of the system are made and the location of the log file appears. Note the path and name of the file. The default location of the log file is C:\Windows\System32\LogFiles\SRT\SRTTrail.txt. Click **Advanced options**. You are returned to the Windows Startup Menu.

(continues)

3. To view the log file from the Windows RE command prompt, click **Troubleshoot** and click **Command Prompt**.

4. In the command prompt window, enter the command **c:** to access the hard drive. (You might need to use a different drive depending on the log file location reported in Step 2.)

5. Use the following command to go to the directory where the log file is located:

   `cd \Windows\System32\LogFiles\SRT`

6. To use Notepad to view the file contents, enter the following command:

   `notepad.exe SRTTrail.txt`

7. In the log file, look for information about a failed test.

6

>> REAL PROBLEMS, REAL SOLUTIONS

REAL PROBLEM 6-1 Sabotaging a Windows System

In a lab environment, follow these steps to find out if you can corrupt a Windows system so that it will not boot, and then repair the system. (This problem can be done using a Windows installation in a virtual machine.) Don't forget about the takeown and icacls commands discussed in this chapter.

1. Rename or move one of the program files listed in Table 6-1. Which program file did you select? In what folder did you find it?

2. Restart your system. Did an error occur? Check in Explorer. Is the file restored? What Windows feature repaired the problem?

3. Try other methods of sabotaging the Windows system, but carefully record exactly what you did to sabotage the boot. Can you make the boot fail?

4. Now recover the Windows system. List the steps you took to get the system back to good working order.

REAL PROBLEM 6-2 Creating a Stop Error

This project is more difficult than it might first appear. Using a VM with Windows 10 installed, create a BSOD or stop error. Take a screenshot of the BSOD. List the steps you took to make Windows 10 crash. Tip: Search the web on **Windows 10 stop error** and try to reproduce the problem.

REAL PROBLEM 6-3 Recovering Data from a Hard Drive

To practice recovering data from a hard drive that won't boot, create a folder on a VM with Windows 10 installed. Put data files in the folder. What is the name of your folder? Move the hard drive to another working VM and install it as a second hard drive in the system. Copy the data folder to the primary hard drive in this second VM. Now return the hard drive to the original VM and verify that the VM starts with no errors. List the steps you used in this project.

REAL PROBLEM 6-4 Preparing a Corrupted Hard Drive for a Clean Windows Installation

You can use a VM to practice using the diskpart command to prepare a corrupted hard drive for a clean installation of Windows. Do the following:

1. Using a VM you have already created in this course, add a second hard drive to the VM. Start the VM and open an elevated command prompt window.

2. Enter the diskpart command. At the diskpart prompt, enter the commands shown in Table 6-4 to clean all partitions off the drive, create a new partition, and format it using the NTFS file system. Then open File Explorer in your VM and verify that the second hard drive is present and available for use.

Diskpart Command	Description
list disk	List the hard drives installed. Select the one to clean based on the size of the drive.
select disk 1	Make Disk 1 the selected hard drive.
clean	Clean the partition table and all partitions from the drive.
convert gpt	Install the GPT partitioning system.
create partition primary	Create the primary partition.
list partition	List the partitions. Note the number of the primary partition.
select partition 2	Select the primary partition.
format fs=ntfs quick	Format using the NTFS file system.
Assign letter W	Assign a drive letter to the volume.
detail partition	Display partition details.
detail volume	Display volume details.
exit	Exit diskpart.

Table 6-4 Diskpart commands to partition and format a GPT hard drive

Notes For a complete list of diskpart commands, go to the Microsoft support site (*technet.microsoft.com*) and search on "Diskpart Command-Line Options."

Securing and Sharing Windows Resources

After completing this chapter, you will be able to:

• Secure a Windows personal computer using Windows tools on the local computer

• Share and secure files and folders on a network

• Support network resources using Active Directory

In this chapter, you learn about some tools and techniques to secure the resources on a personal computer, small network, and Windows domain. Later in your career as a support technician, you can build on the skills learned in this chapter to implement even more security, such as controlling how Windows stores its passwords. However, keep in mind that even the best security will eventually fail. As a thief once said, "Locks are for honest people," and a thief will eventually find a way to break through. Security experts tell us that security measures basically make it more difficult and time consuming for a thief to break through so that she gets discouraged and moves on to easier targets.

This chapter also explains how to lock down a personal computer from unauthorized access. Because security is always a huge concern when dealing with networks, you learn how to share resources on the network while protecting them from people who should not have access. Finally, you'll learn how to use Active Directory to manage users and resources on a network.

SECURING A WINDOWS PERSONAL COMPUTER

**A+
CORE 2
1.4, 1.5,
1.6, 1.8,
2.2, 2.6,
2.7**

When you have a choice in the security measures that you use, keep in mind two goals, which are sometimes in conflict. One goal is to protect resources, and the other goal is not to interfere with the functions of the system. A computer or network can be so protected that no one can use it, or so accessible that anyone can do whatever they want with it. The trick is to provide enough security to protect resources while still allowing users to work unhindered (see Figure 7-1). Also, too much security can sometimes force workers to find insecure alternatives. For example, if you require users to change their passwords weekly, more of them might start writing their passwords down to help remember them.

📝 **Notes** The best protection against attacks is layered protection. If one security method fails, the next might stop an attacker. When securing a workstation, use as many layers of protection as you reasonably can that are justified by the value of the resources you are protecting. These layers of defense are collectively called **defense in depth**.

© Source: Phil Marden/Getty Images

Figure 7-1   Security measures should protect resources without hindering how users work

USING WINDOWS TO AUTHENTICATE USERS

**A+
CORE 2
1.4, 1.5,
1.6, 2.2,
2.5, 2.6,
2.7**

Access to computer resources is controlled by authenticating and authorizing a user or process. A user is authenticated when he proves he is who he says he is. When a computer is on a Windows domain, Active Directory (AD) is responsible for authentication. For a peer-to-peer network, authentication must happen at the local computer. Normally, Windows authenticates a user with a Windows password.

As an administrator, when you first create an account, be sure to assign it a password. It's best to give the user the ability to change the password at any time. In this part of the chapter, you learn how to create strong passwords and how to use Local Group Policy and Local Security Policy to control how users can authenticate to Windows.

CREATE STRONG PASSWORDS

A password needs to be a strong password, which means it should not be easy to guess either by people or by computer programs using various methods, including a simple brute force attack, which tries every single combination of characters until it discovers your password.

A strong password, such as *y*3Q1693pEWJaTz1!*, meets all of the following criteria:

- Use 16 or more characters, which is the best protection against a password attack.
- Combine uppercase and lowercase letters, numbers, and symbols.
- Use at least one symbol in your password.
- Don't use consecutive letters or numbers, such as "abcdefg" or "12345."
- Don't use adjacent keys on your keyboard, such as "qwerty."
- Don't use your sign-in name in the password.

▲ Don't use words in any language. Don't even use numbers or symbols for letters (as in "p@ssw0rd") because programs can easily guess those as well.

▲ Don't use the same password for more than one system.

Studies have proven that the most secure criterion of those listed above is the length of the password. Passwords of 16 characters or more that use letters, numbers, and symbols are the most difficult to crack.

> 🖊 **Notes** How secure is a password? Go to *howsecureismypassword.net* and find out how long it will take a computer to crack the password.

In some situations, a blank Windows password might be more secure than an easy-to-guess password such as "1234." That's because you cannot authenticate to a Windows computer from a remote computer unless the user account has a password. A criminal might be able to guess an easy password and authenticate remotely. For this reason, if a computer is always in a protected room such as a home office and the user doesn't intend to access it remotely, she might choose not to use a password. However, if the user travels with a laptop, always recommend that the user create a strong password.

Although it's not recommended you write your password down, if you do write it down, keep it in as safe a place as you would the data you are protecting. Don't send your passwords over email or chat. Change your passwords regularly, and don't type them on a public computer. For example, computers in hotel lobbies or Internet cafés should only be used for web browsing—not for signing in to your email account or online banking account. These computers might be running keystroke-logging software put there by criminals to record each keystroke. Several years ago, while on vacation in a foreign country, I entered credit card information on a computer in a hotel lobby. Months later, I was still protesting $2 or $3 charges to my credit card from that country. Trust me. Don't do it—I speak from experience.

> 🖊 **Notes** Rather than writing down passwords, consider storing your passwords with a password manager app such as Dashlane (*dashlane.com*), Sticky Password (*stickypassword.com*), or LastPass (*lastpass.com*). These apps can keep your passwords in the cloud or on your own device, and the passwords they create are longer and stronger than those you would be able to memorize.

Next, let's see how Local Group Policy and Local Security Policy tools can be used to enforce security best practices on a workstation.

LOCAL GROUP POLICY AND LOCAL SECURITY POLICY EDITORS

You need to be aware of three tools for policies that control what users and computers can do with a system or network:

▲ **Group Policy** works in Active Directory on a Windows domain to control the privileges of computers and users on the domain. You learn more about Group Policy and Active Directory later in this chapter.

▲ **Local Group Policy** (gpedit.msc) contains a subset of policies in Group Policy; this subset applies only to the local computer or local user.

▲ **Local Security Policy** (secpol.msc) contains a subset of policies in Local Group Policy, which apply only to the local computer's Windows security settings. Local Security Policy is an Administrative Tools snap-in in Control Panel.

The Local Group Policy and Local Security Policy editors are available with business and professional editions of Windows. Figure 7-2 shows the Local Group Policy Editor window on the left and the Local Security Policy window on the right. Notice that the Local Group Policy editor contains two major categories of policies: Computer Configuration and User Configuration. The list of policy groups selected are for the computer configuration for Windows security settings. Compare this list with the one in the Local Security Policy window; they are the same list of policies. In short, when you are working with the computer configuration in the Windows security settings group of the Local Group Policy editor, know you are working with the same group of policies you can edit when using the Local Security Policy editor.

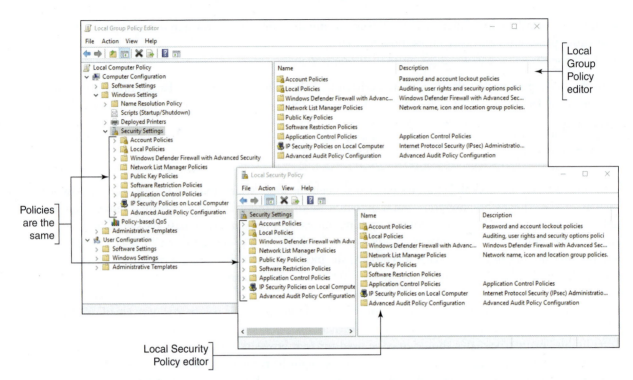

Figure 7-2 The Local Security Policy editor allows you to edit a subset of policies available in the Local Group Policy editor

Now let's see how you can use the Local Group Policy editor to secure a workstation. For example, you can set policies to require all users to have passwords. Once you have enabled a policy, a standard user of the workstation would be required to comply and would not be able to change the policy.

APPLYING | CONCEPTS   APPLYING LOCAL SECURITY POLICIES

Follow these steps to set a few important policies to secure a workstation:

1. Sign in to Windows using an administrator account on a system that uses Windows 10 Pro or Enterprise, Windows 8/8.1 Professional or Enterprise, or Windows 7 Professional, Ultimate, or Enterprise.

2. To start Local Group Policy, enter the **gpedit.msc** command in the Windows 10/7 search box or the Windows 8 Run box. The Local Group Policy Editor console opens.

3. To change a policy, first use the left pane to drill down into the appropriate policy group and then use the right pane to view and edit a policy. Here are important policies you can use to secure a workstation:

   ◢ *Require user passwords and password expiration.* To require that all user accounts have passwords, drill down to the **Computer Configuration**, **Windows Settings**, **Security Settings**, **Account Policies**, **Password Policy** group (see the left side of Figure 7-3). Use the **Minimum password length** policy and set the minimum length to at least eight characters (see the right side of Figure 7-3). Additionally, reduce the password expiration time frame so users must create new passwords frequently. Use the **Maximum password age** policy to require users to reset their password every 60 days. (The best practice is to set the Maximum password age in the range of 30 to 90 days.)

(continues)

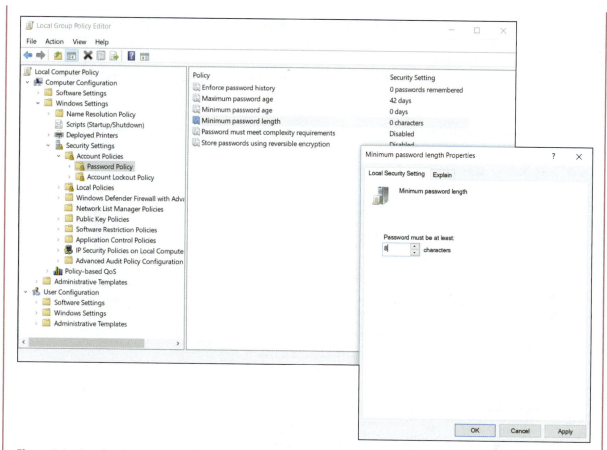

Figure 7-3 Require that each user account have a password by setting the minimum password length policy

▲ *Screen lock timeout.* Windows can monitor for inactivity and run the screen saver after a set amount of time, locking the session. This prevents another person from continuing a Windows session after the user has stepped away from the computer. Drill down to the **Computer Configuration**, **Windows Settings**, **Security Settings**, **Local Policies**, **Security Options** group. Use the **Interactive logon: Machine inactivity limit** policy to set the number of seconds of inactivity before the screen saver runs and locks the workstation until a user signs in.

▲ *Set failed logon restrictions.* Windows can be configured to lock a user account if too many incorrect logons are attempted. Drill down to the **Computer Configuration**, **Windows Settings**, **Security Settings**, **Account Policies**, **Account Lockout Policy** group. Use the **Account lockout threshold** policy to set the number of invalid logon attempts. When the number is exceeded, the account will be locked.

> **✎ Notes** The Properties box for many policies offers the Explain tab. Use this tab to read more about a policy and how it works.

▲ *Disable the Guest account.* For best security, the Guest account should stay disabled; you don't want a user to accidentally enable it. To set a policy to disable the Guest account, first use the left pane to navigate to the **Computer Configuration**, **Windows Settings**, **Security Settings**, **Local Policies**, **Security Options** group. In the Security Options group, right-click **Accounts: Guest account status**, and select **Properties**. Change the status to **Disabled** and click **OK**.

▲ *Change default user names.* A hacker is less likely to hack into the built-in Administrator account or Guest account if you change the names of these default accounts. To change the name of the Administrator account, drill down to the **Computer Configuration**, **Windows Settings**, **Security Settings**, **Local Policies**, **Security Options** group (see the left side of Figure 7-4). In the right pane, double-click **Accounts: Rename administrator account**. In the Properties box for this policy (see the right side of Figure 7-4), change the name and click **OK**. To change the name of the Guest account, use the policy **Accounts: Rename guest account**.

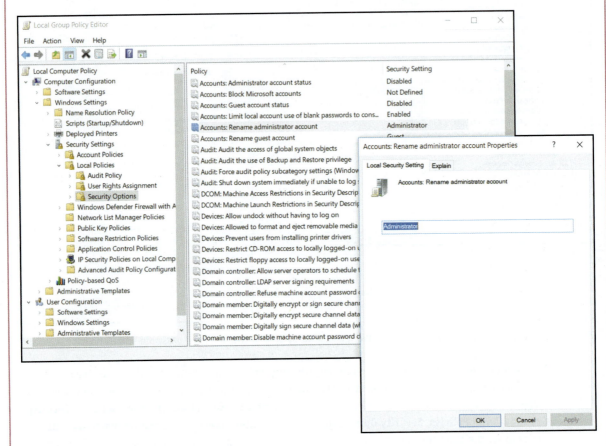

Figure 7-4   Use Group Policy to rename a default user account

> ✎ **Notes** The Administrator account is a built-in account that you might need in an emergency when other user accounts fail. Be sure to create a password for this account. One way to do that is to open an elevated command prompt window and enter the following command:
>
> ```
> net user Administrator <password>
> ```
>
> For added security, open the Computer Management console and change the name of the Administrator account. Because this account and password are extremely valuable and not used very often, don't trust your memory—keep the user account name and password in a protected and secure place.

▲ *Audit logon failures.* Group Policy offers several auditing policies that monitor and log security events. You can then review these Security logs using Event Viewer. For example, to set an audit policy to monitor a failed logon event, drill down to the **Computer Configuration**, **Windows Settings**, **Security Settings**, **Local Policies**, **Audit Policy** group. Use the **Audit logon events** policy. You can audit logon successes and failures. To keep the log from getting too big, you can select **Failure** to log only these events.

(continues)

All the previous policies are also found in the Local Security Policy console. The following policies are available only in Local Group Policy:

▲ *Logon time restrictions.* In many cases, users should only be allowed access to a workstation during specific hours, such as during office hours. The schedule for a user's or group's logon hours is set through Active Directory on the domain. When logon hours set by Active Directory have expired, individual workstations can be configured to disconnect, lock, or log off the user, or to allow the user to continue the current session. To configure what happens when a user's logon hours have expired, drill down to the **User Configuration**, **Administrative Templates**, **Windows Components**, **Windows Logon Options** group. Double-click **Set action to take when logon hours expire**. Select **Enabled** and then choose Lock, Disconnect, or Logoff. If the policy is not enabled, the user's session will continue, but the user will not be able to log on outside of the assigned logon hours once the current session has been terminated.

▲ *Disable Microsoft account resources.* Recall that a Microsoft account is a single sign-on (SSO) account, which means it provides authentication to multiple services and resources. When a user signs in to a Windows 10/8 computer with a Microsoft account, she has access to online resources such as OneDrive and OneNote and can sync settings on the computer with other computers that use the same Microsoft account. Settings include Start screen tiles, desktop personalization, installed apps and app settings, web browser favorites, and passwords to apps, websites, and networks.

> **✎ Notes** To see and edit the sync settings available for a Microsoft account, open the Windows 10 **Settings** app, click the **Accounts** group, and select **Sync your settings** in the left pane. In Windows 8, open the charms bar, click **Settings**, click **Change PC settings**, click **OneDrive**, and click **Sync settings**.

Depending on your company's policy, you might need to restrict access to online resources and sync settings that are linked to a user's Microsoft account. To disable OneDrive, for example, drill down to the **Computer Configuration**, **Administrative Templates**, **Windows Components**, **OneDrive** group. Enable the **Prevent the usage of OneDrive for file storage** policy to prevent users and programs from accessing OneDrive. Additionally, in the **Windows Components** submenu, click the **Sync your settings** group and use these policies to disable syncing apps, app settings, passwords, and other Windows settings (see Figure 7-5).

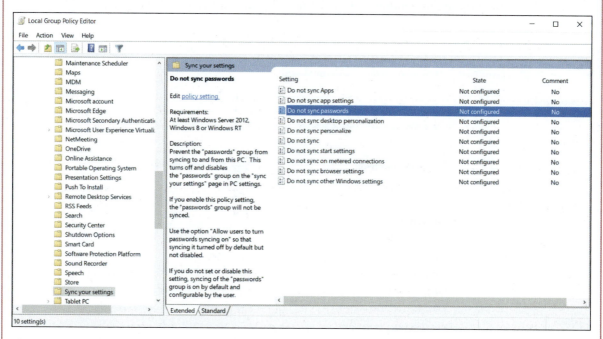

Figure 7-5 Restrict SSO authentication to online resources associated with a Microsoft account

(continues)

◢ *Disable AutoRun and AutoPlay.* When you attach a USB flash drive or external hard drive or insert a disc in the optical drive, Windows automatically accesses the storage media and then requests instructions for what to do next. Media files can be played automatically, which is called AutoPlay. Executable files can be run automatically, which is called AutoRun. You can disable both of these features to add yet another layer of security protection. To disable AutoPlay, drill down to the **Computer Configuration**, **Administrative Templates**, **Windows Components**, **AutoPlay Policies** group. Enable the **Turn off Autoplay** policy. To disable AutoRun, enable **Set the default behavior for AutoRun** and use the **Disabled** option.

4. When you finish setting your local security policies, close the Local Group Policy Editor console. To put your changes into effect, restart the system or open a command prompt window and enter the command **gpupdate /force**. The command might request that you restart the computer for all policies to take effect. The gpupdate command refreshes local group policies as well as group policies set in Active Directory on a Windows domain.

⭐ **A+ Exam Tip**   The A+ Core 2 exam expects you to know how to secure a workstation in a given scenario, including setting a strong password and configuring a workstation so that passwords will expire, knowing that a screen saver requires a password to unlock the workstation, that a logon time is restricted, and that the system locks when sign-in attempts have failed.

MANAGE USER CREDENTIALS

A user might need help managing the passwords and digital certificates stored on a Windows computer. To manage these user credentials, open the **Credential Manager** applet in Control Panel. The tool allows you to manage web credentials and Windows credentials (see Figure 7-6). When you select a website under Web Credentials, you can edit or delete the user name and password to access the site. When you click **Windows Credentials**, you can edit and delete Windows user names, passwords, and digital certificates installed on the system. You can also use this window to install a new digital certificate in Windows.

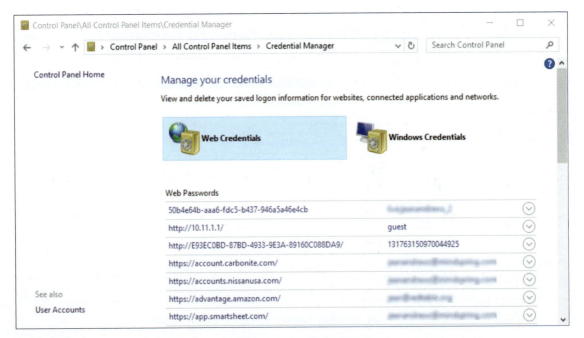

Figure 7-6   Manage passwords and digital certificates in Credential Manager

USING BIOS/UEFI PASSWORDS TO AUTHENTICATE USERS

**A+
CORE 2
2.7**

BIOS/UEFI firmware on the motherboard offers power-on passwords, which include an administrator or supervisor password (required to change BIOS/UEFI setup) and a user password (required to use the system or view BIOS/UEFI setup). Some firmware may also offer a drive lock password, which is required to access the hard drive. The drive lock password is stored on the hard drive so that it will still control access if the drive is removed from the computer and installed on another system. Figure 7-7 shows a BIOS/UEFI setup Security screen where you can set the Administrator and User passwords.

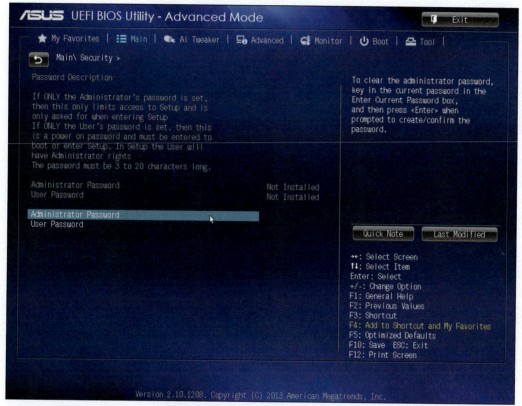

Source: American Megatrends, Inc.

Figure 7-7   BIOS/UEFI passwords can control access to BIOS/UEFI setup and to boot the system

SECURING INTERNET EXPLORER

**A+
CORE 2
1.6**

The Internet Options dialog box can be used to secure Internet Explorer, a browser included with Windows 10/8/7. The latest release of Internet Explorer is version 11, although Windows 10 features a new browser called Microsoft Edge to eventually replace Internet Explorer. Current releases of Windows 10/8/7 come with Internet Explorer 11 installed; for an old installation of Windows, open Windows Update and find and install the Internet Explorer 11 update. You can also go to the *microsoft.com* website and follow links to download and install Internet Explorer 11.

Here are some tips about using Internet Explorer 11:

▲ *Menu bar.* To open the Internet Explorer menu bar, press the **Alt** key or right-click a blank area in the title bar and check **Menu bar** in the shortcut menu. Notice in Figure 7-8 that you can also add the command bar to the Internet Explorer window.

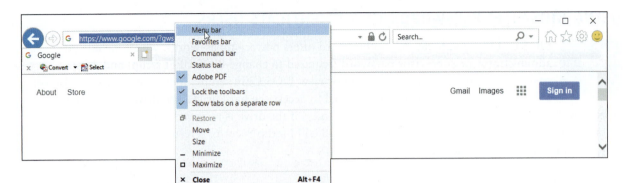

Figure 7-8 Access the shortcut menu from the title bar to control the Internet Explorer window

▲ **HTTP Secure.** Some web servers use HTTP with the SSL or TLS protocols (called HTTP Secure or HTTPS) to secure transmissions to and from the web server. Look for *https* and a padlock icon in the browser address box when HTTPS is used. Click the padlock to get information about the site security.

▲ **Repair or disable.** If you have a problem with Internet Explorer 11, try installing Windows updates, applying a restore point, or refreshing Windows 10/8. If you prefer to use a different browser, you can disable Internet Explorer 11. Open the **Programs and Features** window in Control Panel and click **Turn Windows features on or off**. In the Windows Features box, uncheck **Internet Explorer 11** and click **OK**.

Now let's see how you can use the Internet Options box to secure Internet Explorer. To open the box, click the **Tools** icon on the right side of the Internet Explorer title bar and click **Internet options**. Another method is to press **Alt** to display the menu bar, click **Tools** in the menu, and click **Internet options**. A third method is to click **Internet Options** in the Classic view of Control Panel. The Internet Options box is shown in Figure 7-9.

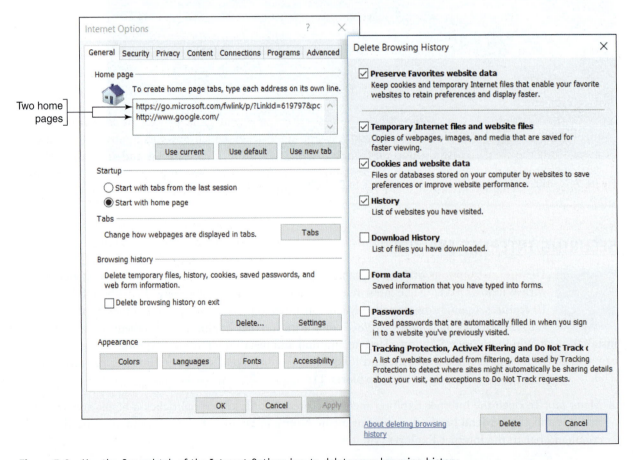

Figure 7-9 Use the General tab of the Internet Options box to delete your browsing history

> **✎ Notes** If you open the Internet Options box through Control Panel, the box is titled *Internet Properties* and the menus and options vary slightly.

> **★ A+ Exam Tip** The A+ Core 2 exam expects you to know how to use the General, Security, Privacy, Connections, Programs, and Advanced tabs in the Internet Options box.

Here are the more important tabs in the Internet Options box and how to use them:

▲ *General tab.* Using the General tab, you can change the home page or add a second home page tab. You can also protect your identity and surfing records:

   ▲ To delete what Internet Explorer has kept about your former browsing, click **Delete**. In the Delete Browsing History box (see the right side of Figure 7-9), uncheck the first item and check all other items. (If you want to keep cookies used by websites in your Favorites list, check the first item, **Preserve Favorites website data.**) Click **Delete**.

   ▲ For future browsing sessions, you can delete your browsing history each time you close Internet Explorer by checking **Delete browsing history on exit** on the General tab of the Internet Options box.

Internet Explorer holds a cache containing previously downloaded content in case it is requested again. The cache is stored in several folders named Temporary Internet Files. On the General tab, click **Settings** to change the maximum allowed space used for temporary Internet files and control the location of these files.

▲ *Security tab.* You can set a zone security level on the Security tab. For the Internet, medium-high is the default value; at this level, Internet Explorer prompts before downloading content and does not download ActiveX controls that are not signed by Microsoft. An ActiveX control is a small app or add-on that can be downloaded from a website along with a webpage and is executed by Internet Explorer to enhance the webpage (for example, to add animation to the page). A virus can sometimes hide in an ActiveX control, but Internet Explorer is designed to catch them by authenticating each ActiveX control it downloads. To customize security settings, click **Custom level**. In the Security Settings box, you can decide exactly how you want to handle downloaded content. For example, you can disable file downloads.

▲ *Privacy tab.* Use the Privacy tab to block cookies that might invade your privacy or steal your identity. You can also use this tab to control the Pop-up Blocker, which prevents annoying pop-ups as you surf the web. To allow a pop-up from a particular website, click **Settings** and enter the URL of the website in the Pop-up Blocker Settings box. See Figure 7-10. Some pop-ups are useful, such as when you're trying to download a file from a website and the site asks permission to complete the download.

▲ *Connections tab.* The Connections tab allows you to configure proxy server settings and create a VPN connection. Many large corporations and ISPs use proxy servers to speed up Internet access. A web browser does not have to be aware that a proxy server is in use. However, one reason you might need to configure Internet Explorer to be aware of and use a proxy server is when you are on a corporate network and are having a problem connecting to a secured website (one using HTTP over SSL or another encryption protocol). The problem might be caused by Windows trying to connect using the wrong proxy server on the network. Check with your network administrator to find out if a specific proxy server should be used to manage secure website connections.

> **★ A+ Exam Tip** The A+ Core 2 exam expects you to know how to configure proxy settings on a client desktop.

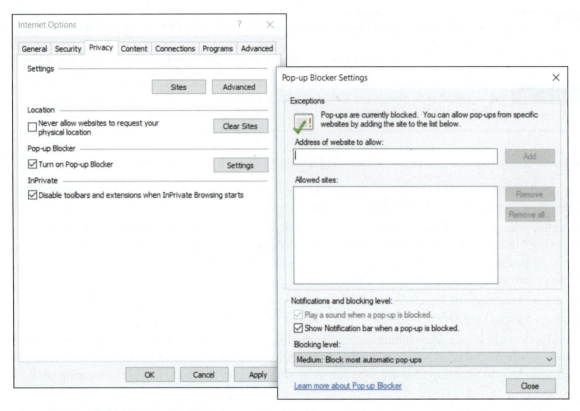

Figure 7-10 Use the Privacy tab to control pop-ups and cookies

If you need to configure Internet Explorer to use a specific proxy server, open the **Connections** tab and click **LAN settings**. In the settings box, check **Use a proxy server for your LAN** and enter the IP address of the proxy server (see Figure 7-11). If your organization uses more than one proxy server, click **Advanced** and enter IP addresses for each type of proxy server on your network (see the right side of Figure 7-11). You can also enter a port address for each server, if necessary. If you are trying to solve a problem of connecting to a server using HTTP over SSL or another secured protocol, use the Secure field to enter the IP address of the proxy server that is used to manage secure connections.

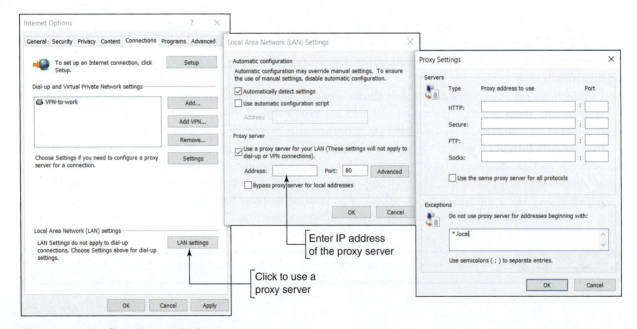

Figure 7-11 Configure Internet Explorer to use one or more proxy servers

▲ *Programs tab.* The Programs tab is used to manage add-ons, also called plug-ins, which are small apps that help Internet Explorer to display multimedia content, manage email, translate text, or other actions. On the Programs tab, click **Manage add-ons** to open the Manage Add-ons box. See Figure 7-12. Here's what you can do with this box:

  ▲ *View all add-ons.* In the left pane under Show, you can select all add-ons installed on the computer, as shown in the figure.

  ▲ *Enable or disable an add-on.* Select an add-on listed in the right pane to see information about it in the lower pane. To enable or disable a selected add-on, click **Enable** or click **Disable**.

  ▲ *Delete an add-on.* Downloaded ActiveX controls can be uninstalled using this window. Select a downloaded ActiveX add-on and click **More information** in the lower pane. If the add-on has been downloaded and can be removed, the Remove button on the More information box will be available. You can also uninstall downloaded add-ons using the Programs and Features window in Control Panel.

7

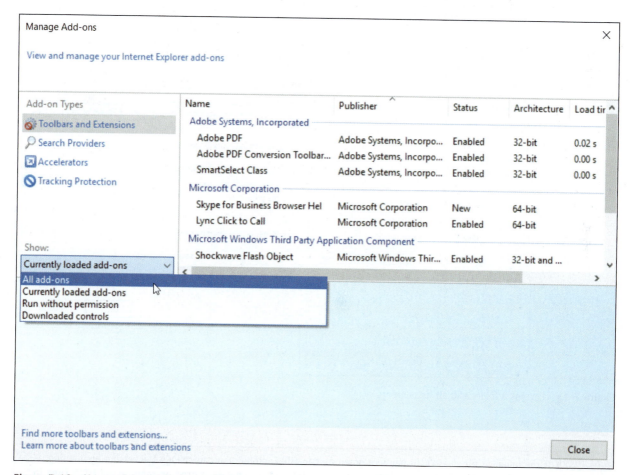

Figure 7-12 Manage Internet Explorer add-ons

✎ **Notes** If you use Control Panel to open the Internet Options box and open the Manage Add-ons box from there, the *Currently loaded add-ons* option is missing in the drop-down list under Show.

▲ *Advanced tab.* The Advanced tab contains several miscellaneous settings used to control Internet Explorer. If you suspect problems are caused by wrong settings, use this tab to reset Internet Explorer to all default settings.

Now let's turn our attention to securing another resource on the network: folders and files.

FILE AND FOLDER ENCRYPTION

A+
CORE 2
2.6
In Windows, files and folders can be encrypted using the Windows Encrypting File System (EFS). This encryption works only with the NTFS file system and business and professional editions of Windows. If a folder is marked for encryption, every file created in the folder or copied to the folder will be encrypted. An encrypted file remains encrypted if you move it from an encrypted folder to an unencrypted folder on the same or another NTFS volume. To encrypt a folder or file, right-click it and open its Properties box (see Figure 7-13). On the General tab, click **Advanced**. In the Advanced Attributes box, check **Encrypt contents to secure data** and click **OK**. In File Explorer or Windows Explorer, encrypted file and folder names are displayed in green by default.

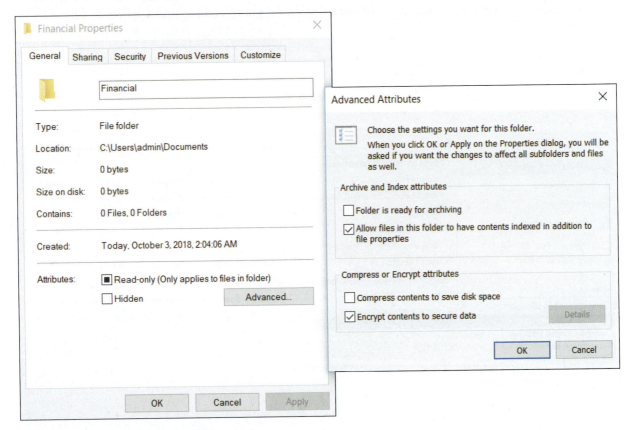

Figure 7-13 Encrypt a folder and all its contents

Notes If the folder or file doesn't display in a green font in File Explorer, you can change the setting by opening **Control Panel** and clicking **File Explorer Options**. On the View tab, check **Show encrypted or compressed NTFS files in color**. Click **OK**.

Caution A user sometimes forgets a password, and an administrator can reset the forgotten password. However, know that if an administrator resets a user password, the user will lose all his EFS encrypted folders and files, personal digital certificates, and passwords stored on the computer. To reset a user password, you can use the **Network Places Wizard** tool (netplwiz.exe), as shown in Figure 7-14. Select the user and click **Reset Password**.

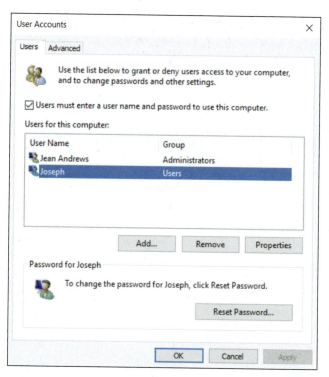

Figure 7-14 Reset a user password

BITLOCKER ENCRYPTION

A+
CORE 2
1.6, 2.6

BitLocker Drive Encryption in Windows professional and business editions locks down a hard drive by encrypting the entire Windows volume and any other volume on the drive and restricts access by requiring one or two encryption keys. A similar feature, BitLocker To Go, encrypts data on a USB flash drive and restricts access by requiring a password. You need to be aware of the restrictions and possible risks before you decide to use BitLocker. It's intended to work in partnership with file and folder encryption to provide data security.

★ **A+ Exam Tip** The A+ Core 2 exam expects you to know when it is appropriate to use BitLocker Drive Encryption and BitLocker To Go in a given scenario.

The three ways you can use BitLocker Drive Encryption depend on the type of protection you need and the computer hardware available:

◢ *Computer authentication.* Many laptop computers have a chip on the motherboard called the TPM (Trusted Platform Module) chip. The TPM chip holds the BitLocker encryption key (also called the startup key). If the hard drive is stolen from the laptop and installed in another computer, the data would be safe because BitLocker would not allow access without the startup key stored on the TPM chip. Therefore, this method authenticates the computer. However, if the motherboard fails and is replaced, you'll need a backup copy of the startup key to access data on the hard drive. (You cannot move the TPM chip from one motherboard to another.)

◢ *User authentication.* For computers that don't have TPM, the startup key can be stored on a USB flash drive (or other storage device the computer reads before the OS is loaded), and the flash drive must be installed before the computer boots. This method authenticates the user. For this method to be the most secure, the user must never leave the flash drive stored with the computer. (Instead, the user might keep the USB startup key on his key ring or a lanyard.)

◢ *Computer and user authentication.* For *best* security, a password can be required at every startup in addition to TPM. Using this method, both the computer and the user are authenticated. This practice is an example of multifactor authentication (MFA), which uses more than one method to authenticate.

BitLocker Drive Encryption provides great security, but security comes with a price. For instance, you risk the chance your TPM will fail or you will lose all copies of the startup key. In these events, recovering the data can be messy. Therefore, use BitLocker only if the risks of using it do not outweigh the risks of stolen data. And, if you decide to use BitLocker, be sure to make extra copies of the startup key and/or password and keep them in a safe location.

> ⚡ **Caution**   In Chapter 8, you learn that some data, such as health-care data, is regulated by the government, and organizations that are negligent to protect it can be held legally responsible for data breaches. For this type of data, encryption and other security measures may be mandated by law.

To start the process of using BitLocker Drive Encryption, first go into BIOS/UEFI setup and enable the TPM chip. Then open the **BitLocker Drive Encryption** applet in Control Panel (see Figure 7-15). Using this window, you can click **TPM Administration** to manage the TPM chip and turn on BitLocker or BitLocker To Go.

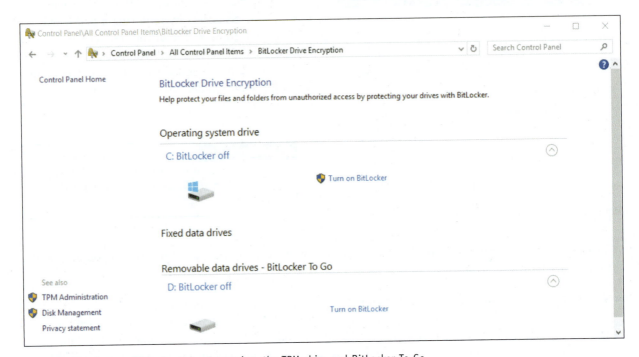

Figure 7-15   Manage BitLocker Drive Encryption, the TPM chip, and BitLocker To Go

> ✏️ **Notes**   For detailed instructions on how to set up BitLocker Drive Encryption, see the Microsoft Windows IT Pro Center article "BitLocker" at *docs.microsoft.com/en-us/windows/security/information-protection/bitlocker/bitlocker-overview*.

WINDOWS FIREWALL SETTINGS

**A+
CORE 2
1.5, 1.6,
1.8**

Recall from Chapter 3 that a SOHO router can serve as a hardware firewall to protect its network from attack over the Internet. Recall that the best protection from attack is layered protection (see Figure 7-16). In addition to a network hardware firewall, a large corporation might use a software firewall, also called a corporate firewall, installed on a computer that stands between the Internet and the network to protect the network. This computer has two network cards installed, and the installed software firewall filters the traffic between the two cards.

A personal firewall, also called a host firewall or application firewall, is software installed on a personal computer to protect it. A personal firewall provides redundant protection from attacks over the Internet, filters inbound traffic to protect a computer from attack from other computers on the same network, and filters outbound traffic to prevent attacks on other computers on the same network. When setting up a SOHO network or a personal computer, configure a personal firewall on each computer.

Windows Firewall is a personal firewall that protects a computer from intrusion and from attacking other computers; it is automatically configured when you set up your security level for a new network

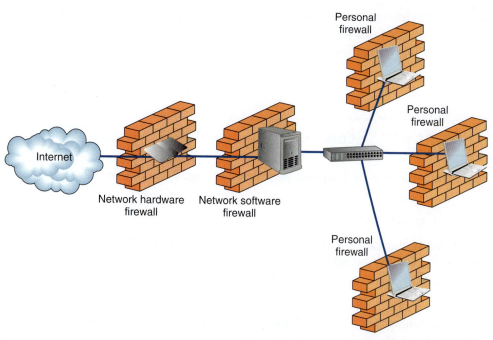

Figure 7-16   Three types of firewalls used to protect a network and individual computers on the network

connection. To set the security for a network connection, open the **Network and Sharing Center** in Control Panel and click **Change advanced sharing settings.** The resulting Windows 10 Advanced sharing settings window is shown in Figure 7-17. (Recall that for Windows 10/8, the options are private and public security, and for Windows 7, the options are home, work, and public security.)

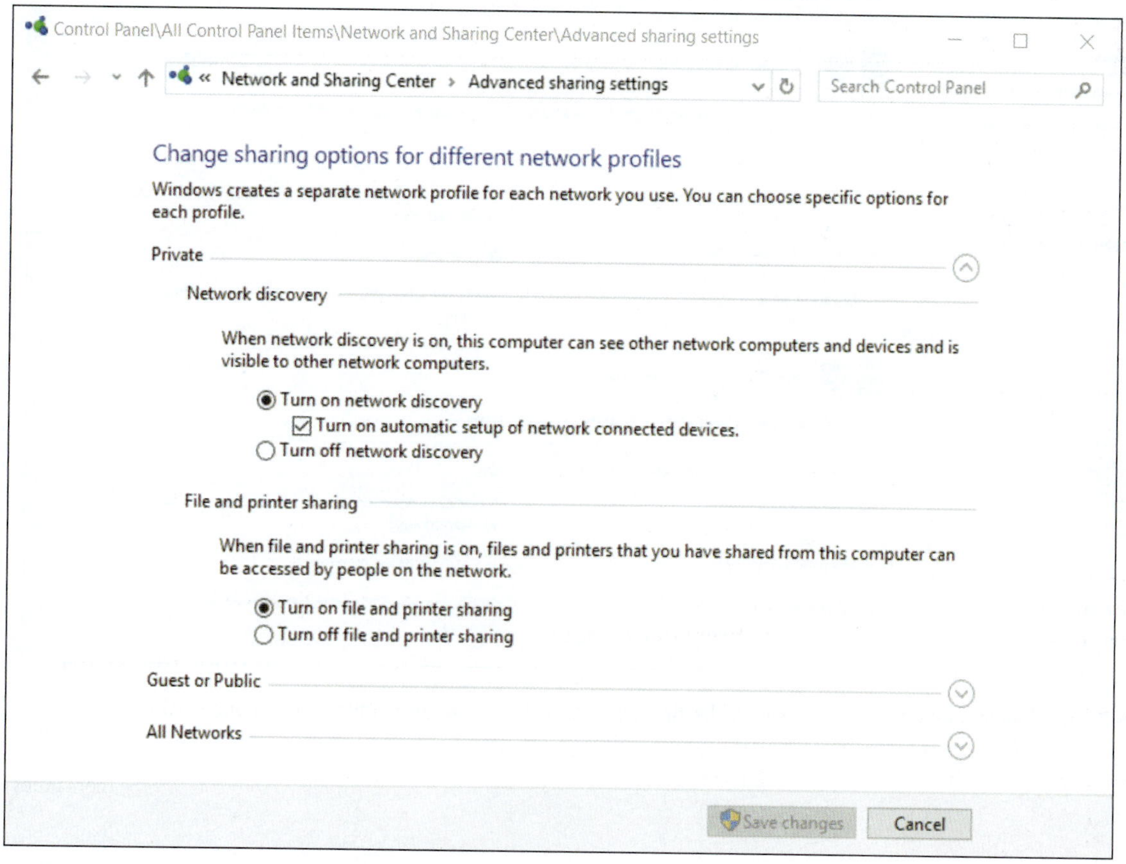

Control Panel\All Control Panel Items\Network and Sharing Center\Advanced sharing settings   —   □   ✕

← → ∨ ↑ « Network and Sharing Center › Advanced sharing settings   ∨ ↻   Search Control Panel   🔎

Change sharing options for different network profiles

Windows creates a separate network profile for each network you use. You can choose specific options for each profile.

Private ⌃

    Network discovery

        When network discovery is on, this computer can see other network computers and devices and is visible to other network computers.

        ◉ Turn on network discovery
          ☑ Turn on automatic setup of network connected devices.
        ◯ Turn off network discovery

    File and printer sharing

        When file and printer sharing is on, files and printers that you have shared from this computer can be accessed by people on the network.

        ◉ Turn on file and printer sharing
        ◯ Turn off file and printer sharing

Guest or Public ⌄

All Networks ⌄

🛡 Save changes   Cancel

Figure 7-17   Configure the security level for network connections

Later in the chapter, you learn how to share folders and printers on a private network. For folder and printer sharing to work, you need to use the Advanced sharing settings window to turn on network discovery and file and printer sharing so that Windows Firewall allows this type of network traffic.

APPLYING | CONCEPTS CONFIGURING WINDOWS FIREWALL

You can use the Windows Firewall window to configure even more firewall settings. Follow these steps to find out how:

1. Use one of these methods to open Windows Firewall:

   ▲ Open the **Network and Sharing Center**. For Windows 10, click **Windows Defender Firewall** in the lower part of the left pane. For Windows 8/7, click **Windows Firewall**.
   ▲ Open Control Panel in Classic view and click **Windows Defender Firewall**. For Windows 8/7, click **Windows Firewall**.

   The Windows Defender Firewall window is shown in Figure 7-18. Although the Windows 8/7 Windows Firewall window looks slightly different, the windows work basically the same way.

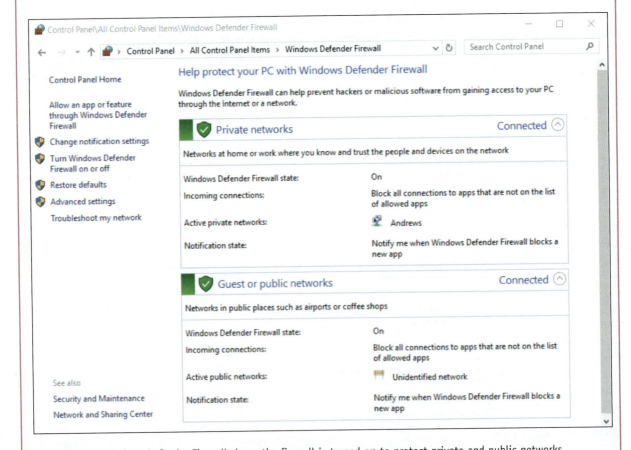

Figure 7-18 Windows Defender Firewall shows the firewall is turned on to protect private and public networks

(continues)

2. In general, Windows Firewall works by allowing or denying network traffic on incoming or outgoing ports. Recall that a port is a number an application on the computer uses to connect to another application on the network or Internet. Here are some basic settings you can configure in Windows Firewall:

a. Use the left pane to turn Windows Firewall on or off. When Windows Firewall is disabled (not a good idea), all traffic is allowed to pass and your computer is unprotected.

b. When Windows Firewall is enabled, all traffic is stopped unless you have specified an exception. To allow or deny a specific app access to the computer, click **Allow an app or feature through Windows Defender Firewall**. You can then select the app from a list of apps and decide how it can use the network connection.

c. To allow or deny all other types of traffic, not just those related to apps, click **Advanced settings**. On the Advanced Security window (see Figure 7-19), you can click Inbound Rules or Outbound Rules to create or edit an inbound or outbound rule and control traffic. A rule can specify how port numbers, TCP/IP protocols, programs, services, computers, and remote users can use the network connection. A rule can apply to public, private, and domain networks.

Figure 7-19 Customize an inbound or outbound rule to control exactly what incoming or outgoing traffic is allowed through the firewall

CONTROLLING ACCESS TO FOLDERS AND FILES

Responsibility for a peer-to-peer network or domain can include controlling access to folders and files for users of a local computer and for remote users accessing shared resources over the network. Managing shared resources is accomplished by (1) assigning privileges to user accounts and (2) assigning permissions to folders, files, and printers.

> ✏️ **Notes** In Windows, the terms *privileges* and *permissions* have different meanings. **Privileges** (also called *rights*) refer to the tasks an account is allowed to do in the system, such as installing software or changing the system date and time. **Permissions** refer to which user accounts or user groups are allowed access to data files and folders. *Privileges are assigned to an account, and permissions are assigned to data files and folders.*

Let's first look at the strategies used for controlling privileges to user accounts and controlling permissions to folders and files. Then you learn the procedures in Windows for assigning these privileges and permissions.

CLASSIFYING USER ACCOUNTS AND USER GROUPS

A+ CORE 2 1.8, 2.2, 2.6

Computer users should be classified to determine the privileges they need to do their jobs. For example, some users need the privilege to sign in to a system remotely and others do not. Other privileges granted to users might include the right to install software or hardware, change the system date and time, change Windows Firewall settings, and so forth. Generally, when a new employee begins work, that employee's job description with exceptions approved by his supervisor determine what privileges the employee needs to perform his job. You, as the support technician, will be responsible to make sure the user account assigned to the employee has these privileges and no more. This approach is called the principle of least privilege.

In Windows, the privileges or rights assigned to a user account are established when you first create the account, which is when you decide the account type. You can later change these privileges by changing the user groups to which the account belongs. Recall from Chapter 2 that user accounts can be created using the User Accounts applet in Control Panel (in any edition of Windows) or the Local Users and Groups utility in the Computer Management console (in business and professional editions of Windows). User accounts can be assigned to different user groups using the Computer Management console in business and professional editions of Windows. Home editions of Windows cannot be used to manage user groups.

TYPE OF USER ACCOUNT

When you use the User Accounts applet in Control Panel to manage user accounts, you can choose between two account types: Administrator or Standard. When you use Local Users and Groups in Computer Management to create an account, the account type is automatically a standard user account.

To create a user account using Computer Management, first open the Computer Management console (compmgmt.msc). Under **Local Users and Groups**, right-click **Users** and select **New User** in the shortcut menu. (Windows Home editions don't include the Local Users and Groups option in the Computer Management console.) Enter information for the new user and click **Create** (see Figure 7-20).

> ⭐ **A+ Exam Tip** The A+ Core 2 exam expects you to be able to compare privileges assigned to the administrator, standard user, power user, and guest user groups.

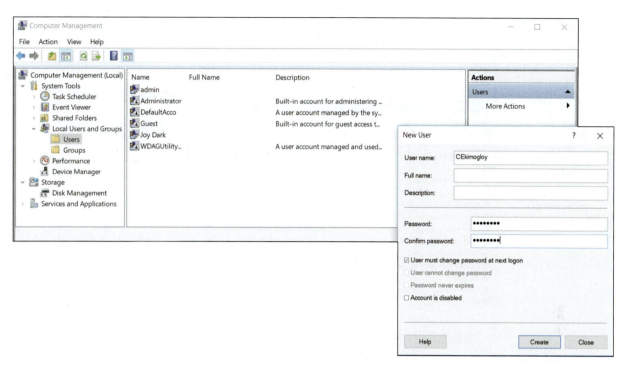

Figure 7-20 Create a new user

BUILT-IN USER GROUPS

A user account can belong to one or more user groups. Windows offers several built-in user groups and you can create your own. Here are important built-in user groups:

▲ *Administrators and Users groups.* By default, administrator accounts belong to the **Administrators group**, and standard user accounts belong to the **Users group**. If you want to give administrator privileges to a standard user account, use the Computer Management console to add the account to the Administrators group.

▲ *Guests group.* The **Guests group** has limited privileges on the system and is given a temporary profile that is deleted when the user signs out. Windows automatically creates one account in the Guests group named the Guest account, which is disabled by default.

▲ *Power Users group.* Older editions of Windows have a **Power Users group** that can read from and write to parts of the system other than its own user profile folders, install applications, and perform limited administrative tasks. Windows 10/8/7 offers a Power Users group only for backward compatibility with legacy applications.

To view user groups installed on a system, open the Computer Management console. Under Local Users and Groups, click **Groups** (see Figure 7-21).

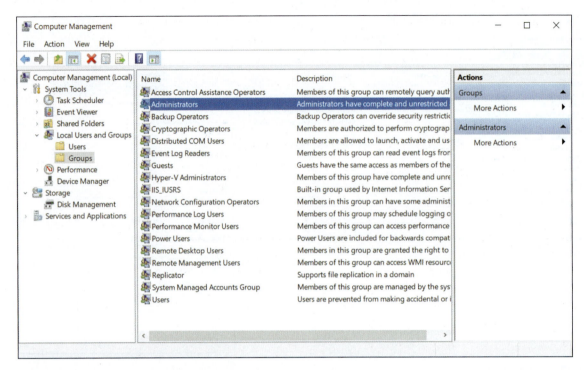

Figure 7-21 User groups installed on a system

To change the groups a user account is in, click **Users** under Local Users and Groups. The list of user accounts appears in the right pane of the console window (see the left side of Figure 7-22). Right-click the user account and select **Properties** in the shortcut menu. In the user account Properties box, click the **Member Of** tab (see the middle of Figure 7-22). Click **Add** and enter the user group name. You must type the user group name exactly as it appears in the list of user groups that you saw earlier (see Figure 7-21). To verify that the group name is correct, click **Check Names**. A verified name is underlined. (Alternately, you can click **Advanced**, click **Find Now**, and select the group name from the list of groups that appears.) Click **OK** twice to close both boxes.

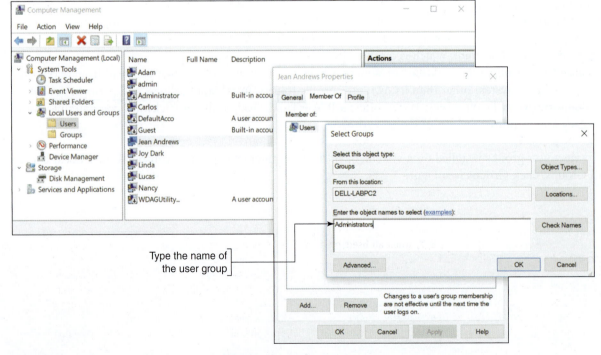

Figure 7-22 Add a user account to a user group

In addition to the groups you can assign to an account, Windows might automatically assign one of these built-in user groups to an account when it is determining permissions assigned to a file or folder:

▲ The Authenticated Users group includes all user accounts that can access the system except the Guest account. These accounts include domain accounts (used to sign in to the domain) and local accounts (used to sign in to the local computer). The accounts might or might not require a password. When you create a folder or file that is not part of your user profile, Windows gives access to all Authenticated Users by default.

▲ The Everyone group includes the Authenticated Users group as well as the Guest account. When you share a file or folder on the network (or to a homegroup in Windows 8/7), Windows gives access to the Everyone group by default.

▲ Anonymous users are users who have not been authenticated on a remote computer. If you sign in to a computer using a local account and then attempt to access a remote computer, you must be authenticated on the remote computer. You will be authenticated if your user account and password match on both computers. If you signed in to your local computer with an account and password that do not match an account and password on the remote computer, you are considered an anonymous user on the remote computer. As an anonymous user, you might be allowed to use File Explorer or Windows Explorer to view shared folders and files on the remote computer, but you cannot access them.

CUSTOMIZED USER GROUPS

Use the Computer Management console or the Local Users and Groups console (lusrmgr.msc) in business and professional editions of Windows to create and manage your own user groups. When managing several user accounts, it's easier to assign permissions to user groups rather than to individual accounts. First create a user group and then assign permissions to this user group. Any user account that you put in this group then acquires or inherits the same permissions.

User groups work especially well when several users need the same permissions. For example, you can set up an Accounting group and a Medical Records group for a small office. Users in the Accounting department and users in the Medical Records department go into their respective user groups. Then you only need to manage the permissions for two groups rather than multiple user accounts.

METHODS TO ASSIGN PERMISSIONS TO FOLDERS AND FILES

**A+
CORE 2
2.2, 2.6**

There are two general strategies for managing shared files and folders, also called directories, in Windows:

▲ *Workgroup sharing.* With workgroup sharing, all privileges and permissions are set up on each local computer so that each computer manages access to its files, folders, and printers shared on the peer-to-peer network. The local user decides which users on the network have access to which shared folder and the type of access they have.

▲ *Domain controlling.* If a Windows computer belongs to a domain instead of a workgroup or homegroup, all security should be managed by the network administrator for the entire network. Although individual users on workstations can share files and folders with other users in the domain, this is not considered a security best practice.

◇ OS Differences For Windows 8/7, when all users on a small network require the same access to all resources, you can use a homegroup. Folders, libraries, files, and printers shared with the homegroup are available to all users on the network whose computers have joined the homegroup. After the homegroup is set up, you can share a file or folder with the homegroup using the Sharing Wizard. To do so, right-click the item and select **Share with** in the shortcut menu. The wizard lists three general options for sharing followed by a list of specific people (see Figure 7-23). Click **Homegroup (view)** or **Homegroup (view and edit)** to assign this permission to the homegroup.

Because of the lack of control over who can access a particular file or folder in a homegroup, Windows 10 Version 1803 and higher does not support homegroups.

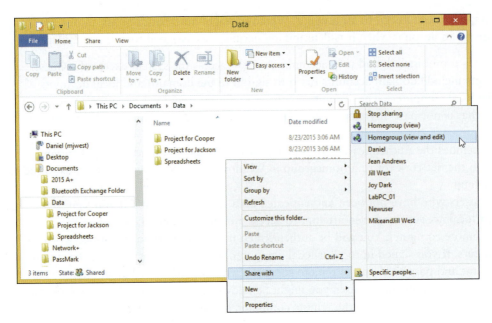

Figure 7-23 Share a folder with the homegroup

On a Windows peer-to-peer network, each workstation shares its files and folders with others in the workgroup, or files and folders on a file server are shared. Here are some tips about which folders to use to hold shared data on a file server or personal computer:

◢ Private data for an individual user is best kept in the C:\Users folder for that user. User accounts with limited or standard privileges cannot normally access these folders because they belong to another user account. However, accounts with administrative privileges do have access.

◢ The C:\Users\Public folder is intended to be used for folders and files that all users share. It is not recommended that you use this folder for controlled access to data.

◢ For best security, create a folder that's not in the C:\Users folder and assign permissions to that folder and its subfolders. You can allow all users access or only certain users or user groups.

Some applications can be shared with others on the network. If you share a folder that has a program file in it, a user on another computer can double-click the program file and execute it remotely on his or her desktop. This is a handy way for several users to share an application that is installed on a single computer. However, know that not all applications are designed to work this way.

Regardless of whether you are sharing to a workgroup or domain, Windows offers two methods to share a folder over the network:

◢ *Share permissions.* Share permissions grant permissions only to network users, and these permissions do not apply to local users of a computer. Share permissions work on NTFS, FAT32, and exFAT volumes and are configured using the Sharing tab in a folder's Properties box. Share permissions apply to a folder and its contents, but not to individual files.

◢ *NTFS permissions.* NTFS permissions apply to local users and network users and apply to both folders and individual files. NTFS permissions work on NTFS volumes only and are configured using the Security tab in a file or folder's Properties box. (The Security tab is missing on the Properties box of a folder or file on a FAT volume.)

Here are some tips when implementing share permissions and NTFS permissions:

◢ If you use both share permissions and NTFS permissions on a folder, the more restrictive permission applies. For NTFS volumes, use only NTFS permissions because they can be customized better. For FAT volumes, your only option is share permissions.

◢ If NTFS permissions are conflicting—for example, when a user account has been given one permission and the user group to which this user belongs has been given a different permission—the more liberal permission applies.

◢ **Permission propagation** is when permissions are passed from parent object to child. **Inherited permissions** are permissions that are attained from a parent. For example, when you create a file or folder in a parent folder, the new object takes on the permissions of the parent folder.

◢ When you move or copy an object to a folder, the object takes on the permissions of that folder. The exception to this rule is when you move (not copy) an object from one location to another on the same volume. In this case, the object retains its permissions from the original folder.

> ✎ **Notes** You can use the xcopy or robocopy command with parameters to change the rules for how inherited permissions are managed when copying and moving files. For more information, see the Microsoft Knowledge Base article cc733145 at *https://technet.microsoft.com/en-us/library/cc733145*.

7

> ★ **A+ Exam Tip** The A+ Core 2 exam expects you to compare NTFS and share permissions, including how allow and deny conflicts are resolved with each and what happens to permissions when you move or copy a file or folder.

HOW TO SHARE FOLDERS AND FILES

A+ CORE 2 1.5, 1.6, 2.2, 2.6 Now that you know about the concepts and strategies for sharing folders and files, let's look at the details of how to use Windows to manage user privileges and file and folder permissions.

APPLYING | CONCEPTS **CREATING USER ACCOUNTS WITH DATA ACCESS**

Nicole is responsible for a peer-to-peer network at a medical doctor's office. Four computers are connected to the small company network; one of these computers acts as the file server for the network. Nicole has created two classifications of data, Financial and Medical. Two workers (Nancy and Adam) require access to the Medical data, and two workers (Linda and Carlos) require access to the Financial folder. In addition, the doctor, Lucas, requires access to both categories of data. Nicole must do the following to set up the users and data:

1. Create folders named Financial and Medical on the file server. Create five user accounts, one each for Lucas, Nancy, Adam, Linda, and Carlos. All the accounts belong to the Windows standard user group. Create two user groups, Financial and Medical.

2. Using NTFS permissions, set the permissions for the Financial and Medical folders on the file server so that only the members of the appropriate group can access each folder.

3. Test access to both folders using test data and then copy all real data into the two folders and subfolders. Set up a backup plan for the two folders, as you learned to do in Chapter 4.

Let's look at how each of these three steps is done.

(continues)

STEP 1: CREATE FOLDERS, USER ACCOUNTS, AND USER GROUPS

Follow these steps to create the folders, user accounts, and user groups on the file server computer that is using Windows 10 Pro:

1. Sign in to the system as an administrator.

2. Using an NTFS volume, create these two folders: **C:\Medical** and **C:\Financial**.

3. Open the Computer Management console or the Local Users and Groups console and create user accounts for **Lucas**, **Nancy**, **Adam**, **Linda**, and **Carlos**. The account types are automatically standard user accounts.

4. To create the Medical user group, right-click **Groups** under Local Users and Groups and select **New Group** in the shortcut menu. The New Group box appears. Enter the name of the group (**Medical**) and its description (**Users have access to the Medical folder**), as shown in Figure 7-24.

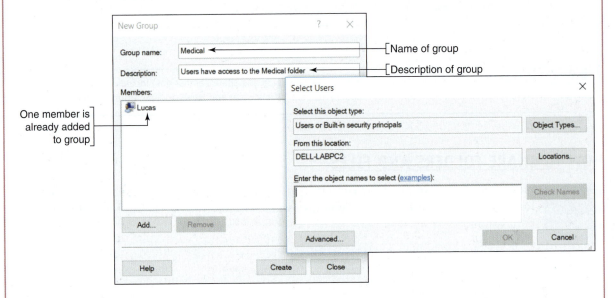

Figure 7-24   Setting up a new user group

5. Add all the users who need access to medical data (Lucas, Adam, and Nancy). To add members to the Medical group, click **Add**. The Select Users box opens, as shown on the right side of Figure 7-24. Under *Enter the object names to select*, enter the name of a user. Click **Check Names** to verify the user. Click **OK**. As each user is added, his or her name appears under Members in the New Group box, as shown in Figure 7-24. To create the group, click **Create** in the New Group box.

6. In the same way, create the Financial group and add Lucas, Linda, and Carlos to the group. Later, you can use the Computer Management console to add or remove users from either group.

7. Close the Computer Management console.

> ⭐ **A+ Exam Tip**   The A+ Core 2 exam expects you to be able to set up a user account or group and know how to change the group to which an account is assigned.

STEP 2: SET NTFS FOLDER PERMISSIONS FOR USER GROUPS

Follow these steps to set the NTFS permissions for the two folders:

1. Open File Explorer or Windows Explorer, right-click the **Medical** folder, and select **Properties** in the shortcut menu. The Properties box for the folder appears.

(continues)

2. Click the **Security** tab (see Figure 7-25). Notice in the box that Authenticated Users, SYSTEM, Administrators, and Users all have access to the C:\Medical folder. When you select a user group, the type of permissions assigned to that group appears in the *Permissions* area. Table 7-1 explains the more significant types of permission. Note that the Administrators group has full control of the folder. Also notice the checks under Allow are dimmed. These permissions are dimmed because they have been inherited from the parent object. In this case, the parent object is Windows default settings.

> ✏️ **Notes** For a thorough discussion of how permissions work, see the Microsoft Knowledge Base article cc783530 at *https://technet.microsoft.com/ en-us/library/Cc783530(v=WS.10).aspx.*

> ⭐ **A+ Exam Tip** The A+ Core 2 exam expects you to know that NTFS permissions can be customized better than share permissions.

Figure 7-25 Permissions assigned to the Medical folder

Permission Level	Description
Full control	Can read, change, delete, and create files and subfolders, read file and folder attributes, read and change permissions, and take ownership of a file or folder.
Modify	Can read, change, and create files and subfolders. Can delete the folder or file but cannot delete subfolders and their files. Can read and change attributes. Can view permissions but not change them. Cannot take ownership.
Read & execute	Can read folders and contents and run programs in a folder. (Applies to both files and folders.)
List folder contents	Can read folders and contents and run programs in a folder. (Applies only to folders.)
Read	Can read folders and contents.
Write	Can create a folder or file and change attributes but cannot read data. This permission is used for a drop folder, where users can drop confidential files that can only be read by a manager. For example, an instructor can receive student homework in a drop folder.

Table 7-1 Permission levels for files and folders

3. To remove the inherited status from these permissions so you can change them, click **Advanced**. The Advanced Security Settings box appears (see the left side of Figure 7-26). Click **Disable inheritance**. The Block Inheritance box appears (see the right side of Figure 7-26). To keep the current permissions but remove the inherited status placed on them, click **Convert inherited permissions into explicit permissions on this object**. Click **Apply**.

> ↻ **OS Differences** To remove the inherited status of folder permissions in Windows 7, open the Advanced Security Settings box and click **Change Permissions**. In the new Advanced Security Settings box, you can now uncheck **Include inheritable permissions from this object's parent**. A Windows Security warning box appears. To keep the current permissions but remove the inherited status placed on them, click **Add**.

(continues)

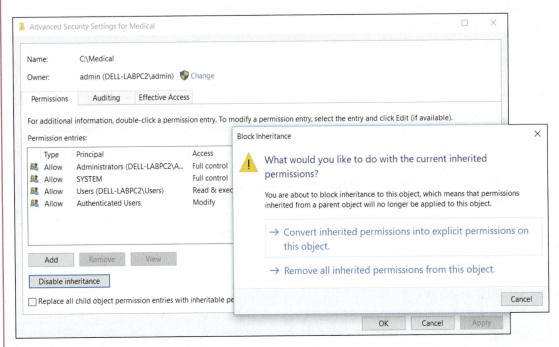

Figure 7-26 Remove the inherited status from the current permissions

4. Close the Advanced Security Settings box.

5. In the Medical Properties box, notice the permissions are now checked in black, indicating they are no longer inherited permissions and can be changed. Click **Edit** to change these permissions.

6. The Permissions box opens (see Figure 7-27). Select the **Authenticated Users** group and click **Remove**. Also remove the **Users** group. Don't remove the SYSTEM group, which gives Windows the access it needs. Also, don't remove the Administrators group. You need to leave that group as is so that administrators can access the data.

7. To add a new group, click **Add**. The Select Users or Groups box opens. Under *Enter the object names to select*, type **Medical**, as shown in Figure 7-28. Click **Check Names** to verify the group. Click **OK**. The Medical group is added to the list of groups and users for this folder.

Figure 7-27 Change the permissions to a folder

(continues)

8. In the Permissions box, make sure the **Medical** group is selected. Under *Permissions for Medical*, check **Allow** under *Full control* to give that permission to this user group. Click **OK** twice to close the Properties box.

9. In a similar way, change the permissions of the C:\Financial folder so that Authenticated Users and Users are not allowed access and the Financial group is allowed full control.

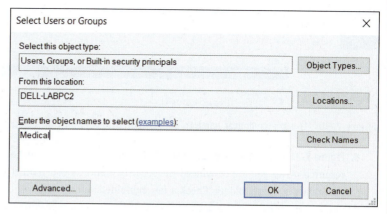

Figure 7-28 Add a user or group to shared permissions

STEP 3: TEST, SET SHARE PERMISSIONS, AND GO LIVE

It's now time to test your security measures. Do the following to test the NTFS permissions and implement your shared folders:

1. Test a user account in each user group to make sure the user can read, write, and delete in the folder he needs but cannot access the other folder. Put some test data in each folder. Then sign in to the system using an account you want to test and try to access each folder. Figure 7-29 shows the box that appears when an unauthorized user attempts to access a local folder. When you click **Continue**, entering an administrator password in the resulting UAC box gives you access.

Figure 7-29 Access to a folder is controlled

2. Now that NTFS permissions are set correctly for each local and network user, you are ready to allow access over the network. To do that, both NTFS and share permissions must allow network access. (Share permissions apply only to network access, not local access.) The best practice is to allow full access using share permissions and restrictive access using NTFS permissions. Remember that the most restrictive permissions apply. To allow full access using share permissions, click the **Sharing** tab of each folder's properties box, and click **Advanced Sharing**.

3. In the Advanced Sharing box, check **Share this folder** if it is not already checked. Then click **Permissions**. To add a new group, click **Add**. The Select Users or Groups box opens. Under *Enter the object names to select*, type **Everyone** and click **OK**. The Everyone group is added to the list of groups and users for this folder.

4. With **Everyone** selected, check **Allow** under *Full control* to give that permission to the Everyone user group. Click **OK** twice and then close the Properties box.

5. Now that you have the security settings in place for one computer, go to each computer on the network and create the user accounts that will be using this computer. Then test the security and make sure each user can or cannot access the \Financial and \Medical folders as you intend. To access shared folders, you can drill down into the Network group in File Explorer or Windows Explorer. Another method is to type the IP address (for example, **\\192.168.1.112**) or computer name (for example, **\\DELL-LABPC2**) in the address bar of the Explorer window, as shown in Figure 7-30.

(continues)

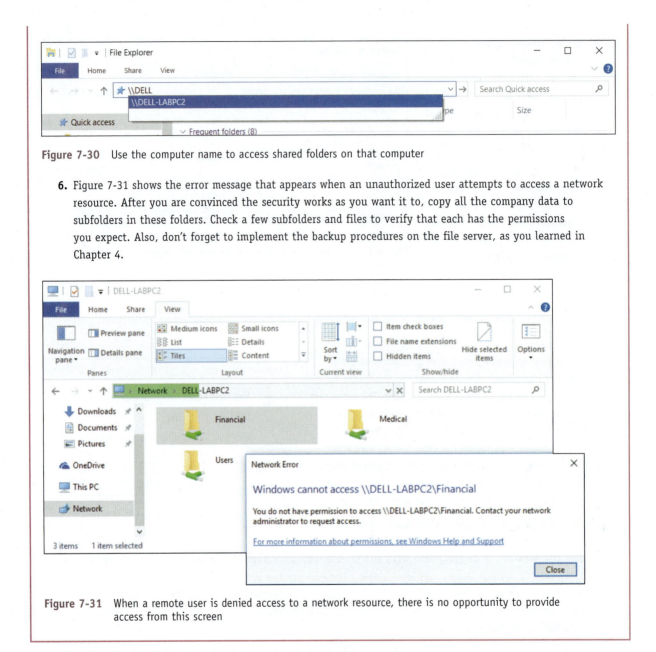

Figure 7-30 Use the computer name to access shared folders on that computer

6. Figure 7-31 shows the error message that appears when an unauthorized user attempts to access a network resource. After you are convinced the security works as you want it to, copy all the company data to subfolders in these folders. Check a few subfolders and files to verify that each has the permissions you expect. Also, don't forget to implement the backup procedures on the file server, as you learned in Chapter 4.

Figure 7-31 When a remote user is denied access to a network resource, there is no opportunity to provide access from this screen

USER AND GROUP INFORMATION WITH THE GPRESULT COMMAND

You can pull a list of all the groups a user belongs to with the **gpresult** command. This information can be helpful when troubleshooting user group issues or Group Policy problems; the command displays user groups a user belongs to and all the currently applied policies set by Group Policy. To retrieve information about a user other than the one signed in, open an elevated command prompt window and enter the command **gpresult /scope user /user** *username* **/r**. Figure 7-32 shows output for the user Adam; you can verify that he belongs to the Medical group. You learn more about the gpresult command later in this chapter.

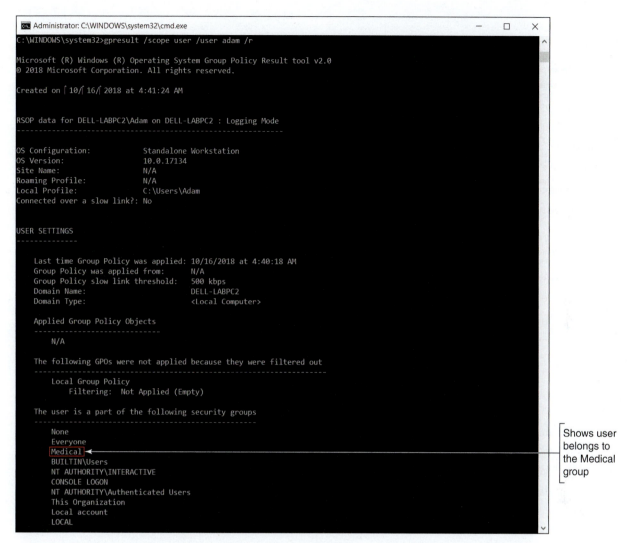

Figure 7-32 The /r parameter requests a summary of the gpresult information instead of more verbose (/v) output

HOW TO USE SHARE PERMISSIONS

Although you can mix NTFS permissions and share permissions on the same system, life is simpler if you use one or the other. For NTFS volumes, NTFS permissions are the way to go because they can be customized better than share permissions. However, you must use share permissions on FAT volumes. To do so, follow these steps:

1. Open the Properties box for the folder (*Personnel* in this case). Notice in Figure 7-33 that the Security tab is missing because the folder is on a FAT volume. Select the **Sharing** tab and click **Advanced Sharing**. The Advanced Sharing box opens (see the right side of Figure 7-33).

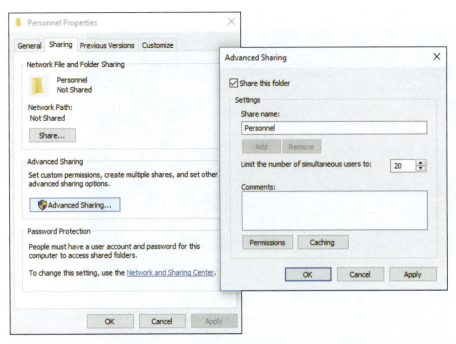

Figure 7-33 Use the Sharing tab of a folder Properties box to set up share permissions on a FAT volume

2. Check **Share this folder**. Then click **Permissions**. The Permissions box opens (see the left side of Figure 7-34). Initially, the folder is shared with Everyone. Also notice that share permissions offer only three permission levels: Full Control, Change, and Read.

3. Click **Add**. The Select Users or Groups box appears (see the right side of Figure 7-34). Enter a user account or user group and click **OK**.

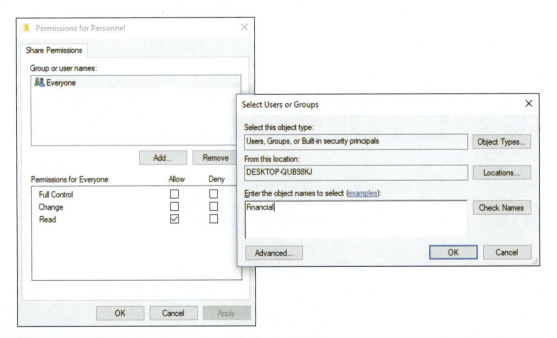

Figure 7-34 Add a user or user group to assign share permissions

4. To delete the Everyone group, select it in the Permissions box and click **Remove**. Click **OK** to close each open box in turn.

SUPPORT AND TROUBLESHOOT SHARED FOLDERS AND FILES

You have just seen how to set up user groups and folder permissions assigned to these groups. If you have problems accessing a shared resource, follow these steps:

1. Windows might be able to solve the problem for you. In Control Panel, click **Troubleshooting**. The Troubleshooting window presents a list of troubleshooters for addressing problems in the categories of Programs, Hardware and Sound, Network and Internet, or System and Security. Click **Access shared files and folders on other computers** and walk through the Shared Folders troubleshooter.

2. Open the Network and Sharing Center. Make sure your network location is set to Private (Home or Work for Windows 7).

3. In the left pane, click **Change advanced sharing settings**. The Advanced sharing settings window opens (refer back to Figure 7-17).

4. Verify that the settings here are the default settings for a Private network profile:

   ◢ Select **Turn on network discovery** and make sure **Turn on automatic setup of network connected devices** is checked.

   ◢ Select **Turn on file and printer sharing**.

> ★ **A+ Exam Tip** The A+ Core 2 exam expects you to know the difference between a shared printer and a network printer. A printer installed locally on a computer can be shared with other computers. This is different from a network printer, which is accessed by each networked computer directly through the network.

> ↻ **OS Differences** If you want a Windows 8/7 computer to access Homegroup resources, select **Allow Windows to manage homegroup connections (recommended)** under HomeGroup connections.
> If you are using NTFS permissions along with less restrictive share permissions to share resources on a network, disable homegroup sharing, which can cause conflicts.

   ◢ If you want to share the Public folder to the network, go to the Public folder sharing section under All Networks and select **Turn on sharing so anyone with network access can read and write files in the Public folders**.

   ◢ If you want the added protection of requiring that all users on the network must have a valid user account and password on this computer, select **Turn on password protected sharing**.

   After you have made your changes, click Save changes at the bottom of the window.

5. In the Network and Sharing Center, click **Change adapter settings**. The Network Connections window appears. Right-click the network connection icon and select **Properties** in the shortcut menu. In the Properties box, verify that **File and Printer Sharing for Microsoft Networks** is checked (see Figure 7-35).

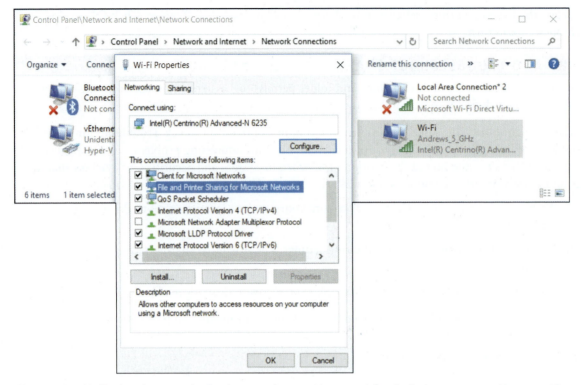

Figure 7-35 Verify that the properties for the network connection are set for sharing resources over the connection

6. The user account name and password on the remote computer must match the user account and password on the host computer. If these accounts and passwords don't match, the user is considered an anonymous user and is denied access to resources shared on the remote computer. To verify that account names and passwords match, open the Computer Management console, where you can view user account names, create new accounts, and set passwords.

Here are a few tips about managing shared folders and files:

▲ *Use advanced permissions settings.* If you need further control of the permissions assigned to a user or group, click **Advanced** on the Security tab of a folder's Properties box. The Advanced Security Settings box appears (see Figure 7-36A). You can see that the Medical user group was given full control. To change these permission details, double-click the user group. In this example, the Medical group is being edited. The Permission Entry box opens (see Figure 7-36B). On Windows 10/8 systems only, click **Show advanced permissions**.

Detailed permissions can now be changed. For example, to prevent users in the Medical group from deleting the Medical folder, its subfolders, and its files, uncheck **Delete subfolders and files** and uncheck **Delete**. Click **OK** to close each box. The resulting change means that users of the Medical group cannot delete or move a file or folder. (They can, however, copy the file or folder.)

★ **A+ Exam Tip** The A+ Core 2 exam expects you to be able to implement permissions so that a user can copy but not move a file or folder and understand how to apply Allow and Deny permissions.

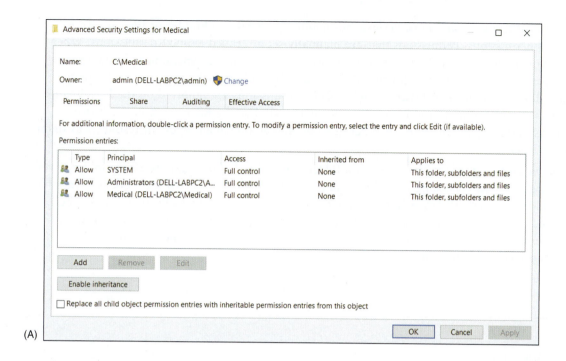

Figure 7-36 Advanced permissions settings

▲ *Manage permissions using the parent folder.* When a subfolder is created, it is assigned the permissions of the parent folder. Recall that these inherited permissions appear dimmed. The best way to change inherited permissions is to change the permissions of the parent object. In other words, to change the permissions of the C:\Financial\QuickBooks folder, change the permission of the C:\Financial folder. Changing permissions of a parent folder affects all its subfolders.

▲ *Check the effective permissions.* Permissions manually set for a subfolder or file can override inherited permissions. Permissions that are manually set are called explicit permissions. When a folder or file has inherited an explicit permission set, it might be confusing to know exactly which permissions are in effect for the file or folder. To find out, see the Advanced Security Settings box. (Look back at Figure 7-36A.) NTFS permissions are reported on the Permissions tab and share permissions are reported on the Share tab. Use the Effective Access tab (for Windows 7, the tab is called Effective Permissions) to get a detailed report of resources available to a particular user.

▲ *Take ownership of a folder.* The owner of a folder always has full permissions for the folder. If you are having a problem changing permissions and you are not the folder owner, try taking ownership of the folder. To do that, click **Advanced** on the Security tab of the folder's Properties box. The Advanced Security Settings box appears. Next to the name of the owner, click **Change**. You can then enter the name of the new owner (see Figure 7-37). Click **Check Names** to confirm the name is entered correctly and click **OK** twice.

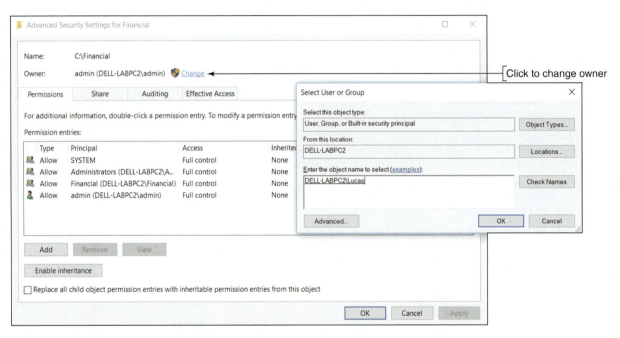

Figure 7-37 Change the owner of a folder

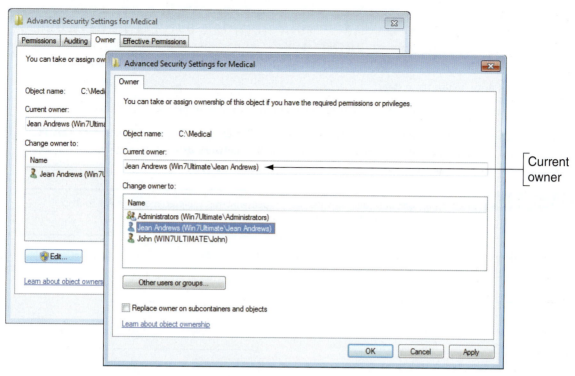

Figure 7-38 Change the owner of a folder in Windows 7

▲ *Use only one workgroup.* It is not necessary that all computers belong to the same workgroup in order to share resources. However, performance improves when they are all in the same workgroup.

▲ *Require passwords for all user accounts.* Don't forget that for best security, each user account needs a password. In a workgroup, the policy to require that all accounts have passwords is set using Local Group Policy. On a domain, Group Policy is used.

▲ *Use a mapped network drive.* For the convenience of remote users, map network drives for shared folders that are heavily used. How to do that is coming up next.

HOW TO MAP A NETWORK DRIVE OR NETWORK PRINTER

**A+
CORE 2
1.8**

A **network share** is one of the most powerful and versatile methods of communicating over a network. A network share makes one computer (the client) appear to have a new hard drive, such as drive E:, that is really hard drive space on another host computer (the server). The client computer creates and saves a shortcut associated with a drive letter that points to the host computer's shared folder or drive. This is called **mapping** the drive. This client/server arrangement is managed by a Windows component, the **Network File System (NFS)**, which makes it possible for files on the network to be accessed as easily as if they are stored on the local computer. NFS is a type of distributed file system (DFS), which is a system that shares files on a network. Even if the host computer uses a different OS, such as macOS or Linux, the network share still functions. In addition to mapping a network drive, you can also map a network printer to a computer.

> ✏ **Notes** A network-attached storage (NAS) device provides hard drive storage for computers on a network. Computers on the network can access this storage using a mapped network drive.

APPLYING | CONCEPTS MAPPING A NETWORK DRIVE AND NETWORK PRINTER

To set up a network drive, follow these steps:

1. On the host computer, share the folder or entire volume to which you want others to have access.

2. On the remote computer that will use the network drive, open File Explorer. In the left pane, click **This PC**. At the top of the window, click the **Computer** tab and click **Map network drive**. (Alternately, you can right-click a folder you see shared on the network and click **Map network drive**.)

> **OS Differences** On a remote computer running Windows 7, open Windows Explorer and press **Alt** to display the menu bar. Click the **Tools** menu and select **Map network drive**.

3. The Map Network Drive dialog box opens, as shown on the left side of Figure 7-39. Select a drive letter from the drop-down list.

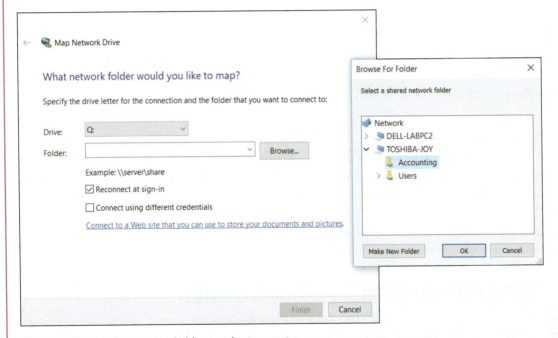

Figure 7-39 Mapping a network drive to a host computer

4. Click the **Browse** button and locate the shared folder or drive on the host computer (see the right side of Figure 7-39). Click **OK** to close the Browse For Folder dialog box, and click **Finish** to map the drive. The folder on the host computer now appears as one more drive in Explorer on your computer.

> ✎ **Notes** When mapping a network drive, you can type the path to the host computer rather than clicking the Browse button to navigate to the host. To enter the path, open the Map Network Drive dialog box and use two backslashes followed by the name of the host computer, followed by a backslash and the drive or folder to access on the host computer. For example, to access the Projects folder on the computer named Win8, enter **\\Win8\ Projects** and then click **Finish**.

If a network drive does not work, go to the Network and Sharing Center and verify that the network connection is good. You can also use the net use command to solve problems with mapped network drives. You learned about the net use command in Chapter 3.

(continues)

✎ Notes A host computer might be in sleep mode or powered down when a remote computer attempts to make a mapped drive connection at startup. To solve this problem, configure the host computer for Wake-on-LAN, as you learned in Chapter 3.

Recall from Chapter 5 that you can connect a network printer to a server and the server can share the printer on the network. The Print Management console can be used to manage all shared printers on the network from a single workstation. You can also map a network printer directly to your computer, eliminating a print server or printer sharing from the process. Here's how:

1. In Windows 10, open the **Settings** app, select the **Devices** group, and then click **Printers & scanners**. A list of installed printers and scanners appears. Click **Add a printer or scanner**. Windows searches for available printers and scanners, but probably will not find the network printer. Click **The printer that I want isn't listed**. In the Add Printer box (see Figure 7-40), select **Add a printer using a TCP/IP address or hostname** and click **Next**.

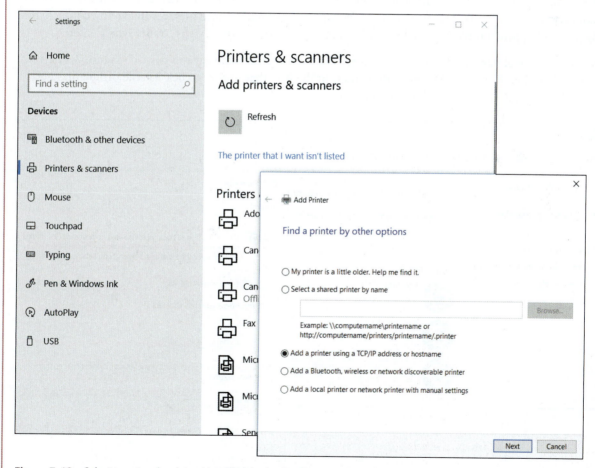

Figure 7-40 Select a network printer identified by its IP address or host name

2. Enter the printer's IP address and click **Next**. Windows searches the network for the printer. If it finds the printer, the installation proceeds and you can select the printer manufacturer and model. Alternately, you can provide printer drivers that you can download to your computer. After the printer is installed, be sure to print a test page.

> **⟨⟩ OS Differences** To install a network printer for Windows 8/7 systems, open **Control Panel** in Classic view and click **Devices and Printers**. Click **Add a printer**. Windows 8/7 will most likely find and list the network printer. Be sure to select a printer that shows its IP address; otherwise, you are connecting to a computer that has shared the printer to the network. If the printer doesn't appear in the list, click **The printer that I want isn't listed**, enter the name of the printer or its IP address, and click **Next**.

If you have problems mapping to a network printer, download the printer drivers from the website of the printer manufacturer and follow the manufacturer's directions to install the printer.

SYNC CENTER AND OFFLINE FILES

A+
CORE 2
1.6

Sync Center, an applet in Control Panel, allows two computers to sync the contents of a shared folder or volume. When you set up a folder to work offline, your computer can work with the folder even when your computer is not connected to the remote computer that holds the share because Sync Center keeps a copy of the files on the local computer. Later, when the computer reconnects to the network, Sync Center can sync up the local and remote files, resolving any conflicts that might have happened if files were edited at both locations. Follow these steps to use Sync Center:

1. Go to **Control Panel** and open **Sync Center**. The Sync Center window appears (see Figure 7-41). To enable offline files, click **Manage offline files**. In the box that appears, click **Enable offline files** and click **OK**. You must restart the computer.

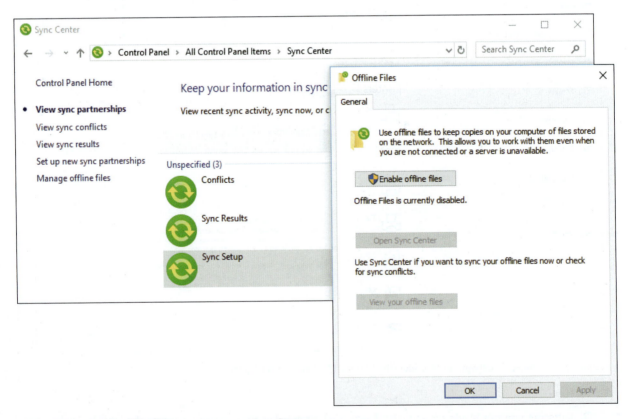

Figure 7-41 Enable offline files so you can use Sync Center

2. Using File Explorer or Windows Explorer, right-click a shared folder on the network and click **Always available offline** (see Figure 7-42). Alternately, you can select the folder, open the **Home** menu, click **Easy access**, and click **Always available offline**.

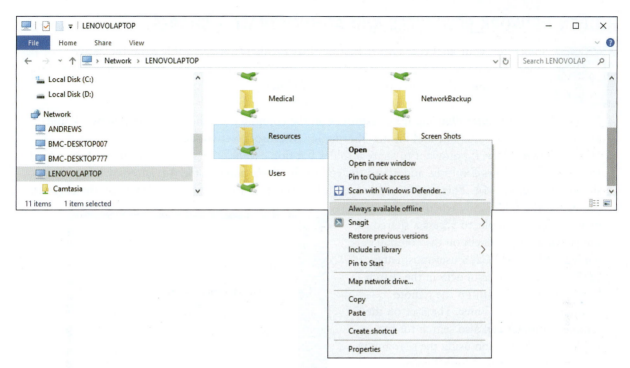

Figure 7-42 Configure a network share as an offline folder

3. The folder will sync on your computer and the remote computer. (On your computer, offline files are stored in the C:\Windows\CSC folder.) When your network connection is slow or disconnected, you can continue to use the folder on your computer.

4. Later, when your computer and the remote computer are connected, you can force a manual sync of the files in the folder. In File Explorer, select the folder, open the **Home** menu, click **Easy access**, and click **Sync**. See Figure 7-43.

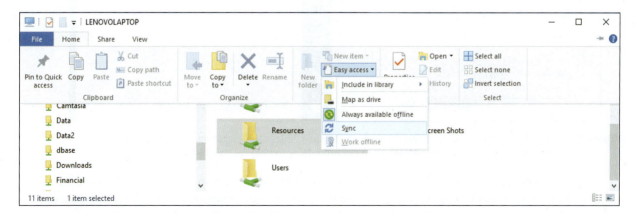

Figure 7-43 Manually force an offline folder to sync with the network share

> ✏️ **Notes** OneDrive is cloud storage associated with your Microsoft account and stored in the Microsoft Cloud. To make OneDrive folders available offline when you are not connected to the Internet, right-click a folder in OneDrive and click **Always available offline**.

HIDDEN NETWORK RESOURCES AND ADMINISTRATIVE SHARES

**A+
CORE 2
1.8, 2.6**

Sometimes your goal is to ensure that a folder or file is not accessible from the network or by other users, or is secretly shared on the network. When you need to protect confidential data from users on the network, you can do the following:

▲ *Disable File and Printer Sharing.* If no resources on the computer are shared, use the Network and Sharing Center to disable File and Printer Sharing for Microsoft Networks.

▲ *Hide a shared folder.* If you want to share a folder but don't want others to see the shared folder in File Explorer or Windows Explorer, add a $ to the end of the share name in the Advanced Sharing box, as shown in Figure 7-44A. This shared and hidden folder is called a hidden share. Others on the network can access the folder only when they know its name. For example, to access a shared folder named Personnel$ on the computer named DELL-LABPC2, a user must enter *DELL-LABPC2***Personnel$** in the search box (see Figure 7-44B) on the remote computer and press **Enter**. The user on the remote computer can also search for the hidden share's location using the search box in File Explorer or Windows Explorer.

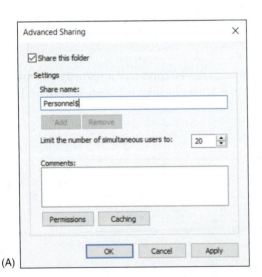

(A)   (B)

Figure 7-44   (A) A $ at the end of the share name hides the share unless the exact name is used to locate it; (B) access a hidden, shared folder on the network by searching for its exact name

So far in this chapter, you have learned about folders and files on a computer that are shared with other users on the network; these shares are called local shares. For computers that belong to a domain, you need to be aware of another way folders are shared, called administrative shares. Administrative shares are folders shared by default that administrator accounts at the domain level can access. You don't need to manually share these folders because Windows automatically does so by default. Two types of administrative shares are:

▲ *The %systemroot% folder.* Enter the path *computername***admin$** to access the *%systemroot%* folder (most likely the C:\Windows folder) on a remote computer in order to work with that computer's system folders and files. For example, to connect to the ws14 workstation shown in Figure 7-45, the entry in the Explorer address bar is **\\ws14\\***admin$*. The authenticate box appears; enter **Administrator** as the user name and the password to the Administrator account. The admin$ administrative share is called the **Remote Admin share**.

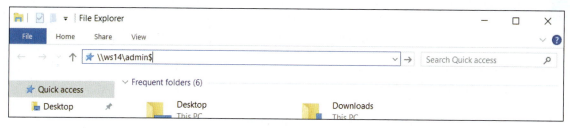

Figure 7-45 Access an administrative share on a domain

◢ *Any volume or drive*. To access the root level of any volume or drive on the network, enter the computer name and drive letter followed by a $—for example, **\\ws14\C$**.

⭐ **A+ Exam Tip** The A+ Core 2 exam expects you to understand the difference between administrative shares and local shares.

✏️ **Notes** To see a list of all shares on a computer, open the Computer Management console and drill down to **System Tools**, **Shared Folders**, **Shares** (see Figure 7-46).

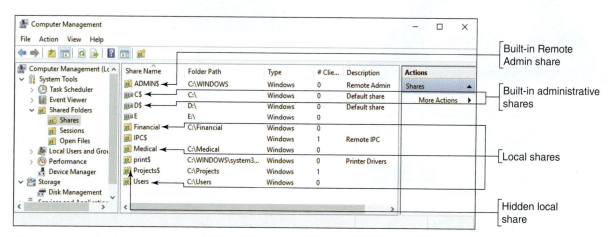

Figure 7-46 Use the Computer Management console to view all shares

---

⚡ **Caution** When supporting a workgroup, you might be tempted to share all the drives on all computers so that you can have easy access remotely. However, using local shares in this way is not a good security practice. Don't share the \Windows folder or an entire drive or volume on the network. These local shares appear in everyone's Explorer window. You don't want your system files and folders exposed like this.

7

USING ACTIVE DIRECTORY DOMAIN SERVICES

Active Directory (AD) is a suite of services and databases provided by Windows Server that is used to manage Windows domains, including access to the domain and what users and computers can do in the domain. AD incorporates five groups of services:

▲ **Active Directory Domain Services (AD DS)** authenticates accounts and authorizes what these accounts can do.
▲ AD Certificate Services (AD CS) secures identities of services, computers, and users.
▲ AD Federation Services (AD FS) secures trust relationships with outside organizations.
▲ AD Rights Management Services (AD RMS) secures data.
▲ AD Lightweight Directory Services (AD LDS) secures applications.

Active Directory organizes resources in a top-down hierarchical structure, as shown in Figure 7-47. Users and resources of a company or school managed by AD are organized into a **forest** (the entire enterprise), which contains a domain (for example, *mycompany.com*). For a few very large enterprises, domains can contain subdomains (for example, *mycompany.com* and *mycompany-dev.com*), but in most situations, a forest contains only a single domain. Domains can contain sites (for example, a New York branch office and a San Francisco branch). Domains are also organized into organizational units and sub-organizational units.

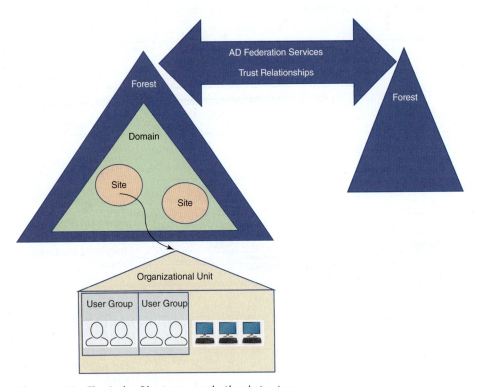

Figure 7-47 The Active Directory organizational structure

An **organizational unit (OU)** is created to make it easier for technicians to assign privileges to users and computers in the OU; privileges are assigned using policies created by Group Policy. These policies are contained in **Group Policy Objects (GPOs)** that are applied to each user and computer in the OU.

An OU also can contain user groups, which contain users. Permissions assigned to folders work much the same way as they do in Windows 10/8/7. NTFS and share permissions are assigned to a folder on a server in the domain by assigning permissions to a user group, and the users in this group inherit these assigned permissions. In summary, managing resources in AD revolves around the tools shown in Figure 7-48.

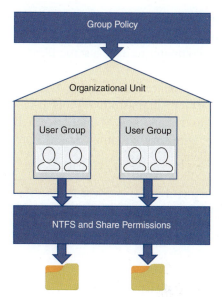

Figure 7-48 Group policies apply to OUs, and NTFS and share permissions apply to folders to control access to the resources in a domain

In this chapter, we focus on the skills an IT technician needs to manage user accounts with Active Directory Domain Services, including creating, resetting, unlocking, enabling, and disabling user accounts and resetting user account passwords. You also learn how Group Policy can be used to assign privileges to an OU and the groups and users in the OU.

CREATING AND MANAGING USER ACCOUNTS IN AD

**A+
CORE 2
2.2, 2.7**

Before we discuss how to manage a user account on a Windows domain, let's pause to see how you can access Domain Services on the domain controller to get to the tools you need. You'll need a local administrator account for a Windows Server computer that is a domain controller. Then you can use one of these methods to access the domain controller:

▲ *Sitting at the computer.* While physically seated at the Windows Server computer, sign in to Windows Server with an administrator account. Then click **Start** and click **Server Manager** in the Start menu. The Server Manager console is shown in Figure 7-49 with the Tools menu open. The Server Manager console contains the tools used to manage Active Directory and is included in Windows Server. It can also be installed in Windows 10.

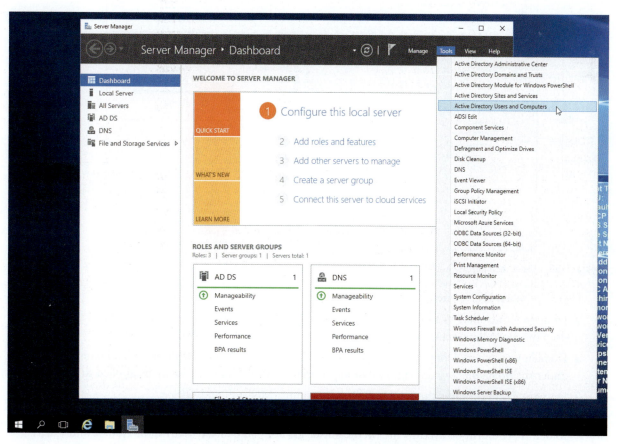

Figure 7-49 The Windows Server desktop with the Server Manager console showing the Tools menu

▲ *Remote access to Windows Server.* You can use Remote Desktop from anywhere on the Internet to connect to a Windows Server computer, sign in, and open Server Manager. How to use Remote Desktop is covered in Chapter 4. Recall that Remote Desktop requires the host computer to have a static IP address; you can expect a domain controller to have one.

▲ *AD Administrative Center and PowerShell.* Administrative Center is an interface for managing Active Directory. In Windows 10/8/7, you can download and install Remote Server Administrative Tools (RSAT) from *microsoft.com*. Administrative Center is one of the tools in this package. Many PowerShell cmdlets apply to Active Directory. To use PowerShell to manage Active Directory, you must first execute the cmdlet **Import-Module ActiveDirectory**, which installs the AD cmdlets.

> ✎ **Notes**   If you don't have access to Active Directory and a Windows domain to practice the skills in this part of the chapter, you can follow the steps in Real Problem 7-2 at the end of this chapter to set up your own Windows domain in Windows Server using the free Google Cloud Platform at *cloud.google.com*.

USE SERVER MANAGER AND CREATE A NEW USER

Let's get started learning to use Server Manager. In Server Manager, follow these steps to view the OU structure and create a new user:

1. Sign in to Windows Server with an administrator account and open **Server Manager.**

2. Click **Tools** (refer back to Figure 7-49) and click **Active Directory Users and Computers.** (The utility is also available in Control Panel under Administrative Tools.) The Active Directory Users and Computers window displays. Figure 7-50 shows the sample domain *homerun.com*, which belongs to our fictitious company, Homerun Sports Medicine, Inc.

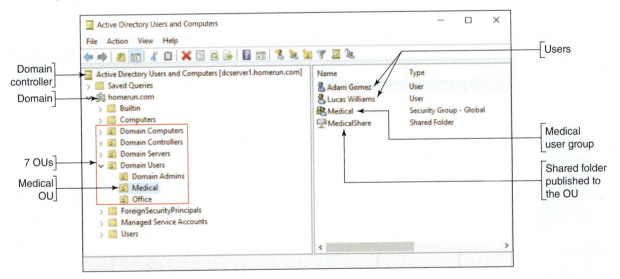

Figure 7-50   Users, computers, and OUs in the domain

There are seven OUs currently in the domain:

▲ Domain Controllers is a default OU created when the domain was created. It contains all the domain controllers managing Active Directory. Our controller is named dcserver1.

▲ Domain Computers, Domain Servers, and Domain Users were created by the system administrator directly under the *homerun.com* domain so that appropriate policies can more easily be applied to these OUs.

▲ Domain Users contains three OUs: Domain Admins, Medical, and Office.

▲ The Medical OU is selected, and you can see it contains two users, one user group, and one shared folder. (If you drill down into the Medical user group, you can see that Adam Gomez and Lucas Williams are members of the group.) It's okay to give a user group the same name as an OU, but it can sometimes get confusing, depending on the situation.

> **Notes** To share a folder in Active Directory, first set the folder's NTFS and share permissions for the user group, as you learned to do earlier in the chapter. Then, to publish the folder in AD, right-click the OU to which you want to include the folder, click **New**, click **Folder**, and point to the folder. The folder is published in AD and can be found by users signed in to the domain on client computers.

3. To add a new user, right-click the OU to which you want to add the user, point to **New**, and click **User** (see Figure 7-51).

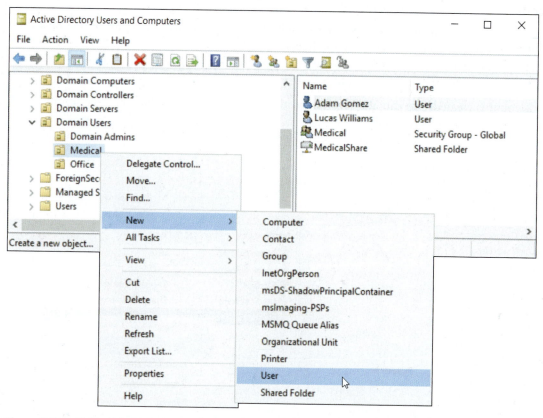

Figure 7-51 Right-click the OU to create a new user

4. Enter the user's first name, last name, and user name (see Figure 7-52A). Click **Next**. On the next screen, decide how to handle the password (see Figure 7-52B).

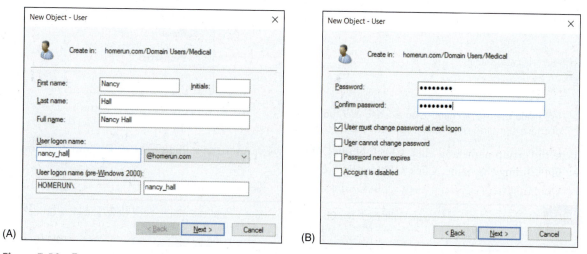

Figure 7-52 To create a new user, (A) enter a name and logon name, and (B) decide how to handle the password

Here are the best practices for these password options:

◢ Always require a password.

◢ By default, the password you enter must meet AD's complexity requirements: It must have at least eight lowercase and uppercase letters, numbers, and symbols, and it cannot contain any three consecutive letters in the user name or display name.

◢ The best practice is to require the user to change the password at next logon.

◢ Don't check *Password never expires*. It's a good idea for the user to occasionally change the password.

◢ Notice you can select *Account is disabled*. This might be appropriate when you are setting up an account well in advance of the account actually being used.

5. Click **Next** and click **Finish**. The account is created. To confirm that the account is created in the correct OU, click the OU; the account should be listed in the right pane.

6. After the account is created, you can add it to an existing user group. Right-click the user account and click **Add to a group** (see Figure 7-53).

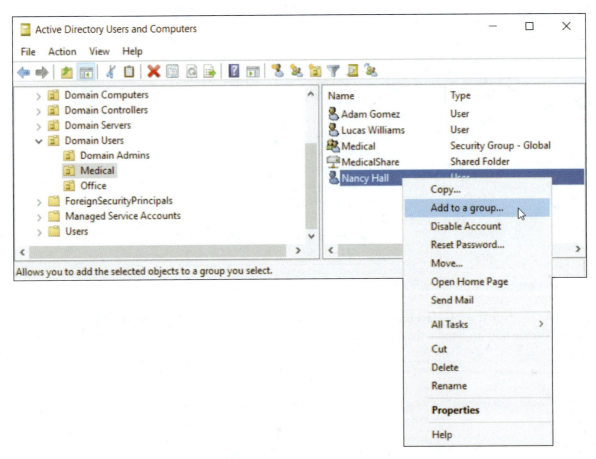

Figure 7-53 Add the user account to an existing user group

7. Type the group name and click **Check Names**. Windows verifies the name of the group and confirms it by underlining the name. Click **OK** (see Figure 7-54).

> ✏️ **Notes** To create a new user group, right-click the OU where you want to add the group, click **New**, and click **Group**. You can then name the group.

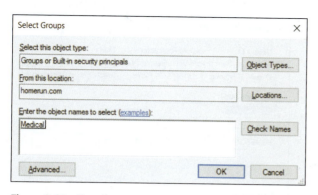

Figure 7-54 Type the user group name and click Check Names

Recall that users belong to user groups and users and user groups belong to OUs. When a policy is applied to an OU, it is applied to all users and user groups in the OU. When folder permissions are assigned to a user group, they are assigned to all users in the user group.

MANAGE ACCOUNTS AND PASSWORDS

An account might get locked after too many failed attempts to sign in. If the user says she knows the password but the account is locked, do the following to unlock the account:

1. An enterprise domain is likely to have hundreds if not thousands of user accounts. Do one of the following to locate the account:

   ◢ If you don't know where to find the account, you can use the search utility. Click the search icon in the Active Directory Users and Computers window (see Figure 7-55).

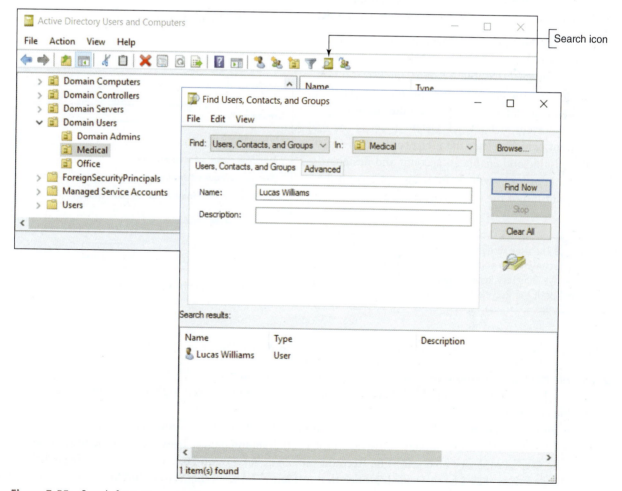

Figure 7-55 Search for a user account

At the top of the Find Users, Contacts, and Groups box, notice you can filter the search using the drop-down menus. Enter the name of the account and click **Find Now**. Double-click the account in the list of matches that appears. The account's Properties box appears.

▲ If you know where to find the account, drill down to it, right-click it, and select **Properties**.

2. In the Properties box for the account, select the **Account** tab (see Figure 7-56), check **Unlock account**, and click **Apply**. The user should then be able to sign in.

Follow these steps to reset a forgotten password and disable, enable, or delete an account:

1. Locate the account and right-click it. In the shortcut menu, click **Reset Password** (refer back to Figure 7-53). In the Reset Password box (see Figure 7-57), enter a new password twice. It's a good idea to leave the *User must change password at next logon* box checked. If the account has been locked, check **Unlock the user's account**. Click **OK**.

2. In the account's shortcut menu in Figure 7-53, note the options to disable and delete an account. When you click **Disable Account**, the user cannot sign in, but the account's user profile still exists and you can later enable the account using the same shortcut menu. Click **Delete** to delete the account, which deletes the user profile. You can also disable and enable an account and designate when an account will expire using options on the Account tab of the user's Properties box.

> **Notes** The user account is considered an object in Active Directory. When you delete an AD object, it goes to the Active Directory Recycle Bin, where it can be recovered until the Recycle Bin is emptied.

Figure 7-56 Unlock a locked account

Figure 7-57 Reset the user password

Here are a few other tips to help you manage accounts in Active Directory:

▲ *Disable the Guest account.* In Active Directory, the Guest account is disabled by default. For best security, leave the account disabled. If you find the Guest account enabled, right-click it and select **Disable Account**.

▲ *Logon time restrictions.* By default, a user can sign in to AD at any time. Suppose, however, that midnight to 8:00AM every Sunday is restricted for routine maintenance. To set logon time restrictions, open the user's Properties box, select the **Account** tab, and click **Logon Hours** (see Figure 7-58). Click an hour and then click **Logon Denied**. Notice that in Figure 7-58, midnight to 8:00AM on Sunday is denied.

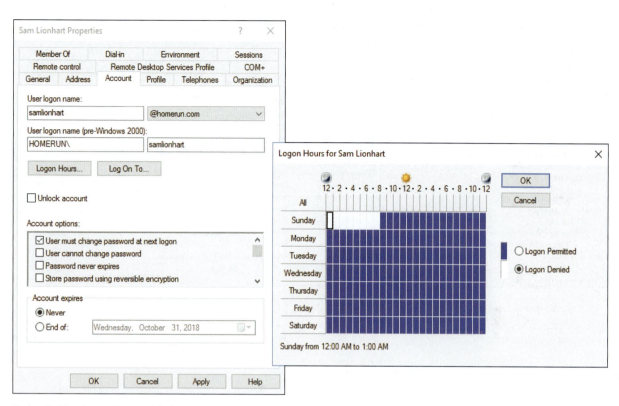

Figure 7-58 Logon time restrictions

- *Timeout and screen lock.* On the Sessions tab of the user's Properties box, you can limit how long a session remains disconnected before it ends (never or up to 2 days), how long an active session stays up (never or up to 2 days), and how long an idle session stays up. After you have made your selections, click **Apply** to save changes.

- *Administrator password.* Before AD Domain Services can be configured to be a domain controller on the network, the Administrator account on its computer must have a strong password (including lowercase and uppercase letters, numbers, and symbols). To manage the properties of the Administrator account, open **Users** in the **Active Directory Users and Computers** window, right-click **Administrator**, and click **Properties**. See Figure 7-59. To change the password of the Administrator account, you can use the following command in an elevated command prompt window in Windows Server:

```
net user Administrator <password>
```

- *Home folder.* The Home folder is the default folder that is presented to the user whenever she is ready to save a file. On a peer-to-peer network, the Home folder in Windows is normally the Documents folder in the user profile at C:\Users*username*\Documents. Active Directory is able to change this Home folder location to a share on the network, which is called folder redirection. Two reasons to apply folder redirection to the Home folder are:

  - On a domain, a user might sign in to different computers. When his Home folder is stored on the network, it's always available and does not need to be copied to each computer he uses.

  - It's easier for backups to be maintained when all Home folders are on a network server rather than on individual workstations. In an organization, individual workstations are generally not backed up regularly, but servers on the network are backed up at least every night.

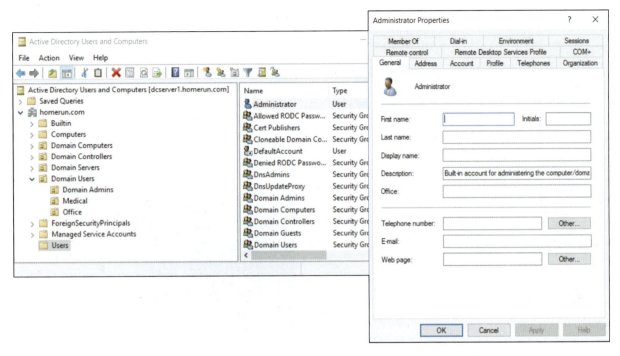

Figure 7-59   Manage the properties of the Administrator account

To see if a user's Home folder is on his local computer or on the network, select the **Profile** tab of the user's Properties box (see Figure 7-60). For this user, the Home folder is in a network share.

> ✎ **Notes**   Many corporations are beginning to use cloud services rather than managing data on their premises. One way to do this is to set up OneDrive in the Microsoft cloud for each user in the Windows domain. Users are then encouraged to use their OneDrive for personal files rather than their Home folders stored on a network share.

▲ *Logon scripts.* A logon script is a list of commands stored in a script file that is performed each time a user signs in to Windows. In Active Directory, logon scripts are normally stored on the domain controllers in a network share named Netlogon. Types of logon scripts supported by Active Directory include Windows batch files (.bat file extension), VBScript files (.vbs file extension), and PowerShell scripts (.ps2 file extension). After the script file is stored in the Netlogon share, select the **Profile** tab in the user's Properties box. See Figure 7-60. Under Logon script, enter the name of the script file along with its file extension.

Figure 7-60   This user's Home folder is contained in a network share

Normally, when you want to change a setting for a single user, you use the user's Properties box, as just explained. If you need to change settings for all the users in an OU, the best tool to use is Group Policy because these policies affect multiple users.

GROUP POLICY OBJECTS

A+
CORE 2
2.2, 2.7

Group Policy can be used on the domain controller to create Group Policy Objects, which contain policies that apply to an OU. These OU policies apply to users, computers, shared folders, and printers in the OU.

Using Group Policy to manage GPOs is beyond the scope of this text. However, let's take a quick look at how you would get started to create and edit a GPO.

CREATE AND EDIT A GPO

You learned earlier that you can use the user account Properties box to set a logon script for a single user. Here is how to create a GPO to set a policy to run a startup script for all users in the domain or an OU:

1. In the Server Manager window, click **Tools** and click **Group Policy Management**. (The tool is also available in Administrative Tools in Control Panel.)

2. In the Group Policy Management window (see Figure 7-61), drill down into the OUs to find the one to which you want to apply the GPO. Right-click the OU and click **Create a GPO in this domain, and Link it here**. You can then name the GPO, as shown in the figure, and click **OK**.

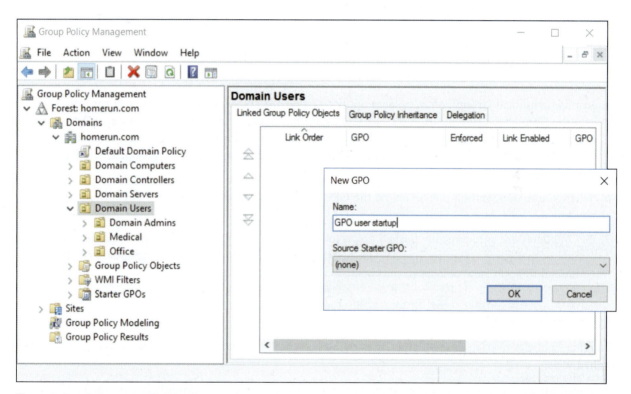

Figure 7-61 Create a new GPO for the Domain Users OU

3. The new GPO appears in the list under the OU and in the Group Policy Objects list. To display details about the GPO, click it and click **OK**. The GPO details display in the right pane with the Settings tab selected.

4. To edit a GPO, right-click it in the left pane and click **Edit**. The Group Policy Management Editor window opens so you can edit the GPO. You can see the GPO name at the top of the left pane of the editor (see Figure 7-62).

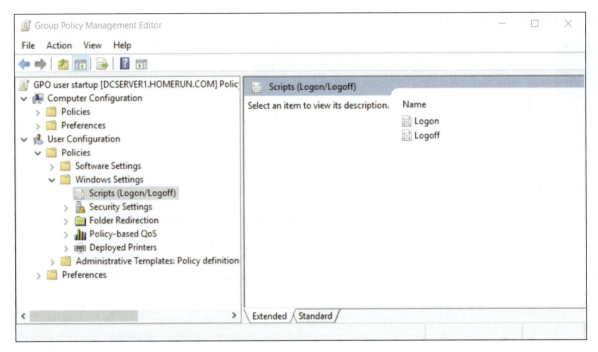

Figure 7-62 Drill down into the policies to find the ones you need

5. Just as with Local Group Policy, policies apply to either the computer or the user. You can drill down into the Computer Configuration or User Configuration policies and find and set the ones you want. For example, to add a login script for all users in the OU to which the GPO belongs, drill down in the **User Configuration, Policies, Windows Settings, Scripts (Logon/Logoff)** group, as shown in Figure 7-62.

6. When you're done setting policies, close the GPO editor to return to the Group Policy Management window.

7. GPO updates are automatically pushed down to clients on the domain in the same site in just a few minutes. On a client computer, just as with Local Group Policy, you can use the **gpupdate /force** command to apply new policies to the client.

WHICH POLICY WINS

Sometimes policies overlap or conflict. Here is the order in which policies are applied; the last policy to be applied wins:

1. *Local.* All local policies are applied first. As you learned earlier, Local Group Policy on the local computer can create policies that apply to the local computer or users.

2. *Site.* Policies for sites are applied next.

3. *Domain.* Policies for a domain are applied next.

4. *OU.* Policies for an OU are applied next and then policies for sub-OUs are applied next.

5. *Enforced.* Policies that are tagged as Enforced policies are applied last and always win over other policies.

✎ **Notes** To tag a GPO as Enforced, right-click the GPO in the Group Policy Management window and click **Enforced**.

Where there is a conflict of policies, the last policy applied wins. It's important to remember the order in which policies are applied, and the acronym LSDOE (usually pronounced "LS-doe") can help: Local, Site, Domain, OU, and Enforced.

Figure 7-63 shows what can happen when there are conflicting policies. In the figure, you see that policies A, B, C, and D are applied; to understand which policy is applied at each level, follow the diagram from left to right. First, notice that local policy A wins because policy A does not exist at the site, domain, OU, or enforced level. For policy B, domain policy B wins over site policy B. For policy C, site policy C wins over local policy C. Although OU policy D would have won over local policy D, the OU policy D was not applied because it was overridden by enforced policy D. Therefore, the resultant policies are local policy A, domain policy B, site policy C, and enforced policy D.

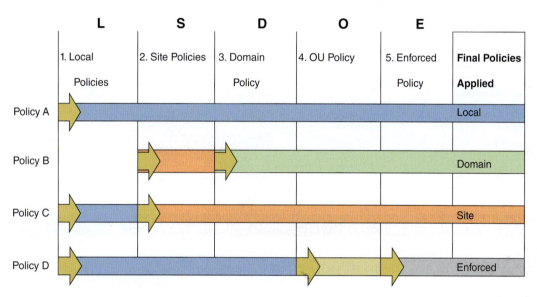

Figure 7-63 Resulting policies applied when conflicting policies exist

To find out the resulting policies for the computer or user, do one of the following:

◢ In a command prompt window, enter the **rsop.msc** command. The **Resultant Set of Policy (RSoP)** window opens, where you can drill down to see the policies set for the computer or user. For example, Figure 7-64 shows the RSoP for the Password Policy.

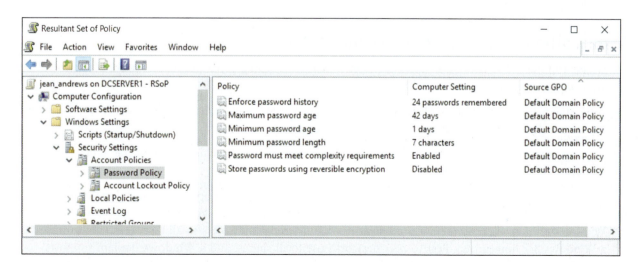

Figure 7-64 The Resultant Set of Policy for the Password Policy

▲ In a command prompt window, enter the **gpresult /v** command, which displays the policies currently applied to the computer and user. The report is very long; you can save it to an HTML file so you can later search it. For example, use this command: **gpresult /h C:\myfile.html**. To view the file, double-click it in File Explorer. The HTML file opens in Internet Explorer. Figure 7-65 shows a snip of the file that includes the Password Policy.

Figure 7-65 The gpresult output displayed as an HTML file in Internet Explorer

>> *CHAPTER SUMMARY*

Securing a Windows Personal Computer

▲ A long password is a strong password.

▲ Use Local Group Policies (gpedit.msc) and Local Security Policies (secpol.msc) to secure a Windows computer.

▲ The Internet Options dialog box is used to manage many Internet Explorer settings. Proxy settings are managed using the Connections tab, and add-ons are managed using the Programs tab.

▲ Encrypting File System (EFS) encrypts files and folders on an NTFS file system. BitLocker Drive Encryption encrypts an entire volume on a hard drive. Both are available on business and professional editions of Windows.

Controlling Access to Folders and Files

▲ Access to folders and files on a network is controlled by assigning privileges to user accounts and assigning permission to folders and files.

▲ Apply the principle of least privilege when assigning privileges to users. You can change the privileges of an account by adding it to or removing it from a user group.

▲ You can create customized user groups to make it easier to manage privileges to multiple user accounts.

▲ Two ways to share files and folders on the network are to use workgroup sharing and domain controllers. With workgroup sharing, you can use share permissions and/or NTFS permissions. For Windows 8/7, when all users on a small network require the same access to all resources, you can use a Windows 8/7 homegroup. Peer-to-peer networks use local shares, and a Windows domain supports administrative shares. You can also hide network resources so that a user must know the name of the resource to access it.

◢ A mapped network drive makes it easier for users to access drives and folders on the network.

Using Active Directory Domain Services

◢ Active Directory (AD) is a suite of services and databases provided by Windows Server that is used to manage Windows domains.

◢ Active Directory organizes resources in a top-down hierarchical structure. A forest contains a domain. Domains can contain sites. Domains are also organized into organizational units (OUs) and sub-organizational units.

◢ Managing resources in AD revolves around the OU, user groups, and NTFS and share permissions. Group Policies apply to OUs, and NTFS and share permissions apply to folders to control access to the resources in a domain.

◢ Active Directory is able to change the Home folder location to a share on the network, which is called folder redirection.

◢ The order in which group policies are applied are: local, site, domain, OU, and enforced. Where there is a conflict in policies, the last policy applied wins.

>> KEY TERMS

For explanations of key terms, see the Glossary for this text.

Active Directory (AD)
Active Directory Domain
   Services (AD DS)
ActiveX control
administrative shares
Administrators group
Anonymous users
Authenticated Users group
BitLocker Drive Encryption
BitLocker To Go
brute force attack
defense in depth
Encrypting File System
   (EFS)

Everyone group
folder redirection
forest
gpresult
gpupdate
Group Policy
Group Policy Object
   (GPO)
Guests group
hidden share
Home folder
inherited permissions
Internet Options
Local Group Policy

Local Security Policy
local shares
Local Users and Groups
mapping
multifactor authentication
   (MFA)
Network File System (NFS)
Network Places Wizard
network share
NTFS permissions
organizational unit (OU)
permission propagation
permissions
Power Users group

principle of least privilege
privileges
Remote Admin share
Resultant Set of Policy
   (RSoP)
Server Manager
share permissions
strong password
Sync Center
TPM (Trusted Platform
   Module)
Users group
Windows Firewall

>> THINKING CRITICALLY

These questions are designed to prepare you for the critical thinking required for the A+ exams and may use content from other chapters and the web.

1. Your organization has set up three levels of classification for data accessed by users on a small network:

   ◢ Low security: Data in the C:\Public folder

   ◢ Medium security: Data in a shared folder that some, but not all, user groups can access

   ◢ High security: Data in a shared and encrypted folder that requires a password to access. The folder is shared only to one user group.

Classify each of the following sets of data:

a. Directions to the company's Fourth of July party

b. Details of an invention made by the company president that has not yet been patented

c. Résumés presented by several people applying for a job with the company

d. Payroll spreadsheets

e. Job openings at the company

2. You work in the Accounting department and have been using a network drive to post Excel workbook files to your file server as you complete them. When you attempt to save a workbook file to the drive, you see the error message: "You do not have access to the folder 'J:\'. See your administrator for access to this folder." What should you do first? Second? Explain the reasoning behind your choices.

a. Ask your network administrator to give you permission to access the folder.

b. Check File Explorer to verify that you can connect to the network.

c. Save the workbook file to your hard drive.

d. Using File Explorer, remap the network drive.

e. Reboot your PC.

3. Which type of server can function as a firewall?

a. Mail server

b. Proxy server

c. Print server

d. FTP server

4. What is the command to launch each of the following tools?

a. Local Group Policy

b. Local Security Policy

c. Computer Management console

d. Local Users and Groups console

e. Resultant Set of Policy (RSoP)

5. What hardware component is needed to set up BitLocker Encryption so that you can authenticate the computer?

6. Where in Group Policy can you locate the policy that requires a smart card to be used to authenticate a user to Windows?

a. Computer Configuration, Windows Settings, Security Settings, Local Policies, Biometrics

b. Computer Configuration, Administrative Templates, System, Logon

c. Computer Configuration, Windows Settings, Security Settings, Local Policies, Security Options

d. User Configuration, Administrative Templates, System, Logon

7. You open a folder Properties box to encrypt the folder, click Advanced, and discover that *Encrypt contents to secure data* is dimmed. What is the most likely problem?

a. Encryption has not been enabled. Use the Computer Management console to enable it.

b. You are not using an edition of Windows that supports encryption.

c. Most likely a virus has attacked the system and is disabling encryption.

d. Encryption applies only to files, not folders.

8. You have shared a folder, C:\DenverCO, with your team. The folder contains information about your company branch in Denver, Colorado. Your company decides to reorganize into zones, so you move the folder as a subfolder in the folder G:\Zone3. When your team members try to access G:\Zone3\DenverCO, they get an error message saying they have been denied access. What happened to the permissions when you moved the folder to its new location?

9. What command do you enter in the Explorer search box to access the Remote Admin share on the computer named Fin?

10. In your organization, each department has a folder on a shared drive. Your boss frequently copies the folder to his local computer to run reports. You have noticed that the folder for your department keeps disappearing from the shared drive. You discover that the folder isn't being deleted and often gets moved into a random, nearby folder. You suspect that coworkers in other departments are being careless with their mouse clicks while accessing their own folders on the shared drive and are dragging and dropping your department folder into other folders without noticing. How can you prevent this folder from being moved, but still allow it to be copied? What steps do you take?

11. If you are having a problem changing the permissions of a folder that was created by another user, what can you do to help solve the problem?

12. When setting up OUs in a new domain, why might it be useful to put all computers in one OU and all users in another?

   a. It will be easier to inventory computers in the domain.

   b. It will help organize users into user groups.

   c. An OU must contain either users or computers, but not both.

   d. Policies generally apply to either computers or users.

13. You have set up a user group named Accounting and have put all employees in the Accounting department in this group, which has been given permission to use the Financial folder on a file server. You are now asked to create a subfolder under Financial named Payroll. Megan, the payroll officer, is the only employee in the Accounting department allowed to access this folder. What is the best way to configure the new share?

   a. Assign Megan read/write permissions to the Payroll folder, and explain to your boss that it is not a best practice to give only one employee access to an important folder.

   b. Assign Megan read/write permissions to the Payroll folder.

   c. Create a new user group named Payroll, put Megan in the group, and assign the group read/write permissions to the Payroll folder.

   d. Ask your boss to allow you to put the folder outside of the Financial folder so you can assign a new user group read/write permissions to this folder that will not conflict with the Accounting user group.

14. Which of the following is true about NTFS permissions and share permissions? Select all that apply.

   a. Share permissions do not work on an NTFS volume.

   b. NTFS permissions work only on an NTFS volume.

   c. If share permissions and NTFS permissions are in conflict, NTFS permissions win.

   d. If you set NTFS permissions but do not set share permissions, NTFS permissions apply.

15. Which security features are available on Windows 10 Home? Select all that apply.

   a. Local Group Policy

   b. NTFS permissions

   c. Active Directory

   d. Internet Options

>> HANDS-ON PROJECTS

Hands-On | Project 7-1   Exploring Password Management Software

Password management software, also called password vault software, such as KeePass (*keepass.info*), LastPass (*lastpass.com*), and Dashlane (*dashlane.com*), can hold your passwords safely so that you don't forget them or have to write them down. Choose two of these programs and a third of your own selection that interests you, then answer the following questions about each one:

1. Which platforms are supported?
2. Which web browsers are supported?
3. From how many competitors can the program import passwords?
4. What types of authentication are supported (e.g., master password, fingerprint, etc.)?
5. Where are the passwords stored? Are they synced across devices? How is the information protected?
6. What are some of the differences between the free edition of each program and the paid versions?
7. What happens to the user's account if the user dies or is incapacitated?

Hands-On | Project 7-2   Using Group Policy to Secure a Workstation

Using Windows 10/8 Professional or Enterprise, or Windows 7 Professional, Ultimate, or Enterprise, set local security policies to require a password for each account, to audit failed logon events, and to create a logon script that displays the message, "The Golden Pineapple Was Here!" when anyone signs in to the system. Test your policies by verifying that a password is required, your script executes when you sign in, and a failed sign-in event using an invalid password is logged and can be viewed in Event Viewer. Answer the following questions:

1. Which policies did you set and what setting was applied to each policy?
2. What software did you use to create your script? What is the exact path and file name (including the file extension) to your script?
3. Which log in Event Viewer shows the logon failure event?
4. List three more policies you find in Group Policy that can make a workstation more secure but are not discussed in this chapter.

Hands-On | Project 7-3   Using Google Chrome

Internet Explorer is not the only browser available, and many users prefer others such as Mozilla Firefox (*mozilla.org*) or Google Chrome (*google.com*). Go to the Google website and download and install Google Chrome. Use it to browse the web. How does it compare with Internet Explorer? What do you like better about it? What do you not like as well? When might you recommend that someone use Chrome rather than Internet Explorer? What security features does Google Chrome offer? What are the steps to import your favorites list from Internet Explorer into Chrome?

Hands-On | Project 7-4   Researching a Laptop with a TPM Chip

Many laptops sold today have a TPM chip, and some have encryption-enabled hard drives that don't require encryption software such as BitLocker. Research the web for a laptop that offers a TPM chip and answer these questions:

1. What is the brand and model of laptop that has the TPM chip? Print the webpage that lists the laptop specifications for the chip.
2. Is the chip optional? If so, what is the cost of including the chip?
3. Does the laptop have an encryption-enabled hard drive?
4. Does the laptop come bundled with encryption software? If so, what is the name of the software?
5. Does the laptop offer a drive lock password?
6. What is the cost of the laptop, including the TPM chip?

Hands-On | Project 7-5   Sharing and Securing a Folder

Using two computers networked together, do the following to practice sharing and securing folders using Windows:

1. Create a user account named **User1** on Computer 1. In the My Documents folder for that account, create a folder named **Folder1**. Create a text file named **File1** in the folder. Edit the file and add the text **Golden Egg**.
2. On Computer 2, create a user account named **User2**. Try to read the Golden Egg text in File1 on Computer 1. What is the result?
3. Configure the computers so that User1 signed in to Computer 2 can open File1 and edit the text "Golden Egg," but User2 cannot view or access the contents of Folder1. List the steps you took to share and secure the folder and to test this scenario to make sure it works.
4. Now make the folder private so that it cannot be seen from Computer 2 in File Explorer or Windows Explorer but can be accessed if User1 knows the folder name. Describe how you did that.

>> REAL PROBLEMS, REAL SOLUTIONS

REAL PROBLEM 7-1 Recovering a Windows Password

You can use freeware to discover a forgotten Windows password, and hackers can use the software to steal a password. The stronger the password, the more difficult it is to discover. Follow these steps to learn more:

1. Create three user accounts on a system and assign the accounts an easy password (use only lowercase letters), a moderately easy password (use lowercase letters and numbers, but no symbols), and a strong password (see the rules given earlier in the chapter for strong passwords).
2. Go to **ophcrack.sourceforge.net** by Geeknet, Inc., and download the free ISO file that contains ophcrack Vista/7 LiveCD. (The software works in Windows 10/8/7.) Use the ISO file to burn the ISO image to a CD-R. Label the CD.

3. Boot from the CD. As it boots, it automatically searches for and lists the user accounts and passwords on the system. Answer the following questions:

   a. What is the name of the operating system the ophcrack software uses on the CD?

   b. Which user account passwords did ophcrack discover?

   c. If ophcrack did not discover a password, perhaps another freeware utility can. List three other password-cracking products that receive positive online reviews.

Keep the ophcrack LiveCD in your computer repair toolkit in case a client in the field asks you to help recover a forgotten Windows password.

REAL PROBLEM 7-2 Setting Up a Windows Domain in Google Cloud

You can use Google Cloud Platform to create a VM with Windows Server installed and then use the VM to create a Windows domain. Do the following:

1. Go to **cloud.google.com**. If you have not already set up a free trial, click **Try free**. You will need to sign in using a Google account. If you don't have an account, you can create one with any valid email address. When you first set up an account, you must enter payment information, which Google promises not to use during your free trial period. Create an individual account type, enter your information, and click **START MY FREE TRIAL**. Google automatically sets up your first project, aptly named My First Project.

2. In the left pane of the Google Cloud Platform page, click **Compute Engine**. If you don't already have a VM created with Windows Server, do the following:

   a. Click **CREATE INSTANCE** in the VM instances menu to create a VM.

   b. Use the default settings, except:
      - Change the name of the VM to **dcserver**.
      - Change the Boot disk to **Windows Server 2016 Datacenter**.

   c. Click **Create** and then wait for Google to create the instance.

3. In the VM instances list, click the **dcserver** instance, which takes you to the VM instance details page. Click **Set Windows password** and assign a user name to your VM instance. Note the user name and click **SET**. Google Cloud assigns a password, which displays on the screen. Copy the password, save it somewhere safe, then click **CLOSE**.

4. A domain controller needs a static IP address on the domain. To set the Primary internal IP address to a static address, follow these steps:

   a. On the VM instance details page, in the *Network interfaces* group under *Network*, click **default**. The VPC network details page appears.

   b. Click **Static internal IP addresses**. Then click **Reserve static address**.

   c. Under Name, enter **dcserver**. Click **RESERVE**.

5. To return to the list of VM instances, click the back arrow to the left of *VPC network details*. The VM instance details page appears. In the left pane, under *Compute Engine*, click **VM instances**. Your list of VMs appears.

6. For the dcserver VM instance, write down the Internal IP and External IP addresses.

7. You are now ready to use Remote Desktop with screen and file sharing to access your VM. Follow these steps:

   a. Enter the **mstsc** command in the Windows 10/7 search box or the Windows 8 Run box. In the Remote Desktop Connection box, enter the External IP address of your VM, which is its public IP address available on the Internet. Click **Connect**.

b. In the *Enter your credentials* box, your Windows user name appears. If your VM's user name is not the same as your Windows user name, click **More choices** and then click **Use a different account.** You can then enter the VM's user name and password. Click **OK** to connect.

8. The Windows Server desktop appears in the Remote Desktop window with the Server Manager window open. In the Networks pane on the right, click **Yes** to turn on network discovery.

9. You are now ready to set up your Windows domain. Follow these steps:

    a. In the Server Manager window, under *Configure this local server*, click **Add roles and features**. The Add Roles and Features Wizard opens. Click **Next**.

    b. On the *Select destination server* page, accept the default values and click **Next**.

    c. Under *Select server roles*, check **Active Directory Domain Services** and click **Add Features**.

    d. Under *Select server roles*, check **DNS Server** and click **Add Features**. A warning message appears. Click **Continue**. (The message was caused by Google Cloud handling tasks that the domain controller would normally handle.)

    e. Click **Next** four times to step through pages in the wizard, accepting default values. The *Confirm installation selections* page appears. Click **Install**. Wait while the installation happens. You can click the flag in the upper-right corner of the Server Manager window to view the progress. See Figure 7-66.

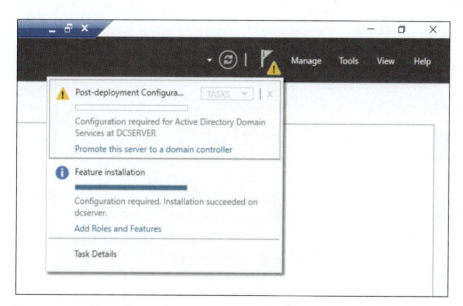

Figure 7-66   The notification flag reports installation progress

10. Although AD Domain Services is now installed, you cannot promote the server to a domain controller until you first set a password for the all-powerful Administrator account. (Recall that this account is different from your user name account, which has Administrative privileges.) To set the password, do the following:

    a. To open an elevated command prompt window, right-click **Start** and click **Command Prompt (Admin)**. Click **Yes**.

    b. Use a password that satisfies AD complexity requirements. For example, in the command prompt window, enter this command:

```
net user Administrator Passw0rd /passwordreq:yes
```

    c. Close the command prompt window.

11. Click the notification flag in the Server Manager window and then click **Promote this server to a domain controller**. The *Deployment Configuration* window appears. Select **Add a new forest**. Enter your root domain name. You can use **homerun.com** or another domain name. Click **Next**.

12. Wait while the Domain Controller Options window loads—it can take some time. Then enter a password twice and click **Next**. Ignore any warning messages and click **Next** several times to step through the wizard. Finally, click **Install**.

13. After the system reboots, you will need to connect again through Remote Desktop. At this point, you have a working domain controller and can practice the skills you learned in this chapter to manage Active Directory. Here is how to get started:

    a. If Server Manager is not already open, click **Start** and click **Server Manager**.

    b. The Server Manager window appears. To manage OUs, user groups, and users, click **Tools** and then click **Active Directory Users and Computers**. Refer back to Figure 7-50.

    c. By default, your domain has one OU: Domain Controllers. To create another OU directly under the domain, right-click the domain name, point to **New**, and click **Organizational Unit** (see Figure 7-67). You can then name the OU.

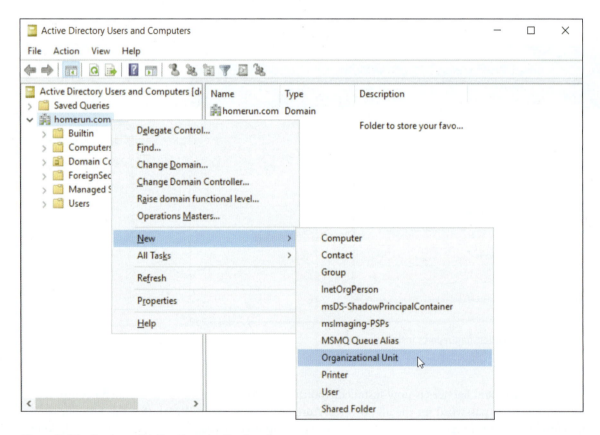

Figure 7-67 Create an OU directly under the domain

14. Have fun poking around and learning to use Active Directory! Every great IT technician needs to have a working knowledge of AD, and you have started that in this chapter. When you're finished working with AD, avoid accumulating any charges against your free quota by shutting down the server VM in the Remote Desktop Connection box.

> **✎ Notes** You will use the Google Cloud Platform service for another project in Chapter 10. Do not disable your Google Cloud Platform account until after you have completed that project.

REAL PROBLEM 7-3 Using Chrome Remote Desktop

Chrome Remote Desktop by Google lets users sign in to remote computers through a Chrome browser. This blend of cloud computing technology and remote desktop access can be handy when you need to support computers that use operating systems other than Windows. Complete the following steps to install and use Chrome Remote Desktop:

1. On Computer 1, download and install Google Chrome, and sign in. Then add the Chrome Remote Desktop add-in.

2. Configure Chrome Remote Desktop to allow access to your computer over the Internet. Run the Chrome Remote Desktop Host Installer after it is downloaded. Be sure to record your PIN in a safe place.

3. On Computer 2, download and install Google Chrome, and sign in. Then add the Chrome Remote Desktop add-in.

4. Configure Chrome Remote Desktop to allow access to your computer over the Internet. Run the Chrome Remote Desktop Host Installer after it is downloaded. Be sure to record your PIN in a safe place.

5. Use Chrome Remote Desktop to create a remote connection to Computer 2. Can you use the utility to view the desktop of Computer 2? Can you control Computer 2 from Computer 1? Can you control Computer 2 directly from its own desktop? What options are available from the Remote Desktop menu on Computer 1?

6. What other operating systems will Chrome Remote Desktop work with?

7. List three reasons why a user might find Chrome Remote Desktop useful. Be sure to consider the advantages of using it with Google Cloud Platform.

7

Security Strategies and Documentation

In Chapter 7, you learned the concepts and principles of securing Windows resources on workstations and networks by classifying users and data, and you learned how to protect resources by applying appropriate permissions so that only authorized users can access the data. In this chapter, you learn about additional tools and techniques to secure the resources on a personal computer and network. You also learn how to recognize that a personal computer is infected with malware and how to clean an infected system and keep it clean. Finally, you learn what your employer might expect of you when dealing with issues of change management, regulated data, software licensing, incident response, and data destruction and disposal.

Chapter 7 and this chapter give you the basics of securing a personal computer or network. Later in your career as a support technician, you can build on the skills learned in these chapters to implement even more security, such as controlling how Windows stores its passwords.

PROTECTING NETWORK RESOURCES

> **A+**
> **CORE 2**
> **2.1, 2.2,**
> **2.3, 2.4,**
> **2.10, 4.1**

In this part of the chapter, you learn both physical and logical methods of protecting computer resources, securely authenticate users on a large network, and educate users to understand their roles to protect and secure network resources by carefully following established best practices.

PHYSICAL SECURITY AND ACCESS CONTROLS

> **A+**
> **CORE 2**
> **2.1, 2.2**

Physically protecting access to a computer's resources is often seen by security experts as the most important—and most overlooked—form of security. Here are some best practices for physical security:

▲ *If the data is really private, keep it behind a locked door or under lock and key.* You can use all kinds of security methods to encrypt, password protect, and hide data, but if it really is that important, one obvious thing you can do is to keep the computer behind a locked door. Sounds simple, but it works. You can also store the data on a removable storage device such as an external hard drive and, when you're not using the data, put the drive in a fireproof safe. (And, of course, keep two copies that are stored in different locations.) Don't forget that printouts of sensitive documents should be kept under lock and key, as well as any passwords you might have written down. Door locks and safes come in several types, including keyed locks, combination locks, and biometric locks. Biometric locks require special input called biometric data to identify a person by her fingerprint, handprint, face, retina, iris, voice, or handwritten signature. Figure 8-1 shows a biometric input device: a fingerprint scanner. Many mobile devices, such as iPads and some laptops, have fingerprint scanners built in.

▲ *Use server locks or cable locks.* Some computer cases allow you to add a lock so that you can physically prevent others from opening the case (see Figure 8-2A). These locks, called server locks, might be used on computers that hold corporate data. You can also use a cable lock, or Kensington lock, to secure a laptop or other computer to a table so someone can't walk away with it (see Figure 8-2B). Most laptops have a security slot on the case to connect the cable lock; this slot is called a Kensington Security Slot or K-Slot. Many thefts occur in private offices or hotel rooms, so even if you're not sitting in a public area with your laptop, consider keeping it locked to a nearby table or post. Be sure to choose a cable lock that resists tampering with pliers or cable cutters.

Source: iStockphoto.com/viiwee

Figure 8-1   This access control device accepts typed code, fingerprint, or smart card input

Figure 8-2 To physically secure a computer, (A) use a computer case lock and key for a desktop to prevent intrusion, or (B) use a cable lock system for a laptop to prevent theft

▲ *Secure ports with port locks.* Any exposed port on a device, such as an RJ-45 port or a USB port, can be used to access the device and compromise its security. USB ports in particular are security risks due to the ease of uploading malware or downloading sensitive data using a small flash drive carried in someone's pocket. If you can't restrict access to the device itself, you might install a port lock to restrict physical access to the exposed ports. The USB lock by PadJack, Inc., consists of three pieces, as shown in Figure 8-3. The smaller two pieces are inserted into the USB port, sealed into place with the wire loop, and cannot be removed without damaging the port or destroying the lock. Other port lock designs can lock a cable into the port so it can't be easily removed.

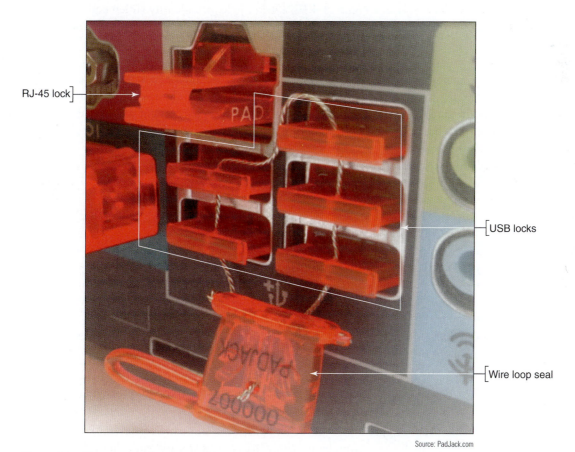

Source: PadJack.com

Figure 8-3 These port locks are reusable, but the wire loop seal can be used only once

▲ *Use privacy screens.* To keep other people from viewing a monitor screen, you can install a privacy screen, also called a privacy filter, that fits over the screen to prevent it from being read from a wide angle. This is especially useful in tight quarters, such as on an airplane, bus, or subway, or other exposed locations such as a receptionist's desk.

▲ *Install a theft-prevention plate.* As an added precaution, physically mark a computer case or laptop so it can be identified if it is later stolen. You can embed a theft-prevention plate into the case and engrave or tattoo your ID information into it. The numbers or barcode identify you as the owner and can clearly establish to police that the laptop has been stolen. Two sources of theft-prevention plates and cable locks are Flexguard Security System (*flexguard.com*) and Computer Security Products, Inc. (*computersecurity.com*). See Figure 8-4. To further help you identify stolen equipment, record serial numbers and model numbers in a safe place separate from the equipment. This information can also be included in an inventory management system.

Source: computersecurity.com/stop/

Figure 8-4   The security plate and the tattoo beneath it serve as an asset management tag and theft-prevention plate

▲ *Use a mantrap and security guard.* The ultimate in physical security is a mantrap, which consists of two doors on either end of a small entryway where the first door must close and/or lock before the second door can open. A separate form of identification might be required for each door, such as a badge for the first door and a fingerprint scan for the second door. A security guard might also maintain an entry control roster, which is a list of people allowed into the restricted area and a log of any approved visitors.

LOGICAL SECURITY AND ACCESS CONTROLS

A+ CORE 2 2.2, 2.10

Software, such as Windows Firewall, can make up a significant portion of your defense resources. Other types of software-based security measures include:

▲ *Antivirus/anti-malware.* Antivirus software or anti-malware software monitors a device for activity that is recognized to be harmful to data or other resources. The software then attempts to block the activity, identify the source of the problem, and remove any malicious files that have infected the computer. You'll learn more about viruses, malware, and antivirus/anti-malware software later in this chapter.

▲ *Email filtering.* Email providers often offer email filtering to filter out suspicious messages based on databases of known scams, spammers, and malware. Corporations might route incoming and outgoing email through a proxy server for filtering with the following goals in mind:

  ▲ Incoming email is inspected for scams or spam that might trick an employee into introducing malware into the corporate network.

  ▲ Outgoing email from employees might be filtered for inappropriate content. This lawful interception is intended to verify that an employee is complying with privacy laws (for example, laws that protect confidential medical records) and is not accidentally or intentionally leaking corporate data and secrets. Email filtering software used in this way is an example of data loss prevention (DLP) software, which helps protect against leaking corporate data.

▲ *Trusted software sources.* It's important to download software only from trusted publishers and providers. Even software from a trusted publisher can be filled with destructive extras if the software is obtained from an untrusted provider. Also know that a website might be trying to trick you into thinking you're downloading applications, software updates, or drivers from a trusted source when you're actually downloading malware. Be careful which sites you use for software downloads.

▲ *Access control lists.* An access control list (ACL) includes which user, device, or program has access to a particular resource, such as a printer, folder, or file, on a corporate network or computer. As you learned in Chapter 7, larger corporate networks manage access control through Active Directory on a Windows domain, and, on smaller peer-to-peer networks, each computer controls access to its own resources. For both types of networks, Group Policy can control user rights, and NTFS permissions and share permissions control access to files and folders.

▲ *Port security and MAC address filtering.* A switch is a network device that provides multiple Ethernet ports used to connect other devices to the local network. A switch is either unmanaged (a simple pass-through device) or managed. A managed switch has embedded web-based firmware to configure it by way of a browser on a local computer connected to the switch. See Figure 8-5. By default, any device can connect to any port; however, you can enable port security to control which devices can use any port or a specific port on the switch. Most managed switches can provide MAC address filtering, which allows you to specify how many MAC addresses a port can accept or to provide a whitelist of MAC addresses the switch will accept. Because it's so easy to spoof, or counterfeit, a legitimate MAC address, MAC address filtering is not considered a recommended best practice as your only layer of defense against attack.

8

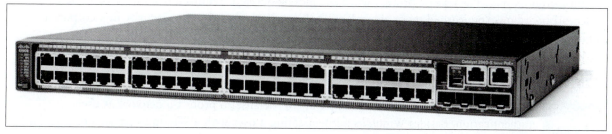

Figure 8-5 This managed switch by Cisco allows for MAC address filtering on its Ethernet ports

> ✎ **Notes** MAC address filtering can also be implemented on a SOHO router, and can easily be hacked as part of your defenses against attack. Therefore, MAC address filtering should only serve as one layer of defense among many. These various layers of defense are collectively called **defense in depth**.

▲ *VPN.* Recall from Chapter 3 that a VPN (virtual private network) protects data by encrypting it over a remote connection to a private network. When you set up a VPN, the VPN software (for example, OpenVPN at *openvpn.net* and *privatetunnel.com*) creates a virtual tunnel between the client computer and a VPN server behind the private network's firewall. Network packets are encrypted at one end of the tunnel and decrypted as they exit the tunnel. VPN connections are used for telecommuters to securely connect to their corporate networks (see Figure 8-6) or for individuals to securely surf the web. In the latter use, all transmissions are sent between the client computers and web servers through a VPN service center that manages the VPN connection. Managed switches, including the one shown earlier in Figure 8-5, sometimes have VPN services embedded in their firmware so they can provide VPN connections for remote users of the private network to which they belong.

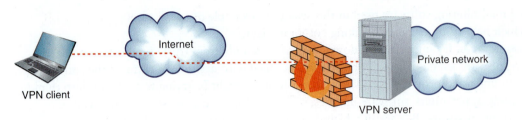

Figure 8-6   A VPN connection secures all traffic between the VPN client and VPN server on the private network

▲ *Mobile device management.* Corporate or personal mobile devices present a particular set of security challenges because they hold sensitive company data while traveling outside of the company network's physical perimeter. **Mobile device management (MDM)** software provides tools for tracking mobile devices—even when they're turned off—and managing the data on those devices. **MDM policies** typically include:

  ▲ Security policy enforcement, such as applying patches or enforcing password requirements

  ▲ Data encryption requirements, to protect data on the mobile device even if it falls into the wrong hands

  ▲ Remote wipe capabilities, to erase all data on the device

To do all this, MDM installs a small app called an **agent** on a managed mobile device, which communicates through various Wi-Fi or cellular connections back to the MDM server in the company data center. The initial installing of the agent and the agent checking the device for security compliance is called **on-boarding**. The reverse process when the mobile device is removed from the MDM fleet is called **off-boarding**. You learned more about BYOD (Bring Your Own Device) security in a corporate environment in Chapter 9.

USER AUTHENTICATION

In Chapter 7, you learned that the first line of defense to protect a network is user authentication. Besides Windows authenticating a user with a Windows password, you can increase authentication security using these methods:

▲ Enforce a **password policy**, which is a set of rules that defines the minimum length of a password, complexity requirements, and how frequently a password must be reset, for example.

▲ Enforce **multifactor authentication**, which requires at least one more factor or action to authenticate beyond the single-factor password. **Two-factor authentication (2FA)** is most often used, and the two factors normally involve what the user:

  ▲ Knows (such as a Windows or Facebook password)

  ▲ Possesses, which is called a token (such as a smart card or key fob)

  ▲ Does (such as typing a certain way)

  ▲ Is, which is called biometric data (such as a fingerprint)

One warning to keep in mind is that factors such as a smart card or biometric data should be used in addition to, and not as a replacement for, a Windows password on a personal computer or domain.

Next, let's look at hardware and software security tokens and authentication services that can work together to provide multifactor authentication.

HARDWARE SECURITY TOKENS

Two types of hardware security tokens are a smart card and a key fob:

▲ *Smart card.* A smart card used as a security token has an embedded microprocessor, which is usually installed on the card under a small gold plate. For example, most current credit cards have a gold plate and microprocessor and are smart cards, as opposed to earlier credit cards that used only a magnetic strip with no internal processor. The microprocessor contains information that is read by a smart card reader or badge reader when the device is inserted into the reader or transmitted wirelessly. See Figure 8-7. At the same time, most smart cards can receive information from the card reader to confirm that the reader is authentic. This is called mutual authentication, which occurs when authentication goes in both directions at the same time and both entities confirm the identity of the other. Because a smart card contains a microprocessor and data, it's considered both a hardware token and a software token.

Source: istock.com/humonia

Figure 8-7 A smart card is read by a wireless smart card reader

> ✎ **Notes** A common use of mutual authentication is sending a confirmation code by text to your smartphone using a phone number the server already has on file. This gives you reassurance that the server to which you're authenticating is what it says it is.

▲ *Key fob.* A key fob is a hardware token that fits conveniently on a keychain, such as the one shown in Figure 8-8. The number on the key fob changes every 60 seconds. When a user signs in to the network, he must enter the number on the key fob, which is synchronized with the network

Source: iStockphoto.com/David Clark

Figure 8-8 A security token such as this key fob is used to authenticate a user gaining access to a secured network

authentication service. Entering the number proves that the user has the key fob in hand. Because the device doesn't actually make physical contact with the system, it is called a contactless token or disconnected token.

SOFTWARE SECURITY TOKENS

Software tokens can be security tokens stored as an app or digital certificate. Here's how each works:

◢ *Software token apps.* These apps, sometimes called authenticator apps, are installed on your smartphone or other computing device and can perform the same service as a key fob, providing a counter or number generator that serves as one factor in multifactor authentication. The app is synchronized with the same calculations on the server so that the app and the server expect the same number at the same time. Software token providers for 2FA include Google Authenticator (*google.com*), Twilio Authy (*authy.com*), and LastPass Authenticator (*lastpass.com/auth*). Many online accounts, such as banking accounts, Facebook, Google, and Amazon, can be set to use 2FA and software tokens. For example, the Authy app by Twilio can be used to require 2FA to sign in to Facebook (see Figure 8-9).

In general, to set up 2FA with an online account, you would:

1. Sign up for and configure the 2FA service with a 2FA provider such as Twilio. You'll need to download and install its authenticator app to your phone or computer.

2. Enable 2FA with a Facebook, Google, banking, or other account you want to secure.

3. Configure the account to use the 2FA service.

4. Now, each time you sign in to the account, you must provide your password and the number generated by the authenticator app.

Source: https://authy.com/features/setup/ by Twilio, Inc.

Figure 8-9 When you sign in to your account, Facebook requests the token generated by the 2FA app

◢ *Digital certificates.* Think of a digital certificate as a digital signature that proves a person or entity, such as a web server, is who they say they are; it's a small file that holds information about the identity of the person or entity. In addition, a public encryption key is used to prove the certificate is legitimate, and is similar to a notary verifying that a signature is legitimate. The digital certificate and public encryption key are assigned by a Certificate Authority (CA) that has confirmed your identity in a separate process. VeriSign (*verisign.com*) and GlobalSign (*globalsign.com*) are two well-known CAs. You purchase a digital certificate from a CA and then install it on your desktop, laptop, or other computing device; in some cases, you can install it on a smart card or flash drive that you can use on any computer.

Digital certificates are used to authenticate individuals (such as to digitally sign and encrypt email or to connect to a corporate network via a VPN), software (Windows can require that device drivers be digitally signed), or server applications (many web servers are digitally signed). For example, to see a web server's digital certificate, navigate to the webpage in your browser and then click the lock icon, as shown in Figure 8-10. Click **View certificate**.

Source: google.com

Figure 8-10 Google's digital certificate is provided by GlobalSign, Inc.

AUTHENTICATION SERVICES

For large networks, you learned in Chapter 7 that Active Directory on a Windows domain is used to authenticate users to the domain and authorize what users can do with domain resources. For added security, everything users attempt to do or do once they are authenticated to the network can be tracked or logged for future auditing. These three security measures are generally known in networking as **AAA (authenticating, authorizing, and accounting)** or **triple A**. Two popular solutions to provide AAA services for large networks are RADIUS and TACACS+:

▲ **RADIUS (Remote Access Dial-In User Service)** was originally developed to authenticate end users accessing resources on a network through dial-up connections and has evolved to other types of connections to a network, including wired, wireless, and VPN.

▲ **TACACS+ (Terminal Access Controller Access Control System Plus)** was developed by Cisco to improve on RADIUS for AAA services specifically designed for network administrators and technicians to remotely connect to a network to configure and manage Cisco network devices, such as routers, switches, and firewalls.

RADIUS and TACACS+ each can work with Active Directory or some other type of directory server to authenticate and authorize users, and sometimes both services are used on the same network. RADIUS and TACACS+ can each support wireless, wired, and VPN connections. Notice in Figure 8-11 the similarities of how each service works; both use a client, server, and user directory:

▲ **Client**. A RADIUS or TACACS+ client can be a wireless access point (WAP) or switch that receives the initial connection from the user's laptop or other device. The client is responsible for querying the RADIUS or TACACS+ server to authenticate the user before allowing the user on the network.

▲ **Server**. A RADIUS or TACACS+ server authenticates the user by querying a user directory. Cisco calls its TACACS+ server the Identify Service Engine server (ISE server).

▲ **User directory**. The RADIUS to ISE server queries a user directory or database, where user credentials are stored. Active Directory is the most popular user directory for today's large networks.

> ✎ **Notes** Often, a basic WAP isn't smart enough to act as the RADIUS or TACACS+ client. In an enterprise environment, many WAPs are connected to a wireless controller device in the data closet, which in turn does the work of managing client requests to the RADIUS or ISE server.

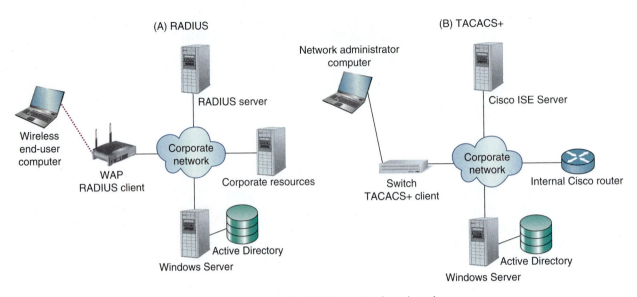

Figure 8-11   AAA services provided by (A) RADIUS and (B) TACACS+ protocols and services

In summary, Table 8-1 compares RADIUS and TACACS+.

Characteristic	RADIUS	TACACS+
Primary use	Intended for end-user network access	Intended for Cisco network device administrative access
Encryption	Encrypts user passwords only	Encrypts every message
Underlying protocol	The RADIUS protocol uses UDP, which does not guarantee transmissions over the corporate network	The TACACS+ protocol uses TCP to guarantee transmissions over the corporate network
Network types	Works on wireless, wired, and VPN network connections	Works on wireless, wired, and VPN network connections

Table 8-1   RADIUS and TACACS+ characteristics

USER EDUCATION

A+
CORE 2
2.4, 2.5, 4.1

Generally speaking, people are the weakest link in setting up security in a computer environment. That's because people can often be tricked into giving out private information. Even with all the news and hype about identity theft and criminal websites, it's amazing how well they still work. Many users naively download a funny screen saver, open an email attachment, or enter credit card information on a website without regard to security. In the IT arena, social engineering is the practice of tricking people into giving out private information or allowing unsafe programs into the network or computer.

A good support technician is aware of the criminal practices used, and is able to teach users how to recognize and avoid this mischief. A document that can help educate users is an acceptable use policy (AUP), which explains what users can and cannot do on the corporate network or with company data, and explains the penalties for violations. The AUP might also describe how these measures help protect the network's security. Important security measures that users need to follow to protect passwords and the computer system are:

◢ Never give out your passwords to anyone, not even a supervisor or tech support person who calls and asks for it.
◢ Don't store your passwords on a computer unless you use company-approved password vault software (for example, KeePass or LastPass). Some organizations even forbid employees from writing down their passwords.

- Don't use the same password on more than one computer, network, application, or website.
- Be aware of shoulder surfing, which is when other people secretly peek at your monitor screen as you work. A privacy filter can help.
- Lock down your workstation each time you step away from your desk.
- Users need to be on the alert for tailgating, which is when an unauthorized person follows an employee through a secured entrance to a room or building. Another form of tailgating is when a user steps away from a computer that's not properly locked and another person continues to use the Windows session.

Hackers might obtain information or trick people into giving information that can be used to hack a computer or network by:

- *Dumpster diving.* Dumpster diving is looking for useful information in someone's trash to help create a convincing impersonation of an individual or company to aid in a malicious attack. Even something that might appear harmless, such as an organizational chart, can help a thief create a convincing email hoax message. For best security, shred all papers and printouts before recycling and educate users about the importance of shredding.
- *Phishing, spear phishing, impersonation, and spoofing.* Phishing (pronounced "fishing") is a type of identity theft in which the sender of an email hoax scams you into responding with personal data about yourself. Even more plausible is spear phishing, where the email appears to come from companies you already do business with. The scam artist baits you by asking you to verify personal data on your bank account, ISP account, credit card account, or something of that nature. Often a convincing impersonation of an individual or company tricks you into responding to the email or clicking a link in the email message, which takes you to an official-looking site complete with corporate or bank logos, where you are asked to enter your user ID and password to enter the site. This tactic is called spoofing, which means the scam artist makes both the email and website look like the real thing. For example, when the user who received the email shown in Figure 8-12 scanned the attached file using antivirus software, the software reported that the file contained malware.

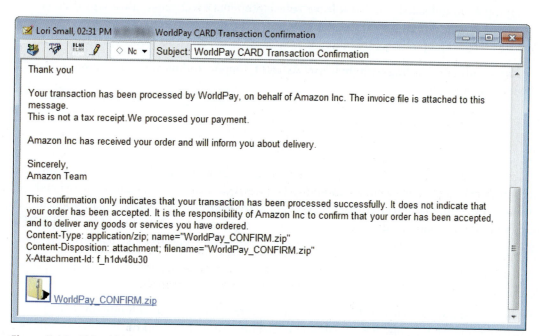

Figure 8-12 This phishing technique using an email message with an attached file is an example of social engineering

An email message might contain a link that leads to a malicious script. If you think an email is legitimate, be on the safe side and don't click the link. To keep a script from running, type the website's home page into your browser address bar and navigate to the relevant page on the website.

Good sites to help you debunk a virus hoax or email hoax are:

▲ *snopes.com* by Barbara and David Mikkelson
▲ *securelist.com* by Kaspersky Lab
▲ *virusbtn.com* by Virus Bulletin, Ltd

Don't forward an email hoax. If you get a hoax from a person you know, do us all a favor and send that person some of the preceding links!

> 🖊 **Notes** A helpful tool to combat phishing attacks is a **Secure DNS** service (sometimes written as SecureDNS), which monitors requests for websites and redirects your browser when it attempts to visit a known malicious site. Popular providers include the free SecureDNS service by Comodo (*comodo.com*) and the enterprise-grade SecureDNS service by RiskAnalytics (*riskanalytics.com*). To use Secure DNS on a personal computer, go to the Network Connections window, open the active connection's TCP/IPv4 properties box, and change the DNS server settings so your computer uses Secure DNS server addresses listed on the provider's website.

> ⭐ **A+ Exam Tip** The A+ Core 2 exam expects you to recognize and distinguish among examples of social engineering situations that might compromise security, such as tailgating, phishing, spear phishing, impersonation, shoulder surfing, and dumpster diving.

A study by Dell showed that 65 percent of business travelers have not secured the corporate data on their hard drives, and 42 percent don't back up that data. Here are some commonsense rules to help protect a laptop when traveling:

▲ When traveling, always know where your laptop is. If you're standing at an airport counter, tuck your laptop case securely between your ankles. At security checkpoints, pay attention to your belongings; tell yourself to stay focused. When flying, never check your laptop as baggage, and don't store it in airplane overhead bins; keep it at your feet.
▲ Never leave a laptop in an unlocked car. If you leave your laptop in a hotel room, use a laptop cable lock to secure it to a table.
▲ When at work, lock your laptop in a secure place or use a laptop cable lock to secure it to your desk.

Next, we turn our attention to dealing with malware. As an IT support technician, you will most certainly be called on to handle it.

DEALING WITH MALICIOUS SOFTWARE ON PERSONAL COMPUTERS

Malicious software, also called **malware**, is any unwanted program that is intended for harm and is transmitted to your computer without your knowledge. **Grayware** is any annoying and unwanted program that might or might not intend harm—for example, adware that produces all those unwanted pop-up ads. In this part of the chapter, you learn about the different types of malware and grayware, what to do to clean up an infected system, and how to protect a system from infection.

WHAT ARE WE UP AGAINST?

You need to know your enemy! In 2017, it was reported that more than 8 million new malware programs were discovered. Different categories of malware and scamming techniques are listed next:

▲ *Viruses.* A **virus** is a program that replicates by attaching itself to other programs. The infected program must be executed for a virus to run. The program might be an application, a macro in a document, a Windows system file, or a boot loader program.

◢ *Spyware.* Spyware spies on you to collect personal information that it transmits over the Internet to web-hosting sites. An example of spyware is a keylogger that tracks all your keystrokes and can be used to steal your identity, credit card numbers, Social Security number, bank information, passwords, email addresses, and so forth.

◢ *Worms.* A worm is a program that copies itself throughout a network or the Internet without a host program. A worm creates problems by overloading the network as it replicates and can even hijack or install a server program such as a web server.

◢ *Trojans.* A Trojan does not need a host program to work; rather, it substitutes itself for a legitimate program. In most cases, a user launches it thinking she is launching a legitimate program. A Trojan is often embedded in the files of legitimate software that is downloaded from an untrustworthy website, or a user is tricked into opening an email attachment (refer back to Figure 8-12).

◢ *Rootkits.* A rootkit loads itself before the OS boot is complete. It can hide in boot managers, boot loader programs, or kernel mode device drivers. UEFI secure boot is especially designed to catch rootkits that launch during the boot. Because a rootkit is already loaded when most anti-malware software loads, it is sometimes overlooked by the software. A rootkit can hide folders that contain software it has installed, cause Task Manager to display a different name for its process, hide registry keys, and can operate in user mode or kernel mode. This last trick helps it remain undetected (see Figure 8-13).

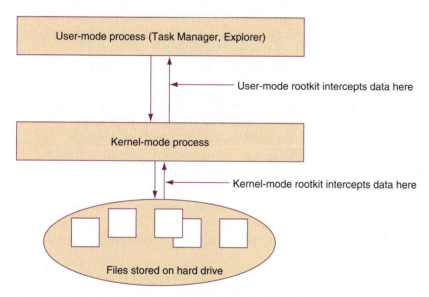

Figure 8-13　A rootkit can run in user mode or kernel mode

A rootkit running in user mode intercepts the API calls between the time the API retrieves the data and when it is displayed in a window. A rootkit running in kernel mode actually interferes with the Windows kernel and substitutes its own information in place of the raw data read by the Windows kernel. Because most anti-malware software to one degree or another relies on Windows tools and components to work, the rootkit is not detected or cannot be deleted if the Windows tools themselves are infected.

> ⚡ **Caution**　If anti-malware software reports that a rootkit is present but cannot delete it, the best solution is to immediately disconnect the computer from the network (if you have not already done so), back up your important data, format your hard drive, and reinstall Windows.

▲ *Ransomware.* Ransomware holds your computer system hostage until you pay money. For example, the CryptoLocker Trojan program that did damage in 2014 was embedded in email attachments and was known to work on Windows, Android, and even some iOS systems. When the user clicked the attachment, the program encrypted the computer's personal files. If the user didn't pay within a 24-hour period, all the files were lost. Many users who did not have backups of their data chose to pay the ransom. A computer infected with ransomware can infect all computers on the network and even cloud servers to which the computer connects.

> **⚡ Caution** The best defense against ransomware is to keep backups of data file versions in a location that is not accessible from File Explorer. A ransomware attack can infect any storage device connected or mapped to your computer, and a single layer of data file backups might be replaced with the encrypted files before you're able to clean your computer and restore the backed-up data. Use a backup method that retains multiple file versions (indefinitely, if possible) and that is not directly accessible from your computer. Many cloud backup services meet these requirements, such as Carbonite (*carbonite.com*), Backblaze (*backblaze.com*), or IDrive (*idrive.com*). After a ransomware attack, you can wipe the computer, reinstall software from original sources, and restore unaffected file versions from your online backups.

▲ *Zero-day attack.* A zero-day attack can happen in two ways: a hacker discovers a security hole in software that is unknown to the developer of the software, or a hacker takes advantage of a recently reported gap in software security before users apply patches released by the developer. The race is on for the vendor to provide a patch to the software and for users to apply those patches before hackers have even one day to use the hole to infect systems and steal user data. Microsoft normally publishes security patches on the second and fourth Tuesday of each month (known as patch Tuesday), but sometimes releases patches off schedule so that hackers have less time to attack customers.

▲ *Man-in-the-middle attack.* In a man-in-the-middle attack, the attacker intercepts communication between two parties and reads and/or alters the content of messages. The attacker can impersonate a legitimate website, network, FTP site, or person in a chat session. For example, a user might connect to an "evil twin" Wi-Fi hotspot, thinking it's a legitimate hotspot, and attempt to start a chat session with a business associate. The attacker pretends to be the business associate and continues the chat with the intention of obtaining private information. The best protection against man-in-the-middle attacks is to use digital certificates to identify a person or service before transmitting sensitive information.

▲ *Denial of service.* A denial-of-service (DoS) attack overwhelms a computer or network with requests or traffic until new connections can no longer be accepted. A distributed denial-of-service (DDoS) attack happens when multiple computers are involved in the attack. DDoS attacks are sometimes performed by botnets, which are described next.

▲ *Zombies and botnets.* A zombie is a computer that has been hacked, and the hacker is using the computer to run repetitive software in the background without the knowledge of its user. For example, the zombie might be email spamming or performing DDoS attacks. A hacker might build an entire network of zombies, which is called a botnet (a network of robots). The CryptoLocker Trojan program was distributed by a botnet and ultimately isolated when the botnet was taken down.

▲ *Dictionary attack.* A dictionary attack can be used to crack a password by trying words in a dictionary. Password cracker software might combine a brute force attack (systematically trying every possible combination of letters, numbers, and symbols) with a dictionary attack to guess the password. A dictionary attack is usually more efficient than using brute force.

▲ *Rainbow tables.* A rainbow table contains a long list of plaintext passwords, just as users would enter, and the password hash list (after it is encrypted). Organizations store only hashed passwords and not plaintext passwords. When a hacker obtains a stolen list of hashed passwords, she can compare this list with those in her rainbow tables to find a match. When two hashed passwords match, she can use the plaintext password in the rainbow table to sign in to the system, impersonating the user.

Rainbow tables make cracking passwords faster than dictionary cracking or brute force cracking. The best defenses against rainbow table attacks are for an organization to use the very best hashing techniques to encrypt their passwords and to add extra characters to the password hash (called salting the passwords).

◢ *Noncompliant systems and violations of security best practices.* A system administrator needs techniques in place to routinely scan BYOD and corporate-owned smartphones, tablets, laptops, desktops, and servers for noncompliant systems that violate security best practices, such as out-of-date anti-malware software or cases where it's not installed. One software product designed to scan devices for noncompliance is System Center Configuration Manager by Microsoft, which works with Microsoft Intune. Intune focuses specifically on mobile devices that connect to a corporate network.

> ★ **A+ Exam Tip** The A+ Core 2 exam might give you a scenario that requires you to detect, remove, or prevent viruses, Trojans, worms, spyware, keyloggers, ransomware, rootkits, and botnet software. You also need to identify and describe zero-day attacks, man-in-the-middle attacks, zombies, dictionary attacks, brute force attacks, phishing, spear phishing, impersonation, shoulder surfing, tailgating, dumpster diving, DoS/DDoS attacks, rainbow tables, spoofing, and noncompliant systems.

STEP-BY-STEP ATTACK PLAN

> **A+ CORE 2 3.3**

This section is a step-by-step attack plan to clean up an infected system. We use anti-malware software, also called antivirus software, to remove all types of general malware, including viruses, spyware, worms, and rootkits. Then we'll use some Windows tools to check out the system, making sure all remnants of malware have been removed and the system is in tip-top order.

> ⚡ **Caution** If a system is highly infected and will later hold sensitive data, a fresh start might be in order. In fact, Microsoft recommends reinstalling Windows as the safest way to deal with highly infected systems. If you have recent backups of data, format the hard drive, reinstall or reimage Windows, and restore data from backups.
>
> If you don't have recent backups for a Windows 10 system, you can try a repair upgrade, a fresh start, or a reset without losing user data. For Windows 8, a refresh can be an excellent option if you have a recent custom refresh image. For Windows 7, consider applying a system image. In Chapter 6, you learned about all of these options to reinstall Windows.

STEP 1: IDENTIFYING AND RESEARCHING MALWARE SYMPTOMS

> **A+ CORE 2 3.3**

An IT support technician needs to know how to recognize that a system is infected. Here are some warnings that suggest malicious software is at work:

◢ *Pop-up ads and browser redirection.* Basically, a user is losing control of his system. For example, Figure 8-14 shows the desktop immediately after a user signed in. Pop-up ads are randomly appearing and the browser home page has changed. A browser might also have an uninvited toolbar. Security alerts—real or spoofed—regularly interrupt the user's activity.

Figure 8-14 A hijacked home page, security alerts, and pop-up ads indicate an infected system

▲ *Rogue antivirus software.* When the user tries to run Windows Defender (anti-malware software embedded in Windows 8), it refuses to run. She opens the Action Center to find that Defender has been disabled because other antivirus software she did not install is running. See Figure 8-15.

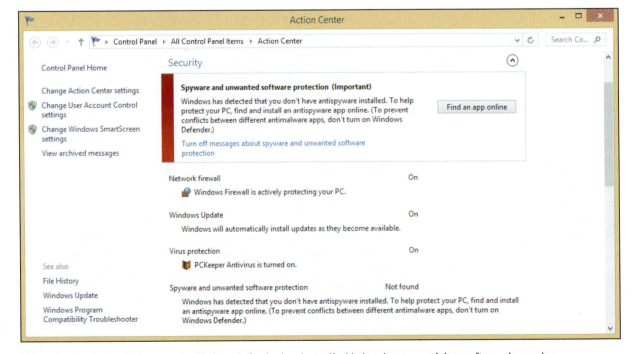

Figure 8-15 Action Center reports Windows Defender has been disabled and rogue antivirus software is running

Windows allows only one anti-malware product to run at a time. You can use Task Manager to stop the rogue antivirus software and then start Windows Defender.

▲ *Slow performance or lockups.* Generally, the system works much slower than before. Programs take longer than normal to load. Strange or bizarre error messages appear. Programs that once worked now give errors. Task Manager shows unfamiliar processes running. The computer's operating system might lock up.

▲ *Internet connectivity issues, application crashes, and OS update failures.* These types of problems seem to plague the system with no reasonable explanation that is specific to the network, application, or Windows update.

▲ *System and application log errors.* The Administrative Events logs in Event Viewer report system and application errors, system crashes, application crashes, and failed OS updates.

▲ *Problems with files.* File names now have weird characters or their file sizes seem excessively large. Executable files have changed size or file extensions change without reason. Files mysteriously disappear or appear. Windows system files are renamed. Files constantly become corrupted. Files you could once access now give access-denied messages, and file permissions change.

▲ *Email problems.* You receive email messages from other users saying you have sent someone spam or an infected message, or you receive automated replies indicating you sent email you didn't know about. This type of attack indicates that your email address or email client software on your computer has been hijacked. Extra spam you're not accustomed to seeing shows up.

▲ *Problems updating your anti-malware software.* Even though you can browse to other websites, you cannot access anti-malware software sites such as *symantec.com* or *mcafee.com*, and you cannot update your anti-malware software.

▲ *Invalid digital certificates.* An OS is responsible for validating certificates used to secure communication. For Windows, Microsoft maintains a database of trusted root certificates issued by Certificate Authorities (CAs). A root certificate is the original certificate issued by the CA. When a Windows system opens a secure email or visits a secure website and encounters a new digital certificate, it requests Microsoft's trusted root certificate, which is downloaded to the computer. The download happens seamlessly without the user's knowledge unless there's a problem. If Windows cannot obtain the root certificate to validate the email or website, it displays an error (see Figure 8-16). Don't trust websites or email whose certificates have expired or been revoked.

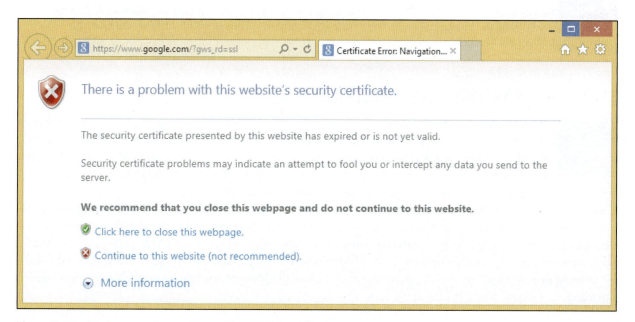

Figure 8-16 Windows reports a problem with a digital certificate

> ✎ **Notes** If a computer gives invalid certificate errors, check that the Windows date is correct. A wrong Windows date before the certificate was issued can cause the problem.

You can use the Certificate Manager (*certmgr.msc*) to view and delete root certificates, as shown in Figure 8-17. For example, the Superfish virus injects a rogue root certificate into the Microsoft store of trusted certificates on the local computer so that it can perform a man-in-the-middle attack to display adware on secure websites a user visits. If you see a Superfish certificate listed among trusted root certificates, be sure to delete it.

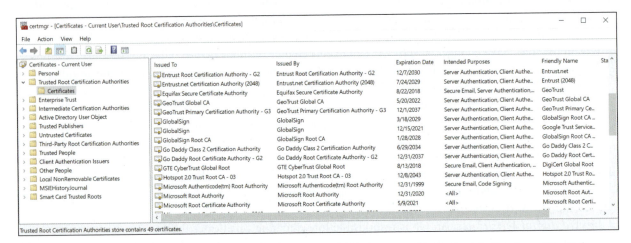

Figure 8-17 Windows Certificate Manager can be used to view and delete root certificates kept in the store of trusted certificates

> ⭐ **A+ Exam Tip** The A+ Core 2 exam might give you a scenario that requires you to recognize the common symptoms of malware listed previously and know how to quarantine and remediate an infected system.

> ✎ **Notes** Malicious software is designed to do varying degrees of damage to data and software, although it does not damage computer hardware. However, when partition table information is destroyed on a hard drive, the drive can appear to be physically damaged.

STEP 2: QUARANTINING AN INFECTED SYSTEM

> **A+**
> **CORE 2**
> **3.3**

If an infected computer is connected to a wired or wireless network, immediately disconnect the network cable or turn off the wireless adapter. You don't want to spread a virus or worm to other computers on your network. A quarantined computer is not allowed to use the regular network that other computers use. If you need to use the Internet to download anti-malware software or its updates, take some precautions first. Consider your options. Can you disconnect other computers from the network while the infected computer is connected? Can you isolate the computer from your local network and connect it directly to the ISP or a special quarantined network? If neither option is possible, try downloading the anti-malware software updates while the computer is booted into Safe Mode with Networking or after a clean boot. (Safe Mode doesn't always allow downloads.) Malware might still be running in Safe Mode or after a clean boot, but it's less likely to do so than when the system is started normally.

Always keep in mind that data on the hard drive might not be backed up. Before you begin cleaning up the system, back up data to another media.

STEP 3: DISABLING SYSTEM RESTORE

In Windows, some malware hides its program files in restore points stored in the System Volume Information folder that's maintained by System Protection. If System Protection is on, anti-malware software can't clean this protected folder. To get rid of the malware, turn off System Protection so that anti-malware software can clean the System Volume Information folder (see Figure 8-18). Realize that when you turn off System Protection, all your restore points are lost, so first consider whether you might need those restore points to troubleshoot the malware infection before you disable System Protection.

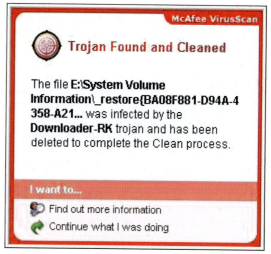

Source: McAfee VirusScan

Figure 8-18   Malware found in a restore point

8

> ⚡ **Caution**   Some highly infected systems will not allow anti-malware software to run. In this situation, you can boot the computer into Safe Mode and use System Restore to apply a restore point that was taken before the infection. Applying a restore point cannot be counted on to completely remove an infection, but it might remove startup entries the malware is using, making it possible to run the anti-malware software from the normal Windows desktop or to run the software in Safe Mode. Consider that you might need to apply a restore point before you disable System Protection, which deletes all your restore points.

To turn off System Protection, go to **Control Panel**, open the **System** window, and click **System protection**. Later, when you are sure the system is clean, turn System Protection back on and create a new restore point that you can use in the future if problems arise.

STEP 4: REMEDIATING THE INFECTED SYSTEM

Table 8-2 lists popular anti-malware software for personal computers and the programs' websites, which also provide information about malware. Before selecting a product, be sure to read some reviews about it and check out some reliable websites that rate anti-malware software.

Anti-Malware Software	Website
Maximum, Internet, or Antivirus+ Security by Trend Micro (for home use)	*trendmicro.com*
Avast Ultimate, Premium, or Free Antivirus (for home use)	*avast.com*
Bitdefender Antivirus Plus, Internet Security, or Total Security	*bitdefender.com*
ClamWin Free Antivirus (open source and free)	*clamwin.com*
F-Secure Total, Safe, Anti-Virus, or Online Scanner (Online Scanner is free)	*f-secure.com*
Kaspersky Internet Security, Anti-Virus, or Security Cloud (Security Cloud is free)	*kaspersky.com*
Malwarebytes for Windows (free version available)	*malwarebytes.com*
McAfee Total Protection	*mcafee.com*
Symantec Endpoint Protection	*symantec.com*
Panda Dome Essential, Advanced, or Complete	*pandasecurity.com*
SUPERAntiSpyware (free edition available)	*superantispyware.com*
Windows Defender (included in Windows 10/8), Microsoft Security Essentials (free for Windows 7)	*microsoft.com*

Table 8-2   Anti-malware software and websites

> ⚡ **Caution**   Beware of websites that appear as sponsored links at the top of search results for anti-malware software. These sites might appear to be the home site for the software, but they are really trying to lure you into downloading adware or spyware.

> ✎ **Notes**   **Windows Defender** anti-malware software is embedded in Windows 10/8 and can be accessed through the Windows 10 Settings app or Windows 8 Control Panel. Windows 7 includes Windows Defender, but the Windows 7 version finds only spyware, not viruses and other malware. For Windows 7, you can download and install Microsoft Security Essentials, which is free anti-malware software.

Now let's look at different situations you might encounter when attempting to run anti-malware software.

WHEN AN INFECTED COMPUTER WILL NOT BOOT

If an infected computer will not boot, the boot manager, boot loaders, or kernel mode drivers launched at startup might be infected or damaged. Launch the computer into Windows Recovery Environment (Windows RE) and use the Startup Repair process to repair the system. Chapter 6 gives more information about solving boot problems. You can also install the hard drive as a second drive in another system and use that system to scan the drive for malware.

UPDATE AND RUN ANTI-MALWARE SOFTWARE THAT'S ALREADY INSTALLED

If anti-malware software is already installed on a system and you suspect an infection, update the software and perform a full scan on the system. Do the following:

1. Make sure the anti-malware software is up to date. These updates download the latest malware definitions, also called malware signatures, which the software uses to define or detect new malware as it gets into the wild (becomes available on the Internet).

2. Use the anti-malware software to perform a full scan of the system. As it scans, the software might ask you what to do with an infected program, or it might log the event in an event viewer or history log it keeps. For example, Windows Defender reports a threat, as shown in Figure 8-19. When you click **Clean PC**, you can decide what to do with the threat. In most situations, select **Remove** to delete the program.

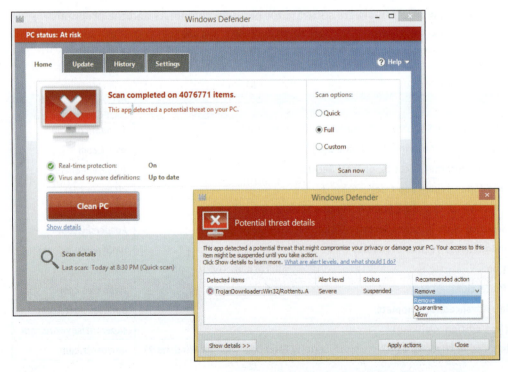

Figure 8-19   Decide what to do with a program that Windows Defender has identified as a severe threat to the system

3. After the scan is complete and you have decided what to do with each suspicious file, reboot the system, allow the software to update itself again, and then scan the system again. Most likely, some new malware will be discovered. Keep rebooting and rescanning until a scan comes up clean.

> ✎ **Notes** If you ever encounter a virus that your updated anti-malware software did not find, be sure to let the manufacturer of the software know so they can research the problem.

RUN ANTI-MALWARE SOFTWARE FROM A NETWORKED COMPUTER

If anti-malware software is not already installed, the most effective way to clean the computer is to run the software from another computer. Follow these steps:

1. Make sure the remote computer has its software firewall set for maximum protection and its installed anti-malware software is up to date and running.

2. Network the two computers and share drive C: on the infected computer. (Don't connect the infected computer to the entire network. If necessary, you can connect the two computers using a crossover cable or using a small switch and network cables.)

3. To make your work easier, you can map a network drive from the remote computer to drive C: on the infected computer.

4. Perform an anti-malware scan on the remote computer, pointing the scan to drive C: on the infected computer.

INSTALL AND RUN ANTI-MALWARE SOFTWARE ON THE INFECTED COMPUTER

If you don't have another computer that you are willing to risk connecting to the infected computer, you can use another computer to purchase and download anti-malware software and then copy the downloaded files to a CD or flash drive that you can insert in the infected computer. Don't make the mistake of using the infected computer to purchase and download anti-malware software because keyloggers might be spying and collecting credit card information. During the installation process, the anti-malware software updates itself and performs a scan. You can also run free online anti-malware software without downloading and installing it, but be careful to use only reputable websites.

INSTALL AND RUN ANTI-MALWARE SOFTWARE IN SAFE MODE

Some malware prevents anti-malware software from installing or running. In this situation, try booting the system in Safe Mode or performing a clean boot and installing the anti-malware software. Some viruses still load in Safe Mode or after a clean boot, and some anti-malware programs will not install in Safe Mode. Recall that to launch Windows in Safe Mode, also called Safe boot, enter the **msconfig** command in the Windows 10/7 search box or the Windows 8 Run box. In the System Configuration box, click the **Boot** tab and check **Safe boot** (see Figure 8-20). To launch Safe Mode with Networking so that you can update your anti-malware software, select **Network** in the list of options. Then restart the system.

> ✎ **Notes** If viruses are launched even after you boot in Safe Mode and you cannot get the anti-malware software to work, try searching for suspicious entries in the Windows registry subkeys under HKLM\System\CurrentControlSet\ Control\SafeBoot. Subkeys under this key control what is launched when you boot into Safe Mode. How to edit the registry is covered in Chapter 5.

8

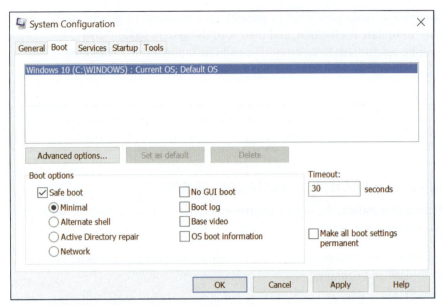

Figure 8-20   Use the Safe boot option to boot the system in Safe Mode and prevent malware from launching at startup

RUN AN ANTI-MALWARE SCAN BEFORE WINDOWS BOOTS

Microsoft offers a specialized scanning utility called Windows Defender Offline (WDO) that loads before Windows and performs a scan in the Windows Preinstallation Environment (WinPE). WinPE is a limited version of Windows that can be used for customizing Windows installations, modifying the Windows installation while it's not running, or performing recovery tasks. WDO can be started from the Windows 10 Settings app:

1. Click **Update & Security**, **Windows Security**, and **Virus & threat protection**.

2. In the Windows Defender Security Center window that opens, click **Run a new advanced scan**. Select **Windows Defender Offline scan**, as shown in Figure 8-21. Make sure all apps and files are saved and closed, then click **Scan now**.

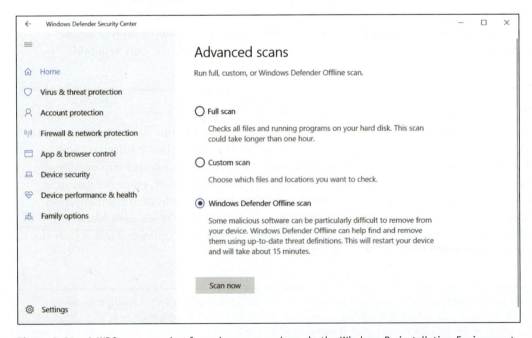

Figure 8-21   A WDO scan searches for and removes malware in the Windows Preinstallation Environment

3. After the scan completes, find information about the scan in the Virus & threat protection window by clicking **Threat history**.

If you're unable to boot into Windows 10, or if you're working with an earlier version of Windows, use an uninfected computer to create a bootable CD or flash drive with the WDO tool, and then boot from that device:

1. Depending on the architecture of the infected machine, download the 32-bit or 64-bit version of WDO from the Microsoft support website at the following link and save it to a CD or flash drive:

   support.microsoft.com/en-us/help/17466/windows-defender-offline-help-protect-my-pc

2. Boot from the WDO device, perform the scan, and check the results.

Other anti-malware companies, such as those listed in Table 8-2, offer preinstallation scanning tools, also called rescue disks or bootable antivirus tools. Two examples are the Bitdefender Rescue CD (*bitdefender.com*) and Kaspersky's Rescue Disk (*kaspersky.com*).

RUN MORE THAN ONE SCAN OF ANTI-MALWARE SOFTWARE

After you've scanned the system using one of the methods just discussed, reboot and install anti-malware software on the hard drive. Update the software, and then keep scanning and rebooting until the scan report is clean.

If a second or third scan doesn't remove all symptoms of malware, consider installing and running a second anti-malware program. What one anti-malware program cannot detect or remove, another one might. For example, Windows Defender on one system removed malware it detected, but did not detect or remove the downloader *dnsatlantic.exe*, which hijacked a browser and is still running in the background (see Figure 8-22).

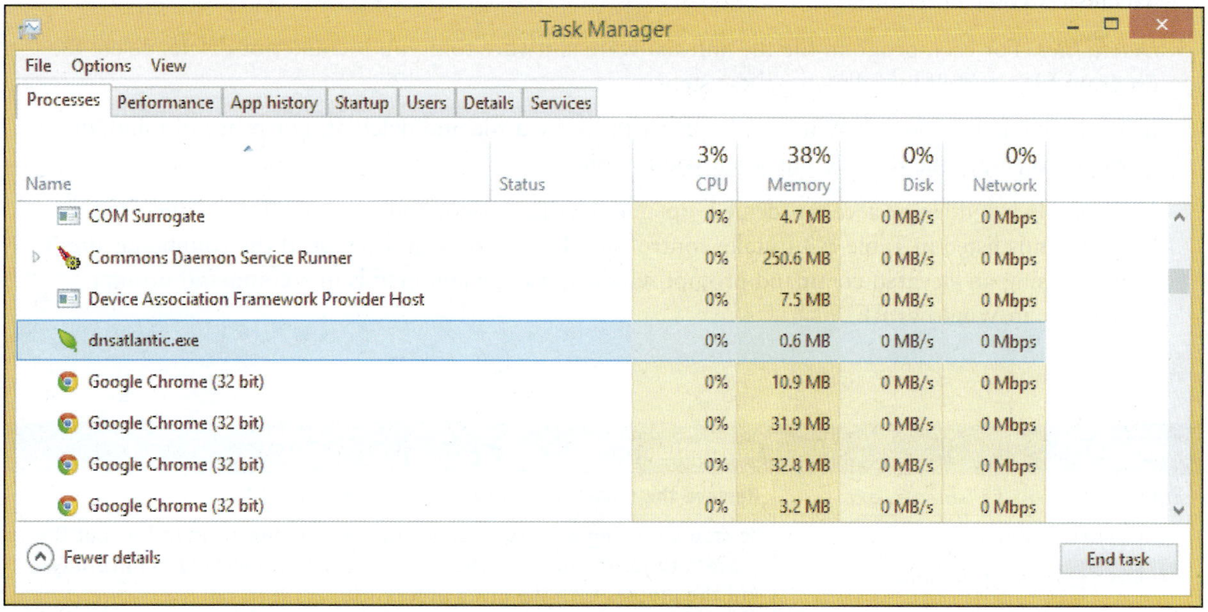
Task Manager
File Options View
Processes Performance App history Startup Users Details Services
Name Status 3% CPU 38% Memory 0% Disk 0% Network
COM Surrogate 0% 4.7 MB 0 MB/s 0 Mbps
Commons Daemon Service Runner 0% 250.6 MB 0 MB/s 0 Mbps
Device Association Framework Provider Host 0% 7.5 MB 0 MB/s 0 Mbps
dnsatlantic.exe 0% 0.6 MB 0 MB/s 0 Mbps
Google Chrome (32 bit) 0% 10.9 MB 0 MB/s 0 Mbps
Google Chrome (32 bit) 0% 31.9 MB 0 MB/s 0 Mbps
Google Chrome (32 bit) 0% 32.8 MB 0 MB/s 0 Mbps
Google Chrome (32 bit) 0% 3.2 MB 0 MB/s 0 Mbps
Fewer details
End task

Figure 8-22 The malware downloader *dnsatlantic.exe* is still running after multiple scans of anti-malware software

In this situation, try another anti-malware program. For example, Microsoft Safety Scanner (*docs.microsoft.com/en-us/windows/security/threat-protection/intelligence/safety-scanner-download*) is not designed for ongoing malware prevention but can sometimes remove malware that Windows Defender did not find. Download and run the latest version of the software.

CLEAN UP WHAT'S LEFT OVER

Next, you'll need to clean up anything the anti-malware software left behind. Sometimes anti-malware software tells you it is not able to delete a file, or it deletes an infected file but leaves behind an orphaned entry in the registry or startup folders. If the anti-malware software tells you it was not able to delete or clean a file, first check the anti-malware software website for any instructions you might find to manually clean things up. Here are some general actions you can take to clean up what the software left behind:

1. *Respond to any startup errors.* On the first boot after anti-malware software has declared a system clean, you might still find some startup errors caused by incomplete removal of the malware. Use System Configuration and/or Task Manager to find out how a startup program is launched. If the program is launched from the registry, you can back up and delete the registry key. If the program is launched from a startup folder, you can move or delete the shortcut or program in the folder. See Chapter 5 for the details of how to remove unwanted startup programs.

2. *Research malware types and program files.* Your anti-malware software might alert you to a suspicious program file that it quarantines, and then ask you to decide if you want to delete it. Also, Task Manager and other tools might find processes you suspect are malware. The web is your best tool to use when making your decision about a program. Here are some websites that offer malware encyclopedias that are reliable and give you symptoms and solutions for malware:

   ◢ Process Library by ProcessLibrary at *processlibrary.com*

   ◢ DLL Library by Uniblue Systems Limited at *liutilities.com*

   ◢ All the anti-malware software sites listed earlier in the chapter in Table 8-2

   Beware of using other sites! Much information on the web is written by people who are just guessing, and some of the information is put there to purposefully deceive. Check things out carefully, and learn which sites you can rely on.

3. *Delete files.* For each program file the anti-malware software told you it could not delete, delete the program file yourself by following these steps:

   a. First try File Explorer or Windows Explorer to locate a file and delete it. For peace of mind, don't forget to empty the Recycle Bin when you're done.

   b. If the file is hidden or access is denied, open an elevated command prompt window and use the commands listed in Table 8-3 to take control of a file so you can delete it. If the commands don't work using an elevated command prompt window, use the commands in a command prompt window in Windows RE.

Command	Description
`attrib -r -s filename.ext`	**Remove the read-only and system attributes to a file.**
`tasklist	more`  `taskkill /f /pid:9999`	**To stop a running process, first use the tasklist command to find out the process ID for the process. Then use the taskkill command to forcefully kill the process with the given process ID.**
`takeown /f filename.ext`	**Take ownership of a file.**
`icacls filename.ext /grant administrators:f`	**Take full access of a file.**

Table 8-3   Commands used to take control of a malware file so you can delete it

c. To get rid of other malware files, delete all Internet Explorer temporary Internet files. Use the Disk Cleanup process in the Drive C: properties box, or delete the browsing history using the Internet Options box.

d. Delete all subfolders and files in the C:\Windows\Temp folder. Figure 8-23 shows where Windows Defender lists potentially unwanted programs (PuPs) that a Trojan downloader put in this folder.

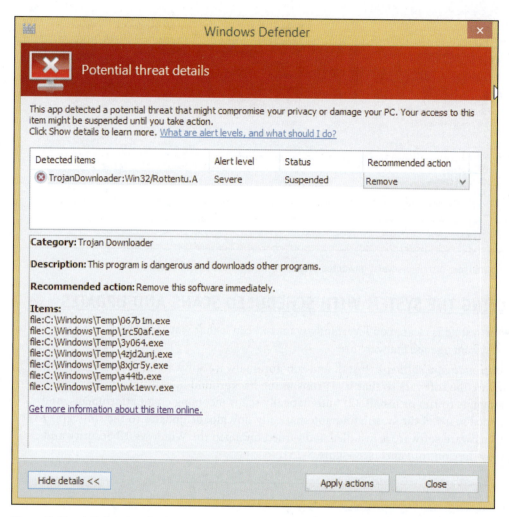

Figure 8-23   A Trojan downloader put programs in the C:/Windows/Temp folder, which must be manually deleted

4. *Clean the registry.* Appendix B lists folders and registry keys that can affect startup. You can search these folders and keys and delete entries you don't want. After you have finished cleaning startup folders and the registry, don't forget to restart the system and make sure all is well before you move on.

5. *Clean up your browsers and uninstall unwanted programs.* Adware and spyware might install add-ons to a browser (including toolbars you didn't ask for), install cookie trackers, and change your browser security settings. Anti-malware software might have found all these items, but as a good defense, take a few minutes to find out for yourself. Chapter 7 covered how to use the Internet Options box to search for unwanted add-ons and delete ActiveX controls. You can uninstall unwanted toolbars, plug-ins, and other software using the Programs and Features window (see Figure 8-24).

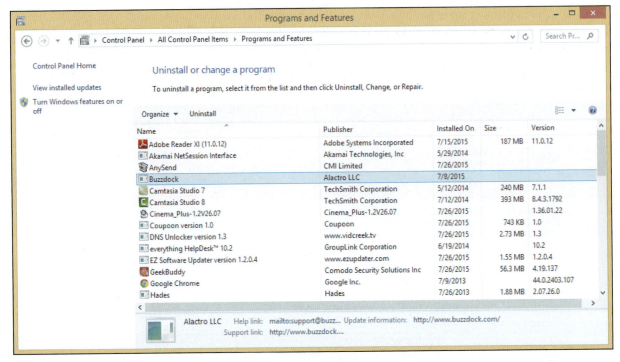

Figure 8-24　A Trojan downloader installed several unwanted programs, which must be uninstalled

STEP 5: PROTECTING THE SYSTEM WITH SCHEDULED SCANS AND UPDATES

A+
CORE 2
3.3

Once your system is clean, you'll certainly want to keep it that way. The three best practices to protect a system against malware are:

▲ *Use anti-malware software.* Install and run anti-malware software and keep it current. Configure the software so that it (1) runs in the background in real time to alert users of malware that attempts to run or install, (2) automatically scans incoming email attachments, and (3) performs scheduled scans of the system and automatically downloads updates to the software. To find out what anti-malware software is installed and turned on, open the Windows 10 Security and Maintenance window in Control Panel (see Figure 8-25).

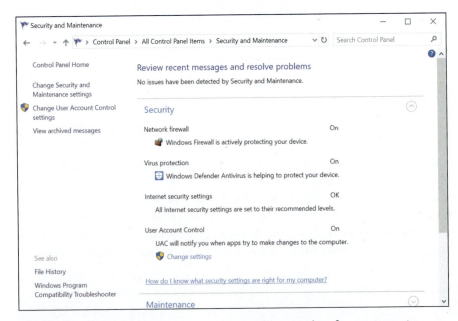

Figure 8-25　Check which apps are providing security protections for your computer

> **⟳ OS Differences** In Windows 8/7, open the Action Center to see what anti-malware software is installed and running.

▲ *Always use a software firewall.* Never, ever connect your computer to an unprotected network without using a firewall. Windows Firewall is turned on by default. Recall that you can configure Windows Firewall to allow no uninvited communication or to allow the exceptions that you specify.

▲ *Keep Windows updates current.* Microsoft continually releases updates to plug vulnerable entrances in Windows where malware might attack and updates to Windows Defender and Microsoft Security Essentials. Recall that you can verify Windows Update settings in the Settings app (Windows 10 only) or by clicking **Windows Update** in the System window in Control Panel (Windows 8/7).

STEP 6: ENABLING SYSTEM PROTECTION AND CREATING A RESTORE POINT

Now that the system is clean, you can turn System Protection back on if necessary and create a restore point. You learned how to do this in Chapter 4.

STEP 7: EDUCATING THE END USER

Now would be a good time to sit down with the user and go over the tips presented earlier in this chapter to keep the system free from malware. Sometimes the most overlooked step in preventing malware infections is to educate the user. Even with all your security measures in place, a user can still download and execute a Trojan, which can install more malware in the system.

> **★ A+ Exam Tip** The A+ Core 2 exam might give you a scenario that requires you to perform one or more of the seven steps to remove malware. Memorize these seven steps and know how to use them in the correct order.

BEST PRACTICES FOR DOCUMENTATION AND SECURITY POLICIES

Well-run IT departments rely on good documentation and security policies to set expectations and standards for security in the entire organization. In this part of the chapter, you learn about the types of documentation and security policies you might encounter in your IT career and what is generally expected of you as an IT technician to follow these best practices and policies.

TYPES OF DOCUMENTATION

Earlier in this text, you learned about ticketing software that tracks, manages, and documents customer service in an IT organization, acceptable use policies (AUP) that document what users can and cannot do with corporate resources, and password policies that document how to create strong passwords. Other types of documentation and documentation software an IT technician might encounter in an organization are described next:

▲ *Knowledge base.* A knowledge base is a collection of articles containing text, images, or video that give information about a network, product, or service. Here are two examples of how a knowledge base might be used:

  ▲ *Customer service.* To better support customers, a company might publish a knowledge base about its products or services on its website. Technical support specialists usually have access to a knowledge base to aid in helping customers during support calls; the knowledge base might be integrated into a ticketing system.

▲ *IT training and troubleshooting.* As IT personnel install, configure, and troubleshoot devices and software, the information they learn can be documented in the IT department's knowledge base so it's readily available for future troubleshooting and for training new IT personnel.

Source: MyAssetTag.com

Figure 8-26 The print on this tag is embedded under a protective surface so it can't be easily damaged

▲ *Inventory management.* Inventory management documents inventory, including end-user devices, network devices, IP addresses, software licenses, and related licenses. Hardware inventory might track equipment by using asset tags and theft-prevention plates, as you learned earlier in the chapter. These tags and plates contain barcodes that are easily read by a laser scanner. See Figure 8-26. Asset tracking software can scan the barcodes to report on existing inventory, track equipment, report needed maintenance, and help with identifying and returning stolen property.

▲ *Password policy.* In Chapter 7, you learned what is required to create a strong password and best practices for passwords (for example, allowing one to expire so that the user must occasionally change it). These requirements are sometimes documented as a password policy.

▲ *Network topology diagrams.* Network documentation should contain a map of a network's topology, which is called a network topology diagram. In networking, topology refers to the pattern in which devices on a network are connected with each other. For example, devices connected in a line are using a bus topology, and devices connected to a single, centralized device are using a star topology. Most Ethernet networks today use a design called a star bus topology, which means that nodes are connected to one or more centralized devices that are connected to each other (see Figure 8-27).

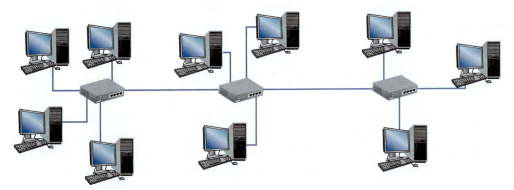

Figure 8-27 A star bus network formed by nodes connected to multiple switches

A network topology diagram might show how nodes on a network are physically connected, such as the one in Figure 8-27, or it might show the logical network topology. For example, the diagram shown earlier in Figure 8-11 shows the logical connection among clients and servers to indicate how data flows among them.

On small networks, a network topology diagram can be hand drawn, but for larger networks, inventory data is usually compiled automatically through network scans. For example, Spiceworks (*spiceworks.com*) offers a free Network Inventory product that probes devices on the network and presents a list of detected devices along with any information gathered about them, such as IP addresses, installed operating systems, and shared folders.

You learn about other types of documentation, such as that involved with change management, later in this chapter.

CHANGE MANAGEMENT

A+ CORE 2 4.2

As an IT support technician, you will undoubtedly be involved in new projects, such as installing hardware or software, upgrading networks, moving IT operations from onsite services to cloud-based services, rolling out virtualized desktops across the organization, implementing a VoIP communication platform, and much more. A project is temporary—it has a beginning, an end, and a singular, well-defined goal. A successful project depends on expert project management to direct a project team through specific tasks and deliver results on time, within the agreed-to budget, and with complete customer satisfaction.

When a project is implemented, change happens. Change managed well means that people affected by the change can make a smooth transition from their current state to the project goal or end result. In most situations, change management is closely integrated with project management and often involves the same teams. For example, a project manager works with a team to plan, develop, test, and implement new software. A change manager might work with the same team to define how the software will affect people and manage all communication, scheduling, training, and support required so that affected people are satisfied, embracing and accepting the end result.

A high-level change process is diagrammed in Figure 8-28. Know, however, that change processes vary widely. Let's look at the basic elements of change management and how they might relate to you as an IT support technician.

DOCUMENTED BUSINESS PROCESSES

A business is complex and well-run organizations know they must understand and document their core business goals and processes. Documented business processes are related activities that lead to a desired business goal, such as an efficient and cost-effective service, excellent customer satisfaction, or a superior product. For example, if customer satisfaction is a defined business goal, IT operational processes might describe how customers are taken care of, support tickets are documented, and customer satisfaction is measured.

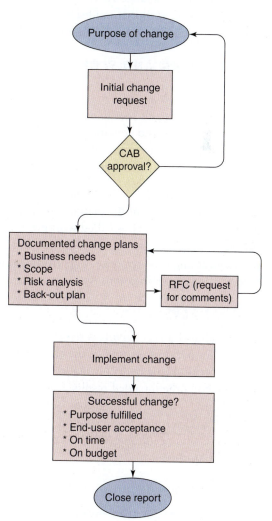

Figure 8-28 The general flow of change management

As change happens, be aware of how this change affects documented business processes. For example, suppose help-desk software is changed so that the customer's electronic signature is required when a ticket is closed. If you forget the electronic signature, your company may not be able to collect payment or follow up with the customer for a satisfaction survey.

PURPOSE OF CHANGE

The starting point for every proposed change is a clear and concise purpose for the change. What will change? What is the current situation and expected outcome? Why is the change needed? What happens if the organization does not initiate this change? How will the success of the change be measured?

> ✎ **Notes** IT technicians often communicate with people impacted by change. Therefore, it's important that you have a firm understanding of the purpose for the change so that you can maintain a positive, helpful attitude.

A proposed change is formally submitted using a change request process. A change request states what needs to be updated or changed but does not indicate how the change will be executed. A simple change request might require only preapproval from a manager. Complex changes, with higher impact and risks, are submitted to a change advisory board. The **change advisory board (CAB)** meets on a regular basis to assess, prioritize, authorize, and schedule changes. The change manager and other representatives approve changes based on the recommendations of the change advisory board.

CHANGE PLAN AND SCOPE

The change plan defines the **scope of change**, which may outline:

▲ Key components of the change and how they will be addressed
▲ Skill sets, tasks, and activities required to carry out the change
▲ Individuals or departments that will participate in the change
▲ How the success of change is measured and when the change is completed

The scope of change defines your responsibilities in the change plan. It's important that you understand exactly your assignment for planning, implementing, and supporting the change and then work within these boundaries, which is called working "in scope." The scope of change might evolve through the feedback process of change management, but until the scope changes, it's important to work in scope. Although it might be tempting to perform yet one more step while implementing a change, don't make "out of scope" modifications, which might result in major disruption.

RISK ANALYSIS

Change almost always involves risk, which refers to a problem (event, situation, or condition) that may or may not occur as a result of the change. For example, a change might be half-finished when the change manager realizes the budget is inadequate. Other risks are alienating customers, not finishing on time, or not delivering the intended results. **Risk analysis** is the process of identifying potential problems so there are no surprises or crisis situations once the change begins. For each potential problem identified, the team attempts to determine the likelihood it may occur, its impact, and what to do if it does occur. As an IT technician, you need to be aware of the risks involved and how to execute the response plan if the problem actually happens.

BACK-OUT PLAN

What if a change goes bad—really bad? Suppose all users lose network connectivity for hours or all database servers that log all online sales orders spontaneously crash. The **back-out plan** defines the activities needed to recover to the original state in the event of an aborted or failed change implementation.

The back-out plan is created and sometimes tested even before the change starts, and includes detailed steps to restore service to users. Obviously, you need to be aware of the back-out plan prior to implementing a change.

END-USER ACCEPTANCE

Recall that change management is responsible for people impacted by change being able to make a smooth transition during the change. End-user acceptance to change often fails because the focus of the change is on the technical side rather than the people side. To gain end-user acceptance, users must know:

1. The purpose of the change, especially the business reasons for the change

2. That the leadership of the company agrees with the change

3. How the change will affect them and their job

4. How to get their individual concerns and questions answered and how their voices will be heard

5. That they will receive end-user training for the changes that impact them

Before a change begins, an organization might request user feedback to the change in a **request for comments (RFC)**. Technical users often have valuable input in the RFC process that may affect the entire change process. IT technicians often play a major role in end-user acceptance. Users who struggle with change will appreciate your empathetic and positive outlook. When a proposed change has been clearly communicated and the user understands "what's in it for me," you have made a significant contribution to a successful change.

DOCUMENT CHANGES

No part of change management should rely on spoken communication. Everything related to changes must be documented, including how the change management process itself works. Change plans are documented and updated throughout the entire change management process. Many larger organizations use change management software, such as Alloy Software (*alloy-software.com*), to manage all stages of change management from the change request form to the final close report. Smaller organizations may manually document change using MS Word or Excel documents or database software. Regardless of the size of the organization, you will be expected to maintain proper documentation for all stages of a change in which you participate.

REGULATED DATA, LICENSING, AND SECURITY POLICIES

An IT technician is expected to follow company security policies for regulated data and software licensing. You also need to know what to do when you discover an incident where these policies have been violated.

REGULATORY AND COMPLIANCE POLICIES

Certain types of data are protected by special governmental regulations and are called **regulated data**. Each industry must comply with a variety of regulations, policies, and laws, which are collectively called **regulatory and compliance policies**. For example, in the health-care industry, patient data is highly regulated, and most hospitals employ one or more regulatory and compliance officers to ensure that the hospital is compliant. Other regulated industries include the copyright laws regulated by the U.S. Copyright Office, workplace safety regulated by the Occupational Safety and Health Administration (OSHA), and consumer protection regulated by the Federal Trade Commission (FTC). Many of these policies directly affect IT operations. When you're first hired by a company, you should receive training on how these issues affect your work and what is expected of you.

Let's look at some specific types of regulated data:

◢ *Personal identity.* PII (personally identifiable information) is a legal term to describe data that can uniquely identify a person, including a Social Security number, email address, physical address, birthdate, birth place, mother's maiden name, marital status, phone numbers, race, and biometric data. Some PII is more sensitive than other information and should be protected more vigilantly.

◢ *Health information.* PHI (protected health information) includes any data about a person's health status or health care. This data is protected by regulations defined by HIPAA (the Health Insurance Portability and Accountability Act), passed in 1996. HIPAA gives patients the rights to monitor and restrict the sharing of their medical information. Hospitals, medical personnel, and other entities covered by HIPAA regulations risk steep penalties for privacy breaches.

◢ *Credit card data.* The Payment Card Industry (PCI) standards were defined to help prevent credit card fraud and are backed by all the major credit card brands (Visa, MasterCard, and others). PCI standards apply to how credit card data is transmitted (such as when receiving payments) and stored (such as when keeping records for recurring billing) by vendors, retailers, and financial institutions.

◢ *Citizens of the EU.* The GDPR (General Data Protection Regulation) is a group of regulations implemented in 2018 in the European Union (EU) to protect personal data of EU citizens, giving them more control over how their data is collected, stored, and shared. The GDPR also includes requirements for how individuals should be notified in the event their data is hacked. Covered personal data includes name, address, photos, IP address, genetic information, and biometric data that uniquely identifies a person.

✎ **Notes** Organizations and individuals who have access to regulated data are at risk legally and financially if they do not comply with the legal requirements regarding the security of this data. When you work in an organization that handles regulated data, ensure your own protection by making certain you understand and comply with all laws regarding this data.

SOFTWARE LICENSING

As an IT support technician, you need to be especially aware of the issues surrounding software licensing. As you have learned, open source software can be freely distributed and installed, but closed source software is owned by the creator (developer) and a license is required to use the software. When someone purchases software from a software developer, that person or organization has only purchased a commercial license for the software, which is the right to use it. The buyer does not legally *own* the software and therefore does not have the right to distribute it. The right to copy the work, called a copyright, belongs to the creator of the work or others to whom the creator transfers this right. Copyrights are intended to legally protect the intellectual property rights of organizations or individuals to creative works, which include books, images, and software. Your rights to use or copy software are clearly stated in the End User License Agreement (EULA) that you agree to when you install the software (see Figure 8-29).

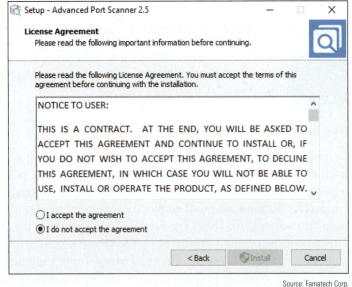

Source: Famatech Corp.

Figure 8-29 Agreeing to the EULA is required before software installs

Making unauthorized copies of original software violates the Federal Copyright Act of 1976 and is called software piracy or, more officially, software copyright infringement. (This act allows for one backup copy of software to be made.) Making a copy of software and then selling it or giving it away is a violation of the law. Normally, only the employee who violates the copyright law is liable for infringement; however, in some cases, an employer or supervisor is also held responsible, even when the copies were made without the employer's knowledge.

> 🖊 **Notes** When an individual or organization purchases the right to install one instance of software, the license is called a **personal license**. By purchasing a **site license**, also called an **enterprise license**, a company can obtain the right to multiple installations of software.

Many software companies, including Microsoft, have implemented measures to control the use of their software, which is called digital rights management (DRM). For example, recall that the retail release of Windows 10 requires a valid product key or a digital license for activation, and Microsoft carefully verifies and monitors that this product key is used only in one installation.

INCIDENT RESPONSE FOR PROHIBITED CONTENT AND ACTIVITIES

As you know, employees in an organization are often asked to agree to an acceptable use policy (AUP) that documents a code of conduct when using corporate resources. For example, the AUP may prohibit an employee from accessing pornographic material on company computers, using company computers and time for personal shopping, or installing pirated software on these computers.

An incident is when an employee or other person has negatively affected safety or corporate resources, violated the code of conduct for the organization, or committed a crime. When you start a new job, ask your employer what procedures you follow for an incident response. If you're the first person to discover an incident, such as use of prohibited content or other activities, you're responsible to perform certain first response duties. Here are some things you need to know:

▲ *Identify and go through proper channels.* When you identify what you believe to be an infringement of the law or the company's code of conduct, where do you turn to report the issue? Make sure you go only through proper channels; don't spread rumors or accusations.

▲ *Preserve data and devices.* What data or device should you immediately preserve as evidence for what you believe has happened? For example, if you believe you have witnessed a customer or employee using a company computer for a crime, should you remove and secure the hard drive from the computer, or should you remove and secure the entire computer?

▲ *Incident documentation.* Incident documentation surrounding the evidence of an incident is important to prevent future incidents and crucial to a criminal investigation. What documentation are you expected to submit and to whom is it submitted? This documentation might track the chain of custody for the evidence, which includes exactly what, when, and from whom it was collected, the condition of this evidence, and how the evidence was secured while it was in your possession. It also includes a paper trail of each person to whom the evidence has been passed on and when. For example, suppose you suspect that a criminal act has happened and you hold a flash drive that you believe contains evidence of this crime. You need to carefully document exactly when and how you received the flash drive. Also, don't pass it on to someone else in your organization unless you have the person's signature on a chain-of-custody document so that you can later prove you handled the evidence appropriately. You don't want the evidence to be disallowed in a court of law because you have been accused of misconduct or tampering with the evidence. Also know that more information than a signature, such as a copy of a driver's license, might be required to identify people in the chain of custody.

8

⭐ **A+ Exam Tip**　The A+ Core 2 exam expects you to be able to explain the process of an incident response, which includes reporting prohibited content or activity through the proper channels, preserving relevant data and evidence, and tracking evidence through an appropriate chain-of-custody document.

DATA DESTRUCTION AND DISPOSAL

A+ CORE 2 2.9

Besides dumpster diving, consider the impact of digital dumpster diving. You need to totally destroy data before you throw out a hard drive, flash drive, CD, DVD, tape, or other media that might have personal or corporate data on it, unless you know the data can't be stolen off the device. Trying to wipe a drive clean by deleting files or even by using Windows to format the drive does not completely destroy the data. Here are some ways to destroy printed documents and sanitize storage devices:

◢ *Overwrite data on the drive.* A drive needs to be wiped clean before you recycle or repurpose it. With older magnetic hard drives, an end user could perform a low-level format of a drive to redefine the sector marks on the drive's platters, making the existing data inaccessible. (This is different from a standard Windows format that configures a file system on the drive.) Today's devices receive a low-level format at the factory that can't be changed later. However, end users can wipe the drive using a zero-fill utility that overwrites all data on the drive with zeroes; sometimes this is inaccurately called a low-level format. You can download a zero-fill utility or so-called low-level format utility from many hard drive manufacturers' websites. This method works for most low-security situations, but professional thieves know how to break through it. If you use one of these utilities, run it multiple times to write zeroes on top of zeroes. Data recovery has been known to reach 14 levels of overwrites because each bit is slightly offset from the one under it.

✏ **Notes**　An app called a file shredder can permanently delete an individual file or folder by overwriting it multiple times. Check the reviews before downloading and using one of these apps.

◢ *For solid-state devices, use a Secure Erase utility.* As required by government regulations for personal data privacy, the American National Standards Institute (ANSI) developed the ATA Secure Erase standards to wipe clean a solid-state device such as a USB flash drive or SSD. You can download a Secure Erase utility from the manufacturer of the device and run it to sanitize the drive, or you can securely erase all data on the device and then reuse or dispose of it.

◢ *Physically destroy the storage media.* Use a drill to drill many holes all the way through the drive housing. Break CDs and DVDs in half and do similar physical damage with a hammer to flash drives or tapes, even to the point of setting them on fire to incinerate them. Again, expert thieves can still recover some of the data.

◢ *For magnetic devices, use a degausser.* A degausser exposes a storage device to a strong electromagnetic field to *completely* erase the data on a magnetic hard drive or tape drive (see Figure 8-30). A degaussed drive can't be reused, but for the best destruction, use the degausser and

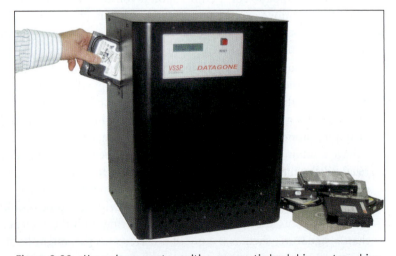

Figure 8-30　Use a degausser to sanitize a magnetic hard drive or tape drive

physically destroy the drive. Degaussing does not erase data on a solid-state hard drive or other flash media because these devices don't use magnetic surfaces to hold data.

▲ *Use a shredder.* Recall you can use a paper shredder to destroy all documents that contain sensitive data. The best paper shredders apply multiple passes to cross-cut the paper instead of strip-cutting; this cuts the paper into smaller pieces that can't be easily reassembled. Many paper shredders can handle credit cards or thin cardboard. Multimedia shredders can also destroy optical discs. Disk drive shredders, such as the one shown in Figure 8-31 from Whitaker Brothers (*whitakerbrothers.com*), can destroy magnetic hard drives, solid-state drives, flash drives, optical discs, and even mobile devices such as smartphones or small tablets.

▲ *Use a secure data-destruction service.* For the very best data destruction, consider a secure data-destruction service. To find a service, search the web for "secure data destruction." However, don't use a service unless you have thoroughly checked its references and guarantees of legal compliance that your organization is required to meet. The service should provide you with a digital certificate of destruction, which verifies that the data has been destroyed beyond recovery. Paper certificates can be forged, but digital certificates produced by the software that performs the destruction will provide auditable results of the destruction process.

Source: whitakerbrothers.com

Figure 8-31   This drive shredder pulverizes small storage devices such as hard drives, flash drives, and smartphones

> ★ **A+ Exam Tip**   The A+ Core 2 exam might give you a scenario that requires you to implement data-destruction techniques, including using a shredder, degausser, incineration, drill, hammer, and recycling or repurposing techniques (low-level formats, overwriting, and drive wipes).

>> CHAPTER SUMMARY

Protecting Network Resources

▲ Physical security can include a locked door, a server lock and cable lock, port lock, privacy filter, theft-prevention plate, mantrap, and security guard.

▲ Logical security can include anti-malware software, a VPN connection, email filtering, qualifying software distributors, an access control list, MAC address filtering, and mobile device management.

◢ Large networks might require additional user authentication other than a Windows password, which can include a password policy and multifactor authentication using hardware or software tokens.

◢ AAA (authenticating, authorizing, and accounting) services include RADIUS and TACACS+.

◢ Security methods include educating users against social engineering and protecting a laptop when traveling.

Dealing with Malicious Software on Personal Computers

◢ Malware includes viruses, spyware, keyloggers, worms, Trojans, rootkits, ransomware, zero-day attacks, man-in-the-middle attacks, DoS attacks, DDoS attacks, zombies, and botnets. Attacks on passwords include dictionary, brute force, and rainbow table attacks. Noncompliant systems open a network up to attack.

◢ Symptoms that indicate malware is present include pop-up ads, slow performance, error messages and logs, file errors, email problems, and invalid digital certificates.

◢ Some systems become so highly infected that the only solution is to format the hard drive, reinstall Windows, and restore data from backups.

◢ To clean up an infected system, (1) know how to identify common malware symptoms, (2) quarantine the infected system, (3) disable System Restore, (4) remediate the system, (5) protect the system with scheduled scans and updates, (6) enable System Protection and create a restore point, and (7) educate the end user.

Best Practices for Documentation and Security Policies

◢ Types of security documentation include ticketing software to document customer service, a knowledge base, acceptable use policies, password policies, inventory management, network topology diagrams, and the documentation needed for change management.

◢ Change management includes identifying the purpose and scope of change, developing a change plan and back-out plan, getting approval from a change board, acquiring end-user acceptance, performing a risk analysis, and documenting the entire change process.

◢ Regulatory and compliance policies help protect regulated data, which can include PII, PHI, PCI, and GDPR data regulated by governmental agencies.

◢ Commercial licensing of software can be a personal license or enterprise license. Terms of the licensing agreement are found in the EULA.

◢ A chain-of-custody document is part of incident documentation and provides a paper trail of the evidence in response to an incident that is suspected to be criminal.

◢ Data can be partly or completely destroyed using a paper shredder, multimedia shredder, low-level format, zero-fill utility, drill, hammer, incinerator, or degausser.

◢ Professional data destruction services may provide a certificate of destruction for legal purposes.

>> KEY TERMS

For explanations of key terms, see the Glossary for this text.

AAA (authenticating, authorizing, and accounting)	access control list (ACL)	ATA Secure Erase	biometric data
	agent	back-out plan	biometric lock
acceptable use policy (AUP)	anti-malware software	badge reader	botnet
	antivirus software	barcode	brute force

cable lock
Certificate Authority (CA)
certificate of destruction
chain of custody
change advisory board (CAB)
change management
commercial license
copyright
data loss prevention (DLP)
defense in depth
degausser
denial-of-service (DoS)
dictionary attack
digital certificate
digital rights management (DRM)
disk drive shredders
distributed denial-of-service (DDoS)
documented business processes
dumpster diving
email filtering
email hoax
End User License Agreement (EULA)
enterprise license
entry control roster
first response

GDPR (General Data Protection Regulation)
grayware
impersonation
incident
incident documentation
incident response
inventory management
Kensington lock
Kensington Security Slot
key fob
keylogger
knowledge base
low-level format
MAC address filtering
malicious software
malware
malware definitions
malware encyclopedias
malware signatures
man-in-the-middle attack
mantrap
MDM policies
mobile device management (MDM)
multifactor authentication
multimedia shredders
mutual authentication
network topology diagram
noncompliant systems
off-boarding

on-boarding
password policy
Payment Card Industry (PCI)
personal license
PHI (protected health information)
phishing
PII (personally identifiable information)
port lock
port security
privacy filter
privacy screen
quarantine computer
RADIUS (Remote Access Dial-In User Service)
rainbow table
ransomware
regulated data
regulatory and compliance policies
request for comments (RFC)
risk analysis
root certificate
rootkit
scope of change
Secure DNS
server lock
shoulder surfing
shredder

site license
smart card
smart card reader
social engineering
software piracy
software token
spear phishing
spoofing
spyware
TACACS+ (Terminal Access Controller Access Control System Plus)
tailgating
topology
triple A
Trojan
two-factor authentication (2FA)
USB lock
virus
VPN (virtual private network)
Windows Defender
Windows Defender Offline (WDO)
Windows Preinstallation Environment (WinPE)
worm
zero-day attack
zero-fill utility
zombie

>> THINKING CRITICALLY

These questions are designed to prepare you for the critical thinking required for the A+ exams and may use content from other chapters and the web.

1. Why is PINE963$&apple not a strong password?

2. What type of employee badge does not have to be swiped by a card reader in order to allow the employee through a door?

   a. RFID badge

   b. Smart card badge

   c. A badge containing a digital certificate

   d. Key fob

3. What tool is best to use when destroying data on an SSD?

   a. Zero-fill utility

   b. Low-level format

   c. Degausser

   d. ATA Secure Erase

4. What device can be installed on a laptop to prevent shoulder surfing?

5. Define and explain the differences between a virus, worm, and Trojan.

6. What is the best way to determine if an email message warning about a virus is a hoax?

   a. Check websites that track virus hoaxes.

   b. Scan the message for misspelled words or grammar errors.

   c. Open the message and see what happens.

   d. Scan your email inbox for malware.

7. What is the first thing you should do when you discover a computer is infected with malware? The second thing?

   a. Turn off system protection.

   b. Update installed anti-malware software.

   c. Format the hard drive.

   d. Quarantine the computer.

8. What does anti-malware software look for to determine that a program or a process is a virus?

9. What registry key keeps information about services that run when a computer is booted into Safe Mode?

10. What folder is used by Windows to hold restore points?

11. What must you do to allow anti-malware software to scan and delete malware it might find in the data storage area where restore points are kept?

12. A virus has attacked your hard drive. Instead of seeing the Windows Start screen when you start up Windows, the system freezes and you see a blue screen of death. You have important document files on the drive that are not backed up and you cannot afford to lose. What do you do first? Explain why this is your first choice.

   a. Try a data-recovery service even though it is expensive.

   b. Remove the hard drive from the computer case and install it in another computer.

   c. Try GetDataBack by Runtime Software (*runtime.org*) to recover the data.

   d. Use Windows utilities to attempt to fix the Windows boot problem.

   e. Run antivirus software to remove the virus.

13. You sign in to your personal computer with your Microsoft account and then you want to set up your computer as a trusted device to make changes to the account settings. Microsoft sends a code to your cell phone in a text message. You enter the code on a Windows screen. This type of authentication is called:

   a. Multifactor authentication

   b. Mutual authentication

   c. Biometric authentication

   d. None of the above

14. At a restaurant, you overhear people discussing an interesting case they treated while working in a dental office that day. Which type of regulated data policies are most likely to have been violated?

a. PII

b. PHI

c. PCI

d. GDPR

15. As a bank employee, you often work from home and remotely access a file server on the bank's network to correct errors in financial data. Which of the following services is most likely the one you are using to authenticate to the network and track what you do on the network?

a. RADIUS

b. Secure DNS

c. Active Directory

d. TACACS+

16. Among the following, which is the best protection against ransomware?

a. Windows File History

b. Carbonite

c. Keylogger software

d. Authy by Twilio

17. Your boss asks you to work through the weekend to install new software on the applications server that serves up applications to 20 users. The following Monday, all users report they cannot open their data files. After speaking with technical support for the new application, you discover it is not compatible with the old data files. Which type of documentation should you refer to first to address this problem?

a. Risk analysis documents

b. Back-out plan documents

c. Change management documents

d. Scope of change documents

>> HANDS-ON PROJECTS

Hands-On | Project 8-1   Creating and Using an Anti-Malware Software Rescue Disc

When an infected computer does not have anti-malware software installed, one method to clean the infection is to create and use an anti-malware rescue disc. Select anti-malware software that offers a free download to create a bootable USB flash drive or CD. For example, you can use Windows Defender Offline or Bitdefender Rescue CD. Create a bootable USB flash drive or CD and use it to scan a computer. Answer the following questions:

1. What is the URL where you found the download to create a rescue disc or drive?

2. List the files in the root directory of the USB flash drive or CD that the software created.

3. Describe the menu or screen that appeared when you booted from the rescue media.

Hands-On | Project 8-2   Downloading and Using Anti-Malware Software

A free trial of AVG Protection software is available on the AVG site at *avg.com*. Do the following to download, install, and run the software:

1. Download the free trial version of AVG Protection software from *avg.com* and install the software.
2. Update the software with the latest malware signatures.
3. Perform a complete scan of the system. Were any suspicious programs found?
4. Set the software to scan the system daily.
5. Set the software to scan incoming email.

Hands-On | Project 8-3   Using the Web to Learn About Malware

One source of information about malware on the web is F-Secure Corporation. Go to the website *f-secure.com* and find information about the latest malware threats. Answer the following questions:

1. Name and describe a recent Trojan downloader. How does the Trojan install and what is its payload (the harm it does)?
2. Name and describe a recent rootkit. How does the rootkit install and what is its payload?
3. Name a recent worm. How does it get into the network and what is its payload?

Hands-On | Project 8-4   Scanning a Network for Connected Devices

To help document devices connected to your network, you can use Advanced IP Scanner. Do the following to install and use the software:

1. Go to **advanced-ip-scanner.com** and then download and install Advanced IP Scanner by Famatech Corp. The software launches automatically.
2. Make sure the range of IP addresses includes all the IP addresses on your network. Click **Scan**. Figure 8-32 shows the results of one scan. Notice the software reports nodes on the network, their IP addresses, services they are running, and shared folders.

(continues)

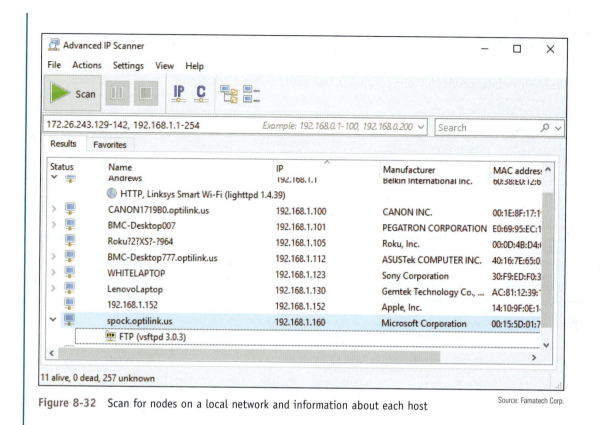

Figure 8-32 Scan for nodes on a local network and information about each host

Source: Famatech Corp.

>> REAL PROBLEMS, REAL SOLUTIONS

REAL PROBLEM 8-1 Using a Port Scanner

Port scanning software can be used to find out how vulnerable a computer is with open ports. This project requires the use of two computers on the same network to practice using port scanning software. Do the following:

1. On Computer 1, download and install Advanced Port Scanner by Famatech at **advanced-port-scanner.com**. (Be careful not to accept other software offered while downloading.)

2. If your Computer 2 is a Windows 10/8 system, open the **Network and Sharing Center**, click **Change advanced sharing settings**, and turn off network discovery and file and printer sharing. (For Windows 7, open the **Network and Sharing Center** and click the network location to change the settings.)

3. On Computer 1, start Advanced Port Scanner and make sure that the range of IP addresses includes the IP address of Computer 2. Change the default port list to 0 through 6000. Then click **Scan**.

4. Browse the list and find Computer 2. List the number and purpose of all open ports found on Computer 2.

5. On Computer 2, turn on network discovery and file and printer sharing. Open the **System** window, click **Remote settings**, and allow Remote Assistance connections to this computer. Close all windows.

6. On Computer 1, rescan and list the number and purpose of each port now open on Computer 2. Figure 8-33 shows the results for one computer, but yours might be different.

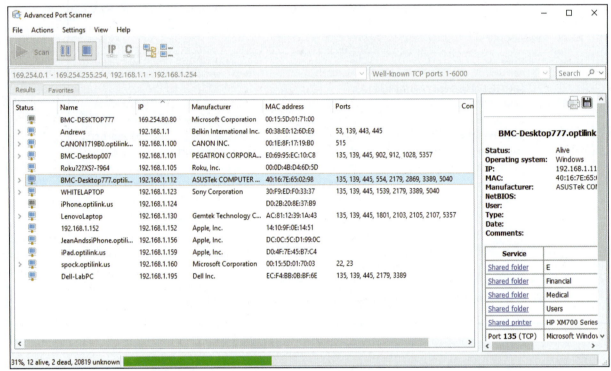

Source: Advanced Port Scanner by Famatech Corp.

Figure 8-33 Advanced Port Scanner shows open ports on networked computers

REAL PROBLEM 8-2 Implementing More Security for Remote Desktop

When Jacob travels on company business, he finds it's a great help to be able to access his office computer from anywhere on the road using Remote Desktop. However, he wants to make sure his office computer and the corporate network are as safe as possible. One way you can help Jacob add more security is to change the listening port that Remote Desktop uses. Knowledgeable hackers know that Remote Desktop uses port 3389, but if you change this port to a secret port, hackers are less likely to find the open port. Search the Microsoft Knowledge Base articles (*support.microsoft.com* and *technet.microsoft.com*) for a way to change the port that Remote Desktop uses. Practice implementing this change by doing the following:

1. Set up Remote Desktop on a computer using a business or professional edition of Windows. This computer is your host computer. Use another computer (the client computer) to create a Remote Desktop session to the host computer. Verify that the session works by transferring files in both directions.

2. Next, change the port that Remote Desktop uses on the host computer to a secret port. Save or print a screenshot showing how you made the change. Use the client computer to create a Remote Desktop session to the host computer using the secret port. Print a screenshot showing how you made the connection using the secret port. Verify that the session works by transferring files in both directions.

3. What secret port did you use? What link on the Microsoft websites gave you the information you needed?

Supporting Mobile Devices

Previous chapters have primarily focused on supporting Windows personal computers. This chapter moves on to discuss operating systems on mobile devices such as smartphones and tablets. As mobile devices become more common, many people use them to surf the web, access email, and manage apps and data. This chapter is intended to show you how to support a device that you might not own or normally use. Technicians are often expected to do such things! As an IT support technician, you need to know about the operating systems and hardware used with mobile devices and how to help a user configure and troubleshoot these devices.

Many employees expect to be able to use their mobile devices to access, synchronize, and edit data on the corporate network. Therefore, to protect this data, corporations require that employee mobile devices be secured and that data, settings, and apps be synchronized to other storage locations. In this chapter, you learn how you can synchronize content on mobile devices to a personal computer or to storage in the cloud (on the Internet). You learn how to secure mobile devices. You also learn about some connection technologies specific to the Internet of Things, which includes many non-computing devices such as door locks and security cameras. Finally, in this chapter, you learn about tools and resources available for troubleshooting mobile operating systems.

> ★ **A+ Exam Tip** Much of the content in this chapter applies to both the A+ Core 1 220-1001 exam and the A+ Core 2 220-1002 exam.

TYPES OF MOBILE DEVICES

Mobile devices vary considerably by size, functionality, available connection types, and primary purpose(s), not to mention cost. Here's a list of the mobile devices that you might be called on to support as an IT support technician:

▲ *Smartphone.* A smartphone is primarily a cell phone that also includes abilities to send text messages with photos, videos, or other multimedia content attached; surf the web; manage email; play games; take photos and videos; and download and use small apps. Most smartphones use touch screens for input (see Figure 9-1) and a few have a physical keyboard plus a touch screen. Many smartphones allow for voice input.

Source: iStockphoto.com/Hocus-focus

Figure 9-1   Most smartphones don't have a physical keyboard and use a touch screen with an on-screen keyboard for input

▲ *Tablets and lightweight laptops.* A tablet is a computing device with a touch screen that is larger than a smartphone and has functions similar to a smartphone. As you can see in Figure 9-2, it might come with a detachable keyboard or a stylus. Most tablets can connect to Wi-Fi networks and use Bluetooth or NFC (Near Field Communication), which you'll learn about later in this chapter, to wirelessly connect to nearby devices. Some tablets have the ability to use a cellular network for data transmissions and phone calls. Installed apps, such as Skype, can make voice phone calls, send text, and make video calls. When a tablet can be used to make a phone call, the distinction between a smartphone and a tablet is almost nonexistent, except for size.

Source: Samsung

Figure 9-2   Tablets are larger than smartphones and smaller than laptops

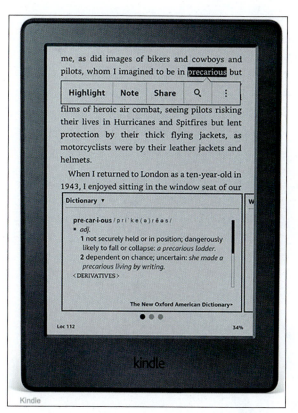

me, as did images of bikers and cowboys and pilots, whom I imagined to be in **precarious** but

| Highlight | Note | Share | 🔍 | ⋮ |

films of heroic air combat, seeing pilots risking their lives in Hurricanes and Spitfires but lent protection by their thick flying jackets, as motorcyclists were by their leather jackets and helmets.

　　When I returned to London as a ten-year-old in 1943, I enjoyed sitting in the window seat of our

Dictionary ▼

pre·car·i·ous /prɪˈke(ə)rēəs/
• *adj.*
　1 not securely held or in position; dangerously likely to fall or collapse: *a precarious ladder.*
　2 dependent on chance; uncertain: *she made a precarious living by writing.*
　< DERIVATIVES >

The New Oxford American Dictionary▸

● ● ●

Loc 112   34%

kindle

Kindle

Source: amazon.com

Figure 9-3　An e-reader includes tools optimized for reading, making notes, and looking up definitions of words

◢ *E-readers.* An **e-reader**, as shown in Figure 9-3, is a mobile device that holds digital versions of books, newspapers, magazines, and other printed documents, which are usually downloaded to the device from the web. An e-reader can connect to the Internet using a Wi-Fi wireless connection or a wired connection to a computer that is connected to the Internet. In addition, content can be stored on a flash memory card, which is inserted in the e-reader. Some e-readers, such as Amazon's Kindle Fire, have other apps that allow for surfing the web, playing games, handling email, and more. Devices such as these blur the line between e-readers and tablets.

◢ *GPS.* A **GPS (Global Positioning System)** feature is often embedded in many mobile devices, including smartphones, smart watches, tablets, and even automobiles, making it possible to identify the device's location in relation to multiple satellites in orbit around the Earth. Dedicated GPS devices are also available from Garmin (*garmin.com*), TomTom (*tomtom.com*), and a few others. A mobile device determines its location by using Bluetooth and GPS information as well as crowd-sourced Wi-Fi and cellular databases built from anonymous, encrypted, geotagged locations of Wi-Fi hotspots and cell towers.

◢ *Wearable technology devices.* **Wearable technology devices,** including smart watches (see Figure 9-4), wristbands, arm bands, eyeglasses, headsets, clothing, tracking tags, and even action cameras can be used as computing devices to make phone calls, send text messages, transmit data, and/or check email. Wearable technology often includes **fitness monitoring** capability where the device can measure heart rate, calculate calories burned, count pool laps or miles jogged or biked, and a host of other activities. These devices can sync up with a computer for power and communication, similar to how other mobile devices work. Many people believe smart watches will eventually replace smartphones as the personal communication device of choice.

Source: iStockphoto.com/Mutlu Kurtbas

Figure 9-4　The app screen on a smart watch by Apple, Inc.

◢ *VR/AR headsets.* A special type of wearable technology, **virtual reality (VR) headsets,** can help a user feel immersed in a virtual experience even to the point of moving physically through 3D space. Devices are used primarily for extreme gaming experiences, and are also used in military and medical training. The two main categories of VR headsets are mobile, which is basically a headset shell to hold a smartphone behind the lenses, or tethered, which requires a wired connection to a robust computer. Mobile VR headsets are inexpensive (as low as $30) and, accordingly, the experience leaves much to be desired.

9

Tethered VR headsets, such as the Oculus Rift in Figure 9-5, are much more expensive (around $400) and often come with a variety of accessories to maximize the VR experience. Microsoft has also developed a line of **augmented reality (AR) headsets** with native compatibility to Windows 10 that tend to fall in the middle ground between mobile and tethered VR headsets.

Source: amazon.com

Figure 9-5 The Oculus Rift communicates with a computer through a wired connection

MOBILE DEVICE OPERATING SYSTEMS

The operating system for a mobile device is installed at the factory. Here are the four most popular ones:

◢ **Android** OS by Google (*android.com*) is based on Linux and is used on various smartphones and tablets. At the time of this writing, Android is the most popular OS for smartphones in the world. Nearly 80 percent of smartphones sold today use Android. Combining both smartphones and tablets, Android holds over 70 percent of the worldwide market.

◢ **iOS** by Apple (*apple.com*) is based on macOS and is currently used on the iPhone and iPad. Almost 20 percent of smartphones sold today are made by Apple and use iOS, and over 20 percent of smartphones and tablets combined use iOS.

◢ **Windows 10 Mobile** by Microsoft (*microsoft.com*) is based on Windows 10 and is used on various smartphones. (Tablets use the 32-bit version of the same Windows 10 operating system used on desktop and laptop systems.) About half a percent of smartphones sold today use Windows 10 Mobile or one of its predecessors, such as Windows Phone 8.1.

◢ **Chrome OS** by Google is built on the open source Chromium OS (*chromium.org*). **Open source** means the source code for the operating system is available for free and anyone can modify and redistribute the source code. Chrome OS is designed solely for use on Google's Chromebook (*google.com/chromebook*), which is available from many different manufacturers as a lightweight laptop, a tablet, or a convertible laptop-tablet. Chrome OS looks and works like the familiar Chrome browser and relies heavily on web-based apps and storage. While technically a desktop OS, Chrome OS on Chromebooks bridges both the desktop and mobile markets, and it's rising in popularity due to increased availability of compatible apps, decreasing prices, quick response times in the OS, and reliable security features.

> ✏ **Notes** You can see current statistics for specific markets and operating systems at *gs.statcounter.com/os-market-share*. The chart can be edited for a variety of different factors, including device type, OS version, geographic market, and time frame.

> ★ **A+ Exam Tip** The A+ Core 2 exam expects you to understand the similarities and differences among the Android, iOS, Windows Mobile, and Chrome OS operating systems used with mobile devices.

ANDROID MANAGED BY GOOGLE

> **A+ CORE 1 3.9**
>
> **A+ CORE 2 1.1**

The Android operating system is based on the Linux OS and uses a Linux kernel. Linux and Android are both open source. Google (*google.com* and *android.com*) manages but does not own Android, and assumes a leadership role in development, quality control, and distributions of the Android OS and Android apps. Ongoing development of the Android OS code by Google and other contributors is released to the public as open source code.

GET TO KNOW AN ANDROID DEVICE

Releases of Android are named after desserts and include Honeycomb (version 3.x), Ice Cream Sandwich (version 4.0.x), Jelly Bean (version 4.1-4.3.x), KitKat (version 4.4+), Lollipop (version 5.0-5.1.1), Marshmallow (version 6.0), Nougat (versions 7.0 and 7.1), Oreo (versions 8.0 and 8.1), and the recently released Pie (version 9.0). Future releases of Android will follow in alphabetic order. At the time of this writing, most new phones and tablets ship with Oreo installed, although Android Pie is released on some phone models.

Android's graphical user interface (GUI) starts with multiple home screens and supports windows, panes, and 3D graphics. The Android OS can use an embedded browser, manage a database using SQLite, and connect to Wi-Fi, Bluetooth, and cellular networks. Most current Android mobile devices have a power button and volume control buttons on the side, and no physical buttons on the front of the device. However, three soft buttons on the navigation bar at the bottom of the screen include back (goes back to the previous screen), home (goes directly to the home screen), and overview (shows all running apps—swipe an app to the side to close it). See Figure 9-6.

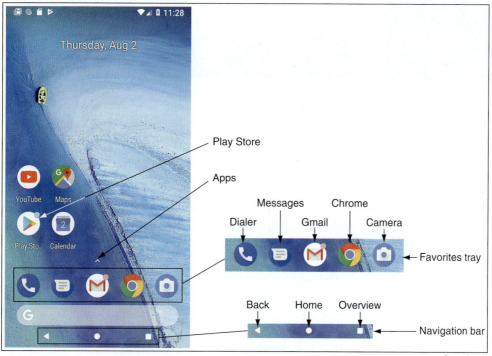

Source: Android

Figure 9-6 This Nexus smartphone has the Android Oreo OS installed

On Android phones, up to five apps or groups of apps can be pinned to the favorites tray just above the navigation bar. Apps in the favorites tray stay put as you move from home screen to home screen by swiping left or right. Tap the small arrow above the favorites tray or swipe up anywhere on the screen to access the app drawer, which lists and manages all apps installed on the phone. Press and hold an app in the app drawer to add it to an existing home screen or to add more home screens.

Notifications provide alerts and related information about apps and social media. Notifications are accessed by swiping down from the top of the screen, as shown in Figure 9-7A. The notifications shade provides access to the quick settings panel, such as Wi-Fi, Bluetooth, and Brightness. Tap the **Settings** gear icon near the upper-right corner to open the Settings app (see Figure 9-7B), or tap the **back** button in the navigation bar to return to the home screen.

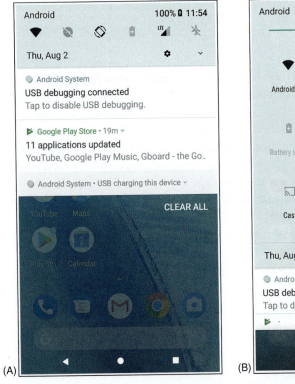
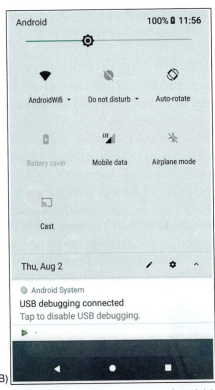

Source: Android

Figure 9-7   (A) The notifications shade includes quick access to the Settings app; (B) swipe down again to access quick settings on the notifications shade

A digital assistant service or app, also called a personal assistant, responds to a user's voice commands with a personable, conversational interaction to perform tasks and retrieve information. Popular examples are Apple's Siri (*apple.com*), Amazon's Alexa (*amazon.com*), Microsoft's Cortana (*microsoft.com*), and the Google Assistant (*assistant.google.com*). Google Assistant can be accessed on most Android devices with the voice command "Ok Google" or "Hey Google," or by touching and holding the Home button. See Figure 9-8. Give Google Assistant voice commands to send a message, start a phone call, look up information, and do many other tasks.

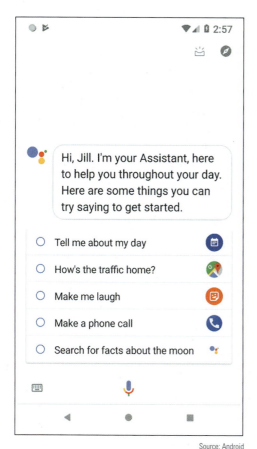

Figure 9-8 Google Assistant responds to voice commands

ANDROID APPS

Android apps are sold or freely distributed from any source or vendor. For example, you can open the Chrome browser and download an app from a website, such as the Amazon Appstore for Android at *amazon.com* or directly from the website of a developer. However, the official source for apps is Google Play at *play.google.com*. A Google account is required to download content from Google Play and can be associated with any valid email address.

To download an app using the Play Store app, tap the **Play Store** app on the home screen. (If you don't see the app icon on the home screen, tap the **app drawer** and then tap **Play Store**.) The app takes you to Google Play, where you can search for apps, games, movies, music, e-books, and magazines (see Figure 9-9A). You can also use the Play Store app to manage updates to installed apps, as shown in Figure 9-9B.

To develop Android apps, an app developer can download Android Studio to his computer from *developer.android.com*. Included in the download are Android SDK tools and an Android emulator. An SDK (Software Development Kit) is a group of tools that developers use to write apps, and an Android emulator is software that creates a virtual Android device complete with virtual hardware (buttons, camera, and even device orientation), a working installation of Android, and native apps. Android Studio is free and is released as open source. In a project at the end of this chapter, you'll download and install Android Studio and then use it to create virtual Android devices.

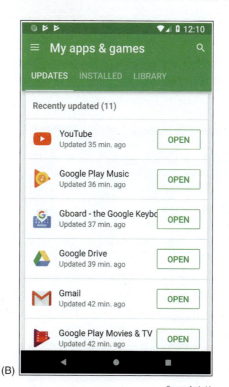

Figure 9-9 Use the Play Store app to (A) search Google Play for apps, music, e-books, movies, and more that you can download, as well as (B) updates to installed apps

IOS BY APPLE

A+
CORE 1
3.9

A+
CORE 2
1.1

Apple, Inc. (*apple.com*) develops, manufactures, and sells the Apple iPhone (a smartphone) and iPad (a handheld tablet). Both of these devices use the iOS operating system, also developed and owned by Apple. iOS is based on macOS, the operating system used by Apple desktop and laptop computers. The latest release at the time of this writing is iOS 12. Apple maintains strict standards on its products, which means iOS is exceptionally stable and bug free. Apple's iOS is also a very easy and intuitive operating system to use. As with macOS, iOS makes heavy use of icons.

GET TO KNOW AN IOS DEVICE

Because Apple is the sole owner and distributor of iOS, the only devices that use it are Apple devices (currently the iPhone and iPad). iPhones and iPads each have a physical Side button on the upper-right side of the device. All iPads and older models of iPhones have a Home button on the bottom front, but the newer iPhone X (pronounced *iPhone ten*) models don't have a Home button (see Figure 9-10). The iOS user interface as it appears on an iPad is shown in Figure 9-11. Apps can be pinned to the dock at the bottom of the screen.

iPhone X series

iPhone 8

Home button

Source: https://www.apple.com/iphone/compare/

Figure 9-10 The iPhone X series does not have the Home button that comes on all previous models of iPhones

Source: iOS

Figure 9-11 Access the dock on an iPad by swiping up from the bottom of the screen

Knowing a few simple navigation tips on an iOS device can help you get around a little more easily:

▲ *Open and close apps.* Tap an app icon to open it. Use the app switcher to switch to a different open app or to close apps. On an iPad, swipe up on the screen or double-click the Home button to show the app switcher and control center on the same screen (see Figure 9-12). On an older iPhone, double-click the Home button to see the app switcher. On an iPhone X, swipe up from the bottom and briefly hold to see the app switcher, or you can swipe side to side to move among open apps. In the app switcher, swipe up to close an app. Closing apps you're not using can save battery life.

Source: iOS

Figure 9-12 Access the app switcher and control center from any screen

▲ *Control center.* Use the control center to change basic settings such as brightness, volume, Wi-Fi, and Bluetooth. For the iPad and older iPhones, swipe up to show the control center (see the right side of Figure 9-12 for an iPad). On an iPhone X, swipe down from the upper-right corner to show the control center. Use the Settings app to adjust which settings are available in the control center.

▲ *Notification screen.* Swipe down from the top of the screen to see the notifications screen. The types of notifications shown and other notification settings can be customized in the Settings app, which you can open from the Home screen by tapping the Settings icon.

▲ *Delete and move apps.* To delete or move an app icon on the screen, press and hold the icon until all icons start to jiggle. As the icons jiggle, press the **X** beside the icon to delete it. To move an icon, press and drag it to a new location. You can add new home screens by dragging an app icon off the screen to the right. To stop the jiggling, press the Home button on the iPad and older iPhones. For iPhone X, press the **Done** button that appears in the upper-right corner of the screen.

▲ *Siri.* For iPhone X, press and hold the Side button to open Siri, iOS's digital assistant service, as shown in Figure 9-13. For all other iPhones and iPads, press and hold the **Home** button to open Siri. Siri was the first of the digital assistant services and has been around long enough to have become quite sophisticated. Siri uses information within the user's account to provide a customized experience.

Source: iOS

Figure 9-13   Siri follows voice commands

IOS APPS

You can get Android apps from many sources, but the only place to go for an iOS app is Apple. Apple is the sole distributor of iOS apps at its **App Store**. Other developers can write apps for the iPhone or iPad, but these apps must be sent to Apple for close scrutiny. If they pass muster, they are distributed by Apple on its website. Apple offers app development tools, including the iOS SDK (Software Development Kit) at *developer. apple.com*.

When you first purchase an iPad or iPhone, you activate it by signing into the device with an **Apple ID**, or user account, using a valid email address and password, and associating the account with a credit card number. Here are options for obtaining apps and other content:

▲ *App Store*. Use the App Store app on your mobile device (see Figure 9-14 for an iPad example) to search, purchase, and download apps, games, e-books, and periodical content such as newspapers and magazines. Some downloads are free.

Source: iOS

Figure 9-14   Use Apple's App Store app to download new apps

▲ *iTunes*. Use the iTunes Store app to search, purchase, and download media content, including music, movies, TV shows, and podcasts. (Again, some downloads are free.) You also have the option to download and install the iTunes software on a Mac or Windows personal computer. When you connect your mobile device to the computer by way of a USB port, you can use the iTunes software to sync the device to iOS updates downloaded from *iTunes.com* and to content on your computer, which can be a helpful troubleshooting option, as you'll see later.

WINDOWS MOBILE BY MICROSOFT

A+
CORE 1
3.9

A+
CORE 2
1.1

The Windows Mobile operating system by Microsoft is more or less a simplified version of the Windows operating system designed for desktop computers, laptops, and tablets. Windows Mobile and Windows version numbers correspond: Windows Mobile 10 corresponds to Windows 10. One of the biggest differences between Windows and Windows Mobile is that Windows Mobile does not have a desktop screen. Everything is accessed from the Start screen.

GET TO KNOW A WINDOWS MOBILE DEVICE

Most Windows phones have three buttons below the screen (see Figure 9-15). These buttons might be physical buttons or software buttons. The start button accesses the Start screen, the back button goes back one screen, and the search button opens a Cortana search box. (Recall that Cortana is the Windows digital assistant app.) Also, if you press and hold the **back** button, it displays recent apps. For most phones, these buttons aren't true software buttons, but they're also not true physical buttons because they might not work when the OS is malfunctioning.

Windows phones rely primarily on the Start screen for accessing apps. Just as with Windows 10, the Start screen is full of live tiles; each represents an app and many show live data on the tile from that app. Here are some tips for getting around Windows Mobile:

▲ Tap a tile on the Start screen to open its app. Scroll up or down to see more tiles. Press and hold to resize or reposition tiles. On many smartphones, pressing and holding a link functions like right-clicking with a mouse on a Windows desktop computer.

▲ Swipe down from the very top of the screen to see notifications in the Action Center (Figure 9-16A), similar to both Android and iOS. Like Android, there is also a Settings icon here to open the Settings app, shown in Figure 9-16B. Settings can also be accessed via the Settings tile on the Start screen.

Figure 9-15 Press and hold the search button to activate Cortana, the Windows digital assistant

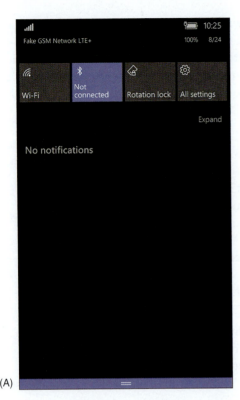 

Figure 9-16   (A) Notifications appear in the Action Center; (B) the Settings app provides an extensive toolkit for customizing a Windows smartphone

▲ Swipe from the right to see the apps list. Press and hold an app on the list to pin the app to the Start screen (see Figure 9-17). On the Start screen, you can press and hold the app tile and then change its size and other characteristics. Tap the **Store** tile on the Start screen to find more apps.

▲ While a menu is displayed in the Settings app, you can sometimes swipe from the right to see a submenu. Windows Mobile is rich with settings options, making it easier to integrate Windows phones in an enterprise environment.

▲ Windows Mobile 10 has a digital assistant called Cortana that also customizes the user's experience.

WINDOWS MOBILE APPS

The availability of apps for Windows mobile devices is much more limited than that for Android or iOS. Windows apps are obtained through the **Microsoft Store** app. Additionally, like Android apps, Windows Mobile apps can be obtained from third-party websites via the browser on the mobile device.

CHROME OS BY GOOGLE

Figure 9-17   To pin an app to the Start screen, press and hold the app's icon and then tap *Pin to Start*

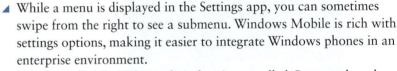

Chrome OS is deeply integrated with Google's Chrome browser: Most of Chrome OS's native apps open directly in the Chrome browser and rely heavily on having an active Internet connection. While there are some apps that will function offline, such as Gmail, Docs, and Calendar, functionality is limited to data that is temporarily stored on the Chromebook until it can again be synced with the user's online account. Chrome OS functions exclusively on Chromebooks, although

Figure 9-18 A Chromebook can be a lightweight laptop, a tablet, or a hybrid laptop-tablet

many manufacturers build and sell Chromebooks. See Figure 9-18.

GET TO KNOW A CHROMEBOOK

Chromebooks come with a variety of external ports, depending on the manufacturer and model. Many feature USB and USB-C ports as well as HDMI. Some include SD card slots for adding extra storage space. The keyboard on a Chromebook (see Figure 9-19) looks similar to the typical laptop keyboard, with a few notable differences. The unique keys mostly run along the top of the keyboard and include these keys: search, previous and next pages, refresh, immersive mode (hides tabs and launcher), and overview mode (shows all open apps). Keyboard shortcuts, a popular feature with Chromebooks, use combinations of key presses to accomplish tasks such as opening a new Chrome window (**ctrl+n**) or tab (**ctrl+t**), taking a screenshot (**ctrl+overview**), locking the screen (**search+L**), and showing all keyboard shortcuts (**ctrl+alt+/**).

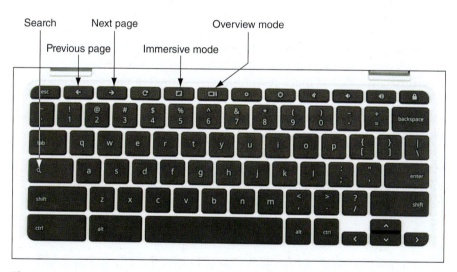

Figure 9-19 A Chromebook keyboard

Figure 9-20 shows the Chrome OS desktop with the Settings app and Chrome browser open. Also notice the shelf on the bottom left and the open status tray on the bottom right. The app launcher is in the shelf. To open the Settings app, click anywhere in the status tray, which opens the tray, and then click the **Settings app** gear icon in the open status tray.

Source: Google

Figure 9-20 The Chrome OS desktop

Chrome OS is automatically updated about every six weeks and includes some significant security measures to protect the computer from malware, including built-in virus protection. Google took a four-pronged approach to security with Chrome OS:

▲ *Sandboxing.* Each tab in the Chrome browser is isolated from the underlying OS and from processes in other tabs.

▲ *Verified boot.* Similar to the Windows Secure boot, it protects the OS from changes being made to its underlying system files, automatically entering recovery mode if modifications are detected.

▲ *Power washing.* The user can perform a simple and quick reset to factory settings in the event a malware infection does manage to take hold.

▲ *Quick updates.* The OS updates itself in the background without user intervention about every six weeks. If an update is needed for a security patch, it can happen within 48 hours.

The end effect is a very stable and secure OS that even security professionals rely on when traveling to techie, hacker, or security conferences, where the persistent threat of hacking attacks is an integral part of the overall experience.

CHROME OS APPS

The Chrome shelf contains icons for important apps; tap an icon to open the app. To view and open any installed app, tap the app launcher icon in the shelf (refer back to Figure 9-20) and tap an app in the launcher (see Figure 9-21). Most apps open in the Chrome browser, and several apps offer Chrome extensions that add functionality to the Chrome browser even when the app is not open. Users can get more apps through the Chrome Web Store app, and some newer Chromebooks also support Android apps downloaded through the Google Play Store app.

⚡ **Caution** Know that if you download Android apps to the Chromebook and then turn off the Play Store app, you'll lose all the Android apps' data and settings from the Chromebook.

Download Android apps from Google Play Store app

Download Chrome apps from Chrome Web Store app

Source: Google

Figure 9-21 Open apps from the Chrome OS app launcher

COMPARING OPEN SOURCE AND CLOSED SOURCE OPERATING SYSTEMS

A+
CORE 1
3.9

A+
CORE 2
1.1, 4.6

Open source operating systems (such as Android and Chrome OS) and closed source operating systems (such as iOS and Windows Mobile) have their advantages and disadvantages. Closed source systems are also called vendor-specific or commercial license operating systems. Here are some key points to consider about releasing or not releasing source code:

◂ Apple carefully guards its iOS source code and internal functions of the OS. Third-party developers of apps have access only to APIs, which are requests to the OS to perform a function, such as to access data provided by the embedded GPS. An app must be tested and approved by Apple before it can be sold in Apple's online App Store. These policies assure users that apps are high quality. It also assures developers they have a central point of contact for users to buy their apps, and their copyrights are better protected.

◂ In the interest of openness and innovation, the Android and Chrome OS source code and the development and sale of apps are not as closely guarded. Apps can be purchased or downloaded from Google Play or Chrome Web Store, but they can also be obtained from other sources such as *amazon.com* or directly from a developer. This freedom comes with a cost because users are not always assured of high-quality, bug-free apps, and developers are not always assured of a convenient market for their apps.

◂ For Android, because any smartphone or tablet manufacturer can modify the source code, many variations of Android exist. These variations can make it difficult for developers to write apps that are compatible with any given Android platform. These inconsistencies can also make it difficult for users to learn to use new Android devices.

CONFIGURING AND SYNCING A MOBILE DEVICE

A+
CORE 1
1.5, 1.6,
1.7, 2.4,
3.1, 3.9

A+
CORE 2
1.1

In this part of the chapter, you learn to configure network connections and to update and back up data, content, and settings on mobile devices. You don't need to memorize these steps—it's sufficient to be familiar with the general idea of where these features are located in the OS and how to use them, especially because the specific steps change with almost every new version of any mobile OS. We'll use examples of both Android and iOS because they're by far the most popular mobile OSs.

> ✎ **Notes** You can follow along with the steps given in the following sections using a real smartphone or tablet (Android or iOS) or you can use an Android emulator. Real Problem 9-1 at the end of this chapter gives you step-by-step instructions to install and configure the free Android Studio, which includes an Android emulator. You can then create emulated Android devices on your screen with real features that work like those on a physical device, including a power button, rotate capability, camera function, and much more.

> ✎ **Notes** Because the Android operating system is open source, manufacturers can customize the OS and how it works. Therefore, specific step-by-step directions will vary from device to device, even when the devices all use the same Android release. Remember that you don't need to memorize the steps—just learn general procedures for supporting a variety of mobile devices.

When you are called on to support a device that you don't own or normally use, it's helpful to begin by looking for how to change settings. Most of the settings you need to use to support a mobile device are contained in the Settings app. Figure 9-22 shows the Settings apps for Android and iOS. Basically, you can open the Settings app and search through its menus and submenus until you find what you need. If you get stuck, check the user guide for the device, which you can download from the device manufacturer's website. The user guide is likely to tell you the detailed steps of how to connect to a network, configure email, update the OS, sync and back up settings and data, secure the device, and what to do when things go wrong. So let's get started.

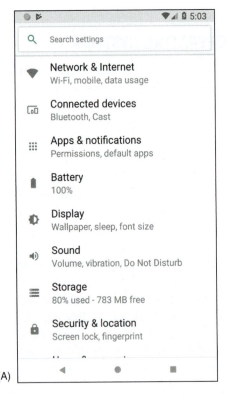

Source: Android, iOS

Figure 9-22   (A) The Android Settings app, and (B) the iOS Settings app

> ✎ **Notes** Most of us rarely follow step-by-step directions when learning to use a new device until when "all else fails, read the directions." This part of the chapter can give you an idea of what to look for, and you can likely figure out the specific steps for yourself.

MOBILE DEVICE LAN/WAN CONNECTIONS

A mobile device might have several antennas—primarily Wi-Fi, GPS, Bluetooth, NFC, and cellular. The device uses a Wi-Fi or cellular antenna to connect to a LAN (local area network) or WAN (wide area network) and uses Bluetooth or NFC to connect to a PAN (personal area network). Settings on the device allow you to enable or disable each antenna. Network connections are configured using the Settings app. Let's look at LAN and WAN network connections first, then we'll look at technologies used for connecting mobile device accessories in PANs.

> **✎ Notes** You can automatically disable the antennas in a mobile device that can transmit signals by enabling **airplane mode** so that the device can neither transmit nor receive the signals. Many newer devices do not disable the GPS or NFC antennas; GPS only receives and never transmits, and NFC signals don't reach very far. While airplane mode is on, you can manually enable some wireless connections, such as Bluetooth or Wi-Fi.

> **★ A+ Exam Tip** The A+ Core 1 exam might give you a scenario that expects you to decide how to configure a Wi-Fi, cellular data, Bluetooth, or VPN connection on a mobile device.

WI-FI CONNECTION

Most mobile devices have Wi-Fi capability and can connect to a Wi-Fi local wireless network. On the Wi-Fi settings screen, you can add a Wi-Fi connection, manage existing networks, view available Wi-Fi hotspots, see which Wi-Fi network you are connected to, turn Wi-Fi off and on, and decide whether the device should ask the user before joining a Wi-Fi network. When the device is within range of Wi-Fi networks, it displays the list of networks. Select one to connect. If the Wi-Fi network is secured, enter the security key to complete the connection. To change a network's settings, tap the name of the network (see Figure 9-23). Searching for a Wi-Fi network can drain battery power. To make a battery charge last longer, disable Wi-Fi when you're not using it.

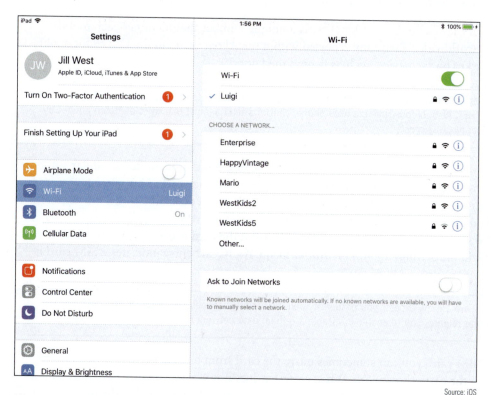

Source: iOS

Figure 9-23 Configure Wi-Fi connection settings

TETHERING AND MOBILE HOTSPOTS

When a mobile device is connected to the Internet by way of its cellular network, recall from Chapter 3 that you can allow other computers and devices to use this same connection. For example, in Figure 9-24, the smartphone is tethered by USB to a laptop so that the laptop can use the cellular network to connect to the Internet. If the smartphone has Wi-Fi capabilities, it can create its own Wi-Fi hotspot for other computers

Figure 9-24 Tether your smartphone to your laptop using a USB cable

and devices to connect to wirelessly. An app on the smartphone controls these connections. To use your phone for tethering and for providing mobile hotspots, your carrier subscription must allow it.

CELLULAR DATA CONNECTION

Smartphones and some laptops, tablets, and wearable mobile devices can connect to a cellular network if they have cellular capability and a subscription to the cellular network carrier. Recall from Chapter 3 that a cellular network provided by a carrier (for example, AT&T or Verizon) is used for voice, text, and data communication.

A cellular network uses GSM or CDMA for voice and another layer of technology for data transmissions, such as 3G, 4G, 5G, and LTE. GSM and LTE require a SIM card installed in the device, and CDMA does not use a SIM card unless the network is also using LTE, which does require a SIM card. To make a cellular data connection, you must have a subscription with your carrier that includes a cellular data plan.

Here is information that might be used when a connection is first made to the network:

▲ The **IMEI (International Mobile Equipment Identity)** is a unique number that identifies each mobile phone or tablet device worldwide. It's usually reported within the *About* menu in the OS, and it might also be printed on a sticker on the device, such as behind the battery.

> **✎ Notes** If your phone gets stolen and you notify your carrier, the carrier can block its use based on the IMEI and alert other carriers to the stolen IMEI. Also, before buying a used phone, check its IMEI against blacklists of stolen phones by doing a Google search on *imei blacklist check*.

▲ The **IMSI (International Mobile Subscriber Identity)** is a unique number that identifies a cellular subscription for a device or subscriber, along with its home country and mobile network. This number is stored on the SIM card for networks that use SIM cards. For networks that don't use SIM cards, the number is kept in a database maintained by the carrier and is associated with the IMEI.

▲ The ICCID (Integrated Circuit Card ID) identifies the SIM card if the card is used. To know if a device is using a SIM card, look in the Settings app on the *About* menu. An ICCID entry indicates a SIM card is present.

> **★ A+ Exam Tip** The A+ Core 1 exam expects you to identify and distinguish between the IMEI and the IMSI, and might give you a scenario that requires you to enable or disable a cellular data network connection.

When a carrier uses a SIM card, you can sometimes move the card from one device to another and the new device can connect to the carrier's network. When a carrier does not use a SIM card, you must contact the carrier and request permission to switch devices. If the carrier accepts the new device, the new IMEI will be entered in the carrier's database.

The carrier typically configures the phone to make calls on its network; however, you might find that you want to disable cellular data at times, or disable cellular roaming. The advantage of disabling cellular data and using Wi-Fi for data transmissions is that these transmissions are not charged against your cellular data subscription plan. Also, Wi-Fi is generally faster than most cellular connections. Disabling roaming can prevent roaming charges on your bill incurred from using other carriers' cellular networks when you travel outside your home territory.

To disable roaming on an Android device, go to the Network & Internet menu in the Settings app, tap **Mobile network**, then turn off **Mobile data** or **Roaming**. On an iOS device, open the Settings app, tap **Cellular Data**, then turn off **Cellular Data**. Next, tap **Cellular Data Options**, then turn off roaming.

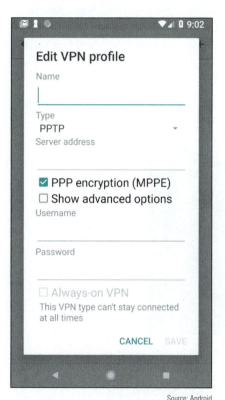

Edit VPN profile

Name

Type
PPTP
Server address

☑ PPP encryption (MPPE)
☐ Show advanced options
Username

Password

☐ Always-on VPN
This VPN type can't stay connected at all times

CANCEL SAVE

Source: Android

Figure 9-25 Configure a VPN connection

If you have roaming enabled, especially for a CDMA device, you'll want to keep the PRL (Preferred Roaming List) updated. The PRL is a database file that lists the preferred service providers or radio frequencies your carrier wants the device to use when outside your home network. You can reset or update the list in the Settings app. For Android devices, go to the **System updates** menu and tap **Update PRL**. For an iOS device, open the Settings app, tap **General**, then scroll down and tap **Reset**, **Subscriber Services**, and **Reprovision Account**.

VPN CONNECTION

Like desktop computers, a mobile device can be configured to communicate information securely over a virtual private network (VPN) connection. To create a VPN connection in the Settings app, tap **VPN** and then add a new VPN connection. Follow directions to complete the connection, which will require you to know the type of encryption protocol used (PPTP, L2TP, or IPsec), the IP address or domain name of the VPN server, and the user name and password to the corporate network. Figure 9-25 shows the configuration options on an Android smartphone. In addition to the built-in Android VPN client shown in the figure, some Android devices also provide proprietary VPN configuration options. To access VPN settings in iOS, open the Settings app, tap **General**, and then tap **VPN**.

MOBILE DEVICE ACCESSORIES AND THEIR PAN CONNECTIONS

**A+
CORE 1
1.5, 1.6,
2.4, 3.1,
3.9**

You can buy all kinds of accessories for mobile devices, such as wireless keyboards, speakers, earbuds, headsets, game pads, docking stations, printers, extra battery packs and chargers, USB adapters, memory cards (usually the microSD form factor) to expand storage space, credit card readers for accepting payments by credit card, and protective covers for waterproofing. For example, Figure 9-26 shows a car docking station for a smartphone. Using this car dock, the smartphone serves as a GPS device giving driving directions.

Figure 9-26 A smartphone and a car docking station

When buying accessories for a mobile device, be sure to check what ports and slots are available on the device. For example, many mobile devices no longer include replaceable batteries. Current iPhones no longer have audio ports—to use a wired headset, you have to plug a dongle into the Lightning port. Some mobile devices have a slot for a memory card, which might be located on the side of the case or inside it; however, Apple mobile devices and many others don't offer this feature. Figure 9-27 shows a memory card slot on an Android tablet, and Figure 9-28 shows a MicroSD card.

Figure 9-27   An Android device might provide a memory card slot to allow for extra storage

Figure 9-28   A mobile device might use a MicroSD card to add extra flash memory storage to the device

WIRED CONNECTIONS FOR ACCESSORIES

Smartphones, tablets, and wearable devices can make a wired connection to a computer. This connection can be used to charge the device, download software updates, upload data to the computer, back up data, and restore software or data. The device's port used for power and communication may be a type of USB port or a proprietary, vendor-specific port. Some USB connectors used for this purpose include microUSB (see Figure 9-29A), the smaller miniUSB (see Figure 9-29B), and the newer USB-C (see Figure 9-29C). Newer Apple iPhones, iPods, and iPads use the proprietary Lightning port and connector for power and communication (see Figure 9-30).

(A)

(B)

(C)

Figure 9-29   Some mobile devices may connect to a computer's USB port by way of a (A) microUSB, (B) miniUSB, or (C) USB-C cable

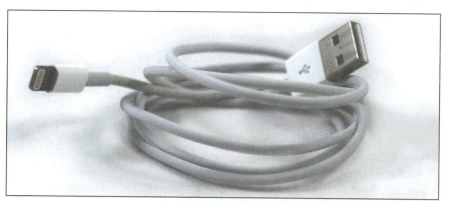

Figure 9-30 A Lightning cable by Apple, Inc., has a USB connector for the computer end and a Lightning connector for an iPhone or iPad

WIRELESS CONNECTIONS FOR ACCESSORIES

Mobile devices typically have the capability to connect to other nearby wireless devices and accessories using a Bluetooth, IR, or NFC wireless connection:

Figure 9-31 An iPad and a wireless keyboard can connect using Bluetooth

▲ *Bluetooth.* Bluetooth is a short-range wireless technology to connect two devices in a small PAN. To create a Bluetooth connection, the two devices must be paired, a process you'll learn more about later in this chapter. Figure 9-31 shows an iPad connected to a keyboard using Bluetooth.

▲ *Infrared.* Infrared (IR) is a wireless connection that requires an unobstructed "line of sight" between transmitter and receiver, which must be within about 30 m of each other. IR relies on light waves just below the visible red-light portion of the spectrum. This means you can't see infrared light, but you can feel it as heat. TV or other multimedia devices and a remote control often use an IR wireless interface. Apps on smartphones and tablets that support IR can be used in place of an IR remote control.

▲ *NFC.* Near Field Communication (NFC) is a wireless technology that establishes a communication link between two NFC devices that are within 10 cm (about 4 inches) of each other. For example, when two smartphones get within close range, they can use NFC to exchange contact information. NFC connections are also used for contactless credit card payments at a store. An NFC tag (see Figure 9-32) contains a small microchip that can be embedded in just about anything, including a key chain tag, printed flyer, or billboard (see Figure 9-32). The NFC tag dispenses information to any NFC-enabled smartphone or other device that comes within 4 inches of the tag. Learn more about NFC at *nearfieldcommunication.org*.

Figure 9-32 These programmable NFC tags have sticky backs for attaching to a flat surface like a wall, desk, or car dashboard

APPLYING | CONCEPTS   PAIRING BLUETOOTH DEVICES

To configure a Bluetooth connection, complete the following steps:

1. Turn on the Bluetooth device, such as a speaker, headset, or keyboard, to which you want to connect your mobile device.

2. Enable Bluetooth on that device and enable pairing mode. Sometimes just turning on Bluetooth enables pairing automatically for a limited period of time. The device might have a pairing button or combination of buttons to enable pairing. When you press this button, a pairing light blinks, indicating the device is ready to receive a Bluetooth connection. This makes the device discoverable, which means it's transmitting a signal to identify itself to nearby Bluetooth devices.

3. On your mobile device, turn on Bluetooth. The mobile device searches for Bluetooth devices. If it discovers the Bluetooth device, tap it to connect. The two Bluetooth devices now begin the pairing process.

4. The devices might require a code to complete the Bluetooth connection. For example, in Figure 9-33, an iPad and Bluetooth keyboard are pairing. To complete the connection, enter the four-digit code on the keyboard.

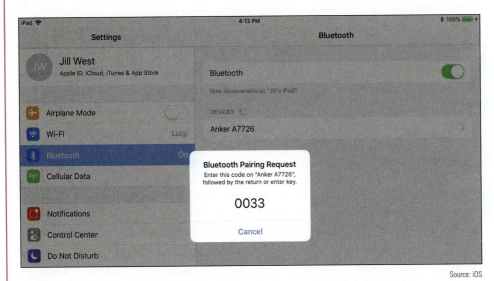

Source: iOS

Figure 9-33   A code is required to pair these two Bluetooth devices

5. Test the connection. For an audio device, play a video or audio recording on the mobile device, and for a keyboard, type into a notes application or text box.

> ★ **A+ Exam Tip**   The A+ Core 1 exam might give you a scenario that requires you to pair Bluetooth devices and then test connectivity after the connection is established.

CONFIGURING MOBILE DEVICE EMAIL

A+ CORE 1 1.6, 3.9

Using a personal computer or mobile device, email can be managed in one of two ways:

- ◢ *Using a browser.* In a browser, go to the website of your email provider and manage your email on the website. In this situation, your email is never downloaded to your computer or mobile device, and your messages remain on the email server until you delete them.
- ◢ *Using an email client.* An email client application, such as Microsoft Outlook, can be installed on your personal computer or on your mobile device. The app can either download

email messages to your device (using the POP3 protocol) or can manage messages on the server (using the IMAP protocol). When the app downloads messages, you can configure the server to continue to store these messages for later use or delete the messages from the server.

Email providers include Gmail (by Google), iCloud (by Apple), Yahoo! (owned by Verizon), or Outlook/Hotmail/Live (Microsoft's public email services for individuals). Microsoft also offers Exchange, its private enterprise email service that is hosted on corporation or ISP servers, or Exchange Online, which is hosted on Microsoft servers. As for apps on your mobile device, Android includes the Gmail app, which can be used with any email provider, and iOS includes its Mail app. In either OS, a different email app can be installed, such as Microsoft Outlook, Google Inbox, Yahoo Mail, or K-9 Mail.

To configure email on a mobile device, open the email app and add an email account directly in the app. Here is the information you'll need to configure an email app on a mobile device:

▲ *Your email address and password.* If your email account is with Google, Microsoft, Apple, or Yahoo!, your email address and password are all you need because the OS can automatically set up these accounts.

If your email account is with any other provider, you'll also need the following information:

▲ *Names of your incoming and outgoing email servers.* To find this information, check the support page of your email provider's website. For example, the server you use for incoming mail might be *imap.mycompany.com*, and the server you use for outgoing mail might be *smtp.mycompany.com*. The two servers might have the same name.

▲ *Type of protocol your incoming server uses.* The incoming server will use POP3 or IMAP4. Using IMAP4, you are managing your email on the server. For example, you can move a message from one folder to another and that change happens on the remote server. Using POP3, the messages are downloaded to your device where you manage them locally. Most POP3 mail servers give you the option to leave the messages on the server or delete them after they are downloaded.

▲ *Security used.* Most likely, if email is encrypted during transmission, the configuration will happen automatically without your involvement. However, if you have problems, you need to be aware of these possible settings:

   ▲ An IMAP server uses port 143 unless it is secured and using SSL. IMAP over SSL (IMAPS) uses port 993.

   ▲ A POP3 server uses port 110 unless it is secured and using SSL. POP3 over SSL uses port 995.

   ▲ Outgoing email is normally sent using the protocol SMTP. A more secure alternative is S/MIME (Secure/Multipurpose Internet Mail Extensions), which encrypts the email message and includes a digital signature to validate the identity of the sender. This feature is enabled after the email account is set up on the device. The activation process is automated for accounts through Microsoft Exchange and can be set up manually for other types of accounts. Look for this security option on the Advanced settings screen.

> ★ **A+ Exam Tip** The A+ Core 1 exam expects you to know about POP3 and IMAP4, and the SSL and port settings they use, and might require you to use this information in configuring email on a mobile device. Before you sit for the exam, memorize the ports (including secure ports) and protocols discussed in this section and understand how this information is used to configure email on a mobile device. A project at the end of this chapter will give you practice with this process.

SYNCING AND BACKING UP MOBILE DEVICES

A+ CORE 1 1.6, 1.7, 3.9

A+ CORE 2 1.1

Synchronization, backup, and restore functions are much simpler now than they were in the past and require almost no attention from the user. Also, compatibility concerns between operating systems are less of an issue now as manufacturers continue to standardize file types and communication protocols. In this part of the chapter, you learn to sync with online accounts or third-party apps, sync with your desktop, update the OS, and back up settings. First, here's the difference between syncing and backups:

   ▲ Syncing mirrors app data and other content among your devices and/or the cloud that use the same Apple or Google account. A photo taken or a calendar event created on one device is available in the cloud and all other devices. As another example, when you sync email, the Gmail app on your phone will show the same email messages and configuration settings as the Gmail interface in your browser on your computer.

▲ Backups are copies of app data, configuration settings, and other content stored in case you need it to recover from a failed, lost, or corrupted device.

SYNC TO THE CLOUD

Syncing data to the cloud means that you can access your data from any device or any computer with a web browser connected to the Internet. (Google products work best in Google Chrome, of course.) You can sync contacts, application purchases and installations, email, pictures, music, videos, calendars, bookmarks, documents, location data on map apps, social media data, e-books, and even passwords.

> ⚡ **Caution** It's not safe to store passwords in your browser. It's much more secure to use a password manager app, such as KeePass or LastPass. KeePass stores passwords only on the local computer, which is more secure but less convenient. LastPass can store passwords in the cloud and sync passwords across devices, which is more convenient but less secure.

When you're signed in to your Google or Apple account, both Google's cloud and Apple's iCloud can automatically sync nearly all content created in their OS-native apps across your devices. (You can choose whether to sync only over Wi-Fi so syncing doesn't use up your cellular data allotment.) Here's how it works:

▲ *Google storage in the cloud.* Android syncs Google apps or third-party apps on your device to your Google storage at *google.com*; the first 15 GB of cloud storage is free. Use the Settings app on your device to manage what is synced. To access your content in the cloud, use any browser to go to *google.com* and sign in to your Google account. A single sign-on (SSO), also called mutual authentication for multiple services, gives access to Gmail, Google Drive, Calendar, Contacts, and all other Google apps. Click the **Google apps** icon to select different apps, as shown in Figure 9-34. Many third-party apps can also sync their data through the Google account the mobile device is registered to, although the sync settings might be managed within the app rather than through the device's Settings app.

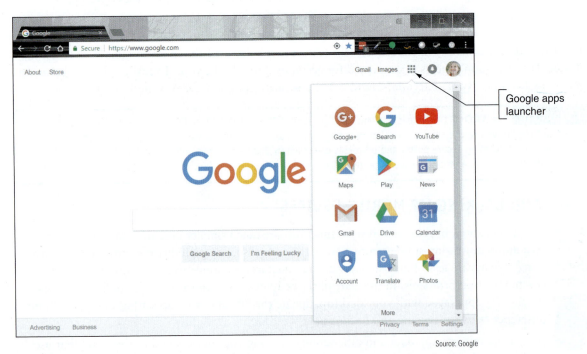

Source: Google

Figure 9-34   Access Android content at *google.com*

▲ *iCloud storage in the cloud*. iOS syncs content to the Apple website at *icloud.com*; the first 5 GB of cloud storage is free. To set up iCloud syncing, go to the **Settings** app on your iPad or iPhone, tap the user name, and tap **iCloud** to go to the screen (see Figure 9-35) where you can decide which apps and data get synced and manage your iCloud storage.

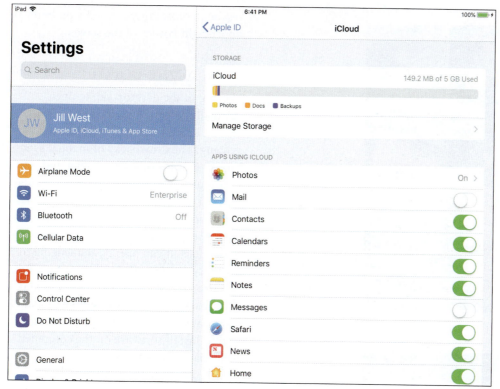

Source: iOS

Figure 9-35   Manage iCloud synchronization on a mobile device

You can access synced data in the cloud from your computer by signing in to your Apple account at *icloud.com*. For example, the Launchpad or home page for your iCloud content (see Figure 9-36) shows synced apps, including Mail, Contacts, Calendar, iCloud Drive, and Photos.

Source: iCloud.com

Figure 9-36   Access iOS content at *icloud.com*

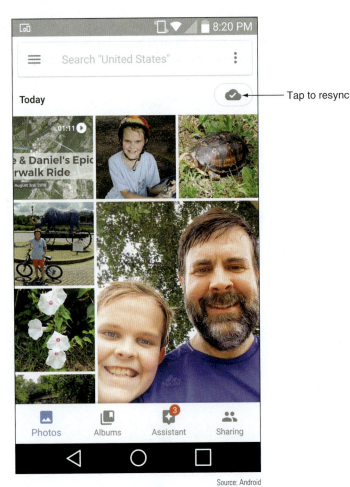

Tap to resync

Figure 9-37   If content fails to sync automatically, resync manually

Source: Android

If you notice an account is not syncing correctly, resync information for the account through the app that holds the data. For example, Figure 9-37 shows the Photos app on an Android phone. To resync photos, tap the cloud icon in the upper-right corner of the screen.

SYNC TO THE DESKTOP

Syncing to the desktop can happen manually as you think to do it or you can set up your device for automatic syncing. The drawbacks of manual syncing are that it's time consuming and the user must remember to do it on a regular basis. If it's been six months since the last sync and the phone or tablet dies, the user loses six months' worth of photos and videos. It can also be challenging to set up syncing to cover all that you might want to sync, such as text messages and third-party app data and settings. Manual or automatic syncing might require you to install software on the computer to manage the syncing.

Here are some manual syncing options:

▲ *USB connection and File Explorer.* The tried-and-true method for syncing photos and videos from a phone or tablet directly to the desktop is to plug the device into a USB connection with the computer (or a Lightning to USB connection on a Mac) and copy files from the device to the computer. For a Windows computer, you can use File Explorer to copy files from the device to your computer, which preserves the original quality of the media files, unlike some cloud-based sync services, which reduce resolution before storing in the cloud. An advantage of this type of syncing to a computer is that no extra software needs to be installed on your computer.

▲ *iTunes with iOS.* For iOS devices, you can install iTunes on a computer and use it to sync and back up the mobile device. After you install and start iTunes, connect your mobile device through a USB connection and iTunes will then recognize the device. For example, Figure 9-38 shows the iTunes window on a Mac with backup options at the top right and sync options at the lower right. After selecting the sync or backup settings you want, click **Sync** to sync the device and computer or **Back Up Now** to back up the device to your computer.

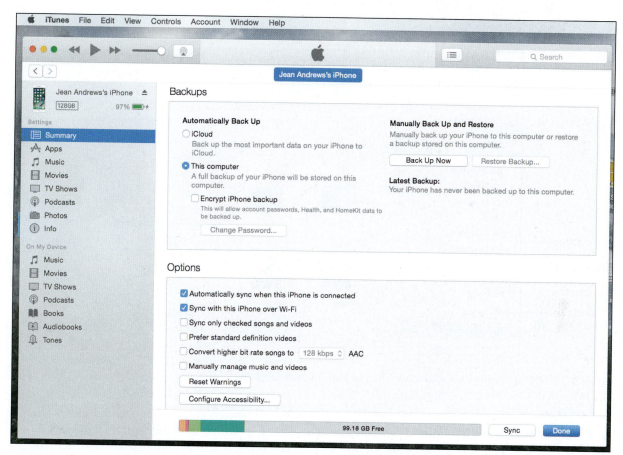

Figure 9-38 iTunes can sync or back up a mobile device with a Mac or Windows computer

The following three options provide automatic syncing to the desktop. Each option requires you to install an application on the computer and configure the sync settings. Before you install the app, make sure the computer meets the minimum hardware and OS requirements needed to support the app:

▲ *Third-party syncing apps.* OneDrive, Dropbox, and other apps provide cloud-based file storage services and will sync entire folders in the background with no user intervention required to any computer or device that has the app installed and signed in. Make a change on one device and you immediately see it on another or in the cloud. OneDrive, Dropbox, and other syncing apps can install in Android and iOS mobile devices and in Windows and Linux on the desktop. Figure 9-39 shows File Explorer on a Windows 10 computer with synced folders for iCloud Photos, iCloud Drive, Google Drive, Dropbox, and OneDrive, all of which are also installed on one or more of the user's mobile devices.

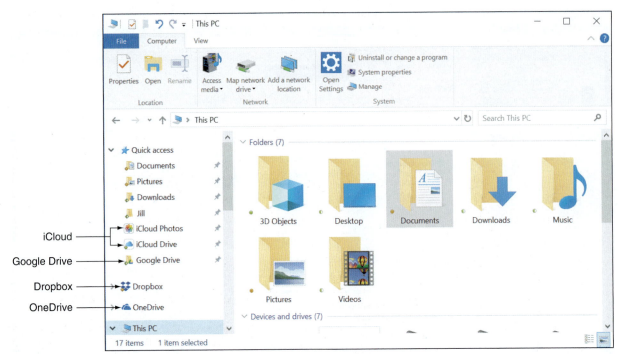

Figure 9-39   Use synchronization apps to sync files to your Windows computer

▲ *Backup & Sync app with Android.* Sync an Android device to a Windows or Mac computer using the Backup & Sync app. When you install the app on your computer, it installs a Google Drive folder and can automatically sync files to the mobile device, the computer, and the cloud.

▲ *iCloud Drive with iOS.* As you know, you can sync app settings and other data on your iOS device to the Apple cloud at *icloud.com*. In addition, when you turn on iCloud Drive, the Files app on an iPad or iPhone syncs files across devices and you can share these files with people in your contacts list. You can also install the iCloud Drive app on a computer so that files can sync to your desktop (refer back to Figure 9-39), which is similar to the way Dropbox works. To turn on iCloud Drive on a device, open the **Settings** app, tap the user name, then tap **iCloud**. Verify that **iCloud Drive** is turned on and syncing the apps you want to sync. If iCloud Drive is installed on your Windows computer, content will also sync there.

SYNC AN ACTIVITY WITH HANDOFF AND CONTINUE ON PC

In addition to syncing files and other content, you can sync activity in progress. For example, suppose you're visiting a webpage on your smartphone, and you want to open that webpage in your desktop's browser without searching for it again. Or suppose you're working on a document on one device, and you want to continue your work on the other device. You can transfer the activity from the mobile device to the desktop and back, picking up on one device where you left off on the other.

▲ *Apple Handoff.* In macOS and iOS, the feature is called Handoff. Enable Handoff in the Settings menu on the iPhone or iPad and in the System Preferences menu on the Mac. When the device and computer are on the same Wi-Fi or Bluetooth network and signed in to the same Apple account, the Handoff icon appears on each device for activities transferrable from the other. Tap or click the icon to pick up an activity from the other device.

▲ *Microsoft Launcher or Continue on PC.* Windows 10 offers an Android app called Microsoft Launcher or an iOS app called Continue on PC. Both of these apps add a share option, called Continue on PC, into certain activities you perform on your phone and send to a Windows computer (see Figure 9-40A).

Android **launchers** are apps that can replace Android's default home screen (called the Pixel Launcher) to add different features and functionality. In the case of Microsoft Launcher, as shown in Figure 9-40B and Figure 9-40C, the app makes the Android's home screen look and function more like a Windows Mobile phone, including synchronization with your Windows desktop. Compare the home screen in Figure 9-40B with the home screen in Figure 9-6 to identify subtle differences. To get started with Windows 10, open the **Settings** app and click **Phone**.

(A)   (B)   (C)

Source: Android

Figure 9-40 (A) Tap Continue on PC to pick up an Android activity on your Windows desktop; (B) the Microsoft launcher has made subtle changes to the Android home screen; (C) the launcher's All apps screen is similar to the Windows Start screen

> ✏️ **Notes** Many apps also include the ability to sync activities between devices, either within one user's account or between accounts. Google Chrome, for example, syncs browsing history, settings, and bookmarks with all devices signed into Chrome using the same account. Microsoft's OneNote syncs notes across devices and can sync notes to devices that belong to other people when you share a notebook.

Source: Android Auto

Figure 9-41 Android Auto lets users check the weather, send a Hangouts message, or make a phone call using their vehicle's touch screen

SYNC TO AN AUTOMOBILE

Many newer automobiles offer the option to use Bluetooth to pair a smartphone with the car's computer for easy access to the phone's music, navigation, and call features through the car's media screen. While this is not true synchronization because most of the phone's content stays on the phone and is not stored on the car's computer, it does allow the user to control the phone through the car's control panel or touch screen. Figure 9-41 shows information from an Android phone on a Kia Sedona's touch screen using the Android Auto app. Apple devices use the Apple CarPlay app instead. Both apps include navigation, music, phone, and text message activities to interact with the user directly on the car's screen.

> **✎ Notes** You can emulate a car's touch screen in Android Studio for testing apps in the Android Auto interface. You'll need to download and install the testing tool Desktop Head Unit (DHU) in the SDK Manager, and you'll need a real smartphone to connect with the DHU (not an emulated one). Learn more at *developer.android.com/training/auto/testing/*.

UPDATE THE OS

Updates to the Android OS are automatically pushed to the device from the manufacturer. Because each manufacturer maintains its own versions of Android, these updates might not come at the same time Google announces a major update, which limits availability of updates for some devices. Also, vendors don't continue to make these modifications indefinitely—eventually a device ages out of the vendor's updates in what's called an end-of-life limitation. When the device does receive notice of an update, it might display a message asking permission to install the update. With some devices, you can also manually check for updates at any time, although not all devices provide this option.

To see if manual updates can be performed on your device, go to the **Settings** app and tap **About**. On the About screen, tap **System updates**, **Software update**, or a similar item. The device turns to the manufacturer's website for information and reports any available updates.

Before installing an OS update, you might want to go to the website and read the release instructions about the update, called Product Release Instructions (PRI), which typically describe new features or patches the update provides and how long the update will take. Later, if a device is giving problems after an OS update, check the PRI for information that might help you understand the nature of the problem.

To check for and install updates on an iOS device, you must first be signed in to your device with an Apple ID, which requires an associated credit card number. Then open the **Settings** app and tap **General** in the left pane. On the right side, tap **Software Update**. Any available updates will be reported here and can be installed.

It's a good idea to back up your mobile device's files, settings, configurations, and profiles before performing an update. How to back up a device is discussed next.

BACK UP AND RECOVERY

Suppose your mobile device is lost, stolen, or damaged beyond repair. Backups and recovery options need to be in place to prepare for these events. Here are some options:

- *File-level backup.* Syncing emails, contacts, calendars, photos, and other data through online accounts or to your computer is called a file-level backup, because each file is backed up individually. File-level backups, however, don't include your app data or OS settings, such as your Wi-Fi passwords, account profile, or device and app configuration.
- *Partial image-level backup.* A true image-level backup includes everything on the device and can completely restore the device to its previous state. However, a mobile device OS offers only a partial image-level backup that includes settings, native app data, Wi-Fi passwords, the account profile, and device and app configuration. Third-party app configurations and their data are not included in the OS backup.
- *Combination of file-level and partial image-level backups.* To prepare for catastrophic failure or loss, you need to use both backup methods: Sync data files to your computer or the cloud and use the OS backup for other types of data and settings. Make sure that syncing and backups include critical apps, their configuration, and data. In reality, though, backups for mobile devices will miss a few configurations, such as app installations or third-party app configurations. For this reason, you might need to use an additional method of backing up data and settings for any critical third-party applications.

Generally, you can back up to the cloud or to your computer. Android provides a way to back up to Google Drive:

- *Google Drive backup.* To enable Android's backup feature, open the **Settings** app, go to **System**, and then tap **Backup**. Make sure that **Back up to Google Drive** is turned on and change the backup account if needed. You can also fine-tune what content is included in the backup. Your backup data is stored on Google's servers and is associated with your Google account.

◢ *Back up to computer.* You need a third-party app or a manufacturer's app to create a detailed backup of the device configuration and content to your computer.

iOS can back up to a computer using iTunes or to the cloud using iCloud. The best practice is to use both methods:

◢ *iCloud Backup.* Go to **Settings** and tap the user name, then tap **iCloud**. Scroll down and tap **iCloud Backup**. When you turn on iCloud Backup, it backs up whenever the device is plugged into a power source and connected to Wi-Fi, the screen is locked, and there's enough unused iCloud storage to hold the backup. However, you can also create a new backup at any time by clicking **Back Up Now**. iCloud backs up app data, call history, device settings, text, photos, and videos unless these items are already included in iCloud syncing.

◢ *iTunes backup.* Open iTunes on your computer and connect your mobile device to the computer. You might have to enter your device passcode. In iTunes, select your device and click **Back Up Now**.

When deciding whether to back up to the cloud or a computer, consider that cloud backups using Google Drive or iCloud are readily accessible from any computer and happen automatically when you're connected to Wi-Fi. The disadvantages are that you have less control over security of your data and you have to pay for cloud storage.

Here are two situations when you might want to recover from a backup:

◢ *To the original mobile device.* If you have reset the device while troubleshooting a problem and have a backup in the cloud, sign in to the device using your Google or Apple account. You will then be given the option to recover from backup or to set up the device as a new device. You'll learn more about resetting a device later in this chapter. For iOS, if you have a backup on your computer and connect the device to your computer, iTunes gives you the option to recover from backup.

◢ *To a new device.* The same recovery options are offered when you first sign in to a new mobile device using your Google or Apple account—or, for iOS, when you connect a new device to your computer and the iTunes app.

> 🖉 **Notes** If you're about to buy a new phone or tablet, be sure to back up your old device before you switch your carrier service or your Google or Apple account to the new device. If possible, also back up your phone or tablet before taking it in for repair at a service center.

Whatever backup method you use, it's important to occasionally test the backup recovery process to verify that you know how to use it, the recovery works, and you know exactly what's being recovered. After you test the recovery process, you might realize you need additional backup methods in place to make sure everything is covered.

SECURING A MOBILE DEVICE

Because smartphones and tablets are so mobile, they get stolen more often than other types of computers. Therefore, protecting data on a mobile device is especially important. Consider what might be revealed about your life if someone stole your smartphone or tablet and the data on it.

◢ Your apps and personal data could expose email, calendars, call logs, voice mail, text messages, Dropbox, iCloud Drive, Google Maps, Hangouts, Gmail, QuickMemo, YouTube, Amazon, Facebook, videos, photos, notes, contacts, and bookmarks and browsing history in web browsers.

◢ Videos and photos might reveal private information and be tagged with date and time stamps and GPS locations.

◢ Network connection settings include Wi-Fi security keys, email configuration settings, user names, and email addresses.

◢ Purchasing patterns and history as well as credit card information might be stored—or at least accessible for use—in mobile payment apps, in apps developed by retailers, through membership card databases, or through email records.

To keep your data safe, consider controlling access to your devices and consider what apps you can use to protect the data. These methods are discussed in this part of the chapter along with BYOD (Bring Your Own Device) policies that might be used in an enterprise environment to secure corporate data stored on a device.

DEVICE ACCESS CONTROLS

Consider the following lock methods to control access to the device.

A+
CORE 2
2.8

◢ *Screen lock.* A screen lock requires the correct input to unlock the device. Mobile devices provide a variety of options for unlocking the screen. As the complexity of a lock code increases, so does the security of the device:

  ◢ *Swipe lock.* Swipe your finger across the screen to unlock the device. (This is not very secure but it prevents a pocket dial.)

  ◢ *PIN lock.* Enter a numeric code with numbers.

  ◢ *Passcode lock.* Enter an alphanumeric code with letters and/or numbers.

  ◢ *Pattern lock.* Draw a pattern across a display of dots on the screen.

  ◢ *Fingerprint lock.* Use a specialized scanner that collects an optical, electrical, or ultrasonic reading of a person's fingerprint and then compares this information to stored data.

  ◢ *Face lock.* Use the device's camera to perform facial recognition.

Figure 9-42A shows screen lock options on an Android smartphone, including a swipe lock, pattern lock, PIN lock, and passcode lock. Android also allows the user to set exceptions to the screen lock, as shown in Figure 9-42B. Using these options, the smartphone might stay unlocked when it detects it's being carried or when it detects its location, such as the user's home or office.

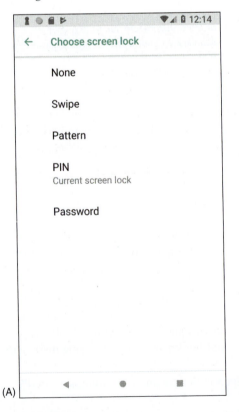
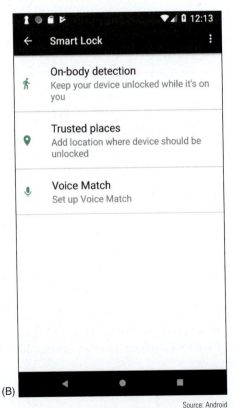

Source: Android

Figure 9-42   (A) Screen lock options on an Android smartphone; (B) Smart Lock exceptions to keep the screen unlocked

> **Notes** Fingerprint and facial recognition are both forms of biometric authentication. **Biometric authentication** collects biological data about a person's fingerprints, handprints, face, voice, retina, iris, and handwritten signatures to confirm the person's identity. In some states, you cannot legally be forced to give your phone's password to investigators, but you can be required to give your fingerprint.

▲ *Restrict failed login attempts.* When you set a screen lock, you can specify that data be erased after a certain number of failed login attempts, or you can simply block further attempts. With iOS, the device locks after six failed attempts and you must wait before you can try again. If the device permanently locks and you've created a backup in iTunes, you can sync to the backup to access the phone. Otherwise, you'll have to use recovery mode, which erases the device. With Android devices, login attempt restriction options vary by manufacturer. You can change the lock code online using the device's associated Google account on the Find My Device website (*google.com/android/find*), which also locates the device.

> **Caution** If you set your device to erase data after failed login attempts, be sure to keep backups of your data and other content. A small child can pick up your smartphone and accidentally erase all your data with a few finger taps.

▲ *Full device encryption.* Both Android and iOS devices offer full device encryption, which encrypts all the stored data on a device. Encrypting a device's stored data makes it essentially useless to a thief. However, encryption might slow down device performance and data is only as safe as the strength of the password keeping the data encrypted. Also, data might be vulnerable again when it's being viewed or transmitted because device encryption only encrypts data while it's stored on the device, not when it's in motion or in use. When enabling encryption for the first time, it might take an hour or more to complete the encryption. Also, if the encryption process is interrupted during that time, some or all of the data will be lost.

▲ *Multifactor authentication.* Smartphones can be used to authenticate to services and networks (for example, email, cloud services, corporate network accounts, VPNs, or even Facebook) as one of the two or more techniques required for multifactor authentication. For example, you might first enter a password on a computer as the first authentication and then a code is sent as a text message to your smartphone; you must then enter the code in the computer as the second authentication. Another example might be that you enter a code in a computer that is at a certain location and the system you're signing in to checks the GPS location of your smartphone to make sure it is near the computer. In addition, authenticator applications can be installed on your smartphone and configured to provide multifactor authentication support for a huge variety of account types. Popular examples are Google Authenticator or Microsoft Authenticator, both of which work on either Android or iOS devices, or an independent competitor like Authy (*authy.com*), which also works in Chrome OS.

SOFTWARE SECURITY

A+ CORE 2 2.8

In addition to controlling access to a device, software can help secure data. Most of the methods discussed here require the user to understand the importance of a security measure and how to use it:

▲ *OS updates and patches.* Apply OS updates and patches to plug up security holes. Android automatically pushes updates to many of its devices, but iOS devices and many other mobile devices require manual updates.

▲ *Antivirus/anti-malware.* Because Apple closely protects iOS and its apps, it's unlikely an Apple device will need anti-malware software. The Android OS and apps are not as closely guarded, so Android anti-malware apps are recommended. Before installing one, be sure to read reviews about it. Most of the major anti-malware software companies provide Android anti-malware apps.

▲ *Trusted sources.* iOS devices are limited to installing apps only from Apple's App Store. Android and Windows devices can download and install apps from other sources, only some of which are trustworthy. Trusted sources generally include well-known app stores, such as Amazon Appstore for Android (*amazon.com/appstore*) or SlideME (*slideme.org*). Other trusted sources might include your bank's website, your employer, or your school, although often their apps are posted in Google Play (*play.google.com*) as well. Before downloading an app, look for lots of reviewer feedback as one measure of safety.

Android versions before Oreo allow you to limit app sources to only the Google Play Store, which can help reduce the threat of untrusted sources for apps. In the **Settings** app, tap **Security** and make sure that **Unknown sources** is unchecked. Beginning with Oreo, you can decide which apps are allowed to install other apps. To choose, go to **Settings > Apps & notifications > Advanced > Special app access > Install unknown apps** (see Figure 9-43A). If you decide to use third-party app sources, be sure you already have a good anti-malware program and a firewall running on your device.

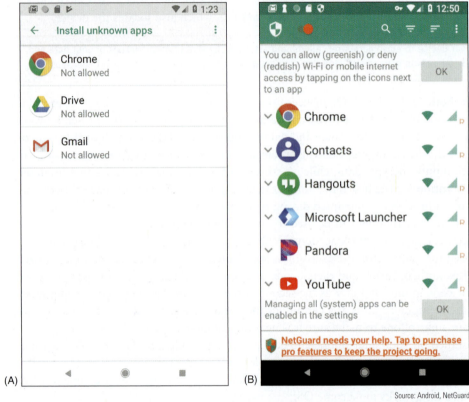

Source: Android, NetGuard

Figure 9-43 (A) Choose which apps can install apps from sources other than the Play Store; (B) choose which apps can access the Internet

▲ *Firewalls.* As with Windows computers, a firewall on a mobile device helps control which apps or services can use network connections. When you install an app, you're required to agree to the permissions it requests in order to get the app. A firewall gives you more control over an app's network access. For example, a firewall can prevent the Facebook app from sending SMS messages.
Most firewall apps for mobile devices mimic a VPN connection, which forces all network communication to be routed through the firewall. Figure 9-43B shows an example of one firewall app, NetGuard (*netguard.me*), on an Android smartphone; the app allows you to decide which other apps can use the networks.

▲ *Android locator application and remote wipe.* You can use Find My Device (*google.com/android/find*), Android's built-in locator application, to locate your phone on a map, force it to ring at its highest volume, change the device password, or remotely erase all data from the device to protect your privacy, which is called a remote wipe. See Figure 9-44. To use the locator app to locate your device or perform a remote wipe, Find My Device must already be turned on in the **Security & location** menu in the Settings app. Third-party locator applications are also available in the Play Store.

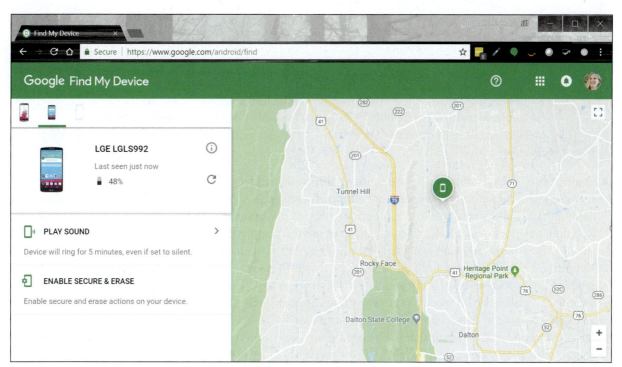

Figure 9-44 Locate a lost Android device using any web-enabled computer or mobile device and your Google account

◢ *iOS locator application and remote wipe.* Similar to Android's Find My Device, iCloud offers the ability to locate a lost iOS device if the feature is already enabled on the device before it's lost. On an iPad or iPhone, open the Settings app, tap the *user name*, tap **iCloud**, and then turn **Find my iPad** or **Find my iPhone** on or off. Besides using a browser on a computer to find your device, you can also download Find My iPhone or Find My iPad to another Apple device and use it to locate your lost device. Both apps are free. If your device was stolen or you have given up on finding your device, you can use iCloud to perform a remote wipe.

MOBILE SECURITY IN CORPORATE ENVIRONMENTS

**A+
CORE 2
2.8**

Corporations and schools might provide corporate-owned devices, which are secured and managed by corporate policies and procedures, or the organization might have **BYOD (Bring Your Own Device)** policies and procedures. With BYOD, an employee or student is allowed to connect his own device to the corporate network. For security purposes, an organization configures the person's device before allowing it to connect to the network.

Employees or employee groups in an organization are assigned **security profiles**, which are a set of policies and procedures to restrict how a user can access, create, and edit the organization's resources. **Profile security requirements** can be partially implemented by configuration requirements placed on BYOD and corporate-owned devices an employee uses. These device requirements, such as full device encryption, remote wipes, location apps, access control, authenticator apps, multifactor authentication, firewalls, anti-malware measures, or use of VPN connections, must be clearly outlined. Users must be educated on how to use them, and they must include assurance that devices continue to meet the baseline requirements.

Part of these requirements will likely include installation of a **remote backup application**, which remotely backs up the device's data to a company file server. For example, Canopy Remote Backup by Atos (*canopy-cloud.com*) provides cloud-based backups for laptops, tablets, and smartphones.

COMMON MOBILE DEVICE MALWARE SYMPTOMS

**A+
CORE 1
5.5**

**A+
CORE 2
3.4, 3.5**

Android and Windows mobile devices are more susceptible to malware than iOS devices because apps can be downloaded from sites other than Google or Microsoft. With iOS devices, apps can be obtained only from the Apple App Store and are therefore more strictly vetted. However, for any mobile device, malware can be introduced by a Trojan that a user accepts (for example, as an email attachment) or by macros embedded in shared documents.

Here are some symptoms that indicate malware might be at work on an Android, iOS, or Windows Mobile device:

◄ *Power drain, slow data speeds, high resource utilization, leaked personal files or other data, strange text messages, and data transmission over limits.* Battery power draining faster than normal or slow data upload or download speeds can indicate that apps are running in the background to leak your data to online servers. For example, when the XAgent malware app installs on an Apple device with iOS version 7 or below, the app icon is hidden, and the app runs in the background. When you close the app, it restarts. The malware not only uses resources, it steals personal data and makes screenshots, which it sends to a remote command-and-control (C&C) server. A C&C server might send coded text messages back to the phone. If you receive strange text messages, suspect malware. Another indication of malware at work is a spike in data usage charges on your phone bill.

◄ *Dropped phone calls or weak signal.* Dropped phone calls can happen when malware is interfering and trying to eavesdrop on your conversations or is performing other background activities.

◄ *Unintended Wi-Fi and Bluetooth connections.* Malicious Wi-Fi hotspots and Bluetooth devices can hijack a device or inject it with malware. When a mobile device connects to a malicious Wi-Fi hotspot, the device can receive a malicious script that repeatedly reboots the device, which makes it unusable. To prevent this type of attack, avoid free Wi-Fi hotspots or use a VPN connection. To prevent a device from pairing with a malicious Bluetooth device, turn off Bluetooth when it's not in use.

◄ *Unauthorized account access.* A malicious app can steal passwords and data from other apps and can pretend to be a different app to get access to online accounts. If you suspect an online account has been hacked, consider malware might be on the mobile device that uses this account.

◄ *Unauthorized location tracking.* Spyware apps installed on a mobile device can report its location to a C&C server.

◄ *Unauthorized use of camera or microphone.* Unauthorized surveillance is a sure sign of malware. Stalker spyware apps have been known to take photos and send them to a C&C server; send a text alert to a hacker and then add the hacker to a live call; use the microphone to record live conversations and then send the recording to a C&C server; report Facebook, Skype, Viber, and iMessage activity, including passwords and location data; and upload all photos, videos, and text messages to a C&C server.

> 🖉 **Notes** When is spyware legal? Parents can legally install spyware (politely called monitoring software) on a minor child's phone, tablet, or computer, and employers can monitor employee devices when they are company owned. One example is FlexiSPY (*flexispy.com*), an app that runs in the background to monitor text, email, Facebook and other visited websites, apps, photos, videos, contacts, bookmarks, location tracking, and phone calls. It can also record calls and surrounding sounds. It comes with a mobile viewer app installed on the parent's or employer's smartphone.

MOBILE DEVICE MALWARE REMOVAL

**A+
CORE 2
2.8**

Here are general steps for removing malware from a mobile device, listed from least to most invasive:

◄ *Uninstall the offending app.* If you can identify the malware app, close the app and uninstall it. If the app won't uninstall, you can force stop the app or any background processes that belong to the app. For Android apps running in the background, open the Settings app, tap **Apps,** and tap a running app to force it to stop. Then try again to uninstall the app.

◢ *Update the OS.* Check to see if any updates are available for the device. For an iOS device, consider using iTunes on your computer to perform the update rather than updating iOS directly from the device.

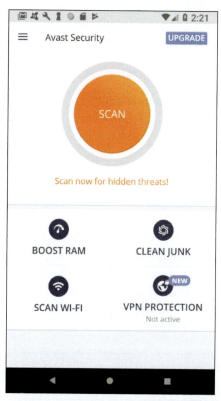

Figure 9-45 Avast performs regular scans on an Android device

Source: Avast

◢ *Perform a factory reset.* The most surefire way to remove malware is to back up data and other content, reset the device to its factory default state, and then restore the content from backup. Reset options for Android and iOS are discussed later in this chapter.

After you have removed malware on a mobile device, you will want to keep it clean. Here are a few tips:

◢ Keep OS updates current.
◢ Educate users about the importance of privacy settings (for example, disable cookies and turn off Bluetooth when it's not in use). Also, users should not open email attachments or download shared files from untrusted sources.
◢ Consider installing an anti-malware app. Apple claims that an iOS device cannot be infected with malware and does not make anti-malware apps available in the App Store. However, you can get an app from the App Store that monitors your device and scans for malware that might be in stored files, but is not installed. For Android and Windows Mobile devices, search online reviews and consider the features offered before deciding on an anti-malware app. An anti-malware app, such as Avast shown in Figure 9-45, can scan apps and files for malware, scan for unauthorized surveillance, monitor security and privacy settings, find the device when it's lost, lock and remote wipe it, and maintain automatic updates. It might even include a firewall or a VPN feature.

APPLYING | CONCEPTS   ROOTING AND JAILBREAKING

To get more control over what can be done with an Android or iOS device, some people have discovered they can get root or administrative privileges to the OS and the entire file system (all files and folders), and complete access to all commands and features. For Android, the process is called **rooting**, and for iOS, the process is called **jailbreaking**. After jailbreaking, an iOS phone can get apps from any source, but Apple has the right to void the warranty or refuse to provide support. Rooting and jailbreaking might also violate BYOD policies in an enterprise environment. In addition, rooting or jailbreaking makes a device more susceptible to malware. Here is how you can tell if a device is rooted or jailbroken:

◢ *Rooted Android device.* Use one of these methods to find out if an Android device has been rooted:
  ◢ Download and run a root checker app from Google Play, which will tell you if the device is rooted.
  ◢ Download and run a terminal window app from Google Play. (A terminal window in Linux is similar to a command prompt window in Windows.) When you open the app, look at the command prompt. If the prompt is a #, the device is rooted. If the prompt is a $, the device is likely not rooted. With the $ prompt showing, try the **sudo su root** command, which in Linux allows you root access. If the prompt changes to #, the device is rooted.

🖉 **Notes** In Linux, the # command prompt displays when a user has root access and the $ command prompt displays when a user does not.

(continues)

▲ *Jailbroken iOS device.* To find out if an iOS device has been jailbroken, look for an unusual app on the home screen—for example, the Electra, Meridian, Cydia, or Icy app. If any of these apps is present, the device has been jailbroken. If you have any app icon on your home screen that is not available in the App Store, the app is most likely a jailbreak app or other malware. When you update iOS using iTunes, the jailbreak will be removed.

Mobile devices and their reliance on wireless communication are closely related to another set of technologies, the Internet of Things or IoT. You might have heard of smart lights, smart TVs, and even smart houses. Let's take a look at what the IoT is all about and begin exploring the special technologies developed for these purposes.

THE INTERNET OF THINGS (IOT)

A+ CORE 1 2.3, 2.4

There's some debate on what makes up the Internet of Things (IoT). Most people define IoT to be devices connected to the Internet for a specific purpose, such as a smart thermostat, that normally would not be connected to the Internet. Generally, it's agreed that traditional computing devices, such as desktops, laptops, and smartphones, or traditional networking devices, such as routers, firewalls, and cable modems, are not IoT devices. However, as the line between "computer" and "Internet-connected non-computer" blurs, this distinction will become less relevant.

✎ **Notes** For a device to be considered part of the IoT, the device or its controller or bridge must have an IP address. After all, a node can't connect to the Internet without an IP address.

In this part of the chapter, you learn about the wireless technologies used by IoT devices and how to set up a smart home network of IoT devices.

IOT WIRELESS TECHNOLOGIES

In most cases, IoT devices are monitored and controlled by wireless connections. Besides Wi-Fi and Bluetooth, Z-Wave and Zigbee are two other wireless technologies commonly used by smart locks, smart light bulbs, and other IoT smart home devices. Here are the primary facts about Z-Wave and Zigbee:

▲ **Z-Wave** transmits around the 900-MHz band and requires less power than Wi-Fi. It has a larger range than Bluetooth, reaching a range of up to 100 m in open air (though significantly less inside buildings).

▲ **Zigbee** operates in either the 2.4-GHz band or the 900-MHz band, requires less power than Wi-Fi, and generally reaches a range of about 20 m inside but can reach much farther.

▲ Z-Wave and Zigbee are not compatible. Zigbee is faster than Z-Wave. Z-Wave and Zigbee use encryption and are considered safe from hackers.

▲ Both Z-Wave and Zigbee devices can connect in a mesh network, which means that devices can "hop" through other devices to reach the destination device. Z-Wave and Zigbee devices don't inherently use TCP/IP without another protocol at work, such as Z/IP or Zigbee IP, that manages TCP/IP networking.

▲ Typically, Zigbee and Z-Wave compete about equally for the smart home device wireless standard of choice. Zigbee is the choice for large-scale commercial or industrial use because it is more robust.

✎ **Notes** When worker honeybees return to their nest, they do a dance that looks like a zig-zag pattern. Zigbee was named after this phenomenon: *zig bee*.

Another wireless standard used in the IoT industry is RFID (radio-frequency identification), which is traditionally used in small tags that attach to and identify clothing inventory, car keys, bags, luggage, pets, cattle, hospital patients, and much more. An RFID tag contains a microchip and antenna and can be a passive or active tag. Active RFID tags have built-in batteries and transmitters to respond to commands or requests for information. Passive RFID tags, which cost much less, are essentially electronic barcodes that can be read from a few feet away without requiring line-of-sight access. Recently, RFID has been used for real-time IoT inventory management. RFID readers placed in manufacturing plants, warehouses, transportation systems, and stores can track inventory in real time to get products to customers faster and with less overhead.

SETTING UP A SMART HOME

As an IT support technician, you might be called on to set up and support a smart home that uses IoT devices. For the most basic of smart homes, you'll need:

▲ *Smartphone or tablet and Wi-Fi home network with Internet access.* Use a smartphone or tablet to set up and control smart devices by way of the device manufacturer's app you install on the phone or tablet. Internet access is often required to use the app.

▲ *Smart home devices.* Examples are smart light bulbs, thermostats, security cameras, door locks, doorbells, refrigerators, televisions, and sound systems. Smart devices can be controlled by the manufacturer's app installed on a phone or tablet. Some smart devices, such as a smart thermostat by Nest (*nest.com*), can connect directly to a Wi-Fi network via an embedded Wi-Fi radio (see Figure 9-46). Alternately, devices such as a door lock or thermostat might use Bluetooth to communicate with a phone or tablet within Bluetooth range or might use a bridge to connect to the Wi-Fi network. Other devices, such as smart light bulbs or a door lock, might use Zigbee, Z-Wave, or another wireless technology that the phone or tablet does not use. Such devices require a bridge device to connect them to the Wi-Fi network, as shown in Figure 9-46.

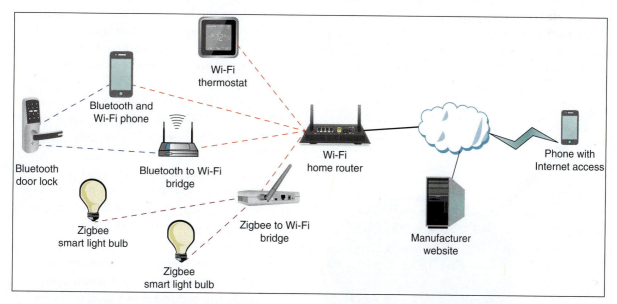

Figure 9-46   IoT devices connected to a smart home network may use a variety of wireless technologies

For smart devices to truly be IoT devices, you must be able to control them over the Internet. For that to happen, they must connect directly or through a bridge to a home Wi-Fi network that has Internet access. Notice in Figure 9-46 that the manufacturer's website is involved when managing many IoT devices. For example, Figure 9-47 shows the webpage where two exterior webcams and two thermostats by Nest (*nest.com*) can be monitored and managed from anywhere on the web.

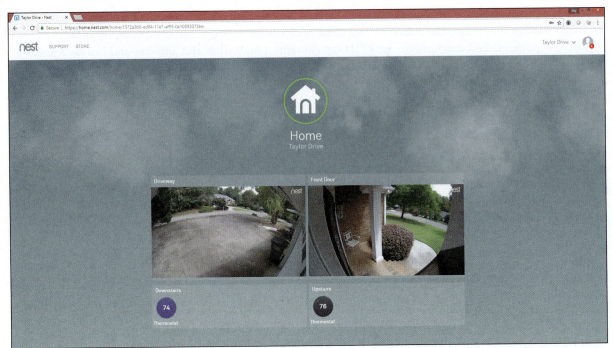

Source: *nest.com*

Figure 9-47 IoT device manufacturers provide websites to manage their devices

You can enhance a smart home network with smart speakers and controller hubs:

▲ *Smart speaker.* A smart speaker includes digital assistant software that is voice activated. Amazon, Google, and Apple offer competing smart speakers, which connect by Wi-Fi to the Internet and include a search engine. For example, you can command a smart speaker to play music available over Pandora radio on the web. You can also ask it to tell you the capital of Myanmar. When you sign in to your Amazon, Google, or Apple account on the web, you can set up smart devices so that a smart speaker can turn them on or off and tell you information the devices provide. For example, you can ask a smart speaker with a screen, such as an Echo Show, to show you the live feed from a security camera at your front door. Here are three options for smart speakers:

Figure 9-48 The orange light indicates the Echo Dot is on but not connected to a Wi-Fi network

▲ *Alexa and Echo devices by Amazon.* An Echo smart speaker is voice activated and may include a screen. The embedded digital assistant is called Alexa. You can say, "Alexa, turn on the lights," and the app does it. One low-end Echo product is the Echo Dot shown in Figure 9-48. You'll need the Alexa app on an Android or iOS device to set up an Echo device.

▲ *Google Assistant and Google Home.* Google Assistant is an app on an Android phone and is also embedded in a Google Home smart speaker. You control Google Assistant by starting with the spoken command "OK Google." You set up the Google Home smart speaker using an app on your phone (see Figure 9-49). You can also install the Google Assistant app on an iPhone or iPad so it can control smart devices set up to use the app.

Figure 9-49   Use a smartphone to set up a Google Home smart speaker

Source: google.com

▲ *Siri and HomePod by Apple.* Siri is the digital assistant included with an iPhone or iPad and is also embedded in a HomePod smart speaker. A HomePod is set up using an iPhone or iPad.

▲ *Controller hub.* A smart speaker can access the web and turn Wi-Fi-connected smart devices on or off, but for a completely automated smart home experience, you need a controller hub. A controller hub, also called a smart home hub, can control smart devices that use different manufacturer apps and different wireless technologies, such as Wi-Fi, Bluetooth, Zigbee, or Z-Wave, to create an integrated smart home experience. For example, you can use a controller hub to coordinate dinner:

When you approach your home, the garage door opens, the range turns on to warm up the soup, the room temperature is raised, and the kitchen lights are turned on. Two examples of hubs are Wink Hub (*wink.com*) and Samsung SmartThings (*smartthings.com*). In addition, software hubs such as Yonomi (*yonomi.co*) install as apps on smartphones and tablets.

Some people start a smart home by installing one or two smart devices controlled from a smartphone. Later they add a smart speaker and other smart devices to manage lighting, climate, convenience features, security, and entertainment. They also add controller hubs to make all the devices work together.

APPLYING | CONCEPTS   SETTING UP A DIGITAL ASSISTANT AND SMART SPEAKER

One significant goal of manufacturers of IoT smart home devices is to make them easy to set up and connect to the home's Wi-Fi network. However, the steps for setting up these devices vary somewhat among manufacturers, their products, and product models. Here, we'll look at the general steps for configuring an Echo Dot from Amazon; you should use the more specific steps from your product's manufacturer.

1. The Echo Dot and Alexa are set up and controlled from the Alexa app on a smartphone. Download and install the Alexa app first and sign in to your Amazon account. After Alexa is set up, you can also control Alexa from your Amazon account at *amazon.com*.

2. Plug the Echo Dot into a wall outlet. After it powers up and the light turns orange, it's ready to be paired with a smartphone. Refer back to Figure 9-48.

3. On the smartphone in the Alexa app, choose the Echo Dot from the device setup menu (see Figure 9-50A).

(continues)

9

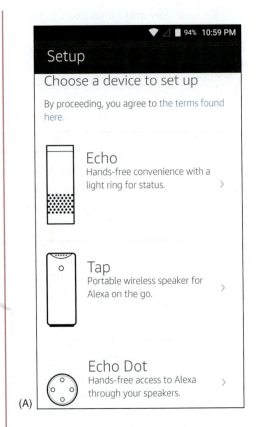

Source: amazon.com

Figure 9-50 (A) Choose the Echo Dot in the setup options; (B) connect the phone to the Dot's Wi-Fi hotspot

4. Echo Dot provides its own Wi-Fi hotspot to do the initial setup for another Wi-Fi network. First, connect the phone to the Dot's Wi-Fi hotspot (see Figure 9-50B). You can then configure the Dot to connect to your home's Wi-Fi network.

5. Once the Dot is communicating with your local network, it's ready to respond to voice commands. Use the wake word "Alexa" to activate the Dot, then say your command or request. You can change the wake word in the Alexa app. If you're setting up a smart home network, you're ready to add smart home devices to your Alexa account.

✎ **Notes** Some people like to use Alexa when traveling. In late 2018, Amazon introduced Echo Auto, which connects to your smartphone and vehicle for the Alexa experience on the road. Be aware, however, that Echo Auto uses data on your smartphone's cellular data plan.

APPLYING | CONCEPTS SETTING UP AN IOT SMART HOME DEVICE

The following general steps apply to setting up many types of IoT devices:

1. Download the manufacturer's app.

2. Open the app to follow the instructions for installation and configuration and to control the device from your smartphone. You might also need to install a bridge for devices that don't use Wi-Fi.

3. To control the device with voice communication, enable the smart home device in your digital assistant account.

Using these general steps, we're adding a smart door lock, the August Smart Lock Pro (see Figure 9-51), to a smart home network. This smart lock by default is controlled via Bluetooth by your smartphone within Bluetooth range. In addition, we're installing the August Connect, which is a bridge to connect the smart lock to your home Wi-Fi network so that you can control the smart lock from anywhere on the Internet or through a smart speaker such as Alexa.

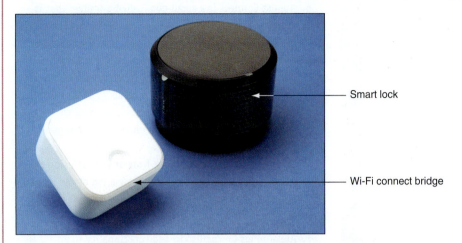

Smart lock

Wi-Fi connect bridge

Figure 9-51   The August Smart Lock Pro automatically unlocks or locks as the user's Bluetooth-enabled smartphone moves closer or farther away

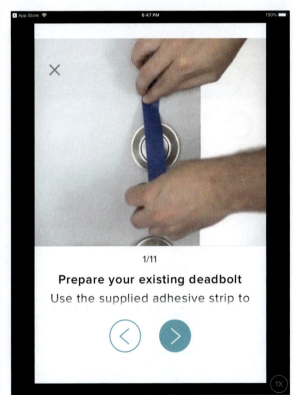

1/11

Prepare your existing deadbolt
Use the supplied adhesive strip to

Source: August Home Inc.

Figure 9-52   Install the smart lock on existing deadbolt hardware

The steps above are general steps; you should follow the more specific directions provided by your device's manufacturer:

1. Smart home device manufacturers usually provide their own app to control the device. Download and install the August Home app on your smartphone and create an account. This process might include security measures such as providing a photo of yourself, verifying your phone number with a texted security code, and verifying your email with an emailed security code.

2. Set up your smart lock in the app. The August Home app gives step-by-step video instruction for the lock installation (see Figure 9-52). You can also search YouTube for demonstrations of this process for your device. A good video for the August Smart Lock is posted by Silver Eagle Locksmith at *youtube.com/watch?v=omrbvCVOcI8*.

3. With your smartphone within Bluetooth range of the door lock, the app will connect to the lock via Bluetooth and continue setup. You can name your house and the specific location of the lock, such as "Front Door." The app might also install a firmware update at this time.

4. Calibrate the lock if instructed to do so. This involves setting the lock to "locked" and "unlocked" multiple times so the detectors inside the lock know how far to turn the latch.

(continues)

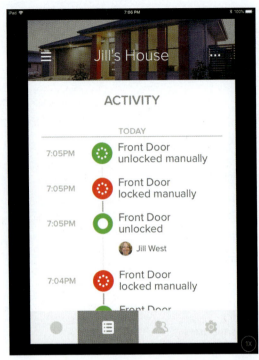

Source: August Home Inc.

Figure 9-53 See the lock's recent activity, including which users have locked or unlocked the door

5. Next, if you're using an iPhone or iPad, you have the option to link the lock to HomeKit, which is the software used by HomePod, Apple's smart speaker that works with Siri. We're going to use Alexa, so we skip this step.

6. August Connect is a small box, called a bridge, that is mounted near the door lock and connects to the lock via Bluetooth and to your Wi-Fi home network so that you can control the lock from your smartphone anywhere on the Internet. To install the Connect, make sure your smartphone is connected to the home Wi-Fi network, then plug the Connect into a wall outlet near the lock's location. The app detects the Connect and configures it for your home Wi-Fi network.

You can now control the lock from anywhere using the August Home app, and you can view a log of the lock's activity, as shown in Figure 9-53. However, we want to also link it to the Alexa app.

7. Alexa relies on "skills" to add functionality to an Alexa account. Think about skills as apps within the Alexa app. To add smart home devices to Alexa, use the Alexa app to first enable Smart Home Skills (see Figure 9-54A), then enable the August Smart Home skill (see Figure 9-54B).

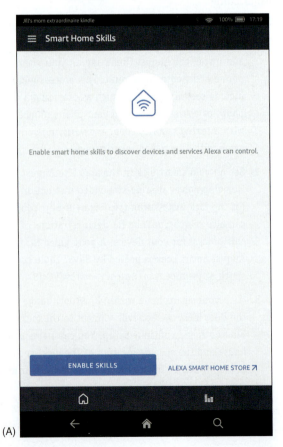

(A)

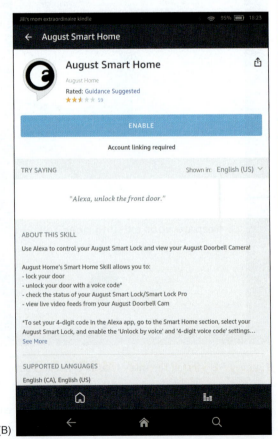

(B)

Source: amazon.com

Figure 9-54 Using the Alexa app, (A) enable Smart Home Skills; (B) enable the August Smart Home skill

Figure 9-55 Install this smart light switch to remotely control a room's light, fan, or electric outlets

8. After you link your August account and give Alexa permission to manage the lock, Alexa will discover the lock. Alexa will now respond to voice commands such as, "Alexa, tell August to lock the front door" and "Alexa, tell August to unlock the front door," in which case you'll also need to tell Alexa your PIN.

Let's look at a couple more examples of IoT smart devices. The smart light switch by Meross (*meross.com*), shown in Figure 9-55, uses Wi-Fi and the Meross app and can be controlled by Amazon Alexa or Google Assistant. The Honeywell wireless thermostat in Figure 9-56 uses Honeywell proprietary RedLINK wireless transmissions and can communicate with a Wi-Fi network via the RedLINK-to-Wi-Fi bridge, also shown in the figure, so that it can interact with Honeywell's Total Comfort Care app. Both devices can also link to Amazon Alexa or Google Assistant.

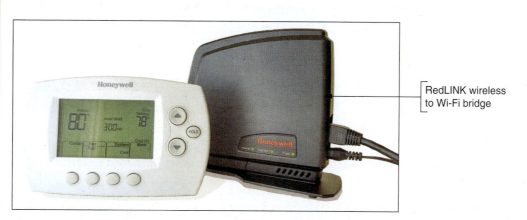

RedLINK wireless to Wi-Fi bridge

Figure 9-56 Use your phone, an Echo Dot, or a Google Home smart speaker to control this wireless thermostat

The setup for both the Wi-Fi smart light switch and the thermostat using RedLINK wireless is similar to how the Bluetooth thermostat was set up:

1. Install the app.

2. Install the device in the app. If the device does not use Wi-Fi, install an optional bridge device.

3. Connect the device to a smart speaker.

TROUBLESHOOTING MOBILE DEVICES

**A+
CORE 1
1.6, 5.5**

As an IT support technician for mobile devices, know that they contain few **field replaceable units (FRU)**, or hardware that can be replaced by field technicians. The cost of replacement, including parts and labor, generally exceeds the value of fixing the device. Although it is possible to replace the screens in some mobile devices, a support technician is generally not expected to take the time to do so.

There are, however, many problems with a device that you can troubleshoot using tools within the OS. When learning to troubleshoot any OS or device, remember the web is a great source of information. Depend on the *support.google.com/googleplay* and *support.apple.com* websites to give you troubleshooting tips and procedures for their respective mobile devices. In this section, we'll first explore troubleshooting tools for mobile device OSs, and then we'll consider many common symptoms and problems and what to do about them.

TROUBLESHOOTING TECHNIQUES

The following steps are ordered to solve a problem while making the least changes to the system (i.e., try the least invasive solution first). Try the first step; if it does not solve the problem, move on to the next step. With each step, first make sure the device is plugged in or already has sufficient charge to complete the step. After you try one step, check to see if the problem is solved before you move on to the next step. Here are the general steps we're following, although some might not be possible, depending on the situation:

1. Close, uninstall, and reinstall an app. Too many open apps can shorten battery life and slow down device performance. If you suspect an app is causing a problem, uninstall it and use the app store to reinstall it.

2. Restart the device (also called a soft boot) and reboot the device (also called a hard boot).

3. Update, repair, or reinstall the OS, or recover the system from the last backup.

4. Start over by resetting the device to its factory state (all data and settings are lost).

Earlier in the chapter, you learned how to close, uninstall, and reinstall an app. Let's look at the last three steps in a little more detail. For more specific instructions, search the website of the device manufacturer.

RESTART OR REBOOT THE DEVICE

A restart powers down the device and restarts it, which is similar to a Windows restart. A reboot, also called a hard boot, is similar to a Windows shutdown and performs a full clean boot. First try a restart, and if that doesn't fix the problem, try a hard boot:

1. *Restart the device, also called a soft boot.* To restart an Android device, press and hold the power button, and select **restart**. To restart an iOS device, press and hold the Side button and slide the power-off message to the right. To turn the device back on, press and hold the Android power button or iOS Side button. Power cycling a smartphone every few days is a good idea to keep the phone functioning at peak efficiency.

2. *Reboot the device using a hard boot.* When the menus in a device don't work or the device freezes entirely, a full clean boot might help. For most Android devices, hold down the power button and volume-down button at the same time. (Check Android device manufacturers for details.) To reboot an iPhone X, hold down either volume button and the Side button until the Apple logo appears; for an iPad or older iPhone, press and hold the Side button and the Home button.

If the device has a removable battery and it refuses to hard boot, you can open the back of the device and then remove and reinstall the battery as a last resort (unless the device is under warranty).

UPDATE, REPAIR, OR RESTORE THE SYSTEM

As you progress through troubleshooting steps, try these options to update, repair, or restore a device:

1. *Back up content and settings.* Before you try any of the techniques in this section, first try to back up data and settings using one or more of the methods discussed earlier in the chapter.

2. *Update the OS.* Try installing any updates, if available.

For Android devices, you can try these options to repair and restore your system:

1. *Boot into Android Safe Mode.* Similar to Windows computers, Android offers a Safe Mode for trouble-shooting. In Safe Mode, only the original software installed on the phone will run so that you can eliminate third-party software as the source of the problem. Be aware, however, that booting to Safe Mode might result in the loss of some settings, such as synchronization accounts. The combination of buttons to access Safe Mode varies by device, so see the manufacturer's website for specific instructions. For Google's Pixel smartphone, you access Safe Mode by holding down the power button until the power menu appears. Tap and hold the **Power Off** option until the pop-up shown in Figure 9-57A appears. Tap **OK** to restart the phone in Safe Mode, as shown in Figure 9-57B. Notice the *Safe mode* flag at the bottom of the screen. In Safe Mode, only apps native to the Android installation can run, and troubleshooting tools can be accessed through the Settings app to back up data, test configuration issues, or reset the device. To exit Safe Mode, restart the phone normally.

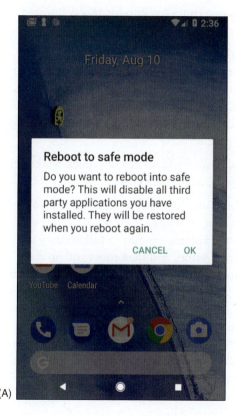

Source: Android

Figure 9-57 (A) Restart in Safe Mode; (B) in Safe Mode, third-party apps don't load

2. *Restore from backup.* If you have used Google Drive or a third-party app to back up the Android OS, its data or settings, now is the time to restore the system from this backup.

Several troubleshooting apps have been developed to help resolve Android problems. Most of these apps work only if they have already been installed before the problem occurs. If you have not already installed a troubleshooting app, your best resource at this point is to do a Google search on the problem and depend as much as possible on the device manufacturer's website.

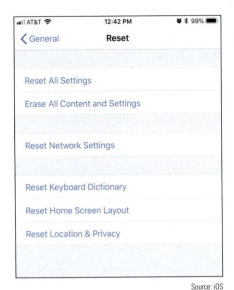

Source: iOS

Figure 9-58 The Reset screen on an iPhone

For iOS devices, you have several options for repairing and restoring your system, which are listed beginning with the least invasive:

1. *Reset all iOS settings.* To erase settings, open the **Settings** app and tap **General** and **Reset**. On the Reset screen (see Figure 9-58), tap **Reset All Settings**.

2. *Restore from backup.* Use one of these methods to restore from backup:

   ▲ *Restore the device from iCloud.* If you have an iCloud backup, open the **Settings** app and tap **General, Reset,** and **Erase All Content and Settings** (see Figure 9-58). Then tap **Restore** and **iCloud backup.** You'll need to sign in to iCloud.

   ▲ *Restore the device from iTunes.* If you have used iTunes to back up the device, connect the device to your computer, start **iTunes,** and click **Restore Backup.** Refer back to Figure 9-38. In the figure, notice the option is grayed out because there is no iTunes backup for this connected iPhone.

3. *Reinstall iOS.* If an iOS device won't turn on or start up, first consider that the battery might be dead. Try to charge it for at least an hour. If you still can't turn it on, you can use iTunes to try to reinstall iOS without losing your data. (You can use iTunes on any computer, even if you have not previously used it to back up your device.)

   a. If necessary, download and install iTunes. Make sure iTunes is updated and then close it.

   b. Connect the iPhone or iPad to the computer and start iTunes. For an iPhone X or iPhone 8, press and release the volume-up button followed by the volume-down button, and then press and hold the Slide button until you see the recovery mode screen (see Figure 9-59A). For older iPhones or iPads, press and hold the Home button and Side button. Follow the directions until you see the screen shown in Figure 9-59B, and then click **Update.** The latest version of iOS that works on your device should install and keep your data.

(A)   (B)

Source: https://support.apple.com/en-us/HT201412

Figure 9-59 Use recovery mode with iTunes to reinstall iOS on an iOS device that will not start

START OVER WITH A FACTORY RESET

As a last resort, you can perform a factory reset. The reset erases all data and settings and resets the device to its original factory default state. You can then apply a backup if you have one, so try to back up all data and settings before performing the reset, if possible.

1. *Factory reset from the Settings app.* In Android, open the **Settings** app, tap **System**, tap **Reset options**, and then tap **Erase all data (factory reset)**. In iOS, open the **Settings** app, and then tap **General** and **Reset**. On the Reset screen, tap **Erase All Content and Settings**.

2. *Factory reset from a hard boot (Android only).* If you cannot start Android or cannot get to the Settings app after a reboot, you can perform a factory reset from a hard boot. For most Android devices, hold down the power button and volume-down button at the same time until you see the Android bootloader menu. Select **Recovery Mode** and then check the device manufacturer's website for other options on the Recovery Mode screen that you can try before a full factory reset. If you decide that you have no other options, select **Factory reset** on the Recovery Mode screen.

3. *Factory reset and restore from iTunes backup (iOS only).* If an iOS device won't turn on and you've already tried to reinstall iOS using iTunes, as discussed above, you can perform a factory reset using iTunes. Connect the device to a computer that has iTunes installed and go to recovery mode in iTunes, as you learned to do earlier. Then click **Restore** (see Figure 9-59B). All data and settings on the device are erased and iOS is reinstalled. If you have previously used iTunes on this computer to back up your device, the device is restored from the backup. If you have an iCloud backup, you will be given the opportunity to restore from iCloud the first time you sign on to the device with your Apple ID.

> **Notes** If you have forgotten your iOS passcode, you are given six attempts to enter it before the device is disabled. You will need to use iTunes to reinstall iOS and you will lose all your data and settings unless you have an iTunes backup to restore the device from backup. If you have backed up to iCloud and you sign into iOS for the first time with your Apple ID, you are given the chance to restore the device from the iCloud backup.

If you've tried the previous steps and your device is still not working properly, search for more troubleshooting tips online, review the list of common problems below, or take the device to the place of purchase for repair.

COMMON PROBLEMS AND SOLUTIONS

Several common problems with mobile devices can be addressed with a little understanding of what has gone wrong behind the scenes. Here's a description of how to handle some common problems:

▲ *Short battery life or power drain.* Too many apps or malware running in the background will drain the battery quickly, as will Wi-Fi, Bluetooth, or other wireless technologies. Disable wireless connections and close apps when you're not using them to save battery juice. Consider that malware might be at work; how to address malware is covered earlier in the chapter. If the battery charge still lasts an extremely short time, try exchanging the AC adapter (charger). If that doesn't work, exchange the battery unless the device is under warranty. Many Android devices have replaceable batteries, so if a battery is performing poorly, consider replacing it.

▲ *Inaccurate touch screen response.* A cover on the screen can result in inaccurate touch screen responses. Also, accessibility settings can alter a touch screen's performance. Check accessibility settings in the Settings app. Hold duration is a particular suspect, as are touch location assistance and screen auto-rotate.

▲ *Touch screen nonresponsive.* Here are some tips to try when a touch screen is giving you problems:

▲ Clean the screen with a soft, lint-free cloth.

▲ Don't use the touch screen when your hands are wet or you are wearing gloves.

▲ Restart the device.

▲ Remove any plastic sheet or film protecting the touch screen. Some screen protectors are too thick and interfere with the touch screen interface, or bubbles and debris under the screen protector can cause problems. Use a screen protector that is approved for your device and carefully follow instructions for installing it. Turn on the screen protector's touch sensitivity setting if available.

▲ If you recently installed a third-party app when the touch screen became unresponsive, try uninstalling that app. Sometimes third-party apps can cause a touch screen to freeze.

▲ *No sound or distorted sound from speakers*. This might seem obvious, but first make sure the volume is turned up by pressing the device's physical **Up** volume button. Also, the problem could be that the sound output for the device is being misdirected. Check to see if Bluetooth is on; if it is, turn it off to make sure the device is not inadvertently connected to a Bluetooth headset or car stereo system. Also check Accessibility settings. Some of the Accessibility audio settings can interfere with normal operation of the device's built-in speaker system.

▲ *Dim display*. Try increasing the brightness. This is especially helpful when trying to view the screen in bright daylight, but increasing the brightness level will also drain the battery more quickly. For Android, open the notifications shade, then slide the brightness slider to the right to brighten the screen. Make sure the Auto option is not selected so that you have more control over the screen's brightness level.

For the iPad and older iPhones, swipe up to show the control center; on an iPhone X, swipe down from the upper-right corner to show the control center. In the control center, you can adjust the screen brightness.

Sometimes individual apps will control the screen brightness separately from the OS, so also check brightness settings within an app. Also check color and contrast settings on the accessibility menu in the Settings app (for Android, see Figure 9-60).

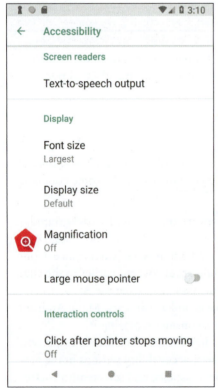

Source: Android

Figure 9-60 Accessibility settings can make a mobile device act in unexpected ways

▲ *Cannot broadcast to external monitor*. Many mobile devices can wirelessly mirror, or cast, their displays to a TV, monitor, projector, or to a dongle attached to one of these display devices. Android devices rely on Miracast technology, while iOS devices use AirPlay. When troubleshooting, first confirm that both devices are turned on (and not in sleep mode), placed closely enough to each other, casting is enabled where needed, and devices are connected to the same Wi-Fi network. You can also check for available updates on each device. Next, consider sources of interference, such as crowded Wi-Fi bands, and check that the Wi-Fi router is set to prioritize Wi-Fi multimedia (WMM) traffic. A VPN app on the device sometimes disables the casting feature because of the way cast technology seems to pose a threat to VPN security. It might be necessary to uninstall third-party VPN apps for casting to work properly.

▲ *Bluetooth connectivity issues.* Turn the Bluetooth radio off and then back on again. Devices typically limit the time they're available for pairing, so reactivating Bluetooth restarts the pairing process. In Bluetooth settings, you might be able to adjust the visibility timeout so devices have more time to discover each other. You can also delete all known Bluetooth devices in the Settings app to try the pairing process from the beginning. Sometimes an OS update will cause issues with Wi-Fi network connectivity or Bluetooth pairings. In this case, reset network settings in the Settings app. This restores network settings to factory defaults, and then you can attempt pairing again.

▲ *Wi-Fi connectivity problems.* Intermittent connectivity problems or no wireless connectivity might be caused by problems with the signal that is being broadcast from the router or access point. First make sure the access point and router are working correctly, that they're positioned closely enough to each other, that the Wi-Fi network you want to connect to is visible to the device (not hidden), and that you're using the correct security key. For Wi-Fi issues on the device side, first start with Wi-Fi settings in the Settings app for the network to which you're trying to connect. Try renewing the IP address, and if that doesn't work, tell the device to forget the network and then retry connecting to the network. Finally, try resetting the network settings. By default, many mobile devices stop attempting to reconnect to a weak Wi-Fi signal to conserve battery power, but you can sometimes change this setting so the device will attempt to maintain a connection even with a weak signal.

▲ *Signal drop/weak signal.* Sometimes updating the device's firmware can solve problems with dropped calls or network connections due to a weak signal because the update might apply to the radio firmware, which manages the cellular, Wi-Fi, and Bluetooth radios. This is sometimes referred to as a baseband update. For most of today's mobile devices, firmware updates are pushed out by the manufacturer at the same time as OS updates. If your device allows for managing firmware updates separately, usually that option will be available in the Settings app (see Figure 9-61) in the same place as the OS update option. You might also be able to download software from the device's manufacturer that can apply updates to the device through a USB connection with your computer. Examples are iTunes (*apple.com/itunes*) for Apple devices, LG PC Suite (*lg.com/us/support/software-firmware-drivers*) for LG devices, and HTC Sync Manager (*htc.com/us/software/htc-sync-manager*) for HTC devices. These apps can also be used for synchronization and backup functions. Be careful when applying a firmware update, as a failed update can "brick" the device, which means to make it useless.

▲ *GPS not functioning.* Geotracking, which is the identification of a device's location to track the device's movements, relies heavily on GPS location information. For example, Siri checks the device's current location before recommending Italian restaurants in the area. Many apps can only access this information if Location services are enabled on the device (however, emergency calls can use location information even if Location services are not enabled). If an app is having trouble accessing location-specific information, check the Location services settings in the Settings app, as shown in Figure 9-62.

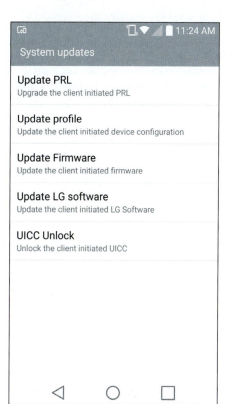

Source: Android

Figure 9-61 This LG phone lists several options for applying updates

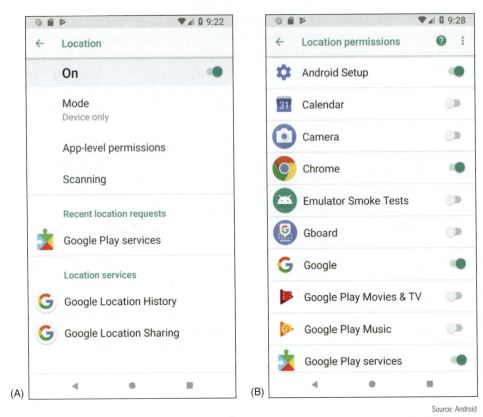

Source: Android

Figure 9-62   (A) Manage Location services in the Settings app, and (B) fine-tune which apps can use Location services

▲ *Unable to decrypt email.* Email encryption is done using a public key and a private key. You distribute your public key to those who want to send you encrypted email and you keep the private key on your device. If your device is unable to decrypt email, most likely you'll need to generate a new public key and private key and then distribute your new public key to those who send you encrypted email. Search the website of the email app you are using for encryption to find instructions for setting up new public and private keys and for other tips on troubleshooting decrypting problems.

▲ *Apps not loading.* When apps load slowly or not at all, a hot or failing battery might be the problem. Having too many apps open at once will use up memory and slow down overall performance. Close apps you're not using, clean cached data, and disable live wallpapers. Try to update the app or uninstall it and install it again. The device might be short on storage space; uninstall unused apps and delete files that are no longer needed. The Settings app displays how much storage space is available (see Figure 9-63A) and what content can be removed (see Figure 9-63B). Consider downloading an app to clean up storage space or monitor how apps are using memory. Consider performing a factory reset and start over by installing only the apps you actually use.

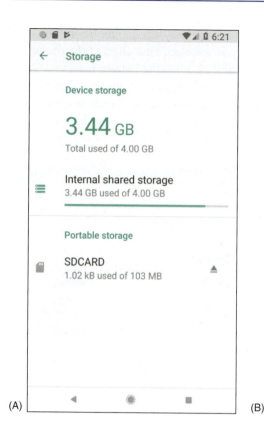
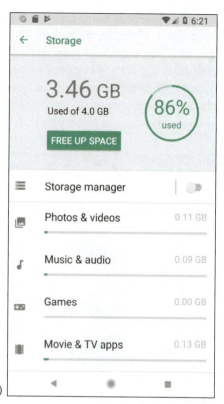

(A)   (B)

Source: Android

Figure 9-63 (A) Android reports how storage is used and (B) makes suggestions to free some storage space

▲ *App log errors.* Some apps maintain logs of errors that can be useful to technical support staff for the app. When helping you troubleshoot a problem, an app support technician might give you specific steps for accessing those logs.

▲ *Frozen system.* Consider that the battery may be low. Try recharging the battery for at least an hour. Then follow directions given earlier to reboot the device using a hard boot. If that doesn't work, move on to reinstall the OS, recover the system from backup, and finally reset the device to its factory state.

▲ *System lockout.* If a device is locked because of too many failed attempts to sign in (such as when a child has attempted to unlock your device or you have forgotten the passcode), wait until the timer on the device counts down and try to sign in again. With Android devices, you might also be able to sign in using your Google account and the password associated with the device. After you have entered the account and password, you must reset your passcode or screen swipe pattern. If you still can't unlock the device, know that Google offers many solutions to this problem. Go to *accounts.google.com* and search for additional methods and tools to unlock your device.

If you have forgotten the passcode for an iOS device, Apple advises that your only solution is to reset the device, which erases all data and settings, and then restore the device from a backup. You can restore from a backup stored in iTunes on your computer or from iCloud.

▲ *Overheating.* For a true overheating problem where the device is too hot to touch safely, power off and replace the device. However, all devices can get fairly warm if the display is left on for too long, if the surrounding environment is particularly hot, if the device is sitting on a blanket or other soft surface, if the case is not properly vented, if the battery is going bad, or if the device remains plugged in to a power source for a long period of time. Don't use a mobile device for too long in direct sunlight, turn off the display when you're not using it, and close apps that you're not using. This will also help conserve battery power.

If you know where the battery is located inside a mobile device, check for heat originating from that area of the device. If the area is hot, replacing the battery might be your solution. First check if the phone is under warranty. If the phone is not under warranty, open the case and examine the battery for damage. Is it swollen or warped? If so, replace the battery. For most mobile devices, you can find teardown instructions, videos, tools, and replacement parts for purchase online at various websites, such as *ifixit.com* (see Figure 9-64). If the phone is under warranty, you might be able to tell if the battery is swollen or warped by laying the phone on a flat surface. If the phone itself appears warped, take it in for repair.

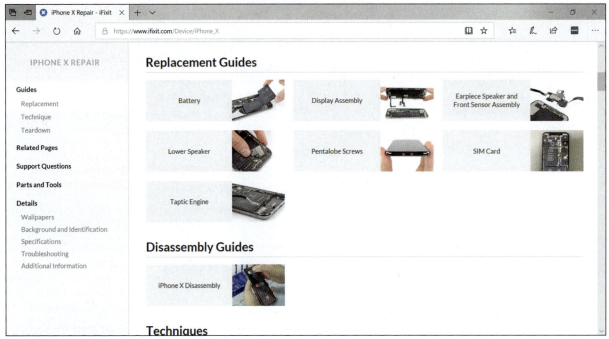

Source: ifixit.com

Figure 9-64 At *ifixit.com*, you can find instructions and purchase tools or parts to replace an iPhone battery

> **✎ Notes** Some Android smartphones provide information about the device when you enter ***#*#4636#*#*** in the phone's dialer keypad. In the screen that appears, select **Battery Information**. If the Battery Health screen reports "unknown," suspect a bad battery. The screen also reports the temperature of the battery, which should be less than 40° C.

>> CHAPTER SUMMARY

Types of Mobile Devices

◢ Mobile devices an IT support technician might be called on to service include smartphones, tablets, lightweight laptops, e-readers, GPS devices, and wearable technology devices such as smart watches, fitness monitors, and VR or AR headsets.

Mobile Device Operating Systems

◢ The most popular operating systems used on mobile devices include Android by Google, iOS by Apple, Windows and Windows Mobile by Microsoft, and Chrome OS by Google.

◢ Android is an open source OS, and anyone can develop and sell Android apps or variations in the Android OS. Google is the major distributor of Android and Android apps are available on its Google Play website.

◢ iOS by Apple is used only on Apple devices, including the iPhone and iPad. Apps for iOS are distributed solely by Apple.

◢ Windows Mobile by Microsoft installs on smartphones and uses the same version numbers as Windows for desktops, laptops, and tablets.

◢ Chrome OS is designed solely for use on Google's Chromebook, which is a tablet, lightweight laptop, or convertible laptop-tablet available from many different manufacturers. Chrome OS relies heavily on the Chrome browser and an active Internet connection. Chrome OS apps are distributed through the Chrome Web Store, and apps for the newer Chromebooks are distributed from the Google Play Store.

Configuring and Syncing a Mobile Device

◢ A mobile device might have several antennas for wireless connections—primarily Wi-Fi, GPS, Bluetooth, NFC, and cellular. The device uses a Wi-Fi or cellular antenna to connect to a LAN (local area network), a WAN (wide area network), or to create its own hotspot, and it uses Bluetooth or NFC to connect to a PAN (personal area network). A wired connection might use a microUSB, miniUSB, USB-C, or proprietary port, such as the Lightning port by Apple, for syncing with a computer or tethering to provide the computer with cellular WAN access.

◢ Email can be accessed on a mobile device through a browser or an email client. Email providers include Gmail (by Google), iCloud (by Apple), Yahoo! (owned by Verizon), or Outlook/Hotmail/Live (Microsoft's public email services for individuals). Microsoft also offers Exchange, its private enterprise email service that is hosted on corporation or ISP servers, or Exchange Online, which is hosted on Microsoft servers.

◢ Syncing mirrors app data and other content among your devices and/or the cloud that use the same Apple or Google account. Backups are copies of app data, configuration settings, and other content in case you need it to recover from a failed, lost, or corrupted device.

Securing a Mobile Device

◢ Control access to a mobile device by restricting failed login attempts, encrypting the device, and configuring a screen lock such as a swipe lock, PIN lock, passcode lock, pattern lock, fingerprint lock, or face lock. You can also use the mobile device as an authentication factor to increase security for access to other services and networks.

◢ Secure mobile device data and resources by regularly updating and patching the OS, using an anti-malware app, getting apps only from trusted sources, implementing a firewall, and configuring a locator app and the ability to remote wipe the device.

◢ In corporate environments, profile security might require the use of full device encryption, remote backups, remote wipes, access control to the device, firewalls, anti-malware measures, and VPN connections to protect company resources on the mobile device.

◢ Symptoms of malware on mobile devices include slow performance, short battery life, power drain, slow data speeds, leaked personal files or data, data transmission over limits, signal drops, weak signal, unintended Wi-Fi connections, unintended Bluetooth pairing, unauthorized account access, unauthorized location tracking, unauthorized camera or microphone activation, and high resource utilization.

◢ To remediate an infected device, uninstall the offending app, update the OS, and/or do a factory reset on the device.

The Internet of Things (IoT)

◢ The IoT is made up of any device connected to a network or to the Internet, including a plethora of devices from thermostats and light switches to security cameras and door locks, but not including traditional computing devices, such as desktops, laptops, and smartphones, or traditional networking devices, such as routers, firewalls, and cable modems.

9

▲ Wireless technologies used by IoT devices include Wi-Fi, Bluetooth, Z-Wave, and Zigbee. RFID is used to passively or actively track items and inventory, such as shipped packages, clothing inventory, hospital patients, and your car keys, and can be used in an automated IoT inventory system.

▲ Zigbee is faster and more robust than Z-Wave and is better suited for industrial and large-scale commercial use.

▲ A smart home requires a Wi-Fi network with Internet access, a smartphone or tablet, smart home devices, and optional smart speakers, controller hubs, and bridges.

Troubleshooting Mobile Devices

▲ To troubleshoot a mobile device using tools in the OS, you can close running apps, uninstall and reinstall an app, reboot the device, update the OS, reset all settings (iOS only), use Safe Mode (Android only), use Recovery mode, or perform a factory reset.

▲ To address specific, common symptoms on a mobile device, you might need to check accessibility settings, replace the battery if it's not under warranty, change the way a device is used, remove protective coverings that are causing interference, check wired or wireless connection configurations, adjust device settings, or consult with tech support for the device manufacturer or app.

>> KEY TERMS

For explanations of key terms, see the Glossary for this text.

airplane mode
Android
app drawer
App Store
Apple ID
AR (augmented reality) headset
authenticator application
baseband update
biometric authentication
Bluetooth
BYOD (Bring Your Own Device)
cast
Chrome OS
commercial license
controller hub
digital assistant
dock
emulator
end-of-life limitation
e-reader
Exchange Online

favorites tray
file-level backup
fitness monitoring
FRU (field replaceable unit)
full device encryption
geotracking
Gmail
Google account
Google Play
GPS (Global Positioning System)
Home button
iCloud
iCloud Drive
image-level backup
IMEI (International Mobile Equipment Identity)
IMSI (International Mobile Subscriber Identity)
iOS
IoT (Internet of Things)
iPad
iPhone

IR (infrared)
iTunes
jailbreaking
launcher
Lightning port
locator application
macOS
Microsoft Store
microUSB
miniUSB
multifactor authentication
NFC (Near Field Communication)
notification
open source
paired
PRI (Product Release Instructions)
PRL (Preferred Roaming List)
profile security requirements
radio firmware
remote backup application

remote wipe
RFID (radio-frequency identification)
rooting
SDK (Software Development Kit)
security profile
Side button
smartphone
smart speaker
S/MIME (Secure/Multi-purpose Internet Mail Extensions)
SSO (single sign-on)
tablet
trusted source
USB-C
VR (virtual reality) headset
wearable technology device
Windows 10 Mobile
Yahoo!
Zigbee
Z-Wave

>> THINKING CRITICALLY

These questions are designed to prepare you for the critical thinking required for the A+ exams and may use content from other chapters and the web.

1. Which of these network connections would allow your smartphone to sync your photos to your online account? Choose all that apply.

  a. Wi-Fi

  b. Bluetooth

  c. GPS

  d. Cellular

2. While visiting a coffee shop, you see a poster advertising a concert for a music group you'd love to see. You notice there's an NFC tag at the bottom with additional information about the concert. Which of the following devices would likely be able to read the NFC tag?

  a. GPS

  b. Smartphone

  c. E-reader

  d. VR headset

3. Which of the following mobile device OSs are open source? Choose all that apply.

  a. iOS

  b. Windows 10 Mobile

  c. Chrome OS

  d. Android

4. A smart speaker has no screen or keypad for changing its settings. Order three steps to configure the speaker.

  a. Connect the smartphone to the speaker's Wi-Fi hotspot.

  b. Download the speaker's app to a smartphone.

  c. Enter the password to the home Wi-Fi network.

  d. Enter the password to the speaker's Wi-Fi hotspot.

5. Which Chromebook security feature ensures that malware can't change the OS's system files?

  a. Quick updates

  b. Power washing

  c. Sandboxing

  d. Verified boot

6. You work for a company that provides dozens of the same smartphone model for its employees. While troubleshooting one smartphone that won't connect to the cellular network, you call the provider's tech support number for some assistance. The technician asks for the device's IMEI. What is she trying to determine?

  a. The OS version on the phone

  b. The specific device you're calling about

  c. The SIM card installed in the device

  d. The IP address of the phone on the cellular provider's data network

7. Which encryption protocols might be used to secure a VPN connection? Choose all that apply.

  a. L2TP

  b. SSH

  c. PPTP

  d. IPsec

8. You're at the store to buy a car charger for your dad's iPhone. There are several options with many different types of connectors. Which of these connectors should you choose?

   a. USB-C

   b. microUSB

   c. Lightning

   d. VGA

9. Place the following information in the correct fields in Figure 9-65 to add an email account to a smartphone using port 143 for the incoming mail server and port 25 for the outgoing mail server (not all information will be used):

   imap-mail.sample.com

   p@ssw0rd

   pop-mail.sample.com

   mjones@sample.com

   smtp-mail.sample.com

   Mary Jones

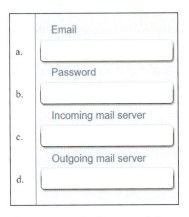

Figure 9-65 Configure email for a smartphone

10. Congratulations! You just bought a new-to-you car, and it comes with a media system that can sync with your iPhone. You're concerned about data usage on your cell phone, so before you go pick up your car, you decide to download the necessary app at home while you're connected to Wi-Fi. What app do you need to download?

11. You're traveling across the country for a much-anticipated vacation. When you get there, your smartphone seems to be having trouble connecting to the local cellular network. You call the provider, and the technician suggests you update the PRL. Why might this help? Where would you find this option on your Android smartphone to perform the update?

12. Your company has recently been hired to install a smart security system for a large office building. The system will include security cameras, voice-controlled lights, smart locks, and smart thermostats. Some of the security cameras will be installed outdoors throughout the parking lot. Which wireless IoT protocol should your company use for the installation?

a. Wi-Fi because it is always encrypted

b. Zigbee because it is always encrypted

c. Z-Wave because it is the fastest wireless standard

d. Bluetooth because it is easiest to configure

13. You're trying to cast a video presentation from your tablet to a projector for a training session with some new hires. Although you tested it successfully yesterday, today the connection is not cooperating. You've closed apps you're not using, and you've checked that the projector and the tablet are working otherwise. Of the following troubleshooting steps, which should you try first? Second?

a. Restart the projector.

b. Restart the tablet.

c. Reinstall the presentation app.

d. Verify that you have Internet access on the tablet.

14. An app that cost you $4.99 is missing from your Android. What is the best way to restore the missing app?

a. Go to backup storage and perform a restore to recover the lost app.

b. Purchase the app again.

c. Go to the Play Store where you bought the app and install it again.

d. Go to the Settings app and perform an application restore.

15. Suppose you and your friend want to exchange lecture notes taken during class. She has an iPhone and you have an iPad. What is the easiest way to do the exchange?

a. Copy the files to an SD card and move the SD card to each device.

b. Drop the files in OneDrive and share notebooks with each other.

c. Send a text to each other with the files attached.

d. Transfer the files through an AirDrop connection.

16. You have set up your Android phone using one Google account and your Android tablet using a second Google account. Now you would like to download the apps you purchased on your phone to your tablet. What is the best way to do this?

a. Set up the Google account on your tablet that you used to buy apps on your phone and then download the apps.

b. Buy the apps a second time from your tablet.

c. Back up the apps on your phone to your SD card and then move the SD card to your tablet and transfer the apps.

d. Call Google support and ask them to merge the two Google accounts into one.

17. Of the 10 devices shown earlier in Figure 9-46, how many of them are assigned IP addresses?

a. Four: two phones, a web server, and a router

b. Three: two phones and a web server

c. Seven: a thermostat, a router, two phones, two bridges, and a web server

d. All 10 are assigned IP addresses.

>> HANDS-ON PROJECTS

Hands-On | Project 9-1   Selecting a Mobile Device

Shop for a new smartphone or tablet that uses iOS or Android. Be sure to read some reviews about a device you are considering. Select two devices that you might consider buying and answer the following questions:

1. What is the device brand, model, and price?

2. What is the OS and version? Amount of storage space? Screen size? Types of network connections? Battery life? Camera pixels?

3. What do you like about each device? Which would you choose and why?

Hands-On | Project 9-2   Exploring *ifixit.com*

Replacing the battery in a smartphone or tablet is a handy skill for an IT support technician to have. If you have a smartphone or tablet or know a friend who has one, find out the brand and model of the device, or use one of the devices you researched for Hands-On Project 9-1. Search the *ifixit.com* website, which is a wiki-based site with tons of guides for tearing down, repairing, and reassembling all kinds of products, including smartphones, tablets, and laptops.

Does the site offer a guide for replacing the battery in your device or your friend's device? If so, list the high-level steps for the repair. If not, choose another device and list the high-level steps for that device. What tools would you need to actually make the repair?

Hands-On | Project 9-3   Researching Apps for Mobile Payment Services

iPhone and Android phones both offer some kind of mobile payment service, which allows you to use your smartphone to pay for merchandise or services at a retail checkout counter. iPhone has Apple Pay, and Android uses Google Pay. Mobile payment services rely on NFC (Near Field Communication) technology to exchange financial information between your phone and the reader at the checkout counter. You might want to pay with a credit card stored on your phone or get discounts with a store rewards account reported by your phone as you check out. But how secure is your sensitive financial information?

Research the following topics and answer the following questions:

1. Research how mobile payment systems use NFC technology. How does NFC work? How can you activate NFC on an Android phone for making a payment with Google Pay? On an iPhone for making a payment with Apple Pay?

2. Find and read some articles online or watch videos that describe the details of storing financial information for mobile payment systems, accessing the information when needed, and transmitting the information securely. What security measures are in place? Where is the data actually stored? What information is actually transmitted at the point of transaction?

3. List three third-party mobile payment apps available either in Apple's App Store or in Google's Play Store. On which mobile OS versions will the apps work? What are advantages and disadvantages of each app? How much do the apps cost? What security measures do the apps use?

4. If you were to purchase one of these apps, which one would it be? Why?

Hands-On | Project 9-4 Practicing Locating Your iOS or Android Device

Whether you have an Android device or an iOS device, knowing how to locate it when it gets lost or stolen or how to perform a remote wipe can be crucial skills in an emergency. Using your own device or a friend's, complete the following steps to find out how these tasks work:

1. If you have an iOS device, go to *iCloud.com/#find*. If you have an Android device, go to *google.com/android/find*.

2. Sign in and make sure the correct device is selected. Was the website able to locate your device? If not, check your device settings and make any adjustments necessary until the website successfully locates the device.

3. Explore the site to see how to make the device ring, how to lock the device by changing the passcode, and how to erase the device. What did you learn about your device?

One potential snag in finding or remotely wiping your device would be relying on passwords stored in your device to access your Google or iCloud account. Be sure to store your sign-in information for these accounts in password vault software or memorize the information.

9

>> REAL PROBLEMS, REAL SOLUTIONS

REAL PROBLEM 9-1 Using Android Studio to Run an Android Emulator

For this project, you might want to work with a partner so that you will have someone with whom to discuss the project in case the installation requires some troubleshooting. Make sure you're using a computer that meets the minimum requirements. While Android Studio works on macOS and Linux platforms, these instructions apply specifically to Windows 10. Here are the Windows system requirements:

▲ Microsoft Windows 10/8/7 (32- or 64-bit)

▲ 3 GB RAM minimum, 8 GB RAM recommended; plus 1 GB for the Android Emulator

▲ 2 GB of available storage space minimum, 4 GB recommended

▲ 1280 × 800 minimum screen resolution

Complete the following steps:

1. Make sure that your computer does not have Hyper-V enabled. To check this, open **Control Panel**, click **Programs and Features**, and click **Turn Windows features on or off**. Make sure that **Hyper-V** is not checked. If it is, uncheck it. Click **OK**. If you had to disable Hyper-V, restart your computer.

2. Make sure that hardware virtualization is enabled in your motherboard's BIOS/UEFI. The name and steps to access this feature vary by motherboard. Check your motherboard's documentation to determine how to enable this feature. What steps did you take to check or enable virtualization on your motherboard?

3. Download the current stable version of Android Studio at *developer.android.com/studio*. You might need to use Chrome to download the file, as the Edge browser is more likely to cause an error. Run the .exe file that you downloaded. At the time of this writing, the file name is android-studio-ide-173.4907809-windows.exe. What is the name of the file you downloaded?

4. Follow the setup wizard and accept all default settings, installing any SDK packages that it recommends. When you reach the SDK Components Setup window shown in Figure 9-66, click to select

Android SDK Platform with **API 28** (or a more current version, if available) and **Android Virtual Device**. If your computer has an Intel CPU, be sure that **Performance (Intel ® HAXM)** is also selected. Click **Next** and continue the setup with all default selections.

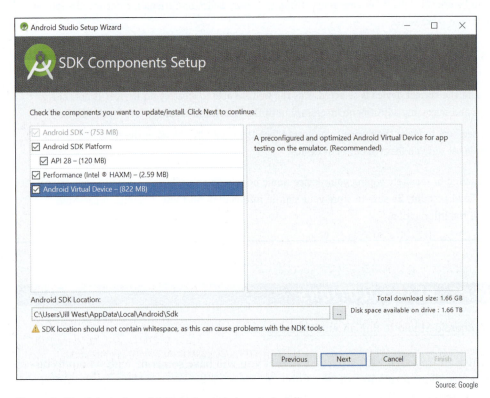

Source: Google

Figure 9-66   Select all available components here to install

5. When installation is complete, run **Android Studio**. The user interface is shown in Figure 9-67.

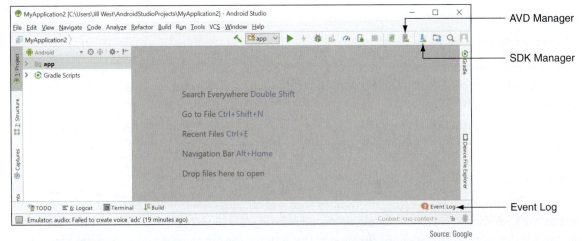

Source: Google

Figure 9-67   Android Studio is designed for app developers to build and test their products

6. Click to launch the AVD Manager, which is shown in Figure 9-68.

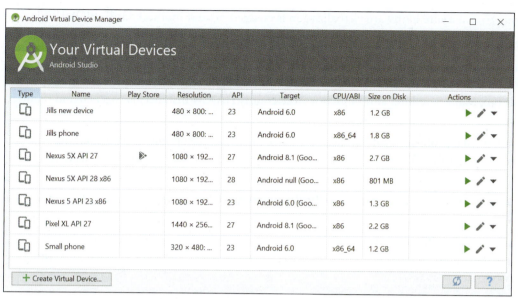

Figure 9-68   Use an existing virtual device or create a new one

9

7. To make sure everything is working so far, click a green **Launch** arrow next to an existing virtual device. If it works, you should see an emulated Android phone (see Figure 9-69A), although it might take a minute or two to fully launch. If you get an error message at this point, use the troubleshooting tips below or search online for possible solutions to your specific error message, which you can see in the Event Log.

(A)   (B)

Figure 9-69   (A) An emulated Nexus 5 with Android Marshmallow, and (B) an emulated Pixel XL with Android Oreo

    a. Check again to make sure hardware virtualization is enabled in your motherboard's BIOS/UEFI.

    b. Check again to make sure Hyper-V is disabled in Windows.

    c. If your computer is using an Intel CPU, make sure HAXM is updated and installed properly. To check this, click to launch the **SDK Manager**. With **Android SDK** selected in the left pane, click the **SDK Tools** tab. Make sure **Intel x86 Emulator Accelerator (HAXM Installer)** is checked and reported as **Installed**.

    d. If you're still having problems or if you had to change anything during this troubleshooting, you might need to reinstall HAXM. To do this, close Android Studio. In **File Explorer**, navigate to the following location:

    C:\Users*username*\AppData\Local\Android\sdk\extras\intel\Hardware_Accelerated_Execution_ Manager

    Run the file named **intelhaxm-android.exe** and respond to any prompts to complete the installation. Restart Android Studio, and try again to launch the AVD Manager and then to launch an existing virtual device.

8. What troubleshooting did you have to perform? What did you learn from this process?

9. Close the virtual device so you can create a new one with an updated OS. In the AVD Manager, click **Create Virtual Device**. Choose the **Pixel XL** phone and click **Next**. Choose the **Oreo Android 8.1** release. You might have to download the system image from the Play Store. If so, click **Download**, then select the release and click **Next**. If desired, give the device a name and then click **Finish**. Your new device should appear in your list of devices. Click its green **Launch** arrow to launch the device, as shown in Figure 9-69B.

10. Play around with the UI to see how well it emulates a real smartphone. Try some of the features discussed in this chapter. Which features did you test?

REAL PROBLEM 9-2 Configuring Email on a Mobile Device

For this project, use your own Android device or an emulated Android device. If you've not already set up Android Studio's phone emulator, complete Real Problem 9-1 before completing this project. You'll need a legitimate email account for this project. If you don't already have one you can use, you can create a free email account using *mail.google.com*, *outlook.live.com*, or *mail.yahoo.com*.

    Follow these steps to manually configure the email client on a mobile device:

1. Open the **Gmail** app and then tap **Add another email address**. Gmail can automatically configure email from many providers. Because it's essential that you know how to manually configure email on a mobile device, tap **Other**.

2. Add your email address and tap **MANUAL SETUP**. Check with your email provider to determine whether to use POP3 or IMAP. What's the main difference between these two protocols? What are the ports for these two protocols? What are the secure ports for these protocols?

3. Enter the password, check **Keep me signed in**, and tap **Sign in**. On the next screen, tap **Yes** to agree to the needed permissions.

4. Add the incoming server settings for your email provider, or check the server suggested by the Gmail app. Which incoming email server are you required to use? When you're ready, tap **NEXT**.

5. Add the outgoing server settings for your email provider, or check the server suggested by the Gmail app. Which outgoing email server are you required to use? When you're ready, tap **NEXT**.

6. Set your account options as desired, then tap **NEXT**.

7. If you were successful, you'll get a notice confirming your account is set up. Set the account name and your name as desired, then tap **NEXT**. If you weren't successful, backtrack and troubleshoot to solve the problem.

8. When you're finished, send an email to a classmate, and check an email sent from someone else to confirm your email account is working on your smartphone.

9. You need to know how to change the settings on an account. What steps are required to change the server settings for the account you just added?

10. You should also know how to remove an email account from a mobile device. What steps are required to remove the email account you just added?

9

macOS, Linux, and Scripting

After completing this chapter, you will be able to:

- Use and support macOS for Apple computers

- Use and support Linux distributions with graphical and command-line interfaces

- Identify basic scripting methods and scripting software

I n this chapter, you learn about two more operating systems for desktops and laptops other than Windows: macOS and Linux. As you will see, understanding Windows gives you a solid foundation to approach learning and supporting other operating systems. IT technicians are expected to be familiar with a variety of operating systems and operating environments, and this chapter equips you for these skills. In addition, you learn the fundamentals of scripting used in all scripting software and environments. IT technicians customarily use scripts to automate repetitive tasks.

macOS FOR MACINTOSH COMPUTERS

macOS, formally called Mac OS X, is a proprietary operating system that is only available for Macintosh computers by Apple Inc. (*apple.com*). Like Linux, macOS is built on a UNIX foundation and has been evolving and improving since its original release in 1984. (UNIX is a popular OS used to control networks and to support server applications available on the Internet.) At the time of this writing, macOS Mojave was just released, and some users are converting to it from the last release, macOS High Sierra.

The Mac keyboard has some special keys. See Figure 10-1. However, don't depend on these special keys because a customer might have a regular keyboard connected via a USB port. The touch pad on a Mac laptop is called the trackpad, and is a touch pad on steroids; you can use multiple fingers and actions called **gestures**, which you learn about as you read through this part of the chapter.

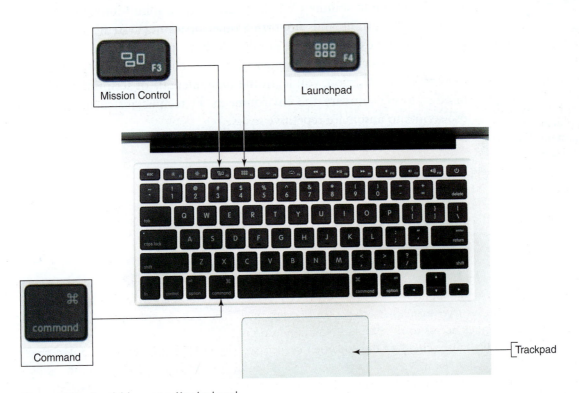

Figure 10-1   Special keys on a Mac keyboard

Now let's get to know the macOS interface, including the desktop with its dock and Apple menu, Finder, Launchpad, System Preferences, Spotlight, Mission Control, multiple desktops, iCloud Drive, Keychain, Screen Sharing, Remote Disc, and Terminal.

GETTING TO KNOW THE macOS DESKTOP

The macOS desktop, with its major components labeled, is shown in Figure 10-2. The **Finder** application, which can help you find applications and data files, is open and active. Because Finder is the currently active application, the menu bar for the Finder window is displayed at the top of the screen. The menu bar provides drop-down menus that contain options for working with applications, files, and the interface.

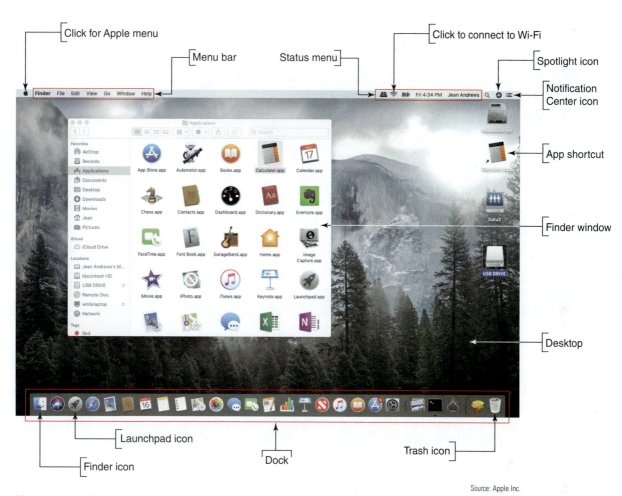

Source: Apple Inc.

Figure 10-2 The macOS desktop with a Finder window showing the Applications pane

By default, the dock appears at the bottom of the desktop. It contains shortcut icons to access frequently used applications. To open an application from its icon in the dock, click it once. The icons in the dock that represent open applications have a small, black dot underneath them. The macOS desktop can also include shortcuts that provide quick access to files, folders, and applications.

When a window is open, three circles in the upper-left corner (see Figure 10-3A) let you manipulate the window. The red circle closes the window, the yellow circle minimizes the window to the dock in the lower-right corner of the screen (see Figure 10-3B), and the green circle maximizes the window to full-screen size. To restore a maximized window to its original size, move your pointer to the top of the screen. When the circle icons appear, click the green circle.

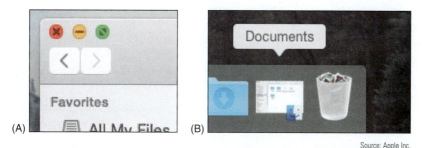

Source: Apple Inc.

Figure 10-3 (A) Close, minimize, or expand a window; (B) this Finder window has been minimized, but the app is still running and is easily accessible in the dock

Closing an app's window does not close the app. To quit an app that is active, click the name of the app in the menu bar and click **Quit** at the bottom of the drop-down menu. See Figure 10-4.

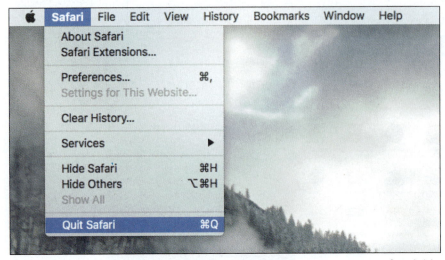

Figure 10-4   To close an app, select Quit in the app's menu

FINDER

The Finder window, shown earlier in Figure 10-2 and again in Figure 10-5, functions something like File Explorer in Windows; use it to find and access files, applications, and macOS utility programs. To open the Finder window, click it in the dock. Note that the Finder is always running; you can close the Finder window, but you can't end the Finder utility. Here are useful things you can do with Finder:

▲ *Files and folders.* To open files and folders, click **Documents** or some other storage location, such as iCloud Drive or Downloads. Double-click a folder to drill down into it and double-click a document file to open it. You can drag and drop a file or folder into and out of a folder or location window.

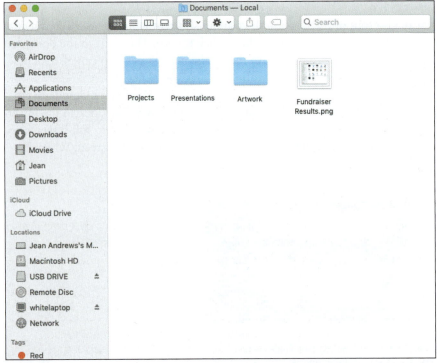

Figure 10-5   The Finder window showing the Documents folder contents

◢ *Applications*. To open an app, click **Applications** in the sidebar, scroll to the app, and click it. You can also open apps from Launchpad.

◢ *macOS utilities*. macOS offers several utility programs that are accessed from the Finder window. Click **Applications**, scroll down to the **Utilities** folder, and click it. See Figure 10-6. You learn to use several of these utilities later in this chapter.

Source: Apple Inc.

Figure 10-6 Utilities to support a Mac are in the Utilities folder under Applications in the Finder window

◢ *Locations*. As shown on the left side of Figure 10-6, available locations are the Mac, the internal hard drive (Macintosh HD), a USB drive, Remote Disc, and the network. Drill down into any of these locations to see available resources. When you drill down into Network, you see network devices and their shared resources. When you drill down into Remote Disc, you can see a shared optical drive that has been shared by another computer on the network.

◢ *Finder menu bar*. To use the Finder menu bar to list devices and other resources, click **Go** in the Finder menu bar and click **Computer**. The Computer window shows all locations and storage devices, and you can drill down into them. To control what appears in the Finder sidebar or on the desktop, click **Finder** in the menu bar and then click **Preferences**.

◢ *Tags*. Tags are used to assign a tag or color to a file or folder to make it easier to find later. For example, you can secondary-click a file and use the shortcut menu to assign it a blue tag. (A **secondary-click** is a tap of the trackpad with two fingers.) Later, click the blue tag in the left column of Finder to see all items with blue tags.

✎ **Notes** If you use an app frequently, such as GarageBand, you can add it to the dock or desktop. In Finder, click **Applications** and then click and drag the app's icon to the dock or desktop. To remove an icon from the dock or desktop, click and drag the icon to the Trash icon.

LAUNCHPAD

Launchpad (see Figure 10-7), which is somewhat similar to a combination of the Windows Start menu and Programs and Features window, shows all apps installed on the computer. Use one of these methods to open Launchpad:

◢ *Use the dock.* Click the Launchpad icon in the dock.
◢ *Use a gesture.* Pinch with three fingers and your thumb on the trackpad.
◢ *Use a key.* Press the Launchpad key at the top of the Mac keyboard.

In the Launchpad window shown in Figure 10-7, notice the two dots above the dock, which indicate that Launchpad requires two screens to show all installed apps. Swipe left or right with two fingers to move through the screens.

Source: Apple Inc.

Figure 10-7 View all installed apps in Launchpad; when more apps are installed, Launchpad creates additional screens to the side

Here are tips on how to use Launchpad:

◢ Click an app to open it, which also closes Launchpad.
◢ To uninstall an app, press and hold the **option** key, which causes the app icons to jiggle. Click an **X** on an icon to uninstall its app. You can also rearrange jiggling icons, similar to how an iPad and iPhone work. Release the option key when you're done.
◢ To close Launchpad and return to the desktop, use a pinch gesture with three fingers and your thumb spread apart.

APPLE MENU

The menu at the top of the macOS screen changes with each application that is active except for the Apple icon, which is always shown at the far left of the menu bar. The Apple menu (see Figure 10-8) opens when you click the Apple icon. Use the Apple menu to put the computer to sleep, log out, restart, or shut down the system.

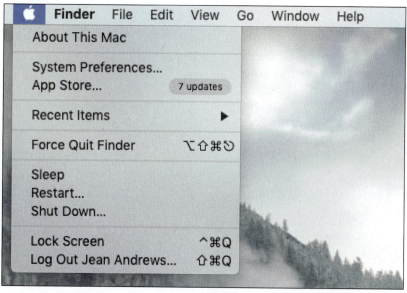

Source: Apple Inc.

Figure 10-8   The Apple menu is always available no matter which application is active

The Apple menu also provides access to system information, system preferences, the App Store, recent items, and the Force Quit option. Similar to ending a task from Task Manager in Windows, you can **force quit** an app by clicking **Force Quit**. In the Force Quit Applications window (see Figure 10-9), select the app and click **Force Quit**. The application closes. You can also access the Force Quit Applications window by pressing **command (⌘)-option-esc**.

Figure 10-9   Force Quit can be used to close an app that is not responding

Source: Apple Inc.

SYSTEM PREFERENCES

The System Preferences window is used to change and customize macOS settings and is similar to the Settings app in Windows 10. It can be opened from the Apple menu (refer back to Figure 10-8) or from the System Preferences icon in the dock (see Figure 10-10). The System Preferences window is shown in Figure 10-11.

Source: Apple Inc.

Figure 10-10   The System Preferences icon in the dock shows the app is open

Click at any time to return to this screen in System Preferences

Source: Apple Inc.

Figure 10-11 The System Preferences window is used to customize the macOS interface

Click an icon in System Preferences to change settings for that tool, feature, or app. As an IT technician, here are a few important tools you might use in System Preferences:

- ◢ *Trackpad*. Click Trackpad to adjust trackpad gestures.
- ◢ *iCloud*. Set up an iCloud account on this computer, choose what content to sync to iCloud and iCloud Drive, and adjust account details.
- ◢ *Time Machine*. Use Time Machine to configure backups.
- ◢ *Users & Groups*. Add and remove users and change startup items for a user.
- ◢ *Sharing*. Share the Mac's screen, files, and printers, and allow remote login and management of the computer.
- ◢ *Network*. Change network settings, including TCP/IP settings for Bluetooth, Wi-Fi, and Ethernet connections. (For Mac laptops, Ethernet connections are often made via the multipurpose Thunderbolt port using a Thunderbolt to Gigabit Ethernet adapter.)
- ◢ *Spotlight*. Change settings for Spotlight, the macOS search utility. You can control where Spotlight searches and its keyboard shortcuts.

SPOTLIGHT

If you're having a problem locating a file or folder, Spotlight can search for it. To open Spotlight, click the search icon on the right side of the menu bar or press **command** (⌘) **+ spacebar**. In the Spotlight search box (see Figure 10-12), type the name of the file, folder, or text you want to find. For example, if you type **Projects**, Spotlight lists a folder named Projects as the Top Hit (see Figure 10-13).

> ✎ **Notes** When you no longer need a file or folder, drag its icon to the Trash icon until the Trash is highlighted, and release the icon. When an item is in the Trash, you can recover it: Click **Trash** to open it and drag an item in the Trash to another location. To empty the trash, click **Finder** in the menu bar and click **Empty Trash**.

Figure 10-12 Spotlight searches the local computer and online resources

Source: Apple Inc.

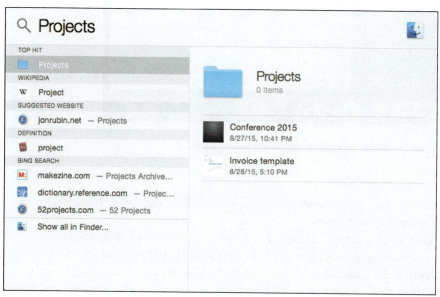

Figure 10-13 Use Spotlight to search for files and folders

Source: Apple Inc.

MISSION CONTROL AND MULTIPLE DESKTOPS

Mission Control gives you a quick view of all open windows and desktops and lets you switch among them. The macOS includes a feature called **multiple desktops**, which as its name indicates, is several desktop screens, each with its own collection of open windows. Suppose you're working with several windows for a school project, and you have a few more windows open for a project at work. You can place the school project windows on one desktop, called a **Space**, and place the work project windows on a separate desktop or Space.

To accomplish this, first open Mission Control using one of these methods:

- Press the Mission Control key.
- Click **Mission Control** in the Launchpad window.
- Swipe up with three or four fingers on your trackpad.

A Mission Control window is shown in Figure 10-14. Three desktops have been created on the system, as you can see in the Spaces bar at the top of the window. Also, when an app is in full-screen mode, it acts as a separate Space and shows up in the Spaces bar along with desktops. To create a new desktop, drag an open window into the Spaces bar or click + on the right side of the Spaces bar. To delete a desktop, hover over it in the Spaces bar and click the X. Desktop configurations apply to each user and remain in place even when the computer is rebooted.

10

Drag an open window here to create a new desktop

Source: Apple Inc.

Figure 10-14   Mission Control allows you to create multiple desktops to contain windows

Here are a few more tips about multiple desktops:

▲ *Move among desktops.* To move among desktops as you work, swipe left or right with three fingers or press **control + left arrow** or **control + right arrow**.

▲ *Organize desktops.* To help keep your desktops organized, it helps to customize each desktop with a different wallpaper. Go to a desktop and secondary-click. In the menu that appears on the desktop background, click **Change Desktop Background** (see Figure 10-15A). The Desktop & Screen Saver window opens. (This window is one of the tools in System Preferences.) Select your wallpaper and close the window. Wallpaper settings in other existing desktops won't be affected.

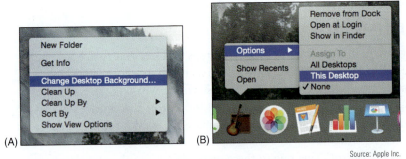

(A)   (B)

Source: Apple Inc.

Figure 10-15   (A) Set a different background for each desktop, and (B) assign different apps in the dock of each desktop

▲ *Organize apps in desktops.* To help keep your apps organized, you can assign an app to a specific desktop. Go to that desktop and secondary-click the app's icon in the dock (see Figure 10-15B). Select **Options** and then click **This Desktop**. Later, when you open the app, the selected desktop will appear with the app's open window.

iCLOUD AND iCLOUD DRIVE

Looking back at the Finder window shown earlier in Figure 10-5, notice that iCloud Drive is listed in the sidebar along with other storage locations such as Desktop, Documents, and Downloads. When a user signs in to macOS for the first time, she is given the opportunity to set up iCloud with her Apple ID, or the setup can be done later in System Preferences. In System Preferences, you can also control which apps store their data in iCloud (see Figure 10-16).

Figure 10-16 Choose what content to sync with iCloud

Source: Apple Inc.

To open iCloud Drive, click it in the Finder window or in Launchpad. Drag and drop files in and out of the iCloud Drive window. The contents are synced with any iPhone, iPad, or Windows desktop that has the iCloud Drive app installed, or with another device that is set up with your Apple ID. (On iPhone and iPad, recall that you can manage iCloud Drive using the Files app.) You can also access your iCloud content, including iCloud Drive, from any device with a browser by going to *icloud.com* and signing in with your Apple ID.

KEYCHAIN

Keychain is the macOS built-in password manager. To open Keychain, go to the Finder window, drill down into the **Applications** list, and then click **Utilities** (refer back to Figure 10-6). Double-click **Keychain Access app**. From the Keychains window (see the left side of Figure 10-17), you can view, edit, and remove accounts for applications, websites, and servers. You can also manage personal accounts that you've added, such as credit card and bank accounts.

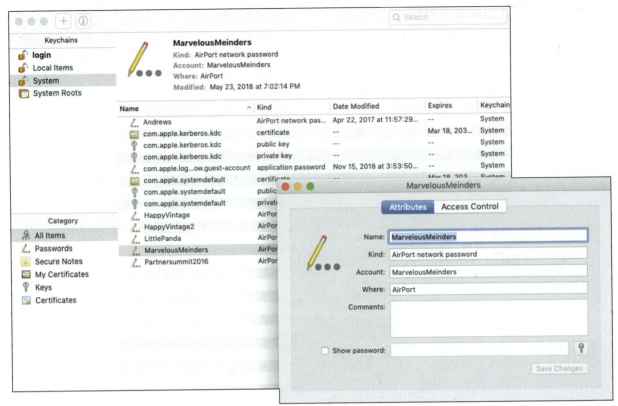

Source: Apple Inc.

Figure 10-17   The data stored in Keychain is encrypted

If you have problems with Keychain, you can delete all saved passwords and restore from backup. In the **Keychain Access** menu, click **Preferences**. In the Preferences box, click **Reset My Default Keychains**. New, empty Login and Local Items keychains are created. If you have Time Machine backups, try to restore the keychains from backup.

SCREEN SHARING

In System Preferences, click **Sharing** to open the Sharing window, where you can set up file and folder sharing on the network, printer sharing, remote access, and screen sharing. Screen Sharing works like Remote Desktop in Windows. In the Sharing window (see Figure 10-18), turn on Screen Sharing and set it up to allow all users or only certain users that you add.

To use screen sharing, a user of another Mac on the network should be able to see your shared Mac in his Finder window in the Shared group. He can click your computer and then click **Share Screen**. He then has the opportunity to sign in to your computer with a user name and password recognized by your computer. Using screen sharing, he can move files and folders between the two computers.

> ✎ **Notes**   Screen Sharing uses incoming port 5900. To access a Mac from the Internet, set up port forwarding on your router to allow incoming traffic on port 5900.

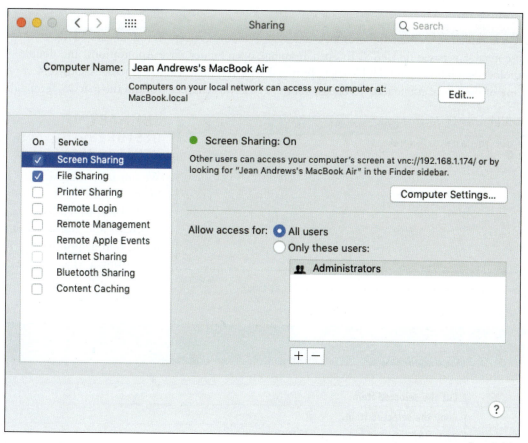

Source: Apple Inc.

Figure 10-18 Screen Sharing makes it easier to collaborate on projects or to help other users with their computers

How secure is macOS screen sharing? Some of the content moved between computers is encrypted and some is not, and you must open an incoming port on your router. Therefore, macOS screen sharing is not as secure as other types of remote access software. Also, as you'll recall from Chapter 4, third-party remote access apps that use a browser are considered more secure than OS tools that open ports for incoming traffic initiated from the Internet. Two examples of apps that use browsers and provide encrypted communication are join.me (*join.me*) and Zoom (*zoom.us*).

REMOTE DISC

If your Mac has an optical drive, the Sharing window includes the option *DVD or CD Sharing*. This feature, called Remote Disc, gives other Mac computers on the network access to the computer's optical drive. Remote Disc is especially useful when you need to install software or drivers from a disc on a Mac that doesn't have an optical drive. After you turn on *DVD or CD Sharing* on a Mac that has an optical drive, go to the Mac that doesn't have an optical drive and open **Finder**. In Finder, click **Remote Disc** in the sidebar under Locations (refer back to Figure 10-5).

> **Notes** You can enable remote disc sharing on a Windows computer. To share a Windows computer's optical drive with Macs on your network, download and install **DVD or CD Sharing Update 1.0 for Windows**, which is available at *support.apple.com/kb/DL112?locale=en_US*.

TERMINAL

Terminal in macOS is similar to a command prompt window in Windows, except Terminal uses UNIX commands because macOS is based on UNIX. To open Terminal, open **Finder**, click **Applications**, and double-click the **Utilities** folder. Scroll down and double-click **Terminal**. The Terminal window opens, as shown in Figure 10-19. Many of the Linux commands you learn about later in this chapter work in the macOS Terminal.

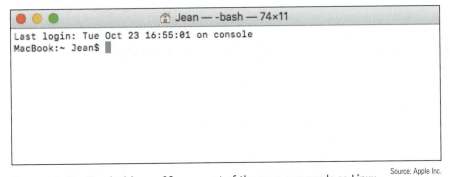

Source: Apple Inc.

Figure 10-19　Terminal in macOS uses most of the same commands as Linux

SUMMARY OF GESTURES AND KEYSTROKES

We finish up this part of the chapter with Table 10-1, which lists shortcuts and gestures you might find helpful when supporting a Mac. You've already learned to use several of these.

Keystrokes, Substitute Keys, and Gestures	Description
Keystrokes	
command-x	Cut the selected item.
command-c	Copy the selected item.
command-v	Paste the selected item.
command-a	Select all items.
option-command-esc	Force quit an app.
command-spacebar	Open Spotlight.
shift-command-5	Take a screenshot of the entire screen or part of the screen. By default, screenshots are saved to the desktop.
Substitute keys when using a regular keyboard instead of a Mac keyboard	
command key	The Windows logo key or Control key is the substitute.
option key	The Alt key is the substitute.
Gestures (gesture actions can be changed in the trackpad app's System Preferences)	
Secondary-click	Tap the trackpad with two fingers. Optional actions are: ◢ Tap the bottom-right corner of the trackpad. ◢ Tap the bottom-left corner of the trackpad. ◢ With a mouse, right-click.
Swipe	Swipe left or right with three fingers to move among desktops. On a keyboard, press control + right arrow and control + left arrow.
Scroll	Swipe up or down with two fingers.
Zoom	Pinch in or out with two fingers.
Pinch	Pinch in with three fingers and thumb to show Launchpad. Do a spread-apart pinch with three fingers and thumb to return to the desktop. If you are already on the desktop, a spread-apart pinch pushes all open windows to the edges to clear the desktop.

Table 10-1　Useful keystrokes, substitute keys, and gestures

MAINTAINING AND SUPPORTING macOS

**A+
CORE 2
1.3, 1.9**

In addition to working with files and applications, you also need to know how to support and maintain macOS, including updates, backups, and hard drive maintenance. This section will give you a good foundation for these skills. To dig deeper into how to support a Mac, search the documentation on the Apple website (*support.apple.com*).

> ⚡ **Caution**   Many Apple computers are covered by an Apple Care warranty, which provides excellent coverage for Macs. Always be absolutely certain that a Mac is not covered by Apple Care before opening the case or doing anything else that might void the warranty.

macOS DIRECTORY STRUCTURES

You need to be familiar with the directory structure in macOS so you know where to look for what. Here are some tips:

▲ To see the directory structure, click **Go** on the Finder menu bar and then click **Computer.** In the Finder window, click the hard drive, which is labeled Macintosh HD in most systems. In Figure 10-20, you can see the five folders at the root level. (Other folders in the root are hidden.) User data is in the Users folder.

10

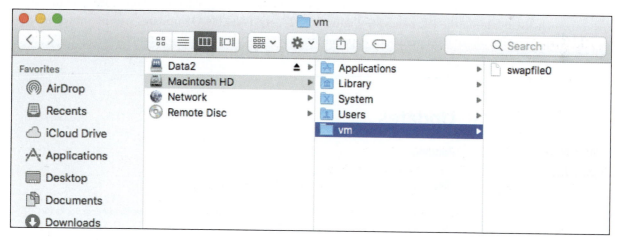

Figure 10-20   Folders visible in the root of the hard drive

Source: Apple Inc.

▲ Notice the vm folder is selected, and it contains a single file, swapfile0. This swapfile is used to hold virtual memory, similar to pagefile.sys in Windows.

▲ You can also browse the directory structure using the Terminal and Linux commands. In **Finder,** open **Applications,** open **Utilities,** and double-click **Terminal.** Use the cd command to move through the directory structure and the ls command to list files and directories. For example, Figure 10-21 shows the root directory of the Macintosh HD. Compare Figure 10-20 with Figure 10-21 and notice that some folders that appear in the Terminal window are hidden in the Finder window. You learn more about these directories later in this chapter.

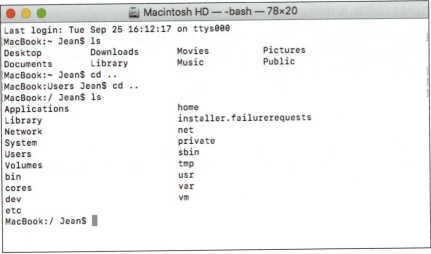

Figure 10-21 Contents of the root directory on a Mac hard drive

Source: Apple Inc.

UPDATE macOS, DRIVERS, AND FIRMWARE

Just like Windows, macOS needs regular updates. Updates often address zero-day vulnerabilities, which makes these updates important to maintaining a healthy system. However, sometimes the updates themselves introduce bugs, which is why many Mac experts advise against setting macOS updates to install automatically. Instead, wait a few days after a macOS update is released before manually installing the update; this gives you a chance to see if the update introduces any significant issues.

macOS updates come from the App Store. To manually update macOS, click the **App Store** icon in the dock, then click **Updates** in the left pane. See Figure 10-22. Any available OS updates will be shown near the top of the screen. Additional updates to apps might also be available in this window.

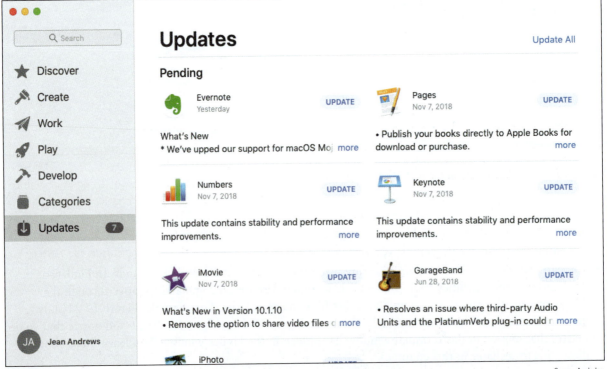

Source: Apple Inc.

Figure 10-22 The Updates window shows available updates and recently installed updates

> **Notes** Printer, scanner, and graphics driver updates are usually included in macOS updates. Other devices that require drivers, if not included in macOS, can be downloaded from the manufacturer's website and installed. These drivers will not be updated through macOS updates. If any problems are encountered with these devices, you'll need to check the manufacturer's website for updates.

To change the settings for automatic updates, open **System Preferences** and click **Software Update**. The OS checks for and reports available updates. For automatic updates, check **Automatically keep my Mac up to date**. To change detailed update settings, click **Advanced** (see Figure 10-23). Here is an explanation of each option:

- ▲ *Check for updates*. Automatically check for updates.
- ▲ *Download new updates when available*. Download updates without installing them.
- ▲ *Install macOS updates*. Install all updates to the operating system without first requiring user approval.
- ▲ *Install app updates from the App Store*. Install all updates to App Store applications without first requiring user approval.
- ▲ *Install system data files and security updates*. Install critical system patches that address known vulnerabilities.

Source: Apple Inc.

Figure 10-23   Manage how automatic updates are handled

Usually any needed firmware updates are included in the macOS update. Occasionally, however, Apple has released a firmware update as a stand-alone installation. You can find a list of available firmware updates in the Apple Knowledge Base Article at *support.apple.com/en-us/HT201518*.

To determine whether a Mac computer needs a firmware update, first check the current firmware version on the computer. This and a great deal more information is available in the System Information app. Open **Finder**, navigate to the **Utilities** folder, and double-click **System Information**. In the System Information window (see Figure 10-24), select **Hardware** in the sidebar and look under Hardware Overview for the *Model Identifier*, *Boot ROM Version*, and *SMC Version (system)*. Compare the information in the System Information window with the information for the latest firmware update available on the *support.apple.com* website. Install a firmware update only if the version listed on Apple's website is newer than what's installed on the computer.

> **Notes** The System Information app can also be opened from the Apple menu. Click the **Apple** icon, then click **About This Mac**, which gives an overview of the computer's system information, as shown in Figure 10-25. Then click **System Report** to open the System Information window that you saw in Figure 10-24.

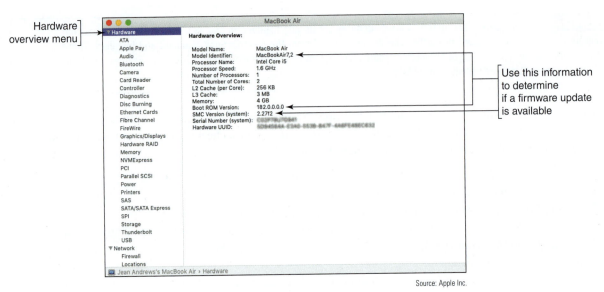

Source: Apple Inc.

Figure 10-24 The System Information window gives detailed information about the computer

Source: Apple Inc.

Figure 10-25 Click System Report to go to the System Information window for more detailed information

> **✎ Notes** Although Macs are not attacked by malware as often as Windows systems, it's still important to protect a Mac by installing and maintaining anti-malware software. Products to consider are Avast Free Mac Security (*avast.com*), Sophos Home Premium for Mac (*sophos.com*), and Trend Micro Antivirus for Mac (*trendmicro.com/mac*).

BACK UP AND RESTORE WITH TIME MACHINE

Like iOS mobile devices, Mac computers can use iCloud Drive to store files and folders in the cloud and sync this content across all of your devices. Unlike the mobile devices you learned about in Chapter 9, iCloud is not sufficient for backing up a Mac. For this purpose, macOS includes Time Machine, which is a built-in backup utility that automatically backs up user-created data, applications, and the entire macOS system. You can back up to:

- An external USB or Thunderbolt hard drive or a USB flash drive
- Another Mac on the local network
- Network-attached storage (NAS) devices that support Time Machine

Once Time Machine is set up, backups are updated in the background. Depending on the space available on the backup drive, Time Machine keeps hourly backups for 24 hours, daily backups for a month, and weekly backups until the disk is full. The oldest backups are deleted to make space for new backups. You can also set up multiple backup schedules to more than one backup device.

To set up Time Machine in macOS, open **System Preferences** and click **Time Machine**. The Time Machine window appears, as shown in Figure 10-26.

Figure 10-26 Configure Time Machine backups

Source: Apple Inc.

Follow the on-screen directions to select a backup disk and configure backup options. Everything on the disk will be erased. The original backup will be at least 20 GB, includes the entire macOS volume, and takes some time to complete.

> **Notes** When your Mac is not connected to the backup disk, Time Machine stores backup copies, called local **snapshots**, of created, modified, or deleted files on the hard drive. When you reconnect the computer to the backup disk, the local snapshots are copied to the backup disk. Local snapshots stay on the hard drive as long as they don't take up too much space, and can be restored from the hard drive if needed. Time Machine saves one snapshot each day and one weekly snapshot for each week the backup disk is disconnected.

You can use the backups to recover files, folders, or the entire macOS volume. To recover a file or folder from Time Machine, open **Finder**. In the **Applications** group, double-click **Time Machine**. The timeline and available backups in Finder appear (see Figure 10-27). Use the Finder window to locate the file or folder. Then go back through time to find the version of the file or folder you want to restore. To move through time, you can use the timeline on the right, the arrow buttons, or click a Finder window in the stack of available windows. Select the item and click **Restore**.

Figure 10-27　Locate an item and then go back through time to find the version to restore

Later in this chapter, you learn how to use Time Machine to restore the entire macOS startup disk, which is the volume on which macOS is installed.

DRIVE MAINTENANCE TOOLS

Hard drives in Mac computers require very little maintenance. However, performing a few simple tasks on a regular basis can help keep things running smoothly:

▲ **Empty the trash.** To empty the Trash, click the **Trash** icon in the dock. Trash contents appear in a Finder window (see Figure 10-28). Click **Empty** and then click **Empty Trash** in the warning box. Items are permanently deleted.

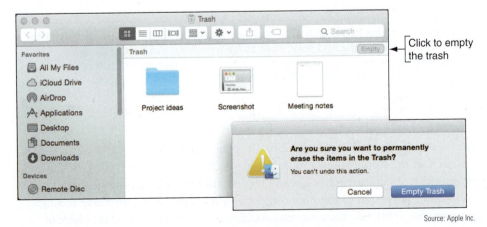

Figure 10-28　Check the contents of the Trash Can before emptying it

◢ *Free up space.* Maintain at least 15–20 percent free space on the hard drive for optimal performance. To see how much free space is available on the drive, open the Apple menu, click **About This Mac**, and then click the **Storage** tab, as shown in Figure 10-29.

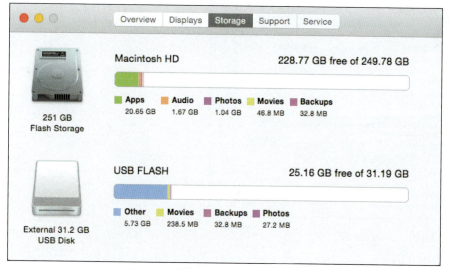

Source: Apple Inc.

Figure 10-29   Maintain at least 15 percent free space on the hard drive

◢ *Install updates.* Regularly check for and install macOS and app updates, which you learned to do earlier in this chapter.
◢ *Verify no startup items.* Programs that automatically launch at startup are called startup items and programs that automatically launch after a user logs in are called login items. Apple discourages the use of startup items because they slow down the startup process and items in the startup folder might be malware. You can verify that the system doesn't have startup items by looking in two directories that can contain them: /Library/StartupItems and /System/Library/StartupItems (see Figure 10-30).

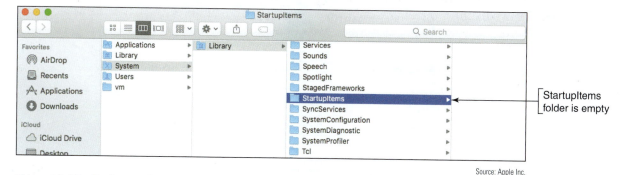

Source: Apple Inc.

Figure 10-30   For best performance, the StartupItems folder should remain empty

◢ *Remove login items.* Launching too many programs at login slows down the boot process and uses up valuable RAM. To adjust login items, open **System Preferences** and click **Users & Groups**. Select a user account in the sidebar, and then click the **Login Items** tab (see Figure 10-31). Use the + and – buttons at the bottom of the items list to add or remove login items.

Figure 10-31 A list of login items applies to each user

▲ *Restart the computer.* Power cycle the computer at least once a week. A quick way to do so is to click **Restart** in the Apple menu (refer back to Figure 10-8).

▲ *Uninstall unneeded apps.* Uninstall apps you no longer need. Apps obtained from the App Store are uninstalled from Launchpad. For apps installed from other sources besides the App Store, locate the app in Finder and drag the app to the Trash. Empty the trash to complete the uninstall.

REPAIRS USING THE DISK UTILITY APP

The Disk Utility app can be used to repair file system errors and hard drive corruptions. To open Disk Utility, open **Finder** and navigate to the **Utilities** folder. Double-click **Disk Utility**. In the sidebar, select **Macintosh HD** (see Figure 10-32) and click **Info** in the menu bar to view information about the drive.

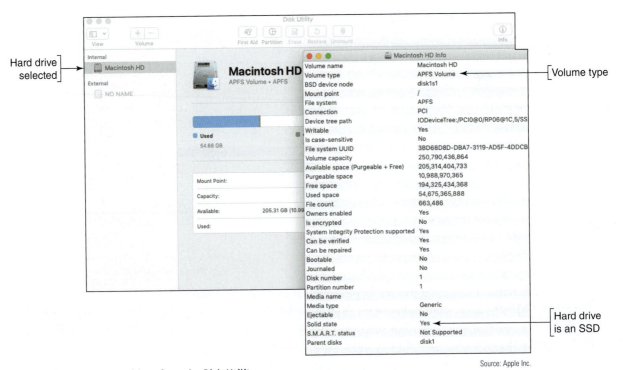

Figure 10-32 Manage drives from the Disk Utility app

In the Info box shown on the right side of Figure 10-32, you can see the drive is using the APFS file system. Here are the file systems macOS supports:

▲ **APFS (Apple File System)** is the default file system for SSDs and can also be used for magnetic hard drives. APFS allocates free space as needed for each volume on the drive. APFS uses the GUID (also called GPT) partitioning system.

▲ **Mac OS Extended** file system, also called **HFS+ (Hierarchical File System Plus)**, is an older file system in macOS 10.12 and earlier versions that uses a proprietary Apple partitioning system. If the Mac OS Extended file system is installed on an SSD and the system is upgraded to High Sierra, the upgrade converts the file system to APFS because it better manages an SSD. When upgrading to Mojave, the file system is always upgraded to APFS. However, APFS is not compatible with some earlier versions of macOS.

▲ The FAT32 and exFAT file systems are supported for compatibility with Windows and Linux.

> ✎ **Notes** Windows cannot read from storage devices that are using the APFS or Mac OS Extended file system unless third-party drivers are installed in Windows. For example, HFS Explorer can be installed to allow Windows to read a volume using the Mac OS Extended (also called HFS) file system.

You can use **First Aid** in Disk Utility to scan the hard drive for file system errors and repair them. In Disk Utility, select the drive in the sidebar, click **First Aid**, and click **Run** in the box that appears. A warning box reports that apps will be frozen while the drive is repaired. Click **Continue**. The process can take some time. Click **Done** when it completes.

> ✎ **Notes** If you plug in an external hard drive and macOS does not recognize the drive, you can use Disk Utility to fix the problem. In the Disk Utility window, select the drive and click **Mount**. If the mount does not work, click **First Aid** and then try to mount the drive again. When you mount a drive, it can be viewed by the OS, the drive is listed in the sidebar of the Finder window, and its icon appears on the desktop.

TROUBLESHOOTING macOS STARTUP

**A+
CORE 2
1.9**

When you have problems with macOS startup, use the options discussed in this part of the chapter to diagnose and fix the problems. These options are summarized in Table 10-2. Turn on the Mac and press certain keys at startup to launch tools or boot from other media. Release the keys as soon as you see the Apple logo.

Keys to Press as a Mac Boots	Tools Launched
Hold down shift key	Boots into Safe Mode
Hold down option key	Displays the Startup Manager so you can choose to boot from different media (for example, the external hard drive, USB flash drive, or network locations)
Hold down d key	Launches Apple Diagnostics to perform tests on hardware
Hold down command+r	Launches macOS Recovery to reinstall macOS from a Time Machine backup or the Internet

Table 10-2 Keys to press to access Mac startup options

> ✎ **Notes** Many of these same steps can also help when troubleshooting kernel panics. A **kernel panic** is similar to a BSOD in Windows. It might be caused by something simple, such as a crashed app or a network communication issue, or it might result from a corrupted macOS installation. macOS restarts automatically when experiencing a kernel panic. If the kernel panic continues to prompt restarts, macOS will stop trying after five attempts and shut down the computer.

SAFE MODE

Starting the computer in Safe Mode can solve problems when the computer won't start due to file system errors or corrupted startup or login items. Safe Mode in macOS loads essential kernel components, prevents startup items and login items from launching, and loads a minimum of user processes. It also verifies the startup disk and repairs any file system errors it finds.

To boot into Safe Mode, hold down the **shift** key as a Mac starts up. To verify that the computer booted into Safe Mode, open **System Information**. In the Software group, look for Boot Mode, which should report Safe (see Figure 10-33).

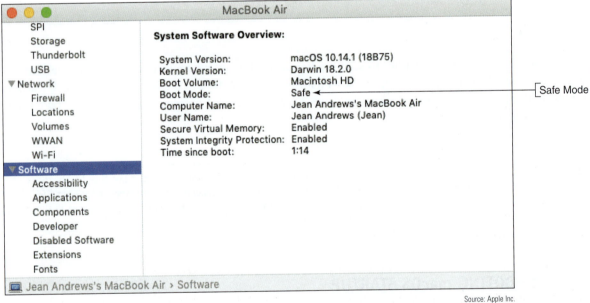

Source: Apple Inc.

Figure 10-33 Boot Mode indicates the computer is booted into Safe Mode

Do these things in Safe Mode:

▲ When Safe Mode starts, it automatically attempts to fix many problems. Restart the computer normally and see whether the problem is solved.

▲ Delete startup and login items that you suspect are causing a problem.

macOS RECOVERY

Using the macOS Recovery tools, you can reinstall macOS from a Time Machine backup or from the Internet. You can also erase the hard drive before you perform the image recovery. Turn on the Mac and press and hold **command+r** until you see the Apple logo. macOS Recovery launches and you see the macOS Utilities menu (see Figure 10-34).

Figure 10-34 Boot into macOS Recovery to reinstall macOS

Source: Apple Inc.

After you select an option, click **Continue**. Here are the options you'll see:

▲ *Restore From Time Machine Backup.* Plug in the external hard drive that holds the Time Machine backup, then select this option and follow the on-screen directions.

▲ *Reinstall macOS.* The latest macOS that was installed on the computer is downloaded from the Internet and reinstalled. As you follow the on-screen directions, the computer will reboot several times. If errors occur during the process, try erasing the hard drive and reinstalling again. After the new installation of macOS boots up, any data backed up with Time Machine can be restored.

▲ *Disk Utility.* If you need to erase the hard drive (for example, before you give away a Mac), select **Disk Utility** and follow the on-screen directions.

Suppose you are attempting to reinstall macOS from the Internet and you are not able to get an Internet connection through Wi-Fi or Ethernet. In this situation, you can use another Mac to create a bootable installation device and use it to reinstall macOS. This bootable device is created using commands in the Terminal window and is not covered in this text. The commands and process can be found at *support.apple.com/en-us/HT201372.*

STARTUP MANAGER AND NETBOOT

When you press the option key at startup, the Startup Manager screen appears and allows you to select your boot device. See Figure 10-35.

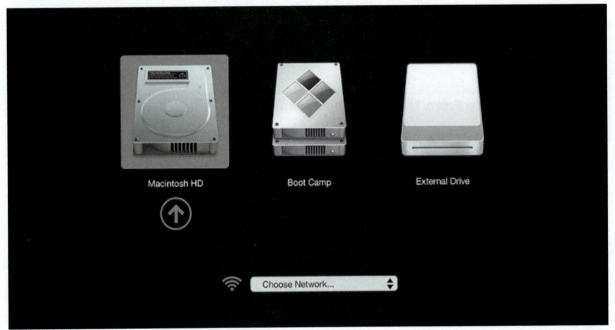

Source: *https://support.apple.com/en-us/HT202796*

Figure 10-35 Startup Manager allows you to select a startup disk or network startup

If you want to boot to a deployment server on the network to reinstall macOS from a disk image, you will use the Apple technology called NetBoot. NetBoot searches for a disk image stored in a DMG file on the server. A DMG file is a disk image file for a Mac and is similar to WIM or ISO files in Windows. In addition to storing clones of the macOS, DMG files are often used to hold app installers, as are EXE files in Windows.

BOOT CAMP

Notice in Figure 10-35 the option to start the computer using Boot Camp, which is an Apple technology that allows you to install and run Windows on a Mac. If the hard drive on a Mac is using a single partition with at least 40 GB of free space, Boot Camp can split the partition and install Windows in the new partition for a dual boot. Access the Boot Camp Assistant through the Utilities folder; Figure 10-36 shows the first screen, which includes a warning to first back up your disk before installing Windows on a Mac. After Windows is installed, you can choose which OS to use as your default for the computer, or you can press and hold the **option** key when starting the computer to reach the Startup Manager, which lets you choose from the installed operating systems. (Although you can install Windows on a Mac, you cannot install macOS on a non-Apple computer.)

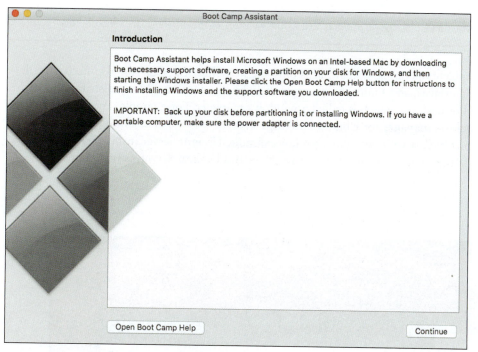

Source: Apple Inc.

Figure 10-36 Use Boot Camp Assistant to install Windows on a Mac and manage the Windows installation

LINUX OPERATING SYSTEM

> **A+**
> **CORE 2**
> **1.3, 1.9,**
> **4.9**

A variation of UNIX is **Linux** (pronounced "Lih-nucks"), an OS created by Linus Torvalds when he was a student at the University of Helsinki in Finland. Basic versions of this OS are open source, and all the underlying programming instructions (called source code) are freely distributed. Linux is popular because it's inexpensive and very stable (it seldom crashes). Linux is used as an OS for desktops, servers, mobile devices, and IoT devices. It's the most popular OS for server applications such as web servers and email servers. In addition, Android and Chrome OS for mobile devices are based on Linux, and bootable CDs and flash drives that contain utility software often use Linux. Versions of Linux are called distributions or flavors; the more popular ones for desktops and servers are listed in Table 10-3. Hardware requirements for Linux vary widely by distribution.

Name	Comments	Website
Arch Linux	Arch Linux must be manually configured. It has excellent online documentation and community support, and Linux professionals appreciate its simplicity.	*archlinux.org*
Fedora	Fedora has been around for a long time and is backed by a stable company. When updates are released, they tend to work well without errors. It's a great distribution for just about any OS purpose.	*getfedora.org*
Linux Mint	Linux Mint is based on Ubuntu with several features added.	*linuxmint.com*
openSUSE	openSUSE is made for servers, desktops, and mobile devices. Applications install without a hassle; go to *software.opensuse.org*, select an app, and perform a Direct Install.	*opensuse.org*
Red Hat Enterprise Linux	Designed for enterprise use on servers and workstations, this commercial distribution is stable and comes with long-term support. The free version of Red Hat Enterprise is CentOS, which comes with no support.	*redhat.com*
Ubuntu	Ubuntu is one of the most popular distributions of Linux for desktops and servers, and it comes with tons of online tutorials and help.	*ubuntu.com*

Table 10-3 Popular Linux distributions for desktops and servers

✏️ **Notes** For more information on Linux, see *linux.org* as well as the websites of the different Linux distributors.

Linux itself is not a complete operating system but is only the kernel for the OS. You also need a shell for user and application interfaces, and Linux shells vary widely by distributions. Many distributions of Linux include a GUI shell or desktop, which is called a windows manager. For example, Figure 10-37 shows the desktop or windows manager for Ubuntu Desktop. Some distributions of Linux designed for server applications don't have a windows manager. For example, Ubuntu Server installs with only a command-line interface. In this chapter, we use Ubuntu Desktop and Ubuntu Server as our sample Linux distributions.

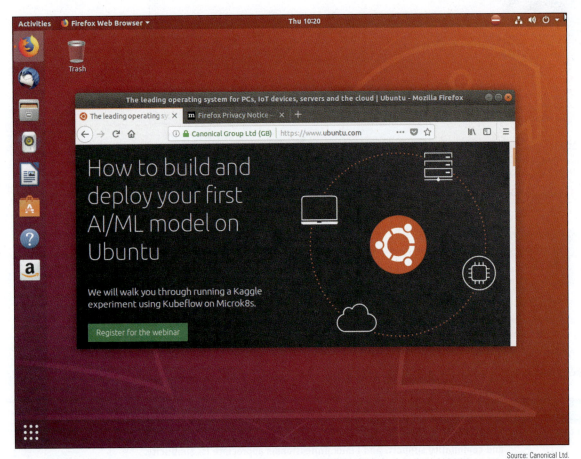

Source: Canonical Ltd.

Figure 10-37 Ubuntu Desktop with the Mozilla Firefox browser window open

You can install Ubuntu Desktop or Ubuntu Server in a VM or on a hard drive, CD, or USB flash drive. When you install Ubuntu on a CD or USB flash drive, it is called a **Live CD** or **Live USB**. A Live CD or USB can boot up a live version of Linux, complete with Internet access and all the tools you normally have available in a hard drive installation of Linux, but without installing the OS on the hard drive. To create a Live CD or Live USB, you can follow the directions given at *linuxliveusb.com/en/home*. This bootable CD or USB drive can be useful when testing a computer that cannot boot from the hard drive where Windows is installed.

Let's first install and explore Ubuntu Desktop with its graphical interface, and then you'll learn to install and use Ubuntu Server with its command-line interface.

APPLYING | CONCEPTS   INSTALLING UBUNTU DESKTOP IN A VM

Follow these steps to install Ubuntu Desktop in a VM:

1. Recall that you learned how to install a hypervisor and create a VM in Chapter 2. If you don't already have a hypervisor installed, install one that you can use to manage VMs. For example, in 64-bit Windows 10 Pro, you can use the Programs and Features window to enable Client Hyper-V, which comes embedded in the OS. Alternately, you can download and install one of these free hypervisors:

   ◢ Oracle VirtualBox at *virtualbox.org/wiki/Downloads*
   ◢ Windows Virtual PC at *microsoft.com/en-us/download/details.aspx?id=3702*
   ◢ VMware Workstation Player at *my.vmware.com/web/vmware/free#desktop_end_user_computing/vmware_ workstation_player/12_0*

2. Go to **ubuntu.com/download/desktop** and download the free Ubuntu Desktop OS to your hard drive. The file that downloads is an ISO file.

> ✎ **Notes** Ubuntu Desktop is only available as a 64-bit OS. To install a 64-bit guest OS in a VM, the host OS must also be 64-bit.

3. Open the Hyper-V Manager, Oracle VM VirtualBox, Virtual PC Manager, or VMware Workstation Player manager. Create a new VM with at least 2 GB of RAM and at least a 25-GB virtual hard drive capacity. Mount the ISO file that contains the Ubuntu Desktop download to a virtual DVD in your VM.

4. Start up the VM and install Ubuntu Desktop in the VM, accepting all default settings. Be sure to write down the name of the VM and your Ubuntu host name, Ubuntu user name, and password. When given the option, decline to install any extra software bundled with the OS. If needed, the software can be installed later.

> ✎ **Notes** If you need help learning to use your hypervisor of choice, try searching for some tutorial videos at *youtube.com* or on the hypervisor manufacturer's website.

5. When asked to restart the VM, first dismount (remove) the ISO file from the optical drive so that the VM boots to the hard drive. After Ubuntu Desktop launches, log in with your user name and password. Figure 10-38 shows the desktop with the Settings window active and the Network setting selected. To open this window, click the **Apps** button and then click **Settings**. When a window is active, its menu appears at the top of the screen. Also notice the System menu is displayed. To open the System menu, click the system icons area in the upper-right corner of the screen.

6. Take a few minutes to poke around the desktop. You'll see how it resembles macOS in many ways. For example, to open a Terminal window where you can enter Linux commands, click **Activities** and type **terminal** in the search box. Then click **Terminal** in the list that appears. Using the Terminal, you can enter Linux commands to manage and support the OS.

7. To shut down Ubuntu Desktop, click the system icons area in the upper-right corner of the screen. The System menu opens. Click the **Power** icon and click **Power Off**.

To learn more about using Ubuntu Desktop, an excellent source of information is the Ubuntu Desktop Guide at *help.ubuntu.com/stable/ubuntu-help/*.

10

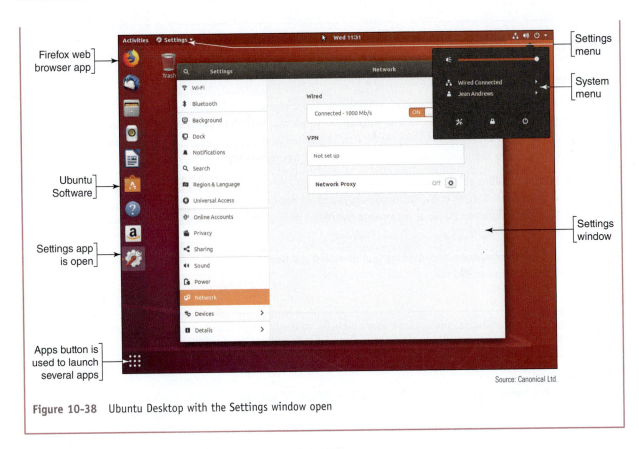

Firefox web browser app

Ubuntu Software

Settings app is open

Apps button is used to launch several apps

Settings menu

System menu

Settings window

Source: Canonical Ltd.

Figure 10-38 Ubuntu Desktop with the Settings window open

LINUX INSTALLS, UPDATES, AND BACKUPS

A+
CORE 2
1.3, 1.9,
4.9

When supporting a Linux system, an IT technician needs to know how to install software, update the OS and apps, and create and maintain scheduled backups. Here are a few details to get you started:

▲ *Install software.* To install software, click the **Ubuntu Software** button. Ubuntu Desktop software appears. Click an item and then click **Install** to start its installation. You can also install an app by clicking a setup file you have downloaded from the web.

▲ *Update Ubuntu and apps.* To update, click **Updates** in the Ubuntu Software window. Updates for Ubuntu are listed first, followed by app updates. Click **Install** beside the updates you want to install. Figure 10-39 shows that no updates are available.

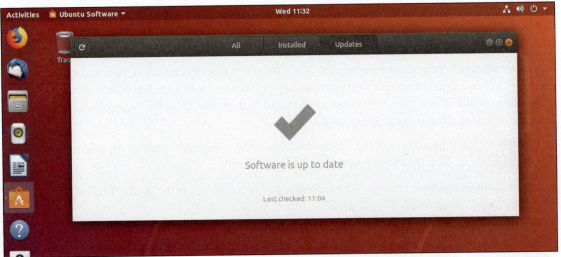

Source: Canonical Ltd.

Figure 10-39 Ubuntu Desktop is up to date

◢ *Change update settings.* To change update settings, open the **Software & Updates** menu and click **Software & Updates** in the drop-down list. Then click the **Updates** tab in the Software & Updates window (see Figure 10-40).

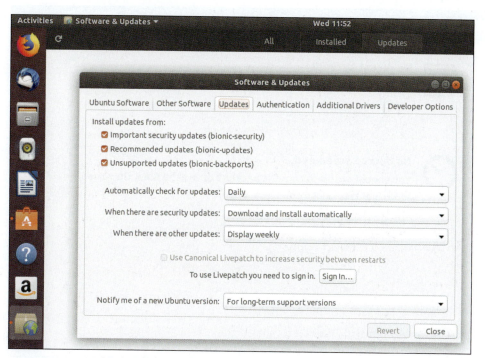

Figure 10-40 Change how Ubuntu Desktop handles updates

Source: Canonical Ltd.

10

Figure 10-41 Ubuntu Desktop utilities

Source: Canonical Ltd.

◢ *Configure backups.* Click the **Apps** button. In the list of apps, scroll down and click **Utilities** (see Figure 10-41). Click the **Backups** utility. Using the Backups window (see Figure 10-42), you can schedule backups, decide where the backups are stored, and select which items are included in the backup.

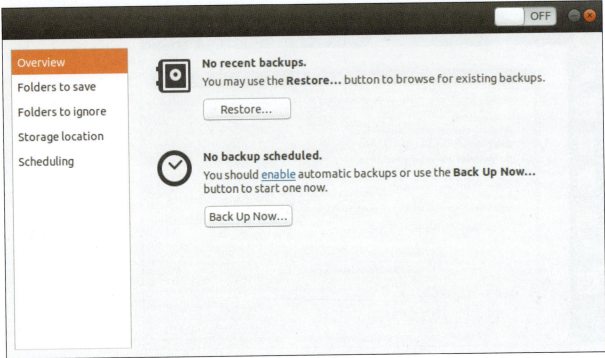

Source: Canonical Ltd.

Figure 10-42   Schedule an Ubuntu Desktop backup

Now that you know about Ubuntu Desktop, let's turn our attention to Ubuntu Server.

INSTALLING AND EXPLORING UBUNTU SERVER

A+
CORE 2
1.3, 1.9,
4.9

Ubuntu Server does not include a windows manager but uses a command-line interface called the terminal. The default shell for the terminal is the Bash shell, which stands for "Bourne Again Shell" and takes the best features from two previous shells, the Bourne and Korn shells. In this chapter, we use Ubuntu Server and its default Bash shell. In Linux, a command prompt in the terminal is called a shell prompt.

> 🖊 **Notes** To find out what shell is the default shell for the Linux system, enter the **echo $SHELL** command. To find out which shell you are currently using, enter the **echo $0** command.

As an IT support technician, you should know a little about Linux and its command-line interface. In this chapter, you learn about root and user accounts, file structure, some common commands, and how to use the vi text editor. As you work, be aware that the organization of files and directories and the way each command works might be slightly different with the distribution and version of Linux you are using.

> 🖊 **Notes** As you learn to use Ubuntu, know that the *help.ubuntu.com* website contains a wealth of information about Ubuntu and links to even more help.

APPLYING | CONCEPTS   INSTALLING UBUNTU SERVER IN A VM

To practice Linux skills covered in this chapter, you need an installation of Ubuntu Server. Before you continue with this chapter, follow these steps to install Ubuntu Server in a VM on a Windows computer:

1. Go to **ubuntu.com/download/server** and download the Ubuntu Server OS to your hard drive. The file that downloads is an .iso file.

2. Open the Hyper-V Manager, Oracle VM VirtualBox, Virtual PC Manager, or VMware Workstation Player manager, and then create a new VM. For Ubuntu Server, you'll need at least 2 GB of RAM and at least a 25-GB virtual hard drive. Mount the ISO file that contains the Ubuntu Server download to a virtual DVD in your VM.

3. Start up the VM and install Ubuntu Server, accepting all default settings until you get to the Filesystem setup screen (see Figure 10-43). To improve Ubuntu performance, you can set up a **swap partition**, which is used to hold virtual memory. In Linux, a swapfile or swap partition can hold virtual memory, but a swap partition yields better performance. Select **Manual**, as shown in the figure, so that you can create two partitions on the hard drive.

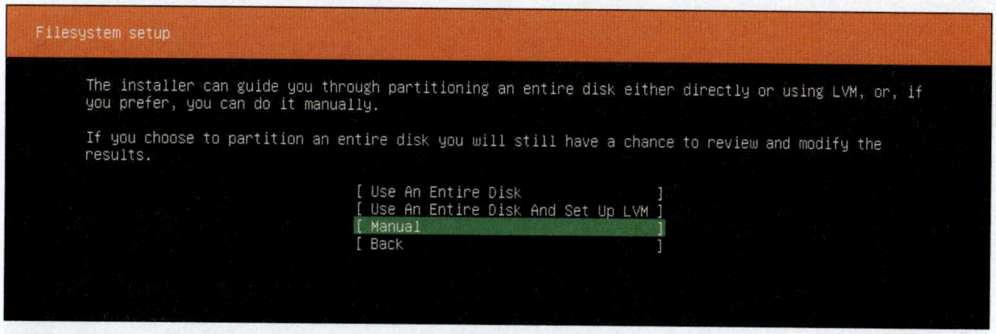

Figure 10-43   Partition the hard drive to include a swap partition

Source: Canonical Ltd.

> **Notes** When installing Ubuntu, use the arrow keys to navigate menus and press **Enter** to make a selection. The **Esc** key takes you back one level in a menu.

4. On the next screen, under AVAILABLE DEVICES, point to the local disk and press **Enter**. In the drop-down menu, select **Add Partition**, as shown in Figure 10-44.

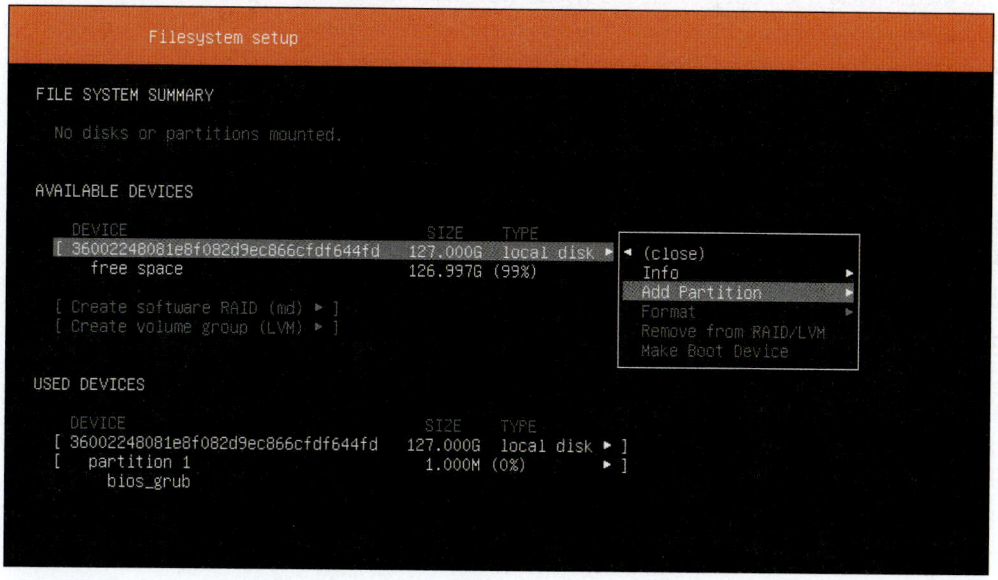

Figure 10-44   Create a new partition on the drive

Source: Canonical Ltd.

(continues)

5. In the Adding partition box, enter the size of the boot partition (at least 50 GB) and select the file system type **ext4**, as shown in Figure 10-45.

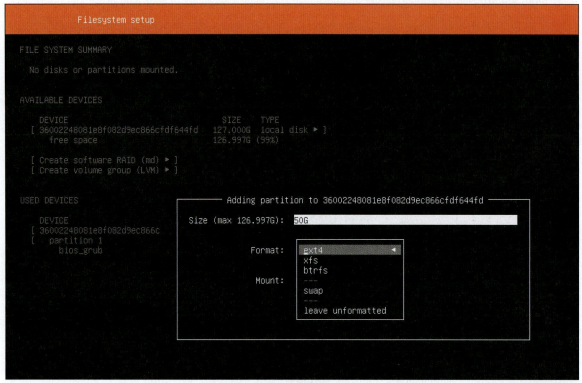

Source: Canonical Ltd.

Figure 10-45   Select ext4 for the file system of the new Ubuntu partition

6. Add a second partition and select **swap** as the file system type. Make the partition size a little larger than the amount of installed memory. Figure 10-46 shows the resulting Filesystem setup screen with three partitions created. Notice that not all of the hard drive is partitioned in our example:

   ◢ **Partition 1.** The small bios_grub partition is automatically created and is used to boot the system in a dual-boot environment. **GRUB (GR and Unified Bootloader)** is a boot loader used to manage dual-boot systems.
   ◢ **Partition 2.** The 50-GB partition that will hold the OS uses the ext4 file system.
   ◢ **Partition 3.** The 4-GB swap partition is used to hold virtual memory. A swap partition does not have a file system installed.

7. Select **Done** to complete the installation, accepting all defaults. Be sure to write down the name of the VM and your Ubuntu host name, Ubuntu user name, and password. When given the option, decline to install any extra software bundled with the OS. Notice this software includes add-ons to be used when Ubuntu Server is installed in the cloud at Amazon Web Services or Google Cloud. If needed, the software can be installed later.

8. After the VM restarts, Ubuntu Server launches, and you should see the terminal shell in the VM. See Figure 10-47.

(continues)

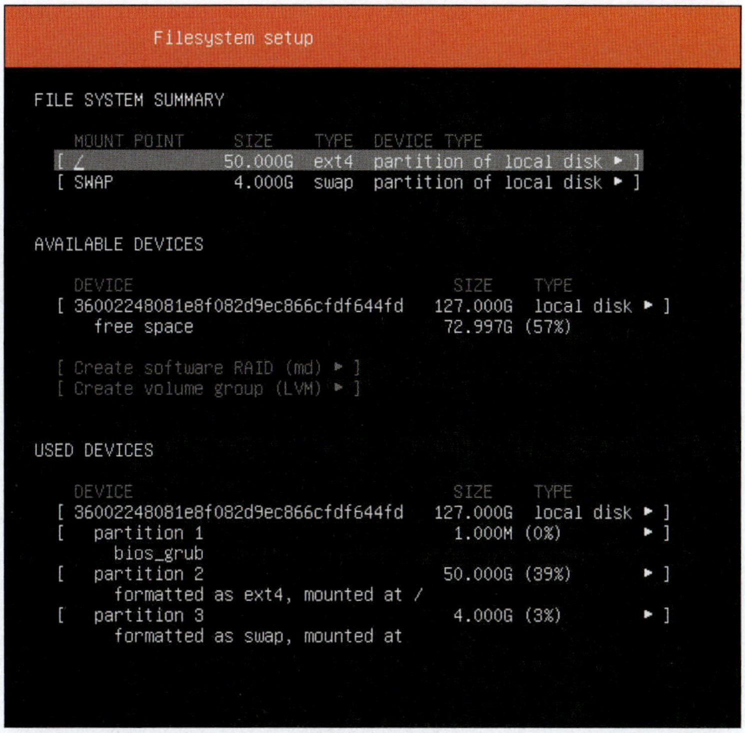

Source: Canonical Ltd.

Figure 10-46   Partitions are created to hold the Ubuntu installation

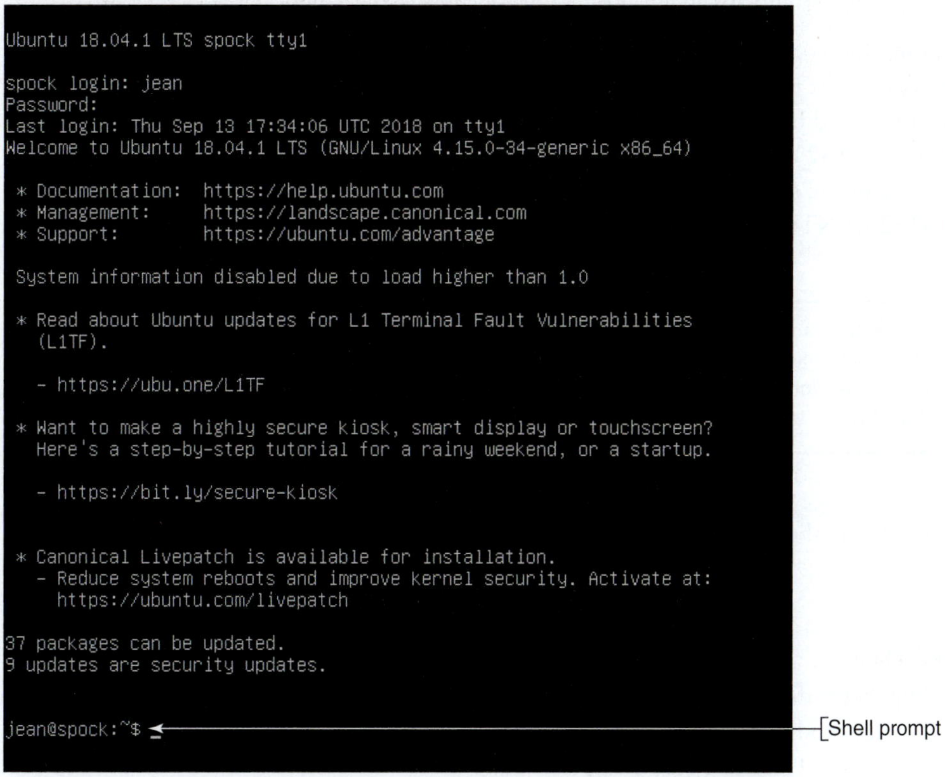

Source: Canonical Ltd.

Figure 10-47   When you log in to Ubuntu Server, available updates are listed

(continues)

9. You might need to press **Enter** to see the shell prompt. Then enter your user name and password, and you're logged in to Ubuntu Server. In the figure, the server is named spock and the logged-in user is jean. Notice Ubuntu reports that 37 packages can be updated. In Ubuntu, a **package** is the collection of files needed to install software.

10. Whenever you're ready to shut down Ubuntu Server, use the **sudo shutdown now** command.

Normally, the shell prompt includes the user name, host name, and the current directory, followed by a $. For example, in Figure 10-47, the shell prompt shows the user name is jean, the host name is spock, and the ~ character indicates the user's home directory, which for the jean account is /home/jean. When you first log in to Linux, the current directory is always the home directory of the logged-in user. (In Linux, directories in a path are separated with forward slashes, in contrast to the backward slashes used by Windows.)

It's easiest to install a swap partition when you install Ubuntu. If Ubuntu is installed on a single partition on the hard drive and you want to improve performance later, you can shrink the Ubuntu partition and create a swap partition in the free space. How to do that is not covered in this text.

> ★ **A+ Exam Tip** The A+ Core 2 exam expects you to know that a swap partition improves performance and that you can create one during or after the installation. You also need to know about the ext4 and ext3 file systems.

Recall that each OS has file systems it can support. Linux file systems include:

▲ *ext4.* The current Linux file system is ext4 (fourth extended file system).
▲ *ext3.* The ext3 file system was the first to support journaling, which is a technique that tracks and stores changes to the hard drive and helps prevent file system corruption.
▲ *FAT32 and NTFS.* The FAT32 and NTFS file systems are supported for compatibility with Windows and macOS. Windows can use either FAT32 or NTFS, and macOS can use FAT32. Ubuntu should not be installed on a FAT32 or NTFS volume.

> 🖉 **Notes** On a local network or in a dual boot with Windows and Linux, you might want to access files in either volume from either OS. Know that Linux can access the NTFS file system on the Windows volume, but Windows cannot access the ext4 file system on the Linux volume. You can, however, install third-party software, such as Paragon ExtFS for Windows (*paragon-software.com*), to access the ext4 volume.

As you read along and learn about Linux commands, you can use your Ubuntu VM to practice these commands.

DIRECTORY STRUCTURES

Table 10-4 lists some important directories that are created in the root during a typical Linux installation. (Some distributions of Linux modify the directory structure.) Not all directories in the root are listed in the table.

Directory	Description
/bin	Contains programs and commands necessary to boot the system and perform other system tasks not reserved for the administrator, such as shutdown and reboot
/boot	Consists of components needed for the boot process, such as boot loaders
/dev	Holds device names, which consist of the type of device and a number identifying the device; actual device drivers are located in the /lib/modules /[*kernel version*]/ directory
/etc	Contains system configuration data, including configuration files and settings and their subdirectories; these files are used for tasks such as configuring a user account, changing system settings, and configuring a domain name resolution service
/home	Contains user data; every user of the system has a directory in the /home directory, such as /home/jean or /home/scott, and when a user logs in, that directory becomes the current working directory
/lib	Stores common libraries used by applications so that more than one application can use the same library at one time; an example is the library of C programming code, without which only the kernel of the Linux system could run
/lost+found	Stores data that is lost when files are truncated or when an attempt to fix system errors is unsuccessful
/opt	Contains installations of third-party applications such as web browsers that do not come with the Linux OS distribution
/root	Serves as the home directory for the root user and contains only files specific to the root user; don't confuse this directory with the root, which contains all the directories listed in this table
/sbin	Stores commands required for system administration
/tmp	Stores temporary files, such as the ones that applications use during installation and operation
/usr	Contains executable programs, libraries, and shared resources that are not critical to the Ubuntu system
/var	Holds variable data such as logs, email, news, print spools, and administrative files

Table 10-4 Important directories in a typical Linux root directory

APPLYING | CONCEPTS   EXPLORING DIRECTORIES AND FILES

Let's learn a few Linux commands that we can use to explore directories and files. As shown in Figure 10-48, use these commands:

1. Use the **clear** command to clear the screen of all its clutter.

2. Use the **pwd** command (print working directory) to display the full path to the current directory, which is /home/jean in the figure.

3. Use the **cd ..** command to move up one directory to /home. (There's a space after d.)

4. Use the **ls** command to display the list of files and subdirectories in the /home directory. Notice in the figure that the one subdirectory in the /home directory is jean.

5. Use the **ls -l** command to display the results using the long format. (There's a space after the s.) As you can see in the figure, the results are:

```
drwxr-xr-x 4 jean jean 4096 Sep 12 16:56 jean
```

(continues)

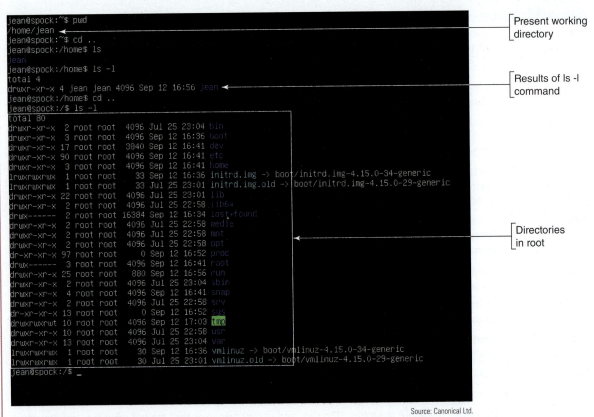

Figure 10-48   Directories in the root

Here is an explanation of the types of information in the list:

▲ *Attributes*. The first 10 characters (drwxr-xr-x) define the file or directory attributes. The first character identifies the type of item: A d is a directory, a - is a regular file, and a 1 indicates the item is a link to another location. The other nine characters (rwxr-xr-x) define the read, write, and execute permissions assigned to the file or directory; these permissions are explained in detail later in the chapter.

▲ *Links*. The second column lists the number of links the item has, which is 4 in our example. In Linux, a link is similar to a Windows shortcut to a file or directory.

▲ *Owners*. The third column lists the user owner and the fourth column lists the group that owns the file or directory. In Figure 10-48, the owner is jean and the owner group is also jean.

▲ *Size, date, and name*. The last columns list the size of the file or directory in bytes, the date the item was last modified, and the name of the file or directory. The name of directory jean is listed in blue.

6. When you use the **cd ..** command again, you move up to the main directory in Linux, called the root directory, which is indicated with a forward slash. The **ls -l** command lists the files and subdirectories in the root.

ROOT ACCOUNT AND USER ACCOUNTS

A Linux system administrator is responsible for installing updates to the OS (called patches), managing backups, installing software and hardware, setting up user accounts, resetting passwords, and generally supporting the OS and users. To accomplish this, she requires root privileges or access to all the functions of the OS. Two ways Linux allows for root privileges are:

▲ *Superuser*. The principal user account is called the **root account**. Notice in Figure 10-48 that all the directories and files in the root directory belong to the root account. When logged in to the root account, the user is called the **superuser**. Because the root account is so powerful, Ubuntu disables login to this account by default. The root account is similar to the Windows Administrator account.

◢ *Regular user account with root privileges.* Any user account can be assigned root privileges. If the user has root privileges, she can execute any command that requires root access by adding sudo to the beginning of the command line. An account with root privileges is similar to a Windows account that has been assigned Administrative rights.

The command to switch users is su. For a user to switch to the root account, she uses the command **sudo su root,** as shown in Figure 10-49. Notice in the figure that the shell prompt changes to

root@spock:/#. The Linux command prompt for the root user is different from the command prompt for regular users. The root command prompt is #, and other users have the $ command prompt. To switch back to the jean account, use the command **su jean.** As a general practice, never log in to Linux as root unless you have no other option; you can do a lot of damage as root.

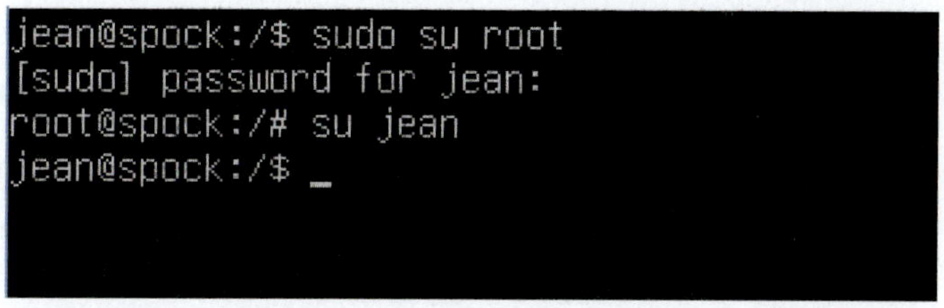

```
jean@spock:/$ sudo su root
[sudo] password for jean:
root@spock:/# su jean
jean@spock:/$ _
```

Source: Canonical Ltd.

Figure 10-49 The user account, host name, and current directory appear in the shell prompt along with a # or $ to indicate the root account or other account

LINUX COMMANDS

Table 10-5 describes some basic Linux commands, together with simple examples of how some are used. As you read along, be aware that all commands entered in Linux are case sensitive, meaning that uppercase and lowercase matter.

Command	Description
adduser	**Add a user to a system:** adduser <username>
apt-get	**Install and remove applications and other programs (called packages) in Linux. When you first install Linux, it installs with only a bare-bones set of commands and utilities and includes a library of packages that you can install as needed. For example, to install the SSH (Secure Shell) package so you can remote in to your Linux server, use this command:** sudo apt-get install ssh **The apt-get command requires root access, which means you must precede the command with sudo.**
cat	**View the contents of a file. Many Linux commands can use the redirection symbol > to redirect the output of the command. For example, use the redirection symbol with the cat command to copy a file:** cat /etc/shells > newfile **The content of the shells file is written to newfile.**
cd	**Change the directory.** **To change the directory to /etc:** cd /etc **To move up one level in the directory tree:** cd .. **To go to the root:** cd /
chmod	**Change modes (or permissions) for a file or directory. You'll see several examples of this command later in the chapter.**
chown	**Change the owner of a file or directory.**
clear	**Clear the screen. This command is useful when the screen has become cluttered with commands and data that you no longer need to view.**

Table 10-5 Some common Linux commands (continues)

Command	Description
`cp`	Copy a file: `cp <source> <destination>`

`dd`	Copy and convert files, directories, partitions, and even entire DVDs or hard drives. It's a powerful command with many practical uses and parameters, and only a superuser can use it. The basic format of the command is:
	
	`dd if=<source> of=<destination>`
	
	For example, use this command to create an ISO file from the contents of a CD:
	
	`dd if=/dev/cdrom of=/tmp/cdimage.iso`

`deluser`	Remove a user from a system:
	
	`deluser <username>`
	
	Remove the user and his home directory:
	
	`deluser -remove-home <username>`

`df`	The command stands for *disk filesystem* and displays the amount of free space on the hard drive. To see the file system the drive is using: `df -T`
`echo`	Display information on the screen. You can also save the information to a file. For example, to create a new file that contains text, enter this command: `echo "Hello World" > myfile`
`exit`	Log out; the login shell prompt appears, where you can log in again.
`grep`	Search for a specific pattern in a file or in multiple files. This command is useful when searching through long log files: `grep <pattern> <file>`

`ifconfig`	Troubleshoot problems with TCP/IP network connections. This command can disable and enable network adapters and assign a static IP address to an adapter. For example, to show all configuration information:
	
	`ifconfig –a`
	
	To enable or disable an adapter, use the up or down parameter. For example, to enable eth0, the first Ethernet interface:
	
	`sudo ifconfig eth0 up`
	
	To assign a static IP address to the eth0 interface:
	`ifconfig eth0 192.168.1.90`

`iwconfig`	This command works like ifconfig but applies only to wireless networks. Use it to display information about the wireless adapter's configuration or to change the configuration. To set the wireless NIC to Ad-Hoc mode so that other devices within range can connect directly to it, use this command, where wlan0 identifies the wireless adapter:
	
	`iwconfig wlan0 mode Ad-Hoc`
	
	To force the NIC to use channel 3:
	
	`iwconfig wlan0 channel 3`

`kill`	Kill a process instead of waiting for it to terminate. Use the ps command to list process IDs. To end a process, use the kill command followed by the PID. For example, to kill the process with a PID of 984: `kill 984` The command sends a signal to the process to end itself in an orderly way. If the process doesn't die peacefully, you can get the kernel involved to forcefully end the process; this is called a **forced kill**: `kill -kill 984`

Table 10-5   Some common Linux commands (continues)

Command	Description
`ls`	Like the Windows dir command, ls displays a list of directories and files. For example, to list files in the /etc directory, use the long parameter for a complete listing: `ls -l /etc` **To include hidden files in the list:** `ls -la /etc` (In Linux, hidden files begin with a period.)
`man`	Display the online help manual, called man pages. For example, to get information about the echo command: `man echo` The manual program displays information about the command. To exit the manual program, type q.
`mkdir`	Make a new directory: `mkdir <directory>`

`mv`	Move a file or rename it, if the source and destination are the same directory:
	
	`mv <source> <destination>`
	
	To move myfile from the jean directory to the home directory:
	
	`sudo mv /home/jean/myfile /home/myfile`
	
	Because the /home directory is owned by the root account, the sudo command is required.

`passwd`	Change a password. When a user enters the command, he is asked for the old password and then can change it. The superuser can change the password for any account and does not need to enter the account's old password, making it possible to reset a forgotten password.
`ping`	Test network connections by sending a request packet to a host. If a connection is successful, the host will return a response packet. For example: `ping 192.168.1.100` The ping results continue until you manually stop the process. Press Ctrl+C to break out of the process. **To specify the number of pings:** `ping 192.168.1.100 -c 4`
`ps`	The command stands for *process status* and displays the process table so that you can identify process IDs for currently running processes. (Once you know the process ID, you can use the kill command to terminate a process.) **To list processes of the current user:** `ps` **To list processes owned by all users:** `ps aux`
`pwd`	Show the name of the current or present working directory. **When you first log in to Linux, the directory is /home/***username***.**
`rm`	Remove or delete the file or files that are specified: `rm <file>`
`rmdir`	Remove or delete an empty directory: `rmdir <directory>`
`shutdown`	Automatically shut down the system. **To shut down now:** `sudo shutdown now` **To warn users and then shut down:** `sudo shutdown -h +10 "Everyone log out now. The system will shut down in 10 minutes for maintenance."` **To reboot now:** `sudo shutdown -r now`

10

Table 10-5   Some common Linux commands (continues)

Command	Description
su	The command stands for *substitute user* or *switch user* and changes to a different user account. When switching to superuser, add sudo to the command.
	To switch to the root account: `sudo su root`
	To switch back to the jean account: `su jean`
sudo	The command stands for *substitute user to do the command* and is pronounced "sue-doe" or "sue-doo." When logged in as a normal user with an account that has the right to use root commands, you can start a command with sudo to run the command as the superuser. A user password may be required.
	For example: `sudo shutdown now`
touch	Create a blank file in the current directory. For example:
	`touch myfile`
vi	Launch a full-screen editor that can be used to edit a file:
	`vi <file>`

Table 10-5 Some common Linux commands (continued)

> ★ **A+ Exam Tip** The A+ Core 2 exam expects you to be familiar with these Linux commands: ls, grep, cd, shutdown, pwd, passwd, mv, cp, rm, chmod, chown, iwconfig, ifconfig, ps, su, sudo, apt-get, vi, dd, and kill.

Here are a few tips when using commands at a shell prompt:

▲ *Retrieve previous commands.* Press the arrow-up key to retrieve previously entered commands and then edit a command that appears.

▲ *Use wildcard characters.* Linux can use the * and ? wildcard characters in command lines, similar to Windows. For example, the **ls *.???** command lists all files with a file extension of three characters. In addition, Linux provides a third wildcard: Brackets can give a choice of characters. For example, the **ls *.[abc]*** command lists all files whose file extension begins with a, b, or c.

▲ *Redirect output.* Normally, output from a command displays on the screen. To redirect that output to a file, use the redirection symbol >. For example, to redirect the output of the ifconfig command to myfile, use this command: **ifconfig > myfile**

▲ *Page the output.* Append |more to the end of a command line to display the results of the command on the screen one page at a time. For example, to page the ls command: **ls -l |more**

▲ *Use Ctrl+C.* To break out of a command or process, press **Ctrl+C**. Use it to recover after entering a wrong command or to stop a command that requires a manual halt.

THE VI EDITOR

The **vi editor** (visual editor) is a text editor that works in command mode (to enter commands) or in insert mode (to edit text). In this section, you learn how to create a text file in the vi editor, edit text, and save your changes. All vi commands are case sensitive.

Let's create and work with a file called mymemo:

1. You can save a file to your home directory because you own that directory. If you are not already in your home directory, use the cd command to go there. For example:

   `cd /home/jean`

2. To open the vi editor and create the new file, enter the command **vi mymemo**. The vi editor screen appears and the file name is shown at the bottom of the screen.

3. When you first open the vi editor, you are in command mode. Type **i** to switch to insert mode. When you are in insert mode, the word INSERT is shown at the bottom of the screen.

4. Type the contents of Step 3 as the text for your memo (see Figure 10-50). Use your arrow keys to move over the text to edit it. You can also use the Insert key to switch between inserting text and overwriting text.

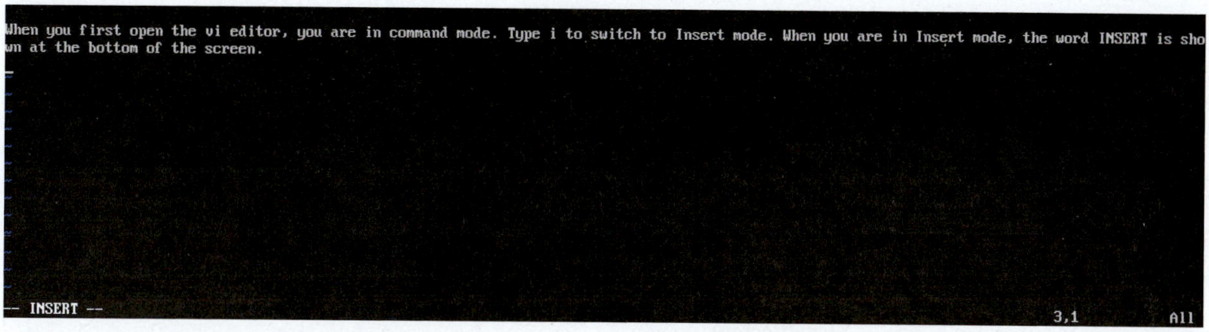

When you first open the vi editor, you are in command mode. Type i to switch to Insert mode. When you are in Insert mode, the word INSERT is shown at the bottom of the screen.

-- INSERT --   3,1   All

Figure 10-50 The vi text editor in Insert mode

Source: Canonical Ltd.

10

5. To switch back to command mode, first press the **Esc** key and then type a **:**. The colon command prompt appears and your pointer goes to the bottom of the screen. Type **wq** to save (write) the file and exit (quit) the editor.

Here is a list of enough vi commands to get you started with the editor. You can find other commands online:

:w   Save your changes but don't exit the editor.

:q   Exit the editor after you have just saved your changes with the :w command.

:wq   Save your changes and exit the editor.

:q!   Quit without saving your changes.

APPLYING | CONCEPTS   INSTALLING FTP SERVER IN UBUNTU

In the following steps, you learn to use several Linux commands to install and configure software and examine a log file. Follow these steps to set up an FTP server in Ubuntu:

1. Log in to Ubuntu Server with your user name and password.

2. To create a short file to test the FTP server, you can use the echo command with redirection. Create mymemo in your /home/*username* directory using this command:

```
echo "my typing" > /home/username/mymemo
```

3. To install the FTP program named vsftpd, enter this command:

```
sudo apt-get install vsftpd
```

4. Respond to the prompts and then wait for the package to install.

(continues)

5. Now you need to configure the FTP program by editing the /etc/vsftpd.conf text file. Before you edit the file, go to the /etc directory and make a backup copy of the file just in case you need it later. The sudo command is needed because files in the /etc directory belong to root:

```
cd /etc
sudo cp vsftpd.conf vsftpd.backup
```

6. Use the vi editor to edit the FTP configuration file:

```
sudo vi vsftpd.conf
```

7. Verify and/or change three lines in the file to create the settings listed below. Part of the file, including the three lines, is shown in Figure 10-51.

anonymous_enable=NO	Disable anonymous logins.
local_enable=YES	If necessary, remove the # to uncomment the line and allow local users to log in.
write_enable=YES	If necessary, remove the # to uncomment the line and allow users to write to a directory.

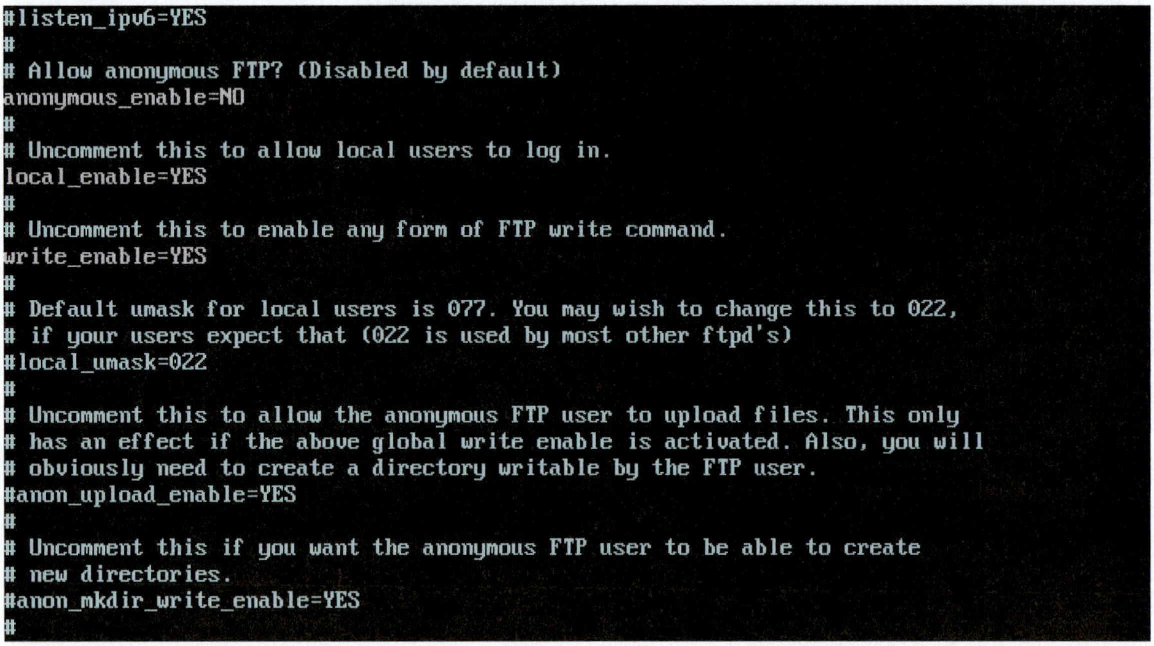

```
#listen_ipv6=YES
#
# Allow anonymous FTP? (Disabled by default)
anonymous_enable=NO
#
# Uncomment this to allow local users to log in.
local_enable=YES
#
# Uncomment this to enable any form of FTP write command.
write_enable=YES
#
# Default umask for local users is 077. You may wish to change this to 022,
# if your users expect that (022 is used by most other ftpd's)
#local_umask=022
#
# Uncomment this to allow the anonymous FTP user to upload files. This only
# has an effect if the above global write enable is activated. Also, you will
# obviously need to create a directory writable by the FTP user.
#anon_upload_enable=YES
#
# Uncomment this if you want the anonymous FTP user to be able to create
# new directories.
#anon_mkdir_write_enable=YES
#
```

Source: Canonical Ltd.

Figure 10-51 Part of the vsftpd.conf text file

8. Exit the vi editor, saving your changes. Restart the FTP service using this command:

```
service vsftpd restart
```

9. To find out the IP address of the server, type **ifconfig**.

10. On your host Windows computer, open a command prompt window and go to a directory on your Windows computer where you have a file stored. To test your FTP server, open an FTP session using the IP address of the server—for example, **ftp 192.168.1.110** (your IP address may be different). Then enter your user name and password. The ftp> prompt appears. See Figure 10-52.

(continues)

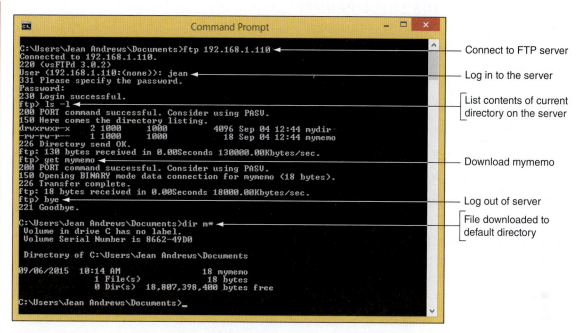

Figure 10-52 Use FTP to transfer files between a Windows and Ubuntu system

11. Next use the **ls -l** command to see a list of directories and files. You should see the file mymemo that you created in your /home/*username* directory earlier.

12. If you want to transfer files with FTP commands, use the **get** and **put** commands. To download the mymemo file, use the command **get mymemo**. To transfer a file from your Windows computer to your Ubuntu server, use the **put** command.

13. Type **bye** to disconnect from the FTP server. At the Windows command prompt, you can use the **dir m*** command, as shown in Figure 10-52, to verify that the file was received on the Windows computer.

14. Return to Ubuntu Server and examine the FTP log file, /var/log/vsftpd.log. Because the file is short, you can use the cat command to display the entire log. The sudo command is required because /var files belong to root:

```
sudo cat /var/log/vsftpd.log
```

15. After much activity, log files can get quite long. The grep command can help you find a specific action, user, IP address, file name, or directory name. For example, to display lines in the log file that contain the text "LOGIN," use this grep command:

```
sudo grep "LOGIN" /var/log/vsftpd.log
```

The results of the cat and grep commands are shown in Figure 10-53.

```
jean@VM50:~$ cd /var/log
jean@VM50:/var/log$ sudo cat vsftpd.log
Fri Sep  4 12:42:29 2015 [pid 1420] CONNECT: Client "127.0.0.1"
Fri Sep  4 12:42:38 2015 [pid 1419] [jean] OK LOGIN: Client "127.0.0.1"
Fri Sep  4 12:45:48 2015 [pid 1428] CONNECT: Client "192.168.1.124"
Fri Sep  4 12:45:58 2015 [pid 1427] [jean] OK LOGIN: Client "192.168.1.124"
Fri Sep  4 12:46:24 2015 [pid 1429] [jean] OK DOWNLOAD: Client "192.168.1.124", "/home/jean/mymemo", 18 bytes, 19.93Kbyte/sec
jean@VM50:/var/log$ sudo grep "LOGIN" /var/log/vsftpd.log
Fri Sep  4 12:42:38 2015 [pid 1419] [jean] OK LOGIN: Client "127.0.0.1"
Fri Sep  4 12:45:58 2015 [pid 1427] [jean] OK LOGIN: Client "192.168.1.124"
jean@VM50:/var/log$ _
```

Figure 10-53 The grep command can be used to search for specific text in log files

Source: Canonical Ltd.

UPDATE LINUX FROM THE SHELL PROMPT

In general, Linux updates don't come as often as Windows or macOS updates. The creator of your Linux distribution publishes updates to packages in the current release of a distribution and publishes new releases of a distribution. When you first log in to the system, Linux reports the package updates that are available (refer back to Figure 10-47).

Use these commands to update the packages previously installed in your system:

1. To refresh the list of all available updates:

   `sudo apt-get update`

2. To update only the installed packages:

   `sudo apt-get upgrade`

A new release of a distribution contains all updates since the last release. As a Linux administrator, you need to stay aware of the latest release of the distribution you are using and decide when or if it's appropriate to upgrade to that release. Before you upgrade to a new release, be sure you have backups of your data and a disk image (called a clone) of the entire Linux partition.

Here's how to upgrade to a new release for Ubuntu Server:

1. Follow the previous steps to update all packages installed in the system.

2. To make sure the latest update manager program is installed:

   `sudo apt-get install update-manager-core`

3. To install the latest release of Ubuntu Server:

   `sudo do-release-upgrade`

If a new release is available, the last command reports it and you can follow directions to install it.

> **✎ Notes** Ubuntu Server does not have an easy-to-use backup service. Normally, the system administrator installs third-party software, such as Bacula, to perform backups. Another option is to write your own **shell scripts**, which are similar to batch files, that include tar commands to create an archive of many files and copy it to other media or network storage. How to set up a backup process for Linux is not covered in this chapter.

ASSIGN PERMISSIONS AND OWNERSHIP OF FILES OR DIRECTORIES

A file or directory can have read, write, and/or execute permissions assigned to it. Permissions can be assigned to (a) the owner, (b) other users in the same group as the owner, and (c) all users. The chmod command is used to manage permissions for files and directories. To see current permissions, examine the 10 characters in the left column that display when you use the ls -l command. For example, suppose the output for the ls -l command on the /home/jean directory is that shown in Figure 10-54.

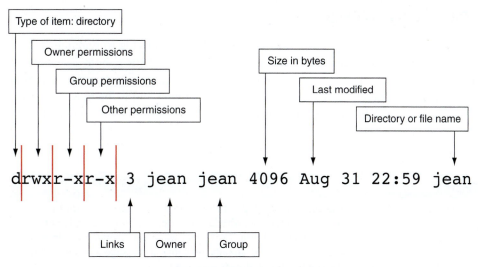

Figure 10-54   Information about the jean directory displayed by ls-l

Here is the explanation of these characters:

▲ The first character identifies the type of item (d is a directory; - is a regular file).
▲ Characters 2–4 show the permissions assigned to the user or owner (for example, rwx means the user has read, write, and execute permissions).
▲ Characters 5–7 show the permissions assigned to the group (for example, r-x means the group has read and execute permissions, but not write permission).
▲ Characters 8–10 show the permissions for others (for example, r-x means other users have read and execute permissions, but not write permission. By contrast, --- would mean others don't have read, write, or execute permission).

The chmod command changes these permissions. For example, in Figure 10-54, if the user jean wants to give read, write, and execute permissions to everyone (group and other), she can use this command:

chmod g=rwx,o=rwx /home/jean

The **g** assigns permission to the group and the **o** assigns permissions to others. (The **u** can assign permissions to the owner.) For a folder, you must move out of the folder before you change its permissions. Also, the command has no space before or after a comma.

Let's look at an example of when you might need to change the ownership of a directory or file. Suppose you are setting up an FTP server so that users who have accounts on the server can use FTP to upload files to their home directories. Table 10-6 lists commands that might be useful to set up the user directories.

Command	Description
sudo adduser carlos	**Creates the user account and its home directory**
sudo mkdir /home/carlos/files	**Creates a directory for carlos to store his files when using FTP; the sudo command is required to create the directory in another user's account, and this new directory belongs to root**
sudo chown carlos:carlos /home/carlos/files	**Makes carlos the owner of the files directory; the carlos group is also assigned to the files directory**
sudo chmod g-w,o-w /home/carlos/files	**Removes write permissions for the files directory for all but the carlos user (the g-w parameter removes write permissions and g+w adds write permissions)**

Table 10-6   Commands to set up user directories with appropriate write permissions

TELNET AND SSH FOR REMOTE ACCESS

Recall that Windows uses Remote Desktop and macOS uses Screen Sharing to remotely access a computer with screen and file sharing. In Linux, the primary utilities for remote access at a shell prompt are Telnet and SSH (Secure Shell). Telnet does not encrypt transmissions, but SSH encrypts all transmissions. Therefore, SSH is more secure than Telnet and is the most common method to remotely access a Linux system. Use the commands in Table 10-7 to install Telnet and SSH in Linux.

Command	Description
`sudo apt-add-repository universe`	Add the universe repository to the list of places Ubuntu can find apps. This is an official repository of apps, but it is not supported by Ubuntu. (Note that when you attempt to add the repository and it is already available, a message appears saying the component is already enabled.)
`sudo apt-get update`	Download and update all apps available to Ubuntu, including the ones in the universe repository.
`sudo apt-get install openssh-server`	Install and run the SSH server in Linux.
`sudo apt install telnetd`	Install and run the Telnet server.

Table 10-7 Install and run Telnet and SSH in Linux

In Windows, SSH is enabled by default and Telnet Client can be turned on using the Windows Features window, which is available in the Programs and Features window. Here are the steps to remotely access a Linux system from a Windows or Linux computer:

1. For Windows, turn on **Telnet Client** in the **Windows Features** window.

2. At a Windows command prompt or Linux shell prompt, use the following command to open a Telnet session, substituting the IP address for the Linux system you want to remote in to:

   telnet 192.168.1.160

3. The Linux login prompt appears. Enter your user name and password. To close the session, use the **logout** command.

4. To use SSH to remote in, enter the following command, substituting your user name and IP address for the remote Linux system:

   ssh jean@192.168.1.160

5. Enter your password to log in to Linux. To close the session, use the **logout** command.

COMPARING WINDOWS, macOS, AND LINUX

Now that you have learned how to use and support Windows, macOS, and Linux, let's take a step back and compare these three types of operating systems. As an IT technician, most likely you'll be called on to help a customer decide which type of OS to use in a given situation. Here are some tips to help you decide between Windows, macOS, and Linux:

▲ *User desktops and laptops.* Windows and macOS are well-suited for user desktops and laptops because each OS has a plethora of applications designed for it. Most often when deciding between the two, it comes down to what a company or individual prefers and knows how to use and support. Linux with a windows manager, on the other hand, comes up short in the number of desktop applications designed for it.

▲ *Server applications.* Linux is popular as a server OS for supporting many types of server applications, such as web servers, email servers, and DNS servers. However, Windows Server with Active Directory is more popular when it comes to controlling and securing access to a network in a corporate environment. Many IT departments use a combination of Windows Server to manage the Windows domain and Linux servers to manage server applications.

▲ *End-of-life vendor limitation.* In practice, computers and their operating systems might stay in service long after manufacturer support for the OS has ended. However, it's important that you know when an OS will no longer be supported by its manufacturer. Here is the rundown:

    ▲ *Windows.* In the past, Microsoft released a new version of Windows about every three years, but with Windows 10, it seems to be heading in the direction of Windows as a service. Microsoft has unofficially said that Windows 10 is its last version of Windows, meaning that it will continue to provide ongoing feature updates (about every six months) and minor updates weekly. Eventually, we expect to think of just Windows, not a particular version, which is the direction that Apple has taken.

    ▲ *macOS.* Over the past 20 years, Apple has released versions of Mac OS X about once a year; it was renamed macOS in 2016. The version a Mac can support depends on the age of the Mac. For example, a MacBook made in 2009 or later should support High Sierra, a current macOS release, and a MacBook made in 2012 or later should support Mojave, the latest macOS release.

    ▲ *Linux.* How long a Linux distribution will be supported depends on the developer. For example, Canonical (*canonical.com*), which makes Ubuntu Desktop and Ubuntu Server, releases a new distribution of Ubuntu about every two years and provides support of that release for about five years.

▲ *Compatibility between OSs.* When selecting an OS, consider how compatible it is with other OSs in the organization. Because macOS and Linux are both built on UNIX, they are more compatible with each other than with Windows. The FAT32 file system can be read and written by Linux, macOS, and Windows, and is therefore the file system of choice when you are concerned with compatibility. Linux can read and write to NTFS file systems used on Windows systems, but macOS cannot.

Now let's turn our attention to the last topic of the chapter, scripting.

SCRIPTING SOFTWARE AND TECHNIQUES

In this text you've learned to use commands in a Windows command prompt window, cmdlets in a PowerShell window, and Linux commands in macOS and Linux terminals. When a technician finds himself repetitively entering the same group of commands, he might decide to store them in a text file and execute them as a batch. The text file containing the list of commands is called a script; using scripts can save time and assures consistency (fewer errors). In this part of the chapter, you learn about the various script file types and then explore the basics of reading and writing scripts, which will help get you started using scripts written by others or writing your own scripts.

SCRIPT FILE TYPES

In Chapter 4, you learned to create a batch file that contains Windows commands. This and other script file types are listed in Table 10-8 with a description of the software that can read and interpret each command in a script file and execute these commands in a run-time environment.

Script File Extension	Description
.bat	A batch file contains a list of Windows commands that can be executed in a command prompt window.
.ps1	A PowerShell script contains cmdlets executed in Windows PowerShell. The script is written using dynamic type checking, which means each cmdlet is checked by the PowerShell interpreter as it is typed to verify that the command can be executed as it is added to the script file. Many scripting and programming applications support dynamic type checking.
.vbs	A .vbs script is written with VBScript, which is modeled after the more complex Visual Basic, a full-fledged programming language.
.sh	A UNIX or Linux script, also called a shell script, contains Linux commands and is executed in a UNIX or Linux shell.
.py	A Python script is a group of Python commands interpreted by Python. Python can also compile the commands into an executable program.
.js	A .js script written in JavaScript is a text file that contains commands normally used with webpages. These scripts can be embedded in an HTML file, which is downloaded from a web server to a browser and used to build an interactive webpage in the browser.

Table 10-8 Types of script files and scripting software

Scripts are simpler to write and use than programs. The difference between a script and a program is:

▲ *A script is interpreted.* A script is read, interpreted, and executed command by command directly from the script file by software called an interpreter. For example, a technician types commands into a script file, and the commands are verified to work by PowerShell or VBScript. When a technician executes the script, PowerShell or VBScript reads, interprets, and executes each command in the file.

▲ *A program is compiled.* A program is first written using a programming language such as Visual Basic or Python, which interprets the code to verify that it can be executed. Then the coding file is compiled by the Visual Basic or Python complier into a binary executable file that has an .exe file extension. The executable file can then be run or executed by an operating system.

BASICS OF SCRIPTING

A+
CORE 2
4.8

Ready to learn a little scripting? Let's get started with some key terms:

▲ An environmental variable (sometimes called a system variable) is information the OS makes available to a script. For example, the Windows and Linux PATH variable lists the paths (drives, directories, and subdirectories) the script can use. Another example is the TEMP variable, which tells a script where it can store its temporary files. To view and edit environmental variables in Windows, open the **System** window and click **Advanced system settings**. On the Advanced tab of the System Properties box, click **Environmental Variables**. See Figure 10-55.

▲ Comments are text you put in a script to document the script. They can include your name, the date, the purpose of the script, and documentation that might help someone understand command lines in the script. Comment syntax refers to how you tag the text as a comment so that it is not interpreted as a command. For example, in PowerShell, a line in the script file can hold a comment if you begin the line with a #.

▲ A basic loop executes the same commands multiple times until some condition is met.

▲ A variable is the name of an unknown data item and can be assigned a value, which is called initializing the variable. In PowerShell, a variable name is preceded by $. You can assign a value to a variable using the equal symbol (=).

▲ A data type determines what type of value a variable can be assigned. Two common data types are integers (whole numbers) and strings (text).

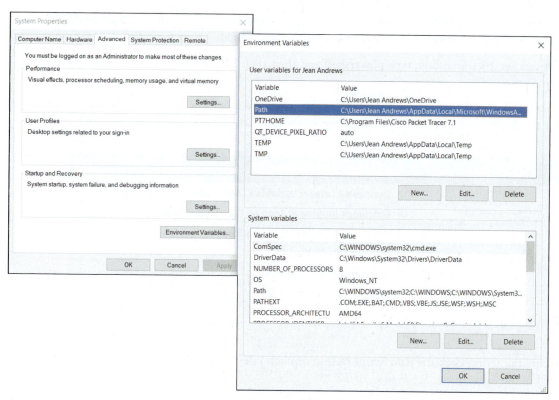

Figure 10-55 View, create, edit, and delete environmental variables

It's a commonly known fact in the world of scripting and programming that the very first script or program a person writes does nothing more than say "Hello World." This proves you know how to create, save, and execute a script. Let's create one in a shell script:

1. At an Ubuntu shell prompt, make sure the current directory is your home directory. Then enter this command, saving the .sh file in your home directory:

   ```
   echo "echo Hello World" > my-script.sh
   ```

2. To assign execute permission to the file, use this command:

   ```
   chmod u=rwx my-script.sh
   ```

3. To execute a shell script, type ./ before the script file name. Enter this command (see Figure 10-56):

   ```
   ./my-script.sh
   ```

```
jean@spock:~$ echo "echo Hello World" > my-script.sh  ◄──────── ⎡Create the
jean@spock:~$ ls -l                                              ⎣script
total 12
drwxrwxr-x 2 jean jean 4096 Sep 27 21:09 Hold
-rw-rw-r-- 1 jean jean   17 Sep 27 21:17 my-script.sh
-rw------- 1 jean jean    4 Sep 12 19:57 MyTestFile.txt
jean@spock:~$ chmod u=rwx my-script.sh
jean@spock:~$ ls -l
total 12
drwxrwxr-x 2 jean jean 4096 Sep 27 21:09 Hold
-rwxrw-r-- 1 jean jean   17 Sep 27 21:17 my-script.sh
-rw------- 1 jean jean    4 Sep 12 19:57 MyTestFile.txt
jean@spock:~$ ./my-script.sh  ◄──────────────────────── ⎡Execute
Hello World                                               ⎣the script
jean@spock:~$ _
                                                         ⎡Script
                                                         ⎣results
```

Figure 10-56 A simple shell script is created and executed

Now let's create a PowerShell script with a loop using Windows 10 **PowerShell ISE**, the PowerShell Integrated Scripting Environment, where scripts are created and tested:

1. In the Windows 10 search box, type **powershell** and then click **PowerShell ISE**. The PowerShell ISE window opens.

2. PowerShell ISE does dynamic type checking. As the command is interpreted, color coding is added to indicate the purpose of what you type. Type the following lines in the script pane (see Table 10-9):

Command	Purpose
`$i = 0`	Defines an integer variable i that is assigned the value 0
`While ($i -lt 3)`	Continues looping as long as the variable is less than 3
`{`	Defines the beginning of the loop
`Write-output "Hello World"`	Displays "Hello World"
`$i++`	Adds one to the i variable
`}`	Defines the end of the loop

Table 10-9 Commands in a script with a basic loop

3. To execute the script, click the **Run Script** button or click **File** and then click **Run**. The script is executed in the lower pane. See Figure 10-57.

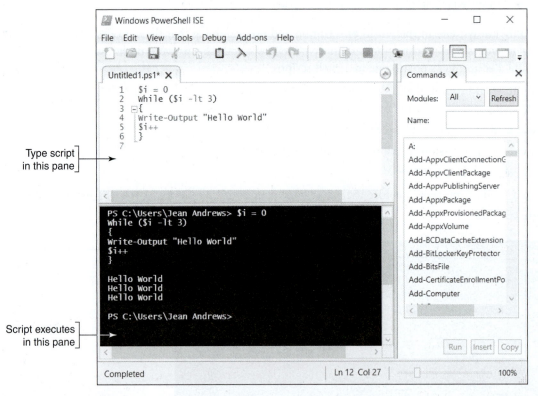

Figure 10-57 A PowerShell script with a basic loop is executed

4. To save your script, click **File**, click **Save**, and save the script to your desktop. Name the script **MyLoopScript**. By default, the .ps1 file extension is assigned to the file.

5. Close the **PowerShell ISE** window and open a standard **PowerShell** window.

6. By default, running PowerShell scripts is disabled. To set the execution policy so that scripts will run except those downloaded from the Internet without a valid digital signature, enter this cmdlet:

   Set-ExecutionPolicy RemoteSigned

7. Use this alias cmdlet to go to your Windows desktop folder:

   cd desktop

8. Use the **dir** alias cmdlet to list the contents of your desktop folder. You should see the script file listed.

9. To execute a PowerShell script, begin with ./. Use this cmdlet to execute your script:

   ./MyLoopScript

So that's the basics of scripting. I hope you love it and write many more scripts in your IT career.

CHAPTER SUMMARY

macOS for Macintosh Computers

◢ macOS is used only for Macintosh computers by Apple Inc. Like Linux, macOS is built on a UNIX foundation.

◢ The dock appears at the bottom of the desktop. The icons in the dock that represent open applications have a small, black circle underneath them.

◢ Important macOS tools used to manage and support a Mac include Finder, Launchpad, the Apple menu, System Preferences, Spotlight, Mission Control, Keychain, Screen Sharing, Remote Disc, Terminal, and gestures on a trackpad.

◢ For IT technicians, the most important tools in System Preferences are accessed through Time Machine, Users & Groups, and Sharing. Screen Sharing, one of the Sharing tools, works like Remote Desktop in Windows.

◢ macOS updates often address zero-day vulnerabilities, which makes these updates important to maintaining a healthy system.

◢ Time Machine is a built-in backup utility that automatically backs up user-created data, applications, and system files to an external hard drive that's attached either directly to the computer or through the local network.

◢ First Aid in Disk Utility can scan and repair file system errors on a hard drive.

◢ Tools to fix macOS startup problems include Safe Mode, macOS Recovery, Startup Manager, and NetBoot.

◢ Boot Camp is a macOS utility that allows you to install Windows on a Mac computer in a dual boot with macOS.

Linux Operating System

◢ Distributions of Linux provide a shell prompt in the Linux terminal and might also provide a desktop with a GUI. The default command-line shell for Linux is the Bash shell.

◢ Ubuntu Desktop with its windows manager offers Ubuntu software to install apps and update Ubuntu.

◢ The root account in Linux has access to all features of the OS. When logged in to the root account, the user is called the superuser.

▲ Important Linux commands include adduser, apt-get, cat, cd, chmod, chown, clear, cp, dd, deluser, df, echo, exit, grep, ifconfig, iwconfig, kill, ls, man, mkdir, mv, passwd, ping, ps, pwd, rm, rmdir, shutdown, su, sudo, touch, and vi.

▲ An app is normally configured in Linux by editing a text file in the /etc directory.

▲ Telnet and SSH can be used to remotely access a Linux computer. Telnet transmissions are not secured, but all SSH transmissions are encrypted.

▲ Windows and macOS are popular OSs for desktops and laptops, and Linux is popular as an application server OS. For compatibility, the FAT32 file system can be used by Windows, macOS, and Linux.

Scripting Software and Techniques

▲ Scripts are executed in a run-time environment without first being compiled, as are programs.

▲ Script file types include batch files, PowerShell scripts, VBScript, shell scripts (for Linux and UNIX), Python scripts, and JavaScript.

>> KEY TERMS

For explanations of key terms, see the Glossary for this text.

APFS (Apple File System)
Apple menu
apt-get
Bash shell
basic loop
batch file
Boot Camp
chmod
chown
clone
comment syntax
dd
DMG file
dock
dynamic type checking
environmental variable
ext3
ext4 (fourth extended file system)
Finder

First Aid
force quit
forced kill
gestures
grep
GRUB (GR and Unified Bootloader)
HFS+ (Hierarchical File System Plus)
ifconfig
integers
iwconfig
JavaScript
kernel panic
Keychain
kill
Launchpad
Linux
Live CD
Live USB
login items

macOS
Mac OS Extended
Mission Control
multiple desktops
NetBoot
package
passwd
PowerShell ISE
PowerShell script
Python script
Remote Disc
root account
run-time environment
Screen Sharing
script
secondary-click
shell prompt
shell script
snapshots
Space

Spotlight
SSH (Secure Shell)
startup disk
startup items
strings
su (substitute user or switch user)
sudo
superuser
swapfile
swap partition
System Preferences
Telnet
terminal
Terminal
Time Machine
variable
VBScript
vi editor
Windows as a service

>> THINKING CRITICALLY

These questions are designed to prepare you for the critical thinking required for the A+ exams and may use content from other chapters and the web.

1. Why is the scrollbar typically hidden from view in macOS?

2. Which app manages multiple desktop screens in macOS?

3. Which app provides tools for customizing the macOS interface?

4. A scanner connected to your Mac is giving problems and you suspect corrupted device drivers. What should you do first? Second?

   a. Download and install drivers from the scanner manufacturer.

   b. Back up the macOS startup disk using Time Machine.

   c. Update macOS.

   d. Uninstall the scanner and install it again.

5. How often does Time Machine create new backups, and how long are these backups kept?

6. Your macOS installation is corrupted and you want to boot from an external Thunderbolt hard drive to repair the installation. Which key(s) do you hold down at startup to boot from the external hard drive?

   a. d key

   b. command+r keys

   c. shift key

   d. option key

7. You are helping your friend troubleshoot a problem with his Linux server. You enter a common Linux command and discover it doesn't work exactly as you expected. What might be the problem and what do you do next?

   a. The Linux installation is corrupted; restore the system from backup.

   b. The Linux shell is not the one you expected; use the echo $SHELL command.

   c. You probably don't know how to use the Linux command; search the web for information about the command.

   d. The Linux shell is not the one you expected; use the echo $0 command.

8. What is the full path to the home directory of the user account lucio in Linux?

9. You are running a web server app in Ubuntu Server. Users complain that their browsers are loading webpages with errors. Where are you likely to find the log file where the web server reports its errors?

   a. /app/log

   b. /bin

   c. /var/log

   d. /root

10. In Linux, when logged in as a normal user with root privileges, which command must precede the apt-get command in the command line in order to install a program?

    a. sudo

    b. sudo user

    c. su

    d. root

11. Which file system does Linux currently use for the volume on which Linux is installed?

12. You have set up an FTP server in Ubuntu Server. Jason, a user, calls to say he gets an error when trying to put a file in his /home/jason/files directory. You look at the directory structure and see that you forgot to give the user ownership of the directory. Which command can fix the problem?

10

    a. `chown jason:jason /home/jason/files`

    b. `sudo chmod u=rwx /home/jason/files`

    c. `sudo chown jason:jason /home/jason/files`

    d. `chmod u-rwx /home/jason/files`

13. What is the Linux vi editor command to save your changes and exit the editor?

14. You are managing an FTP server installed in Ubuntu Server. The server has created a very large log file, vsftpd.log. Which command is appropriate to search the log file for activity of the user charlie?

    a. `sudo cat /var/log/vsftpd.log`

    b. `grep "charlie" /var/log/vsftpd.log`

    c. `sudo grep "charlie" /var/log/vsftpd.log`

    d. `cat /var/log/vsftpd.log`

15. Explain why most Linux commands work about the same on a Mac computer as they do on a Linux system.

16. You work at an IT help desk and have been asked to set up 25 new user accounts in Active Directory. Your boss tells you to save time by using a PowerShell script that's available on a network share. You look at several script files named CreateNewUsers that are stored on the drive. Which one is likely to be the one you want?

    a. The file with a .js file extension

    b. The file with a .bat file extension

    c. The file that is the largest

    d. The file with a .ps1 file extension

>> HANDS-ON PROJECTS

Hands-On | Project 10-1 Practicing Using the macOS Desktop

If you're not used to a Mac, the macOS desktop might feel strange compared with Windows, but with a little practice, you'll find all of the essential functions right at your fingertips. Complete the following steps to explore the macOS desktop:

1. ***Confirm that you have a Wi-Fi connection.*** Look for the Wi-Fi icon in the upper-right corner of the screen. If there is no connection, the icon will look like an empty upside-down triangle (see Figure 10-58). Click the Wi-Fi icon, turn on Wi-Fi if necessary, and connect to the network.

2. ***Install an app from the App Store.*** Click the App Store icon in the dock; sign in if necessary. Select a free app and install it. A good one to try is Evernote. After installation is complete, leave the App Store window open. Use Finder to open the app.

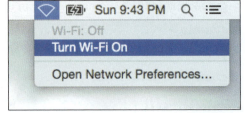

Source: Apple Inc.

Figure 10-58 Click to turn on Wi-Fi or click Open Network Preferences to set other options

(continues)

3. *Switch between windows with Exposé.* Open two more windows, such as Safari and Maps. On a laptop, swipe down with three fingers to open Exposé. On a desktop, press **control + down arrow**. In Exposé, press **tab** to switch between windows. Press **esc** to return to the desktop.

4. *See all open windows with Mission Control.* On a laptop, swipe up with three fingers to open Mission Control. On a desktop, open **Mission Control** by pressing **control + up arrow** or the **F3 Mission Control** key. Click a window to go to that window on the desktop.

5. *Uninstall the app you installed.* Close all open windows on the desktop. You might need to use the Evernote menu on the menu bar to close it, if that is the app you installed. Next, open Launchpad. On a laptop, use a trackpad gesture; on a desktop, press the **F4 Launchpad** key. In Launchpad, locate the icon for the app you installed. Press and hold the icon. All the icons jiggle. Some apps, such as Mission Control, are embedded in macOS and cannot be uninstalled; others that can be uninstalled have an X on the icon (see Figure 10-59). Click the **X** on the app you want to uninstall, then click **Delete** in the message bubble that appears, as shown in the figure. Click an open space on the screen to make the icons stop jiggling. Click the open space again to return to the desktop.

Source: Apple Inc.

Figure 10-59 Use Launchpad to uninstall an app

Hands-On | Project 10-2 Practicing Linux Commands

Practice the Linux commands listed in Table 10-10 using the Ubuntu Server you created earlier. As you do so, you'll examine the directory structure, create a new directory, and put a blank file in it.

(continues)

Task	Command	Description
1	`ls -l`	Lists files and directories in the current directory; in Linux, a directory is treated more like a file than it is in a Windows directory
2	`pwd`	Displays the full path to the current directory; when you first log in to a system, that directory is /home/*username*
3	`mkdir mydir`	Creates a directory named mydir; the directory is created in the current directory
4	`cd mydir`	Goes to the directory you just created in the /home/*username* directory
5	`touch myfile`	Creates a blank file named myfile in the current directory
6	`ls`	Lists the current directory's contents
7	`cd ..`	Moves up one level in the directory tree
8	`cd /etc`	Changes the directory to the /etc directory, where text files are kept for configuring installed programs
9	`ls`	Lists the contents of the /etc directory
10	`cd /home`	Changes the directory to the /home directory
11	`ping 127.0.0.1`	Pings the loopback address; pinging continues until you stop it by pressing Ctrl+C
12	`ifconfig`	Displays TCP/IP configuration data
13	`man ifconfig`	Displays the page from the Linux Manual about the ifconfig command; press q to exit
14	`df -T`	Displays free space on the hard drive and the file system used
15	`exit`	Logs out; the login shell prompt appears, where you can log in again

Table 10-10   Practice using Linux commands

Hands-On | Project 10-3   Changing Permissions for a Ubuntu Directory

Follow these steps to change permissions for your home directory and then create a new user account to test these permissions:

1. Create a new user account named **charlie**. Log in to Ubuntu Server as charlie and try to copy a file to your own home directory. For example, you can use this command to make a new copy of the mymemo file you created earlier:

   cp mymemo mymemo.charlie

   When you do so, permission is denied.

2. Log back in to Ubuntu Server with your own account.

3. To install the chmod command, use this command:

   sudo apt-get install coreutils

4. Use the chmod command to give full read, write, and execute permissions to everyone for your home directory.

5. Log out and log back in to the system as charlie, and verify that the user charlie can now copy a file to your home directory.

Hands-On | Project 10-4 Practicing macOS Commands

To practice using Terminal, repeat the steps in Hands-On Project 10-2 using the macOS Terminal window. (For the df –T command, don't use the –T parameter.) In macOS, the final command of that project, exit, will not produce the same results as it does in Linux. Do research online and answer the following questions about closing the macOS Terminal window:

1. What does the exit command do in the macOS Terminal window?
2. How can you adjust Terminal settings so that the exit command closes the Terminal window?
3. What keyboard shortcut can you use instead to close the Terminal window?

> ✎ **Notes** Even if you don't have a Mac computer to use for completing this project, you can still research the answers to the questions above. The information is readily available online.

Hands-On | Project 10-5 Killing a Process in macOS

macOS Terminal is a powerful tool and can be used to kill a hung process or to kill a process you suspect to be malware. First, try to use Force Quit to end the process. If that doesn't work, use Terminal to end the process. Follow these general directions to practice this skill:

1. Once again, install the Evernote app, but don't launch it.
2. Open **Terminal**. Use the following command to list all running processes (the x option displays all processes, even those not started in this shell):

   `ps x`

3. Leave Terminal open. Launch the Evernote app. Return to the Terminal window and list all running processes again. What are the Evernote app process IDs? Of the two process IDs, which one represents the application itself, and which one represents a login item?
4. The pgrep command combines the functionality of ps and grep. Do research online to find the Apple man page for pgrep. What do the –f and –l options do?
5. Confirm the Evernote app's process IDs with the command **pgrep –f –l Evernote**. (Be sure to capitalize the E in Evernote.) Do the process IDs match the information you found earlier?
6. Use Terminal to kill the Evernote app (not the login item).
7. Return to the macOS desktop and uninstall Evernote.

Hands-On | Project 10-6 Using Telnet and SSH

Following directions given earlier in the chapter, install Telnet and SSH in Ubuntu Server in your VM. If you get an error, Ubuntu Server might need updating. Commands to update Ubuntu are also given in the chapter.

On your Windows host computer, turn on Telnet Client. Open a command prompt window and remote in to your Ubuntu Server VM using both Telnet and SSH.

10

>> *REAL PROBLEMS, REAL SOLUTIONS*

REAL PROBLEM 10-1 Using Google Cloud Platform to Create an Ubuntu VM

Recall that Google Cloud Platform is an example of PaaS that you can use to learn a new operating system or develop apps. To use the service to create an Ubuntu VM, do the following:

1. Go to **cloud.google.com** and click **Free Trial**. You will need to sign in using a Google account. If you don't have an account, you can create one with any valid email address.

2. In the Developers Console, create a new project. Then drill down into **Compute, Compute Engine,** and **VM instances**. Create a VM instance with the latest Ubuntu version (Ubuntu 18.04 LTS at the time of this writing) as the installed OS. Then wait several minutes for Google to create the instance.

3. Note the External IP assigned to the VM instance. Click **SSH**. In the drop-down menu that appears, click **Open in browser window** and remote in to your VM using the SSH utility. The VM opens in a separate window where you can use Ubuntu commands (see Figure 10-60).

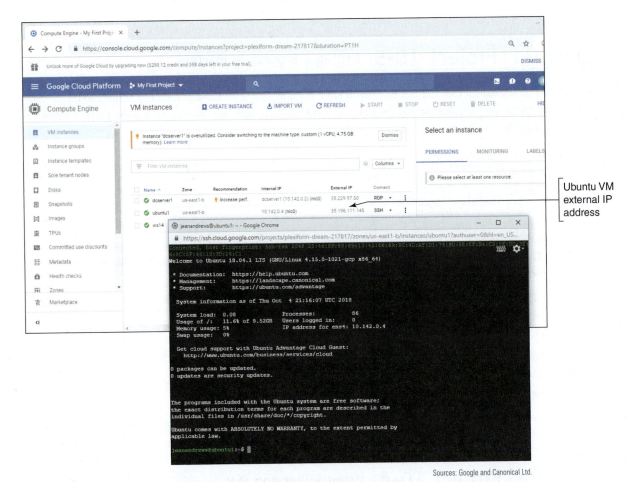

Sources: Google and Canonical Ltd.

Figure 10-60   Google Cloud Platform serves up an Ubuntu VM instance

✎ **Notes** When you set up your Google Cloud account, your credit card information was required. If you're now done with your Google Cloud 60-day free trial, close your billing account so that your credit card will not be accidentally charged at the end of your free trial period. Click the three-bar icon on the far-left side of the blue Google Cloud Platform menu bar and click **Billing**. Then click **CLOSE BILLING ACCOUNT**.

REAL PROBLEM 10-2 Sharing a Folder to the Network from a Mac Computer and Mapping the Drive on a Windows Computer

In Chapter 7, you shared a folder on the network and mapped a network drive. These tasks can also be done in macOS, which makes it easier to share files between computers of various operating systems. Complete the following steps to set up a network share from a Mac computer:

1. *Create a folder to share.* Use Finder to create a subfolder in the Documents folder and name the new folder **MeetingMinutes**.

2. *Set sharing options.* Open **System Preferences** and click **Sharing**. Select **File Sharing** in the sidebar and make sure it's turned on. Click the **Options** button and make sure that *Share files and folders using SMB* is checked. Under Windows File Sharing, check the box to turn on file sharing for your macOS user account with Windows computers. Enter your macOS user account password if necessary and click **OK**. Click **Done**.

3. *Share the folder.* Under Shared Folders, click **Documents** and click the **+** button below the Shared Folders list. Double-click the **MeetingMinutes** folder, which should then be added to the Shared Folders list. Click **MeetingMinutes** to select it. Under Users, make sure the **Everyone** group is set to **Read Only**. Return to the System Preferences main window.

4. *Enable shared folders for the guest account.* Click **Users & Groups**. Click the lock icon in the lower-left corner of the window so you can make changes to user settings, and sign in. Click the **Guest User** account in the sidebar. Check *Allow guest users to connect to shared folders* and return to the main System Preferences window.

5. *Set a static IP address.* In System Preferences, click **Network** and then click **Advanced**. Click the **TCP/IP** tab. Configure the IPv4 address with a manual address as directed by your instructor. Click **OK**.

6. *Map the network share on a Windows computer.* On your Windows computer, open **File Explorer**, right-click **This PC**, and click **Map network drive**. In the **Map Network Drive** box, enter the Mac's IP address and the name of the shared folder, as shown in Figure 10-61, adjusting the specific details to your situation. Check *Connect using different credentials* and then click **Finish**. When asked for a user name and password, enter **Guest** for the user name and leave the password blank. Explorer should open a new window that shows the mapped drive.

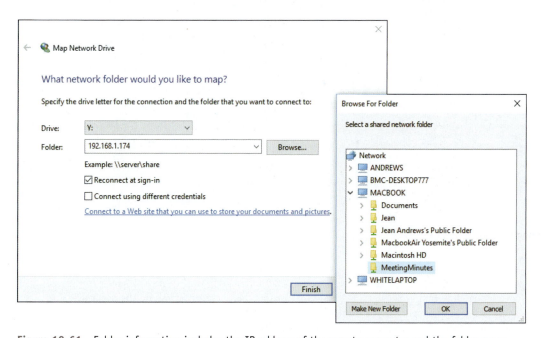

Figure 10-61 Folder information includes the IP address of the remote computer and the folder name

7. *Check the network share.* Create a file on the Mac computer and save it to the shared folder. Does it appear in the mapped network drive on the Windows computer? If not, troubleshoot and fix the problem. Create a file on the Windows computer and save it to the shared folder. Does the file appear in the shared folder on the Mac computer? What do you think went wrong? What setting do you need to change so you can add files to the shared folder from the Windows computer? Did it work? If not, troubleshoot and fix the problem.

8. *Change share permissions.* Currently the folder is shared with anyone on the network. This is fine in certain situations, but it's not a best practice for most corporate networks. What changes can you make to restrict the shared folder to a single user? To a group of users?

9. *Create a new user and a new group.* List the steps to create a new user and a new user group on the Mac computer. What types of user accounts are available? What did you name the new user account and the new user group? Add both the new user and your own user account to the new group. Change the share settings on the MeetingMinutes folder so that the new user group has read and write privileges, and the Everyone group has read-only privileges.

10. *Take a screenshot and share it.* With the sharing window showing the new settings, take a screenshot. Press **command + shift + 4** and then select the Sharing window. The screenshot is saved to the desktop. Drag it from the desktop to the shared folder and email the screenshot to your instructor.

REAL PROBLEM 10-3 Preparing for the A+ Core 2 Exam

This text prepares you for the A+ Core 2 exam. Now that you have completed the text, you are ready to make your final review of the A+ Core 2 objectives and sit for the exam. Read through the objectives listed at the beginning of this text and make sure you understand each objective. Your instructor might suggest other exam-prep tasks. You can go to the CompTIA website at *comptia.org* to sign up for the exam or use another method suggested by your instructor. A+ Certification requires that you pass the A+ Core 1 and A+ Core 2 exams.

Safety Procedures and Environmental Concerns

This appendix covers how to stay safe and protect equipment and the environment as you perform the duties of an IT support technician. We begin by understanding the properties and dangers of electricity.

MEASURES AND PROPERTIES OF ELECTRICITY

In our modern world, we take electricity for granted, and we miss it terribly when it's cut off. Nearly everyone depends on it, but few really understand it. A successful hardware technician does not expect to encounter failed processors, fried motherboards, smoking monitors, or frizzed hair. To avoid these excitements, you need to understand how to measure electricity and how to protect computer equipment from its damaging power.

Let's start with the basics. To most people, volts, ohms, joules, watts, and amps are vague terms that simply mean electricity. All these terms can be used to measure some characteristic of electricity, as listed in Table A-1.

Unit	Definition	Computer Example
Volt (for example, 115 V)	Electrical force is measured in volts. The symbol for volts is V.	A power supply steps down the voltage from 115-V house current to levels of 3.3, 5, and 12 V that computer components can use.
Amp or ampere (for example, 1.5 A)	An amp is a measure of electrical current. The symbol for amps is A.	An LCD monitor requires about 5 A to operate. A small laser printer uses about 2 A. An optical drive uses about 1 A.
Ohm (for example, 20 Ω)	An ohm is a measure of resistance to electricity. The symbol for ohm is Ω.	Current can flow in typical computer cables and wires with a resistance of near zero Ω.
Joule (for example, 500 J)	A joule is a measure of work or energy. One joule (pronounced "jewel") is the work required to push an electrical current of 1 A through a resistance of 1 Ω. The symbol for joule is J.	A surge suppressor (see Figure A-1) is rated in joules—the higher the better. The rating determines how much work a device can expend before it can no longer protect the circuit from a power surge.
Watt (for example, 20 W)	A watt is a measure of the total electrical power needed to operate a device. One watt is one joule per second. Watts can be calculated by multiplying volts by amps. The symbol for watts is W.	The power consumption of an LCD computer monitor is rated at about 14 W. A DVD burner uses about 25 W when burning a DVD.

Table A-1 Measures of electricity

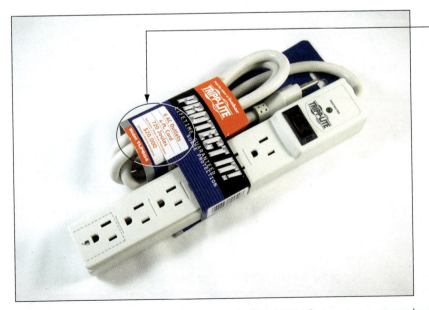

Rating is 720 joules

Figure A-1 A surge suppressor protects electrical equipment from power surges and is rated in joules

Now let's look at how electricity gets from one place to another and how it is used in house circuits and computers.

AC AND DC

Electricity can be either AC or DC. Alternating current (AC) goes back and forth, or oscillates, rather than traveling in only one direction. House current in the United States is AC and oscillates 60 times in one second (60 hertz). Voltage in the system is constantly alternating from positive to negative, which causes the electricity to flow first in one direction and then in the other. Voltage alternates from +115 V to –115 V. AC is the most economical way to transmit electricity to our homes and workplaces. By decreasing current and increasing voltage, we can force alternating current to travel great distances. When alternating current reaches its destination, it is made more suitable for driving our electrical devices by decreasing voltage and increasing current.

Direct current (DC) travels in only one direction and is the type of current that most electronic devices require, including computers. A rectifier is a device that converts AC to DC, and an inverter is a device that converts DC to AC. A transformer is a device that changes the ratio of voltage to current. The power supply used in computers is both a rectifier and a transformer.

Large transformers reduce the high voltage on power lines coming to your neighborhood to a lower voltage before the current enters your home. The transformer does not change the amount of power in this closed system; if it decreases voltage, it increases current. The overall power stays constant, but the ratio of voltage to current changes, as illustrated in Figure A-2.

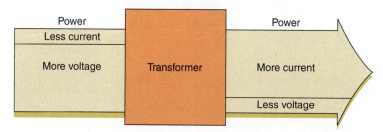

Figure A-2 A transformer keeps power constant but changes the ratio of current to voltage

Again, direct current flows in only one direction. Think of electrical current like a current of water that flows from a state of high pressure to a state of low pressure or rest. Electrical current flows from a high-pressure state (called hot) to a state of rest (called ground or neutral). For a power supply, a power line may be either +5 or –5 volts in one circuit or +12 or –12 volts in another circuit. The positive or negative value is determined by how the circuit is oriented, either on one side of the power output or the other. Several circuits coming from the power supply accommodate different devices with different power requirements.

HOT, NEUTRAL, AND GROUND

AC travels on a hot line from a power station to a building and returns to the power station on a neutral line. When the two lines reach the building and enter an electrical device, such as a lamp, the device controls the flow of electricity between the hot and neutral lines. If an easier path (one with less resistance) is available, the electricity follows that path. This can cause a

A

short, a sudden increase in flow that can also create a sudden increase in temperature—enough to start a fire and injure both people and equipment. Never put yourself in a position where you are the path of least resistance between the hot line and ground!

> ⚡ **Caution**   It's very important that PC components be properly grounded. Never connect a PC to an outlet or use an extension cord that doesn't have the third ground plug. The third line can prevent a short from causing extreme damage. In addition, the bond between the neutral and ground helps eliminate electrical noise (stray electrical signals) within the PC that is sometimes caused by other nearby electrical equipment.

To prevent uncontrolled electricity in a short, the neutral line is grounded. Grounding a line means that the line is connected directly to the earth; in the event of a short, the electricity flows into the earth and not back to the power station. Grounding serves as an escape route for out-of-control electricity because the earth is always capable of accepting a flow of current. With computers, a surge suppressor can be used to protect them and their components against power surges.

> ⚡ **Caution**   Beware of the different uses of black wire. In desktop computers and in DC circuits, black is used for ground, but in home wiring and in AC circuits, black is used for hot!

The neutral line to your house is grounded many times along its way (in fact, at each electrical pole) and is also grounded at the breaker box where the electricity enters your house. You can look at a three-prong plug and see the three lines: hot, neutral, and ground (see Figure A-3).

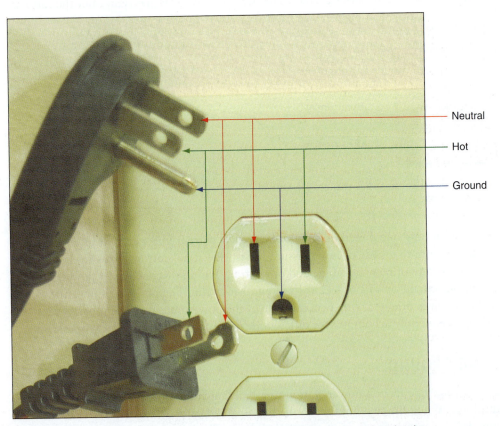

Neutral

Hot

Ground

Figure A-3   A polarized plug showing hot and neutral, and a three-prong plug showing hot, neutral, and ground

✏️ **Notes** House AC voltage in the United States is about 110–120 V, but know that in other countries, this is not always the case. In many other countries, the standard is 220 V. Outlet styles also vary from one country to the next.

Now that you know about electricity, you will learn how to protect yourself against the dangers of electricity and other factors that might harm you as you work around computers.

PROTECTING YOURSELF

To protect yourself against electrical shock when working with any electrical device, including computers, printers, scanners, and network devices, disconnect the power if you notice a dangerous situation that might lead to electrical shock or fire. When you disconnect the power, do so by pulling on the plug at the AC outlet. To protect the power cord, don't pull on the cord itself. Also, don't just turn off the on/off switch on the device; you need to actually disconnect the power. Note that any of the following can indicate a potential danger:

- You notice smoke coming from the computer case or the case feels unusually warm.
- The power cord is frayed or otherwise damaged in any way.
- Water or other liquid is on the floor around the device or was spilled on it.
- The device has been exposed to excess moisture.
- The device has been dropped or you notice physical damage.
- You smell a strong electronics odor.
- The power supply or fans are making a whining noise.

SAFELY WORKING INSIDE COMPUTERS, PRINTERS, AND OTHER ELECTRICAL DEVICES

To stay safe, always do the following before working inside computers, printers, and other electrical devices:

- *Remove jewelry*. Remove any jewelry that might come in contact with components. Jewelry is commonly made of metal and might conduct electricity if it touches a component. It can also get caught in cables and cords inside computer cases.
- *Power down the system and unplug it.* For a computer, unplug the power, monitor, mouse, and keyboard cables, unplug any other peripherals or cables attached, and move them out of your way.
- *For a computer, press and hold down the power button for a moment.* After you unplug the computer, press the power button for about three seconds to completely drain the power supply. Sometimes when you do so, you'll hear the fans quickly start and go off as residual power is drained. Only then is it safe to work inside the case.

ELECTRICAL FIRE SAFETY

Never use water to put out a fire fueled by electricity because water is a conductor and you might get a severe electrical shock. A computer lab needs a fire extinguisher that is rated to put out electrical fires. Fire extinguishers are rated by the type of fires they put out:

- Class A extinguishers can use water to put out fires caused by wood, paper, and other combustibles.
- Class B extinguishers can put out fires caused by liquids such as gasoline, kerosene, and oil.
- **Class C fire extinguishers** use nonconductive chemicals to put out a fire caused by electricity. See Figure A-4.

A

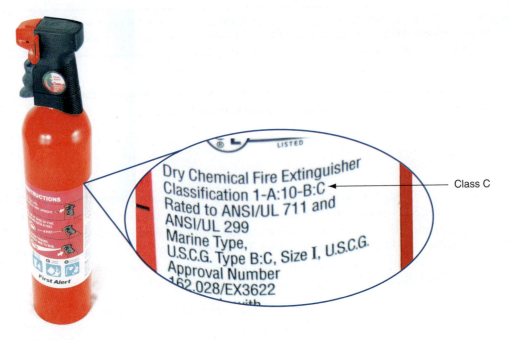

Class C

Figure A-4 A Class C fire extinguisher is rated to put out electrical fires

PROPER USE OF CLEANING PADS AND SOLUTIONS

A+
CORE 2
4.4, 4.5

As a support technician, you'll find yourself collecting different cleaning solutions and cleaning pads to clean a variety of devices, including the mouse and keyboard, CDs, DVDs, Blu-ray discs and their drives, and monitors. Figure A-5 shows a few of these products. For example, the contact cleaner in the figure is used to clean the contacts on the edge connectors of expansion cards; a good cleaning can solve a problem with a faulty connection.

Figure A-5 Cleaning solutions and pads

Most of these cleaning solutions contain flammable and poisonous materials. Take care when using them so that they don't get on your skin or in your eyes. To find out what to do if you are accidentally exposed to a dangerous solution, look at the instructions printed on the can or check out the material safety data sheet (see Figure A-6). A material safety data sheet (MSDS) explains how to properly handle substances such as chemical solvents and how to dispose of them.

An MSDS includes information such as physical data, toxicity, health effects, first aid, storage, shipping, disposal, and spill procedures. The MSDS comes packaged with the chemical; you can also order one from the manufacturer or find one on the Internet (see *ilpi.com/msds*).

Figure A-6 Each chemical you use should have a material safety data sheet available

> ⭐ **A+ Exam Tip** The A+ Core 2 exam expects you to know how to use MSDS documentation to dispose of chemicals and help protect the environment. You also need to know that you must follow all local government regulations when disposing of chemicals and other materials dangerous to the environment.

If you have an accident with cleaning solutions or other dangerous products, your company or organization might require you to report the accident and/or fill out an incident report. Check with your organization to find out how to report these types of incidents.

MANAGING CABLES

People can trip over cables or cords left on the floor, so be careful that cables are in a safe place. If you must run a cable across a path or where someone sits, use a cable or cord cover that can be nailed or screwed to the floor. Don't leave loose cables or cords in a traffic area where people can trip over them; such objects are called trip hazards.

LIFTING HEAVY OBJECTS

Back injury caused by lifting heavy objects is one of the most common work injuries. Whenever possible, put heavy objects, such as a large laser printer, on a cart to move them. If you do need to lift a heavy object, follow these guidelines to keep from injuring your back:

1. Look at the object and decide which side of it to face so that the load will be the most balanced when you lift it.

2. Stand close to the object with your feet apart.

3. Keeping your back straight, bend your knees and grip the load.

A

4. Lift with your legs, arms, and shoulders, not with your back or stomach.

5. Keep the load close to your body and avoid twisting your body while you're holding the load.

6. To put the object down, keep your back as straight as you can and lower the object by bending your knees.

Don't try to lift an object that is too heavy for you. Because there are no exact guidelines for when heavy is too heavy, use your best judgment as to when to ask for help.

SAFETY GOGGLES AND AIR FILTER MASK

If you work in a factory environment where flying fragments, chips, or other particles are about, your employer might require that you wear **safety goggles** to protect your eyes. In addition, if the air is filled with dust or other contaminants, your employer might require you to wear an air-purifying respirator, commonly called an **air filter mask**, which filters out the dust and other contaminants. If safety goggles or a mask is required, your employer is responsible for providing one that is appropriate for your work environment.

PROTECTING THE EQUIPMENT

As you learn to troubleshoot and solve computer problems, you gradually begin to realize that many of them could have been avoided by good computer maintenance, which includes protecting the computer against environmental factors such as humidity, dust, and out-of-control electricity.

PROTECTING THE EQUIPMENT AGAINST STATIC ELECTRICITY OR ESD

Suppose you come indoors on a cold day, pick up a comb, and touch your hair. Sparks fly! What happened? Static electricity caused the sparks. **Electrostatic discharge (ESD)**, commonly known as **static electricity**, is an electrical charge at rest. When you came indoors, this charge built up on your hair and had no place to go. An ungrounded conductor (such as wire that is not touching another wire) or a nonconductive surface (such as your hair) holds a charge until it is released. When two objects with dissimilar electrical charges touch, electricity passes between them until the dissimilar charges become equal.

To see static charges equalizing, turn off the lights in a room, scuff your feet on the carpet, and touch another person. Occasionally, you can see and feel the charge in your fingers. If you can feel the charge, you discharged at least 1500 volts of static electricity. If you hear the discharge, you released at least 6000 volts. If you see the discharge, you released at least 8000 volts of ESD. A charge of only 10 volts can damage electronic components! *You can touch a chip on an expansion card or motherboard, damage the chip with ESD, and never feel, hear, or see the electrical discharge.*

ESD can cause two types of damage in an electronic component: catastrophic failure and upset failure. A catastrophic failure destroys the component beyond use. An upset failure damages the component so that it does not perform well, even though it may still function to some degree. Upset failures are more difficult to detect because they are not consistent and not easily observed. Both types of failures permanently affect the device. Components are easily damaged by ESD, but because the damage might not show up for weeks or months, a technician is likely to get careless and not realize the damage he or she is doing.

⚡ **Caution** Unless you are measuring power levels with a multimeter or power supply tester, *never* touch a component or cable inside a computer case while the power is on. The electrical voltage is not enough to seriously hurt you but is more than enough to permanently damage the component.

Before touching or handling a component (for example, a hard drive, motherboard, expansion card, processor, or memory modules), protect it against ESD by always grounding yourself first. You can ground yourself and the computer parts by using one or more of the following static control devices or methods:

▲ *ESD strap.* An ESD strap, also called a ground bracelet, antistatic wrist strap, or ESD bracelet, is a strap you wear around your wrist. The strap has a cord attached with an alligator clip on the end. Attach the clip to the computer case you're working on, as shown in Figure A-7. Any static electricity between you and the case will be discharged. Therefore, as you work inside the case, you will not damage the components with static electricity. The bracelet also contains a resistor that prevents electricity from harming you.

Figure A-7   A ground bracelet, which protects computer components from ESD, can clip to the side of the computer case and eliminate ESD between you and the case

⚡ **Caution** When working on a laser printer, *don't* wear the ESD strap because you don't want to be the ground for these high-voltage devices.

▲ *Ground mats.* A ground mat, also called an ESD mat, dissipates ESD and is commonly used by bench technicians (also called depot technicians) who repair and assemble computers at their workbenches or in an assembly line. Ground mats have a connector in one corner that you can use to connect the mat to the ground (see Figure A-8). If you lift a component off the mat, it is no longer grounded and is susceptible to ESD, so it's important to use an ESD strap with a ground mat.

A

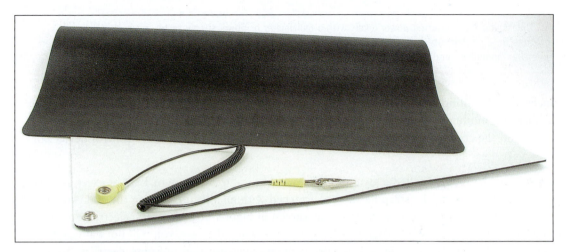

Figure A-8 An ESD mat dissipates ESD and should be connected to the ground

▲ *Static shielding bags.* New components come shipped in static shielding bags, also called antistatic bags. These bags are a type of Faraday cage, named after Michael Faraday, who built the first cage in 1836. A Faraday cage is any device that protects against an electromagnetic field. Save the bags to store other devices that belong in a computer but are not currently installed. As you work on a computer, know that a device is not protected from ESD if you place it on top of the bag; the protection is inside the bag (see Figure A-9).

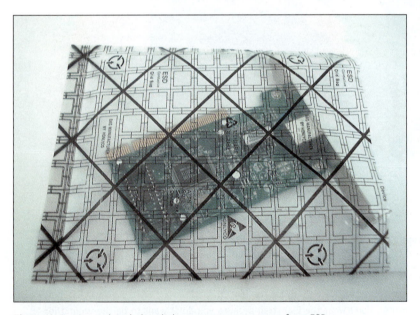

Figure A-9 An antistatic bag helps protect components from ESD

> ⚡ **Caution** An older CRT monitor can also damage components with ESD. Don't place or store expansion cards on top of or next to a CRT monitor, which can discharge as much as 29,000 volts onto the screen.

The best way to guard against ESD is to use an ESD strap together with a ground mat. Consider an ESD strap essential equipment when working on a computer. However, if you are in a situation in which you must work without one, touch the computer case or the power supply before you touch a component in the case, which is called self-grounding. Self-grounding dissipates any charge between you and whatever you touch. Here are some rules that can help protect computer parts against ESD:

◢ When passing a circuit board, memory module, or other sensitive component to another person, ground yourself and then touch the other person before you pass the component.
◢ Leave components inside their protective bags until you are ready to use them.
◢ Work on hard floors, not carpet, or use antistatic spray on the carpet.
◢ Don't work on a computer if you or the computer has just come in from the cold because there is more danger of ESD when the atmosphere is cold and dry.
◢ When unpacking hardware or software, remove the packing tape and cellophane from the work area as soon as possible because these materials attract ESD.
◢ Keep components away from your hair and clothing.

> ★ **A+ Exam Tip** The A+ Core 2 exam emphasizes that you should know how to protect computer equipment as you work on it, including how to protect components against damage from ESD.

PHYSICALLY PROTECTING YOUR EQUIPMENT FROM THE ENVIRONMENT

A+
CORE 2
4.4, 4.5

When you protect equipment from ongoing problems with the environment, you are likely to have fewer problems later, and you will have less troubleshooting and repair to do. Here is how you can physically protect a computer:

◢ *Protect a computer against dust and other airborne particles.* When a computer must sit in a dusty environment, around those who smoke, or where pets might leave hair, you can:

  ◢ Use a plastic keyboard cover to protect the keyboard. When the computer is turned off, protect the entire system with a cover or enclosure.

  ◢ Install air filters over the front or side vents of the case where air flows in. Put your hand over the case of a running computer to feel where the air flows in. For most systems, air flows in from the front vents or vents on the side of the case that is near the processor cooler. The air filter shown in Figure A-10 has magnets that hold the filter to the case when screw holes are not available.

> 🖊 **Notes** When working at a customer site, be sure to clean up any mess you created by blowing dust out of a computer case or keyboard.

  ◢ Use compressed air or an antistatic vacuum (see Figure A-11) to remove dust from inside the case, if you have the case cover open. Figure A-12 shows a case fan that jammed because of dust and caused a system to overheat. While you're cleaning up dust, don't forget to blow or vacuum out the keyboard.

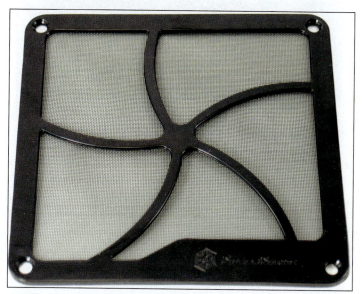

Figure A-10 This air filter is designed to fit over a case fan, power supply fan, or panel vent on the case

A

Figure A-11   An antistatic vacuum is designed to work inside sensitive electronic equipment such as computers and printers

Figure A-12   This dust-jammed case fan caused a system to overheat

▲ *Allow for good ventilation inside and outside the system.* Proper air circulation is essential to keeping a system cool. Don't block air vents on the front and rear of the computer case or on the monitor. Inside the case, make sure cables are tied up and out of the way so as to allow for airflow and not obstruct fans from turning. Put covers on expansion slot openings at the rear of the case and put faceplates over empty bays on the front of the case. Don't set a tower case directly on thick carpet because the air vent on the bottom front of the case can be blocked. If you are concerned about overheating, monitor temperatures inside and outside the case.

> ★ **A+ Exam Tip**   The A+ Core 2 exam expects you to know how to keep computers and monitors well ventilated and to use protective enclosures and air filters to protect the equipment from airborne particles.

▲ *High temperatures and humidity can be dangerous for hard drives.* I once worked in a basement with PCs, and hard drives failed much too often. After we installed dehumidifiers, the hard drives became more reliable. If you suspect a problem with room humidity, you can monitor it using a hygrometer. High temperatures can also damage computer equipment, and you should take precautions not to allow a computer to overheat.

> ✎ **Notes** A server room where computers stay and people don't stay for long hours is usually set to balance what is good for the equipment and to conserve energy. Low temperatures and moderate humidity are best for the equipment, although no set standards exist for either. Temperatures might be set from 65 to 70 degrees F, and humidity between 30 percent and 50 percent, although some companies keep their server rooms at 80 degrees F to conserve energy. A data center where both computers and people stay is usually kept at a comfortable temperature and humidity for humans.

▲ *Protect electrical equipment from power surges.* Lightning and other electrical power surges can destroy computers and other electrical equipment. If a house or office building does not have surge protection equipment installed at the breaker box, be sure to install a protective device at each computer. The least expensive device is a power strip that is also a surge suppressor, although you might want to use an uninterruptible power supply for added protection.

Lightning can also get to your equipment across network cabling coming in through an Internet connection. To protect against lightning, use a surge suppressor such as the one shown in Figure A-13 in line between the ISP device (for example, a DSL modem or cable modem) and the computer or home router to protect it from spikes across the network cables. Notice the cord on the surge suppressor, which connects it to ground.

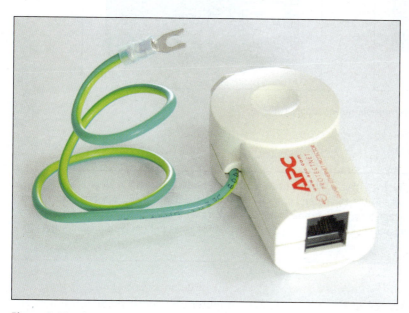

Figure A-13   A surge protector by APC for Ethernet lines

An **uninterruptible power supply (UPS)** is a device that raises the voltage when it drops during **brownouts** or **sags** (temporary voltage reductions). A UPS also does double duty as a surge suppressor to protect the system against power surges or spikes. In addition, a UPS can serve as a battery backup to provide enough power for a brief time during a total blackout so you can save your work and shut down the system. A UPS is not as essential for a laptop computer as it is for a desktop because a laptop has a battery that can sustain it during a blackout. Also, consider using a UPS to protect power to a router, switch, or other essential network device.

A

A common UPS device is a rather heavy box that plugs into an AC outlet and provides one or more electrical outlets and perhaps Ethernet and USB ports (see Figure A-14). It has an on/off switch, requires no maintenance, and is very simple to install. Use it to provide uninterruptible power to your desktop computer, monitor, and essential network devices. It's best not to connect a UPS to nonessential devices such as a laser printer or scanner. The UPS shown in Figure A-14 has a USB port so that a computer can monitor power management and network ports to block harmful voltage on the network.

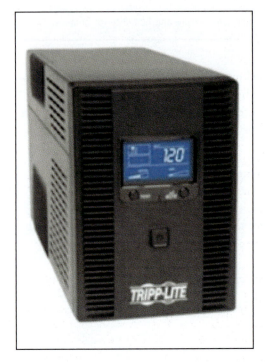

Source: dell.com

Figure A-14　The front and rear of an uninterruptible power supply (UPS)

✎ Notes If a power outage occurs and you don't have a reliable power conditioner installed at the breaker box in your house or building, unplug all power cords to the computers, printers, monitors, and peripherals. Sometimes when the power returns, sudden spikes are accompanied by another brief outage. You don't want to subject your equipment to these surges. When buying a surge suppressor, look for one that guarantees against damage from lightning and that reimburses for equipment destroyed while the surge suppressor is in use.

PROTECTING THE ENVIRONMENT

**A+
CORE 2
4.4, 4.5**

IT support technicians need to be aware that they can do damage to the environment if they dispose of used computer equipment improperly. As a support technician, one day you're sure to face an assortment of useless equipment and consumables (see Figure A-15). Before you decide to trash it all, take a moment and ask yourself if some of the equipment can be donated or at least recycled. Think about fixing up an old computer and donating it to an underprivileged middle school student. If you don't have the time for that, consider donating to the local computer repair class. The class can fix up such computers as a class project and donate them to young students.

Figure A-15   Keep, trash, recycle, or donate?

When disposing of any type of equipment or consumables, make sure to comply with local government environmental regulations. Table A-2 lists some items and how to dispose of them.

Parts	How to Dispose of Them
Alkaline batteries, including AAA, AA, A, C, D, and 9-volt	Dispose of these batteries in the regular trash. First check to see if there are recycling facilities in your area.
Button batteries used in digital cameras and other small equipment; battery packs used in notebooks	These batteries can contain silver oxide, mercury, lithium, or cadmium and are considered toxic waste that require special toxic waste handling. Dispose of them by returning them to the original dealer or by taking them to a recycling center. To recycle, pack them separately from other items. If you don't have a recycling center nearby, contact your county for local disposal regulations.
Cell phones and tablets	Most cell phone carriers will buy back old cell phones to recycle or refurbish. If you can restore the device to factory state, donate it to charity. Before tossing it in the trash, check with local county or environmental officials for laws and regulations in your area that cover proper disposal of the item. E-waste recycling companies, such as Eco-Cell (*eco-cell.com*), receive cell phones for resale or recycling.
Laser printer toner cartridges	Return these to the manufacturer or dealer to be recycled.
Ink-jet printer cartridges, cell phones, tablets, computer cases, power supplies, other computer parts, monitors, chemical solvents, and their containers	Check with local county or environmental officials for laws and regulations in your area that cover proper disposal of these items. The county might have a recycling center that will receive the items. Discharge a CRT monitor before disposing of it. See the MSDS documents for chemicals to know how to dispose of them.
Storage media such as hard drives, CDs, DVDs, and BDs	Do physical damage to the device so it is not possible for sensitive data to be stolen. Then the device can be recycled or put in the trash. Your organization might have to meet legal requirements to destroy data. If so, make sure you understand these requirements and how to comply with them.

Table A-2   Computer parts and how to dispose of them

⭐ **A+ Exam Tip**   The A+ Core 2 exam expects you to know how to follow environmental guidelines to dispose of batteries, laser printer toner, cell phones, tablets, CRT monitors, chemical solvents, and containers. If you're not certain how to dispose of a product, see its MSDS document.

A

Be sure a CRT monitor is discharged before you dispose of it. Most CRT monitors are designed to discharge after sitting unplugged for 60 minutes. They can be manually discharged by using a high-voltage probe with the monitor case opened. Ask a technician who's trained to service monitors to do this for you.

> ✎ **Notes** Go to *youtube.com* and search on "discharge a CRT monitor" to see some interesting videos that demonstrate the charge inside a monitor long after it is turned off and unplugged. As for proper procedures, I'm not endorsing all these videos; just watch for fun.

>> KEY TERMS

For explanations of key terms, see the Glossary for this text.

air filter mask	electrostatic discharge	material safety data sheet	surge suppressor
alternating current (AC)	(ESD)	(MSDS)	transformer
amp	ESD mat	ohm	trip hazard
antistatic bag	ESD strap	rectifier	uninterruptible power
antistatic wrist strap	ground bracelet	safety goggles	supply (UPS)
brownout	ground mat	sag	volt
Class C fire extinguisher	inverter	self-grounding	watt
direct current (DC)	joule	static electricity	

>> HANDS-ON PROJECTS

Hands-On | Project A-1   Practicing Handling Computer Components

Working with a partner, you'll need some computer parts and the antistatic tools you learned about in this appendix. Practice touching and picking up the parts and passing them between you. As you do so, follow the rules to protect the parts against ESD. Have a third person watch as you work and point out any ways you might have exposed a part to ESD. As you work, be careful not to touch components on circuit boards or the gold "fingers" on the edge connector of an expansion card. When you are finished, store the parts in antistatic bags.

Hands-On | Project A-2   Safely Cleaning Computer Equipment

Practice some preventive maintenance tasks by following these steps to clean a computer:

1. Shut down the computer and unplug it. Press the power button to drain power.
2. Clean the keyboard, monitor, and mouse. For a wheel mouse, remove the ball and clean the wheels. Clean the outside of the computer case. Don't forget to clean the mouse pad.
3. Open the case and use a ground bracelet to clean the dust from the case. Make sure all fans move freely.
4. Verify that the cables are out of the way of airflow. Use cable ties as necessary.
5. Check that each expansion card and memory module is securely seated in its slot.
6. Power up the system and make sure everything is working.
7. Clean up around your work area. If you left dust on the floor as you blew it out of the computer case, be sure to clean it up.

Hands-On | Project A-3   Researching Disposal Rules

Research the laws and regulations in your community concerning the disposal of batteries and old computer parts. Answer these questions:

1. How do you properly dispose of a monitor in your community?

2. How do you properly dispose of a battery pack used by a notebook computer?

3. How do you properly dispose of a large box of assorted computer parts, including hard drives, optical drives, computer cases, and circuit boards?

A

Entry Points for Startup Processes

This appendix contains a summary of the entry points that can affect Windows 10/8/7 startup. The entry points include startup folders, Group Policy folders, the Scheduled Tasks folder, and registry keys. To see all the subfolders listed in this appendix, use File Explorer Options or Folder Options in Control Panel to unhide folders that don't normally display in File Explorer or Windows Explorer.

Programs and shortcuts to programs are stored in these startup folders:

▲ C:\Users*username*\AppData\Roaming\Microsoft\Windows\Start Menu\Programs\Startup
▲ C:\ProgramData\Microsoft\Windows\Start Menu\Programs\Startup

Startup and shutdown scripts used by Group Policy are stored in these folders:

▲ C:\Windows\System32\GroupPolicy\Machine\Scripts\Startup
▲ C:\Windows\System32\GroupPolicy\Machine\Scripts\Shutdown
▲ C:\Windows\System32\GroupPolicy\User\Scripts\Logon
▲ C:\Windows\System32\GroupPolicy\User\Scripts\Logoff

Scheduled tasks are stored in this folder:

▲ C:\Windows\System32\Tasks

To see a list of scheduled tasks, enter the **schtasks** command in a command prompt window.

These keys cause an entry to run once and only once at startup:

▲ HKLM\Software\Microsoft\Windows\CurrentVersion\RunOnce
▲ HKLM\Software\Microsoft\Windows\CurrentVersion\RunServiceOnce
▲ HKLM\Software\Microsoft\Windows\CurrentVersion\RunServicesOnce
▲ HKCU\Software\Microsoft\Windows\CurrentVersion\RunOnce

Group Policy places entries in the following keys to affect startup:

▲ HKCU\Software\Microsoft\Windows\CurrentVersion\Policies\Explorer\Run
▲ HKLM\Software\Microsoft\Windows\CurrentVersion\Policies\Explorer\Run

Windows loads many DLL programs from the following key, which is sometimes used by malicious software. Don't delete one unless you know it's causing a problem:

▲ HKLM\Software\Microsoft\Windows\CurrentVersion\ShellServiceObjectDelayLoad

Entries in the keys listed next apply to all users and hold legitimate startup entries. Don't delete an entry unless you suspect it to be bad:

▲ HKLM\Software\Microsoft\Windows\CurrentVersion\Run
▲ HKCU\Software\Microsoft\Windows NT\CurrentVersion\Windows
▲ HKCU\Software\Microsoft\Windows NT\CurrentVersion\Windows\Run
▲ HKCU\Software\Microsoft\Windows\CurrentVersion\Run

These keys and their subkeys contain entries pertaining to background services that are sometimes launched at startup:

▲ HKLM\Software\Microsoft\Windows\CurrentVersion\RunService
▲ HKLM\Software\Microsoft\Windows\CurrentVersion\RunServices

The following key contains a value named BootExecute, which is normally set to autochk. It causes the system to run a type of Chkdsk program to check for hard drive integrity if it was previously shut down improperly. Sometimes another program adds itself to this value, causing a problem. The Chkntfs utility can be used to exclude volumes from being checked by autochk. For more information about this situation, search for "CHKNTFS.EXE: What You Can Use It For" at *support.microsoft.com*.

▲ HKLM\System\CurrentControlSet\Control\Session Manager

Here is an assorted list of registry keys that have all been known to cause various problems at startup. Remember, before you delete a program entry from one of these keys, research the program file name so that you won't accidentally delete something you want to keep:

- HKCU\Software\Microsoft\Command
- HKCU\Software\Microsoft\Command Processor\AutoRun
- HKCU\Software\Microsoft\Windows\CurrentVersion\RunOnce\Setup
- HKCU\Software\Microsoft\Windows NT\CurrentVersion\Windows\load
- HKLM\Software\Microsoft\Windows NT\CurrentVersion\Windows\AppInit_DLLs
- HKLM\Software\Microsoft\Windows NT\CurrentVersion\Winlogon\System
- HKLM\Software\Microsoft\Windows NT\CurrentVersion\Winlogon\Us
- HKCR\batfile\shell\open\command
- HKCR\comfile\shell\open\command
- HKCR\exefile\shell\open\command
- HKCR\htafile\shell\open\command
- HKCR\piffile\shell\open\command
- HKCR\scrfile\shell\open\command

Finally, check out the subkeys in the following key; they apply to 32-bit programs installed in a 64-bit version of Windows:

- HKLM\Software\Wow6432Node

Other ways in which processes can be launched at startup:

- Services can be set to launch at startup. To manage services, use the Services console (services.msc).
- Device drivers are launched at startup. For a listing of installed devices, use Device Manager (devmgmt.msc) or the System Information utility (msinfo32.exe).

B

CompTIA Acronyms

CompTIA provides a list of acronyms that you need to know before you sit for the A+ exams. You can download the list from the CompTIA website at *comptia.org*. The list is included here for your convenience. However, CompTIA occasionally updates the list, so be sure to check the CompTIA website for the latest version.

Acronym	Spelled Out
AC	Alternating Current
ACL	Access Control List
ACPI	Advanced Configuration Power Interface
ADF	Automatic Document Feeder
ADSL	Asymmetrical Digital Subscriber Line
AES	Advanced Encryption Standard
AHCI	Advanced Host Controller Interface
AP	Access Point
APIPA	Automatic Private Internet Protocol Addressing
APM	Advanced Power Management
ARP	Address Resolution Protocol
ASR	Automated System Recovery
ATA	Advanced Technology Attachment
ATAPI	Advanced Technology Attachment Packet Interface
ATM	Asynchronous Transfer Mode
ATX	Advanced Technology Extended
AUP	Acceptable Use Policy
A/V	Audio Video
BD-R	Blu-ray Disc Recordable
BD-RE	Blu-ray Disc Rewritable
BIOS	Basic Input/Output System
BNC	Bayonet-Neill-Concelman
BSOD	Blue Screen of Death
BYOD	Bring Your Own Device
CAD	Computer-Aided Design
CAPTCHA	Completely Automated Public Turing test to tell Computers and Humans Apart
CD	Compact Disc
CD-ROM	Compact Disc-Read-Only Memory
CD-RW	Compact Disc-Rewritable
CDFS	Compact Disc File System
CERT	Computer Emergency Response Team
CFS	Central File System, Common File System, or Command File System
CGA	Computer Graphics and Applications
CIDR	Classless Interdomain Routing
CIFS	Common Internet File System
CMOS	Complementary Metal-Oxide Semiconductor
CNR	Communications and Networking Riser
COMx	Communication port (x = port number)
CPU	Central Processing Unit
CRT	Cathode-Ray Tube
DaaS	Data as a Service
DAC	Discretionary Access Control

Acronym	Spelled Out
DB-25	Serial Communications D-Shell Connector, 25 pins
DB-9	Serial Communications D-Shell Connector, 9 pins
DBaaS	Database as a Service
DC	Direct Current
DDoS	Distributed Denial of Service
DDR	Double Data Rate
DDR RAM	Double Data Rate Random Access Memory
DFS	Distributed File System
DHCP	Dynamic Host Configuration Protocol
DIMM	Dual Inline Memory Module
DIN	Deutsche Industrie Norm
DLP	Digital Light Processing or Data Loss Prevention
DLT	Digital Linear Tape
DMA	Direct Memory Access
DMZ	Demilitarized Zone
DNS	Domain Name Service or Domain Name Server
DoS	Denial of Service
DRAM	Dynamic Random Access Memory
DRM	Digital Rights Management
DSL	Digital Subscriber Line
DVD	Digital Versatile Disc
DVD-R	Digital Versatile Disc-Recordable
DVD-RAM	Digital Versatile Disc-Random Access Memory
DVD-ROM	Digital Versatile Disc-Read Only Memory
DVD-RW	Digital Versatile Disc-Rewritable
DVI	Digital Visual Interface
DVI-D	Digital Visual Interface–Digital
ECC	Error Correcting Code
ECP	Extended Capabilities Port
EEPROM	Electrically Erasable Programmable Read-Only Memory
EFS	Encrypting File System
EIDE	Enhanced Integrated Drive Electronics
EMI	Electromagnetic Interference
EMP	Electromagnetic Pulse
EPP	Enhanced Parallel Port
EPROM	Erasable Programmable Read-Only Memory
ERD	Emergency Repair Disk
eSATA	External Serial Advanced Technology Attachment
ESD	Electrostatic Discharge
EULA	End User License Agreement
EVGA	Extended Video Graphics Adapter/Array
exFAT	Extended File Allocation Table

C

Acronym	Spelled Out
Ext2	Second Extended File System
FAT	File Allocation Table
FAT12	12-bit File Allocation Table
FAT16	16-bit File Allocation Table
FAT32	32-bit File Allocation Table
FDD	Floppy Disk Drive
FPM	Fast Page Mode
FQDN	Fully Qualified Domain Name
FSB	Front-Side Bus
FTP	File Transfer Protocol
GDDR	Graphics Double Data Rate
GDI	Graphics Device Interface
GPS	Global Positioning System
GPT	GUID Partition Table
GPU	Graphics Processing Unit
GSM	Global System for Mobile Communications
GUI	Graphical User Interface
GUID	Globally Unique Identifier
HAL	Hardware Abstraction Layer
HAV	Hardware Assisted Virtualization
HCL	Hardware Compatibility List
HDCP	High-Bandwidth Digital Content Protection
HDD	Hard Disk Drive
HDMI	High Definition Media Interface
HIPS	Host Intrusion Prevention System
HPFS	High Performance File System
HTML	Hypertext Markup Language
HTPC	Home Theater PC
HTTP	Hypertext Transfer Protocol
HTTPS	Hypertext Transfer Protocol Secure
I/O	Input/Output
IaaS	Infrastructure as a Service
ICMP	Internet Control Message Protocol
ICR	Intelligent Character Recognition
IDE	Integrated Drive Electronics
IDS	Intrusion Detection System
IEEE	Institute of Electrical and Electronics Engineers
IIS	Internet Information Services
IMAP	Internet Mail Access Protocol
IMEI	International Mobile Equipment Identity
IMSI	International Mobile Subscriber Identity
IP	Internet Protocol

Acronym	Spelled Out
IPConfig	Internet Protocol Configuration
IPP	Internet Printing Protocol
IPS	Intrusion Prevention System
IPSec	Internet Protocol Security
IR	Infrared
IrDA	Infrared Data Association
IRP	Incident Response Plan
IRQ	Interrupt Request
ISA	Industry Standard Architecture
ISDN	Integrated Services Digital Network
ISO	International Organization for Standardization
ISP	Internet Service Provider
JBOD	Just a Bunch of Disks
KB	Knowledge Base
KVM	Kernel-based Virtual Machine
KVM	Keyboard-Video-Mouse
LAN	Local Area Network
LBA	Logical Block Addressing
LC	Lucent Connector
LCD	Liquid Crystal Display
LDAP	Lightweight Directory Access Protocol
LED	Light-Emitting Diode
LPD/LPR	Line Printer Daemon/Line Printer Remote
LPT	Line Printer Terminal
LVD	Low Voltage Differential
MAC	Media Access Control or Mandatory Access Control
MAN	Metropolitan Area Network
MAPI	Messaging Application Programming Interface
mATX	Micro Advanced Technology Extended
MAU	Media Access Unit or Media Attachment Unit
MBR	Master Boot Record
MBSA	Microsoft Baseline Security Analyzer
MDM	Mobile Device Management
MFA	Multifactor Authentication
MFD	Multifunction Device
MFP	Multifunction Product
MicroDIMM	Micro Dual Inline Memory Module
MIDI	Musical Instrument Digital Interface
MIME	Multipurpose Internet Mail Extension
MIMO	Multiple Input Multiple Output
MMC	Microsoft Management Console
MP3	Moving Picture Experts Group Layer 3 Audio

C

Acronym	Spelled Out
MP4	Moving Picture Experts Group Layer 4
MPEG	Moving Picture Experts Group
MSConfig	Microsoft Configuration
MSDS	Material Safety Data Sheet
MT-RJ	Mechanical Transfer Registered Jack
MUI	Multilingual User Interface
NaaS	Network as a Service
NAC	Network Access Control
NAS	Network-Attached Storage
NAT	Network Address Translation
NetBEUI	Networked Basic Input/Output System Extended User Interface
NetBIOS	Networked Basic Input/Output System
NFC	Near Field Communication
NFS	Network File System
NIC	Network Interface Card
NiCd	Nickel Cadmium
NiMH	Nickel Metal Hydride
NLX	New Low-profile Extended
NNTP	Network News Transfer Protocol
NTFS	New Technology File System
NTLDR	New Technology Loader
NTP	Network Time Protocol
NTSC	National Transmission Standards Committee
NVMe	Non-volatile Memory Express
OCR	Optical Character Recognition
OEM	Original Equipment Manufacturer
OLED	Organic Light-Emitting Diode
OS	Operating System
PaaS	Platform as a Service
PAL	Phase Alternating Line
PAN	Personal Area Network
PAT	Port Address Translation
PC	Personal Computer
PCI	Payment Card Industry
PCI	Peripheral Component Interconnect
PCIe	Peripheral Component Interconnect Express
PCIX	Peripheral Component Interconnect Extended
PCL	Printer Control Language
PCMCIA	Personal Computer Memory Card International Association
PE	Preinstallation Environment
PGA	Pin Grid Array
PGA2	Pin Grid Array 2

Acronym	Spelled Out
PGP	Pretty Good Protection
PHI	Personal Health Information
PII	Personally Identifiable Information
PIN	Personal Identification Number
PKI	Public Key Infrastructure
PnP	Plug and Play
PoE	Power over Ethernet
POP3	Post Office Protocol 3
PoS	Point of Sale
POST	Power-On Self-Test
POTS	Plain Old Telephone Service
PPM	Pages Per Minute
PPP	Point-to-Point Protocol
PPTP	Point-to-Point Tunneling Protocol
PRI	Primary Rate Interface
PROM	Programmable Read-Only Memory
PS/2	Personal System/2 connector
PSTN	Public Switched Telephone Network
PSU	Power Supply Unit
PVA	Patterned Vertical Alignment
PVC	Permanent Virtual Circuit
PXE	Preboot Execution Environment
QoS	Quality of Service
RADIUS	Remote Authentication Dial-In User Server
RAID	Redundant Array of Independent (or Inexpensive) Disks
RAM	Random Access Memory
RAS	Remote Access Service
RDP	Remote Desktop Protocol
RF	Radio Frequency
RFI	Radio Frequency Interference
RFID	Radio Frequency Identification
RGB	Red Green Blue
RIP	Routing Information Protocol
RIS	Remote Installation Service
RISC	Reduced Instruction Set Computer
RJ-11	Registered Jack Function 11
RJ-45	Registered Jack Function 45
RMA	Returned Materials Authorization
ROM	Read-Only Memory
RPO	Recovery Point Objective
RTC	Real-Time Clock
RTO	Recovery Time Objective

C

Acronym	Spelled Out
Saas	Software as a Service
SAN	Storage Area Network
SAS	Serial Attached SCSI
SATA	Serial Advanced Technology Attachment
SC	Subscription Channel
SCP	Secure Copy Protection
SCSI	Small Computer System Interface
SCSI ID	Small Computer System Interface Identifier
SD card	Secure Digital Card
SEC	Single Edge Connector
SFC	System File Checker
SFF	Small Form Factor
SFTP	Secure File Transfer Protocol
SIM	Subscriber Identity Module
SIMM	Single In-Line Memory Module
SLI	Scalable Link Interface, System Level Integration, or Scan-line Interleave
S.M.A.R.T.	Self-Monitoring, Analysis, and Reporting Technology
SMB	Server Message Block
SMTP	Simple Mail Transfer Protocol
SNMP	Simple Network Management Protocol
SoDIMM	Small Outline Dual Inline Memory Module
SOHO	Small Office/Home Office
SP	Service Pack
SPDIF	Sony-Philips Digital Interface Format
SPGA	Staggered Pin Grid Array
SRAM	Static Random Access Memory
SSD	Solid-State Drive
SSH	Secure Shell
SSID	Service Set Identifier
SSL	Secure Sockets Layer
SSO	Single Sign-on
ST	Straight Tip
STP	Shielded Twisted-Pair
SXGA	Super Extended Graphics Array
TACACS	Terminal Access Controller Access Control System
TCP	Transmission Control Protocol
TCP/IP	Transmission Control Protocol/Internet Protocol
TDR	Time Domain Reflectometer
TFTP	Trivial File Transfer Protocol
TKIP	Temporal Key Integrity Protocol
TLS	Transport Layer Security
TN	Twisted Nematic

Acronym	Spelled Out
TPM	Trusted Platform Module
UAC	User Account Control
UDF	User Defined Functions, Universal Disk Format, or Universal Data Format
UDP	User Datagram Protocol
UEFI	Unified Extensible Firmware Interface
UNC	Universal Naming Convention
UPnP	Universal Plug and Play
UPS	Uninterruptible Power Supply
URL	Uniform Resource Locator
USB	Universal Serial Bus
USMT	User State Migration Tool
UTM	Unified Threat Management
UTP	Unshielded Twisted-Pair
UXGA	Ultra Extended Graphics Array
VA	Vertical Alignment
VDC	Volts DC
VDI	Virtual Desktop Infrastructure
VESA	Video Electronics Standards Association
VFAT	Virtual File Allocation Table
VGA	Video Graphics Array
VLAN	Virtual LAN
VM	Virtual Machine
VNC	Virtual Network Computer
VoIP	Voice over Internet Protocol
VPN	Virtual Private Network
VRAM	Video Random Access Memory
WAN	Wide Area Network
WAP	Wireless Access Protocol or Wireless Access Point
WEP	Wired Equivalent Privacy
Wi-Fi	Wireless Fidelity
WINS	Windows Internet Name Service
WLAN	Wireless Local Area Network
WMN	Wireless Mesh Network
WPA	Wireless Protected Access
WPA2	Wi-Fi Protected Access 2
WPS	Wi-Fi Protected Setup
WUXGA	Wide Ultra Extended Graphics Array
WWAN	Wireless Wide Area Network
XGA	Extended Graphics Array
ZIF	Zero-Insertion-Force
ZIP	Zigzag Inline Package

C

GLOSSARY

100BaseT An Ethernet standard that operates at 100 Mbps and uses twisted-pair cabling up to 100 meters (328 feet). *Also called* Fast Ethernet. Variations of 100BaseT are 100BaseTX and 100BaseFX.

10-foot user interface Applications software used on large screens to control output display menus and other clickable items in fonts large enough to read at a distance of 10 feet.

20-pin P1 connector A connector used by an older ATX power supply and motherboard; it provided +3.3 volts, +5 volts, +12 volts, –12 volts, and an optional and rarely used –5 volts.

24-pin P1 connector A connector used by an ATX Version 2.2 power supply and motherboard; it provides additional power for PCI Express slots.

32-bit operating system A type of operating system that processes 32 bits at a time.

3D printer A printer that uses a plastic filament to build a 3D model of a digital image.

3G A third generation cellular wireless Internet connection standard used with CDMA or GSM mobile phone services that allows for transmitting data and video.

4G A fourth generation cellular wireless Internet connection standard typically used with LTE (Long Term Evolution) technology; 4G transmits data and video up to 1 Gbps.

4-pin 12-V connector An auxiliary motherboard connector used for extra 12-V power to the processor.

5G A fifth generation cellular wireless Internet connection standard expected to transmit 10–50 Gbps. 5G is not yet released.

64-bit operating system A type of operating system that processes 64 bits at a time.

802.11 a/b/g/n/ac The collective name for the IEEE 802.11 standards for local wireless networking, which is the technical name for Wi-Fi.

802.11a An outdated Wi-Fi standard that transmitted up to 54 Mbps.

802.11ac *See* IEEE 802.11ac.

802.11b An outdated Wi-Fi standard that transmitted up to 11 Mbps and experienced interference with cordless phones and microwaves.

802.11g An outdated Wi-Fi standard that was compatible with and replaced 802.11b.

802.11n *See* IEEE 802.11n.

8-pin 12-V connector An auxiliary motherboard connector used for extra 12-V power to the processor; it provides more power than the older 4-pin auxiliary connector.

A+ Certification A certification awarded by CompTIA (the Computer Technology Industry Association) that measures an IT technician's knowledge and skills.

AAA (authenticating, authorizing, and accounting) The three major methods used to secure a network and its resources. Authenticating controls access to the network, authorizing controls what a user or computer can do on the network, and accounting tracks what a user or computer has done on the network. *Also called* triple A.

AC adapter A device that converts AC to DC and can use regular house current to power a laptop computer.

accelerometer A type of gyroscope used in mobile devices to sense the physical position of the device.

acceptable use policy (AUP) A document that explains to users what they can and cannot do on the corporate network or with company data, and the penalties for violations.

access control list (ACL) A record or list of the resources (for example, a printer, folder, or file) that a user, device, or program has access to on a corporate network, server, or workstation.

Action bar On an Android device, an area at the bottom of the screen that can contain up to five custom software buttons, called Home touch buttons. The three default buttons are back, home, and overview.

Action Center A tool in Windows 8/7 that lists errors and issues that need attention.

Active Directory (AD) A suite of services and databases provided by Windows Server that is used to manage Windows domains, including five groups of services: Domain Services, Certificate Services, Federation Services, Rights Management, and Lightweight Directory Services.

Active Directory Domain Services (AD DS) A component of Active Directory that is responsible for authenticating accounts and authorizing what these accounts can do.

active hours The range of time during the day when Windows 10 avoids automatic restarts while applying updates.

active partition For MBR hard drives, the primary partition on the drive that boots the OS. Windows calls the active partition the system partition.

active recovery image In Windows 8, the custom refresh image of the Windows volume that will be used during a refresh of the Windows installation. *Also see* custom refresh image.

ActiveX control A small app or add-on that can be downloaded from a website along with a webpage and is executed by a browser to enhance the webpage.

ad hoc mode A peer-to-peer wireless network between computers where each wireless computer serves as its own wireless access point and is responsible for securing each connection.

adapter address *See* MAC (Media Access Control) address.

address reservation When a DHCP server assigns a static IP address to a DHCP client. For example, a network printer might require a static IP address so that computers on the network can find the printer.

ADF (automatic document feeder) scanner A component of a copier, scanner, or printer that can automatically pull individual items of paper, cards, or envelopes from a stack into a roller system for processing.

administrative shares The folders and volumes shared by default on a network that administrator accounts can access but are invisible to standard users. Use the fsmgmt.msc command to view a list of shared folders and volumes.

Administrative Tools A group of tools accessed through Control Panel and used to manage the local computer or other computers on the network.

administrator account In Windows, a user account that grants an administrator rights and privileges to all hardware and software resources, such as the right to add, delete, and change accounts and to change hardware configurations. *Compare with* standard account.

Administrators group A type of user group. When a user account is assigned to this group, the account is granted rights that are assigned to an administrator account.

Advanced Boot Options menu A Windows 7 menu that appears when you press F8 as Windows starts. The menu can be used to troubleshoot problems when loading Windows.

Aero user interface The Windows 7 interface that gives windows a transparent, glassy appearance. *Also called* Aero glass *or* Aero interface.

AES (Advanced Encryption Standard) An encryption standard used by WPA2; it is currently the strongest encryption standard used by Wi-Fi.

AFP (Apple Filing Protocol) An outdated file access protocol used by early editions of macOS by Apple; AFP is one protocol in the suite of AppleTalk networking protocols.

agent A small app installed on a client that communicates with a server. For example, MDM on-boarding might install an agent on a mobile device to verify that the device complies with security measures.

air filter mask A mask that filters the dust and other contaminants from the air for breathing safety. *Also called* air-purifying respirator.

AirDrop A feature of iOS whereby iPhones and iPads can transfer files between nearby devices. The devices use Bluetooth to detect nearby devices and Wi-Fi to establish connectivity and transfer files.

airplane mode A setting within a mobile device that disables the cellular, Wi-Fi, and Bluetooth antennas so the device cannot transmit signals.

AirPrint A technology by Apple that allows Apple computers and mobile devices to print to an AirPrint-capable printer without first installing the printer.

alias A nickname or shortcut for a cmdlet in Windows PowerShell. For example, dir is an alias for the Get-ChildItem cmdlet.

all-in-one computer A computer that has the monitor and computer case built together and uses components that are common to both a notebook and a desktop computer.

alternate IP address When configuring TCP/IP in Windows, the static IP address that Windows uses if it cannot lease an IP address from a DHCP server.

alternating current (AC) Current that cycles back and forth rather than traveling in only one direction. In the United States, the AC voltage from a standard wall outlet is normally between 110 and 115 V. In Europe, the standard AC voltage from a wall outlet is 220 V.

AM3+ A type of pin grid array CPU socket used with AMD Piledriver and Bulldozer processors and the 9-series chipset. AM3+ is typically used in high-end gaming systems.

AM4 A type of CPU socket used with AMD Ryzen and Athlon processors and the AM4 family of chipsets, including the 970, 980G, and 990X chipsets. AM4 is typically used in mainstream desktop systems. The socket has 1331 pins in a pin grid array.

A-Male connector A common type of USB connector that is flat and wide and connects an A Male USB port on a computer or USB hub.

amp (A) A measure of electrical current.

analog A continuous signal with infinite variations, as compared with digital, which is a series of binary values—1s and 0s.

Android An operating system for mobile devices that is based on the Linux OS and supported by Google.

anonymous users User accounts that have not been authenticated on a remote computer.

ANSI (American National Standards Institute) A nonprofit organization dedicated to creating trade and communications standards.

answer file A file of information that Windows requires in order to do an unattended installation.

anti-malware software Utility software that can prevent infection, scan a system, and detect and remove all types of general malware, including viruses, spyware, worms, and rootkits.

antistatic bag A static shielding bag that new computer components are shipped in.

antistatic wrist strap *See* ESD strap.

antivirus software Utility software that can prevent infection, scan a system, and detect and remove viruses.

anycast address Using TCP/IP version 6, a type of IP address used by routers that identifies multiple destinations. Packets are delivered to the closest destination.

APFS (Apple File System) In macOS, the default file system for SSDs; it can also be used for magnetic hard drives. APFS uses the GUID partitioning system.

APIPA (automatic private IP address) *See* automatic private IP address (APIPA).

APK (Android Application Package) The format used to distribute an Android app in a package of files wrapped into one file with an .apk file extension.

app drawer An app embedded in the Android OS that lists and manages all apps installed on the device.

App Store The app on an Apple device (iPad, iPhone, or iPod touch) that can be used to download content from the iTunes Store website (*itunes.apple.com*).

Apple ID A user account that uses a valid email address and password and is associated with a credit card number that allows you to download iOS and macOS updates and patches, apps, and multimedia content.

Apple menu In macOS, the menu that appears when the user clicks the Apple icon in the upper-left corner of the screen.

application streaming A hybrid technique between a cloud-based application that is never installed on the local computer and an application that's downloaded and installed locally. An example is Android Instant Apps.

application virtualization Using this virtualization, a virtual environment is created in memory for an application to virtually install itself.

G

Application Virtualization (App-V)   Software by Microsoft used for application virtualization.

Apps Drawer   An Android app that lists and manages all apps installed on the device. By default, this app's icon is in the favorites tray on an Android screen.

apt-get   A Linux and macOS command to install and remove software packages and install OS updates.

AR (augmented reality) headset   A Microsoft headset with native compatibility with Windows 10 that is a hybrid between a mobile and tethered VR headset.

array   A group of hard drives that work together to provide a single storage volume.

artifact   A horizontally torn image on a computer screen.

ATA Secure Erase   Standards developed by the American National Standards Institute (ANSI) that dictate how to securely erase data from solid-state devices such as a USB flash drive or SSD in order to protect personal privacy.

ATAPI (Advanced Technology Attachment Packet Interface)   An interface standard within the IDE/ATA standards that allows tape drives, optical drives, and other drives to be treated like an IDE hard drive by the system.

ATX (Advanced Technology Extended)   The most common form factor for desktop computer cases, motherboards, and power supplies; it was originally introduced by Intel in 1995. ATX motherboards and cases make better use of space and resources than the earlier AT form factor.

ATX12V power supply   An ATX Version 2.1 power supply that provides an extra 12-V power cord with a 4-pin connector and is used with the auxiliary 4-pin power connector on motherboards to provide additional power for processors.

audio port   A port that can be used by microphone, audio in, audio out, and stereo audio out connections. *Also called* a sound port.

Authenticated Users group   All user accounts that have been authenticated to access the system except the Guest account. *Compare with* anonymous users.

authentication server   A server responsible for authenticating users or computers to the network so they can access network resources.

authenticator application   An app installed on a smartphone to provide multifactor authentication—for example, Google Authenticator, Microsoft Authenticator, and Authy.

autodetection   A feature of BIOS/UEFI that detects a new drive and automatically selects the correct drive capacity and configuration, including the best possible standard supported by both the hard drive and the motherboard.

automatic private IP address (APIPA)   In TCP/IP version 4, an IP address in the address range 169.254.x.y, used by a computer when it cannot successfully lease an IP address from a DHCP server.

auto-switching   A function of a laptop computer's AC adapter that enables it to automatically switch between 110-V and 220-V AC power.

Azure Active Directory (Azure AD)   Microsoft domain services managed by Microsoft servers in the cloud. Windows 10 business and professional editions support joining an Azure domain.

back flash   To revert to an earlier version of BIOS/UEFI after flashing BIOS/UEFI.

back-out plan   A plan that defines the activities needed to recover to the original state in the event of an aborted or failed change implementation.

Backup and Restore   The Windows utility used to create and update scheduled backups of user data and the system image.

Backup Operators group   A type of Windows user account group. When a user account belongs to this group, it can back up and restore any files on the system, regardless of whether it has access to these files.

badge reader   A device that can read the microchip or magnetic stripe on a card, such as a credit card, and transmit the information to a computer.

bandwidth   In relation to analog communication, the range of frequencies that a communications channel or cable can carry. In general use, the term refers to the volume of data that can be transmitted on a bus or over a cable; bandwidth is stated in bits per second (bps), kilobits per second (Kbps), or megabits per second (Mbps). *Also called* data throughput *or* line speed.

barcode   A pattern of numbers and variable-length lines that can be read by a machine; a barcode is often used to identify a manufacturer and product.

barcode reader A device used to scan barcodes on products at the points of sale or when taking inventory.

base station A fixed transceiver and antenna used to create one cell within a cellular network.

baseband update An update to radio firmware on a mobile device that manages cellular, Wi-Fi, and Bluetooth radios. Baseband updates may be included in OS updates.

Bash on Ubuntu on Windows A Windows 10 shell that uses Ubuntu Bash commands. Ubuntu is a popular distribution of Linux. *Also called* Bash on Windows *and* Ubuntu Bash.

Bash shell The default shell used by the terminal for many distributions of Linux.

basic disk The term Windows uses to describe a hard drive when it is a stand-alone drive in the system. *Compare with* dynamic disk.

basic loop A scripting or programming technique to execute the same group of commands multiple times until a condition is met.

batch file A script text file that has a .bat file extension and contains a series of Windows commands.

BCD (Boot Configuration Data) A small Windows database that is structured the same as a registry file and contains configuration information about how Windows is started. The file is stored in the \Boot directory of the hidden system partition.

bcdedit A Windows command used to manually edit the BCD.

BD (Blu-ray disc) An optical disc technology that uses the UDF version 2.5 file system and a blue laser beam, which is shorter than any red beam used by DVD or CD discs. The shorter blue laser beam allows Blu-ray discs to store more data than a DVD.

beamforming A technique supported by the IEEE 802.11ac Wi-Fi standard that can detect the location of connected devices and increase signal strength in that direction.

best-effort protocol *See* connectionless protocol.

biometric authentication To authenticate to a network, computer, or other computing device by means of biometric data, such as a fingerprint or retinal data. Touch ID on an iPhone or face lock on an Android device can perform biometric authentication.

biometric data Data that identifies a person by a fingerprint, handprint, face, retina, iris, voice, or handwritten signature.

biometric device An input device that can identify biological data about a person's fingerprints, handprints, face, voice, eyes, and handwriting.

biometric lock A lock that can be opened by input of biometric data.

BIOS (basic input/output system) Firmware that can control much of a computer's input/output functions, such as communication with the keyboard and the monitor. *Compare with* UEFI.

BIOS setup The program in system BIOS that can change the values in CMOS RAM. *Also called* CMOS setup.

BitLocker Drive Encryption A utility in Windows 10/8/7 that is used to lock down a hard drive by encrypting the entire Windows volume and any other volume on the drive. *Also called* BitLocker Encryption.

BitLocker Encryption *See* BitLocker Drive Encryption.

BitLocker To Go A Windows utility that can encrypt data on a USB flash drive and restrict access by requiring a password.

bitmap Rows and columns of bits that collectively represent an image.

blacklist In filtering, a list of items that are not allowed—for example, a list of websites that computers on a local network are not allowed to access. *Compare with* whitelist.

blue screen of death (BSOD) A Windows error that occurs in kernel mode, is displayed against a blue screen, and causes the system to halt. The error might be caused by problems with devices, device drivers, or a corrupted Windows installation. *Also called* a stop error.

Bluetooth A short-range wireless technology used to connect two devices in a small personal network.

Bluetooth PIN code A code that may be required to complete the Bluetooth connection in a pairing process.

Blu-ray Disc (BD) *See* BD.

G

B-Male connector A USB connector that connects a USB 1.x or 2.0 device such as a printer.

BNC connector An outdated network connector used with thin coaxial cable. Some BNC connectors are T-shaped and are called T-connectors. One end of the T connects to the NIC, and the two other ends can connect to cables or end a bus formation with a terminator.

Bonjour An Apple program that is used to interface between computers and devices and share content and services between them. When iTunes is installed on a Windows computer, the installation includes Bonjour.

Boot Camp A utility in macOS that allows you to install and run Windows on a Mac computer.

Boot Configuration Data (BCD) store *See* BCD.

boot loader menu A startup menu in a dual-boot system that gives the user the choice of which operating system to load, such as Windows 10 or Windows 8. Multiples OSs are installed on a dual-boot system.

boot partition The hard drive partition where the Windows OS is stored. The system partition and the boot partition may be different partitions.

boot priority order A list of devices stored in firmware on the motherboard that BIOS/UEFI startup uses in the order listed to search for and load an operating system.

booting The process of starting up a computer and loading an operating system.

BootMgr The file name of the boot manager program responsible for loading Windows on a BIOS system. The file has no file extension.

bootrec A Windows command used to repair the BCD and boot sectors.

bootsect A Windows command used to repair a dual-boot system.

botnet A network of zombies or robots.

Branchcache A Windows feature to optimize content on a WAN by caching the content on local servers for better access.

bridge A networking device that stands between two segments of a network and manages traffic between them.

broadband A transmission technique that carries more than one type of transmission on the same medium, such as voice and DSL on a regular telephone line.

broadcast message A message sent over a local network to all devices on the network; the message does not contain recipient information.

brownout A temporary reduction in voltage that can sometimes cause data loss. *Also called* sag.

brute force Systematically trying every possible combination of letters, numbers, and symbols to crack a password.

brute force attack A method to hack or discover a password by trying every single combination of characters.

BSOD (blue screen of death) *See* blue screen of death (BSOD).

burn-in When a static image stays on a monitor for many hours, leaving a permanent impression of the image on the monitor.

bus The paths, or lines, on the motherboard on which data, instructions, and electrical power move from component to component.

BYOD (Bring Your Own Device) A corporate policy that allows employees or students to connect their own devices to the corporate network.

BYOD Experience A Microsoft feature that allows a personal device to join an Azure domain and access corporate resources on the domain.

cable Internet A broadband technology that uses cable TV lines and is always connected (always up).

cable lock A cable with a lock used to physically secure a laptop or computer to a table or other stationary device. *Also called* Kensington lock.

cable modem A device that converts a computer's digital signal to analog before sending it over cable TV lines and that converts incoming analog data to digital.

cable stripper A hand tool used to cut away the plastic jacket or coating around the wires of a network cable.

cable tester A tool used to test a cable to find out if it is good or to identify a cable that is not labeled.

calibration The process of checking and correcting the graduations of an instrument or device, such as an inkjet printer.

call tracking software A system that tracks the dates, times, and transactions of help-desk or on-site IT support calls, including the problem presented, the issues addressed, who did what, and when and how each call was resolved.

CAS Latency   A method of measuring access timing to memory, which is the number of clock cycles required to write or read a column of data off a memory module. CAS stands for Column Access Strobe.

case fan   A fan inside a computer case that's used to draw air out of or into the case.

cast   A mobile device feature that allows the device to transmit its display to a television, monitor, or projector.

CAT-5 (Category 5)   A rating used for UTP cables and rated for Fast Ethernet, but seldom used today.

CAT-5e (Category 5e)   A popular rating used for UTP cables and rated for Fast Ethernet and Gigabit Ethernet.

CAT-6 (Category 6)   A rating used for twisted-pair cables that have less crosstalk than CAT-5e cables. CAT-6 cables might contain a plastic cord down the center that helps to prevent crosstalk, but they are less flexible and more difficult to install than CAT-5e.

CAT-6a (Category 6a)   A rating used for twisted-pair cables that are thicker and faster than CAT-6 and rated for 10GBase-T (10-Gigabit Ethernet).

CAT-6e (Category 6e)   An unofficial name for CAT-6a.

CAT-7 (Category 7)   A rating used for twisted-pair cables that have shielding to almost completely eliminate crosstalk and improve noise reduction.

Category view   The default view in Control Panel that presents utilities grouped by category.

cd (change directory)   The Windows command to change the current default directory.

CD (compact disc)   An optical disc technology that uses a red laser beam and can hold up to 700 MB of data.

CDFS (Compact Disc File System)   The 32-bit file system for CD discs and some CD-R and CD-RW discs. *Also see* Universal Disk Format (UDF).

CDMA (Code Division Multiple Access)   A protocol standard used by cellular WANs and cell phones for transmitting digital data over cellular networks.

cellular network   A network that can be used when a wireless network must cover a wide area. The network is made up of cells, each controlled by a base station. *Also called* a cellular WAN *or* wireless wide area network (WWAN).

cellular network analyzer   Software and hardware that can monitor cellular networks for signal strength of cell towers, WAPs, and repeaters, which can help technicians better position antennas in a distributed antenna system (DAS).

central processing unit (CPU)   The component where almost all processing of data and instructions takes place. The CPU receives data input, processes information, and executes instructions. *Also called* a microprocessor *or* processor.

Centrino   A technology used by Intel whereby the processor, chipset, and wireless network adapter are all interconnected as a unit, which improves laptop performance.

Certificate of Authenticity   A sticker that contains the Windows product key.

certificate of destruction   Digital or paper documentation that assures customers their data has been destroyed beyond recovery by a secure service.

Certificate Authority (CA)   An organization, such as VeriSign, that assigns digital certificates or digital signatures to individuals or organizations. *Also called* certification authority.

chain of custody   Documentation that tracks all evidence collected and used in an investigation, including when and from whom the evidence was collected, the condition of the evidence, and how the evidence was secured while in possession of a responsible party.

change advisory board (CAB)   The team in an organization charged with assessing, prioritizing, authorizing, and scheduling change.

change management   The processes for successfully bringing people forward to an end result or goal.

channel   A specific radio frequency within a broader frequency.

charging   In laser printing, the process of placing a high electrical charge on the imaging drum to condition it before an image is exposed to the drum.

charm   A Windows 8 shortcut that appears in the charms bar.

charms bar   A menu that appears on the right side of any Windows 8 screen when you move your pointer to the right corner.

G

chassis   A case for any type of computer.

chassis air guide (CAG)   A round air duct that helps to pull and direct fresh air from outside a computer case to the cooler and processor.

child directory   *See* subdirectory.

chip reader   A device that reads the chip on a smart card or license to pull information from it.

chipset   A group of chips on the motherboard that controls the timing and flow of data and instructions to and from the CPU.

chkdsk (check disk)   A Windows command to verify that the hard drive does not have bad sectors that can corrupt the file system.

chmod   A Linux and macOS command to change modes (or permissions) for a file or directory.

chown   A Linux and macOS command to change the owner of a file or directory.

Chrome OS   An OS by Google that is built on the open source Chromium OS and used on Google Chromebooks. The OS looks and works much like the Chrome browser and relies heavily on web-based apps and storage.

CIDR (Classless Interdomain Routing) notation   A shorthand notation (pronounced "*cider notation*") for expressing an IPv4 address and subnet mask; the IP address is followed by a slash (/) and the number of bits in the IP address that identifies the network—for example, 15.50.35.10/20.

CIFS (Common Internet File System)   A file access protocol and the cross-platform version of SMB used between Windows, Linux, macOS, and other operating systems. CIFS is a spinoff of the SMB2 protocol.

Class C fire extinguisher   A fire extinguisher rated to put out electrical fires.

Classic view   A view in Control Panel that presents utilities as small or large icons that are not grouped.

clean boot   A process of starting Windows with a basic set of drivers and startup programs; a clean boot can be useful when software does not install properly.

clean install   A process used to overwrite the existing operating system and applications when installing an OS on a hard drive.

client/server   Two computers communicating using a local network or the Internet. One computer (the client) makes requests to the other computer (the server), which answers the request.

client/server application   An application where a client program installed on one computer requests information from a server program installed on another computer on the network or Internet.

client-hosted desktop virtualization   When a local computer is used to host a hypervisor and its virtual machines.

client-side desktop virtualization   Using this virtualization, software installed on a desktop or laptop manages virtual machines used by the local user.

client-side virtualization   Using this virtualization, a personal computer provides multiple virtual environments for applications.

clone   In Linux and macOS, an image of the entire partition on which the OS is installed.

closed source   Software owned by a vendor that requires a commercial license to install and use. *Also called* vendor-specific or commercial license software.

cloud computing   A service where server-side virtualization is delegated to a third-party service, and the Internet is used to connect server and client machines.

cloud file storage service   A way of storing files in the cloud. Examples are Google Drive, iCloud Drive, Dropbox, and OneDrive.

cloud printing   Printing to a printer anywhere on the Internet from a personal computer or mobile device connected to the Internet.

cloud-based application   An application installed on a server on the Internet; the user can access the software through a browser. The application is a type of SaaS.

cloud-based network controller   A manager of network resources in the cloud through services that are also in the cloud. These network resources are managed through a browser and might include Wi-Fi access points, network servers, routers, switches, and firewalls. An example of a cloud-based network controller is CloudTrax (*cloudtrax.com*).

cluster   On a magnetic hard drive, one or more sectors that constitute the smallest unit of space on the drive for storing data (also referred to as a file allocation unit). Files are written to a drive as groups of whole clusters.

cmdlets Prebuilt scripts (pronounced "*command-lets*") written for Windows PowerShell, a command-line interface expected to replace the command prompt window.

CMOS (complementary metal-oxide semiconductor) The technology used to manufacture microchips. CMOS chips require less electricity, hold data longer after the electricity is turned off, and produce less heat than earlier technologies. The configuration or setup chip is a CMOS chip.

CMOS battery The lithium coin-cell battery on the motherboard used to power the CMOS chip that holds BIOS setup data so that the data is retained when the computer is unplugged.

CMOS RAM Memory contained on the CMOS configuration chip.

coaxial (coax) cable A cable that has a single copper wire down the middle and a braided shield around it.

cold boot *See* hard boot.

color depth The accuracy of color representation on a monitor screen; color depth is important for editing photographs and in graphic design.

comment syntax The text in a script or program that tags a line as documentation so it is not interpreted as a command in the script or program.

commercial license When applied to software, the rights to use the software, as assigned to the user by the software vendor.

community cloud Online resources and services that are shared between multiple organizations but are not available publicly.

CompactFlash (CF) card A flash memory device that allows for sizes up to 137 GB, although current sizes range up to 64 GB.

compatibility mode A group of settings that can be applied to older drivers or applications so that they might work using a newer version of Windows than the one they were designed to use.

Compatibility Support Module (CSM) A feature of UEFI that allows it to be backward-compatible with legacy BIOS devices and drivers.

Component Services (COM+) A Microsoft Management Console snap-in that can be used to register components used by installed applications.

compressed (zipped) folder A folder with a .zip extension that contains compressed files. When files are put in the folder, they are compressed. When files are moved to a regular folder, they are decompressed.

computer infestation *See* malicious software.

Computer Management A Windows console (compmgmt.msc) that contains several administrative tools used by support technicians to manage the local computer or other computers on the network.

computer name *See* host name.

connectionless protocol A TCP/IP protocol such as UDP that works at the OSI Transport layer and does not guarantee delivery by first connecting and checking where data is received. It might be used for broadcasting, such as streaming video or sound over the web, where guaranteed delivery is not as important as fast transmission. *Also called* a best-effort protocol. *Also see* UDP (User Datagram Protocol).

connection-oriented protocol In networking, a TCP/IP protocol that confirms a good connection has been made before transmitting data to the other end, verifies that data was received, and resends data if it was not received. An example of a connection-oriented protocol is TCP.

console A window that consolidates several Windows administrative tools.

contrast ratio The contrast between true black and true white on a screen.

Control Panel A window containing several small utility programs called applets that are used to manage hardware, software, users, and the system.

controller hub A device that controls the smart devices in an IoT network to create an integrated smart home experience. *Also called* smart home hub.

cooler A cooling system that sits on top of a processor and consists of a fan and a heat sink.

copy The Windows command to copy a single file, a group of files, or a folder and its contents.

G

copyright The right to copy a creative work; a copyright belongs to the creator(s) of the work or others to whom the creator transfers this right.

Cortana A Windows 10 voice-enabled digital assistant and search feature.

CPU *See* central processing unit (CPU).

crimper A hand tool used to attach a terminator or connector to the end of a cable.

critical applications Applications that are required to keep a business functioning and that require alternative solutions if they are not functioning.

crossover cable A cable used to connect two like devices such as a hub to a hub or a computer to a computer (to make the simplest network of all). The transmit connectors at one end of the cable are wired as the receiving connectors at the other end of the cable and vice versa.

custom installation In the Windows setup program, the option used to overwrite the existing operating system and applications, producing a clean installation of the OS. The main advantage is that problems with the old OS are not carried forward.

custom refresh image In Windows 8, an image of the entire Windows volume, including the Windows installation. The image can be applied during a Windows 8 refresh operation.

data loss prevention (DLP) Methods that protect corporate data from being exposed or stolen; for example, software that filters employee email to verify that privacy laws are not accidentally or intentionally being violated.

data source A resource on a network that includes a database and the drivers required to interface between a remote computer and the data.

Data Sources A connection between a local application and a remote database so that the application can manage the database. *Also called* ODBC Data Sources (Open Database Connectivity Data Sources).

data throughput *See* bandwidth.

DB-15 *See* VGA (Video Graphics Array) port.

DB-9 *See* serial port.

DB15 port *See* VGA (Video Graphics Array) port.

DB9 port *See* serial port.

dd In Linux and macOS, the command to copy and convert files, directories, partitions, and entire DVDs or hard drives. You must be logged in as a superuser to use the command.

DDR *See* Double Data Rate SDRAM.

DDR2 Memory that is faster and uses less power than DDR.

DDR3 Memory that is faster and uses less power than DDR2.

DDR3L Memory that is faster and uses less power than regular DDR3.

DDR4 Memory that is faster and uses less power than DDR3.

DE15 port *See* VGA (Video Graphics Array) port.

dead pixel A pixel on an LCD monitor that is not working and can appear as a small white, black, or colored spot on the screen.

default gateway The gateway a networked computer uses to access another network unless it knows to specifically use another gateway for quicker access.

default printer The designated printer to which Windows prints unless another one is selected.

default product key A product key that can be used to fix a problem created when Windows 10 setup installs the wrong edition of the OS.

default program A program associated with a file extension that is used to open the file.

defense in depth Layered protection for a system or network so that, if one security method fails, the next might stop an attacker.

defrag The Windows command that examines a magnetic hard drive for fragmented files and rewrites these files to the drive in contiguous clusters.

Defrag and Optimization tool (defrgui.exe) A Windows utility that defragments a magnetic hard drive and trims an SSD to improve performance. *Also called* Defragment and Optimize Drives utility.

defragment A drive maintenance procedure that rearranges fragments or parts of files on a magnetic hard drive so each file is stored on the drive in contiguous clusters.

Defragment and Optimize Drives *See* Defrag and Optimization tool.

defragmentation tool A utility or command to rewrite a file to a disk in one contiguous chain of clusters, thus speeding up data retrieval.

degausser   A machine that exposes a storage device to a strong magnetic field to completely erase the data on a magnetic hard drive or tape drive.

del   The Windows command to delete a file or group of files. *Also called* the erase command.

denial-of-service (DoS)   An attack that overwhelms a computer or network with incoming traffic until new connections can no longer be accepted.

deployment strategy   A procedure to install Windows, device drivers, and applications on a computer; it can include the process to transfer user settings, application settings, and user data files from an old installation to the new installation.

desktop case   A computer case that lies flat and sometimes serves double duty as a monitor stand. A tower case is sometimes called a desktop case.

destination network address translation (DNAT)   When a firewall using NAT allows uninitiated communication to a computer behind the firewall through a port that is normally closed. *Also see* port forwarding.

device driver   A small program stored on the hard drive and installed in Windows that tells Windows how to communicate with a specific hardware device such as a printer, network, port on the motherboard, or scanner.

Device Manager   The primary Windows tool (devmgmt.msc) for managing hardware.

DHCP (Dynamic Host Configuration Protocol)   A protocol used by a server to assign a dynamic IP address to a computer when it first attempts to initiate a connection to the network and requests an IP address.

DHCP client   A computer or other device (such as a network printer) that requests an IP address from a DHCP server.

DHCP server   A computer or other device that provides an IP address from a pool of addresses to a client computer that requests an address.

DHCPv6 server   A DHCP server that serves up IPv6 addresses.

dictionary attack   A method to discover or crack a password by trying words in a dictionary.

digital   A signal consisting of a series of binary values—1s and 0s. *Compare with* analog.

digital assistant   A service or app, such as Apple's Siri and Microsoft's Cortana, that responds to a user's voice commands with a personable, conversational interaction to perform tasks and retrieve information. *Also called* personal assistant.

digital certificate   Encrypted data that serves as an electronic signature to authenticate the source of a file or document or to identify and authenticate a person or organization sending data over a network. The data is assigned by a certificate authority such as VeriSign and includes a public key for encryption. *Also called* digital ID *or* digital signature.

digital license   A Windows 10 license assigned to a computer after Windows 10 has been activated on the machine.

digital rights management (DRM)   Software and hardware security limitations meant to protect digital content and prevent piracy.

digital signature   *See* digital certificate.

digitizer   *See* graphics tablet.

digitizing tablet   *See* graphics tablet.

DIMM (dual inline memory module)   A miniature circuit board installed on a motherboard to hold memory.

dir   The Windows command to list files and directories.

direct current (DC)   Current that travels in only one direction (the type of electricity provided by batteries). Computer power supplies transform AC to low DC.

direct thermal printer   A type of thermal printer that burns dots onto special coated paper, as older fax machines did.

DirectX   A Microsoft software development tool that developers can use to write multimedia applications such as games, video-editing software, and computer-aided design software.

disc image   *See* ISO image.

discolored capacitor   An indicator of a failing motherboard; such capacitors might have bulging heads or crusty corrosion at their base.

Disk Cleanup   A Windows utility to delete temporary files and free up space on a drive.

disk cloning   *See* drive imaging.

disk drive shredder   A device that can destroy magnetic hard drives, SSDs, flash drives, optical discs, and mobile devices so that sensitive data on the device is also destroyed.

G

diskpart   A Windows command to manage hard drives, partitions, and volumes.

DISM (Deployment Image Servicing and Management)   A set of commands to create, capture, and manage a Windows 10 standard image. The commands can also be used to repair a corrupted Windows 10 installation.

DisplayPort   A port that transmits digital video and audio (not analog transmissions) and can be used in the place of VGA and DVI ports on personal computers.

distorted geometry   Images that are stretched inappropriately on a monitor.

distributed denial-of-service (DDoS)   A DoS attack performed by multiple computers and sometimes by botnets, even when users of the botnet computers are not aware of the attack.

distribution server   A file server holding Windows setup files that are used to install Windows on computers networked to the server.

distribution share   The collective files in an installation that include Windows, device drivers, and applications. The package of files is served up by a distribution server.

DMG file   In macOS, a disk image file similar to WIM or ISO files in Windows.

DMZ (demilitarized zone)   A computer or network that has limited or no firewall protection within a larger organization of protected computers and networks.

DNS (Domain Name System or Domain Name Service)   A distributed pool of information (called the namespace) that keeps track of assigned host names and domain names and their corresponding IP addresses. DNS also refers to the system that allows a host to locate information in the pool and the protocol the system uses.

DNS client   When Windows queries the DNS server for name resolution, which means to find an IP address for a computer when the fully qualified domain name is known.

DNS server   A Domain Name Service server that uses a DNS protocol to find an IP address for a computer when the fully qualified domain name is known. An Internet service provider is responsible for providing access to one or more DNS servers as part of the service it provides for Internet access.

dock   (1) For the Android OS, the area at the bottom of the Android screen where up to four apps can be pinned. (2) For macOS, a bar that appears by default at the bottom of the screen and contains program icons and shortcuts to files and folders.

docking port   A connector on the bottom of the laptop that connects to a port replicator or docking station.

docking station   A device that receives a laptop computer and provides additional secondary storage and easy connection to peripheral devices.

documented business processes   Stated goals of a business, including how the business achieves these goals.

domain   In Windows, a logical group of networked computers, such as those on a college campus, that share a centralized directory database of user account information and security.

domain account   *See* global account.

domain name   A name that identifies a network and appears before the period in a website address, such as *microsoft.com*. A fully qualified domain name is sometimes loosely called a domain name. *Also see* fully qualified domain name.

domain user account   An account assigned to a user by Active Directory that identifies the user and defines user rights on the domain. *Also called* network ID.

Double Data Rate SDRAM (DDR SDRAM)   A type of memory technology used on DIMMs that runs at twice the speed of the system clock, has one notch, and uses 184 pins. *Also called* DDR SDRAM, SDRAM II, *and* DDR.

double-sided   A DIMM feature whereby memory chips are installed on both sides of a DIMM.

drive imaging   Making an exact image of a hard drive, including partition information, boot sectors, operating system installation, and application software, to replicate the hard drive on another system or recover from a hard drive crash. *Also called* disk cloning *or* disk imaging.

driver rollback   To undo a device driver update by returning to the previous version.

driver store   The location where Windows stores a copy of the driver software when first installing a device.

DSL (Digital Subscriber Line)   A telephone line that carries digital data from end to end and is used as a type of broadband Internet access.

DSL modem   A device that converts a computer's digital signal to analog before sending it over telephone lines and converts incoming analog data to digital.

dual boot   The ability to boot using either of two different OSs, such as Windows 10 and Windows 7. *Also called* multiboot.

dual channels   A motherboard feature that improves memory performance by providing two 64-bit channels between memory and the chipset. DDR, DDR2, DDR3, and DDR4 DIMMs can use dual channels.

dual processors   Two processor sockets on a server motherboard.

dual rail   A power supply with a second +12 V circuit or rail used to ensure that the first circuit is not overloaded.

dual ranked   Double-sided DIMMs that provide two 64-bit banks. The memory controller accesses one bank and then the other. Dual-ranked DIMMs do not perform as well as single-ranked DIMMs.

dual voltage selector switch   A switch on the back of the computer case where you can change the input voltage to the power supply to 115 V (in the United States) or 220 V (in other countries).

dumb terminal   *See* zero client.

dump   In Linux, a collection of data that is copied to backup media.

dumpster diving   Looking for useful information in someone's trash to help create an impersonation of an individual or company to aid in a malicious attack.

duplex printer   A printer that is able to print on both sides of the paper.

duplexing assembly   In a duplex printer, an assembly of several rollers that enables printing on both sides of the paper.

DVD (digital versatile disc or digital video disc)   A technology for optical discs that uses a red laser beam and can hold up to 17 GB of data.

DVD-ROM   Stands for DVD read-only memory.

DVD-RW   Stands for DVD rewriteable memory.

DVD-RW DL   Stands for DVD rewriteable memory, dual layers. It doubles storage capacity.

DVI (Digital Video Interface) port   A port that transmits digital or analog video.

DVI-A   A DVI (Digital Video Interface) video port that only transmits analog data.

DVI-D   A DVI video port that works only with digital monitors.

DVI-I   A DVI video port that supports both analog and digital monitors.

DXDiag (DirectX Diagnostics Tool)   A Windows command (dxdiag.exe) used to display information about hardware and diagnose problems with DirectX. The command returns the version of DirectX installed.

dxdiag.exe   *See* DXDiag (DirectX Diagnostics Tool).

dynamic disk   A way to partition one or more hard drives so that they can work together to increase space for data storage or to provide fault tolerance or improved performance. *Also see* RAID. *Compare with* basic disk.

dynamic IP address   An IP address assigned by a DHCP server for the current session only, and leased when the computer first connects to a network. When the session is terminated, the IP address is returned to the list of available addresses. *Compare with* static IP address.

dynamic RAM (DRAM)   The most common type of system memory; it requires refreshing every few milliseconds.

dynamic type checking   A technique in scripting and programming whereby each command line is checked by the command interpreter software to verify that the command can be executed.

dynamic volume   A volume type used with dynamic disks by which you can create a single volume that uses space on multiple hard drives.

ECC (error-correcting code)   A chipset feature on a motherboard that checks the integrity of data stored on DIMMs or RIMMs and can correct single-bit errors in a byte. More advanced ECC schemas can detect, but not correct, double-bit errors in a byte.

EFI (Extensible Firmware Interface)   The original version of UEFI, which was first developed by Intel.

EFI System Partition (ESP)   For a GPT hard drive, the bootable partition used to boot the OS; ESP contains the boot manager program for the OS.

electrostatic discharge (ESD)   Another name for static electricity, which can damage chips and

G

destroy motherboards, even though it might not be felt or seen with the naked eye.

elevated command prompt window   A Windows command prompt window that allows commands requiring administrator privileges.

email filtering   To search incoming or outgoing email messages for matches kept in databases that can identify known scams and spammers and protect against social engineering.

email hoax   An email message that tries to tempt you to give out personal information or tries to scam you.

embedded MMC (eMMC)   Internal storage used instead of an SSD in mobile devices such as cell phones, tablets, and laptops.

emergency notifications   Government alerts, such as AMBER alerts, that are sent to mobile devices in an emergency.

emulator   A virtual machine that emulates hardware, such as the hardware buttons on a smartphone.

Encrypting File System (EFS)   A way to use a key to encode a file or folder on an NTFS volume and protect sensitive data. Because it is an integrated system service, EFS is transparent to users and applications.

End User License Agreement (EULA)   A digital or printed statement of your rights to use or copy software, which you agree to when the software is installed.

end-of-life limitation   The point when the manufacturer of software or hardware stops providing updates or patches for its product.

endpoint device   A computer, laptop, smartphone, printer, or other host on a network.

endpoint management server   A server that monitors various endpoint devices on the network to ensure that endpoints are compliant with security requirements such as anti-malware and that OS updates are applied.

enterprise license   A license to use software that allows an organization to install multiple instances of the software. *Also called* site license.

entry control roster   A list of people allowed into a restricted area and a log of approved visitors; the roster is used and maintained by security guards.

environmental variable   Data the OS makes available to a script or program for use during its execution. *Also called* a system variable.

EoP (Ethernet over Power)   The technology that allows Ethernet transmissions over power lines in a building. A powerline adapter is plugged into the electrical circuit(s) at both ends and the adapters connect to the Ethernet network. Because the transmissions are not contained, encryption is required for security. *Also called* powerline networking.

erase   *See* del.

e-reader   A mobile device that holds digital versions of books, newspapers, magazines, and other printed documents, which are usually downloaded to the device from the web.

eSATA (external SATA)   A standard and port used to connect external SATA drives to a computer. eSATA uses a special shielded SATA cable up to 2 meters long.

escalate   To assign a problem to someone higher in the support chain of an organization. This action is normally recorded in call tracking software.

ESD mat   A mat that dissipates ESD and is commonly used by technicians who repair and assemble computers at their workbenches or in an assembly line. *Also called* ground mat.

ESD strap   A strap worn around your wrist and attached to a computer case, ground mat, or another ground so that ESD is discharged from your body before you touch sensitive components inside a computer. *Also called* antistatic wrist strap *or* ground bracelet.

Ethernet over Power (EoP)   *See* powerline networking.

Ethernet port   *See* network port.

Event Viewer   A Windows tool (Eventvwr.msc) useful for troubleshooting problems with Windows, applications, and hardware. It displays logs of significant events, such as a hardware or network failure, OS failure, OS error messages, a device or service that has failed to start, and General Protection Faults.

Everyone group   In Windows, the Authenticated Users group as well as the Guest account. When you share a file or folder on the network, Windows gives access to the Everyone group by default.

Exchange Online   An email service provided by Microsoft that is hosted on Microsoft servers.

executive services   In Windows, a group of components running in kernel mode that interfaces between the subsystems in user mode and the HAL.

exFAT A file system suitable for large external storage devices and compatible with Windows, macOS, and Linux.

expand The Windows command that extracts files from compressed distribution files, which are often used to distribute files for software installation.

expansion card A circuit board inserted into a slot on the motherboard to enhance the capability of the computer. *Also called* an adapter card.

expert system Software that uses a database of known facts and rules to simulate a human expert's reasoning and decision-making processes.

ext3 The Linux file system that was the first to support journaling, which is a technique that tracks and stores changes to the hard drive and helps prevent file system corruption.

ext4 (fourth extended file system) The current Linux file system, which replaced the ext3 file system.

extended partition On an MBR hard drive, the only partition that can contain more than one logical drive. In Windows, a hard drive can have only a single extended partition. *Compare with* primary partition.

extender A device that amplifies and retransmits a wireless signal to a wider coverage area and retains the original network name.

extension magnet brush A long-handled brush made of nylon fibers that are charged with static electricity to pick up stray toner inside a laser printer.

external enclosure A housing designed to store hard drives outside the computer.

external SATA (eSATA) port A port for external drives based on SATA that uses a special, external shielded SATA cable up to 2 meters long.

F connector A connector used with an RG-6 coaxial cable for connections to a TV; it has a single copper wire.

factory default The state of a mobile device or other computer at the time of purchase. The operating system is reinstalled and all user data and settings are lost.

Fast Ethernet *See* 100BaseT.

FAT (file allocation table) A table on a hard drive or other storage device used by the FAT file system to track the clusters used to contain a file.

fat client *See* thick client.

FAT32 A file system suitable for low-capacity hard drives and other storage devices and supported by Windows, macOS, and Linux.

fault tolerance The degree to which a system can tolerate failures. Adding redundant components, such as disk mirroring or disk duplexing, is a way to build in fault tolerance.

favorites tray On Android devices, the area above the Action bar that contains up to seven apps or groups of apps. These apps stay put as you move from home screen to home screen.

ferrite clamp A clamp installed on a network cable to protect against electrical interference.

fiber optic As applied to Internet access technologies, a dedicated, leased line that uses fiber-optic cable from the ISP to a residence or place of business.

fiber-optic cable Cable that transmits signals as pulses of light over glass or plastic strands inside protected tubing.

field replaceable unit (FRU) A component in a computer or device that can be replaced with a new component without sending the computer or device back to the manufacturer. Examples include a power supply, DIMM, motherboard, and hard disk drive.

file allocation unit *See* cluster.

file association The association between a data file and an application to open the file; this association is determined by the file extension.

file attributes The properties assigned to a file. Examples of file attributes are read-only and hidden status.

File Explorer The Windows 10/8 utility used to view and manage files and folders.

File Explorer Options applet The Windows 10 applet used to determine how files and folders are displayed in File Explorer. In Windows 8/7, the applet is called Folder Options.

file extension A portion of the file name that indicates how the file is organized or formatted, the type of content in the file, and what program uses the file. In command lines, the file extension follows the file name and is separated from it by

G

a period—for example, in Msd.exe, exe is the file extension.

File History A Windows 10/8 utility that can schedule and maintain backups of data. It can also create a system image for backward compatibility with Windows 7.

file name The first part of the name assigned to a file, which does not include the file extension. In Windows, a file name can be up to 255 characters.

file server A computer dedicated to storing and serving up data files and folders.

file system The overall structure that an OS uses to name, store, and organize files on a disk. Examples of file systems are NTFS and FAT32. Windows is always installed on a volume that uses the NTFS file system.

file-level backup A process that backs up and restores individual files.

Finder The macOS utility used to find and view applications, utilities, files, storage devices, and network resources available to macOS. Finder is similar to Windows File Explorer.

firewall Hardware and/or software that blocks unwanted Internet traffic from a private network and can restrict Internet access for local computers.

firmware Software that is permanently stored in a chip. The BIOS on a motherboard is an example of firmware.

First Aid A macOS tool in the Disk Utility group of tools that scans a hard drive or other storage device for file system errors and repairs them.

first response The duties of the person who first discovers an incident, which may include identifying and going through proper channels to report the incident, preserving data or devices, and documenting the incident.

fitness monitor A wearable computer device that can measure heart rate, count pool laps or miles jogged or biked, and a host of other activities.

flashing BIOS/UEFI The process of upgrading or refreshing the programming stored on a firmware chip.

flatbed scanner A scanner with a flat, glass surface that holds paper to be scanned. The scan head moves under the glass and the scanner might have feeders to scan multiple copies.

flat-panel monitor *See* LCD (liquid crystal display) monitor.

folder *See* subdirectory.

Folder Options applet In Windows 8/7, an applet accessed through Control Panel that manages how files and folders are displayed in File Explorer or Windows Explorer. *Compare with* File Explorer Options applet.

folder redirection The technique in Active Directory of using a shared folder on the network instead of a user's Home folder on the local computer.

force quit In macOS, to abruptly end an app without allowing the app to go through its close process.

forced kill In Linux, to abruptly end an app without allowing the app to go through its close process.

forest The entire enterprise of users and resources that is managed by Active Directory.

form factor A set of specifications for the size, shape, and configuration of a computer hardware component such as a case, power supply, or motherboard.

format The Windows command to prepare a hard drive volume, logical drive, or USB flash drive for use (for example, format d:). This process erases all data on the device.

formatting *See* format.

FPC (flexible printed circuit) connectors Flat and flexible ZIF and non-ZIF connectors used for tight locations in electronic equipment.

FQDN (fully qualified domain name) A host name and domain name that identifies a computer and the network to which it belongs. For example, *joesmith.mycompany.com* is an FQDN. An FQDN is sometimes loosely referred to as a domain name.

fragmented file A file that has been written to different portions of the disk so that it is not in contiguous clusters.

Fresh Start The Windows 10 process to perform a clean installation of the OS using the most recent version of Windows 10 available from Microsoft.

front panel connector A group of wires running from the front or top of the computer case to the motherboard.

front panel header A group of pins on a motherboard that connect to wires at the front panel of the computer case.

Front Side Bus (FSB) *See* system bus.

FRU (field replaceable unit)   *See* field replaceable unit (FRU).

FTP (File Transfer Protocol)   A TCP/IP protocol and application that uses the Internet to transfer files between two computers.

FTP server   A server using the FTP or Secure FTP protocol to download or upload files to remote computers.

full device encryption   A process that encrypts all the stored data on a device, such as a smartphone or tablet.

full duplex   Communication that happens in two directions at the same time.

full format   The process of creating an empty root directory, checking each sector for errors, marking bad sectors so they will not be used by the file system, and installing a file system and drive letter to a storage device or volume.

fully qualified domain name (FQDN)   *See* FQDN (fully qualified domain name).

fuser assembly   A component in laser printing that uses heat and pressure to fuse the toner to paper.

gadget   A mini-app that appears on the Windows 7 desktop.

gateway   Any device or computer that network traffic can use to leave one network and go to a different one.

GDPR (General Data Protection Regulation)   A group of regulations implemented by the European Union (EU) to protect personal data of EU citizens.

geotracking   A mobile device's routine reporting of its position to Apple, Google, or Microsoft at least twice a day, making it possible for these companies to track your device's whereabouts.

gesture   An action performed on the Mac trackpad using one or more fingers.

ghost cursor   A trail on the screen left behind when you move the mouse.

Gigabit Ethernet   A version of Ethernet that supports rates of data transfer up to 1 gigabit per second.

gigahertz (GHz)   One thousand MHz, or one billion cycles per second. *Also see* hertz *and* megahertz.

global account   An account used at the domain level, created by an administrator, and stored in the SAM (security accounts manager) database on a Windows domain controller. *Also called* a domain account *or* network ID. *Compare with* local account.

global address   *See* global unicast address.

global unicast address   In TCP/IP version 6, an IP address that can be routed on the Internet. *Also called* global address.

Globally Unique Identifier Partition Table (GUID or GPT)   *See* GUID Partition Table (GPT).

Gmail   An email service provided by Google at *mail.google.com*.

Google account   A user account identified by a valid email address that is registered on the Google Play website (*play.google.com*) and used to download content to an Android device.

Google Play   The official source for Android apps (also called the Android marketplace), at *play.google.com*.

gpresult   The Windows command to find out which group policies are currently applied to a system for the computer or user.

GPS (Global Positioning System)   A receiver that uses the system of 24 or more satellites orbiting Earth. The receiver locates four or more of these satellites and uses their locations to calculate its own position in a process called triangulation.

gpupdate   The Windows command to refresh local group policies as well as group policies set in Active Directory on a Windows domain.

graphical user interface (GUI)   An interface that uses graphics as opposed to a command-driven interface.

graphics processing unit (GPU)   A processor that manipulates graphic data to form the images on a monitor screen. A GPU can be embedded on a video card, on the motherboard, or integrated within the processor.

graphics tablet   An input device that can use a stylus to hand draw. It works like a pencil on the tablet and uses a USB port. *Also called* digitizing tablet *and* digitizer.

grayware   A program that is potentially harmful or potentially unwanted.

grep   A Linux and macOS command to search for and display a specific pattern of characters in a file or multiple files.

ground bracelet   *See* ESD strap.

G

ground mat *See* ESD mat.

Group Policy A console (gpedit.msc) available in Windows Server and Windows 10/8/7 professional and business editions that is used to control what users can do and how the local and network computers on the Windows domain can be used.

Group Policy Object (GPO) A named set of policies that have been created by Group Policy and are applied to an OU.

GRUB (GRand Unified Bootloader) The current Linux boot loader, which can handle dual boots with another OS installed on the system.

GSM (Global System for Mobile Communications) An open standard for cellular WANs and cell phones that uses digital communication of data and is accepted and used worldwide.

Guests group A type of user group in Windows. User accounts that belong to this group have limited rights to the system and are given a temporary profile that is deleted after the user logs off.

GUID Partition Table (GPT) A method for partitioning hard drives that allows for drives of any size. For Windows, a drive that uses this method can have up to 128 partitions. The GPT partitioning system is required to use a Secure boot with UEFI firmware.

gyroscope A device that contains a disc that can move and respond to gravity as the device is moved.

HAL (hardware abstraction layer) The low-level part of Windows, written specifically for each CPU technology, so that only the HAL must change when platform components change.

half duplex Communication between two devices whereby transmission takes place in only one direction at a time.

Handoff A technique of Apple devices and computers that lets you start a task on one device, such as an iPad, and then pick up that task on another device, such as a Mac desktop or laptop.

hard boot A restart of the computer by turning off the power or pressing the Reset button. *Also called* a cold boot.

hard disk drive (HDD) *See* hard drive.

hard drive The main secondary storage device of a computer. Two technologies are currently used by hard drives: magnetic and solid state. *Also called* hard disk drive (HDD).

hard reset (1) For Android devices, a factory reset, which erases all data and settings and restores the device to its original factory default state. (2) For iOS devices, a forced restart similar to a full shutdown, followed by a full clean boot of the device.

hardware address *See* MAC (Media Access Control) address.

hardware RAID One of two ways to implement RAID. Hardware RAID is more reliable and performs better than software RAID, and is implemented using BIOS/UEFI on the motherboard or a RAID controller card.

hardware signature Information kept on Microsoft activation servers along with a digital license to identify a machine that has activated a Windows installation.

hardware-assisted virtualization (HAV) A processor feature that can provide enhanced support for hypervisor software to run virtual machines on a system. The feature must be enabled in BIOS/UEFI setup.

HAV (hardware-assisted virtualization) *See* hardware-assisted virtualization (HAV).

HD15 port *See* VGA (Video Graphics Array) port.

HDMI (High Definition Multimedia Interface) port A digital audio and video interface standard currently used on desktop and laptop computers, televisions, and other home theater equipment. HDMI is often used to connect a computer to home theater equipment.

HDMI connector A connector that transmits both digital video and audio and is used on most computers and televisions.

HDMI mini connector A smaller type of HDMI connector used for connecting devices such as smartphones to a computer. *Also called* mini-HDMI connector.

header On a motherboard, a connector that consists of a group of pins that stick up on the board.

heat sink A piece of metal with cooling fins that can be attached to or mounted on an integrated chip package (such as the CPU) to dissipate heat.

help A Windows command that gives information about any Windows command.

hertz (Hz) A unit of measurement for frequency calculated in terms of vibrations or cycles per second. For example, for 16-bit stereo sound, a frequency of 44,000 Hz is used. *Also see* megahertz *and* gigahertz.

HFS+ (Hierarchical File System Plus) An older macOS file system for macOS 10.12 and earlier versions that uses a proprietary Apple partitioning system. *Also called* the Mac OS Extended file system.

hibernation A power-saving state that saves all work to the hard drive and powers down the system.

hidden share A folder whose folder name ends with a $ symbol. When you share the folder, it does not appear in the File Explorer or Windows Explorer window of remote computers on the network.

high-level formatting A process performed by the Windows Format program (for example, FORMAT C:/S), the Windows installation program, or the Disk Management utility. The process creates the boot record, file system, and root directory on a hard drive volume or other storage device. *Also called* formatting, OS formatting, *or* operating system formatting. *Compare with* low-level formatting.

high-touch using a standard image A strategy to install Windows that uses a standard image for the installation. A technician must perform the installation on the local computer. *Also see* standard image.

high-touch with retail media A strategy to install Windows where all the work is done by a technician sitting at the computer using Windows setup files. The technician also installs drivers and applications after the Windows installation is finished.

HKEY_CLASSES_ROOT (HKCR) A Windows registry key that stores information to determine which application is opened when the user double-clicks a file.

HKEY_CURRENT_CONFIG (HKCC) A Windows registry key that contains information about the hardware configuration that is used by the computer at startup.

HKEY_CURRENT_USER (HKCU) A Windows registry key that contains data about the current user. The key is built when a user logs on using data kept in the HKEY_USERS key and data kept in the Ntuser.dat file of the current user.

HKEY_LOCAL_MACHINE (HKLM) An important Windows registry key that contains hardware, software, and security data. The key is built using data taken from the SAM hive, the Security hive, the Software hive, the System hive, and from data collected at startup about the hardware.

HKEY_USERS (HKU) A Windows registry key that contains data about all users and is taken from the Default hive.

Home button A hardware button on the bottom of Apple's iPhone or iPad.

Home folder The default folder presented to a user when she is ready to save a file. On a peer-to-peer network, the Home folder is normally the Documents folder in the user profile.

Home Theater PC (HTPC) A PC that is designed to play and possibly record music, photos, movies, and video on a television or extra-large monitor screen.

homegroup In Windows 8/7, a type of peer-to-peer network where each computer shares files, folders, libraries, and printers with other computers in the homegroup. Access to the homegroup is secured using a homegroup password. Windows 10 does not support a homegroup, as it is considered a security risk.

host A device, such as a desktop computer, laptop, or printer, on a network that requests or serves up data or services to other devices.

host name A name that identifies a computer, printer, or other device on a network; the host name can be used instead of the computer's IP address to address the computer on the network. The host name together with the domain name is called the fully qualified domain name. *Also called* computer name.

Hosts file A file in the C:\Windows\System32\drivers\etc folder that contains computer names and their associated IP addresses on the local network. The file has no file extension.

hot-plugging Plugging in a device while the computer is turned on. The computer will sense the device and configure it without rebooting. In addition, the device can be unplugged without an OS error. *Also called* hot-swapping.

G

hotspot   A small area that offers connectivity to a wireless network, such as a Wi-Fi network.

hot-swappable   The ability to plug in or unplug devices without first powering down the system. USB devices are hot-swappable.

hot-swapping   *See* hot-plugging.

HTTP (Hypertext Transfer Protocol)   The TCP/IP protocol used for the World Wide Web and used by web browsers and web servers to communicate.

HTTPS (HTTP secure)   The HTTP protocol working with a security protocol such as Secure Sockets Layer (SSL) or Transport Layer Security (TLS) to create a secured socket that includes data encryption. TLS is better than SSL.

hub   A network device or box that provides a central location to connect cables and distributes incoming data packets to all other devices connected to it. *Compare with* switch.

hybrid cloud   A combination of public, private, and community clouds used by the same organization. For example, a company might store data in a private cloud but use a public cloud email service.

hybrid hard drive (H-HDD)   A hard drive that uses both magnetic and SSD technologies. The bulk of storage uses the magnetic component, and a storage buffer on the drive is made of an SSD component. Windows ReadyDrive supports hybrid hard drives.

HyperTransport   The AMD technology that allows each logical processor within the processor package to handle an individual thread in parallel; other threads are handled by other processors within the package.

HyperThreading   The Intel technology that allows each logical processor within the processor package to handle an individual thread in parallel; other threads are handled by other processors within the package.

hypervisor   Software that creates and manages virtual machines on a server or on a local computer. *Also called* virtual machine manager (VMM).

I/O shield   A plate installed on the rear of a computer case that provides holes for I/O ports coming off the motherboard.

IaaS (Infrastructure as a Service)   A cloud computing service that provides only hardware, which can include servers, storage devices, and networks.

iCloud   A website by Apple (*www.icloud.com*) used to sync content on Apple devices in order to provide a backup of the content.

iCloud Backup   A feature of an iPhone, iPad, or iPod touch that backs up the device's content to the cloud at *icloud.com*.

iCloud Drive   Storage space at *icloud.com* that can be synced with files stored on any Apple mobile device or any personal computer, including a macOS or Windows computer.

IDE (Integrated Drive Electronics or Integrated Device Electronics)   A hard drive whose disk controller is integrated into the drive, eliminating the need for a controller cable and thus increasing speed as well as reducing price.

IDS (intrusion detection system)   Software that monitors all network traffic and creates alerts when suspicious activity happens. IDS software can run on a UTM appliance, router, server, or workstation.

IEEE 802.11ac   The latest Wi-Fi standard; it supports up to 7 Gbps (actual speeds are currently about 1300 Mbps) and uses 5.0-GHz radio frequency and beamforming.

IEEE 802.11n   A Wi-Fi standard that supports up to 600 Mbps, uses 5.0-GHz or 2.4-GHz radio frequency, and supports MIMO.

ifconfig (interface configuration)   A Linux and macOS command similar to ipconfig that displays details about network interfaces and can enable and disable an interface. When affecting the interface, the command requires root privileges.

image deployment   Installing a standard image on a computer.

image-level backup   A process that backs up and restores everything on a device, such as a hard drive, smartphone, or tablet. The restore process restores the device to a previous state.

imaging drum   An electrically charged rotating drum found in laser printers.

IMAP4 (Internet Message Access Protocol, version 4)   A TCP/IP protocol used by an email server and client that allows the client to manage email stored on the server without downloading the email. *Compare with* POP3.

IMEI (International Mobile Equipment Identity)   A unique number that identifies a mobile phone or tablet device worldwide. The number can usually be found imprinted on the device or reported in the About menu of the OS.

impact paper Paper used by impact printers that comes in a box of fanfold paper or in rolls (used with receipt printers).

impact printer A type of printer that creates a printed page by using a mechanism that touches or hits the paper.

impersonation Pretending to be another individual or company to aid in a malicious attack.

IMSI (International Mobile Subscriber Identity) A unique number that identifies a cellular subscription for a device or subscriber, along with its home country and mobile network. Some carriers store the number on a SIM card installed in the device.

incident When an employee or other person has negatively affected safety or corporate resources, violated the code of conduct for an organization, or committed a crime.

incident documentation Documentation, including chain-of-custody documents, surrounding the evidence of an incident that may be used to prevent future incidents and as evidence in a criminal investigation.

incident response Predefined corporate procedures that are to be followed when an incident occurs.

Infrared (IR) An outdated wireless technology that has been mostly replaced by Bluetooth to connect personal computing devices.

infrastructure mode A mode in which Wi-Fi devices connect to a Wi-Fi access point, such as a SOHO router, which is responsible for securing and managing the wireless network.

inherited permissions Permissions assigned by Windows that are obtained from a parent object.

initialization files Text files that keep hardware and software configuration information, user preferences, and application settings and are used by the OS when first loaded and when needed by hardware, applications, and users.

ink cartridge A cartridge in inkjet printers that holds different colors of ink.

inkjet printer A type of ink dispersion printer that uses cartridges of ink. The ink is heated to a boiling point and then ejected onto the paper through tiny nozzles.

in-place upgrade A Windows installation that is launched from the Windows desktop. The installation carries forward user settings and installed applications from the old OS to the new one. A Windows OS is already in place before the installation begins.

In-Plane Switching (IPS) A class of LCD monitor that offers truer color images and better viewing angles, although it is expensive and has slower response times.

integer In scripting and programming, a type of data that is a whole number.

integrated print server A printer feature that allows it to connect to a network, manage print jobs from multiple computers, monitor printer maintenance tasks, and perhaps send email alerts when a problem arises.

interface In TCP/IP version 6, a node's attachment to a link. The attachment can be a physical attachment (for example, when using a network adapter) or a logical attachment (for example, when using a tunneling protocol). Each interface is assigned an IP address.

interface ID In TCP/IP version 6, the last 64 bits or 4 blocks of an IP address that identify the interface.

internal components The main components installed in a computer case.

Internet Options A dialog box used to manage Internet Explorer settings.

Internet service provider (ISP) *See* ISP (Internet service provider).

intranet Any private network that uses TCP/IP protocols. A large enterprise might support an intranet that is made up of several local networks.

inventory management In an IT organization, the methods used to track end-user devices, network devices, IP addresses, software licenses, and other software and hardware equipment.

inverter An electrical device that converts DC to AC.

iOS The operating system owned and developed by Apple and used for their various mobile devices.

IoT (Internet of Things) Any device that can connect to the Internet for a specific purpose, such as a smart thermostat or door lock.

IP (Internet Protocol) The primary TCP/IP protocol, used by the Internet layer, that is

G

responsible for getting a message to a destination host. In the OSI model, the Internet layer is called the Network layer.

IP address   A 32-bit or 128-bit address used to uniquely identify a device or interface on a network that uses TCP/IP protocols. Generally, the first numbers identify the network; the last numbers identify a host. An example of a 32-bit IP address is 206.96.103.114. An example of a 128-bit IP address is 2001:0000:B80::D3:9C5A:CC.

iPad   A handheld tablet developed by Apple.

ipconfig (IP configuration)   A Windows command that displays TCP/IP configuration information and can refresh TCP/IP assignments to a connection, including its IP address.

iPhone   A smartphone developed by Apple.

IPS (intrusion prevention system)   Software that monitors and logs suspicious activity on a network and can prevent the threatening traffic from burrowing into the system. *Compare with* IDS (intrusion detection system).

IPv4 (Internet Protocol version 4)   Version 4 of the TCP/IP protocols and standards that define 32-bit IP addresses and how they are used.

IPv6 (Internet Protocol version 6)   Version 6 of the TCP/IP protocols and standards that define 128-bit IP addresses and how they are used.

IR (infrared)   A wireless connection that requires an unobstructed line of sight between transmitter and receiver and uses light waves just below the visible red-light spectrum.

ISATAP   In TCP/IP version 6, a tunneling protocol that has been developed for IPv6 packets to travel over an IPv4 network; ISATAP stands for Intra-Site Automatic Tunnel Addressing Protocol.

ISDN (Integrated Services Digital Network)   A broadband telephone line that can carry data at about five times the speed of regular telephone lines. Two channels (telephone numbers) share a single pair of wires. ISDN has been replaced by DSL.

ISO file   *See* ISO image.

ISO image   A file format that has an .iso file extension and holds an image of all the data that is stored on an optical disc, including the file system. ISO stands for International Organization for Standardization.

ISP (Internet service provider)   An organization, such as Charter, that provides individuals and organizations access to the Internet via a technology such as cable Internet, DSL, or cellular.

iTunes   Software by Apple installed on a Mac or Windows computer to sync an iPhone or iPad to iOS updates downloaded from *itunes.com* and to troubleshoot problems with the Apple device.

iTunes Store   The Apple website at *itunes.com* and the Apple app on an Apple mobile device, where apps, music, TV shows, movies, books, podcasts, and iTunes U content can be purchased and downloaded to a device.

iTunes U   Content at the iTunes Store website (*itunes.com*) that contains lectures and even complete courses from many schools, colleges, and universities.

ITX   *See* Mini-ITX.

iwconfig   A Linux and macOS command similar to ifconfig that applies only to wireless networks. Use it to display information about a wireless interface and configure a wireless adapter.

jailbreaking   A process to break through the restrictions that only allow apps for an iOS device to be downloaded from the iTunes Store at *itunes.com*. Jailbreaking gives the user root or administrator privileges to the operating system and the entire file system, and complete access to all commands and features.

JavaScript   A scripting language normally used to create scripts for webpages; the scripts are embedded in an HTML file to build an interactive webpage in a browser.

joule   A measure of work or energy. One joule of energy produces 1 watt of power for one second.

jumper   Two small posts or metal pins that stick up side by side on a motherboard or other device and are used to hold configuration information. The jumper is considered closed if a cover is over the wires and open if the cover is missing.

Kensington lock   *See* cable lock.

Kensington Security Slot   A security slot on a laptop case to connect a cable lock. *Also called* K-Slot.

kernel   The portion of an OS that is responsible for interacting with the hardware.

kernel mode   A Windows "privileged" processing mode that has access to hardware components.

kernel panic A Linux or macOS error from which it cannot recover, similar to a blue screen of death in Windows.

key fob A device, such as a type of smart card, that can fit conveniently on a key chain.

keyboard backlight A feature on some keyboards where the keys light up.

Keychain In macOS, a built-in password manager utility.

Key-enrollment Key (KEK) *See* Key-exchange Key (KEK).

Key-exchange Key (KEK) A Secure boot database that holds digital signatures provided by OS manufacturers.

keylogger A type of spyware that tracks your keystrokes, including passwords, chat room sessions, email messages, documents, online purchases, and anything else you type on your computer. Text is logged to a text file and transmitted over the Internet without your knowledge.

keystone RJ-45 jack A jack that is used in an RJ-45 wall jack.

kill A Linux and macOS command used to forcefully end or kill a process.

knowledge base A collection of articles containing text, images, or video that give information about a network, product, or service.

KVM (Keyboard, Video, and Mouse) switch A switch that allows you to use one keyboard, mouse, and monitor for multiple computers. Some KVM switches also include sound ports so that speakers and a microphone can be shared among multiple computers.

LAN (local area network) A network bound by routers or other gateway devices that usually covers only a small area, such as one building.

land grid array (LGA) A socket that has blunt protruding pins in uniform rows that connect with lands or pads on the bottom of the processor. *Compare with* pin grid array (PGA).

laptop A portable computer that is designed for travel and mobility. Laptops use the same technology as desktop computers, with modifications for conserving voltage, taking up less space, and operating while on the move. *Also called* a notebook computer.

laser printer A type of printer that uses a laser beam to control how toner is placed on the page and then uses heat to fuse the toner to the page.

Last Known Good Configuration In Windows 7, registry settings and device drivers that were in effect when the computer last booted successfully. These settings are saved and can be restored during the startup process to recover from errors during the last boot.

latency Delays in network transmissions that result in slower network performance. Latency is measured by the round-trip time it takes for a data packet to travel from source to destination and back to the source.

launcher The Android graphical user interface (GUI) that includes multiple home screens and supports windows, panes, and 3D graphics.

Launchpad The macOS utility used to launch and uninstall applications.

LC (local connector) connector A fiber-optic cable connector that can be used with either single-mode or multimode fiber-optic cables and is easily terminated; it is smaller than an SC connector.

LCD (liquid crystal display) monitor A monitor that uses LCD technology. LCD produces an image using a liquid crystal material made of large, easily polarized molecules. *Also called* a flat-panel monitor.

LDAP (Lightweight Directory Access Protocol) A TCP/IP protocol used by client applications to query and receive data from a database. The LDAP protocol does not include encryption.

LED (Light-Emitting Diode) A technology used in an LCD monitor that requires less mercury than earlier technologies.

Level 1 cache (L1 cache) Memory on the processor die used as a cache to improve processor performance.

Level 2 cache (L2 cache) Memory in the processor package but not on the processor die. The memory is used as a cache or buffer to improve processor performance. *Also see* Level 1 (L1) cache.

Level 3 cache (L3 cache) Cache memory that is further from the processor core than Level 2 cache but still in the processor package.

LGA1150 A CPU socket for Intel processors that works with 4th and 5th generation chipsets and

G

processors. The socket uses a land grid array and 1150 pins.

LGA1151   A CPU socket for Intel processors that uses a land grid array and 1151 pins. Two versions of the socket currently exist; the older version works with 6th and 7th generation chipsets and processors, and the newer version works with 8th generation chipsets and processors. The two sockets are not compatible because the pins are used differently on each version of the socket.

library   A collection of one or more folders that can be stored on different local drives or on the network.

Lightning   *See* Lightning port.

Lightning port   The proprietary Apple connector used on Apple iPhones, iPods, and iPads for power and communication.

Lightweight Directory Access Protocol (LDAP)   *See* LDAP (Lightweight Directory Access Protocol).

line-of-sight wireless connectivity   A type of connection used by satellites that requires an unobstructed path free of mountains, trees, and tall buildings from the satellite dish to the satellite.

link (local link)   In TCP/IP version 6, a local area network or wide area network bounded by routers. *Also called* local link.

link local address   *See* link local unicast address.

link local unicast address   In TCP/IP version 6, an IP address used for communicating among nodes in the same link; this IP address is not allowed on the Internet. *Also called* local address *and* link local address.

Linux   An OS based on UNIX that was created by Linus Torvalds of Finland. Basic versions of this OS are open source, and all the underlying programming instructions are freely distributed.

lite-touch, high-volume deployment   A strategy that uses a deployment server on the network to serve up a Windows installation after a technician starts the process at the local computer.

lithium ion   Currently the most popular type of battery for notebook computers; it is more efficient than earlier types. Sometimes abbreviated as "Li-Ion" battery.

Live CD   In Linux, a CD, DVD, or flash drive that can boot up a live version of Linux, complete with Internet access and all the tools you normally have available in a hard drive installation of Linux; however, the OS is not installed on the hard drive.

live sign in   A way to sign in to Windows 8 using a Microsoft account.

live tiles   On the Windows 10 Start menu or the Windows 8 Start screen, tiles used by some apps to offer continuous real-time updates.

Live USB   In Linux, a live CD stored on a USB flash drive. *Also see* Live CD.

loadstate   A command used by the User State Migration Tool (USMT) to copy user settings and data temporarily stored at a safe location to a new computer. *Also see* scanstate.

local account   A Windows user account that applies only to the local computer and cannot be used to access resources from other computers on the network. *Compare with* global account.

local area network (LAN)   *See* LAN (local area network).

Local Group Policy   A console (gpedit.msc) available in Windows 10/8/7 professional and business editions that applies only to local users and the local computer. *Also see* Group Policy.

local link   *See* link.

local printer   A printer connected to a computer by way of a port on the computer. *Compare with* network printer.

Local Security Policy   A Windows Administrative Tools snap-in in Control Panel that can manage the Security Settings group of policies. This same group can also be found in Group Policy in the Local Computer Policy/Computer Configuration/Windows Settings group.

local shares   Folders on a computer that are shared with others on the network by using a folder's Properties box. Local shares are used with a workgroup and not with a domain.

Local Users and Groups   For business and professional editions of Windows, a Windows utility console (lusrmgr.msc) that can be used to manage user accounts and user groups.

location data   Data that a device can routinely report to a website so that the device can be located on a map.

location independence   A function of cloud computing whereby customers generally don't know the geographical locations of the physical devices providing cloud services.

locator application An app on a mobile device that can be used to locate the device on a map, force the device to ring, change its password, or remotely erase all data on the device.

logical drive On an MBR hard drive, a portion or all of a hard drive's extended partition that is treated by the operating system as though it were a physical drive or volume. Each logical drive is assigned a drive letter, such as drive F, and contains a file system. *Compare with* volume.

logical topology The logical way computers connect on a network.

login item In macOS, a program that automatically launches after a user logs in. Login items are managed in the Users & Groups utility in System Preferences.

LoJack A technology by Absolute Software that tracks the whereabouts of a laptop computer and, if the computer is stolen, locks down access to it or erases data on it. The technology is embedded in the BIOS/UEFI of many laptops.

Long Term Evolution (LTE) *See* LTE (Long Term Evolution).

loopback address An IP address that indicates your own computer and is used to test TCP/IP configuration on the computer.

loopback plug A device used to test a port in a computer or other device to make sure the port is working; it might also test the throughput or speed of the port.

low-level format A type of formatting, usually done at the factory, where sector marks are added to the platters of a magnetic hard drive.

low-level formatting A process (usually performed at the factory) that electronically creates the hard drive tracks and sectors and tests for bad spots on the disk surface. *Compare with* high-level formatting.

LPT (Line Printer Terminal) Assignments of system resources that are made to a parallel port and used to manage a print job. Two possible LPT configurations are referred to as LPT1: and LPT2:.

LPT port *See* parallel port.

LTE (Long Term Evolution) In telecommunications, a set of wireless communication standards that define data and voice transmissions over cellular networks; LTE is expected to replace GSM and CDMA.

M.2 connector A motherboard or expansion card slot that connects to a mini add-on card. The slot uses a PCIe, USB, or SATA interface with the motherboard chipset, and several variations of the slot exist. *Also called* a Next Generation Form Factor (NGFF) connector.

MAC (Media Access Control) address A 48-bit (6-byte) hardware address unique to each NIC or onboard network controller; the address is assigned by the manufacturer at the factory and embedded on the device. The address is often printed on the adapter as hexadecimal numbers. An example is 00 00 0C 08 2F 35. *Also called* a physical address, an adapter address, *or a* hardware address.

MAC address filtering A technique used by a router or wireless access point that allows computers and devices to access a private network if their MAC addresses are on a list of approved addresses.

Mac OS Extended *See* HFS+ (Hierarchical File System Plus).

macOS The proprietary desktop operating system by Apple. macOS is based on UNIX and used only on Apple computers. macOS was formerly called Mac OS X.

magnetic hard drive One of two technologies used by hard drives where data is stored as magnetic spots on disks that rotate at a high speed. *Compare with* solid-state drive (SSD).

magnetic stripe reader A device that can read the magnetic stripe on a card, such as a credit card, and transmit the information to a computer.

main board *See* motherboard.

malicious software Any unwanted program that is transmitted to a computer without the user's knowledge and that is designed to do varying degrees of damage to data and software. Types of infestations include viruses, Trojan horses, worms, adware, spyware, keyloggers, browser hijackers, dialers, and downloaders. *Also called* malware, infestation, *or* computer infestation.

malware *See* malicious software.

malware definition Information about malware that allows anti-malware software to detect

G

and define malware. *Also called* a malware signature.

malware encyclopedias Lists of malware, including symptoms and solutions, often maintained by manufacturers of anti-malware software and made available on their websites.

malware signatures *See* malware definition.

MAN (metropolitan area network) A type of network that covers a large city or campus.

managed switch A switch that has firmware that can be configured to monitor, manage, and prioritize network traffic.

man-in-the-middle attack An attack that pretends to be a legitimate website, network, FTP site, or person in a chat session in order to obtain private information.

mantrap A physical security technique of using two doors on either end of a small entryway where the first door must close before the second door can open. A separate form of identification might be required for each door, such as a badge for the first door and a fingerprint scan for the second door. In addition, a security guard might monitor people as they come and go.

mapping A process in which the client computer creates and saves a shortcut (called a network drive) to a folder or drive shared by a remote computer on the network. The network drive has an associated drive letter that points to the network share.

Master Boot Record (MBR) A partitioning system used by hard drives with a capacity less than 2 TB. On an MBR hard drive, the first sector is called the MBR; it contains the partition table and a program motherboard that firmware uses to boot an OS from the drive.

master file table (MFT) The database used by the NTFS file system to track the contents of a volume or logical drive.

Material Safety Data Sheet (MSDS) A document that explains how to properly handle substances such as chemical solvents; it includes information such as physical data, toxicity, health effects, first aid, storage, disposal, and spill procedures.

mATX *See* microATX.

MBR (Master Boot Record) *See* Master Boot Record (MBR).

md (make directory) The Windows command to create a directory.

MDM policies Policies that establish compliance standards used by MDM and may include various forms of security enforcement, such as data encryption requirements and remote wipes.

measured service When a cloud computing vendor offers services that are metered for billing purposes or to ensure transparency between vendors and customers.

Media Center In some editions of Windows 8/7, a digital video recorder and media player; it is not available in Windows 10.

Media Creation Tool Software downloaded from the Microsoft website and used to download Windows setup files, which in turn are used to create setup media or to install Windows.

megahertz (MHz) One million Hz, or one million cycles per second. *Also see* hertz *and* gigahertz.

memory bank The memory a processor addresses at one time. Today's desktop and laptop processors use a memory bank that is 64 bits wide.

Memory Diagnostics A Windows 10/8/7 utility (mdsched.exe) used to test memory.

Metro User Interface (Metro UI) *See* modern interface.

micro USB A smaller version of the regular USB connector.

Micro-A connector A USB connector that has five pins and is smaller than the Mini-B connector. It is used on digital cameras, cell phones, and other small electronic devices.

microATX (mATX) A smaller version of the ATX form factor. MicroATX addresses some technologies that were developed after the original introduction of ATX. *Also called* mATX.

Micro-B connector A USB connector that has five pins and a smaller height than the Mini-B connector. It is used on digital cameras, cell phones, and other small electronic devices.

microprocessor *See* central processing unit (CPU).

Microsoft account For Windows 10/8, an email address registered with Microsoft that allows access to several types of online accounts, including Microsoft OneDrive, Facebook, LinkedIn, Twitter, Skype, and Outlook.

Microsoft Assessment and Planning (MAP) Toolkit Software that can be used by a system administrator from a network location to query hundreds of computers in a single scan and determine if a computer qualifies for a Windows upgrade.

Microsoft Deployment Toolkit (MDT) A suite of Microsoft tools that can automate a Windows installation.

Microsoft Exchange A popular server application used by large corporations for employee email, contacts, and calendars.

Microsoft Management Console (MMC) A Windows utility to build customized consoles. These consoles can be saved to a file with an .msc file extension.

Microsoft Store The official source for Windows apps at *microsoftstore.com*.

Microsoft Terminal Services Client *See* mstsc (Microsoft Terminal Services Client).

MIDI (musical instrument digital interface) A set of standards that are used to represent music in digital form. A MIDI port is a 5-pin DIN port that looks like a keyboard port, only larger.

MIMO (multiple input/multiple output) *See* multiple input/multiple output (MIMO).

Mini DisplayPort A smaller version of DisplayPort that is used on laptops or other mobile devices.

Mini PCI The PCI industry standard for desktop computer expansion cards; it is applied to a much smaller form factor for notebook expansion cards.

Mini PCI Express (Mini PCIe) A standard used for a notebook's internal expansion slots that follows the PCI Express standards. *Also called* Mini PCIe.

Mini PCIe *See* Mini PCI Express (Mini PCIe).

Mini-B connector A USB connector that has five pins and is often used to connect small electronic devices, such as a digital camera, to a computer.

minicartridge A tape drive cartridge that is only $3\frac{1}{4} \times 2\frac{1}{2} \times 3/5$ inches. It is small enough to allow two drives to fit into a standard 5-inch drive bay of a PC case.

Mini-DIN-6 connector A 6-pin variation of the S-Video port that looks like a PS/2 connector; it is used by a keyboard or mouse.

mini-HDMI connector *See* HDMI mini connector.

Mini-ITX A smaller version of the microATX form factor. *Also called* ITX *and* mITX.

miniUSB A smaller version of the regular USB connector; it is also smaller than microUSB.

Miracast A wireless display-mirroring technology that requires a Miracast-capable screen or dongle in order to mirror a smartphone's display to a TV, a wireless monitor, or a wireless projector.

mirrored volume The term used by Windows for the RAID 1 level that duplicates data on one drive to another drive and is used for fault tolerance. *Also see* RAID 1.

mirroring Copying one hard drive to another as a backup. *Also called* RAID 1.

Mission Control In macOS, a utility and screen that gives an overview of all open windows and thumbnails of the Dashboard and desktops.

mITX *See* Mini-ITX.

mobile device management (MDM) Software that includes tools for tracking mobile devices and managing the security of data on the devices according to established MDM policies.

mobile hotspot A location created by a mobile device so that other devices or computers can connect by Wi-Fi to the device and to the Internet.

mobile payment service An app that allows you to use your smartphone or other mobile device to pay for merchandise or services at a retail checkout counter.

modem port A port used to connect dial-up phone lines to computers.

modern interface In Windows 10/8, an interface that presents the Windows 10 live tiles and their apps or the Windows 8 Start screen to the user. In Windows 8, it was called the Metro User Interface or Metro UI.

Molex connector A 4-pin power connector used to provide power to a PATA hard drive, optical drive, or other internal component.

motherboard The main board in the computer. The CPU, ROM chips, DIMMs, and interface cards are plugged into the motherboard. *Also called* the system board.

mount point A folder that is used as a shortcut to space on another volume, which effectively increases the size of the folder to the size of the other volume. *Also see* mounted drive.

G

mounted drive A volume that can be accessed by way of a folder on another volume so that the folder has more available space. *Also see* mount point.

mstsc (Microsoft Terminal Services Client) A command (mstsc.exe) that allows you to remote in to a host computer using Remote Desktop Connection.

MT-RJ (mechanical transfer registered jack) connector A type of connector that can be used with either single-mode or multimode fiber-optic cables and is more difficult to connect than the smaller LC connector.

multiboot *See* dual boot.

multicast address In TCP/IP version 6, an IP address used when packets are delivered to a group of nodes on a network.

multicasting In TCP/IP version 6, the transmission of messages from one host to multiple hosts, such as when the host transmits a videoconference over the Internet.

multicore processing A processor technology whereby the processor housing contains two or more processor cores that operate at the same frequency but independently of each other.

multifactor authentication (MFA) The use of more than one method to authenticate access to a computer, network, or other resource.

multimedia shredder A device that can destroy optical discs, flash drives, SSDs and other devices so that sensitive data stored on the device is also destroyed.

MultiMediaCard (MMC) A compact storage card that looks like an SD card, but the technology is different and they are not interchangeable. Generally, SD cards are faster than MMC cards.

multimeter A device used to measure the various attributes of an electrical circuit. The most common measurements are voltage, current, and resistance.

multiple desktops A feature of Mission Control in macOS, where several desktop screens, each with its own collection of open windows, are available to the user.

multiple input/multiple output (MIMO) A feature of the IEEE 802.11n/ac standards for wireless networking whereby two or more antennas are used at both ends of transmissions to improve performance.

multiple monitor misalignment When the display is staggered across multiple monitors, making the display difficult to read. Fix the problem by adjusting the display in the Windows Screen Resolution window.

multiple monitor orientation The aligned orientation of dual monitor screens. When the display does not accurately represent the relative positions of multiple monitors, use the Windows Screen Resolution window to move the display for each monitor so they are oriented correctly.

multiplier The factor by which the bus speed or frequency is multiplied to get the CPU clock speed.

multiprocessing Two processing units installed within a single processor; it was first used by the Pentium processor.

multiprocessor platform A system that contains more than one processor. The motherboard has more than one processor socket and the processors must be rated to work in this multiprocessor environment.

multitouch A touch screen on a computer or mobile device that can handle a two-finger pinch.

mutual authentication To authenticate in both directions at the same time as both entities confirm the identity of the other.

name resolution The process of associating a character-based name with an IP address.

NAND flash memory The type of memory used in SSDs. NAND stands for "Not AND" and refers to the logic used when storing a 1 or 0 in the grid of rows and columns on the memory chip.

NAS (network attached memory) A group of hard drives inside an enclosure that connects to a network via an Ethernet port and is used for storage on the network.

NAT (Network Address Translation) A technique that substitutes the public IP address of the router for the private IP address of a computer on a private network when the computer needs to communicate on the Internet.

native resolution The actual (and fixed) number of pixels built into an LCD monitor. For the clearest display, always set the resolution to the native resolution.

navigation pane   In File Explorer or Windows Explorer, a pane on the left side of the window where devices, drives, and folders are listed. Double-click an item to drill down into it.

nbtstat (NetBIOS over TCP/IP Statistics)   A Windows TCP/IP command that is used to display statistics about the NetBT protocol.

Near Field Communication (NFC)   *See* NFC.

neighbors   In TCP/IP version 6, two or more nodes on the same link.

net localgroup   A Windows TCP/IP command that adds, displays, or modifies local user groups.

net use   A Windows TCP/IP command that connects or disconnects a computer from a shared resource or can display information about connections.

net user   A Windows TCP/IP command used to manage user accounts.

NetBIOS   A legacy suite of protocols used by Windows before TCP/IP.

netbook   A low-end, inexpensive laptop with a 9- or 10-inch screen and no optical drive that is generally used for web browsing, email, and word processing by users on the go.

NetBoot   A technology that allows a Mac to boot from the network and then install macOS on the machine from a clone DMG file stored on a deployment server.

NetBT (NetBIOS over TCP/IP)   A feature of Server Message Block (SMB) protocols that allows legacy NetBIOS applications to communicate on a TCP/IP network.

netdom (network domain)   A Windows TCP/IP command that allows administrators to manage Active Directory domains and trust relationships for Windows Server from the command prompt on the server or remotely from a Windows 8/7 workstation.

netstat (network statistics)   A Windows TCP/IP command that displays statistics about TCP/IP and network activity and includes several parameters.

network adapter   *See* network interface card (NIC).

Network and Sharing Center   The primary Windows 10/8/7 utility used to manage network connections.

Network Attached Storage (NAS)   A device that provides multiple bays for hard drives and an Ethernet port to connect to the network. The device is likely to support RAID.

network drive map   Mounting a drive to a computer, such as drive E:, that is actually hard drive space on another host computer on the network.

Network File System (NFS)   *See* NFS (Network File System).

network ID   The leftmost bits in an IP address. The rightmost bits of the IP address identify the host.

network interface card (NIC)   An expansion card that plugs into a computer's motherboard and provides a port on the back of the card to connect a computer to a network. *Also called* a network adapter.

network multimeter   A multifunctional tool that can test network connections, cables, ports, and network adapters.

Network Places Wizard   *See* User Accounts.

network port   A port used by a network cable to connect to the wired network. *Also called* an Ethernet port.

network printer   A printer that any user on the network can access, either through the printer's own network card and connection to the network, through a connection to a stand-alone print server, or through a connection to a computer as a local printer that is shared on the network.

network share   A networked computer (the client) that appears to have a hard drive, such as drive E:, which is actually hard drive space on another host computer (the server). *Also see* mapping.

network topology diagram   A documented map of network devices that includes the patterns or design used to connect the devices, either physically or logically.

next-generation firewall (NGFW)   A firewall that combines firewall software with anti-malware software and other software that protects resources on a network.

NFC (Near Field Communication)   A wireless technology that establishes a communication link between two NFC devices (for example, two smartphones or a smartphone and an NFC tag) that are within 4 inches (10 cm) of each other.

G

NFS (Network File System)   A client/server distributed file system that supports file sharing over a network across platforms. For example, a Linux-hosted NFS server can serve up file shares to Windows workstations on the network. Windows 10 supports NFS client connections.

NIC (network interface card)   *See* network interface card (NIC).

node   Any device that connects to the network, such as a computer, printer, or router.

noncompliant system   A system that violates security best practices, such as out-of-date anti-malware software or cases where it's not installed.

nonvolatile RAM (NVRAM)   Flash memory on the motherboard that UEFI firmware uses to store device drivers and information about Secure boot. Contents of NVRAM are not lost when the system is powered down.

North Bridge   The portion of the chipset hub that connects faster I/O buses (for example, the video bus) to the system bus. *Compare with* South Bridge.

notebook   *See* laptop.

Notepad   A text editing program.

notification area   An area to the right of the taskbar that holds the icons for running services; these services include the volume control and network connectivity. *Also called* the system tray *or* systray.

notifications   Alerts and related information about apps and social media sent to mobile devices and other computers.

nslookup (namespace lookup)   A TCP/IP command that lets you read information from the Internet namespace by requesting information about domain name resolutions from the DNS server's zone data.

NTFS (New Technology file system)   A file system that supports encryption, disk quotas, and file and folder compression; it is required for the volume that holds a Windows installation.

NTFS permissions   A method to share a folder or file over a network; these permissions can be applied to local users and network users. The folder or file must be on an NTFS volume. *Compare with* share permissions.

NVMe (Non-Volatile Memory Express or NVM Express)   An interface standard used to connect an SSD to the system and that uses the PCI Express ×4 interface to communicate with the processor. NVMe is about five times faster than SATA3.

octet   In TCP/IP version 4, each of the four numbers that are separated by periods and make up a 32-bit IP address. One octet is 8 bits.

off-boarding   The established process used when a mobile device is removed from the MDM fleet of devices allowed to connect to a corporate network and its resources. *Compare with* on-boarding.

Offline Files   A utility that allows users to work with files in a designated folder when the computer is not connected to the corporate network. When the computer is later connected, Windows syncs up the offline files and folders with those on the network.

ohm (Ω)   The standard unit of measurement for electrical resistance. Resistors are rated in ohms.

OLED (organic light-emitting diode) monitor   A type of monitor that uses a thin LED layer or film between two grids of electrodes and does not use backlighting.

onboard NIC   A network port embedded on the motherboard.

onboard port   A port that is directly on the motherboard, such as a built-in keyboard port or onboard network port.

on-boarding   The established process used when a mobile device is added to the MDM fleet of devices allowed to connect to a corporate network and its resources. *Compare with* off-boarding.

on-demand   A service that is available to users at any time. On-demand cloud computing means the service is always available.

OneDrive   A file hosting service from Microsoft that offers free and purchased storage space in the cloud.

Open Database Connectivity (ODBC)   A technology that allows a client computer to create a data source so that the client can interface with a database stored on a remote (host) computer on the network. *Also see* data source.

open source   Source code for an operating system or other software that is available for free; anyone can modify and redistribute the source code.

operating system (OS) Software that controls a computer. An OS controls how system resources are used, and it provides a user interface, a way of managing hardware and software, and ways to work with files.

optical connector A connector used with a fiber-optic cable.

organizational unit (OU) An object that defines a collection of user groups and/or computers in Active Directory.

Original Equipment Manufacturer (OEM) license A Microsoft Windows license available for purchase only by manufacturers or builders of personal computers and intended to be installed only on a computer for sale.

OS X *See* macOS.

OSI (Open Systems Interconnection) Model A model for understanding and developing computer-to-computer communication that divides networking functions among seven layers: Physical, Data Link, Network, Transport, Session, Presentation, and Application.

overclocking Running a processor at a higher frequency than that recommended by the manufacturer. Overclocking can result in an unstable system, but it is a popular practice when a computer is used for gaming.

overheat shutdown When a device, such as a projector, overheats and automatically powers off. Allow it to cool down before powering it up again.

PaaS (Platform as a Service) A cloud computing service that provides hardware and an operating system and is responsible for updating and maintaining both.

package A collection of files needed to install software.

packet A message sent over a network as a unit of data; the information at the beginning of the packet identifies the type of data, where it came from, and where it's going. *Also called* data packet *or* datagram.

pagefile.sys The Windows swap file used to hold virtual memory, which enhances physical memory installed in a system.

paired When two Bluetooth devices have established connectivity and are able to communicate.

pairing The process of two Bluetooth devices establishing connectivity.

PAN (personal area network) A small network consisting of personal devices at close range; the devices can include smartphones, PDAs, and notebook computers.

parallel ATA (PATA) An older IDE cabling method that uses a 40-pin flat or round data cable or an 80-conductor cable and a 40-pin IDE connector. *Also see* serial ATA.

parallel port An outdated female 25-pin port on a computer that transmitted data in parallel, 8 bits at a time, and was typically used with a printer. Parallel ports have been replaced by USB ports. *Also called* an LPT1 port, LPT2 port, *and* LPT port.

parity An older error-checking scheme used with SIMMs in which a ninth, or "parity," bit is added. The value of the parity bit is set to either 0 or 1 to provide an even number of 1s for even parity and an odd number of 1s for odd parity.

parity error An error that occurs in parity error-checking when the number of 1s in the byte is not in agreement with the expected number.

partition A division of a hard drive that can hold a volume. MBR drives can support up to four partitions on one hard drive. In Windows, GPT drives can have up to 128 partitions.

partition table A table that contains information about each partition on the drive. For MBR drives, the partition table is contained in the Master Boot Record. For GPT drives, the partition table is stored in the GPT header and a backup of the table is stored at the end of the drive.

passive CPU cooler *See* fanless CPU cooler.

passwd A Linux and macOS command to change a password. A superuser can change the password for another user.

password policy A set of rules that defines the minimum length of a password, complexity requirements, and how frequently the password must be reset.

patch A minor update to software that corrects an error, adds a feature, or addresses security issues. *Also called* an update. *Compare with* service pack.

patch cable *See* straight-through cable.

G

patch panel   A device that provides multiple network ports for cables that converge in one location such as an electrical closet or server room.

path   A drive and list of directories pointing to a file, such as C:\Windows\System32.

Payment Card Industry (PCI)   Regulated credit card and debit card data and the standards that regulate how this data is transmitted and stored to help prevent fraud; PCI applies to vendors, retailers, and financial institutions.

PCI (Peripheral Component Interconnect)   A bus common to personal computers that uses a 32-bit wide or 64-bit data path. Several variations of PCI exist. On desktop systems, one or more notches on a PCI slot keep the wrong PCI cards from being inserted in the slot.

PCI Express (PCIe)   An evolution of PCI that is not backward-compatible with earlier PCI slots and cards. PCIe slots come in several sizes, including PCIe ×1, PCIe ×4, PCIe ×8, and PCIe ×16.

PCIe 6/8-pin connector   A power cord connector used by high-end video cards with PCIe ×16 slots to provide extra voltage to the card; the connector can accommodate a 6-hole or 8-hole port.

PCI-X   The second evolution of PCI, which is backward-compatible with conventional PCI slots and cards, except 5-V PCI cards. PCI-X is focused on the server market.

PCL (Printer Control Language)   A printer language developed by Hewlett-Packard that communicates instructions to a printer.

PCMCIA card   A card used with older laptops that was one or more variations of a PC Card to add memory to the laptop or provide ports for peripheral devices—for example, modem cards, network cards for a wired or wireless network, sound cards, SCSI host adapters, FireWire controllers, USB controllers, flash memory adapters, TV tuners, and hard disks.

PDU (protocol data unit)   A message on a TCP/IP network. A PDU might be called a packet or frame, depending on the complexity of the PDU.

peer-to-peer (P2P)   As applied to networking, a network of computers that are all equals, or peers. Each computer has the same amount of authority, and each can act as a server to the other computers.

Performance Monitor   A Microsoft Management Console snap-in that can track activity by hardware and software to measure performance.

permission propagation   When Windows passes permissions from parent objects to child objects.

permissions   Varying degrees of access assigned to a folder or file and given to a user account or user group. Access can include full control, write, delete, and read-only.

personal license   A license that gives a user the right to install and use one or two instances of software.

PHI (protected health information)   Regulated data about a person's health status or health care as defined by HIPAA (the Health Insurance Portability and Accountability Act), which includes steep penalties and risks for noncompliance.

phishing   Sending an email message with the intent of getting the user to reveal private information that can be used for identity theft. *Also see* spear phishing.

physical address   *See* MAC (Media Access Control) address.

physical topology   The physical arrangement of connections between computers.

pickup roller   A part in a printer that pushes a sheet of paper forward from the paper tray.

PII (personally identifiable information)   Regulated data that identifies a person, including a Social Security number, email address, physical address, birthdate, birth place, mother's maiden name, marital status, phone numbers, race, and biometric data.

pin grid array (PGA)   A socket that has holes aligned in uniform rows around it to receive the pins on the bottom of the processor. *Compare with* land grid array (LGA).

ping (Packet InterNet Groper)   A TCP/IP command used to troubleshoot network connections. It verifies that the host can communicate with another host on the network.

pinning   Making a frequently used application more accessible by adding its icon to the taskbar on the desktop.

pixel   A small spot on a fine horizontal scan line. Pixels are illuminated to create an image on the monitor.

pixel pitch   The distance between adjacent pixels on the screen.

plasma monitor   A type of monitor that provides high contrast with better color than LCD monitors. It works by discharging xenon and neon plasma on flat glass, and it doesn't contain mercury.

platform   The hardware, operating system, runtime libraries, and modules on which an application runs.

Platform Key (PK)   A digital signature that belongs to the motherboard or computer manufacturer. The PK authorizes turning Secure boot on or off and updating the KEK database.

plenum   The area between floors of a building.

PoE injector (Power over Ethernet)   A device that adds power to an Ethernet cable so the cable can provide power to a device.

POP or POP3 (Post Office Protocol, version 3)   The TCP/IP protocol that an email server and client use when the client requests the downloading of email messages. The most recent version is POP version 3. *Compare with* IMAP4.

port   (1) As applied to services running on a computer, a number assigned to a process on a computer so that the process can be found by TCP/IP. *Also called* a port address *or* port number. (2) A physical connector, usually at the back of a computer, that allows a cable to be attached from a peripheral device, such as a printer, mouse, or modem.

port address   *See* port.

port filtering   To open or close certain ports so they can or cannot be used. A firewall uses port filtering to protect a network from unwanted communication.

port forwarding   A technique that allows a computer on the Internet to reach a computer on a private network using a certain port when the private network is protected by NAT and a firewall that controls the use of ports. *Also called* port mapping.

port lock   A physical lock, such as a USB lock, that prevents use of a computer port.

port mapping   *See* port forwarding.

port number   *See* port.

port replicator   A nonproprietary device that typically connects to a laptop via a USB port and provides ports to allow the laptop to easily connect to peripheral devices, such as an external monitor, network, printer, keyboard, mouse, or speakers. *Also called* a universal docking station.

port security   Controlled access to ports on a managed switch, which is usually done through MAC address filtering for one or more ports.

port triggering   When a firewall opens a port because a computer behind the firewall initiates communication on another port.

POST (power-on self test)   A self-diagnostic program used to perform a simple test of the CPU, RAM, and various I/O devices. The POST is performed by startup BIOS/UEFI when the computer is first turned on.

POST card   A test card installed in a slot on the motherboard or plugged in to a USB port that is used to help discover and report computer errors and conflicts that occur when a computer is first turned on and before the operating system is launched.

POST diagnostic card   *See* POST card.

PostScript   A printer language developed by Adobe Systems that tells a printer how to print a page.

Power Options applet   An applet accessed through Control Panel that manages power settings to conserve power.

Power over Ethernet (PoE)   A feature that might be available on high-end wired network adapters that allows power to be transmitted over Ethernet cable to remote devices.

power supply   A box inside the computer case that receives power and converts it for use by the motherboard and other installed devices. Power supplies provide 3.3, 5, and 12 volts DC. *Also called* a power supply unit (PSU).

power supply tester   A device that can test the output of each power cord coming from a power supply.

power supply unit (PSU)   *See* power supply.

Power Users group   A type of user account group. Accounts assigned to this group can read from and write to parts of the system other than their own user profile folders, install applications, and perform limited administrative tasks.

powerline networking   *See* EoP (Ethernet over Power).

G

PowerShell A command-line interface (CLI) that processes objects called cmdlets, which are pre-built programs built on the .NET Framework, rather than processing text in a command line.

PowerShell ISE Software used to create, edit, and test PowerShell scripts. ISE stands for Integrated Scripting Environment.

PowerShell script A text file of PowerShell commands that can be executed as a batch.

Preboot eXecution Environment (PXE) Programming contained in the BIOS/UEFI code on the motherboard that is used to start up the computer and search for a server on the network to provide a bootable operating system. *Also called* Pre-Execution Environment (PXE).

Pre-Execution Environment (PXE) *See* Preboot eXecution Environment (PXE).

presentation virtualization Using this virtualization, a remote application running on a server is controlled by a local computer.

PRI (Product Release Instructions) Instructions about an update to an OS or other software published by the product manufacturer to alert users about what to expect from the update.

primary partition A hard disk partition that can be designated as the active partition. An MBR drive can have up to three primary partitions. In Windows, a GPT drive can have up to 128 primary partitions. *Compare with* extended partition.

principle of least privilege An approach where computer users are classified and the rights assigned are the minimum rights required to do their job.

print head The part in an inkjet or impact printer that moves across the paper, creating one line of the image with each pass.

Print Management A utility in the Administrative Tools group of Windows professional and business editions that allows you to monitor and manage printer queues for all printers on the network.

print server Hardware or software that manages the print jobs sent to one or more printers on a network.

print spooler A queue for print jobs.

printer maintenance kit A kit purchased from a printer manufacturer that contains the parts, tools, and instructions needed to perform routine printer maintenance.

printer self-test page A test page that prints by using controls at the printer. The page allows you to eliminate a printer as a problem during troubleshooting and usually includes test results, graphics, and information about the printer, such as its resolution and how much memory is installed.

printui The Windows Printer User Interface command, which is used by administrators to manage printers on local and remote computers.

privacy filter *See* privacy screen.

privacy screen A device that fits over a monitor screen to prevent other people from viewing it from a wide angle. *Also called* privacy filter.

private cloud Services on the Internet that an organization provides on its own servers or that are established virtually for a single organization's private use.

private IP address In TCP/IP version 4, an IP address used on a private network that is isolated from the Internet.

privileges The access to data files and folders given to user accounts and user groups. *Also called* rights.

PRL (Preferred Roaming List) A list of preferred service providers or radio frequencies your carrier wants a mobile device to use; it is stored on a Removable User Identity Module (R-UIM) card installed in the device.

process A program that is running under the authority of the shell, together with the system resources assigned to it.

processor *See* central processing unit (CPU).

processor frequency The speed at which the processor operates internally, usually expressed in GHz.

processor thermal trip error A problem when the processor overheats and the system restarts.

product activation The process that Microsoft uses to prevent software piracy. For example, once Windows 10 is activated for a particular computer, it cannot be legally installed on another computer.

product key A series of letters and numbers assigned by Microsoft that is required to activate a license to use Windows.

Product Release Instructions (PRI) Information published by the manufacturer of an operating system that describes what to expect from a published update to the OS.

profile security requirements A set of policies and procedures that define how a student or employee's profile settings are configured for security purposes. For example, a policy might require encryption and backup software to be installed on the student or employee's personal devices that connect to the organization's network.

Programs and Features A Control Panel applet that lists the programs installed on a computer; you can use it to uninstall, change, or repair programs.

projector A device used to shine a light that projects a transparent image onto a large screen; a projector is often used in classrooms or with other large groups.

protocol A set of rules and standards that two entities use for communication. For example, TCP/IP is a suite or group of protocols that define many types of communication on a TCP/IP network.

provisioning package A package of settings, apps, and data specific to an enterprise that is downloaded and installed on a device when it first joins Azure Active Directory.

proxy server A computer that intercepts requests that a client (for example, a browser) makes of a server (for example, a web server). A proxy server can serve up the request from a cache it maintains to improve performance or it can filter requests to secure a large network.

PS/2 port A round 6-pin port used by an older keyboard or mouse.

public cloud Cloud computing services provided over the Internet to the general public. Google or Yahoo! email services are examples of public cloud deployment.

public IP address In TCP/IP version 4, an IP address available to the Internet.

pull automation A Windows installation from a deployment server that requires the local user to start the process. *Compare with* push automation.

punchdown tool A hand tool used to punch individual wires from a network cable into their slots to terminate the cable.

push automation An installation automatically pushed by a server to a computer when a user is not likely to be manning the computer. *Compare with* pull automation.

PVC (polyvinyl chloride) The product used to cover Ethernet cables; it is not safe to be used in a plenum because it gives off toxic fumes when burned.

Python script A text file of Python commands that can be executed as a batch.

QoS (Quality of Service) *See* Quality of Service (QoS).

quad channels Technology used by a motherboard and DIMMs that allows the memory controller to access four DIMMS at the same time. DDR3 and DDR4 DIMMs can use quad channels.

Quality of Service (QoS) A feature used by Windows and network hardware devices to improve network performance for an application. For example, VoIP requires a high QoS.

quarantined computer A computer that is suspected of infection and not allowed to use the network, is put on a different network dedicated to such computers, or is allowed to access only certain network resources.

quick format A format procedure for a hard drive volume or other drive that doesn't scan the volume or drive for bad sectors; use it only when a drive has been previously formatted and is in healthy condition. *Compare with* full format.

Quick Launch menu The menu that appears when the Windows Start button is right-clicked.

QuickPath Interconnect (QPI) The technology used first by the Intel X58 chipset for communication between the chipset and the processor; it uses 16 serial lanes, similar to PCI Express. QPI replaced the 64-bit wide Front Side Bus used by previous chipsets.

radio firmware Firmware on a device that manages wireless communication, such as cellular, Wi-Fi, and Bluetooth radio communication.

radio frequency (RF) The frequency of waves generated by a radio signal, which are electromagnetic frequencies above audio and below light. For example, Wi-Fi 802.11n transmits using a radio frequency of 5 GHz and 2.4 GHz.

RADIUS (Remote Access Dial-in User Service) A standard to authenticate and authorize users to wired, wireless, and VPN network connections. Authentication is made to a user database such as Active Directory.

G

RAID (redundant array of inexpensive disks or redundant array of independent disks) Several methods of configuring multiple hard drives to store data to increase logical volume size and improve performance, or to ensure that if one hard drive fails, the data is still available from another hard drive.

RAID 0 Using space from two or more physical disks to increase the disk space available for a single volume. Performance improves because data is written evenly across all disks. Windows calls RAID 0 a striped volume. *Also called* striping *or* striped volume.

RAID 1 A type of drive imaging that duplicates data on one drive to another drive and is used for fault tolerance. Windows calls RAID 1 a mirrored volume. *Also called* mirrored volume.

RAID 1+0 *See* RAID 10.

RAID 10 A combination of RAID 1 and RAID 0 that requires at least four disks to work as an array of drives and provides the best redundancy and performance.

RAID 5 A technique that stripes data across three or more drives and uses parity checking, so that if one drive fails, the other drives can re-create the data stored on the failed drive. RAID 5 drives increase performance and provide fault tolerance. Windows calls these drives RAID-5 volumes.

RAID-5 volume The term used by Windows for RAID 5. *See* RAID 5.

rainbow table A list of plaintext passwords and matching password hashes (encrypted passwords) used by hackers for reverse lookup. When the password hash is known, a hacker can find the plaintext password and use it to hack into a computer or network.

RAM (random access memory) Memory modules on the motherboard that contain microchips used to temporarily hold data and programs while the CPU processes both. Information in RAM is lost when the computer is turned off.

ransomware Malware that holds your computer system hostage with encryption techniques until you pay money or a time period expires and the encrypted content is destroyed.

rapid elasticity A cloud computing service that is capable of scaling up or down as a customer's need level changes.

raw data Data sent to a printer without any formatting or processing.

RCA connector A connector used with composite and component cables that is round and has a single pin in the center.

rd (remove directory) The Windows command to delete a directory (folder) or group of directories (folders).

RDP (Remote Desktop Protocol) *See* Remote Desktop Protocol (RDP).

read/write head A sealed, magnetic coil device that moves across the surface of a disk in a hard disk drive (HDD), either reading data from or writing data to the disk.

ReadyBoost A Windows utility that uses a flash drive or secure digital (SD) memory card to boost hard drive performance.

recover The Windows command that can recover a file when part of it is corrupted.

recovery drive A Windows 10/8 bootable USB flash drive that can be used to recover the system when startup fails; the drive can be created using the Recovery applet in Control Panel. The drive can hold an OEM recovery partition copied from the hard drive.

recovery partition A partition on a hard drive that contains a recovery utility and installation files.

Recovery System In macOS, a lean operating system that boots from a hidden volume on the macOS startup disk and is used to troubleshoot macOS when startup errors occur.

rectifier An electrical device that converts AC to DC. A computer power supply contains a rectifier.

Recycle Bin A location on the hard drive where deleted files are stored.

refresh A Windows 8 technique to recover from a corrupted Windows installation using a custom refresh image, a recovery partition, or the Windows setup DVD. Depending on the health of the system, the user settings, data, and Windows 8 apps might be restored from backup near the end of the refresh operation.

refresh rate As applied to monitors, the number of times in one second the monitor can fill the screen with lines from top to bottom. *Also called* vertical scan rate.

registry   A database that Windows uses to store hardware and software configuration information, user preferences, and setup information.

Registry Editor   The Windows utility (Regedit.exe) used to edit the Windows registry.

Regsvr32   A utility for registering component services used by an installed application.

regulated data   Data that is protected by special governmental laws or regulations; industry must comply with these regulations or face penalties.

regulatory and compliance policies   The governmental policies or rules that an industry must follow to protect regulated data.

reliability history   *See* Reliability Monitor.

Reliability Monitor   A Windows utility that provides information about problems and errors that happen over time. *Also called* reliability history.

Remote Admin share   A default share that gives the Administrator user account access to the Windows folder on a remote computer in a Windows domain.

remote application   An application that is installed and executed on a server and is presented to a user working at a client computer.

Remote Assistance   A Windows tool that allows a technician to remote in to a user's computer while the user remains signed in, retains control of the session, and can see the screen. This is helpful when a technician is troubleshooting problems on a computer.

remote backup application   A cloud backup service on the Internet that backs up data to the cloud and is often used for laptops, tablets, and smartphones.

Remote Desktop Connection (RDC)   A Windows tool that gives a user access to a Windows desktop from anywhere on the Internet.

Remote Desktop Protocol (RDP)   The Windows protocol used by Remote Desktop and Remote Assistance utilities to connect to and control a remote computer.

Remote Disc   A feature of macOS that gives other computers on the network access to the Mac's optical drive.

remote network installation   An automated installation where no user intervention is required.

remote printing   Printing from a computer or mobile device to a printer that is not connected directly to the computer or device.

remote wipe   An operation that remotely erases all contacts, email, photos, and other data from a device to protect your privacy.

ren (rename)   The Windows command to rename a file or group of files.

repair upgrade   A nondestructive installation of Windows 10 over an existing Windows installation; the upgrade can repair the existing installation.

repeater   A networking device that amplifies and retransmits a wireless signal to a wider coverage area and uses a new network name for the rebroadcast.

request for comments (RFC)   Feedback to a proposed change that is requested by an organization of its customers or users.

resiliency   In Windows Storage Spaces, the degree to which the configuration can resist or recover from drive failure.

Resilient File System (ReFS)   A file system that offers excellent fault tolerance and compatibility with virtualization and data redundancy in a RAID system; ReFS is included in Windows 10 Pro for Workstations.

resolution   The number of pixels on a monitor screen that are addressable by software (for example, 1024 × 768 pixels).

Resource Monitor   A Windows tool that monitors the performance of the processor, memory, hard drive, and network.

resource pooling   Cloud computing services to multiple customers that are hosted on shared physical resources and dynamically allocated to meet customer demand.

restore point   A snapshot of the Windows system, usually made before installation of new hardware or applications. Restore points are created by the System Protection utility.

Resultant Set of Policy (RSoP)   A Windows command and console (rsop.msc) that displays the policies set for a computer or user.

REt (Resolution Enhancement technology)   The term used by Hewlett-Packard to describe the way a laser printer varies the size of the dots used to create an image. This technology partly accounts for the sharp, clear image created by a laser printer.

G

retinal scanning   As part of the authentication process, some systems acquire biometric data by scanning the blood vessels on the back of the eye; this method is considered the most reliable of all biometric data scanning.

reverse lookup   A way to find the host name when you know a computer's IP address. The nslookup command can perform a reverse lookup.

revoked signature database (dbx)   A Secure boot database that is a blacklist of signatures for software that has been revoked and is no longer trusted.

RFID (radio-frequency identification)   A wireless technology used on small tags that contain a microchip and antenna; RFID is often used to track and identify car keys, clothing, animals, and inventory.

RFID badge   A badge worn by an employee and used to gain entrance into a locked area of a building. An RFID token transmits authentication to the system when the token gets within range of a query device.

RG-59 coaxial cable   An older and thinner coaxial cable once used for cable TV.

RG-6 coaxial cable   A coaxial cable used for cable TV that replaced the older and thinner RG-59 coaxial cable.

RIMM   An older type of memory module developed by Rambus, Inc.

riser card   A card that plugs into a motherboard and allows for expansion cards to be mounted parallel to the motherboard. Expansion cards are plugged into slots on the riser card.

risk analysis   The process of identifying potential problems that might arise as a change plan is implemented; this process is done before the change begins.

RJ-11   *See* RJ-11 jack.

RJ-11 jack   A phone line connection or port found on modems, telephones, and house phone outlets. *Also called* RJ-11 port.

RJ-11 port   *See* RJ-11 jack.

RJ-45   A port that looks like a large phone jack and is used with twisted-pair cable to connect to a wired network adapter or other hardware device. RJ stands for registered jack. *Also called* RJ-45 port *or* Ethernet port.

RJ-45 port   *See* RJ-45.

robocopy (robust file copy)   A Windows command that is similar to and more powerful than the xcopy command; it is used to copy files and folders.

root account   In Linux and macOS, the account that gives the user access to all the functions of the OS; the principal user account.

root certificate   The original digital certificate issued by a Certificate Authority.

root directory   The main directory, at the top of the top-down hierarchical structure of subdirectories, created when a hard drive or disk is first formatted. In Linux, it's indicated by a forward slash. In Windows, it's indicated by a backward slash.

rooting   The process of obtaining root or administrator privileges to an Android device, which then gives you complete access to the entire file system and all commands and features.

rootkit   A type of malicious software that loads itself before the OS boot is complete and can hijack internal OS components so that it masks information the OS provides to user-mode utilities such as Windows File Explorer or Task Manager.

router   A device that manages traffic between two or more networks and can help find the best path for traffic to get from one network to another.

RS-232   A 9-pin serial connector used with rack server consoles and older mice, keyboards, dial-up modems, and other peripherals.

run-time environment   The environment provided by the operating system in which commands contained in a script file are interpreted and executed.

S1 state   On the BIOS/UEFI power screen, one of the five S states used by ACPI power-saving mode to indicate different levels of power-saving functions. In the S1 state, the hard drive and monitor are turned off and everything else runs normally.

S2 state   On the BIOS/UEFI power screen, one of the five S states used by ACPI power-saving mode to indicate different levels of power-saving functions. In S2 state, the hard drive and monitor are turned off and everything else runs normally. In addition, the processor is also turned off.

S3 state   On the BIOS/UEFI power screen, one of the five S states used by ACPI power-saving mode to indicate different levels of power-saving functions. In S3 state, everything is shut down except RAM and enough of the system to respond to a wake-up. S3 is sleep mode.

S4 state On the BIOS/UEFI power screen, one of the five S states used by ACPI power-saving mode to indicate different levels of power-saving functions. In S4 state, everything in RAM is copied to a file on the hard drive and the system is shut down. When the system is turned on, the file is used to restore the system to its state before shutdown. S4 is hibernation mode.

S5 state On the BIOS/UEFI power screen, one of the five S states used by ACPI power-saving mode to indicate different levels of power-saving functions. S5 is the power-off state after a normal shutdown.

SaaS (Software as a Service) A cloud computing service that is responsible for hardware, the operating systems, and the applications installed.

Safe Mode The technique of launching Windows with a minimum configuration, eliminating third-party software, and reducing Windows startup to only essential processes. The technique can sometimes launch Windows when a normal Windows startup is corrupted.

safety goggles Eye goggles worn while working in an unsafe environment such as a factory, where fragments, chips, or other particles might cause eye injuries.

sag *See* brownout.

SATA (Serial Advanced Technology Attachment or Serial ATA) An interface standard used mostly by hard drives, optical drives, and other storage devices. Current SATA standards include SATA3, SATA2, and eSATA.

SATA Express An interface standard that uses a unique SATA connector and combines PCIe and SATA to improve on the performance of SATA3. SATA Express is three times faster than SATA3 but not as fast as NVMe.

SATA power connector A 15-pin flat power connector that provides power to SATA drives.

SC (subscriber connector or standard connector) A type of snap-in connector that can be used with either single-mode or multimode fiber-optic cables. It is not used with the fastest fiber-optic networking.

scanstate A command used by the User State Migration Tool (USMT) to copy user settings and

data from an old computer to a safe location such as a server or removable media. *Also see* loadstate.

scope of change Part of a change plan that defines the key components of change and how they will be addressed, the people, skills, tasks, and activities required to carry out the change, how the results of the change will be measured, and when the change is complete.

screen orientation The layout or orientation of the screen, which is either portrait or landscape.

screen resolution The number of dots or pixels on the monitor screen, expressed as two numbers such as 1680 × 1050.

Screen Sharing In macOS, a utility to remotely view and control a Mac; it is similar to Remote Desktop in Windows.

script A text file that contains a list of commands that can be interpreted and executed by the OS.

SCSI (Small Computer System Interface) An interface between a host adapter and the CPU that can daisy-chain as many as 7 or 15 devices on a single bus.

SD (Secure Digital) card A group of standards and flash memory storage cards that come in a variety of physical sizes, capacities, and speeds.

SDK (Software Development Kit) A group of tools that developers use to write apps. For example, Android Studio is a free SDK that is released as open source.

secondary logon Using administrator privileges to perform an operation when you are not logged on with an account that has these privileges.

secondary-click An action in macOS applied to an item on the macOS screen, such as displaying a shortcut menu for a file; it is similar to a right-click in Windows. By default, the action is a tap with two fingers on the Mac trackpad.

sector On a hard disk drive or SSD, the smallest unit of bytes addressable by the operating system and BIOS/UEFI. On hard disk drives, one sector usually equals 512 bytes; SSDs might use larger sectors.

Secure boot A UEFI and OS feature that prevents a system from booting up with drivers or an OS that is not digitally signed and trusted by the motherboard or computer manufacturer.

Secure Digital (SD) card A type of memory card used in digital cameras, tablets, cell phones, MP3

G

players, digital camcorders, and other portable devices. The three standards used by SD cards are 1.x (regular SD), 2.x (SD High Capacity or SDHC), and 3.x (SD eXtended Capacity or SDXC).

Secure DNS   A security service offered by providers such as Comodo to interrupt a phishing attack by monitoring a browser's requests for websites and redirecting the browser when it attempts to visit a known malicious site. To implement Secure DNS, use the provider's DNS server addresses for your DNS service.

Secure FTP (SFTP)   A TCP/IP protocol used to transfer files from an FTP server to an FTP client using encryption.

Secure Shell (SSH)   A protocol used to pass login information to a remote computer and control that computer over a network using encryption.

security profile   A set of policies and procedures that restrict how a student or employee can access, create, and edit the organization's resources.

security token   A smart card or other device that is one factor in multifactor authentication or can serve as a replacement for a password.

self-grounding   A method to safeguard against ESD that involves touching the computer case or power supply before touching a component in the computer case.

separate pad   *See* separation pad.

separation pad   A printer part that keeps more than one sheet of paper from moving forward.

serial ATA (SATA)   *See* SATA (Serial Advanced Technology Attachment or Serial ATA).

serial port   A male 9-pin or 25-pin port on a computer system used by slower I/O devices such as a mouse or modem. Data travels serially, one bit at a time, through the port. Serial ports are sometimes configured as COM1, COM2, COM3, or COM4. *Also called* DB-9 *or* DB9 port.

server lock   A physical lock that prevents someone from opening the computer case of a server.

Server Manager   A Windows Server console, also available in Windows 10, that contains the tools used to manage Active Directory.

Server Message Block (SMB)   A protocol used by Windows to share files and printers on a network.

server-side virtualization   Using this virtualization, a server provides a virtual desktop or application for users on multiple client machines.

service   A program that runs in the background to support or serve Windows or an application.

service pack   A collection of several patches or updates that is installed as a single update to an OS or application.

Service Set Identifier (SSID)   The name of a wireless access point and wireless network.

Services console   A console used by Windows to stop, start, and manage background services used by Windows and applications.

Settings app   In Windows 10, an app to view and change many Windows settings.

setup BIOS/UEFI   Firmware used to change motherboard settings. For example, you can use it to enable or disable a device on the motherboard, change the date and time that is later passed to the OS, and select the order of boot devices for startup BIOS/UEFI to search when looking for an operating system to load.

shadow copy   A copy of open files made so that they are included in a backup.

share permissions   A method to share a folder (not individual files) to remote users on the network, including assigning varying degrees of access to specific user accounts and user groups. These permissions do not apply to local users of a computer; they can be used on an NTFS or FAT volume. *Compare with* NTFS permissions.

sheet battery   A secondary battery that fits on the bottom of a laptop to provide additional battery charge.

shell   The portion of an OS that relates to the user and applications.

shell prompt   In Linux and macOS, the command prompt in the terminal.

shell script   A text file of Linux commands that can be executed as a batch.

shielded twisted-pair (STP) cable   A cable that is made of one or more twisted pairs of wires and is surrounded by a metal shield.

Short Message Service (SMS)   A technology that allows users to send a test message using a cell phone.

shoulder surfing   As you work, other people secretly peeking at your monitor screen to gain valuable information.

shredder   A device, such as a paper shredder or multimedia shredder, that destroys sensitive data by destroying the paper or storage device that holds the data.

shutdown The Windows command to shut down the local computer or a remote computer.

Side button The physical button on the upper-right side of an iPhone or iPad.

signature database (db) A Secure boot database that holds a list of digital signatures of approved operating systems, applications, and drivers that can be loaded by UEFI.

signature pad A device with a touch screen used to capture a handwritten signature made with a stylus or finger.

SIM (Subscriber Identity Module) card A small flash memory card that contains all the information a device needs to connect to a GSM or LTE cellular network, including a password and other authentication information needed to access the network, encryption standards used, and the services that a subscription includes.

SIMM (single inline memory module) An outdated miniature circuit board used to hold RAM. SIMMs held 8, 16, 32, or 64 MB on a single module. SIMMs have been replaced by DIMMs.

Simple Network Management Protocol (SNMP) *See* SNMP (Simple Network Management Protocol).

simple volume A type of volume used on a single hard drive. *Compare with* dynamic volume.

single channel The memory controller on a motherboard that can access only one DIMM at a time. *Compare with* dual channel, triple channel, *and* quad channel.

single sign-on (SSO) An account that accesses multiple independent resources, systems, or applications after signing in one time to one account. An example is a Microsoft account.

single-core processing An older processor technology whereby the processor housing contains a single processor or core that can process two threads at the same time. *Compare with* multicore processing.

single-sided A DIMM that has memory chips installed on one side of the module.

site license A license that allows a company to install multiple copies of software or allows multiple employees to execute the software from a file server.

slack Wasted space on a hard drive caused by not using all available space at the end of a cluster.

sleep mode A power-saving state for a computer when it is not in use. *Also called* standby mode *or* suspend mode. *Also see* S3 state.

sleep timer The number of minutes of inactivity before a computer goes into a power-saving state such as sleep mode.

SLP (Service Location Protocol) A TCP/IP protocol used by AFP to find printers and file sharing devices on a local network.

small form factor (SFF) A motherboard used in low-end computers and home theater systems. An SFF is often used with an Intel Atom processor and sometimes purchased as a motherboard-processor combo unit.

S.M.A.R.T. (Self-Monitoring Analysis and Reporting Technology) A BIOS/UEFI and hard drive feature that monitors hard drive performance, disk spin-up time, temperature, distance between the head and the disk, and other mechanical activities of the drive in order to predict when it is likely to fail.

smart camera A digital camera that has embedded computing power to make decisions about the content of the photos or videos it records, including transmitting alerts over a wired or wireless network when it records certain content. *Also called* a vision sensor.

smart card Any small device that contains authentication information that can be keyed into a sign-in window or read by a reader to authenticate a user on a network.

smart card reader A device that can read a smart card to authenticate a person onto a network.

smart speaker A speaker that includes voice-activated digital assistant software and connects by Wi-Fi or other wireless technology to the Internet.

smart TV A television that has the ability to run apps, store data, and connect to the Internet.

smartphone A cell phone that can send text messages with photos, videos, and other multimedia content, surf the web, manage email, play games, take photos and videos, and download and use small apps.

SMB (Server Message Block) A file access protocol originally developed by IBM and used

G

by Windows to share files and printers on a network. The current SMB protocol is SMB3.

SMB2 *See* CIFS (Common Internet File System).

S/MIME (Secure/Multipurpose Internet Mail Extensions) A protocol that encrypts an outgoing email message and includes a digital signature; S/MIME is more secure than SMTP, which does not use encryption.

SMTP (Simple Mail Transfer Protocol) A TCP/IP protocol used by email clients to send email messages to an email server and on to the recipient's email server. *Also see* POP *and* IMAP.

SMTP AUTH (SMTP Authentication) An improved version of SMTP used to authenticate a user to an email server when the email client first tries to connect to the email server to send email. The protocol is based on the Simple Authentication and Security Layer (SASL) protocol.

snap-in A Windows utility that can be installed in a console window by Microsoft Management Console.

snapshot In macOS, a backup created by Time Machine that is stored on the hard drive when the computer is not connected to backup media and copied to backup media when connectivity is restored.

SNMP (Simple Network Management Protocol) A versatile TCP/IP protocol used to monitor network traffic and manage network devices. The SNMP server works with SNMP agents installed on devices being monitored.

social engineering The practice of tricking people into giving out private information or allowing unsafe programs into the network or computer.

socket (1) In computer hardware, a rectangular connector with pins or pads and a mechanism to hold the CPU in place; it is used to connect a CPU to the motherboard. (2) In networking, an established connection between a client and a server, such as the connection between a browser and web server.

SO-DIMM (small outline DIMM) A type of memory module for laptop computers that uses DIMM technology. A DDR4 SO-DIMM has 260 pins, and a DDR3 SO-DIMM has 204 pins. A DDR2 or DDR SO-DIMM has 200 pins.

soft boot To restart a computer without turning off the power; for example, in Windows 10/8,

press Win+X, point to Shut down or sign out, and click Restart. *Also called* warm boot.

soft reset (1) For Android, to forcefully reboot the device (full shut down and cold boot) by pressing and holding the power button. (2) For iOS, to put the device in hibernation and not clear memory by pressing the Wake/sleep button.

software piracy The act of making unauthorized copies of original software, which violates the Federal Copyright Act of 1976.

software RAID Using Windows to implement RAID. The setup is done using the Disk Management utility.

software token An app or digital certificate that serves as authentication to a computer or network.

solid-state device (SSD) An electronic device with no moving parts. An SSD is a storage device that uses memory chips to store data instead of spinning disks (such as those used by magnetic hard drives and CD drives). Examples of solid-state devices are jump drives (also known as key drives or thumb drives), flash memory cards, and solid-state disks used as hard drives in notebook computers designed for the most rugged uses. *Also called* solid-state disk (SSD) *or* solid-state drive (SSD). *Compare with* magnetic hard drive.

solid-state drive (SSD) *See* solid-state device (SSD).

solid-state hybrid drive (SSHD) *See* hybrid hard drive (H-HDD).

Sound applet An applet accessed through Control Panel to select a default speaker and microphone and adjust how Windows handles sounds.

sound card An expansion card with sound ports.

South Bridge The portion of the chipset hub that connects slower I/O buses (for example, a PCI bus) to the system bus. *Compare with* North Bridge.

Space In macOS, one desktop screen. Multiple desktops or Spaces can be open and available to users.

spacer *See* standoff.

spanning A configuration of two hard drives that hold a single Windows volume to increase the size of the volume. Sometimes called JBOD (just a bunch of disks).

SPDIF (Sony-Phillips Digital InterFace) sound port A port that connects to an external home theater audio system, providing digital audio output and the best signal quality.

spear phishing A form of phishing where an email message appears to come from a company you already do business with.

spoofing Tricking someone into thinking an imitation of a website or email message is legitimate. For example, a phishing technique tricks you into clicking a link in an email message, which takes you to an official-looking website where you are asked to enter your user ID and password to access the site.

spooling Placing print jobs in a queue so that an application can be released from the printing process before printing is completed. Spool is an acronym for simultaneous peripheral operations online.

Spotlight In macOS, the search app that can be configured to search the local computer, Wikipedia, iTunes, the Maps app, the web, and more.

spudger A metal or plastic flat-head wedge used to pry open casings without damaging plastic connectors and cases when disassembling a notebook, tablet, or mobile device.

spyware Malicious software that installs itself on your computer or mobile device to spy on you. It collects personal information about you and transmits it over the Internet to web-hosting sites that intend to use the information for harm.

SSD (solid-state drive or solid-state device) *See* solid-state device (SSD).

SSH (Secure Shell) A protocol and application that encrypts communication between a client and server and is used to remotely control a Linux computer.

SSID (Service Set Identifier) *See* Service Set Identifier (SSID).

SSO (single sign-on) *See* single sign-on (SSO).

ST (straight tip) connector A type of connector that can be used with either single-mode or multimode fiber-optic cables. The connector does not support full-duplex transmissions and is not used on the fastest fiber-optic systems.

standard account The Windows 10/8/7 user account type that can use software and hardware and make some system changes, but cannot make changes that affect the security of the system or other users. *Compare with* administrator account.

standard image An image that includes Windows, drivers, applications, and data, which are standard to all the computers that might use the image.

standby mode *See* sleep mode.

standoff Round plastic or metal pegs that separate the motherboard from the case so that components on the back of the motherboard do not touch the case.

Start screen In Windows 8, a screen with tiles that represent lean apps, which use few system resources and are designed for social media, social networking, and the novice end user.

startup BIOS/UEFI Part of UEFI or BIOS firmware on the motherboard that is responsible for controlling the computer when it is first turned on. Startup BIOS/UEFI gives control to the OS once the OS is loaded.

startup disk In macOS, the entire volume on which macOS is installed.

startup items In macOS, programs that automatically launch at startup. Apple discourages the use of startup items, which are stored in two directories: /Library/StartupItems and /System/Library/StartupItems. Normally, both directories are empty.

startup repair A Windows 10/8/7 utility that restores many of the Windows files needed for a successful boot.

static electricity *See* electrostatic discharge (ESD).

static IP address A permanent IP address that is manually assigned to a computer or other device.

static RAM (SRAM) RAM chips that retain information without the need for refreshing, as long as the computer's power is on. They are more expensive than traditional DRAM.

storage card An adapter card used to manage hardware RAID rather than using the firmware on the motherboard.

Storage Spaces A Windows utility that can create a storage pool using any number of internal or external backup drives. The utility is expected to replace Windows software RAID.

STP (shielded twisted-pair) cable Twisted-pair networking cable that shields or covers each pair of wire in the cable to prevent electromagnetic interference.

G

straight-through cable   An Ethernet cable used to connect a computer to a switch or other network device. *Also called* a patch cable.

string   In scripting and programming, a type of data that can contain any character but cannot be used for calculations.

striped volume   The term used by Windows for RAID 0. A striped volume is a type of dynamic volume used for two or more hard drives; it writes to the disks evenly rather than filling up allotted space on one and then moving on to the next. *Compare with* spanned volume. *Also see* RAID 0.

striping   *See* RAID 0.

strong password   A password that is not easy to guess.

stylus   A device that is included with a graphics tablet and works like a pencil on the tablet.

su   A Linux and macOS command to open a new terminal shell for a different user account; su stands for "substitute user."

subdirectory   A directory or folder contained in another directory or folder. *Also called* a child directory *or* folder.

subnet   A group of local networks tied together in a subsystem of the larger intranet. In TCP/IP version 6, a subnet is one or more links that have the same 16 bits in the subnet ID of the IP address. *See* subnet ID.

subnet ID   In TCP/IP version 6, the last block (16 bits) in the 64-bit prefix of an IP address. The subnet is identified using some or all of these 16 bits.

subnet mask   In TCP/IP version 4, 32 bits that include a series of ones followed by zeroes—for example, 11111111.11111111.11110000.00000000, which can be written as 255.255.240.0. The 1s identify the network portion of an IP address, and the 0s identify the host portion of an IP address. The subnet mask tells Windows if a remote computer is on the same or different network.

subscription model   A method of licensing software with a paid annual subscription and the software is installed on your local computer. For example, Office 365 uses a subscription model.

sudo   A Linux and macOS command to execute another command as a superuser when logged in as a normal user with an account that has the right to use root commands. Sudo stands for "substitute user to do the command."

superuser   A user who is logged in to the root account.

surge protector   A device that protects against voltage spikes by blocking or grounding excessive voltage. *Also called* surge suppressor.

surge suppressor   *See* surge protector.

suspend mode   *See* sleep mode.

S-Video port   A 4-pin or 7-pin round video port that sends two signals over the cable, one for color and the other for brightness, and is used by some high-end TVs and video equipment.

swap partition   A partition on a Linux hard drive used to hold virtual memory.

swapfile   In macOS, the file used to hold virtual memory, similar to pagefile.sys in Windows.

switch   A device used to connect nodes on a network in a star network topology. When it receives a packet, it uses its table of MAC addresses to decide where to send the packet.

Sync Center   A Control Panel applet that allows two computers to sync the contents of a shared folder or volume.

synchronization app   An app on a mobile device or other computer to sync data and settings to cloud storage accounts such as Google Cloud and iCloud and between devices.

synchronous DRAM (SDRAM)   The first DIMM to run synchronized with the system clock; it has two notches and uses 168 pins.

Syslog   A protocol that collects event information about network devices, such as errors, failures, and users logging in or out, and sends the information to a Syslog server.

Syslog server   A server that receives and analyzes syslog data to monitor network devices and create alerts when problems arise that need attention.

system BIOS/UEFI   UEFI (Unified Extensible Firmware Interface) or BIOS (basic input/output system) firmware on the motherboard that is used to control essential devices before the OS is loaded.

system board   *See* motherboard.

system bus   The bus between the CPU and memory on the motherboard. The bus frequency in documentation is called the system speed, such as 400 MHz. *Also called* the memory bus, FrontSide Bus, local bus, *or* host bus.

system clock   A line on a bus that is dedicated to timing the activities of components connected to it. The system clock provides a continuous pulse that other devices use to time themselves.

System Configuration   A Windows utility (Msconfig.exe) that can identify what processes are launched at startup and can temporarily disable a process from loading.

System File Checker (SFC)   A Windows utility that verifies and, if necessary, refreshes a Windows system file, replacing it with one kept in a cache of current system files or downloaded from the Internet with the help of Windows Updates.

system image   The backup of the entire Windows volume; it can also include backups of other volumes. The system image works only on the computer that created it, and is created using Windows 10/8 File History or the Windows Backup and Restore utility.

System Information   A Windows tool (Msinfo32.exe) that provides details about a system, including installed hardware and software, the current system configuration, and currently running programs.

system partition   The active partition of the hard drive, which contains the boot loader or boot manager program and the specific files required to start the Windows launch.

System Preferences   In macOS, a utility to customize the macOS interface; it is available on the Apple menu.

System Protection   A utility that automatically backs up system files and stores them in restore points on the hard drive at regular intervals and just before you install software or hardware.

system repair disc   A disc you can create in Windows 10/7 to launch Windows RE. The disc is not available in Windows 8.

System Restore   A Windows utility used to restore the system to a restore point.

system state data   In Windows, files that are necessary for a successful load of the operating system.

system tray   *See* notification area.

System window   A window that displays brief but important information about installed hardware and software and gives access to important Windows tools needed to support the system.

systray   *See* notification area.

T568A   Standards for wiring twisted-pair network cabling and RJ-45 connectors; in T568A, the green pair of wires is connected to pins 1 and 2 and the orange pair is connected to pins 3 and 6.

T568B   Standards for wiring twisted-pair network cabling and RJ-45 connectors; in T568B, the orange pair of wires uses pins 1 and 2 and the green pair is connected to pins 3 and 6.

tablet   A computing device with a touch screen that is larger than a smartphone and with functions similar to a smartphone.

TACACS+ (Terminal Access Controller Access Control System Plus)   A Cisco AAA service specifically designed for network administrators to remotely connect to a network and configure and manage Cisco routers, switches, firewalls, and other network devices. The service authenticates, authorizes, and tracks activity on the network and can work with Active Directory.

tailgating   When an unauthorized person follows an employee through a secured entrance to a room or building.

tap pay device   A device in a point-of-sale system that uses an encrypted wireless NFC connection to read and send payment information from a customer's smartphone to a vendor's account.

Task Manager   A Windows utility (Taskmgr.exe) that lets you view the applications and processes running on your computer as well as information about process and memory performance, network activity, and user activity.

Task Scheduler   A Windows tool that can set a task or program to launch at a future time, including at startup.

Task View   A Windows 10 feature used to create and manage multiple desktops.

taskbar   A bar normally located at the bottom of the Windows desktop that displays information about open programs and provides quick access to others.

taskkill   A Windows command that uses the process PID to kill a process.

G

tasklist   A Windows command that returns the process identifier (PID), which is a number that identifies each running process.

TCP (Transmission Control Protocol)   The protocol in the TCP/IP suite of protocols that works at the OSI Transport layer, establishes a session or connection between parties, and guarantees packet delivery.

TCP/IP (Transmission Control Protocol/Internet Protocol)   The group or suite of protocols used for almost all networks, including the Internet. Fundamentally, TCP is responsible for error-checking transmissions and IP is responsible for routing.

TCP/IP model   In networking theory, a simple model used to divide network communication into four layers. This model is simpler than the OSI model, which uses seven layers.

technical documentation   Digital or printed technical reference manuals that are included with software packages and hardware to provide directions for installation, usage, and troubleshooting. The information extends beyond that given in user manuals.

Telnet   A TCP/IP protocol and application used to allow an administrator or other user to control a computer remotely.

Teredo   In TCP/IP version 6, a tunneling protocol to transmit TCP/IPv6 packets over a TCP/IPv4 network; it is named after the Teredo worm that bores holes in wood. Teredo IP addresses begin with 2001, and the prefix is written as 2001::/32.

terminal   In Linux and macOS, the command-line interface. In macOS, the terminal is accessed through the Terminal utility in the Applications group of the Finder window.

tether   To connect a computer to a mobile device that has an Internet cellular connection so that the computer can access the Internet by way of the mobile device.

thermal compound   A creamlike substance that is placed between the bottom of the cooler heat sink and the top of the processor to eliminate air pockets and help draw heat off the processor.

thermal paper   Special coated paper used by thermal printers.

thermal printer   A type of line printer that uses wax-based ink, which is heated by heat pins that melt the ink onto paper.

thermal transfer printer   A type of thermal printer that uses a ribbon containing wax-based ink. The heating element melts the ribbon onto special thermal paper so that it stays glued to the paper as the feeder assembly moves the paper through the printer.

thick client   A regular desktop computer or laptop that is sometimes used as a client by a virtualization server. *Also called* fat client.

thin client   A computer that has an operating system but little computing power and might only need to support a browser used to communicate with a virtualization server.

thin provisioning   A technique used by Storage Spaces whereby virtual storage space can be made available to users who do not have physical storage allotted to them. When the virtual storage space is close to depletion, the administrator is prompted to install more physical storage.

third-party drivers   Drivers that are not included in BIOS/UEFI or Windows and must come from the manufacturer.

thread   Each process that the processor is aware of; a thread is a single task that is part of a larger task or request from a program.

Thunderbolt   *See* Thunderbolt 3 port.

Thunderbolt 3 port   A multipurpose standard and connector used for communication and power. Early versions were limited to Apple products and used a modified DisplayPort. The current version 3 uses modified USB-C ports on Apple and non-Apple devices.

ticket   An entry in a call-tracking system made by the person who receives a call for help. A ticket is used to track and document actions taken, and it stays open until the issue is resolved.

Time Machine   In macOS, a built-in backup utility that can be configured to automatically back up user-created data, applications, and system files to an external hard drive attached either directly to the computer or the local network.

TKIP (Temporal Key Integrity Protocol)   A type of encryption protocol used by WPA to secure a wireless Wi-Fi network. *Also see* WPA (Wi-Fi Protected Access).

tone generator and probe   A two-part kit used to find cables in the walls of a building. The toner connects to one end of the cable and puts out a pulsating tone that the probe can sense. *Also called* a toner probe *or* tone probe.

tone probe   *See* tone generator and probe.

toner probe   *See* tone generator and probe.

toner vacuum   A vacuum cleaner designed to pick up toner used in laser printers; the toner is not allowed to touch any conductive surface.

topology   In networking, the physical or logical pattern or design used to connect devices on a network.

touch pad   A common pointing device on a notebook computer.

touch screen   An input device that uses a monitor or LCD panel as a backdrop for user options. Touch screens can be embedded in a monitor or LCD panel or installed as an add-on device over the monitor screen.

tower case   The largest type of personal computer case. Tower cases stand vertically and can be up to two feet tall. They have more drive bays and are a good choice for computer users who anticipate making significant upgrades.

TPM (Trusted Platform Module)   A chip on a motherboard that holds an encryption key required at startup to access encrypted data on the hard drive. Windows 10/8/7 BitLocker Encryption can use the TPM chip.

TR4 (Threadripper 4)   A land grid array socket for AMD Ryzen processors and X399 chipsets. The socket is used with high-end AMD processors.

trace   A wire on a circuit board that connects two components or devices.

tracert (trace route)   A TCP/IP command that enables you to resolve a connectivity problem when attempting to reach a destination host such as a website.

track   One of many concentric circles on the surface of a hard disk drive.

tractor feed   A continuous feed within an impact printer that feeds fanfold paper through the printer rather than individual sheets; this format is useful for logging ongoing events or data.

transfer belt   A laser printer component that completes the transferring step in the printer.

transfer roller   A soft, black roller in a laser printer that puts a positive charge on the paper. The charge pulls the toner from the drum onto the paper.

transformer   An electrical device that changes the ratio of current to voltage. A computer power supply is basically a transformer and a rectifier.

trim   To erase entire blocks of unused data on an SSD so that write operations do not have to manage the data.

trip hazards   Loose cables or cords in a traffic area where people can trip over them.

triple A   *See* AAA (authenticating, authorizing, and accounting).

triple channels   When the memory controller accesses three DIMMs at the same time. DDR3 DIMMs support triple channeling.

Trojan   A type of malware that tricks you into downloading and/or opening it by substituting itself for a legitimate program.

Troubleshooting applet   A Control Panel applet used to automatically troubleshoot and fix many common Windows problems involving applications, hardware, sound, networking, Windows updates, and maintenance tasks.

trusted source   A source for downloading software that is considered reliable, such as app stores provided by a mobile device manufacturer and websites of well-known software manufacturers.

TV tuner card   An adapter card that receives a TV signal and displays it on the computer screen.

Twisted Nematic (TN)   A class of LCD monitor that has fast response times to keep fast-moving images crisper. TN monitors are brighter, consume more power, and have limited viewing angles.

twisted-pair cabling   Cabling, such as a network cable, that uses pairs of wires twisted together to reduce crosstalk.

two-factor authentication (2FA)   When two tokens or actions are required to authenticate to a computer or network. Factors can include what a person knows (password), what she possesses (a token such as a key fob or smart card), what she does (such as typing a certain way), or who she is (biometric data).

Type 1 hypervisor   Software to manage virtual machines that is installed before any operating system is installed.

Type 2 hypervisor   Software to manage virtual machines that is installed as an application in an operating system.

G

UDF (Universal Disk Format) A file system for optical media used by all DVD discs and some CD-R and CD-RW discs.

UDP (User Datagram Protocol) A connectionless TCP/IP protocol that works at the OSI Transport layer and does not require a connection to send a packet or guarantee that the packet arrives at its destination. The protocol is commonly used for broadcasting to multiple nodes on a network or the Internet. *Compare with* TCP (Transmission Control Protocol).

UEFI (Unified Extensible Firmware Interface) *See* Unified Extensible Firmware Interface (UEFI).

UEFI CSM (Compatibility Support Module) mode Legacy BIOS in UEFI firmware.

ultra-thin client *See* zero client.

unattended installation A Windows installation in which answers to installation questions are stored in a file that Windows calls so that they do not have to be typed in during the installation.

unicast address Using TCP/IP version 6, an IP address assigned to a single node on a network.

Unified Extensible Firmware Interface (UEFI) An interface between firmware on the motherboard and the operating system. UEFI improves on legacy BIOS processes for managing motherboard settings, booting, handing over the boot to the OS, loading device drivers and applications before the OS loads, and securing the boot to ensure that no rogue operating system hijacks the system.

Unified Threat Management (UTM) A computer, security appliance, network appliance, or Internet appliance that stands between the Internet and a private network. A UTM device runs a firewall, anti-malware software, and other software to protect the network, and is considered a next-generation firewall.

uninterruptible power supply (UPS) A device that raises the voltage when it drops during brownouts.

unique local address (ULA) In TCP/IP version 6, an address used to identify a specific site within a large organization. It can work on multiple links within the same organization. The address is a hybrid between a global unicast address that works on the Internet and a link local unicast address that works on only one link.

Universal Plug and Play (UPnP) *See* UPnP (Universal Plug and Play).

unmanaged switch A switch that requires no setup or configuration. *Compare with* managed switch.

unshielded twisted-pair (UTP) cable *See* UTP (unshielded twisted-pair) cable.

upgrade path A qualifying OS required by Microsoft in order to perform an in-place upgrade.

UPnP (Universal Plug and Play) A feature of a SOHO router that enables computers on the local network to have unfiltered communication so they can automatically discover services provided by other computers on the network. UPnP is considered a security risk because hackers might exploit the vulnerability created when computers advertise their services on the network.

USB (Universal Serial Bus) Multipurpose bus and connector standards used for internal and external ports for a variety of devices. Current USB standards are USB 3.2, 3.1, 3.0, and 2.0.

USB port A type of port designed to make installation and configuration of I/O devices easy. It provides room for as many as 127 devices daisy-chained together.

USB 2.0 A version of USB that runs at 480 Mbps and uses cables up to 5 meters long. *Also called* Hi-Speed USB.

USB 3.0 A version of USB that runs at 5 Gbps and uses cables up to 3 meters long. *Also called* SuperSpeed USB.

USB 3.0 B-Male connector A USB connector used by SuperSpeed USB 3.0 devices such as printers or scanners.

USB 3.0 Micro-B connector A small USB connector used by SuperSpeed USB 3.0 devices. The connectors are not compatible with regular Micro-B connectors.

USB lock A type of port lock used to control access to a USB port on a computer.

USB optical drive An external optical drive that connects to a computer via a USB port.

USB to Bluetooth adapter A device that plugs into a USB port on a computer to connect to Bluetooth devices.

USB to RJ-45 dongle An adapter that plugs into a USB port and provides an RJ-45 port for a network cable to connect to a wired network.

USB to Wi-Fi dongle   An adapter that plugs into a USB port and provides wireless connectivity to a Wi-Fi network.

USB-C   A USB connector that is flat with rounded sides and used by smartphones and tablets. The connector is required for USB 3.2 devices to attain maximum speeds.

User Account Control (UAC) dialog box   A Windows security feature that displays a dialog box when an event requiring administrative privileges is about to happen.

User Accounts   A Windows utility (netplwiz.exe) that can be used to change the way Windows sign-in works and to manage user accounts, including changing passwords and changing the group membership of an account. *Also called* Network Places Wizard.

user mode   In Windows, a mode that provides an interface between an application and the OS, and only has access to hardware resources through the code running in kernel mode.

user profile   A collection of files and settings about a user account that enables the user's personal data, desktop settings, and other operating parameters to be retained from one session to another.

user profile namespace   The group of folders and subfolders in the C:\Users folder that belong to a specific user account and contain the user profile.

User State Migration Tool (USMT)   A Windows utility that helps you migrate user files and preferences between computers to help a user make a smooth transition from one computer to another.

Users group   A type of Windows user account group. An account in this group is a standard user account, which does not have as many rights as an administrator account.

usmtutils   A command used by the User State Migration Tool (USMT) that provides encryption options and hard-link management.

UTM (Unified Threat Management)   *See* Unified Threat Management (UTM).

UTP (unshielded twisted-pair) cable   Twisted-pair networking cable commonly used on LANs that is less expensive than STP cable and does not contain shielding to prevent electromagnetic interference.

variable   The name of one item of data used in a script or program.

VBScript   A scripting language that creates scripts modeled after the more complex Visual Basic programming language. VBScripts have a .vbs file extension.

VDI (Virtual Desktop Infrastructure)   *See* Virtual Desktop Infrastructure (VDI).

VGA (Video Graphics Adapter) port   A 15-pin analog video port popular for many years. *Also called* DB-15, DB15 port, DE15 port, *or* HD15 port.

VGA mode   Standard VGA settings, which include a resolution of 640 × 480.

vi editor   In Linux and macOS, a text editor that works in command mode (to enter commands) or in insert mode (to edit text).

video capture card   An adapter card that captures video input and saves it to a file on the hard drive.

video memory   Memory used by the video controller. The memory might be contained on a video card or be part of system memory. When it is part of system memory, the memory is dedicated by Windows to video.

virtual assistant   A mobile device app that responds to a user's voice commands with a personable, conversational interaction to perform tasks and retrieve information. *Also called* a personal assistant *or* digital assistant.

virtual desktop   When a hypervisor manages a virtual machine and presents the VM's desktop to a user. A remote user normally views and manages the virtual desktop via a browser on the local computer.

Virtual Desktop Infrastructure (VDI)   A presentation of a virtual desktop made to a client computer by a hypervisor on a server in the cloud.

virtual LAN (VLAN)   A subnet of a larger network created to reduce network traffic. Managed switches are commonly used to set up VLANs.

virtual machine (VM)   Software managed by a hypervisor that simulates the hardware of a physical computer, creating one or more logical machines within one physical machine.

virtual machine manager (VMM)   *See* hypervisor.

G

virtual memory A method whereby the OS uses the hard drive as though it were RAM. *Also see* pagefile.sys.

virtual NIC A network adapter created by a hypervisor that is used by a virtual machine and emulates a physical NIC.

virtual printing Printing to a file rather than directly to a printer.

virtual private network (VPN) A security technique that uses encrypted data packets between a private network and a computer somewhere on the Internet.

virtualization When one physical machine hosts multiple activities that are normally done on multiple machines.

virtualization server A computer that serves up virtual machines to multiple client computers and provides a virtual desktop for users on these client machines.

virus A program that often has an incubation period, is infectious, and is intended to cause damage. A virus program might destroy data and programs.

vision sensor *See* smart camera.

VM (virtual machine) *See* virtual machine (VM).

Voice over LTE (VoLTE) A technology used on cellular networks for LTE to support voice communication.

VoIP (Voice over Internet Protocol) A TCP/IP protocol and an application that provides voice communication over a TCP/IP network. *Also called* Internet telephone.

volt (V) A measure of potential difference or electrical force in an electrical circuit. A computer ATX power supply usually provides five separate voltages: +12 V, -12 V, +5 V, -5 V, and +3.3 V.

volume A primary partition that has been assigned a drive letter and can be formatted with a file system such as NTFS. *Compare with* logical drive.

VPN (virtual private network) *See* virtual private network (VPN).

VR (virtual reality) headset A device worn on the head that creates a visual and audible virtual experience.

wait state A clock tick in which nothing happens; it is used to ensure that the microprocessor isn't getting ahead of slower components. A 0-wait state is preferable to a 1-wait state. Too many wait states can slow down a system.

Wake-on-LAN Configuring a computer so that it will respond to network activity when the computer is in a sleep state. *Also called* WoL.

WAN (wide area network) A network or group of networks that span a large geographical area.

WAP (wireless access point) *See* wireless access point (WAP).

warm boot *See* soft boot.

watt The unit of electricity used to measure power. A typical computer may use a power supply that provides 500W.

wear leveling A technique used on a solid-state drive that ensures the logical block addressing does not always address the same physical blocks; this technique distributes write operations more evenly across the device.

wearable technology device A device, such as a smart watch, wristband, arm band, eyeglasses, headset, or clothing, that can perform computing tasks, including making phone calls, sending text messages, transmitting data, and checking email.

WEP (Wired Equivalent Privacy) An encryption protocol used to secure transmissions on a Wi-Fi wireless network; however, it is no longer considered secure because the key used for encryption is static (it doesn't change).

whitelist In filtering, a list of items that is allowed through the filter—for example, a list of websites that computers on a local network are allowed to access. *Compare with* blacklist.

Wi-Fi (Wireless Fidelity) The common name for standards for a local wireless network, as defined by IEEE 802.11. *Also see* 802.11 a/b/g/n/ac.

Wi-Fi analyzer Hardware and/or software that monitors a Wi-Fi network to detect devices not authorized to use the network, identify attempts to hack transmissions, or detect performance and security vulnerabilities.

Wi-Fi calling On mobile devices, voice calls that use VoIP over a Wi-Fi connection to the Internet.

Wi-Fi Protected Setup (WPS) A method to make it easier for users to connect their computers to a secured wireless network when a hard-to-remember SSID and security key are used. WPS is considered a security risk that should be used with caution.

wildcard An * or ? character used in a command line that represents a character or group of characters in a file name or extension.

Windows 10 The latest Microsoft operating system for personal computers and tablets and an upgrade to Windows 8.

Windows 10 Mobile A Microsoft OS for smartphones.

Windows 7 A Microsoft OS whose editions include Windows 7 Starter, Windows 7 Home Basic, Windows 7 Home Premium, Windows 7 Professional, Windows 7 Enterprise, and Windows 7 Ultimate. Each edition comes at a different price with different features and capabilities.

Windows 8 reset A clean installation of Windows 8 that first formats the Windows volume. If an OEM recovery partition is present, the system is reset to its factory state. If no recovery partition is present, the installation is performed from a Windows 8 setup DVD.

Windows 8.1 A free update or release of the Windows 8 operating system.

Windows 8.1 Enterprise A Windows 8 edition that allows for volume licensing in a large, corporate environment.

Windows 8.1 Pro for Students A version of Windows 8 that includes all the same features as Windows 8 Pro, but at a lower price. This version is available only to students, faculty, and staff at eligible institutions.

Windows 8.1 Professional (Windows 8.1 Pro) A version of Windows 8 that includes additional features at a higher price. Windows 8.1 Pro supports homegroups, joining a domain, BitLocker, Client Hyper-V, Remote Desktop, and Group Policy.

Windows as a service Beginning with Windows 10, the Microsoft strategy to deploy Windows and then provide ongoing, incremental updates to service the OS with no end-of-life limitation. In comparison, earlier versions of Windows had more discrete and significant updates, and end-of-life limitations required you to eventually upgrade to a new version of Windows.

Windows Assessment and Deployment Kit (ADK) In Windows 8, a group of tools used to deploy Windows 8 in a large organization; the ADK contains the User State Migration Tool (USMT).

Windows Boot Loader One of two programs that manage the loading of Windows 10/8/7. The program file (winload.exe or winload.efi) is stored in C:\Windows\System32, and it loads and starts essential Windows processes.

Windows Boot Manager (BootMgr) The Windows program that manages the initial startup of Windows. For a BIOS system, the program is bootmgr; for a UEFI system, the program is bootmgfw.efi. The program file is stored in the root of the system partition.

Windows Defender Anti-malware Software embedded in Windows 8/7. In Windows 8, the software can detect and remove many types of malware. In Windows 7, the software can detect and remove only spyware.

Windows Defender Antivirus Anti-malware software embedded in Windows 10 that can detect viruses, prevent them, and clean up a system infected with viruses and other malware. In Windows 8/7, a similar tool is called Windows Defender.

Windows Defender Offline (WDO) Scanning software available in Windows 10 or downloaded from the Microsoft website that launches before Windows to scan a system for malware. WDO works in the WinPE environment.

Windows Easy Transfer A Windows tool used to transfer Windows user data and preferences to a Windows installation on another computer.

Windows Explorer The Windows 7 utility used to view and manage files and folders. *Compare with* File Explorer.

Windows Firewall A personal firewall in Windows that protects a computer from intrusion and is automatically configured when you set your network location in the Network and Sharing Center.

Windows pinwheel A Windows graphic that indicates the system is waiting for a response from a program or device.

Windows Preinstallation Environment (Windows PE) A minimum operating system used to start a Windows installation. *Also called* WinPE.

G

Windows Recovery Environment (Windows RE)   A lean operating system installed on the Windows 10/8/7 setup DVD and on the Windows volume that can be used to troubleshoot problems when Windows refuses to start.

Windows RT   A Windows 8 edition that is a lighter version designed for tablets, netbooks, and other mobile devices.

Windows Subsystem for Linux (WSL)   A Windows component that supports the Bash on Ubuntu on Windows shell.

Windows.old folder   When using an unformatted hard drive for a clean installation, this folder is created to store the previous operating system settings and user profiles.

wire stripper   A tool used when terminating a cable. The tool cuts away the plastic jacket or coating around the wires in a cable so that a connector can be installed on the end of the cable.

wireless access point (WAP)   A wireless device that is used to create and manage a wireless network.

wireless LAN (WLAN)   A type of LAN that does not use wires or cables to create connections, but instead transmits data over radio or infrared waves.

wireless locator   A tool that can locate a Wi-Fi hotspot and tell you the strength of the RF signal.

wireless wide area network (WWAN)   A wireless broadband network for computers and mobile devices that uses cellular towers for communication. *Also called* a cellular network.

WLAN (wireless LAN)   *See* wireless LAN (WLAN).

WMN (wireless mesh network)   Many wireless devices communicating directly rather than through a single central device. This technology is commonly used in IoT wireless networks.

workgroup   In Windows, a logical group of computers and users in which administration, resources, and security are distributed throughout the network without centralized management or security.

worm   An infestation designed to copy itself repeatedly to memory, drive space, or a network until little memory, disk space, or network bandwidth remains.

WPA (Wi-Fi Protected Access)   A data encryption method for wireless networks that use the TKIP (Temporal Key Integrity Protocol) encryption method. The encryption keys are changed at set intervals while the wireless LAN is in use. WPA is stronger than WEP.

WPA2 (Wi-Fi Protected Access 2)   A data encryption standard compliant with the IEEE802.11i standard that uses the AES (Advanced Encryption Standard) protocol. WPA2 is currently the strongest wireless encryption standard.

WPA3 (Wi-Fi Protected Access 3)   A standard that offers improved data encryption over WPA2 and allows for Individual Data Encryption, whereby a laptop or other wireless device can create a secure connection over a public, unsecured Wi-Fi network.

wpeinit   The Windows command that initializes Windows PE and enables networking. *Also see* Windows Preinstallation Environment (Windows PE).

WPS (Wi-Fi Protected Setup)   *See* Wi-Fi Protected Setup (WPS).

WWAN (wireless wide area network)   *See* cellular network.

x86 processor   An older processor that first used the number 86 in the model number; it processes 32 bits at a time.

x86-64 bit processor   A hybrid processor that can process 32 bits or 64 bits.

XaaS (Anything as a Service or Everything as a Service)   An open-ended cloud computing service that can provide any combination of functions depending on a customer's exact needs.

xcopy   A Windows command more powerful than the copy command that is used to copy files and folders.

xD-Picture Card   A type of flash memory device that has a compact design and currently holds up to 8 GB of data.

XPS Document Writer   A Windows feature that creates a file with an .xps file extension. The file is similar to a .pdf file and can be viewed, edited, printed, faxed, emailed, or posted on websites.

Yahoo!   An email provider owned by Verizon.

zero client   A client computer that does not have an operating system and merely provides an interface between the user and the server.

zero insertion force (ZIF) socket   A processor socket with one or two levers on the sides that are used to move the processor out of or into the socket so that equal force is applied over the entire socket housing.

zero-day attack   An attack in which a hacker discovers and exploits a security hole in software before its developer can provide a protective patch to close the hole.

zero-fill utility   A hard drive utility that fills every sector on the drive with zeroes.

zero-touch, high volume deployment   An installation strategy that does not require the user to start the process. Instead, a server pushes the installation to a computer when a user is not likely to be manning it.

ZIF connector   A connector that uses a lever or latch to prevent force from being used on a sensitive connection. ZIF stands for zero insertion force.

Zigbee   A wireless standard used by smart devices that works in the 900-MHz band, has a range up to 100 m, and is considered more robust than Z-Wave, a competing standard.

zombie   A computer that has been hacked to run repetitive software in the background without the knowledge of its user. *Also see* botnet.

Z-Wave   A wireless standard used by smart devices that works in the 900-MHz or 2.4-GHz band and has a range up to 20 m. Z-Wave competes with Zigbee but is not considered as robust as Zigbee.

G

INDEX

I